BIJA GANITA

BIJA GANITA

OR THE

ALGEBRA

OF THE

HINDUS

EDWARD STRACHEY

GYAN

Published by

Gyan Publishing House
5, Ansari Road
Daryaganj, New Delhi-110002
Phone: 011-47034999, 9811692060
E-mail: books@gyanbooks.com

Distribution Network
gyanbooks.com
India, USA, Canada, UK, Australia, France

ISBN : 978-81-212-9638-0 (PB)
First Published, 1812

2nd Impression 2023

Printed at: Gyan Press, Delhi.

BIJA GANITA
Author: EDWARD STRACHEY

BIJA GANITA:

OR THE

ALGEBRA

OF THE

HINDUS.

BY

EDWARD STRACHEY,

OF THE

EAST INDIA COMPANY's BENGAL CIVIL SERVICE.

CONTENTS.

CHAPTER III.

CHAPTER IV.

CHAPTER V.

CHAPTER VI.

BOOK 1.

BOOK 2.

BOOK 3.

BOOK 4.

BOOK 5.

MR. DAVIS'S NOTES.

ERRATA.

Page 3, line 4, *for* Heilbronnen *read* Heilbronner.

5, 1, *for* undistinguished *read* undistinguishing.

11, 6, *after* notes *read* at the bottom of the pages.

13, 1, *dele* the inverted commas at the beginning of the line.

17, 5, (at the end), *for* number *read* colour.

29, 25, Suppose $\frac{ax+c}{b}=y$ where a, b, and c are known and x and y unknown.

93, 9, 10, and 11, the character prefixed to the numbers 1 and 2 is here लो which is the first letter of the word *Loheet* (see opposite page); but it should be a different character, viz. the first letter of the word *Roop* रू.

Note—In Mr. Davis's notes the word Ja, Roo, Bha, Ca, &c. which are frequently used, are contractions of Jabut, Roop, Bhady, Canist, &c. They should have been printed with points after them, thus, Ja. Roo. &c.

PREFACE.

It is known that there are Sanscrit books on Astronomy and Mathematics. Whether the Science they contain is of Hindoo Origin and of high antiquity, or is modern and borrowed from foreign sources, is a question which has been disputed. Some of the Advocates for the Hindoos have asserted their pretensions with a degree of zeal which may be termed extravagant; and others among their opponents have with equal vehemence pronounced them to be impostors, plagiaries, rogues, blind slaves, ignorant, &c. &c.

My object in the following paper is to support the opinion that the Hindoos had an original fund of Science not borrowed from foreign sources. I mean to infer also, because of the connexion of the sciences and their ordinary course of advancement, that the Hindoos had other knowledge besides what is established by direct proof to be theirs, and that much of what they had, must have existed in early times.

But with respect to the antiquity of the specimens which I am going to exhibit, nothing seems to be certainly known beyond this, that in form and substance as they are here, they did exist at the end of the 12th or the beginning of the 13th Century.

It is not my purpose to inquire here what parts of Indian science have already been ascertained to be genuine. I only wish to observe that the doubts which have been raised as to the pretensions of the Hindoos are of very recent birth, and that no such doubts have been expressed by persons who were perhaps as well able to judge of the matter as we are.*

* The Edinburgh Review, in criticising Mr. Bentley's Indian Astronomy, in the 20th number, ably contended for the antiquity and originality of Hindoo Science. The writer of that article however seems to have left the field; and his successor, in a Review of Delambre's History of Greek Arithmetic, has taken the other side of the question, with much zeal. This Critic is understood to be Mr. Leslie, who, in his Elements of Geometry, has again attacked the Hindoos. Mr. Leslie, after explaining the rule for constructing the sines by differences, which was given in the 2nd Volume of the Asiatic Researches by Mr. Davis, from the Surya Siddhanta, adds the follownig remarks.

We are told that in early times Pythagoras and Democritus, who taught the Greeks astronomy and mathematics, learnt these sciences in India. The Arabians

---

" Such is the detailed explication of that very ingenious mode which, in certain cases, the Hindoo Astronomers employ for constructing the table of approximate sines. But totally ignorant of the principles of the operation, those humble calculators are content to follow blindly a slavish routine. The Brahmins must therefore have derived such information from people farther advanced than themselves in science, and of a bolder and more inventive genius. Whatever may be the pretensions of that passive race, their knowledge of trigonometrical computation has no solid claim to any high antiquity. It was probably, before the revival of letters in Europe, carried to the East, by the tide of victory. The natives of Hindustan might receive instruction from the Persian Astronomers, who were themselves taught by the Greeks of Constantinople, and stimulated to those scientific pursuits by the skill and liberality of their Arabian conquerors."—(Leslie's Elements, p. 485.)

When scientific operations are detailed, and most of the theorems on which they depend are given in the form of rules, surely it is not to be inferred because the demonstrations do not always accompany the rules, therefore that they were not known; on the contrary, the presumption in such a case is that they were known. So it is here, for the Hindoos certainly had at least as much trigonometry as is assumed by Mr. Leslie to be the foundation of their rule. Mr. Leslie, after inferring that the Hindoos must have derived their science from people farther advanced than themselves, proceeds to shew the sources from which they might have borrowed, namely, the Persians, the Greeks, and the Arabians. Now as for the Persians as a nation, we do not know of any science of theirs except what was originally Greek or Arabian. This indeed Mr. Leslie would seem not to deny; and as for the Greeks and Arabians it is enough to say that the Hindoos could not borrow from them what they never had. They could not have borrowed from them this *slavish routine* for the sines, which depends on a principle not known even to the modern Europeans till 200 years ago. In short the tide of victory could not have carried that which did not exist.

It appears from Mr. Davis's paper that the Hindoos knew the distinctions of sines, cosines, and versed sines. They knew that the difference of the radius and the cosine is equal to the versed sine; that in a right-angled triangle if the hypothenuse be radius the sides are sines and cosines. They assumed a small arc of a circle as equal to its sine. They constructed on true principles a table of sines, by adding the first and second differences.

From the Bija Ganita it will appear that they knew the chief properties of right-angled and similar triangles.

In Fyzee's Lilavati I find the following rules:

(The hypothenuse of a right-angled triangle being h, the base b, and the side s.)

Assume any large number p, then $\frac{\sqrt{((b^2+s^2)p^2)}}{p} = h$.

$$b = \sqrt{(h^2 - s^2)} \text{ and } s = \sqrt{(h^2 - b^2)}.$$
$$\sqrt{((b-s)^2 + 2bs)} = h.$$
$$(h+b)(h-b) = h^2 - b^2.$$

b being given to find h and s in any number of ways; let p be any number; then $\frac{2pb}{p^2-1} = s$, and $ps - b = h$.

$$\frac{\frac{b^2}{p} - p}{2} = s, \text{ and } \frac{\frac{b^2}{p} + p}{2} = h.$$

h being given, $\frac{2ph}{p^2+1} = s$, and $ps - h = b$.

always considered the Indian astrology and astronomy as different from theirs and the Greeks. We hear of Indian astronomy known to them in the time of the Caliph Al Mamun. (See d'Herbelot). Aben Asra is said to have compared the Indian sphere with the Greek and Persian spheres. (Heilbronnen Hist. Math. p. 456). We know that the Arabians ascribe their numeral figures to the

---

Let p and q be any numbers; then

$$2pq = s,\ p^2 - q^2 = b, \text{ and } p^2 + q^2 = h.$$

Given $a = h \pm s$; then $\dfrac{a - \frac{b^2}{a}}{2} = s$, and $\dfrac{a + \frac{b^2}{a}}{2} = h$.

Given $a = b + s$; then $\dfrac{a - \sqrt{(2h^2 - a^2)}}{2} = b$, and $\dfrac{a + \sqrt{(2h^2 - a^2)}}{2} = s$.

There are also rules for finding the areas of triangles, and four-sided figures; among others the rule for the area of a triangle, without finding the perpendicular.

For the circle there are these rules (C being the circumference, D the diameter, c the chord, v the versed sine, a the arch,)

$$C : D :: 22 : 7; \text{ and } C : D :: 3927 : 1250. \text{ (Also see Ayeen Akbery, vol. 3, p. 32.)}$$

$$\frac{D - \sqrt{((D + c)(D - c))}}{2} = v.$$

$$2\sqrt{(D - v) \times v} = c.$$

$$\frac{4aD\,(C - a)}{\frac{5}{4}C^2 - (C - a)a} = c, \text{ and } \frac{C}{2} - \sqrt{\left(\frac{\frac{C^2}{4} - \frac{5}{4}C^2c}{4D + c}\right)} = a.$$

Also formulæ for the sides of the regular polygons of 3, 4, 5, 6, 7, 8, 9 sides inscribed in a circle. There are also rules for finding the area of a circle, and the surface and solidity of a sphere. It will be seen also that Bhascara is supposed to have given these two rules, viz—the sine of the sum of two arcs is equal to the sum of the products of the sine of each multiplied by the cosine of the other, and divided by the radius; and the cosine of the sum of two arcs is equal to the difference between the products of their sines and of their cosines divided by radius.

Is it to be doubted that the Hindoos applied their rule for the construction of the sines, to ascertain the ratio of the diameter of a circle to its circumference?—thus the circumference of a circle being divided into 360 degrees, or 21600 minutes, the sine of 90 degrees which is equal to the radius would be found by the rule 3438. This would give the ratio of the diameter to the circumference $7 : 21\frac{567}{573}$ and $1250 : 3926\frac{402}{573}$, and assuming, as the Hindoos commonly do, the nearest integers, the ratio would be 7 : 22 or 1250 : 3927.

It is not to be denied that there are some remarkable coincidences between the Greek and the Hindoo science; for example, among many which might be given it may be suggested that the contrivances ascribed to Antiphon and Bryso, and that of Archimedes, for finding the ratio of the diameter of a circle to its circumference might have been the foundation of the Hindoo method; that Diophantus's speculations on indeterminate problems might be the origin of the Hindoo Algebra. But there are no truths in the history of science of which we are better assured than that the Surya Siddhanta rule for the sines, with the ratio of the diameter of a circle to its circumference 1250 : 3927; and the Bija Ganita rules for indeterminate problems were not known to the Greeks. Such are the stumbling blocks which we always find in our way when we attempt to refer the Hindoo science to any foreign origin.

Indians; and Massoudi refers Ptolemy's astronomy to them. (See Bailly's preface to his Indian astronomy, where is cited M. de Guignes. Mem. Acad. Ins. T. 36, p. 771). Fyzee, who doubtless was conversant with Greco-arabian learning, and certainly knew the Hindoos well, has never started any doubt of the originality of what he found among them. The preface to the Zeej Mahommed Shahy, or Astronomical Tables, which were published in India in 1728, speaks of the European, the Greek, the Arabian, and the Indian systems as all different. That work was compiled with great learning by persons who were skilled in the sciences of the West, as well as those of the East *. More examples might be given—but to proceed.

The Bija Ganita is a Sanscrit treatise on algebra, by Bhasçara Acharya, a celebrated Hindoo Astronomer and Mathematician.

Fyzee †, who, in 1587, translated the Lilavati, a work of his on arithmetic, mensuration, &c. speaks of an astronomical treatise of Bhascara's, dated in the 1105th year of the Salibahn, which answers to about 1183 of our æra; but Fyzee also says, it was 373 years before 995 Hegira, which would bring it down to A.D. 1225. So that Bhascara must have written about the end of the 12th century, or beginning of the 13th.

A complete translation of the Bija Ganita is a great desideratum; so it has been for more than 20 years, and so it seems likely to remain.

It will be seen however that we have already means of learning, with sufficient accuracy, the contents of this work. I have a Persian translation of the Bija Ganita, which was made in India in 1634, by Ata Allah Rusheedee. The Persian does not in itself afford a correct idea of its original, as a translation should do; for it is an

---

* See Asiatic Researches, 5th vol. on the Astronomical Labours of Jy Singh.

† I will here translate a part of Fyzee's preface:—"By order of king Akber, Fyzee translates into Persian, "from the Indian language, the book Lilavati, so famous for the rare and wonderful arts of calculation and "mensuration. He (Fyzee) begs leave to mention that the compiler of this book was Bhascara Acharya, whose "birth place, and the abode of his ancestors was the city of Biddur, in the country of the Deccan. Though "the date of compiling this work is not mentioned, yet it may be nearly known from the circumstance, that the "author made another book on the construction of Almanacks, called Kurrun Kuttohul, in which the date of "compiling it is mentioned to be 1105 years from the date of the Salibahn, an æra famous in India. From "that year to this, which is the 32d Ilahi year, corresponding with the lunar year 995, there have passed "373 years."

As the Ilahi began in the Hegira (or lunar) year, 992, (see Ayeen Akbery) the date 32 of Ilahi is of course an error. It is likely too that there is an error in the number 373.

Mr. Colebrooke, in the 9th vol. of Asiatic Researches, gives, on Bhascara's own authority, the date of his birth, viz. 1063 Saca. In 1105 Salibahn (or Saca) that is, about A. D. 1183, he was 42 years old.

undistinguished mixture of text and commentary, and in some places it even refers to Euclid. But to infer at once from this that every thing in the book was derived from Greek or Arabian writers, or that it was *inseparably* mixed, would be reasoning too hastily. A little patience will discover evidence of the algebra which it contains, being purely Hindoo*.

The following paper consists of an account of this translation, and some notes which I shall now mention:

Mr. Davis, the well-known author of two papers on Indian Astronomy in the Asiatic Researches, made, many years ago, in India, some abstracts and translations from the original Sanscrit Bija Ganita †, and it is greatly to be regretted that he did not complete a translation of the whole. The papers which contain his notes had long since been mislaid and forgotten. They have been but very lately found, and I gladly avail myself of Mr Davis's permission to make use of them here. The chief part of them is inserted at the end of my account of the Persian translation. To prevent misconception about these notes, it is proper for me to observe that in making them Mr. Davis had no other object than to inform himself generally of the nature of the Bija Ganita; they were not intended probably to be seen by any second person; certainly they were never proposed to convey a perfect idea of the work, or to be exhibited before the public in any shape. Many of them are on loose detached pieces of paper, and it is probable that, from the time they were written till they came into my hands, they were never looked at again. But nevertheless it will be seen that they do, without doubt, describe accurately a considerable portion of the most curious parts of the Bija Ganita; and though they may seem to occupy but a secondary place here, they will be found of more importance than all the rest of this work together.

They shew positively that the main part of the Persian translation is taken from

---

* The late Mr. Reuben Burrow in one of his papers in the Asiatic Researches says, he made translations of the Bija Ganita and Lilavati. Those translations he left to Mr. Dalby. They consist of fair copies in Persian of Ata Allah's and Fyzee's translations, with the English of each word written above the Persian. The words being thus translated separately, without any regard to the meaning of complete sentences, not a single passage can be made out. It is plain, from many short notes which Mr. Burrow has written in the margin of his Bija Ganita, that he made his verbal translation by the help of a Moonshee, and that he had the original Sanscrit at hand, with some opportunity of consulting it occasionally. I am much obliged to Mr. Dalby for allowing me the use of Mr. Burrow's copy which has enabled me to supply deficiencies in mine; and it is otherwise interesting, because it shews that Mr. Burrow had access to the original Sanscrit (probably by means of a Moonshee and a Pundit) and compared it with the Persian.

† It is to be remarked that they were made from the Sanscrit only. Mr. Davis never saw the Persian translation.

the Sanscrit work, and that the references to Euclid are interpolations of the Persian translator they give most of the Hindoo Algebraic notation* which is wanting in the Persian, and they shew that the Astronomy of the Hindoos was connected with their Algebra.

I must however confess, that even before I saw these notes the thing was to my mind quite conclusive. For I found (as will be seen) in this Persian translation of 1634, said to be from the Sanscrit, a perfectly connected structure of science, comprehending propositions, which in Europe were invented successively by Bachet de Mezeriac, Fermat, Euler, and De La Grange†.

---

* The Hindoos have no mark for +, they only separate the quantities to be added by a vertical line thus | or ||, as they separate their slocas or verses.

Their mark for *minus* is a dot over the quantity to be subtracted.

Instead of a mark for multiplication they write the factors together as we do, thus, ab for $a \times b$.

Division they mark as we do by a horizontal line drawn between the dividend and divisor, the lower quantity being the divisor.

For unknown quantities they use letters of the alphabet as we do. They use the first letters of the words signifying colours.

The known quantity (which is always a number) has the word roop (form) or the first letter of the word prefixed.

The square of the unknown quantity is marked by adding to the expression of the simple quantity the first letter of the word which means square, and in like manner the cube.

The sides of an equation are written one above another; every quantity on one side is expressed again directly under it on the other side. Where there is in fact no corresponding quantity, the form is preserved by writing that quantity with the co-efficient 0.

The methods of prefixing a letter to the known number, and using the first letter of the words square and cube are the same as those of Diophantus. I mention it as a curious coincidence; perhaps some people may attach more importance to it than I do.

† The propositions which I here particularly allude to are these:—

1. A general method of solving the problem $\frac{ax \pm c}{b} = y$, a, b and c being given numbers and x and y indeterminate. The solution is founded on a division like that which is made for finding the greatest common measure of two numbers. The rules comprehend every sort of case, and are in all respects quite perfect.

2. The problem $am^2 + 1 = n^2$, (a being given and m and n required) with its solution.

3. The application of the above to find any number of values of $ax^2 + b = y^2$ from one known case.

4. To find values of x and y in $ax^2 + b = y^2$ by an application of the problem $\frac{ax \pm c}{b} = y$. It is unnecessary for me *here* to give any detail of the Hindoo methods.

The first question about this extraordinary matter is, what evidence have we that it is not all a forgery? I answer, shortly, that independently of its being now found in the Sanscrit books, it is ascertained to have been there in 1634 and 1587, that is to say, in times when it could not have been forged.

The following extract from a paper of De La Grange, in the 24th volume of the Memoirs of the Berlin Academy, for the year 1768, contains a summary of that part of the history of Algebra which is now alluded to. As for the 4th of the points abovementioned, the method in detail (however imperfect in some respects) is, as far as I know, new to this day. The first application of the principle in Europe is to be sought in the writings of De La Grange himself.

To maintain that the Bija Ganita rules for the solution of indeterminate problems might have been had from any Greek or Arabian, or any modern European writers before the Mathematicians just named, would be as absurd as to say that the Newtonian Astronomy might have existed in the time of Ptolemy. It is true that Bachet wrote a few years before 1634, but this is no sort of objection to the argument, for that part which might be questioned as a mere copy of Bachet's method, namely, the rules for indeterminate problems of the first degree, is closely connected with matters of latter invention in Europe, and is in Mr. Dalby's copy of Fyzee's translation of the Lilavati, which I have before said was made in 1587; and Mr. Davis's notes shew that it is in the Sanscrit Bija Ganita, which was

---

" La plupart des Géometres qui ont cultivé l'analyse de Diophante se sont, a l'exemple de cet illustre inven-
" tuer, uniquement appliqués à eviter les valeurs irrationelles; et tout l'artifice de leurs méthodes se reduit à
" faire en sorte que les grandeurs inconnues puissent se déterminer par des nombres commensurables.

" L'art de resoudre ces sortes de questions ne demande gueres d'autres principes que ceux de l'analyse
" ordinaire; mais ces principes deviennent insuffisant lors-qu'on ajoute la condition que les quantités cher-
" chées soient non seulement commensurables mais encore égales à des nombres entiers.

" M. Bachet de Mezeriac, auteur d'un excellent commentarie sur Diophante et de différens autres ouvrages
" est, je crois, le premier quit ait tanté de soumettre cette condition au calcul. Ce savant a trouvé une méthode
" générale pour resoudre en nombres entiers toutes les equations du premier degré a deux ou plusieurs incon-
" nues, mais il ne paroit pas avoir été plus loin; et ceux qui aprés lui se sont occupés du même objet, ont
" aussi presque tous borné leurs recherches aux equations indéterminées du premier degré; leurs efforts se
" sont réduits a varier les méthods qui peuvent servir a la resolution de ces sortes d'equations, et aucun, si
" j'ose le dire, n'a donné une methode plus directe, plus générale, et plus ingenieuse que celle de M. Bachet
" qui se trouve dans ses récréations mathématiques intituéles '*Problems plaisans et délectubles qui se font par les*
" *nombres.*' Il est a la vérité assez surprenant que M. de Fermat qui s'etoit si long tems et avec tant de
" succés exercé sur la théorie des nombres entiers, n'ait pas cherché à resoudre généralement les problems
" indeterminés du second degré, et des degrés superieurs comme M. Bachet avoit fait ceux du premier degré;
" on a cependent lieu de croire qu'il s'etoit aussi appliqué a cette recherche, par le probleme qu'il proposa
" comme une espece de défi à M. Wallis et à tous les Geometres Anglois, et qui consistoit à trouver deux
" carrés entiers, dont l'un étant multiplié par un nombre entier donné non carré & ensuite retranché de l'autre,
" le reste fut etre égal à l'unité, car, outre que ce probleme est un cas particulier des équations du second
" dégré à deux inconnués il est comme la clef de la résolution génerale de ces équations. Mais soit que
" M. de Fermat n'ait pas continué ses recherches sur cette matiere, soit qu'elle ne soit parvenue jusqu'à nous,
" il est certain qu'on n'en trouve aucune trace dans ses ouvrages.

" Il paroit même que les Geometres Anglois qui ont résolu le probleme de M. de Fermat n'ont pas connu
" toute l'importance dont il est pour la solution générale des problemes indéterminés du second degré, du
" moins on ne voit pas qu'ils en ayant jamais fait usage, et Euler est si je ne me trompe, le prémier qui ait
" fait voir comment à l'aide de ce probleme on peut trouver une infinité de solutions en nombres entiers de
" toute équation du second dégré à deux inconnues, dont on connoit déja une solution.

" Il résulte de tout ce que nous venons de dire, que depuis l'ouvrage de M. Bachet que a paru en 1613,
" jusqu'a présent, ou du moins jusqu'au mémoire que je donnai l'année passée sur la solution de problems
" indéterminés du sécond dégré, la théorie de ces sortes de problemes n'avoit pas a proprement parler, éte
" poussée au dela du premier dégré."

written four centuries before Bachet. Though we are not without direct proofs from the original, yet, as even the best Sanscrit copies of the Bija Ganita, or any number of such copies exactly corresponding, would still be open to the objection of interpolations, it is necessary in endeavouring to distinguish the possible and the probable corruptions of the text, from what is of Indian origin, to recur to the nature of the propositions themselves, and to the general history of the science. Indeed we have not data enough to reason satisfactorily on other principles. We cannot rely upon the perfect identity or genuineness of any book before the invention of printing, unless the manuscript copies are numerous, and of the same age as the original. Such is the nature of our doubt and difficulty in this case, for old mathematical Sanscrit manuscripts are exceedingly scarce; and our uncertainty is greatly increased by a consideration of this fact, that in latter times the Greek, Arabian, and modern European science has been introduced into the Sanscrit books.

Yet, in cases precisely parallel to this of the Hindoos, we are not accustomed to withhold our belief as to the authenticity of the reputed works of the ancients, and in forming our judgment we advert more to the contents of the book than to the state of the manuscript. When the modern Europeans first had Euclid, they saw it only through an Arabic translation. Why did they believe that pretended translation to be authentic? Because they found it contained a well connected body of science; and it would have been equally as improbable to suppose that the Arabian translator could have invented it himself as that he could have borrowed it from his countrymen. There are principles on which we decide such points. We must not look for mathematical proof, but that sort of probability which determines us in ordinary matters of history.

Every scrap of Hindoo science is interesting; but it may be asked why publish any which cannot be authenticated? I answer, that though this translation of Ata Allah's which professes to exhibit the Hindoo algebra in a Persian dress, does indeed contain some things which are not Hindoo, yet it has others which are certainly Hindoo. By separating the science from the book we may arrive at principles, which if cautiously applied, cannot mislead, which in some cases will shew us the truth, and will often bring us to the probability when certainty is not to be had. On this account I think the Persian translation at large interesting, notwithstanding it contains some trifling matters, some which are not intelligible, and others which are downright nonsense.

I have said that Mr. Davis's notes shew a connexion of the algebra of the

Hindoos with their astronomy. Mr. Davis informs me that in the astronomical treatises of the Hindoos, reference is often made to the algebra; and particularly he remembers a passage where Bhascara says "it would be as absurd for a person "ignorant of algebra to write about astronomy, as for one ignorant of grammar "to write poetry."

Bhascara, who is the only Hindoo writer on algebra whose works we have yet procured, does not himself pretend to be the inventor, he assumes no character but that of a compiler*. Fyzee never speaks of him but as a person eminently skilled in the sciences he taught. He expressly calls him the compiler of the Lilavati.

I understand from Mr. Davis, and I have heard the same in India, that the Bija Ganita was not intended by Bhascara as a separate unconnected work, but as a component part of one of his treatises on astronomy, another part of which is on the circles of the sphere.

I have found among Mr. Davis's papers, some extracts from a Sanscrit book of astronomy, which I think curious, although the treatise they were taken from is modern. Mr. Davis believes it to have been written in Jy Sing's time, when the European improvements were introduced into the Hindoo books. Two of these extracts I have added to the notes on the Bija Ganita. The first of the two shews that a method has been ascribed by Hindoo Astronomers to Bhascara of calculating sines and cosines by an application of the principles which solve indeterminate problems of the second degree. This suggestion is doubtless of Hindoo origin, for the principles alluded to were hardly known in Europe in Jy Sing's time†. I think it very probable that the second extract is also purely Hindoo, and that the writer knew of Hindoo authors who said the square root might be extracted by the cootuk; that is to say, the principle which effects the solution of indeterminate problems of the first degree. From this, and from what is in the Bija Ganita, one cannot but suspect that the Hindoos had continued fractions, and possibly some curious arithmetic of sines. On such matters however, let every one exercise his own judgment.‡

---

* "Almost any trouble and expence would be compensated by the possession of the three copious treatises "on algebra from which Bhascara declares he extracted his Bija Ganita, and which in this part of India are "supposed to be entirely lost."—As. Res. vol. iii. Mr. Davis "On the Indian Cycle of 60 years."

† Jy Sing reigned from 1694 to 1744.

‡ Mr. Reuben Burrow, who, by the bye, it must be confessed is very enthusiastic on these subjects, in a paper

We must not be too fastidious in our belief, because we have not found the works of the teachers of Pythagoras; we have access to the wreck only of their ancient learning; but when we see such traces of a more perfect state of knowledge, when we see that the Hindoo algebra 600 years ago had in the most interesting parts some of the most curious modern European discoveries, and when we see that it was at that time applied to astronomy, we cannot reasonably doubt the originality and the antiquity of mathematical learning among the Hindoos. Science in remote times we expect to find within very narrow limits indeed: its *history* is all we look to in such researches as these. Considering this, and comparing the contents of the Hindoo books with what they might have been expected to contain, the result affords matter of the most curious speculation.

May I be excused for adding a few words about myself. If my researches have not been so deep as might have been expected from the opportunities I had in India, let it be remembered that our labours are limited by circumstances. It is true I had at one time a copy of the original Bija Ganita, but I do not understand Sanscrit, nor had I then any means of getting it explained to me. Official avocations often prevented me from bestowing attention on these matters, and from seizing opportunities when they did occur. Besides, what is to be expected in this way from a *mere amateur*, to whom the simplest and most obvious parts only of such subjects are accessible?

E. S.

The following account of Ata Allah's Bija Ganita is partly literal translation, partly abstract, and partly my own.

The literal translation is marked by inverted commas; that part which consists of my own remarks or description will appear by the context, and all the rest is abstract.

I have translated almost all the rules, some of the examples entirely, and

---

in the appendix of the 2d vol. of the As. Res. speaks of the Lilavati and Bija Ganita, and of the mathematical knowledge of the Hindoos: He says, he was told by a Pundit, that some time ago there were other treatises of algebra, &c. (See the paper.)

others in part; in short, whatever I thought deserving of particular attention, for the sake of giving a distinct idea of the book.

Perhaps some of the translated parts might as well have been put in an abstract; the truth is, that having made them originally in their present form I have not thought it worth while to alter them.

The notes are only a few remarks which I thought might be of use to save trouble and to furnish necessary explanation.

BIJA GANITA.

" After the usual invocations and compliments, the Persian translator begins thus: " By the Grace of God, in the year 1044 Hegira" (or A. D. 1634) " being the " eighth year of the king's reign, I, Ata Alla Rasheedee, son of Ahmed Nadir, " have translated into the Persian language, from Indian, the book of Indian " Algebra, called Beej Gunnit (Bija Ganita), which was written by Bhasker Acharij " (Bhascara Acharya) the author of the Leelawuttee (Lilavati). In the science of " calculation it is a discoverer of wonderful truths and nice subtilties, and it con- " tains useful and important problems which are not mentioned in the Leelawuttee, " nor in any Arabic or Persian book. I have dedicated the work to Shah Jehan, and " I have arranged it according to the original in an introduction and five books."

INTRODUCTION.

" The introduction contains six chapters, each of which has several sections."

CHAPTER I.

On Possession (مال)* and Debt (دين).

" Know that whatever is treated of in the science of calculation is either " affirmative or negative; let that which is affirmative be called *mal*, and that " which is negative *dein*. This chapter has five sections."

Sect. I.

On Addition and Subtraction, that is, to encrease and diminish.

" If an affirmative is taken from an affirmative, or a negative from a negative, " the subtrahend is made contrary; that is to say, if it is affirmative suppose it " negative, and if negative suppose it affirmative, and proceed as in addition.

" The rule of addition is, that if it is required to add two affirmative quantities,

---

* Most of the technical terms here used are Arabic.

" or two negative quantities together, the sum is the result of the addition. If " they are affirmative call the sum affirmative; if negative call the sum negative. " If the quantities are of different kinds take the excess; if the affirmative is " greater, the remainder is affirmative; if the negative is greater, the remainder " is negative; and so it is in subtraction." (Here follow examples).

SECT. II.

On Multiplication *.

" If affirmative is multiplied by affirmative, or negative by negative, the product " is affirmative and to be included in the product. If the factors are contrary " the product is negative, and to be taken from the product. For example, let us " multiply two affirmative by three affirmative, or two negative by three negative, " the result will be six affirmative; and if we multiply two affirmative by three " negative, or the contrary, the result will be six negative."

SECT. III.

On Division.

" The illustration of this is the same as what has been treated of under multi- " plication, that is to say, if the dividend and the divisor are of the same kind " the quotient will be affirmative, and if they are different, negative. For " example, if 8 is the dividend and 4 the divisor, and both are of the same kind, " the quotient will be 2 affirmative; if they are different, 2 negative."

SECT. IV.

On Squares †.

" The squares of affirmative and negative are both affirmative; for to find the

---

* In the Persian translation the product of numbers is generally called the rectangle.

† I had a Persian treatise on Algebra in which there was this passage—" Any number which is to be multiplied " by itself is called by arithmeticians root (جذر), by measurers of surfaces side (ضلع), and by alge- " braists thing (شي). And the product is called by arithmeticians square (مجذور), by measurers " of surfaces square (مربع), and by algebraists possession (مال)." مال is also used for *plus*, and its opposite debt (دين) for *minus*. These terms, all of which are Arabic, are used in the Persian translation of the Bija Ganita, the geometrical more frequently than their corresponding arithmetical or algebraical ones.

" square of 4 affirmative we multiply 4 affirmative by 4 affirmative, and by the rules " of multiplication, as the factors are of the same kind, the product must be 16 " affirmative, and the same applies to negative."

Sect. V.

On the Square Root.

" The square root of affirmative is sometimes affirmative and sometimes nega- " tive, according to difference of circumstances. The square of 3 affirmative or " of 3 negative is 9 affirmative; hence the root of 9 affirmative is sometimes 3 " affirmative and sometimes 3 negative, according as the process may require. " But if any one asks the root of 9 negative I say the question is absurd, for there " never can be a negative square as has been shown."

CHAP. II.

On the Cipher.

" It is divided into four sections."

Sect. I.

On Addition and Subtraction.

" If cipher is added to a number, or a number is added to cipher, or if cipher " is subtracted from a number, the result is that number: and if a number is sub- " tracted from cipher, if it is affirmative it becomes negative, and if negative it " becomes affirmative. For example, if 3 affirmative is subtracted from cipher " it will be 3 negative, and if 3 negative is subtracted it will be 3 affirmative."

Sect. II.

On Multiplication.

" If cipher is multiplied by a number, or number by cipher, or cipher by cipher, " the result will be cipher. For example, if we multiply 3 by cipher, or con- " versely, the result will be cipher"

Sect. III.

On Division.

"If the dividend is cipher and the divisor a number the quotient will be cipher. "For example, if we divide cipher by 3 the quotient will be cipher, for multi-"plying it by the divisor the product will be the dividend, which is cipher: "and if a number is the dividend and cipher the divisor the division is impossible; "for by whatever number we multiply the divisor, it will not arrive at the divi-"dend, because it will always be cipher."

Sect. IV.

On Squares, &c.

"The square, cube, square root, and cube root of cipher, are all cipher; the "reason of which is plain."

CHAP. III.

On Colours.

"Whatever is unknown in examples of calculation, if it is one, call it thing, "(شي), and unknown (مجهول); and if it is more call the second black, "and the third blue, and the fourth yellow, and fifth red. Let these be termed "colours, each according to its proper colour. This chapter has five sections.

Sect. I.

On Addition and Subtraction of Colours.

"When we would add one to another, if they are of the same kind add the "numbers* together; if they are of two or more kinds, unite them as they are, "and that will be the result of the addition." Here follows an example.

"If we wish to subtract, that is to take one from the other, let the subtrahend "be reversed. If then two terms of the same kind are alike in this, that they are "both affirmative or both negative, let their sum be taken, otherwise their dif-"ference, and whatever of the kind cannot be got from the minuend, must be

* Meaning here the co-efficients.

"subtracted from cipher. Then let it be reversed, and this will be the result "exactly." (Here follows an example).

Sect. II.

On Multiplication of Colours.

"If a colour is multiplied by a number the product will be a number*, $x \times x$ "will be x^2, whether the number is the same or different, and the product multi- "plied by x will be x^3. If the colours are different multiply the numbers of both "together, and call the product the rectangle of those two colours." The following is given as a convenient method of multiplying:

	$+ 3x$	$+ 2$
$+5x$	$+ 15x^2$	$+ 10x$
-1	$- 3x$	$- 2$
Product	$+ 15x^2 + 7x - 2$	

which shews the product of $(5x - 1) \times (3x + 2.)$ (Here follow examples).

Sect. III.

On Division of Colours.

"Write the dividend and divisor in one place, find numbers or colours or both, "such that when they are multiplied by the divisor, the product subtracted from "the dividend will leave no remainder. Those numbers or colours will be the "quotient."

* In the Persian translation there is no algebraic notation, I mean to translate "the unknown" by x, "the black" by y, and so on. And in like manner I have used the marks of multiplication, &c. instead of writing the words at length as they are in the Persian.

SECT. IV.

On the square of Colours:

"That is to say, the product arising from any thing multiplied by itself." Examples.

SECT. V.

On the Square Root of Colours.

"To know the square root of a colour, find that which when it is multiplied by "itself the product subtracted from the colour whose root is required, will leave no "remainder. The rule is the same if there are other colours or numbers with "that colour."

Example. Required the square root of $16x^2+36-48x$. The roots of $16x^2$ and 36 are $4x$ and 6, and as $48x$ is $-$ these two roots must have different signs. Suppose one $+$ and the other $-$, multiply them and the product will be $-24x$; twice this is $-48x$ which was required. The root then is $+4x-6$, or $+6-4x$.

Another Example. Required the square root of $9x^2+4y^2+z^2+12xy-6xz-4yz-6x-4y+2z+1$. Take the root of each square; we have $3x$, $2y$, z, and 1. Multiply these quantities and dispose the products in the cells of a square.

	$3x$	$2y$	z	1
$3x$	$9x^2$	$6xy$	$3xz$	$3x$
$2y$	$6xy$	$4y^2$	$2yz$	$2y$
z	$3xz$	$2yz$	z^2	z
1	$3x$	$2y$	z	1

To find what sort of quantities these are: The product of x and y is $+$, therefore the factors are like, suppose them both —. The product of x and z is —, therefore the former having been supposed — the latter must be + because the factors must be different. $3x$ is the product of $3x$ and 1; and x being —, 1 must be +. The sorts thus found are to be placed in the cells accordingly. The sum of the products is the square whose root was required. If x had been supposed + the sorts would have been contrary, the reason of which is plain.

CHAP. IV.

On Surds.

Containing five sections.

Sect. I.

On Addition and Subtraction.

To find the sum or difference of two surds; $\sqrt{a}$ and $\sqrt{b}$ for instance.

Rule. Call $a+b$ the greater surd; and if $a\times b$ is rational call $2\sqrt{ab}$ the less surd. The sum will be $\sqrt{(a+b+2\sqrt{ab})}$ *, and the difference $\sqrt{(a+b-2\sqrt{ab})}$. If $a\times b$ is irrational the addition and subtraction are impossible.

Example. Required the sum of $\sqrt{2}$ and $\sqrt{8}$; $2+8=10$ the greater surd. $2\times 8=16$, $\sqrt{16}=4$, $4\times 2=8$ the less surd. $10+8=18$ and $10-8=2$. $\sqrt{18}$ then will be the sum and $\sqrt{2}$ the difference. If one of the numbers is rational take its square and proceed according to the rule, and this must be attended to in multiplication and division, for on a number square with a number not square the operation cannot be performed.

Another Rule. Divide a by b and write $\sqrt{\frac{a}{b}}$ in two places. In the first place add 1, and in the second subtract 1; then we shall have $\sqrt{((\sqrt{\frac{a}{b}}+1)^2\times b)}=\sqrt{a}+\sqrt{b}$ and $\sqrt{((\sqrt{\frac{a}{b}}-1)^2\times b)}=\sqrt{a}-\sqrt{b}$. If $\frac{a}{b}$ is irrational the addition can only be made by writing the surds as they are, and the subtraction by writing the greater number + and the less —.

---

* For $\sqrt{(a+b\pm 2\sqrt{ab})}=\sqrt{a}\pm\sqrt{b}$.

SECT. II.

On Multiplication.

Proceed according to the rules already given; but if one of the factors has numbers as dirhems or dinars, take their squares and go on with the operation.

Example. Multiply $\sqrt{3}+5$ by $\sqrt{2}+\sqrt{3}+\sqrt{8}$. As 5 is of the square sort take its square, and arrange in a table thus:

	$\sqrt{2}$	$\sqrt{3}$	$\sqrt{8}$
$\sqrt{3}$	$\sqrt{6}$	$\sqrt{9}$	$\sqrt{24}$
$\sqrt{25}$	$\sqrt{50}$	$\sqrt{75}$	$\sqrt{200}$
Product	$3+\sqrt{54}+\sqrt{450}+\sqrt{75}$		

In summing the terms of the product, if any square number is found, take its root. Here 9 is found and its root is 3. The rest of the terms being irrational, add such as can be added. $\sqrt{6}+\sqrt{24}=\sqrt{54}$. If this last were a square number its root should be extracted.

Again, $\sqrt{50}+\sqrt{200}=\sqrt{450}$. No further addition is possible; the complete product therefore is $3+\sqrt{54}+\sqrt{450}+\sqrt{75}$.

Another rule to be observed is, if any of the terms which compose the factors can be added, take their sum and write it in the table instead of the terms of which it is formed. Thus in the last example $\sqrt{2}$ and $\sqrt{8}$ may be added. Write $\sqrt{18}$ which is their sum in the table, and we shall have

	$\sqrt{3}$	$\sqrt{18}$
$\sqrt{3}$	$\sqrt{9}$	$\sqrt{54}$
$\sqrt{25}$	$\sqrt{75}$	$\sqrt{450}$
$3+\sqrt{75}+\sqrt{54}+\sqrt{450}$		

and the result is the same as before.

Another Example. Multiply $\sqrt{3}+\sqrt{25}$ by $\sqrt{3}+\sqrt{12}-5$. Instead of $\sqrt{3}$ and $\sqrt{12}$ write their sum $\sqrt{27}$. Take the square of 5 it is 25, and this is negative notwithstanding the rule which says that whether the root is negative or affirmative the square shall be affirmative. Here the square must be of the same sort as the root. Multiply $\sqrt{27}-\sqrt{25}$ by $\sqrt{3}+\sqrt{25}$.

	$+\sqrt{27}$	$-\sqrt{25}$
$+\sqrt{3}$	$+\sqrt{81}$	$-\sqrt{75}$
$+\sqrt{25}$	$+\sqrt{675}$	$-\sqrt{625}$
	$-16+\sqrt{300}$	

$\sqrt{81}=9$ and $\sqrt{625}=25$. 25 being negative and 9 affirmative their sum is -16, and the sum of $+\sqrt{675}$ and $-\sqrt{75}$ is $+\sqrt{300}$. Therefore $(\sqrt{3}+\sqrt{25})\times(\sqrt{3}+\sqrt{12}-5)=-16+\sqrt{300}$.

SECT. III.

On Division.

Divide the dividend by the divisor, and if the quotient is found without a remainder the division is complete. When this cannot be done proceed as follows: When in the divisor there are both affirmative and negative terms, if there are more of the former make one of them negative; if more of the latter make one of them affirmative. When all the terms are affirmative make one negative, and when all are negative make one affirmative. When the number of affirmative terms is equal to that of the negative, it is optional to change one of them or not. Multiply the divisor (thus prepared) by the original divisor, and add the products rejecting such quantities as destroy each other. Multiply the prepared divisor by the dividend, and divide the product of this multiplication by that of the former the result will be the quotient required.

Example. Let the dividend be that which was the product in the first example under the rule for multiplication, viz. $3+\sqrt{54}+\sqrt{450}+\sqrt{75}$, and the divisor $\sqrt{18}+\sqrt{3}$.

$$\frac{75}{3}=25,\ \frac{450}{18}=25,\ 3^2=9,\ \frac{9}{3}=3,\ \frac{54}{18}=3,\ \sqrt{25}=5,$$

the quotient then is $5+\sqrt{3}$.

Another Example. Divide $\sqrt{9}+\sqrt{54}+\sqrt{450}+\sqrt{75}$ by $5+\sqrt{3}$. Make $\sqrt{3}$ negative, and multiply 5 (or $\sqrt{25}$) $-\sqrt{3}$ by the divisor $\sqrt{25}+\sqrt{3}$.

	$+\sqrt{25}$	$-\sqrt{3}$
$+\sqrt{3}$	$+\sqrt{75}$	$-\sqrt{9}$
$+\sqrt{25}$	$+\sqrt{625}$	$-\sqrt{75}$

$\sqrt{75}$ occurring twice with opposite signs is destroyed. $\sqrt{625}=25$, $\sqrt{9}=-3$, $25-3=22=\sqrt{484}$. Multiply $\sqrt{25}-\sqrt{3}$ by the dividend and we have

	$+\sqrt{9}$	$+\sqrt{54}$	$+\sqrt{450}$	$+\sqrt{75}$
$-\sqrt{3}$	$-\sqrt{27}$	$-\sqrt{162}$	$-\sqrt{1350}$	$-\sqrt{225}$
$+\sqrt{25}$	$+\sqrt{225}$	$+\sqrt{1350}$	$+\sqrt{11250}$	$+\sqrt{1875}$

Here $\sqrt{225}$ and $\sqrt{1350}$ are rejected. Find the sum of $\sqrt{27}$ and $\sqrt{1875}$ in this manner,

$$1875+27=1902,\ 1875\times 27=50625,\ \sqrt{50625}=225$$

$$225\times 2=450,\ 1902-450=1452,\ \sqrt{1452}=\sqrt{1875}-\sqrt{27}.$$

Next find the sum of $\sqrt{162}$ and $\sqrt{11250}$.

$$162+11250=11412,\ 162\times 11250=1822500,$$

$$\sqrt{1822500}=1350,\ 1350\times 2=2700,\ 11412-2700=8712,$$

$\sqrt{8712}=\sqrt{11250}-\sqrt{162}$. By the multiplication of the dividend we have found $\sqrt{1452}$ and $\sqrt{8712}$.

Divide these by $\sqrt{484}$ which was the result of the multiplication of the divisor, and we shall have $\sqrt{18}$, and $\sqrt{3}$ for the quotient required. If $\sqrt{3}$ is retained as correct, and $\sqrt{18}$ is considered as incorrect, instead of $\sqrt{18}$ other numbers may be found by the following rule *.

Divide the incorrect number (meaning the number under the radical sign) by any square number which will divide it without a remainder, and note the quotient. Divide the root of that square number into as many parts as there are numbers required. Take the squares of these parts; multiply them by the quotient above

* To resolve $\sqrt{a}$ into several parts, divide a by any square b^2, and let b be resolved into as many parts, c, d, e, &c. as may be required. Then $\sqrt{a}=\sqrt{\left(\frac{a}{b^2}c^2\right)}+\sqrt{\left(\frac{a}{b^2}d^2\right)}+\sqrt{\left(\frac{a}{b^2}e^2\right)}$ &c. which may be proved by adding the quantities.

found, and the roots of the several products will be the remaining parts of the quotient required.

$\frac{18}{9} = 2$, $\sqrt{9} = 3$, $3 = 1 + 2$, $1^2 = 1$, $2^2 = 4$, $1 \times 2 = 2$, $4 \times 2 = 8$.

$\sqrt{2}$ and $\sqrt{8}$ are the remaining parts of the quotient.

SECT IV.

On the Squares of Surds.

Multiply the surds by themselves.—(Here follow examples).—The squares are found by multiplying the surds in the common way.

SECT. V.

On finding the Square Roots of the Squares of Surds.*

"If the square is of one surd or more, and I would find its root; first I take the "square of the numbers that are with it, and subtract these squares from it. "Accordingly after subtraction something may remain. I take the root of what- "ever remains, add it in one place to the original number, and in another sub- "tract it from the same. Halve both the results, and two roots will be obtained. "I then re-examine the squares of the surds to know whether any square remains

---

* Let $a + \sqrt{b} + \sqrt{c} + \sqrt{d}$, &c. be the square of a multinomial surd, a the sum of the squares of the roots, and $\sqrt{b} + \sqrt{c} + \sqrt{d} +$ &c. the product of the roots taken two and two. The number of roots being n, the number of terms in the square will be n^2, of which n will be the number of rational terms, and $n^2 - n$ the number of surd products. If we call the double products single terms, $\frac{n^2 - n}{2}$ will express the number of surd terms, and considering the sum of the rational terms as one term, the proposed square may be reduced to the form

$$(x + y + z + \&c.) + (2\sqrt{xy} + 2\sqrt{xz} + \&c.) + (2\sqrt{yz} + \&c.\ \&c.)$$

where $\sqrt{x} + \sqrt{y} + \sqrt{z} +$ &c. is the root of the square, and the surd terms of the square are divided into periods of $n - 1$, $n - 2$, $n - 3$, &c. as directed in the Beej Gunnit.

Supposing
$$\begin{aligned} x + y + z + \&c. &= Q \\ y + z + \&c. &= R \\ z + \&c. &= S \\ \&c. \quad &\&c. \end{aligned}$$

$$\sqrt{\frac{Q \pm \sqrt{(Q^2 - 4xR)}}{2}} = \sqrt{x} \text{ or } \sqrt{R}$$

$$\sqrt{\frac{R \pm \sqrt{(R^2 - 4yS)}}{2}} = \sqrt{y} \text{ or } \sqrt{S}$$

$$\sqrt{\frac{S \pm \sqrt{(S^2 - 4zT)}}{2}} = \sqrt{z} \text{ or \&c. and so on.}$$

"after the subtraction or not: if none remains these two are the roots required; "if any remains, that one of these two roots, to which the following rule cannot "be applied, is correct, and the other is the sum of two roots; from that root we "obtain the two roots required. The way of the operation is this, suppose that "root number, and take its square, and subtract from it the square which was "not subtracted at first, and take the root of the remainder; let this be added in "one place to the original number which we supposed, and subtracted from it in "another place, and halve both the results, two roots will be obtained. If then "these three are the roots required, the operation is ended, otherwise go on with "it in the same manner till all the roots are found; and if the first question is "of a number without a square of a surd, it may be solved by the operation "which was described at the end of division. And if in the square there are one "or more surds negative, suppose them affirmative, and proceed to the end with "the operation; and of the two roots found let one be negative."

Required the root of $5+\sqrt{24}$; $5^2=25$, $25-24=1$, $\sqrt{1}=1$, $5+1=6$; $5-1=4$, $\frac{6}{2}=3$ and $\frac{4}{2}=2$; and $\sqrt{3}+\sqrt{2}=\sqrt{(5+\sqrt{24})}$.

Another Example. Required the root of $10+\sqrt{24}+\sqrt{40}+\sqrt{60}$; $10^2=100$, $100-(24+40)=36$, $\sqrt{36}=6$, $10+6=16$, $10-6=4$, $\frac{16}{2}=8$, $\frac{4}{2}=2$, then we have $\sqrt{8}$ and $\sqrt{2}$. As 60 remains to be subtracted, one of these two numbers is one term of the root, and the other is the sum of two remaining terms (should be the root of the sum of the squares of the remaining terms). The rule is not applicable to 2, therefore 8 must be the sum of the terms. $8^2=64$, $64-60=4$, $\sqrt{4}=2$, $8+2=10$, $8-2=6$, $\frac{10}{2}=5$ and $\frac{6}{2}=3$. Wherefore $\sqrt{2}+\sqrt{3}+\sqrt{5}=\sqrt{(10+\sqrt{24}+\sqrt{40}+\sqrt{60})}$.

Another Example. Required the root of $16+\sqrt{24}+\sqrt{40}+\sqrt{48}+\sqrt{60}+\sqrt{72}+\sqrt{120}$; $16^2=256$, $256-(24+40+48)=144$, $\sqrt{144}=12$, $16+12=28$, $16-12=4$, $\frac{28}{2}=14$, $\frac{4}{2}=2$; we have then $\sqrt{14}$ and $\sqrt{2}$. As the rule does not apply to 2, 14 must be the sum of two remaining terms of the root. $14^2=196$, $196-(120+72)=4$, $\sqrt{4}=2$, $14+2=16$, $14-2=12$, $\frac{16}{2}=8$, $\frac{12}{2}=6$. One surd remaining, and the rule not being applicable to 6, 8 must be the sum of two terms. $8^2=64$, $64-60=4$, $\sqrt{4}=2$, $8+2=10$, $8-2=6$, $\frac{10}{2}=5$, and $\frac{6}{2}=3$. All the terms of the square having been brought down, the complete root is $\sqrt{6}+\sqrt{5}+\sqrt{3}+\sqrt{2}$.

Another Example. Required the root of 72: $72^2=5184$, $0^2=0$, $5184-0=5184$, $\sqrt{5184}=72$, $72+72=144$, $72-72=0$, $\frac{144}{2}=72$, $\frac{0}{2}=0$, $\sqrt{72}$ then is the root.

If instead of one term three terms are required, find them by the rule given in the section on division; divide by 36 which is a square number, $\frac{72}{36}=2$, $\sqrt{36}=6$, $6=3+2+1$, $3^2=9$, $2^2=4$, $1^2=1$, $9\times\frac{72}{36}=18$, $4\times\frac{72}{36}=8$, $1\times\frac{72}{36}=2$; therefore $\sqrt{72}=\sqrt{18}+\sqrt{8}+\sqrt{2}$. If three equal terms had been required, the root of the divisor must have been divided into three equal parts.

Another Example. It is required to find the difference of $\sqrt{3}$ and $\sqrt{7}$. The rule not being applicable to this case, suppose $\sqrt{7}$ affirmative, and $\sqrt{3}$ negative, the square of these numbers is $10-\sqrt{84}$. To determine the root of this, suppose 84 to be positive; $10^2=100$, $100-84=16$, $\sqrt{16}=4$, $10+4=14$, $10-4=6$, $\frac{14}{2}=7$, $\frac{6}{2}=3$. We have then $\sqrt{7}$ and $\sqrt{3}$, one of which must be *minus* because $\sqrt{84}$ was *minus*.

Another Example. Whether the root is $+\sqrt{2}+\sqrt{3}-\sqrt{5}$ or $-\sqrt{2}-\sqrt{3}+\sqrt{5}$ the square will be the same, viz. $10+\sqrt{24}-\sqrt{40}-\sqrt{60}$.

Let the root of this square be determined. $10^2=100$, $100-(40+60)=0$, $\sqrt{0}=0$, $10+0=10$, $10-0=10$, $\frac{10}{2}=5$, $\frac{10}{2}=5$. As $\sqrt{24}$ remains, $5^2=25$, $25-24=1$, $\sqrt{1}=1$, $5+1=6$, $5-1=4$, $\frac{6}{2}=3$, $\frac{4}{2}=2$. If $24+40$ is subtracted from 100 there remains 36, $\sqrt{36}=6$, $10+6=16$, $10-6=4$, $\frac{16}{2}=8$, $\frac{4}{2}=2$. As $\sqrt{60}$ remains $8^2=64$, $64-60=4$, $\sqrt{4}=2$, $8+2=10$, $8-2=6$, $\frac{10}{2}=5$, $\frac{6}{2}=3$. If $24+60$ is subtracted from 100 there remains 16. $\sqrt{16}=4$, $10+4=14$, $10-4=6$, $\frac{14}{2}=7$, $\frac{6}{2}=3$, $\sqrt{40}$ yet remaining, $7^2=49$, $49-40=9$, $\sqrt{9}=3$, $7+3=10$, $7-3=4$, $\frac{10}{2}=5$, $\frac{4}{2}=2$. The terms of the root are $\sqrt{2}$ and

$\sqrt{3}$ and $\sqrt{5}$. If 2 and 5, or 3 and 5 are both negative or both affirmative the operation will be the same; the only difference will be in the signs.

"If the root consists of one term* only, its square will be of the kind of "number; if of two terms, its square will be number and one surd; if the root "has three terms, the square will have one number and three surds; if it has four, "the square will have one number and six surds; if five, one number and ten "surds; and if six, one number and fifteen surds. The rule is, add the numbers "in the natural scale, from 1 to the number next below that which expresses "the number of terms in the root, the sum will shew the number of surds. For "the use of beginners is annexed a table in which the first column shews the "number of terms of the roots; the second column shews the number of surd "terms in the squares; and the third the number of rational terms in the "squares, from 1 to 9.

No. of terms in the root.	No. of surds in the square.	No. of rational terms in the squares.
1	0	1
2	1	1
3	3	1
4	6	1
5	10	1
6	15	1
7	21	1
8	28	1
9	36	1

* The number of surd terms in the square being $\frac{n^2 - 2}{2}$, is = the sum of the numbers in the natural scale from 1 to the number next below n.

" For numbers consisting of more terms than 9 the number of surds in the " squares may be found by the rule which has been given. If in the square there " are three surd terms, first subtract two of them from the square of the numbers " and afterwards subtract the third. If there are six surds, first subtract 3, then " 2, and so on; if there are 10 surds, first subtract 4; if 15, first 5; if 21, first 6; " if 28, first 7; if 36, first 8; and in general the number of surds of the square " will be found in the table in the column of roots next above the number " of its root. If they are not subtracted in the regular order, the result will be " wrong. The test of the operation of this: if either of the two numbers found " by the rule is multiplied by 4, and the number which was subtracted from the " square of the rational term is divided by the product, the quotient will be the " other number found, without any remainder. If either of those two numbers " is a correct term of the root, and the other the sum of two roots, the least, or " that which is the correct term, whether in number it be more or less than the " number of the sum of two roots, must be multiplied by 4, and every quantity " that has been subtracted must be divided by the products, the quotient will be " the numbers of the required roots from the second number. If, after this divi- " sion, there is any remainder the operation is wrong.

" The squares of all moofrid numbers* are made up either of rational numbers " alone, or of rational numbers and surds, as has been seen in the examples of the " section on squares.

" If a surd occurs there must be a moofrid number with it, otherwise its root " cannot be found. If a surd is divided into two:—For example, if $\sqrt{18}$ is " divided into $\sqrt{2}$ and $\sqrt{8}$, its root will have one term more than it would have " had regularly; and if two surds are united the root will have one term less. " These two operations of separation and union must be attended to and applied " whenever they are possible."

Example. Required the root of $10+\sqrt{32}+\sqrt{24}+\sqrt{8}$. From the square of 10 which is 100, subtract any two of the numbers under the radical signs, and the remainder will be irrational: the case is, therefore impossible. If we proceed contrary to the rule, by subtracting at once the three terms from 100, we shall have 36 the remainder, then $\sqrt{36}=6$, $10+6=16$, $10-6=4$, $\frac{16}{2}=8$, $\frac{4}{2}=2$. We

* Moofrid means simple as opposed to compound, but in the language of this science it is generally used to express a number having one significant figure.

find then $\sqrt{8}$ and $\sqrt{2}$, but these are not the true roots, for their square is 18. If we proceed contrary to the rule by finding a surd equal to two of the surds, as $\sqrt{72}$, which is the sum of $\sqrt{32}$ and $\sqrt{8}$, and extracting the root of $10+\sqrt{72}+\sqrt{24}$ we shall have for the two roots $\sqrt{6}$ and $\sqrt{4}$, but their square is not equal to the quantity whose root was required. The foregoing rules are illustrated by four more examples, which conclude this chapter.

CHAP. V *.

" To find the value of an unknown number, such that when it is multiplied by " a known number, and the product increased by a known number, and the sum " divided by a known number, nothing remains. Call the number by which the " unknown number is multiplied the dividend, the number which is added the " augment, and that by which the sum is divided the divisor. Find a number " which will divide these three numbers without a remainder. Perform the divi- " sion, and write the three quotients, giving each the same designation as the " number from which it was derived. Divide the dividend by the divisor, and " the divisor by the remainder of the dividend, and the remainder of the divi- " dend by the remainder of the divisor, and so on till one remains. Then let the " division be discontinued. Arrange all the quotients in a line, write the augment " below the line, and a cipher below the augment. Multiply the number above " the cipher; that is to say, the augment, by the number immediately above it, " and to the product add the cipher. Multiply the number thus found by the " number next above in the line, and to the product add the number above the " cipher, and so on till all the numbers in the line are exhausted. If of the two " numbers last found, the lower is applied according to the question, the number " above will be the quotient.

" To find the least values. Divide the value of y by a and call the remainder y. " Divide the value of x by b and call the remainder x. Multiply a by the value " of x and to the product add c. Divide the sum by b and the quotient will be " y without any remainder. And if to the first remainder we add a again and " again, and to the second remainder b as many times, we shall have new values " of x and y.

" This rule is applicable only when the number of quotients is even; when it is

* The rules given in this chapter are in effect the same as those which have been given by the modern European Algebraists for the solution of indeterminate problems of the first degree. Compare them with the process by continued fractions.

" odd proceed as follows. Having performed the operations directed above, sub- " tract the value of y from a and that of x from b. If a number cannot be found " to divide a, b, and c, without a remainder, but a number can be found to divide " a and c without a remainder, (supposing the reduction of these two instead of " that of the three which was directed by the foregoing rule) x will be brought " out right and y wrong. To find y right, multiply its value now found by the " divisor of a and c, and the product will be the true value of y. If c and b only " can be reduced by a common divisor, the value of x must be multiplied by the ' common divisor, and the quotient will be the true value of x. When c is — sub- " tract the value of x from b, and that of y from a."

" If the subtraction is possible let it be done, and the question is solved; if it " is impossible suppose the excess of the subtrahend above the minuend to be " negative. Multiply the minuend by a number, so that the product may be " greater than the negative quantity. From this product subtract the negative " quantity, and the remainder will be the number required.

" When a is — the same rule is to be observed; that is, subtract the values of x " and y from b and a. If c is + and greater than b reject b, and its multiples from " c till a number less than b remains. Note the number of times that b is rejected " from c; if there will be no remainder after rejection it is unnecessary to reject. " Go on with the operation, add the number of rejections to the value of y and " the sum will be its true value. The value of x will remain as before. If c is — " subtract the number of rejections from the value of y. If a and c are greater " than b reject b (or its multiples) from both; call the two remainders a and c " and proceed; x will come out right and y wrong. If there is no augment, or " if c divided by b leaves no remainder, x will be $= 0$, and y the quotient. If " the numbers are not reduced, but the quotients are taken from original num- " bers, x and y will always be brought out right. If the numbers are reduced, " x and y will be brought out right only when both are reduced, and but one of " them will be brought out right when both are not reduced."

Example. $a = 221$, $c = 65$, $b = 195$, dividing these numbers by 13 we have, $a' = 17$, $c' = 5$, $b' = 15$. Divide 17 by 15 (as above directed) continuing the division till the remainder is 1. The quotients are 1 and 7, write these in a line with c' below them, and 0 below c', thus: Multiply 5 by 7 the product is 35, add 0 the sum is 35. Multiply 35 by 1 the product is 35, add 5 the sum is 40. The two last numbers then are 40 and 35. From 40 throw out 17 twice,

1	40
7	35
5	
0	

6 remains; from 35 throw out 15 twice, 5 remains; therefore $x = 5$ and $y = 6$. $\frac{221 \times 5 + 65}{195} = 6$. $17 + 6 = 23$ is a new value of y, and $15 + 5 = 20$ a corresponding value of x, $2 \times 17 + 6 = 40$ is another value of y, and $2 \times 15 + 5 = 35$ a value of x. In like manner we shall have $3 \times 17 + 6 = 57$ and $3 \times 15 + 5 = 50$ new values of y and x, and so on without end.

Another Example. $a = 100$, $b = 63$, $c = 90$; c being $+$ or $-$. Although in this case 10 is a common divisor of a and c, yet as the reduction would give a wrong value of y, write a, b and c as they are, and proceed. We find the quotients 1, 1, 1, 2, 2, 1. Arrange them in a line with c below the last, and 0 below c, in this manner:

$$\begin{array}{c} 1 \\ 1 \\ 1 \\ 2 \\ 2 \\ 1 \\ \hline 90 \\ 0 \end{array}$$

We have then

$$\begin{array}{llll} 1 \times 90 & + 0 & = 90 \\ 2 \times 90 & + 90 & = 270 \\ 2 \times 270 & + 90 & = 630 \\ 1 \times 630 & + 270 & = 900 \\ 1 \times 900 & + 630 & = 1530 \\ 1 \times 1530 & + 900 & = 2430. \end{array}$$

The two last numbers are 1530 and 2430, divide the former by 63 and the latter by 100; the remainders are 18 and 30, therefore $x = 18$ and $y = 30$, $\frac{100 \times 18 + 90}{63} = 30$.

By another method. Divide 100 and 90 by 10, then $a' = 13$, $b = 63$, $c' = 9$; The quotients are now found 0, 6, 3, write them in a line with c' and 0 below; we have

$$\begin{array}{llll} 3 \times 9 & + 0 & = 27 \\ 6 \times 27 & + 9 & = 171 \\ 0 \times 171 & + 27 & = 27. \end{array}$$

The two last numbers are 27 and 171. From 27 throw out 10 twice, 7 remains: from 171 throw out 63 twice, 45 remains. The number of quotients being odd, subtract 45 from 63, the remainder 18 is the value of x. 7 subtracted from 10 gives 3 for y, which is not the true value. To find y correct, multiply 3 by the common divisor 10, the product 30 will be the true value of y.

Another way of solving the same question is this, find a common divisor of b and c, for example, 9. Dividing b and c by 9 we have $a = 100$, $b' = 7$, $c' = 10$. Perform the division and arrange the quotients in a line with c' and 0 below, the quotients will be found 14 and 3, then

$$3 \times 10 + 0 = 30$$
$$14 \times 30 + 10 = 430.$$

From 430 throw out 100 four times, 30 remains. Here we have found a true value of y and a wrong value of x. Multiply 2 by the common divisor 9, and the product 18 is the true value of x. This question may also be solved by first taking a common divisor of a and c, and afterwards a common divisor of b and c, as follows:

Reducing a and c we have $a' = 10$, $c' = 9$, and $b = 63$. Reducing b and c we have $a = 100$, $c' = 10$, $b' = 7$. Unite the reduced numbers thus; $a' = 10$, $b' = 7$; but c having undergone two reductions*, take the difference of the numbers arising from the two operations; then $a' = 10$; $b' = 7$, $c' = 1$, divide and arrange the quotients with c' and 0, as above directed, and we shall have

$$2 \times 1 + 0 = 2$$
$$1 \times 2 + 1 = 3.$$

3 and 2 are now found for x and y, but they are both wrong, for c was reduced both with b and a. 2 must be multiplied by 9 the common divisor of b and c, and 3 must be multiplied by 10 the common divisor of a and c; the true values will be $x = 18$, $y = 30$; and new values of y and x may be had by adding a and b again and again to those already found.

---

* Let $\frac{ax \pm c}{b} = y$, divide a and c by p, then $\frac{\frac{ax}{p} \pm \frac{c}{p}}{b} = \frac{y}{p}$, whence $\frac{b\frac{y}{p} \mp \frac{c}{p}}{\frac{a}{p}} = x$, now divide b and $\frac{c}{p}$ by q, then $\frac{\frac{b}{q} \times \frac{y}{p} \mp \frac{c}{pq}}{\frac{a}{p}} = \frac{x}{q}$. Taking *the difference* is only true in this case, because $pq = c$, and $p - q = 1$.

What has been said is applicable only when c is $+$. When c is $-$, subtract 18, which is the value of x, from 63, the remainder is 45; subtract 30, which is the valueof y from 100, there remains 70. We have in this case $x = 45$, $y = 70$. By adding a and b as above, new values of x and y may be found.

Another Example. Suppose $a = -60$, $b = 13$, and $c = 3 +$ or $-$. Without making any reduction, divide, and place the quotients with c and 0 as before, we have

$$\begin{aligned} 1 \times 3 + 0 &= 3 \\ 1 \times 3 + 3 &= 6 \\ 1 \times 6 + 3 &= 9 \\ 1 \times 9 + 6 &= 15 \\ 4 \times 15 + 9 &= 69. \end{aligned}$$

The last numbers are 69 and 15. From 69 throw out 60, 9 remains; from 15 throw out 13, 2 remains. The number of quotients being odd, subtract the value of x from 13, and that of y from 60, the remainders are 11 and 51. As 60 is $-$ the subtraction must be repeated, by which means we have as before $x = 2$ and $y = 9$. If c is $-$ subtract the value of x from b and that of y from a, and we shall have again $x = 11$ and $y = 51$.

Another Example. $a = 18$, $b = 11$, $c = -10$. Divide and arrange the quotients as before, we have

$$\begin{aligned} 1 \times 10 + 0 &= 10 \\ 1 \times 10 + 10 &= 20 \\ 1 \times 20 + 10 &= 30 \\ 1 \times 30 + 20 &= 50. \end{aligned}$$

From 50 reject 18, and from 30, 11; the remainders are 14 and 8. c being $-$ subtract 8 from 11 and 14 from 18; whence $x = 3$ and $y = 4$.

Another Example. $a = 5$, $b = 3$, $c = 23$. Proceeding as before, we shall have

$$\begin{aligned} 1 \times 23 + 0 &= 23 \\ 1 \times 23 + 23 &= 46. \end{aligned}$$

As 3 can be rejected but 7 times from 23, reject 5, 7 times from 46, the remainders are 2 and 11. If c is $-$ subtract 2 from 3 there remains 1, and 11 from 5 there remains -6. Here twice 5 must be added to -6, the sum 4 is the value of y: and that the numbers may correspond add twice 3 to 1; the sum 7 is the value of x, If c is greater than b, reject b from c. Throw out 3 seven

times from 23, there remains 2. Make $c' = 2$ and place it with 0 under the line of quotients, we find
$$1 \times 2 + 0 = 2$$
$$1 \times 2 + 2 = 4.$$

2 is the true value of x, and 4 which is found for the value of y is wrong. Add 7 the divisor of c to 4, the sum 11 is the true value of y. If c is — subtract 2 from 3, and 4 from 5, and we shall have 1 for the value of x which is right, and 1 for the value of y which is wrong. Subtract 7 from the value of y, the difference is -6; add twice 5 to -6, and we shall have 4 the true value of y.

That the numbers may correspond, twice 3 must in like manner be added to 1, and 7 will be the true value of x.

Another Example. $a = 5$, $b = 13$, $c = 0$, or $c = 65$; the quotients are 0, 2, 1, 1; place them in a line with c and 0 below, we shall have
$$1 \times 0 + 0 = 0$$
$$1 \times 0 + 0 = 0$$
$$2 \times 0 + 0 = 0$$
$$0 \times 0 + 0 = 0.$$

Add 5 to 0, which stands for the value of y, and 13 to that which stands for the value of x, we have then $y = 5$ and $x = 13$. In the second case $a=5$, $b=13$, $c = 65$. As b measures c, x will be found $= 0$ and $y = 0$. To the value of y add 5, which is the number of times b is rejected from c, and this will give a correct value of y, for $\frac{5 \times 0 + 65}{13} = 5$. Adding 13 to 0 which is the value of x, we shall have $x = 13$, and adding 5 to 5 which is the value of y, $y = 10$, for $\frac{5 \times 13 + 65}{13} = 10$.

Another method is to suppose $c = 1$, and proceed as above directed. Multiply the values of x and y, which will be so found by c, rejecting a from the value of y and b from that of x, the remainders will be the numbers required.

Example. $a = 221$, $b = 195$, $c = 65$; dividing these numbers by 13, their common divisor, we have $a' = 17$, $b' = 15$, $c' = 5$. For 5 write one, and finding the quotients as above, arrange them with 1 and 0 below, then
$$7 \times 1 + 0 = 7$$
$$1 \times 7 + 1 = 8$$

Multiply 8 and 7 by 5, the products are 40 and 35; rejecting 17 twice from 40.

and 15 twice from 35, the remainders are 6 and 5; whence $x = 5$ and $y = 6$. If c is — subtract 7 from 15 and 8 from 17, 8 and 9 remain. Multiply these numbers by 5, the products are 40 and 45; 15 and 17 being twice rejected, $x = 10$ and $y = 11$. By subtracting 6 from 17, and 5 from 15, the same numbers will be found.

" Know that the operation of the multiplicand is of use in many examples *, " as, if by the rule I shall have brought it out and any one destroys it, and some " remains; by the operation of the multiplicand, I can determine the numbers " which have been destroyed from that which remains.

" In the operation of the multiplicand of a mixed nature, the multiplicand is " of another kind, and it is called the multiplicand of addition, and that relates " to determining the value of an unknown number, which being multiplied by " a known number, and the product divided by a known number, there will re- " main a known number: and again, if the same unknown number is multiplied " by another number, and the product divided by the former divisor, the re- " mainder after division will be another number. Call the numbers by which the " unknown is multiplied the multiplicand, and that by which it is divided the " divisor, and that which is left after division the remainder. Here then are two " multiplicands, one divisor and two remainders. The method of solution is as " follows: add the two multiplicands together and call the sum the dividend. " Add the two remainders and call the sum the augment negative; leave the " divisor as it is; then proceed according to the rules which have been given: " but the values of x and y must be subtracted from b and a, x will be found " right, and y wrong."

Example. $\text{A} = 5$, $\text{C} = 7$, $a = 10$, $c = 14$, $b = 63$, $\frac{\text{A}x}{b} = y + \text{C}$, and $\frac{ax}{b} = z + c$, $\text{A} + a = 15$, $\text{C} + c = 21$, we have now $a' = 15$, $b' = 63$, $c' =$

* At this place Mr. Burrow's copy has " and besides this it is of great use in determining the signs and " minutes and seconds." And in the margin there is an example by the same commentator, apparently thus: " I give an example which comes under this rule; a star makes 37 revolutions of the heavens in 49 days and " nights; how many will it make in 17 days?" Then the writer goes on to say the answer is 12 rev., 10 s., 1°, 13', 28" $\frac{8}{49}$, which is got I suppose by proportion. Now he adds, " if all this were lost except $\frac{8}{49}$ it might be restored by the rule. He then gives the equation $\frac{60x - 8}{49} = y$ from which x is found $= 23$ and $y = 28''$, then from $\frac{60x' - 23}{49} = y'$ he finds x' and y', and so on till the whole is had.

-21, we find 0 and 4 $\begin{matrix} 4 \times 7 + 0 = 28 \\ 0 \times 28 + 7 = 7 \end{matrix}$, $7 - 5 = 2$, $28 - 21 = 7$, $5 - 2 = 3 = y$ wrong; $21 - 7 = 14 = x$ right; for multiplying 14 by 5 the product is 70, which being divided by 63 leaves the remainder 7; and multiplying 14 by 10, and dividing the product by 63, the remainder 14 is obtained.

CHAP. VI.

"On * the operation of multiplication of the square; and that relates to the "knowing of a square, such that when it is multiplied by a number, and to the "product a number is added, the sum will be a square.

"In this question then there are two squares, one less and the other greater, "and a multiplicand and an augment. From the multiplicand and augment "known, the two unknown squares are to be found. The method of solution "is this: Assume a number and call it the less root; take its square and mul- "tiply it by the multiplicand, and find a number which when added to it or "subtracted from it will be a square; then take its root and call it the greater "root. Write on a horizontal line these three, the less and greater roots, and the "number which was assumed as the augment. And again write such another "line under the former so that every number may be written twice, once "above and below; then multiply crossways the two greater roots by the two "less; then take the sum of the two and call it the less root; then take the "rectangle of the two less roots and multiply it by the multiplicand, add the

---

* The rules at the beginning of this chapter for the general solution of $Ax^2 + B = y^2$ are, as they stand in the Persian, to this purport: Find $Af^2 + \beta = g^2$, where f, β, and g may be any numbers which will satisfy the equation. Make $x' = fg + fg$ and $y' = Aff + gg$, and $\beta' = \beta\beta$. Then $Ax'^2 + \beta' = y'^2$; and making $x'' = x'g + y'f$, and $y'' = Ax'f + y'g$, and $\beta'' = \beta'\beta$, or $x'' = x'g - y'f$ and $y'' = y'g - Ax'f$, we have $Ax''^2 + \beta'' = y''^2$. If $\beta'' > B$ then $\frac{\beta''}{p^2} = B$, and if $\beta'' < B$, then $\beta'' p^2 = B$, but in the first case the values of x'' and y'' must be divided, and in the second case multiplied by p. In this way, by the cross multiplication of the numbers, new solutions are had for $Ax^2 + B = y^2$. When $\beta = 1$ and $\beta' = B$ the rule is the same as Fermat's proposition, which first was applied in this manner by Euler for finding new values of x and y in the equation $Ax^2 + b = y^2$. (See the investigation of this method in his algebra.) If $Ax^2 + B = y^2$, then $x = \frac{2r}{r^2 - A}$, r being any number: this expression is true only when $B = 1$. In that case $A\left(\frac{2r}{r^2 - A}\right)^2 + 1 = \left(\frac{r^2 + A}{r^2 - A}\right)^2$ which is the same as Lord Brouncker's solution of Fermat's problem.

" product to the rectangle of the two greater roots, the result will be the greater " root, and the rectangle of the two augments will be the augment.

" And to find another square in the same condition write on a horizontal line " the less root and the greater root, and the augment, which have been found, " below the less and greater roots, and the agument which were assumed. Per- " form the same operations as before, and what was required will be obtained.

" And another method in the operation is, after multiplying crossways to take " the difference of the two greater roots, it will be the less root. And having " multiplied the rectangle of the two less roots by the multiplicand, note the pro- " duct; then take the rectangle of the two greater roots, and the difference of " these two will be the greater root.

" And know that this augment, that is, the augment of the operation, if it is " the same as the original augment, is what was required. Otherwise, if it is " greater, divide it by the square of an assumed number, that the original aug- " ment may be obtained. If it is less multiply it by the square of an assumed " number, that the original augment may be obtained. And that they may corres- " pond in the first case divide the greater and less roots, by that assumed number, " and in the second case multiply them by the same number.

" And a third method is this: Assume a number and divide its double by the " difference of the multiplicand and its square, the less root will be obtained. " And if we multiply the square of it by the multiplicand, and add the augment " to the result, the root of the sum will be the greater root.

Example *. " What square is that which being multiplied by 8, and the pro- " duct increased by 1, will be a square. Here then are two squares, one less and " one greater, and 8 is the multiplicand and 1 the augment. Suppose 1 the less " root, its square which is 1 we multiply by 8; it is 8. We find 1 which added " to 8 will be a square, that is 9. Let its root which is 3 be the greater " root. Write these three, that is to say, the less and greater roots, and the

---

* To find x and y so that $8x^2+1=y^2$. Suppose $f=1$, and $8f^2+\beta=\square$. Let $\beta=1$, then $8f^2+1=9=3^2$; $3\times1+3\times1=6=x$. $1\times1\times8+3\times3=17=y$, $1\times1=1$ the augment; 1 being the original augment there is no occasion to carry the operation farther. $8\times36+1=289=17^2$. For new values, $3\times6+1\times17=35=x$, $1\times6\times8+3\times17=99=y$. $1\times1=1$ the augment. $8\times35^2+1=9801=99^2$. In like manner more values may be found.

" augment on a horizontal line; and write these numbers below in the same " manner, thus:

Less	Greater	Augment
1	3	1
1	3	1

" Multiply the two greater roots crossways by the two less, it is the same as it " was before; add the two, it is 6; and this is the less root. Take the rectangle of " the two less roots, it is 1. Multiply it by 8, it is the same 8; add it to the rect- " angle of the two greater roots, that is 9; it is 17, and this is the greater root. " Take the rectangle of the two augments; it is 1. As it is according to the ori- " ginal there is no occasion to work for the original augment. The square re- " quired is 36, which multiplied by 8 is 288; adding 1 it becomes 289, and this " is a square whose root is 17. Again, to find a number under the same con- " ditions. Below the less and greater roots and first augment, write the less and " greater roots and augment which have been obtained by the operation, thus:

Less	Greater	Augment
1	3	1
6	17	1

" Multiply crossways the two greater and the two less roots, that is 3 by 6, and 17 by 1, it is thus:

Less	Greater	Augment
1	18	1
6	17	1

"Add the two greater roots; it is 35, and this is the less root. Take the rect-
"angle of the two less roots; it is 6. Multiply it by 8, the multiplicand; add the
"product which is 48 to the rectangle of the two greater roots 3 and 17, which
"is 51, it is 99, and this is the greater root. Take the rectangle of the two
"augments; it is the original augment; for when the square of 35, which is 1225,
"is multiplied by 8, it will be 9800; adding 1 it will be a square, viz. 9801, the
"root of which is 99. In like manner if the two roots and the augment are
"written below the two roots and the other augment; like 6 and 17 and 1, and
"the operation is performed we shall find what we require, and another number
"will be obtained.

Another Example. "What square is that which being multiplied by 11, and
"the product increased by 1, will be a square *? Suppose 1 the less root, and
"multiply its square, which is 1 by 11; it is 11. Find a number which being
"subtracted from it, the remainder will be a square: Let the number be 2; this
"then is the negative augment, and 3 which is the root of 9 is the greater root.
"Write it thus:

Less	Greater	Augment
1	3	2
1	3	2

---

* $11x^2+1=y^2$. Suppose $f=1$ and $11f^2-\beta=\square$. Let $\beta=2$. $11\times1-2=9=3^2$. $3\times1+3\times1=6=x$. $1\times1\times11+3\times3=20=y$. $-2\times-2=+4$. $\frac{4}{2^2}=1$ the original augment.

Therefore $\frac{20}{2}=10=y$. $\frac{6}{2}=3=x$. For $11\times9+1=100=10^2$.

Another way. Suppose $f=1$ and $11f^2+\beta=\square$. Let $\beta=5$. $11\times1+5=16=4^2$. $4\times1+4\times1=8=x$. $1\times1\times11+4\times4=27=y$. $5\times5=25$ the augment. $\frac{8}{5}=x$, $\frac{27}{5}=y$. $11\times\left(\frac{8}{5}\right)^2+1=\frac{729}{25}=\left(\frac{27}{5}\right)^2$.

For new values, $10\times\frac{8}{5}+3\times\frac{27}{5}=\frac{161}{5}=x$. $3\times\frac{8}{5}\times11+10\times\frac{27}{5}=\frac{534}{5}=y$. $1\times1=1$, the augment. $11\times\left(\frac{161}{5}\right)^2+1=\frac{285156}{25}=\left(\frac{534}{5}\right)^2$. By the second method, $\frac{81}{5}-\frac{80}{5}=\frac{1}{5}=x$. $\frac{270}{5}-11\times\frac{24}{5}=\frac{6}{5}=y$. 1 the augment. $11\times\left(\frac{1}{5}\right)^2+1=\frac{36}{25}=\left(\frac{6}{5}\right)^2$. In the same way other values may be found.

" Multiply crossways, and add the two greater, it is 6; and this is the less " root. Take the rectangle of the two less roots; it is 1. Multiply by 11; it is 11. " Add it to the rectangle of the two greater which is 9; it is 20, and this is the " greater root. Take the rectangle of the augments, it is 4 affirmative. Now " we have found a number such that when we divide this number by the square " of that, the quotient will be the original augment. We have found 2 and per- " formed the operation; 1 is obtained. And we divide the greater root which " is 20 by 2, 10 is the greater root. And we divide the less root, 3 is the less " root. For if the square of 3 which is 9 is multiplied by 11, it will be 99, and " when we add 1 it will be 100, and this is the square of 10 which was the " greater root.

" Another method is, suppose 1 the less root, and multiply its square by 11, " it is 11. We find 5 which being added to it will be a square, that is 16; its root " which is 4 is the greater root, thus:

Less	Greater	Augment
1	4	5
1	4	5

" After multiplying crossways, add the two rectangles; it is 8, and this is the " less root, and the rectangle of the two less; which is 1 we multiply by 11, it is " 11; add it to the rectangle of the two greater which is 16; it is 27, and this is " the greater root. And from the rectangle of the augments, 25 augment is " obtained. We have found an assumed number 5, such that when the aug- " ment is divided by its square the quotient will be 1. And for correspondence " we divide 8 by 5; 8 fifths is the less root. And we divide 27 by 5; 27-fifths " is obtained for the greater root. For multiplying the square of 8-fifths, that is " 64 twenty fifth parts by 11, it is 704 twenty fifth parts; add 1 integer that is " 25. It is 729 of the abovementioned denomination. And to find other " numbers under the same conditions, write the two roots and the other augment " below these two roots and augment, and that is on the supposition of 3 and 10 " and 1, which were obtained before, thus:

Less	Greater	Augment
$\frac{8}{5}$	$\frac{27}{5}$	1
		1
3	10	1

" After multiplying crossways, add the two rectangles, it is 161-fifths, and " this is the less root. Multiply the less rectangle, which is 24-fifths, by 11, it is " 264; add it to the rectangle of the two greater, which is 270-fifths, it is 534-" fifths, and this is the greater root. Take the rectangle of the augments, it is 1. " The operation is finished, for multiplying the square of 161-fifths, which is " 25921 twenty-fifth parts, by 11, it is 285131 twenty-fifth parts; add 25 that " is 1 integer, it is 285156, and this is the square of 534-fifths.

" And by the second method. After multiplying crossways it is 81-fifths and " 80-fifths; the difference is 1-fifth, and this 1-fifth is the less root. Multiply the " rectangle of the two less, which is 24-fifths, by 11, it is 264-fifths; and the rect-" angle of the two greater is 270-fifths. Take the difference; it is 6-fifths; and " this is the greater root; and 1 integer is the augment. The square of 1-fifth, " which is 1 twenty-fifth part, multiplied by 11, is 11 twenty-fifth parts; add 25, " it is 36 twenty-fifth parts, the root of which is 6-fifths; and in like manner " any number which is wanted may be obtained.

Example. " Let the first question be solved by the third method *: Suppose " 3 the less root, and take the difference of its square and the multiplicand which " is 8; it is 1. Divide twice 3 by 1; it is 6; and this is the less root. For mul-" tiplying the square of this, which is 36, by 8, it is 288; add 1, it is 289, and " this is a square, the root of which is 17, and this is the greater root.

" Another method is what is called the operation of circulation †. To bring

* To solve the first question by the third method. Suppose $r = 3$, $\frac{2 \times 3}{9 - 8} = 6 = x$. $8 \times 36 + 1 = 289 = 17^2$. $17 = y$.

† تدوير to make to go round, from دور to go round. This rule is, supposing $Ax^2 + B = y^2$. A and B being given to find x and y by the operation of circulation. Find f, β and g so that $Af^2 + \beta = g^2$. Suppose

"out that which is required by the rule of the multiplicand. It is thus: After "supposing the less and greater roots and the augment, suppose the less root the "dividend, and the augment the divisor, and the greater root the augment. "Then by the rule of the multiplicand which is passed, bring out the multipli- "cand and the quotient. If that number by which the questioner multiplied the "square can be subtracted from the square of this multiplicand, let it be done; "otherwise subtract the square of this multiplicand from that number of the mul- "tiplicand. If a small number remains, well; if not increase the multipli- "cand thus: add the divisor again and again to the multiplicand as before "explained, till it is so that you can subtract the number of the multipli- "cand from the square of it, or the square of it from the number of the mul- "tiplicand. Whatever remains we divide by the augment of the operation of "multiplication of the square, and take the quotient which will be the augment "of the operation of multiplication of the square. If then we shall have sub- "tracted the multiplicand from the square, let the quotient remain as it is: and "if we shall have subtracted the square from the multiplicand it will be contrary, "that is, if negative it will become affirmative, and if affirmative negative; and "that quotient which was obtained by adding the dividend to the quotient, as "many times as the divisor was added to the multiplicand, will be the less root;

$\frac{fX+g}{\beta} = Y$ and from the known numbers f, g, β, find X and Y by the rules which have been given. If X^2 be $>$ A take $X^2 - A$, or if not take $A - X^2$. If a small number remains it is well, otherwise take multiples of β, and add them to the found value of X for a new value, till we have $(m\beta + X)^2 - A$, or $A - (m\beta + X)^2$: divide this by β, and if the square has been subtracted change the sign of the quotient. If instead of X the value $m\beta + X$ has been used a corresponding value of Y, $mf + Y$ must be taken: by substituting these values as follows: Y, or $mf + Y = x'$, and $\frac{X^2 \backsim A}{\beta}$ or $\frac{(m\beta + X)^2 \backsim A}{\beta} = \beta'$, we have the solution of this equation $Ax'^2 + \beta' = y'^2$. If β' is neither $=$ B nor to Bp^2 nor to $\frac{B}{p^2}$ proceed as before. Let $Af'^2 + \beta' = g'^2$ be a solution of $Ax'^2 + \beta' = y'^2$ where f', β' and g' are known. Suppose $\frac{f'X' + g'}{\beta'} = Y'$; proceed as before, and solutions will be had for $Ax''^2 + \beta'' = y''^2$, and in like manner for $A\overset{n}{x}{}^2 + \overset{n}{\beta} = \overset{n}{y}{}^2$ till $\overset{n}{\beta}$ is found $=$ B or Bp^2 or $\frac{B}{p^2}$. The truth of this is plain, for as $x' = \frac{fX + g}{\beta}$ and $\beta' = \frac{X^2 - A}{\beta}$, we have $Ax'^2 + \beta' = A\left(\frac{fX + g}{\beta}\right)^2 + \frac{X^2 - A}{\beta}$ which is $= \frac{(Af^2 + \beta)X^2 + 2AfgX + A(g^2 - \beta)}{\beta^2}$; but $Af^2 + \beta = g^2$, and $g^2 - \beta = Af^2$, and therefore $Ax' + \beta' = \frac{g^2X^2 + 2AfgX + A^2f^2}{\beta^2}$ which is $= \left(\frac{gX + Af}{\beta}\right)^2 = y'^2$. This rule, though in some respects imperfect, is in principle the same as that for solving the problem in integers by the application of continued fractions, which was first given in Europe by De La Grange.

" and from the less root and the augment bring out the greater root. If then this " augment shall have been found a square *, the operation is finished; for find " a number by the square of which, if we divide this augment, the result will be " the original augment, when this augment is greater than the original augment; " or otherwise, if we multiply by it, the result will be the original augment, in " the same manner as before. And if it is not a square perform the operation " again in the same manner; that is, supposing the less root the dividend, and " the augment the divisor and the greater root the augment; and work as be- " fore till the original augment or the augment of the square is found.

Example. " What square is that which being multiplied by 67, and the pro- " duct increased by 1, will be a square †. Let us suppose 1 the less root, mul-

---

* I suppose it should be $\text{B}p^2$ or $\frac{\text{B}}{p^2}$. I think it likely that this does not form a part of the original rule which seems to relate to integer values only.

† $67x^2 + 1 = y^2$. Suppose $f = 1$ and $\beta = -3$, then $67 \times 1^2 - 3 = \square = 64 = 8^2$, we have now $\text{A}f^2 + \beta = g^2$, where $f = 1$ and $\beta = -3$, and $g = 8$. Suppose $\frac{f\text{X} + g}{3} = \text{Y}$; that is to say, $\frac{1\text{X} + 8}{3} = \text{Y}$, reject twice β from g we have $8 - 2 \times 3 = 2$ and work for X and Y in $\frac{1\text{X} + 2}{3} = \text{Y}$. Divide 1 by 3, as directed in the last chapter. The quotient is 0, write under it 2 and 0, we find $\text{X} = 2$ and $\text{Y} = 0$. The number of quotients being odd, subtract the value of x from β and that of y from f. $3 - 2 = 1 = \text{X}$, $1 - 0 = 1 = \text{Y}$. As β was rejected twice from g, add 2 to the value of Y. $1 + 2 = 3 = \text{Y}$ we have now $\text{X} = 1$ and $\text{Y} = 3$. As we cannot subtract 67 from 1^2, and as a greater number will remain if we subtract 1^2 from 67, add twice β to X for a new value of X, $2 \times 3 + 1 = 7 = \text{X}$, and for a corresponding value of Y add twice f to Y. $2 \times 1 + 3 = 5 = \text{Y}$. $\text{A} - \text{X}^2$ or $67 - 7^2 = 18$. $\frac{18}{-3} = -6$. As we have taken $\text{A} - \text{X}^2$ we must change the sign of -6, it becomes $+6 = \beta'$, and $\text{Y} = x'$, we have now $\text{A}x'^2 + \beta' = y'^2$, where $\text{A} = 67$, $\beta' = 6$, and $x' = 5$, whence $y' = 41$. Since $\text{B} = 1$ and $\beta' = 6$ we proceed to find $\overset{n}{\beta} = \text{B}$. Let $\text{A}f'^2 + \beta' = g'^2$ where $f' = 5$, $\beta' = 6$, and $g' = 41$. Make $\frac{5\text{X}' + 41}{6} = \text{Y}'$, we shall find $\text{X}' = 41$ and $\text{Y}' = 41$. Subtract f' 6 times from the value of Y', $41 - 6 \times 5 = 11 = \text{Y}'$, and subtract β' the same number of times from the value of X'. $41 - 6 \times 6 = 5 = \text{X}'$. $\text{A} - \text{X}'^2$ or $67 - 5^2 = 42$; $\frac{42}{6} = 7 = \beta''$. As we have taken $\text{A} - \text{X}'^2$ the sign of 7 must be changed, and $-7 = \beta''$, and $11 = \text{Y}'' = x''$; therefore $\text{A}x''^2 + \beta'' = y''^2$, and $y'' = 90$, β'' not being $= \text{B}$ we must proceed as above. Let $\text{A}f''^2 + \beta'' = g''^2$, where $f'' = 1$, $\beta'' = -7$, and $g'' = 90$. Make $\frac{11\text{X}'' + 90}{7} = \text{Y}''$, reject 7 twelve times from 90, $90 - 84 = 6$, we shall find $\text{X}'' = 12$, and $\text{Y}'' = 18$. Subtract f'' from the value of Y'' and β'' from that of X'', $18 - 11 = 7 = \text{Y}''$, $12 - 7 = 5 = x''$. The number of quotients in the division of 11 by 7 being odd, subtract the value of Y'' from f'' and that of X'' from β'', $11 - 7 = 4 = \text{Y}''$, $7 - 5 = 2 = \text{X}''$. As we cannot take 67 from 2^2, and as a greater number remains, if we subtract 2^2 from 67, add β'' once to X'' for a new value of X'', $7 + 2 = 9 = \text{X}''$; $\text{X}''^2 - \text{A}$, or $9^2 - 67 = 14$. $\frac{14}{-7} = -2 = \beta'''$. As β'' was rejected 12 times from g'', 12 must be added to the value of Y, $4 + 12 = 16 = \text{Y}''$.

"tiply it by 67, it is 67. Find 3 the number of the augment, which sub-
"tracted from 67 will leave a square, that is 64, the root of which is 8, and this
"is the greater root. 1 then is the less root, and 8 the greater root, and 3 the
"augment negative. If we wish to bring it out by the operation of circulation, let
"us suppose 1 the dividend, and 8 the augment, and 3 the divisor. As rejection
"of the divisor from the augment is possible, reject it twice, 2 remains. Sup-
"pose this the augment, take the numbers of the line, cipher is obtained. Write
"under it 2 the augment and cipher. Perform the operation, the multiplicand is
"found 2 and the quotient cipher. The number of the line being odd, subtract
"the multiplicand and the quotient from the divisor and the dividend, 1 and 1
"are obtained. As we rejected the divisor which is 3 from the augment which is
"8, add 2 to the quotient, the quotient is 3 and the multiplicand 1. As we
"cannot subtract 67 which is the multiplicand of the operation of multiplication
"of the square, from the square of this multiplicand, and if we subtract the
"square of this from 67 a greater number remains; from necessity we add the
"divisor, which is 3, twice to the multiplicand 1, it is 7; add the dividend to
"the quotient it is 5. Subtract the square of 7, which is 49, from 67, 18 re-
"mains. Divide by the augment of the operation of multiplication of the
"square, which is 3 negative, 6 negative is the quotient. As the square has
"been subtracted from the multiplicand the negative becomes contrary; it is
"6 affirmative, and this is the augment; and 5, which was the number of
"the quotient, is the less root. Then bring out the greater root, from the less
"root and the augment, and the multiplicand 67, it is 41. Write them in order.
"As 6 is the augment of the operation and 1 is the original augment, perform the
"operation again to find the original augment: that is to say, suppose 5 the
"dividend, and 6 the divisor, and 41 the augment, and perform the operation of
"the multiplicand, the multiplicand is found 41 and the quotient also 41. Sub-
"tract 5, the dividend, 6 times from 41, the quotient, 11 remains; and subtract
"6 the same number of times from 41, the multiplicand, 5 remains; take its

---

And as β'' was added once to the value of x'' add f'' to that of y'', $11 + 16 = 27 = y'' = x'''$. Now $Af'''^2 + \beta''' = g'''^2$, because $x''' = 27$, and $\beta''' = -2$, therefore $y''' = 221$. Let $Af'''^2 + \beta''' = g'''^2$, where $f''' = 21$, $\beta''' = -2$, and $g''' = 221$. Having now found β''', which, multiplied by itself will be the augment of the square, (meaning, I suppose, $= Bp^2$) apply the first rule of this chapter. $x'''' = 2f'''g''' = 11934$, $y'''' = g'''^2 + Af'''^2 = 97684$, $\beta'''^2 = 4$, we find $p = 2$ such that $\frac{\beta''''}{p^2} = B = 1$. Dividing $Ax''''^2 + \beta'''' = y''''^2$ by p^2, we have $\left(A\frac{x''''}{p}\right)^2 + 1 = \left(\frac{y''''}{p}\right)^2$, and $67 \times 5967^2 + 1 = 48842^2$.

“ square, it is 25 ; subtract it from 67, 42 remains. Divide it by 6, the augment,
“ 7 is the quotient, and this is the augment. As we subtracted the square of the
“ multiplicand from 67, it is contrary ; 7 then is the augment negative ; and 11
“ which is the quotient, the less root; bringing out the greater root, it is 90.
“ In this case too the original augment is not obtained. Again, perform the oper-
“ ation of the multiplicand ; 11 is the dividend, 90 the augment, and 7 the di-
“ visor. The divisor can be rejected 12 times from the augment ; reject it ; 6
“ remains. Take the line, and perform the rest of the operation ; 18 is the
“ quotient and 12 the multiplicand, thus:

1	18
1	12
1	6
6	

“ Subtract 11, the dividend, from 18, and 7, the divisor, from 12 ; 7 and 5
“ are obtained, the quotient and the multiplicand. As the number of the line
“ was odd subtract 7 from 11 and 5 from 7 ; 4 is the quotient and 2 the multi-
“ plicand. As we cannot subtract 67 from the square of 2 ; and after subtract-
“ ing the square of 2 from 67 a greater number remains, add once the divisor
“ which is 7 to the dividend ; it is 9. Subtract 67 from its square which is 81 ;
“ 14 remains. Divide by 7 the augment negative, 2 negative is the quotient,
“ and this is the augment. Again, as we rejected 7 twelve times from the
“ augment, add 12 to the quotient which is 4 ; it is 16. And as we added 7 to
“ 2 the multiplicand, add 11 to 16 the quotient ; it is 27, and this is the less root.
“ Find the greater root ; it is 221. As an augment is obtained which, after being
“ multiplied into itself, will be the augment of the square, we write this line
“ below that, and multiply crossways in both places. From one cross multiplica-
“ tion it is 5967, add these two ; 11934 is obtained the less root. And the
“ greater root is 97684, and the augment is 4 affirmative. We have found 2 an
“ assumed number, by the square of which, if we divide this augment of the
“ operation, the quotient will be 1, which is the original augment. In like

" manner we divide 11934 by 2, 5967 is the less root, and 48842 is the greater " root.

Another Example. " What square is that which being multiplied by 61, and " the product increased by 1, will be a square*. Let 1 be the less root; 8 is the " greater; and 3 the augment, affirmative. Applying the operation of the multi- " plicand, it is thus:

Dividend.	Divisor.	Augment.
1	3	8

" Reject the divisor twice from the augment, 2 remains; and after the operation " 2 the multiplicand, and cipher the quotient are obtained. As the line is odd " we subtract cipher from the dividend and 2 from the divisor. It is 1 and 1. " As we rejected the divisor twice from the augment, we add 2 to the quotient. " The quotient is 3 and the multiplicand 1. If we subtract the square of the " multiplicand which is 1 from 61, a greater number remains. We therefore add " twice the dividend and the divisor to the quotient and the multiplicand. The

---

* $61x^2+1=y^2$. Let $\text{A}f^2+\beta=g^2$, where $f=1$, $\beta=3$, $g=8$. Make $\frac{fx+g}{\beta}=\text{Y}$ that is $\frac{1\text{X}+8}{3}=\text{Y}$, reject β twice from g, $8-2\times3=2$, we shall find $\text{X}=2$ and $\text{Y}=0$. The number of quotients in the division of 1 by 3 being odd, subtract the value of Y from f, and that of X from β, $1-0=1=\text{Y}$, $2-1=1=\text{X}$. As β was rejected twice from g add 2 to the value of Y, $1+2=\text{Y}$. If we take $\text{A}-\text{X}^2$ a greater number remains; add twice f to the value of Y, and twice β to that of X. $3+2\times1=5=\text{Y}$. $1+2\times3=7=\text{X}$. Take $\text{A}-\text{X}^2$, $61-7^2=12$. Divide by β, $\frac{12}{3}=4$, which becomes $-4=\beta'$, and $5=\text{Y}=x'$. Now $\text{A}x'^2+\beta'=y'^2$, whence $y'=39$. Let $\text{A}f'^2+\beta'=g'^2$ where $f'=5$, $\beta'=-4$, $g'=39$. As β' is not $=\text{B}$, we find a number $p=2$, such that $\frac{\beta'}{p^2}=-1$. Divide x' and y' by p, and we have $\frac{x'}{p}=\frac{5}{2}=x''=f''$, and $\frac{y'}{p}=\frac{39}{2}=y''=g''$, and $\frac{\beta'}{p}=-1=\beta''$. As $\text{B}=+1$, apply the first rule of this chapter, $\beta''\times\beta''=-1\times-1=+1=\text{B}$. $2f''g''=2\times\frac{5}{2}\times\frac{39}{2}=\frac{390}{4}=x$, and $g''^2+\text{A}f''^2=\left(\frac{39}{2}\right)^2+61\times\left(\frac{5}{2}\right)^2=\frac{3046}{4}=y$, $\frac{390}{4}=\frac{195}{2}$, $\frac{3046}{4}=\frac{1523}{2}$ and $61\times\left(\frac{195}{2}\right)^2+1=\left(\frac{1523}{2}\right)^2$. If $\text{A}x^2+\text{B}=y^2$, where $\text{B}=-1$, or $61x^2-1=y^2$, then $\frac{5}{2}=f$, $\frac{39}{2}=g$, and $-1=\beta$. Multiply $\text{A}f^2+\beta=g^2$ crossways with $\text{A}f'^2+\beta'=g'^2$, where $f'=\frac{195}{2}$ and $\beta'=+1$, in order that we may have $\beta\beta'=-1$. Then $x=3805$, and $y=29718$, and $\text{B}=-1$; $61\times(3805)^2-1=(29718)^2$. For new values, where $\text{B}=+1$, multiply $\text{A}f^2+\beta=g^2$ crossways with the values of x and y, which we have just found, $61\times226153980^2+1=1766319049^2$. If B is $-$ take the product of two augments which have unlike signs, and if B is $+$ that of two which have like signs.

"quotient is 5 and the multiplicand 7. Subtract the square of 7 from 61; 12 "remains. Divide by the augment of the operation of multiplication of the "square which is 3 affirmative; 4 affirmative is the quotient; and after reversion "it is 4 negative; and this is the augment; and the quotient which was 5 is the "less root; 39 then will be the greater root. As 4 is not the original augment, "we have found 2 an assumed number; and by its square we divide this augment. "1 the augment negative is the quotient. We also divide 5 and 39 by 2. These "same two numbers, with the denominator 2, are the quotients. As our "question is of the augment affirmative perform the operation of cross multipli-"cation. When we multiply the augment negative by itself it will be affirma-"tive. The less root will be 390 fourth parts; the greater root 3046 fourth "parts; and the augment 1 affirmative. Reduce the less and greater roots to "the denominator 2. The less root is 195 second parts; the greater root 1523 "second parts; and the augment 1 affirmative. And if, for example, the question "was of the subtraction of the augment, the answer would be as above; 5 "second parts being the less root, and 39 second parts the greater root, and 1 the "augment negative. And besides this, if we would obtain another case, let this "be multiplied crossways with that in which 195 second parts is the less root; "for multiplying affirmative by negative, negative is obtained. The less root "then is 3805, and the greater 29718, and the augment 1 negative; and this is "the answer to the question.

"To find another case with the augment affirmative write this below it and "multiply crossways, 226153980 is the less root, and 1766319049 the greater "root, and 1 the augment affirmative. And in like manner wherever the aug-"ment is required negative, we must multiply crossways two augments of dif-"ferent sorts; and if affirmative two of the same sort.

Rule. "If the multiplicand of the question is the sum of two squares, and "the augment 1 negative; it may be solved by the foregoing rules *, and if "wished for, it may be done in another way, viz. Take the root of those two

---

* In $Ax^2+B=y^2$, if $A=p^2+q^2$, and $B=-1$, $x=\frac{1}{p}$ and $x=\frac{1}{q}$; for $(p^2+q^2)\times\left(\frac{1}{p}\right)^2-1=\left(\frac{q}{p}\right)^2$, and $(p^2+q^2)\times\left(\frac{1}{q}\right)^2=\left(\frac{p}{q}\right)^2$.

" squares, and divide the augment by each, the two numbers which are found " will both be the less root; what was required may be obtained from each.

Example. " What square is that which being multiplied by 13, when 1 is sub-" tracted from the product, a square will remain *. 13 then is the sum of 4 and " 9, and 1 the augment negative. Take the roots of 4 and 9, they are 2 and 3. " Divide the augment by these two, the quotients are $\frac{1}{2}$ and $\frac{1}{3}$, both these are " the less roots. What is required may be had from either. For multiplying " the square of $\frac{1}{2}$ which is $\frac{1}{4}$ by 13, it is 13-fourths; and subtracting from it 1, " which is 4, 9-fourths will remain; and this is the square of $1\frac{1}{2}$. Multiplying " the square of $\frac{1}{3}$ which is $\frac{1}{9}$ by 13, it is 13-ninths; and subtracting 1 integer " which is 9, $\frac{4}{9}$ remains; and this is a square."

Here follow solutions of the same question, by the former methods: I omit them because they contain nothing new, and are full of errors in the calculation.

Another Example. Where $8x^2 - 1 = y^2$ is solved by the last rule, is omitted, because it is immaterial.

Another Example. " What square is that which being multiplied by 6, and " 3 added to the product, will be a square. And what number is that which " being multiplied by 6 and 12 added to the product will be a square †. The " operation in the first case is thus. Suppose 1 the less root, and multiply by 6, " it is 6; add 3, it is 9; and this is a square. And for the second case thus: " Multiply 1 by 6, it is 6; and find a number which added to it will be a square;

---

* $13x^2 - 1 = y^2$, here $A = 13 = 9 + 4 = p^2 + q^2$, $p = 2$, $q = 3$; $x = \frac{1}{2}$ and $x = \frac{1}{3}$; for $13 \times \left(\frac{1}{2}\right)^2 - 1 = \frac{9}{4} = (1\frac{1}{2})^2$; and $13 \times \left(\frac{1}{3}\right)^2 - 1 = \frac{4}{9} = \left(\frac{2}{3}\right)^2$.

† $6x^2 + 3 = y^2$, and $6x^2 + 12 = y^2$. First suppose $x = 1$ and $B = 3$, then $6 \times 1 + 3 = 9 = 3^2$, $y = 3$. Second, $6 \times 1 = 6$, find β such that $6 + \beta = \square$. Let $\beta = 3$, $6 + 3 = 9 = 3^2$, 3 being not $= B$, but less than it, find p such that $\beta p^2 = B$, $p = 2$, $3 \times 2^2 = 12 = B$. Now if $\beta' = 3$, $x' = 1$, and $y' = 3$, multiplying $Ax'^2 + \beta' = y'^2$ by p^2, we have $Ax'^2p^2 + \beta'p^2 = y'^2p^2$, and making $x = x'p$, $y = y'p$, and $B = \beta'p^2$, we have $x = 2$, $y = 6$ and $B = 12$. $6 \times 2^2 + 12 = 6^2$.

"we find 3. As this is not the original augment, but is less, find by the rule "which was given above, a number by the square of which when we multiply "this augment the original augment will be obtained. We have found 2. Mul-"tiply 3 by its square which is 4, it is 12; and this is the original augment. "Then that they may correspond, multiply the less and greater roots together; "also by that number, which is 2. The less root is 2, and the greater 6, and "the augment 12. Multiply the square of 2 by 6, it is 24; add 12, it is 36; "and this is a square the root of which is 6."

Here follows another example where, in $\text{A}x^2 + \text{B} = y^2$, $\text{B} = 75$, and $\text{A} = 6$. The solution of this question is like that of the first part of the preceding: f (in $\text{A}f^2 + \beta = g^2$) is assumed $= 5$ and $\beta = 75$.

Another Example. * "300 being the augment the less root is 10; its square "which is 100, we multiply by 6, it is 600. Add 300, it is 900; and this is a "square, the root of which is 30. And know that when the augment is greater "you must bring out what you require by the operation of circulation †, that "the augment may be less. And if you wish to obtain it without the operation "of circulation call to your aid acuteness and sagacity. And when you have "found one case, and the augment is 1, you may find others without end, by "cross multiplication. For however often you multiply 1 by itself, it will still "be one; and the less root and the greater will come out different.

Rule ‡. "If the multiplicand is such that you can divide it by a square with-"out a remainder, divide it; and divide the less and greater roots by the root of "that square, another number will be found. And if you multiply it by a square "and multiply the less and greater by its root, the numbers required will also be "found.

Example. "What square is that which being multiplied by 32, and 1 added to

---

* $6x^2 + 300 = y^2$. Let $x = 10$, then $6 \times 10^2 + 300 = 900 = 30^2$

† When β is a greater number find β', β'', &c. less by the rule of circulation. Solutions of these problems without the rule of circulation, are to be had only by trials judiciously made.

When one case of $\text{A}f^2 + 1 = g^2$ is known any number of cases may be found by cross multiplication; for $1 \times 1 = 1$, and different values of x and y will be found at every new step.

‡ I suspect that this is incorrectly translated; the example does not illustrate the rule. Perhaps it should be, if in $\text{A}x^2 + \text{B} = y^2$, $\text{A} = \text{A}'p^2$, then $\text{A}'x^2 + \frac{\text{B}}{p^2} = \left(\frac{y}{p}\right)^2$. If $\text{A} = \frac{\text{A}'}{p^2}$, then $\text{A}'x^2 + \text{B}p^2 = (yp)^2$.

" the product, will be a square*. The less root then is $\frac{1}{2}$, the square of which $\frac{1}{4}$ " multiplied by 32 will be 8 : add 1, it is 9 ; and this is a square. If we suppose " 2 the less root and divide 32 the multiplicand by 4, 8 will be the multiplicand ; " and dividing the less root by the root of 4 which is 2, 1 is the less root. For " multiplying by 8 and adding 1, it is 9, which is a square, the root of which " is 3.

Rule. " If the multiplicand is a square†, divide the augment by an assumed " number, and write the quotient in two places ; and in one place add to it, and " in the other subtract from it the assumed number, and halve them both ; the " greater number will be the greater root. Divide the less by the root of the " multiplicand, the quotient will be the less root.

Example. " What square is that which when multiplied by 9, and 52 added " to the product, is a square‡. What other square is that which when multiplied " by 4, and 33 added to the product, is a square. In the first case divide 52 by 2, " 26 is the quotient ; write it in two places and add and subtract 2, it is 28 and " 24 : the halves are 14 and 12 ; 14 then is the greater root. And divide the less " number which is 12 by the root of the multiplicand which is 3, 4 is the quo- " tient, and this is the less root : for when the square of 4 which is 16 is multiplied " by 9, it is 144 ; add 52, it is 195, which is the square of 14 : and in the

---

* $32 \times x^2 + 1 = \square$. Let $x = \frac{1}{2}$. $32 \times \left(\frac{1}{2}\right)^2 + 1 = 9 = 3^2$. If $x = 2$. $\frac{A}{p^2} = A'$, $\frac{32}{4} = 8$, $\frac{x}{p} = 1$. $x = 1$; for $8 \times 1 + 1 = 3^2$.

† If $Ax^2 + B = y^2$ and $A = p^2$, take n any number; and we have $\frac{\frac{B}{n} + n}{2} = y$; and $\frac{\frac{B}{n} - n}{\frac{2}{p}} = x$; for $\frac{\frac{B}{n} - n}{\frac{2}{p}} = \frac{B - n^2}{2pn}$ and $\frac{\frac{B}{n} + n}{2} = \frac{B + n^2}{2n}$. But $p^2 \times \left(\frac{B - n^2}{2np}\right)^2 + B = \left(\frac{B + n^2}{2n}\right)^2$; whence the rule.

‡ $9x^2 + 52 = y^2$ and $4x^2 + 33 = y^2$. First $\frac{52}{2} = 26$, $26 + 2 = 28$, $26 - 2 = 24$. $\frac{28}{2} = 14$; $\frac{24}{2} = 12$. $y = 14$, $\frac{12}{\sqrt{9}} = 4 = x$. $9 \times 4^2 + 52 = 196 = 14^2$. Second, $\frac{33}{3} = 11$, $11 + 3 = 14$, $11 - 3 = 8$, $\frac{14}{2} = 7 = y$, $\frac{8}{2} = 4$, $\frac{4}{2} = 2 = x$, $4 \times 2^2 + 33 = 49 = 7^2$. Values of x and y might have been found by taking $n = 4$ in the first case, and $n = 1$ in the second.

"second case divide 33 by 3, 11 is the quotient: after adding and subtracting 3 it "is 14 and 8: after halving, the greater root is 7. Divide 4 by 2, 2 is the quo- "tient; and this is the less root: for multiplying 4 by 4 and adding 33 to the "product, it is 49; and this is the square of 7. And if at first we divide 52 by 4, "and 33 by 1, what is required will be obtained

"*Another Example*, when the multiplicand is equal to the augment. What "square is that which being multiplied by 13 and 13 subtracted from the product, "and in another case added to it, will be a square *. In the first case suppose "1 the less root, its square which is also 1, we multiply by 13, it is 13: subtract "13, their remains cipher, the root of which is cipher. And in the second case "suppose 3 the less root, take its square, it is 9; take the difference between it "and the augment, 4 is the augment. Divide by it the assumed root which is "6, it is 6-fourths, that is $1\frac{1}{2}$, and this is the less root. The square of this "which is 9-fourths we multiply by 13; it is 117-fourths. We see that adding "1 integer, that is 4-fourths to this, it is 121-fourths; and this is a square, the "root of which is 11-second parts: the less root then is 3-second parts, and the "greater root is 11-second parts; and the augment is 1 affirmative. As the "original augment is 13 affirmative, perform the operation of cross multi- "plication with the former which was 13 negative, thus: First multiply 3-second "parts by cipher, it is cipher; and 11-second parts by 1, it is the same:

---

* $13x^2 - 13 = y^2$, and $13x^2 + 13 = y^2$. Let $x = 1$, $13 \times 1 - 13 = 0$. For $13x^2 + 13 = y^2$, let $x' = 3$, $x'^2 = 9$. (Here are two or three errors in the Persian: A case of $Ax'^2 + 1 = y'^2$ is found by the rule $\frac{2r}{A - r^2} = x$). $\frac{6}{4} = \frac{3}{2} = x'$. $13 \times \left(\frac{3}{2}\right)^2 + 1 = \frac{121}{4} = \left(\frac{11}{2}\right)^2$. $x' = \frac{3}{2}$, $y' = \frac{11}{2}$, and $\beta' = 1$. As $B = 13$, multiply crossways with the former case where $13 \times 1 - 13 = 0$. $\frac{3}{2} \times 0 + \frac{11}{2} \times 1 = \frac{11}{2} = x''$; $3 \times 1 \times 13 + \frac{11}{2} \times 0 = \frac{39}{2} = y''$. $13 \times - 1 = - 13 = \beta''$, but $B = + 13$. Suppose then $x''' = \frac{1}{2}$ and $\beta''' = - 1$, $13 \times \left(\frac{1}{2}\right)^2 - 1 = \frac{9}{4} = \left(1\frac{1}{2}\right)^2$. Multiply crossways, $\frac{33}{4} + \frac{39}{4} = \frac{72}{4} = 18 = x$. And $\frac{117}{4} + \frac{143}{4} = \frac{260}{4} = 65 = y$, and $13 = B$. Or by the rule $Aff' - gg' = y$, and $f'g - fg' = x$, $\frac{39}{4} - \frac{33}{4} = \frac{6}{4} = x$, $\frac{143}{4} - \frac{117}{4} = \frac{26}{4} = y$. $13 \times \left(\frac{3}{2}\right)^2 + 13 = \left(6\frac{1}{2}\right)^2$.

" add them together, it is 11-second parts; and this is the less root. Multiply " 3-second parts by 1, it is the same: multiply it by 13, the multiplicand, it is " 39-second parts: add it to the rectangle of the two greater roots which is cipher, " it is the same; and this is the greater root; and 13 is the augment negative; " as it is not the original augment, for 13 affirmative is required; again, suppose " the less root $\frac{1}{2}$ and the augment 1 negative; and multiply $\frac{1}{4}$ which is the square, " by 13; it is 13-fourths. Subtract 1, that is 4-fourths, the augment negative, there " remains 9-fourths, the root of which is $1\frac{1}{2}$. By this we multiply crossways, " thus:

$\frac{11}{2}$	$\frac{39}{2}$	-13
$\frac{1}{2}$	$\frac{3}{2}$	-1

" the less root is 72-fourths, which is 18 integers, and the greater root is 260-" fourths, which is 65 integers, and the augment is 13 affirmative.

" If we would perform the operation of cross multiplication take the dif-" ference of the two, which are 39-fourths, and 33-fourths, that is 6-fourths; " $1\frac{1}{2}$ is the less root; take the difference of the two less, after multiplying by " the multiplicand, and the rectangle of the two greater, it is 26-fourths, that " is $6\frac{1}{2}$; and this is the greater root and 13 is the augment affirmative.

Another Example. " What square is that which being multiplied by 5 nega-" tive, and the product increased by 21 will be a square*. Suppose 1 the less " root, and multiply its square by 5 negative, it is 5 negative: add 21 affirma-" tive, it is 16; 4 then will be the greater root. In another way. Suppose 2 the

* $-5 \times x^2 + 21 = y^2$. Suppose $x = 1$; $-5 \times 1 + 21 = 16$; $y = 4$. Or, suppose $x = 2$, $-5 \times 2^2 + 21 = 1$, $y = 1$. By multiplying crossways when $B = 1$, new values may be found.

" less root and multiply its square by 5 negative, it is 20 negative; add 21 " affirmative, 1 affirmative is obtained, the root of which is 1; the less root then " is 2, and the greater 1, and the augment 21. And if in the place of the multi- " plicand there is 5, and the augment is 1 affirmative, multiply crossways and " numbers without end will be obtained.

" And this which has been written is the introduction to the Indian Algebra. " Now by the help and favour of God we will begin our object."

END OF THE INTRODUCTION.

BOOK I*.

ON THE EQUALITY OF UNKNOWN WITH NUMBER.

"KNOW that whatever is not known in the question, and it is required to bring "it out by a method of calculation, suppose the required number to be one "or two unknown, and with it whatever the conditions of the question in-"volve, and proceed by multiplication and division, and four proportionals and "five proportionals, and the series of natural numbers, and the knowledge of the "side from the diameter, and the diameter from the side, that is the figure of the "bride†, and the knowledge of the perpendicular from the side of the triangle, "and conversely, and the like, so that at last the two may be brought to equa-"lity. If after the operation they are not equal, the question not being about "the equality of the two sides, make them equal by rejection and perfection, and "make them equal. And that is so, that the unknown, and the square of the "unknown of one side is to be subtracted from the other side, if there is an un-"known in it; if not subtract it from cipher: and subtract the numbers and "surds of the other side from the first side, so that the unknown may remain "on one side, and number on the other; the number then, and whatever else is "found, is to be divided by the unknown, the quotient will be the quantity of "the unknown.

"If the question involves more unknown quantities than one, call the first "one unknown, the second two unknown, the third three unknown, and so on. "And the method is this. Suppose the quantity of the lower species less than "that of the higher, and sometimes suppose $\frac{1}{2}$, and $\frac{1}{3}$, and $\frac{1}{4}$ of the unknown

---

* There are many parts of the rules given in the rest of the Work which are unintelligible to me; they are obscured probably by the errors of transcribers and of the Persian translator.—I translate them as exactly as I can from the Persian.

† The Arabs call the 47th proposition of the first book of Euclid, "the figure of the bride." I do not know why.

"and the like: and sometimes suppose the unknown to be a certain number, and "sometimes suppose 1 unknown and the rest certain numbers." The shortest method of solving the question is directed to be observed, and the whole attention to be given to what is required.

The first example is, "A person has 300 rupees and 6 horses; and another "person has 10 horses and 100 rupees debt; and the property of the two is "equal; and the price of the horses is the same; what then is the value of each? "Or, the first person has two rupees more than the property of the first person "in the first question, that is 3 horses and 152 rupees; and the second has the "same as he had before, and the property of both is equal; what then is the "price of one of the horses? Or, in the first question, the property of the first "person is three times the value of that of the second, what then is the value of one "horse? The operation in the first question is this: I suppose the price of a horse "to be the unknown; 6 horses are six unknown. The first person's property then "is 300 rupees affirmative and 6 unknown: and the property of the second is 10 "unknown and 100 rupees negative. As by the question both these sides are "equal there is no occasion for the operation of rejection and perfection. I "make them equal in this manner:

+ 300 Rupees	$6x$
— 100 Rupees	$10x$

"First I write them both, above and below, and I take 100 rupees negative from "300 rupees affirmative, it is 400 rupees affirmative; and I take 6 unknown from "10 unknown, there remains 4 unknown. 400 rupees is equal to 4 unknown. I "divide the first by the second, 100 rupees is the quotient, and this is the price of a horse." The other questions produce also simple equations, in which nothing remarkable occurs.

The second example has three unknown quantities with only one equation; it is solved first by assuming the unknown quantities in the proportion of 3, 2, and 1; and secondly by assuming them as 1, 5, and 4.

In the third example the Mussulman names, Zeid and Omar are introduced. The fourth and fifth examples contain nothing worthy of notice.

The sixth is as follows: "A person lent money to another on condition that he

" should receive 5 per cent. a month. After some months he took from him the " principal and interest, and having subtracted the square of the interest from " principal gave the remainder to another person, on condition that he should " receive 10 per cent. and after the same time had passed, as in the former case, " he took back the principal and interest, and this interest was equal to the first " interest; what sum did he lend to each person, and what was the time for " which the money was lent*?"

The first principal is supposed unknown, and the number of months during which it was lent is supposed 5. The question is solved by the rules of proportion and a simple equation. Another way is given for working this question, viz.

" Divide the interest of the second by that of the first, call the quotient the " multiplicand, and suppose a number the interest for the whole time and take its " square, and from the multiplicand subtract 1, and divide the square by the " remainder; the quotient will be the amount of the second sum, and the second " sum multiplied by the multiplicand, or added to the square of the interest of " the whole, will be equal to the first sum."

The next question is like the preceding, and is solved by means of the rule. I pass over several other examples, which contain nothing new or remarkable. A question in mensuration comes next.

" There is a triangle, one side of which is 13 surd, and another side 5 surd, " and its area 5 direhs; how much is the third side? I suppose the third side " unknown; the side 13 is the base. It is known that when the perpendicular " is multiplied by half the base, or the base by half the perpendicular, the pro- " duct will be the area of the triangle. Here the base and the area are known, " and the perpendicular is unknown. I divide 4 which is the whole area by half " of 13 surd; the quotient is the perpendicular. I perform the operation thus: " As 4 is a number I take its square 16, for the division of a number by a surd " is impossible. I take half of 13 surd thus: I square 2, which is the denomi- " nator of $\frac{1}{2}$, it is 4. I divide 13 by it. The quotient is 13 parts of 4 parts. I

---

* Let P, p, be the principal, I, i, the interest; R, r, the rate, and N, n, the number of the months. If $prn = i$, $PRN = I$, $P = p - i^2$, $N = n$, and $I = i$; we have $(p - i^2).\ RN = i = prn$; or $pRn - i^2RN = prn$; whence $pn \times (R - r) = i^2RN$, and $R - r = \frac{i^2RN}{pn}$, but this is equal to $\frac{ri^2}{P}$, and $P = \frac{ri^2}{R - r} = \frac{i^2}{\frac{R}{r} - 1}$, which is the first part of the rule; the rest is evident.

"divide 16 by 13 parts of 4 parts; it is 64 parts of 13 surd; and this is the "perpendicular. I then require the excess of the square of 5 surd above 64 parts "of 13 surd: First I take the square of 5 surd; it is 5 number; take its square, "it is 25 surd; the root of which is 5. I then take the square of 64 parts of 13 "surd, as above. I take the excess thus: I make 5 of the same sort; it is 65; "I take the excess of 65 above 64; it is one part of 13 surd; and this is from "the place of the perpendicular to the angle formed by the side 5 and the base."

The other segment of the base is found by subtracting this from the whole, by a rule which was given in the 4th chapter of the introduction, for finding the difference of two surds, viz. $\sqrt{a}-\sqrt{b}=\sqrt{\left(\sqrt{\left(\frac{a}{b}\right.}-1)^2\times b\right)}$. The square root of the sum of the squares of this segment and the perpendicular gives the quantity of the unknown side of the triangle.

In the next question, the sides of a triangle being given, its area is required. One of the segments of the base made by a perpendicular, is supposed unknown. From two values of the perpendicular, in terms of the hypothenuses of the two right-angled triangles, and their bases, an equation is formed; from which the unknown quantity is brought out. The equation involves many surds, and they are reduced by the rules laid down in the introduction. The perpendicular is then found by taking the square root of the difference of the squares of a segment of the base, and of the adjacent sides of the triangle. The operation is here concluded. In a marginal note are directions to find the area, as in the foregoing case.

The next is, "What four fractions are those whose denominators are equal, and "whose sum is equal to the sum of their squares. Also what four fractions are "those, the sum of whose squares is equal to the sum of their cubes." For the first part of the question: "Suppose the first fraction one unknown, the second "two unknown, the third three unknown, and the fourth four unknown, and "below each write 1 for the denominator. The sum of the four is 10 unknown. "Their squares are 1 and 4 and 9 and 16, whose sum is 30 square of unknown, "and these two quantities are equal. Divide both by one unknown; the quotients "are 10 number and 30 unknown. Divide 10 by 30 unknown, the quotient is "$\frac{1}{3}$ of unknown. The first fraction then is $\frac{1}{3}$, the second $\frac{2}{3}$, the third $\frac{3}{3}$, and "the fourth $\frac{4}{3}$; and the squares of these fractions are $\frac{1}{9}$ and $\frac{4}{9}$, and $\frac{9}{9}$ and $\frac{16}{9}$; and "the sum of these four is $\frac{30}{9}$, and this is equal to $\frac{10}{3}$." In the same manner the the other fractions are found to be $\frac{3}{10}$, $\frac{6}{10}$, $\frac{9}{10}$, and $\frac{12}{10}$.

The next is to find a right-angled triangle, "the area of which is equal to its "hypothenuse;" and to find a right-angled triangle, "the area of which is equal "to the rectangle of its three sides." For the first part of the problem, one side of the triangle is assumed equal to 4 unknown, and the other side equal to 3 unknown; the hypothenuse is found equal to $5x$, and the area equal to $6x^2$; the equation $5x = 6x^2$ being reduced, gives the value of x. For the second part, the sides are assumed as above, and the value of x is deduced from the equation $60x^3 = 6x^2$.

The next problem is, to find two numbers of which the sum and the difference shall be squares, and the product a cube. The numbers are supposed $5x^2$ and $4x^2$, and the cube to which their product must be equal $1000x^3$, whence x is found.

The next is to find two numbers such that the sum of their cubes shall be a square, and the sum of their squares a cube. One number is supposed x^2, and the other $2x^2$, and the cube $125x^3$ *. In the solution of this the following passage occurs: "The cube of the square of unknown, which in Persian algebra "is termed square of cube." In the margin is this note: "Here is evidently a "mistake; for in Persian algebra the unknown (مجهول) is called thing (شی), "and its square (مربع) square (مال), (literally possession;) and its cube "(مکعب) cube (کعب); and when the cube is multiplied by thing, the "product is called square of square (مال مال); and when the square of "square is multiplied by thing, the product is called square of cube (مال کعب); "and when the square of cube is multiplied by thing, the product is called cube "of cube (کعب کعب), not square of cube. For example, suppose 2 thing "4 is its square, 8 its cube, 16 its square of square, 32 its square of cube, 64 its "cube of cube, not its square of cube, although it is the cube of the square "(مکعب مربع), or the square of the cube (مربع مکعب)."

In the next example the three sides of a triangle are given, and the perpen-

* Sum of the cubes $= x^6 + 8x^6 = 9x^6$ (a square); and the sum of squares $= x^4 + 4x^4 = 5x^4$, assume this $= 125x^3$, or $5x^4 = 125x^3$, whence $5x = 125$, and $x = 25$; therefore 625 and 1250 are the numbers.

dicular is required. It is found in the same way as the perpendicular was found in one of the former questions, when the sides being given the area of the triangle was required.

The three following are different cases of right-angled triangles in which the parts required are found by the principle of the square of the hypothenuse being equal to the sum of the squares of the two sides, and simple equations. In the first the base and the sum of the hypothenuse and the other side are given. In the second the base and the difference of the hyptohenuse and the other side are given; and in the third the base, part of one side, and the sum of the hypothenuse and the other part of that side, are given.

The first book ends with the following example: "Two sticks stand upright "in the ground, one is 10 direhs in height and the other 15 direhs, and the "distance between the two is 20 direhs. If two diameters are drawn between "them, what will be the distance from the place where they meet to the ground*? "Suppose the perpendicular unknown; it is known that as 15 to 20, so is the "unknown to the quantity of the distance from the side 10 to the place where the "unknown stands. We find then by 4 proportionals, 4 thirds of unknown is the said "quantity. In like manner we find the second quantity 20 parts of 10, that is "2 unknown. Take the sum of the two, it is 10-thirds, and this is equal to 20. "Divide 20 by 10-thirds, the quotient is 6; and this is the quantity of the un-"known, that is of the perpendicular. From the place where the perpendicular "stands on the ground, to the bottom of the side 15, is 12; for it is 2 unknown. "The second quantity is 8 direhs; for it is 1 unknown and a third of unknown. "And know that whatever the distance is between the two sticks, the quantity "of the perpendicular will be the same; and so it is in every case. We can also

---

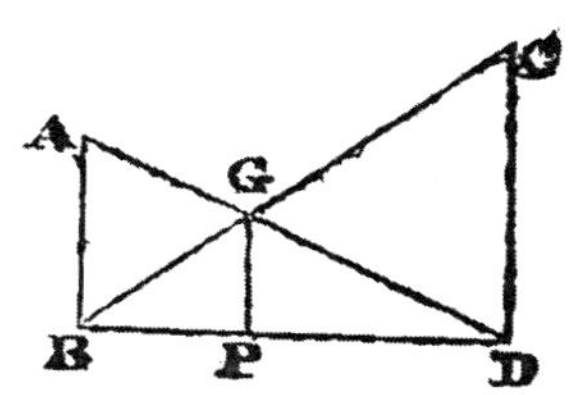

* Let AB = 10, DC = 15, BD = 20.
By similar triangles BD : BP :: DC : PG,
BD : PD :: BA : PG,
whence BP : PD :: BA : DC,
therefore BD is divided in P in the ratio of DC to BA.

By composition BP + PD : BP :: BA + DC : BA; but BP + PD = BD, therefore BA + DC and BA are in the ratio of BD to BP; whence, by the first proportion, BA + DC : BA :: DC : PG, that is, PG is a fourth proportional to BA + DC, BA, and DC, whatever be the length of BD.

Lucas de Burgo has this proposition, (see his Geometry, p. 56.) where the lengths are 4, 6, and 8; or page 60, where they are 10, 15, and 6. The same is in Fyzee's Lilavati, where the rules are

$$GP = \frac{AB \times CD}{AB + CD},\ PD = \frac{BD \times CD}{AB + CD},\ \text{and } BP = \frac{BD \times AB}{AB + CD}.$$

"ascertain these two quantities by another method, and that is the ratio of 25, "(that is the sum of the two sides) to 20, is like the ratio of 15 to the unknown; "that is the quantity towards the side 15. Multiply 15 by 20, it is 300. Divide "300 by 25, it is 12. The ratio of 25 to 20, is like the ratio of 10 to the unknown; "the result is 8, and this is the quantity towards the side 10. By another "method, by four proportionals, we find that the ratio of 20 to 25, is like the "ratio of 8 to the unknown; 6 is the result. In like manner the ratio of 20 to "10, is like that of 12 to unknown; again 6 is the result. Another method is, "divide the rectangle of the two sticks by the sum of the two, the result is the "quantity of the perpendicular, and the quantity of the ground we multiply by "each side separately, and divide both by the sum of the sides. The two quotients "will be the quantities from the place of the perpendicular to the bottom of the "sticks; accordingly divide 150, which is the rectangle of the two sticks, by "25, the quotient is 6. Multiply 20 direhs, which is the quantity of the ground "by both sticks, the products are 300 and 200. Divide both by 25, the quotients "are 12 and 8. In this manner the figure may be found by calculation as "correctly as if it were measured."

END OF THE FIRST BOOK.

BOOK 2.

" ON the interposition of the unknown: where the square of unknown is " equal to number, and that is rejected with the unknown." *(Or divided by the unknown* (انرا رکتند بمجهول). *(I do not know what he means here, perhaps there is some error.)*

" It is intitled, 'Interposition of Unknown,' (توسیط مجهول); because " that which is required is brought out by means (واسطا) of the unknown. It is " called Interposition (توسیط); and Mudhum Uhrun (unknown means) in " Hindee is to be so understood. Its method is this: The square of unknown " being equal to number, multiply both, or divide both by an assumed number, " and add a number to the two results, or subtract it from them that both may " be squares. For if one side is a square the other also will be a square; for they " are equal, and by the equal increase or diminution of two equals, two equals " will be obtained. Take the roots of both, and after equating divide the num- " ber by the root of the square of unknown, that is by unknown; the result will " be what was required. And if there is equality in the cube of the unknown, " or the square of the square, that is after the operation in the thing and cube, " and square of square, if the root cannot be found, nor be brought out by rule, " in that case it can only be obtained by perfect meditation and acuteness*. " And, after equating, if the two sides are not squares, the method of making " them squares is this. Assume the number 4, and multiply it by the number of " the square of the first side, and multiply both sides by the product. And in the

---

* From this place to the end of the rule Mr. Burrow's copy is as follows: " And if in the side which has the " unknown there is a number greater than the unknown, if the number is affirmative make it negative, and if " negative, two numbers will be found in the conditions required, and the way to find the assumed number by " which the two sides should be multiplied, and the number to be added, is extremely easy; for multiply the " multiplicand of the number of the square of the unknown by 4, and let the square of the numbers of the un- " known, of the side in which there is the square of the unknown, be the number added."

" place of number increase both sides by the square of the thing of the unknown, " which is on that side; both sides will be squares. Take the roots of both and " equate them, and the quantity of the unknown will be found.

Example. " Some bees were sitting on a tree; at once the square root of half " their number flew away. Again, eight-ninths of the whole flew away the " second time; two bees remained. How many were there? The method " of bringing it out is this: From the question it appears that half the sum has " a root; I therefore suppose 2 square of unknown, and I take 1 unknown, that " is the root of half. And as the questioner mentions that two bees remain, 1 " unknown and $\frac{8}{9}$ of 2 square of unknown, that is $\frac{16}{9}$ of 1 square of unknown, " and 2 units, is equal to 2 square of unknown. I perform the operation of " equating the fractions in this manner, I multiply both sides by 9, which is the " denominator of a ninth; 16 square of unknown and 9 unknown, and 18 units, " is equal to 18 square of unknown. I equate them thus: I subtract 16 square of " unknown of the first side from 18 square of unknown of the second side; it is " 2 square of unknown affirmative; and in like manner I subtract 9 unknown of " the first side from cipher unknown of the second side; 9 unknown negative " remains. Then I subtract cipher the numbers of the second side from 18 units of " the first side; it is the same. The first side then is 2 square of unknown affirma- " tive and 9 unknown negative, and the second side is 18 units affirmative. In this " example there is equality of square of unknown, and unknown to number; that " is equality of square and thing to number. As the roots of these two sides can- " not be found, suppose the number 4, and multiply it by 2, which is the number " of the square of the unknown, it is 8. I multiply both sides by 8; the first side is " 16 square of thing, and 72 unknown negative; and the second side is 144 " units. I then add the square of the number of the unknown, which is 81, to the " result of both sides; the first side is 16 square of unknown, and 72 unknown " negative, and 81 units; and the second side is 225 units. I take the roots of " both sides: the root of the first side is 4 unknown and 9 units negative; and " the root of the second side is 15 units affirmative. I equate them in this " manner: I subtract cipher unknown of the second side from 4 unknown of the " first side; and 9 units negative of the first side from 15 units affirmative of " the second side; the first is 4 thing, and the second side is 24 units affirma- " tive, I divide, 6 is the result, and this is the quantity of the unknown; and "as we supposed 2 square of unknown, we double 36; the whole number of bees "then was 72."

In the next example arises the equation $\frac{x^2}{2}+4x+10=x^2$; then $x^2-8x=20$, $4x^2-32x+64=4\times 20+64=144$, $2x-8=12$; $x=10$*.

The next example is, "A person gave charity several days, increasing the "gift equally every day. From the sum of the days 1 being subtracted and "the remainder halved, the result is the number of dirhems which he gave the "first day; he increased always by half of that number: and the sum of the "dirhems is equal to the product of these three; that is to say, the number of "days, the number of dirhems the first day, and the number of the increase, "added to $\frac{1}{7}$ of the product." Let the number of days be $4x+1$, $2x$ is the "number of dirhems given the first day, and x is the number of the increase; $(4x+1)\times 2x\times x=2x^2+8x^3$, add $\frac{1}{7}$ of this $\frac{16x^2+64x^3}{7}=$ the sum of the dirhems. Then by a rule of the Leelawuttee, $((4x+1)-1)x+2x=$ the number given the last day; half the sum of what was given the first and last days $=$ what was given the middle day. Multiply this by the number of days; it is $8x^3+10x^2+2x$, which is $=\frac{16x^2+64x^3}{7}$. $8x^2-54x=14$. Multiply by the assumed number 8, for in this case as the co-efficient of x is even, assume the co-efficient itself of x^2, and add the square of half the co-efficient of x, $64x^2-432x+729=841$; $8x-27=29$, $x=\frac{29+27}{8}=7$.

The next is to find x in the equation $\left(\frac{x^2}{0}+\frac{x}{0}\right)\times 0=90$. The solution is, "I suppose, what is required to be *thing*, I divide it by cipher; as the quotient "is impossible, *thing* is obtained, whose denominator is cipher. Its square, which "is the square of *thing*, whose denominator is cipher, I add to *thing*, which is the "root. It is the square of *thing* and *thing*, whose denominator is cipher. I "multiply by cipher; it is the square of *thing* and *thing*. Cipher is thrown out "by a rule of the Leelawuttee, which says, that when the multiplicand is cipher, "and the multiplier a number whose denominator is cipher, the product will be

---

* Part of this example, and most of the rest in this book, are wanting in Mr. Burrow's copy.

" that number, and cipher will be rejected." Whence the equation $x^2 + x = 90$ which is solved in the common way.

The next is; a value of x is required in the case $((x + \frac{x}{2}) \times 0)^2 + 2(x + \frac{x}{2}) \times 0 = 15$. It is brought out in a manner similar to that of the foregoing.

The next example is of a cubic equation, viz. $x^3 + 12x = 6x^2 + 35$. The terms involving the unknown quantity being brought all on the same side, 8 is added to complete the cube. " I take the cube root of the second side 3, and I " write the terms of the first side in the arithmetical manner, thus: 8 units nega- " tive, and 12 unknown affirmative, and 6 square of unknown negative, and 1 " cube of unknown. First, I take the cube root of the last term, it is 1 un- " known. I square it and multiply it by 3, and I divide the term which is last " but one by the product; 2 units negative is the quotient. Its square, which is 4 " affirmative, I multiply by the term first found, viz. 1 *thing*; it is 4 *thing*. I " multiply it by 3, it is 12 unknown. I subtract it from the third term which is " after the first, nothing remains. After that I subtract the term 2 negative from " the first term, nothing remains. The cube root then of the first side is found 1 " *thing* affirmative and 2 units negative." Whence $x - 2 = 3$, which is reduced in the usual way.

In the next a biquadratic is found, $x^4 - 400x - 2x^2 = 9999$. To solve this $400x + 1$ is directed to be added to each side; the equation is then $x^4 - 2x^2 + 1 = 10{,}000 + 400x$. The root of the first side is $x^2 - 1$, but the root of the second side cannot be found. Find a number which being added, the roots of both sides may be found; that is $4x^2 + 400x + 1$. This will give $x^4 + 2x^2 + 1 = 10{,}000 + 4x^2 + 400x$; and extracting the square root, $x^2 + 1 = 100 + 2x$, which is reduced by the rules given in this chapter. At the conclusion of the example are these words: " The solution of such questions as these depends on " correct judgment, aided by the assistance of God.

In the two next examples notice is taken of a quadratic equation having two roots. " When on one side is *thing*, and the numbers are negative, and on the " other side the numbers are less than the negative numbers on the first side, " there are two methods. The first is, to equate them without alteration. The " second is, if the numbers of the second side are affirmative, to make them nega- " tive, and if negative to make them affirmative. Equate them; 2 numbers will " be obtained, both of which will probably answer."

The next example is, " The style of a dial 12 fingers long stands perpendi-

" cular on the ground. If from its shadow, a third of the hypothenuse of these " two sides, viz. the style and the shadow, is subtracted, 14 fingers will remain. " What then are the shadow and the hypothenuse?" In the right-angled triangle 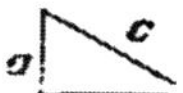

, a being $= 12$, and $b - \frac{c}{3} = 14$; c and b are required. The equation $(3b - 42)^2 = b^2 + 144$ arises, and is reduced to $4b - 63 = 27$. The two values ± 27 are taken notice of. First, $+ 27$ gives $b = 22\frac{1}{2}$, which is declared to be right. From $- 27$, b is found $= 9$; " but here," it is observed, " 9 is not correct; for, after subtracting a third of the hypothenuse, 14 does " not remain." In opposition to this, some one speaking in the first person (the Persian translator, I suppose) says, " I think that this also is right," and goes on " to prove that in this case the hypothenuse will be $= - 15$."

The next problem is to find four numbers such that if to each of them 2 be added, the sums shall be four square numbers whose roots shall be in arithmetical progression; and if to the product of the first and second, and to the product of the second and third, and to the product of the third and fourth, 18 be added, these three sums shall be square numbers; and if to the sum of the roots of all the square numbers 11 be added, the sum shall be a square number, viz. the square of 13.

It is here observed, by way of lemma*, that, in questions like this, the " augment of the products" must be equal to the square of the difference of the roots, multiplied by the " augments of the numbers;" otherwise the case will be impossible.

The following is an abstract of the solution: (Let w, x, y, z be the four numbers required, and r, s, t, v the four roots which must be in arithmetical progression). By the lemma we find the common difference $\sqrt{\frac{18}{2}} = 3$. The first root being r, the second will be $= r + 3$, the third $= r + 6$, and the fourth $= r + 9$.

Now $rs - 2 = \sqrt{(wx + 18)}$, and $st - 2 = \sqrt{(xy + 18)}$, and $tv - 2 = \sqrt{(yz + 18)}$.

---

* In a marginal note, which I suppose to be written by the Persian translator, the application of the Lemma to the problem is illustrated thus: Let a, b, c be three numbers; $(a - b)^2 \times c + (a^2 - c) \times (b^2 - c) = (ab - c)^2$. In this case we have $a - b = 3$, $c = 2$ and b and a two successive roots; and as $w = r^2 - 2$, and $x = s^2 - 2$, &c. the reason of the rule is plain.

We have now $w+2=r^2$; $x+2=(r+3)^2$; $y+2=(r+6)^2$; $z+2=(r+9)^2$;
And $wx+18=(rs-2)^2$; $xy+18=(st-2)^2$, and $yz+18=(tv-2)^2$.

Making $r+s+t+v+(rs-2)+(st-2)+(tv-2)+11=13^2$; a quadratic equation arises, which being reduced r is found $=2$, whence $w=2$, $x=23$, $y=62$, and $z=119$.

Some questions about right-angled triangles occur next; the first is, "Given "the sides of a right-angled triangle 15 and 20; required the hypothenuse. "Although by the figure of the bride the hypothenuse is the root of the sum of "the squares of the two sides, the method of solution by Algebra is this: In this "triangle suppose the hypothenuse unknown, and then divide the triangle into "two right-angled triangles, thus: Suppose the unknown hypothenuse the base "of the triangle, and from the right-angle draw a perpendicular; then 15 is the "hypothenuse of the small triangle, and 20 that of the large one. By four pro-"portionals I find, when the least side about the right angle, whose hypothe-"nuse is 1 unknown, is 15; how much will be the least side about the right "angle whose hypothenuse is 15." In like manner the other segment is to be brought out, whence $x=25$. "If I would find the quantity of the perpen-"dicular, and the segments of the hypothenuse at the place of the perpendicular, "it may be done in various ways; first by four proportionals," &c. They are found on the same principle as above. "And another way which is written "in the Leelawuttee is this; The difference of the two containing sides, that is "to say 5, I multiply by 35, which is the sum of the two sides; it is 175. "I divide by 25 that is the base; the quotient is 7. I add this to the base, it "is 32. I halve it, 16 is obtained; when I subtract 7 from the base, 18 "remains. I halve, 9 is the smaller segment from the place of the perpen-"dicular.

Rule. "The square of the hypothenuse of every right-angled triangle is equal "to twice the rectangle of the two sides containing the right angle, with the "square of the difference of those sides. As the joining of the four triangles "abovementioned is in such a manner that from the hypothenuse of each, the "sides of a square will be formed, and in the middle of it there will be a square, "the quantity of whose sides is equal to the difference of the two sides about the "right-angle of the triangle; and the area of every right-angled triangle is half "the rectangle of the sides about the right triangle. Now twice the rectangle "of the two sides containing *that* is 600, is equal to all the four triangles; and "when I add 25, the small square, it will be equal to the whole square of the "hypothenuse, that is 625, which is equal to the square of thing; and in many "cases an effable root cannot be found, then it will be a surd; and if we do "not suppose thing, add twice the rectangle of one side into the other, to the "square of the difference of the sides, and take the root of the sum, it will be "the quantity of the hypothenuse. And from this it is known that if twice the "rectangle of two numbers is added to the square of their difference, the result "will be equal to the sum of the squares of those two numbers."

The next is in a right-angled triangle 

. Given $\sqrt{(AB - 3)} - 1 = AC - BC$, required the sides. "First, I perform the operation of contrariety and op- "position: let $AC - BC$ be supposed 2. To this add 1, it is 3; take its square, "its is 9; add 3, it is 12. This is the quantity of the less side; its square which "is 144 is $= AC^2 - BC^2$; here then the differences of the two original numbers, "and of the two squares are both known; and the difference of the squares of two "numbers is equal to the rectangle of the sum of the two numbers, into their "difference. Therefore when we divide the difference of the squares by the "difference of the two numbers, the sum of the two numbers will be the quotient; "and if we divide by the sum, the difference will be the quotient: because the "square of a line has reference to a four-sided equiangular figure whose four "sides are equal to that line; for example, the square of 7 direhs is 49. If I "subtract the square of 5 from it, 24 remains; and the difference of 7 and 5 is "2, and their sum 12, and the rectangle of these two is 24, which is the number "remaining. Then it is known that the rectangle of the sum of the two numbers "into their difference, that is 12 multiplied by 2, is equal to the difference of the "squares of the two that is 24," &c. On this principle the sum and difference being found, the numbers themselves are had "by a rule of the Leelawuttee," viz.

$$\frac{a+b}{2} + \frac{a-d}{2} = a, \text{ and } \frac{a+b}{2} - \frac{a-b}{2} = b.$$

By supposing other numbers besides 2 for the difference, and proceeding in the above manner, triangles without end may be found.

As objection is here made (I suppose by the Persian translator) that the above is not algebraical. It is then stated that the translator has found out an easy way of solving the question by Algebra. He directs that the difference $AC - BC$ may be assumed $= 2$, as before; and making $BC = x$, AC will be

$= x + 2$, and AB being $= 12$, the value of x may be found from the equation $x^2 + 12^2 = (x + 2)^2$.

Rule. "The difference of the sum of the squares of two numbers and the "square of their sum is equal to twice the rectangle of the two numbers. For "example, the squares of 3 and 5 are 9 and 25, that is 34, and their sum "is 8 and its square 64, and the difference of these is 30, which is equal to twice "the rectangle of 3 and 5 that is by the 4th figure of the second book thus." In the copy which I now have, the figures are omitted. In Mr. Burrow's copy it is

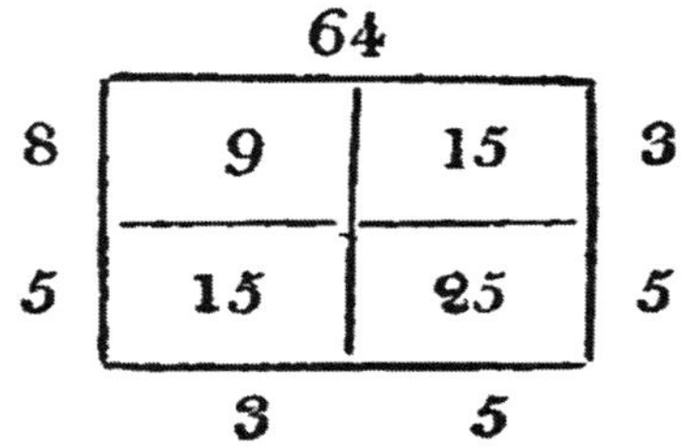

Then follows another rule: $4ab - (a + b)^2 = (a - b)^2$, which may be easily understood by this figure. There is no figure in Mr. Burrow's copy, nor in my present copy, but I had one in which there was a figure for the demonstration of the 8th proposition of the second book of Euclid.

Next come two examples: The first of them is, what right-angled triangle is that "the sum of whose 3 sides is 40, and the rectangle of the two sides about "the right angle 120?

"The method of solution is this: By the first rule take twice 120, it is 240, "and this is equal to the difference of the sum of the squares of the sides about "the right angle, and the square of their sum that is the hypothenuse. Then "the difference of the squares of the two numbers, one of which is the sum of the "two sides and the other the hypothenuse, is 240; and the sum of both is 40. "In the method of finding out the triangle, it was before known that the dif-"ference of the squares of two numbers is equal to the rectangle of their sum and "difference; when the difference of the two squares is divided by the differ-"ence of the two numbers, the quotient is the sum of the numbers; and if it is "divided by the sum, the quotient is the difference. Let then 240 be divided "by the two numbers, which together make 40 by the question, the quotient

" is 6, and this is the difference of the hypothenuse and the sum of the two sides " about the right angle; then add 6 to 40, and take its half, it is 23; this is the " sum of the sides; subtract 6 from 40, and take its half, it is 17, and this is the " hypothenuse, for the sum of the two sides is always greater than the hypothe- " nuse by the asses proposition*. It was stated in the second rule that the " difference of the square of the sum of two numbers, and 4 times their rectangle, " is equal to the square of their difference. Take then the squares of 23, it is " 529, and 4 times the rectangle of the two sides, it is 480; their difference is " 49, which is equal to the square of the difference of the sides, that is 7: then " add 7 to 23, and subtract it from the same, and the halves, are 15 and 8 the " two sides."

The next example is, 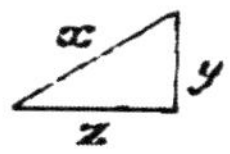

required x, y, z, such that $x + y + z = 56$, and $xyz = 4200$. " I suppose the diameter (*the hypothenuse*) unknown; take its " square it is x^2: This is equal to the sum of the square of the two sides about " the right angle, by the figure of the bride; and as 4200 is the product of the " rectangle of the two sides multiplied by the hypothenuse, I divide 4200 by the " unknown, the quotient $\frac{4200}{x}$ is the rectangle of the two sides. And it was " stated that the excess of the square of the sum of the numbers above the sum " of their squares is equal to twice the rectangle of the two numbers. The sum " of the two sides is $56 - x$; I take its square, it is $x^2 - 112x + 3136$; and the " sum of the squares of the two sides is x^2, for that is the square of the hypothenuse, " which is the same. I take the difference of the two $- 112x + 3136$, and this " is equal to twice the rectangle of the two sides, that is $\frac{8400}{x}$," &c.

The equation is reduced in the common way: the square in the quadratic, which arises, being completed by adding the square of 14, which is half the coefficient of x. In this way the hypothenuse, and thence the other sides are brought out.

---

* Meaning by the asses proposition the 20th of the first book of Euclid, which we are told was ridiculed by the Epicureans as clear even to asses. These passages are only interpolations of the Persian translator.

END OF THE SECOND BOOK.

BOOK 3.

"EXPLAINING THAT MANY COLOURS MAY BE EQUAL TO EACH OTHER."

"THE rule in this case is to subtract the unknown of one side from the un-
" known or cipher of the other side, and all the other colours and the numbers of
" the second side from the first side, from which the unknown was subtracted,
" and divide those colours by the unknown. If, as may happen, the denomi-
" nators are one quantity, perform the operation of the multiplicand; and if the
" denominators are different unknown quantities let them be unknown. Suppose
" the quantity of every one of these unknown the denominator, and put it below
" the colours of the dividend, and reduce the fractions and reject the denomina-
" tors; then the unknown will not remain on any side. After that subtract the
" black of one side from the other side, and subtract the rest of the colours and
" the numbers from the side from which the black was subtracted, and perform
" the same operations as were directed for the unknown, and the quantity of the
" black will be obtained; and in like manner the rest of the colours, and all
" the quantities of the multiplicand will be obtained. Then perform with it the opera-
" tion of the multiplicand; and the multiplicand and quotient will be obtained. The
" multiplicand will be the quantity of the dividend, and the quotient the quantity of
" the divisor. And if in the dividend of the operation of the multiplicand, two
" colours remain; as for example, black and blue, suppose the second in order,
" which is blue, the dividend, and suppose black a number, and add that to the
" augment, and perform the operation; and when the quantity of the two last
" colours is obtained, we shall known by the method which has been explained
" and illustrated in the examples, what are the quantities of the other colours
" which are below it. And when the quantity is known, reject the name of
" colour, and if the quantity of the colour is not obtained in whole numbers,
" again perform the operation of the multiplicand till it comes out whole; and by
" the quantity of the last colour we know the quantities of the other colours, so
" that the quantity of the unknown will be found. If then any one propose a
" question in which there are many things unknown, suppose them different

"colours. Accordingly, suppose the first unknown, and the second black, and "the third blue, and the fourth yellow, and the fifth red, and the sixth green, and "the seventh parti-coloured, and so on, giving whatever names you please to "unknown quantities which you wish to discover. And if instead of these "colours other names are supposed, such as letters, and the like it may be done. "For what is required is to find out the unknown quantities, and the object in "giving names is that you may distinguish the things required."

From the first question in this book arises the equation $5x + 8y + 7z + 90 = 7x + 9y + 6z + 62$. From this is derived $\frac{-y + z + 28}{2x}$ or $\frac{-y + z + 28}{2} = x$. Now z is assumed $= 1$, and from $\frac{-y + 29}{2}$, the multiplicand and the quotient are found by the rules of the fifth chapter of the introduction as follows: The augment being greater than the divisor, the former is divided by the latter. The quotient is retained, and the remainder is written instead of the augment; the quotient is found $= 0$ and the multiplicand $= 1$. As the number of the quotients arising from the division of the dividend by the divisor is in this case odd, and as the dividend is negative; and each of these circumstances requiring the multiplicand to be subtracted from the divisor, and the quotient from the dividend, the quantities remain as they were, viz. 0 and 1. Now adding 14, the quotient of 29 divided by 2, to 0; the true quotient is 14 and the multiplicand $= 1$. Therefore $x = 14$, and $y = 1$, and $z = 1$; and new values may be found by the rules of the 5th chapter of the introduction.

The next question is the same as the third of the 1st book.

In the next we have the four quantities $5x + 2y + 8z + 7w$, and $3x + 7y + 2z + 1w$, and $6x + 4y + 1z + 2w$, and $8x + 1y + 3z + 1w$, all equal to each other; and the values of x, y, z, and w are required. From the first and second is found $2x = 5y - 6z - 6w$; from the second and third $3x = 3y + z - w$; and from the third and fourth $2x = 3y - 2z + w$.

From the two first of these three equations $9y = 20z + 16w$, and from the two last $3y = 8z - 5w$; whence $12z = 93w$; and dividing $\frac{31w + 0}{4} = z$; "and "above, where the rule of the multiplicand was given, it was said that when the "augment is cipher, the multiplicand will be cipher, and the quotient the quotient "of the augment divided by the divisor; here then the multiplicand and quotient "are both cipher." Then adding 31 for a new value of z, and 4 for a new value of w, $31 = z$ and $4 = w$, and the other quantities are brought out in the usual manner.

The next example gives $5x + 7y + 9z + 3w = 100$, and $3x + 5y + 7z + 9w = 100$. From these comes $4y = -8z - 36w + 200$, and for the operation of the multiplicand $\frac{-8z - 36w + 200}{4} = y$. Suppose $w = 4$, then $-8z$ will be the dividend, and $+56$ the augment, and 4 the divisor. As 4 measures 56, 14 times without a remainder, the multiplicand will be $= 0$, and the quotient $= 14$: adding -8 to 14, and 4 to 0, $y = 6$ and $z = 4$. The other quantities are found in the same way as in the former examples. Another method, not materially different from the foregoing, is also prescribed for the solution of this question *.

A great part of the next example is not intelligible to me. What I can make out is this. To find x so that $\frac{x-5}{6} = y$, $\frac{x-4}{5} = z$, $\frac{x-3}{4} = v$, $\frac{x-2}{3} = w$, whole numbers. Taking values of x in these equations the following are found $6y = 5z - 1$, $5z = 4v - 1$, and $4v = 3w - 1$; from this last $w = 3$ and $v = 2$, but these numbers giving $\frac{7}{5}$ a fractional value of z, new values must be sought for w and v. Then after some part which I cannot understand, the author makes $w = 3 + 4u$, and says u is found $= 4$; then $w = 19$, $v = 2 + 3u$, $v = 14$. After more, which I cannot make out, he finds $\frac{4v - 1}{5} = 11 = z$, by means of t which he adds to v and finds $= 15$. After more, which I can make nothing of, he finds $y = 9$ and $x = 59$.

The next example is, what three numbers are those which when the first is multiplied by 5 and divided by 20, the remainder and quotient will be equal; and when the second is multiplied by 7 and divided by 20, the remainder and the quotient will be equal, with an increase of 1, to the remainder and quotient of the first; and when the third is multiplied by 9 and divided by 20, in like manner, the remainder and quotient will be equal with an increase of 1 to the remainder and quotient of the second? The first remainder is called x, the second $x + 1$, and the third, $x + 2$, and these are also the quotients. Let the first number be y. By the

---

* From this place there is a great omission in my copy as far as the question $7x^2 + 8y^2 = \square$, and $7x^2 - 8y^2 - 1 = \square$, in the next book. Mr. Burrows's copy, however, being complete in this part, I shall proceed to supply the omission in mine from his.

question $\frac{5y}{20} = x + \frac{x}{20}$, whence $x = \frac{5y}{21}$. Let the second number be z, then $\frac{7z}{20} = x + 1 + \frac{x+1}{20}$, whence $x = \frac{7z-21}{21}$. Let the third number be v, then $\frac{9v}{20} = x + 2 + \frac{x+2}{20}$, whence $x = \frac{9v-42}{21}$. From the first and second values of x is found $\frac{7z-21}{5} = y$, and from the second and third $\frac{9v-21}{7} = z$. From this last is found by the operation of the multiplicand $z = 6$ and $v = 7$, and 9 is called the augment of z, and 7 the augment of v; as this value of z does not give y integer, other values must be sought. The augment of z is directed to be called w, and the value of w is to be sought; w is found $= 3$, and its augment 5; 33 is found by multiplying 3 by 9 and adding 6; at last the required numbers are found 42, 33, and 28. Most of this example after that part where z is found $= 6$, is unintelligible to me. It appears only that new values of z are found from $6 + 9w$, and that w and its values are found $w = 3$ and $3 + 5u$, and from $w = 3$ the numbers are found. I suppose the question is solved much in the same way as such questions are now commonly done.

The next question gives $\frac{x-1}{2}$, $\frac{x-2}{3}$, $\frac{x-3}{5}$, $\frac{\frac{x-1}{2}-1}{2}$, $\frac{\frac{x-2}{3}-2}{3}$, $\frac{\frac{x-3}{5}-3}{5}$, to find x so that all these numbers shall be integers.

Let the number required be x; let the first quotient be $2y + 1$, this multiplied by the divisor 2 will produce for the dividend $4y + 2$, and 1 being added for the remainder $x = 4y + 3$. In like manner the second quotient being assumed $3z + 2$, $9z + 5 = 4y$; from this last, by the operation of the multiplicand, find $z = 3$ and $y = 8$, and the augment of z is $4v$, and that of y is $9v$; then $x = 4y + 3 = 3 + 4 \times (8 + 9v) = 35 + 36v$. As the value of y, 8 will not answer for x in the third condition, proceed thus: Let the third quotient be $5u + 3$. Multiply by 5 and add 3, $25u + 18 = x$, this is $= 35 + 36v$, hence $25u - 17 = 36v$; then by the operation of the multiplicand $u = 5$ and $v = 3$, $36v = 108$, $25 \times 5 - 17 + 35 = 143 = x$, and as $u = 5 + 36w$ and $v = 3 + 25w$, the augment of x is 900 because $25 \times 36 = 900$.

The next question is to find two numbers r and s such that $\frac{r-1}{5}$, $\frac{s-2}{6}$, $\frac{(s-r)-2}{3}$, $\frac{(r+s)-5}{9}$, and $\frac{rs-6}{7}$ are integers. To find other numbers besides 6 and 8. Let the first number be $5x + 1$, and the second $6x + 2$, the difference is $x + 1$. Divide by 3; suppose the quotient y and the remainder 2; then $x + 1 = 3y + 2$, and $x = 3y + 1$, and $5x + 1$ the first number $= 15y + 6$; and $6x + 2$ the second number $= 18y + 8$; their sum is $33y + 14$. Let $\frac{33y + 14}{9} = z + \frac{5}{9}$; then $\frac{9z - 9}{33} = y = \frac{3z - 3}{11}$; from this is found $y = 3$ and $z = 12$, or $y = 0 + 3w$ and $z = 1 + 11w$; hence $5x + 1 = 45w + 6$, and $6x + 2 = 54w + 8$. "As the product of these taken according to the question involves w^2, and would "be a long work," suppose $45w + 6 = 51$ and let the second number be as it was; throw out 7 from both, the remainders are 2 and $5w + 1$; take their product, it is $10w + 2$. Divide by 7; suppose u the quotient and 6 the remainder; $\frac{10w + 2}{7} = u + \frac{6}{7}$, $10w + 2 = 7u + 6$, $\frac{7u + 4}{10} = w$; from this is found $w = 6$ or $6 + 7v$. The second number being $54w + 8$, it is $54 \times 6 + 8 = 332$, and its augment is $54 \times 7v = 378v$. As the first number is $45w + 6$, and was supposed $= 51$, its augment is $45 \times 7v$.

The next is, what number is that which being multiplied by 9 and 7 and the two products divided by 30, the sum of the two remainders and two quotients will be 26. "Suppose the number x, multiply it by 16, it is $16x$, for if I had "multiplied separately by 7 and 9, by the first figure of the second book, it would "also be $16x$". Let the quotient of $16x$ divided by 30 be y, $16x - 30y$ is the remainder, add the quotient y; $16x - 29y = 26$, and $\frac{29y + 26}{16} = x$. The augment being greater than the divisor, subtract 16 from 26, it is 10. By the operation of the multiplicand, the quotient is found 90 and the multiplicand 50. From 90 subtract the 29^s, and from 50 the 16^s; 3 and 2 remain. Take 3 from 29 and 2 from 16, 26 and 14 remain. As 16 was once rejected from the augment, add 1 to 26, $x = 27$, and the quotient is 14 and the remainder 12. No new values can be had in this case by the augment, for then the quotient and remainder would be greater than 27.

The next is, what number is that which multiplied by 3, 7, and 9, and the products divided by 30, and the remainders added together and again divided by 30, the remainder will be 11. Suppose the number x; let $19x$ be divided by 30, and let the quotient be y, then $19x - 30y = 11$. "If we had multiplied "separately, and divided each number by 30, the sum again divided by 30 would

" also have been equal to 11 ; but this would have been a long operation. The proof " of the rule for such numbers is plain ; for example, if 8 be multiplied by 2, 3, and " 4, it will be 16, 24, and 32, and dividing each by 15, there will remain 1, 9, " and 2. The sum of these, that is 12, divide by 15 ; there remains 12. If 8 is " multiplied by the sum of these that is 9, it will be 72 ; divide this by 15, 12 " remains." From $\frac{30y + 11}{19} = x$ by the operation of the multiplicand is found $x = 29 + 30m$, and $y = 18 + 19m$.

The next is, what number is that which being multiplied by 23, and divided by 60, and again by 80, the sum of the remainders is 100? Let the number be x. Suppose the first remainder 40, and the second 60, and let $\frac{23x}{60} = y + \frac{40}{60}$, then $x = \frac{60y + 40}{23}$. Again, let $\frac{23x}{80} = z + \frac{60}{80}$, then $x = \frac{80z + 60}{23}$. Hence $80z + 20 = 60y$, from which are found $y = 3$ and $z = 2$; these values do not make x integer. $y = 3 + 4m$, $z = 2 + 3m$. Let $y = 7$ and $z = 5$, then $x = 20$. By supposing the remainders 30 and 70, x will be $= 90$, and the question may be worked without supposing the remainders given numbers, and by subjecting the quantities separately to the operation of the multiplicand.

In the next example y being the quotient of $\frac{5x}{13}$, $x + y = 30$. " Here there can " be no multiplicand for no line (of quotients) is found, nor can it be brought " out by interposition" (meaning quadratic equations). Proceed then by another method and the question is solved by position ; the number is supposed 13, and brought out truly $21\frac{2}{3}$; afterwards is added, " I say this too may be done by " Algebra thus :" Call the number x,

$$\frac{5x}{13} + x = \frac{18x}{13} = 30,\quad 18x = 390,\quad x = 21\frac{2}{3}.$$

The next example is. It is said in ancient books that there were three people, of whom the first had 6 dirhems, the second 8, and the third 100. They all went trading and bought pawn leaves at one price, and sold them at one rate, and to each person something remained. They then went to another place where the price of each leaf was 5 dirhems ; they sold the remainder and the property of the three was equal. At what price did they buy first, and at what rate did they sell, and what were the remainders?

Let the number of leaves bought for 1 dirhem be x, and suppose the price they sold for to be a certain number. For example: Suppose 110 leaves sold for 1 dirhem, then the leaves of the first person were $6x$; let the quotient of $6x$, divided by 110 be y, which is the number of dirhems first had; $6x - 110y$ is the number of leaves remaining. Multiply by 5, $30x - 550y$ is their price; add the former result y, $30x-549y$ is the amount of the first person's property. Then by four proportionals is found what the produce of $8x$ and $100x$ will be, that of $6x$ being y; the second person is found to have $y + \frac{y}{3}$ and the third $16y + \frac{2y}{3}$. After working as above, according to the terms of the question, the amount of the second person's property is found $\frac{120x - 2196y}{3}$ and in like manner the third person's $\frac{1500x - 27450y}{3}$. From $30x = 549y$, x is found $= 0$, and its augment 549, this is $= x$, and $y = 30$*. It is added that unless a number is assumed the question cannot be solved without the greatest difficulty.

This book closes with some general remarks about the attention and acuteness requisite for solving questions like these.

---

* Some of these numbers are evidently brought out wrong, for x should be divisible by 5 and by 21. Taking 525 (instead of 549) for x, and putting a, b, c for the leaves sold at 110 per dirhem; we get $b = 1100 + a$, and $c = 51700 + a$; where a may be 110, or the multiples of 110 up to 770.

END OF THE THIRD BOOK.

BOOK 4.

" ON THE INTERPOSITION (توسيط) OF MANY COLOURS."

" AND that relates to making the squares of many colours equal to number. " Its operation is thus: When two sides in the said condition are equal, in the " manner that has been given above for the interposition of one colour, suppose " a number and multiply or divide both sides by it, and add or subtract another " number, so that one of the two sides may be a square. Then the other side " must necessarily have a root, for the two sides are equal, and by the increase or " decrease of equal quantities, equals result; then take the root of that which is " easiest found. And if in the second there is the square of a colour and a " number, suppose the square the multiplicand and the number the augment, " and find the root by the operation of the square which was given above, and " this certainly will be number. Make the first root of colours equal in these " two, and know that you must equate so that the square, or the cube, or the " square of the square, of the unknown may remain. And after the operation of " the multiplication of the square, the less root is the quantity of the root of the " square of the colour of that side which was worked upon; and the greater root " is the root of all that side which was equal to the root of the first side. Equate " then in these two sides. And if in the second side there is the unknown, or " the square of the unknown, the operation of the multiplicand cannot be done. " Then assuming the square of another colour perform the operation. Thus it is. " If there is the unknown with numbers, or the unknown alone, whose root does " not come out by the multiplication of the square, unless by assuming the square " of another colour; when the root of this is obtained, equate in both and find " the quantity of the unknown. The result of this is, that you must apply your " mind with steadiness and sagacity, and perform the operation of multiplication " of the square in any way that you can." Here follow a few lines of general observations not worth translating.

Example. What number is that which being doubled, and 6 times its square added to it, will be a square?

Let the number be x, and let $2x + 6x^2 = y^2$. Multiply by 24, which is 6 multiplied by 4, and add 4; then divide by 4, it is $12x + 36x^2 + 1 = 6y^2 + 1$; $\sqrt{(12x + 36x^2 + 1)} = 6x + 1$. As the root of the other side $6y^2 + 1$ cannot be found, perform the operation of the multiplication of the square. Suppose the less root, or $y = 2$; then $6y^2 + 1 = 5^2$; $5 = 6x + 1$. $x = \frac{2}{3}$. By the rule of cross multiplication for new values $y = 2 \times 10 + 2 \times 10 = 40$ and $6x + 1 = 49$, whence $x = 8$.

The next is: What numbers are those two, the square of the sum of which, and the cube of their sum, is equal to twice the sum of their cubes?

Let the first number be $x - y$; and the second $x + y$, their sum will be $2x$: then $4x^2 + 8x^3 = 2((x - y)^3 + (x + y)^3) = 4x^3 + 12xy^2$; $4x + 4x^2 = 12y^2$; $4x^2 + 4x + 1 = 12y^2 + 1$; whence $2x + 1 = \sqrt{(12y^2 + 1)}$. Then by the multiplication of the square, making 2 the less root, 7 is the greater, $2x + 1 = 7$, $x=3$, $y=2$: $x-y=1$, $x+y=5$. By cross multiplication new values may be found.

The next is: What number is that which, when the square of its square is multiplied by 5, and 100 times its square subtracted from the product, the remainder is a square?

Let the number be x, and let $5x^4 - 100x^2 = y^2$; $5x^2 - 100 = \frac{y^2}{x^2} = \square$. Suppose 10 the less root, then $5 \times 10^2 - 100 = 400 = 20^2$; whence $y = 200$ and $x = 10$.

The next is: What are those two whole numbers whose difference is a square, and the sum of whose squares is a cube?

Let the two numbers be x and y; let $y - x = z^2$, then $x^2 = y^2 - 2yz + z^4$, and as $x^2 + y^2 = ⧈$, let $2y^2 - 2yz^2 + z^4 = z^6$. Then $2y^2 - 2yz^2 = z^6 - z^4$, and $4y^2 - 4yz^2 = 2z^6 - 2z^4$; and $4y^2 - 4yz^2 + z^4 = 2z^6 - z^4$; whence $2y - z^2 = \sqrt{(2z^6 - z^4)} = z^2\sqrt{(2z^2 - 1)}$. Now by the multiplication of the square making 5 the less root, $2 \times 5^2 - 1 = 49$, and 7 is the greater root. Then $\sqrt{(2z^6 - z^4)} = 175 = 2y - z^2$; $2y - 25 = 175$, $y = 100$, $x = y - z^2 = 75$. Or if $z = 29$ new values of x and y will be found as above.

Here follows a Rule. "Know that when both sides are equal and the root of "one side is found, and on the other side there is a colour and its square, make "this side equal to the square of the next colour, that is to say not to x, and let

" its square be to that of y, and if y be its square, make it equal to the square of z, " and multiply or divide both sides by a number, and add or subtract something " so that the root of the side may be found. Here then I have found two roots ; " one the first, which is the root of the first of the first two sides : and the " second, the root of the first of the second two sides, which is not equal to that " root. Perform the operation of the multiplication of the square with that other " side whose root is not found. Let the less root be equal to the first root, and " the greater root be equal to the second root, and the quantity of these colours " will be found."

Example. A person gave to a poor man in one day three units, and gave every day with an increase of two. One day the poor man counted all the money, and asked an accountant when he should receive three times the sum, at the rate paid. Let the number of days passed when he counted his money be x, and the number of days when the sum would be tripled y. First find the amount received in the time x, thus : " By a rule in the Lilavati." $(x - 1) \times 2 + 3 = 2x + 1 =$ the gift of the last day ; $\frac{2x + 1 + 3}{2} = x + 2 =$ the gift of the middle day. Multiply this by the number of days, $x^2 + 2x$ is the sum. In like manner the sum for the time y is $y^2 + 2y$, which by the question is $= 3x^2 + 6x$; whence $9x^2 + 18x + 9 = 3y^2 + 6y + 9$, and $3x + 3 = \sqrt{(3y^2 + 6y + 9)}$. Let $3y^2 + 6y + 9 = z^2$, then will be found $3y + 3 = \sqrt{(3z^2 - 18)}$. By the multiplication of the square, making 9 the less root, $3z^2 - 18 = 15^2$, therefore $3y + 3 = 15$ and $y = 4$; and because $3y^2 + 6y + 9 = z^2 = 81$, and $3x + 3 = 9$, $x = 2$. Thus, on the first day, he got 3, and the second 5, and the sum is 8 ; and on the fourth day he had 24, which is three times 8. In like manner, by making the less root 33, the greater root will be 57, and $y = 18$ and $x = 10$, and other values may be found by assuming other numbers for the less root.

Then follows a Rule, which is so mutilated that I do not know how to translate it. As far I can judge, its meaning appears to be this : If $ax^2 + by^2 = z^2$, the quantities are to be found thus : Either find r such that $ar^2 + b = \square = p^2$, and then x will be $= ry$ and $z = py$, or apply the rule given at the end of the 6th chapter of the introduction for the case, when $a = \square$.

Required* x and y, such that $7x^2 + 8y^2 = \square$, and $7x^2 - 8y^2 + 1 = \square$

* At this place my copy comes in again.

$7x^2 + 8y^2$ is supposed $= z^2$. The operation of multiplication of the square is directed to be performed, $7x^2$ being the multiplicand, and $8y^2$ the augment: "I "suppose 2 the less root, and multiply its square which is four by 7 the multi- "plicand; it is 28; add 8, the square is 36; 6 then is found the greater root; "6 black then is the quantity of blue, and 2 black the quantity of the unknown." Thus z is found $=6y$ and $x = 2y$. The second condition is $7x^2 - 8y^2 + 1 = \square$, whence by substituting $2y$ for x; $28y^2 - 8y^2 + 1$, or $20y^2 + 1 = \square = w^2$. Now by the operation of multiplication of the square, supposing the less root, and $20 \times 2^2+1=81=w^2$; whence $w = 9$. Therefore $x = 4$ and $y = 2$, supposing 36 the less root, x will be $= 72$ and $y = 36$.

In the next Example x and y are required such that $x^2 + y^3 = \square$, and $x + y = \square$. The multiplicand being a square let the augment be divided by y. Then by a rule of the 6th chapter of the introduction $\frac{y^2 - y}{2} = x$*. Let $\frac{y^2 + y}{2} = w^2$, then $y^2 + y = 2w^2$. Multiply by 4 and add 1, $4y^2 + 4y + 1 = 8w^2 + 1$. The root of the first side of the equation is $2y + 1$. Find the root of the second side by the operation of multiplication of the square, supposing 6 the less root, 17 will be the greater; now $2y + 1 = 17$; whence $y = 8$ and $x = 28$ Other values of y and x are $49 = y$, and $1176 = x$.

Another method of solving this question is given. Supposing one of the numbers $2x^2$ and the other $7x^2$; the sum is $9x^2$, which is the square of $3x$. The square of the first added to the cube of the second, is $8x^6 + 49x^4$; let this be $= y^2$; divide by x^4, the quotient is $8x^2 + 49$. Perform the operation of multiplication of the square, supposing 2 the less root, $8 \times 4 + 49 = 81 = 9^2$. Therefore $x = 2$, and the first number $2x^2$ is $=8$, and the second $7x^2$ is $=28$; and supposing 7 the less root, 21 will be the greater root: then $x = 7$, and the first number will be 98 and the second 343.

Rule. "If a square is equal†, the root of which cannot be found‡, and in

---

* Viz. If $A = p^2$ (supposing $Ax^2 + B = y^2$), then $\frac{\frac{B}{n} + n}{2} = y$; and $\frac{\frac{\frac{B}{n} - n}{2}}{p} = x$.

† Here seems to be an omission.

‡ If the number can be reduced to the form $(ax + my)^2 + ry^2$, it becomes rational by making $ax + my = \frac{r-1}{2}y$, for then $\left(\frac{r-1}{2}y\right)^2 + ry^2 = \left(\frac{r+1}{2}y\right)^2$. In Mr. Burrow's copy this rule begins, "If *there are two* "*sides*, the root," &c.

" which there are two squares of two colours, and the rectangle of those two " colours; take the root of one square, and find from the second square a root, so " that from the two squares that rectangle may be thrown out.

" For example: In the second side is 36 square of unknown, and 36 square of " black, and 36 rectangle of unknown and black. Take the root of 36 square of " unknown, 6 unknown; and from 36 square of black, take the root of 9 square " of black, 3 black. When we take twice the rectangle of these two roots, the " rectangle which is also 36 will be thrown out; and from the squares 27 square " of black will remain. Divide whatever remains by the colour, of which this is " the square; and from the number of the colour of the quotient, having sub- " tracted one, halve the remainder, make what is obtained equal to that root " which has been found. After dividing the second by the first, the quantity of " the first colour will be obtained."

In the next example x and y are required such that $x^2 + y^2 + xy = \square$, and $\sqrt{(x^2 + y^2 + xy)} \times (x + y) + 1 = \square$. " The first equation being multiplied by " 36 gives $36x^2 + 36xy^2 + 36xy = 36z^2$. The root of one square and part of the " second square, the rectangle having been thrown out, are found 6 unknown, and " 3 black: there remains 27 square of black." Then applying the rule, x is found $= \frac{5y}{3}$, whence $x^2 = \frac{25y^2}{9}$, and $x^2 + y^2 + xy = \frac{25y^2}{9} + y^2 + \frac{5y}{3}y = \frac{49y^2}{9}$ $= \left(\frac{7y}{3}\right)^2$, and $\sqrt{(x^2+y^2+xy)}\times(x+y)+1 = \frac{7y}{3}\left(\frac{5y}{3} + y\right) + 1 = \frac{56y^2 + 9}{9}$; make this $= w^2$, then $56y^2 + 9 = 9w^2$. Then root of $9w^2$ is $3w$, and by the operation of multiplication of the square, making 6 the less root, 45 will be the greater root. For $56 \times 36 + 9 = 2025 = 45^2$; therefore $y = 6$ and $x = 10$; or making 180 the less root, $y = 180$ and $x = 300$.

The next question is: Required x and y such that $\frac{xy + y}{2} = ⊞$, and $x^2 + y^2 = \square$, and $x + y + 2 = \square$, and $x - y + 2 = \square$, and $x^2 - y^2 + 8 = \square$, and $\sqrt[3]{\frac{x + xy}{2}} + \sqrt{(x^2 + y^2)} + \sqrt{(x + y + 2)} + \sqrt{(x - y + 2)} + \sqrt{(x^2 - y^2 + 8)} = \square$. It is plain that 6 and 8 will answer the above conditions. Pass them and find two others. It is required to find them by means of one unknown quantity only. Suppose the first number $p^2 - 1$, and the second $2p$. Then $\frac{xy + y}{2} = \frac{(p^2 - 1) \times 2p + 2p}{2} = \frac{2p^3 - 2p + 2p}{2} = p^3$. And $x^2 + y^2 = p^4 -$

$2p^2 + 1 + 4p^2 = p^4 + 2p^2 + 1 = (p + 1)^2$. And $x + y + 2 = (p^2 - 1) + 2p + 2 = p^2 + 2p + 1 = (p + 1)^2$. And $x^2 - y^2 + 2 = (p - 1)^2$. And $x^2 - y^2 + 8 = p^4 - 2p^2 + 1 - 4p^2 + 8 = p^4 - 6p^2 + 9 = (p^2 - 3)^2$; and the sum of the roots is equal to $p + (p^2 + 1) + (p + 1) + (p - 1) + (p^2 - 3) = 2p^2 + 3p - 2$. As the root of this cannot be found, make it equal to 9^2: then $2p^2 + 3p = 9^2 + 2$. Multiply by 8 and add 9; $16p^2 + 24p + 9 = 89^2 + 25$. Find the root of the first side $\sqrt{(16p^2 + 24p + 9)} = 4p + 3$. For the root of the second side perform the operation of multiplication of the square. Suppose the less root 5, the greater root will be 15; for $8 \times 25 + 25 = 225 = 15^2$. Make the root of this equal to that of the first side $4p + 3 = 15$, whence $p = 3$. In this case $x = 8$ and $y = 6$; making the less root 30, the greater will be 85; p will then be $\frac{41}{2}$ and $x = \frac{1677}{4}$ and $y = 41$; or making the less root 175, the greater will be 495, $p = 123$, $x = 15128$, and $y = 266$. Or x may be supposed $= p^2 + 2p$, and $y = 2$. Or $x = p^2 - 2p$, and $y = 2p - 2$. Or $x = p^2 + 4p + 3$, and $y = 2p + 4$. And the numbers required may be brought out in an infinite number of ways besides the above.

Here follows an observation, that in calculation, correctness is the chief point; that a wise and considerate person will easily remove the veil from the object; but that where the help of acuteness is wanting, a very clear explication is necessary. "And so it is when there is such a question as this: What two numbers are those, "the sum or difference of which, or the sum or difference of the squares of "which, being increased or lessened by a certain number, called the augment, "will be a square. If examples of this sort are required to be solved by one "colour only, it is not every supposition that will solve them; but first suppose "the root of the difference of the two numbers one unknown, and another "number with it either affirmative or negative. Divide the augment of the "difference of the two squares, by the augment of the sum of the numbers, and "add the root of the quotient to the root of the supposed difference abovemen-"tioned; it will be the root of the two numbers. Take then every one, the "square of the root of the difference of the numbers, and the square of the root "of the sum of the numbers, and write them separately. Afterwards, by the way "of opposition add and subtract, the augment of the difference, and the sum of "the two numbers aforementioned, as is in the example, to and from the squares of "the two, which, by the question, were increased or diminished. The result of "the addition and subtraction will be known, and from that the two numbers

" may be found in this manner, viz. by the rule $\frac{(x+y)+(x-y)}{2} = x$, and " $\frac{(x+y)-(x-y)}{2} = y$."

The next is to find x and y such that $x+y+3 = \square$, and $x-y+3 = \square$, and $x^2+y^2-4 = \square$, and $x^2-y^2+12 = \square$, and $\frac{xy}{2}+y = \boxdot$, and the sum of the roots $+2 = \square$. Exclude 6 and 7, which it is plain will answer. $\sqrt{(x-y)}$ is supposed $= p-1$, then x is made equal to p^2-2 and $y = 2p$, wherefore $x+y+3 = (p^2-2)+2p+3 = (p+1)^2$, and $x-y+3 = (p^2-2)-2p+3 = (p-1)^2$, and $x^2+y^2-4 = (p^4-4p^2+4)+4p^2-4 = (p^2)^2$, and $x^2-y^2+12 = (p^4-4p^2+4)-4p^2+12 = (p^2-4)^2$, and $\frac{xy}{2}+y = \frac{(p^2-2)\,2p}{2}+2p = p^3$, and the sum of the roots $+2 = (p+1)+(p-1)+p^2+(p^2-4)+p+2 = 2p^2+3p-2$; make this $= q^2$; $2p^2+3p-2 = q^2$, and $2p^2+3p = q^2+2$. Multiply by 8 and add 9. $16p^2+24p+9 = 8q^2+25$. The root of the first side is $4p+3$. Find the root of the second side by the operation of multiplication of the square; making the less root 175, the greater root will be 495. Therefore $4p+3 = 495$, and $p = 123$, and $x = 15127$, and $y = 246$.

The next is: Required x and y such that $x^2-y^2+1 = \square$, and $x^2+y^2+1 = \square$. Let $x^2 = 5p^2-1$ and $y^2 = 4p^2$, $x^2-y^2+1 = p^2$ and $x^2+y^2+1 = (3p)^2$. The root of $4p^2$ is $2p$. Find the root of $5p^2-1$ by the operation of multiplication of the square. Supposing the less root 1, the greater will be 2. Supposing 17 the less root, the greater will be 38. Or if $x^2+y^2-1 = \square$, and $x^2-y^2-1 = \square$, let $x^2 = 5p^2+1$ and $y^2 = 4p^2$; and so on as in the first case.

Rule. " When the root of one side is found, and on the second side there is " a colour, whether with or without a number, equate that side with the square " of the colour which is after it and one unit. And bring out the quantity of " the colour of the second side which is first in the equation; and bring out what " is required in the proper manner."

Example. To find x and y such that $3x+1 = \square$, and $5x+1 = \square$. Let $3x+1 = (3z+1)^2$, then $x = 3z^2+2z$, let $5(3z^2+2z)+1 = w^2$, whence $15z^2+10z = w^2-1$; multiply by 15 and add 25; $225z^2+150z+25 = 15w^2+10$. The root of the first side is $15z+5$. Find the root of the second side by the operation of multiplication of the square; making the less root 9, the greater will be 35; $15z + 5 = 35$; therefore $z = 2$ and $x = 16$. By another way: Let $x = \frac{z^2 - 1}{3}$; multiply by 5 and add 1, $\frac{5z^2 - 2}{3}$, make this $= w^2$; $5z^2 = 3w^2 + 2$. Multiply by 5; $25z^2 = 15w^2 + 10$; the root of the first side is $5z$. Find the the root of the second as before, making the less root 9, the greater will be 35; whence z and x. In the above example other values of x are mentioned besides those which I have taken notice of.

The next example is: Required x such that $3x + 1 =$ ⧈, and $3(3x + 1)^{\frac{2}{3}} + 1 = \square$. Let $3x+1=y^3$; then $3x = y^3 - 1$, and $x = \frac{y^3 - 1}{3}$; multiply this by 3 and add 1, the result is y^3, the cube cube root of which is y. Let $3y^2 + 1 = z^2$; making the less root 4, the greater will be 7, whence $x = 21$.

The next is: To find x and y such that $2(x^2-y^2)+3=\square$, and $3(x^2-y^2)+3=\square$. "Know that in bringing out what is required, you must sometimes suppose the "colour in that number which the question involves, and sometimes begin from "the middle, and sometimes from the end, whichever is easiest. Here then "suppose the difference of the squares unknown," &c.

Let $x^2-y^2=p$; make $2p+3=q^2$; then $\frac{q^2 - 3}{2}=p$; multiply this by 3, and add 3, it is $\frac{3q^2 - 3}{2}$; let this be $= r^2$; therefore $3q^2 - 3 = 2r^2$; multiply by 3 and transpose; $9q^2=6r^2+9$; the root of the first side is $3q$. Find that of the second side by the operation of multiplication of the square. Making the less root 6, the greater will be 15. Or making the less 60, the greater will be 147. If $3q=15$, $q=5$; if $3q=147$, $q=49$. In the first case $p=11$, and in the second $p = 1199$. Suppose $x - y = 1$, $x^2 - y^2$ being $= 11$, $\frac{x^2 - y^2}{x - y} = x + y = \frac{11}{1} = 11$; and $x+y$ and $x - y$ being given, x and y may be found. In the first case $x = 6$ and $y = 5$. In the second $x = 600$ and $y = 599$.

Rule. "If the square of a colour is divided by a number and the quotient is "a colour. If after the reduction of the equation its root is not found, make it "equal to the square of a colour, that the quantity of the black may come "out."

The next example which concludes this book is: Required x such that $\frac{x^2 - 4}{7}$ = a whole number. Make $\frac{x^2 - 4}{7} = y$, then $x^2 = 7y + 4$: the root of the first side is x; that of the second side cannot be found. "Then by the above rule" let $7z + 2 = \sqrt{(7y + 4)}$; $49z^2 + 28z + 4 = 7y + 4$; whence $7z^2 + 4z = y$. "As the quantity the of black is 7 square of the blue, and 4 blue; and as 7 blue and "2 units were supposed equal to a root which is equal to the unknown, I make "it equal to the unknown. This same is the quantity of the unknown. I sup- "pose the quantity of the blue a certain number," &c. As $7z+2=x$. If $z=0$, $x=2$. If $z=1$, $x=9$. If $z=2$, $x=16$. Other values of x may be found in the same manner.

"After* equating that the two sides may come out, multiply the first side by "a number and take its root, and keeping the second side as it was, multiply the "number of the second side by the number which the first was multiplied by, "and make it equal to the square of a colour."

Example. What number is that whose square being multiplied by 5, and 3 added, and divided by 16, nothing remains? Let the number be x. Let $\frac{5x^2 + 3}{16} = y$, a whole number; then $5x^2 = 16y - 3$, $5x^2 \times 5 = 25x^2$, $\sqrt{(25x^2)} = 5x$. Then there seems to be assumed $3 \times 5 = z^2 - 1$, and afterwards from $\frac{8z + 1}{5} = x$, the question is prepared for solution.

The next rule is: "If the cube of a colour is divided by a number, and the "quotient is a colour, make it equal to the cube of a colour. The way to find "that, is this: Assume the cube of a number and divide it by the divisor; there "should be no remainder; and add the number with it again nd again to the "divisor, or subtract it from it; or let the cube be a cube of a number, which "join with it; or again multiply that number by the fixed number 3, and the "result multiply into the quotient, and divide it by the dividend; also there

* In Mr. Burrow's copy the fourth book ends with two rules and two examples, which, as far as I can make them out, are as above.

" will be no remainder. If a number can be found with these conditions equate " with its cube."

Example. What number is that from whose cube 6 being taken and the remainder divided by 5 nothing remains? Let the number be x and $\frac{x^3 - 6}{5} = y$ a whole number. Hence $x^3 = 5y + 6$. Then the cube root of this which is $= x$ is assumed $= 5z + 1$, and y is found $= 25z^3 + 15z^2 + 3z - 1$.

END OF THE FOURTH BOOK.

BOOK 5.

"ON THE EQUATION OF RECTANGLES."

"AND that relates to the method of solving questions which involve the "rectangles of colours. Know that when the question is of one number multiplied by another, if the two numbers are supposed colours, it necessarily comes "under rectangle of colours. The solution of that being very intricate and "exceedingly difficult, if one number is required suppose it unknown; and if "two or three, suppose one unknown and the others certain numbers, such that "when they are multiplied together according to the question, no colour will be "obtained except the unknown, and it will not come under rectangle of colours. "And besides multiplication, if the increase or diminution of a number is required, perform the operation according to the question, then it will be exactly "a question of the same sort as those in the first book, which treats of the "equality of unknown and number. By the rules which were given there, what "is required will be found."

The first question is to find x and y such that $4x + 3y + 2 = xy$. Supposing $y = 5$, then $4x + 17 = 5x$, wherefore $x = 17$ and $y = 5$. Supposing $y = 6$, then $x = 10$. In like manner any number whatever being put for y the value of x will be found.

The next is to find w, x, y, z, such that $(w+x+y+z)\,20 = wxyz$. Suppose the first w, the second 5, the third 4, and the fourth 2; then $20w+220=40w$, and $w = 11$. Other values of w, x, y, z, are taken notice of.

The next is to find x and y in integers such that $\sqrt{(x + y + xy + x^2 + y^2)} + x + y = 23$, or $= 53$. In the first case, suppose the first number x, and the second 2, then $\sqrt{(x^2 + 3x + 6)} + x + 2 = 23$, and $\sqrt{(x^2 + 3x + 6)} = 21 - x$, and $x^2 + 3x + 6 = x^2 - 42x + 441$; whence x will be found $= \frac{29}{3}$; this not being an integer, let the operation be repeated. Suppose $y = 3$ then x will be found $= \frac{97}{11}$; this too being a fraction, suppose $y = 5$; then x will be $= 7$. In the second case a number is put for y, and a fractional value of x is found. "And if we suppose the second number 11, the quantity of the unknown will "be 17, and this is contrary; for if the second number is supposed 17, the quan- "tity of the unknown will be 11; and if one is supposed a colour and the other a "certain number, it is probable that the unknown will be brought out a fraction; "and if a whole number is required, it may be found by much search. And if "both are supposed colours, and the question solved by this rule, a whole "number will easily be found,"

*Rule**. "When two sides are equal, the method of equating them is thus: "subtract the rectangle of one side from the other side, and besides that what- "ever is on the second side is to be subtracted from the first; then let both sides "be divided by the rectangle; and on the side where there are colours let those "colours be multiplied together. And let a number be supposed, and let the "numbers which are on that side be added to it; and let the result be divided "by the supposed number; and let the quotient and the number of the divisor "be separately increased or lessened by the number of the colours which were "before multiplication, whichever may be possible. Wherever the unknown is "added or subtracted there will be the quantity of the black; and wherever the "black is added or subtracted there will be the quantity of the unknown. And "in like manner if there is another number, and if both addition and subtraction "are possible, let both be done, and two different numbers will be found. Also "if the number of the colours is greater, and cannot be subtracted, subtract the "quotient and the number of the divisor from the colour if possible, what was "required will be obtained."

Example. x and y are required such that $4x + 3y + 2 = xy$. Multiply 3 by

---

* This rule is very ill expressed; it must mean—The equation being reduced to $ax + by + c = xy$, $a + \frac{ab + c}{p}$ will be $= y$ and $b + p = x$. Because $ax + by + c = xy$, $c = xy - ax - by$, add ab to both sides, then $ab + c = xy - ax - by + ab = (x - b)(y - a)$: and making $p = x - b$, $y - a$ will be $= \frac{ab + c}{p}$. Therefore $x = b + p$, and $y = a + \frac{ab + c}{p}$. More formulæ may be had by resolving $ab + c$ into different factors.

4, and add 2 to the product $3\times4+2=14$. Suppose 1. Divide 14 by 1. Add 4 to the number 1, and add 3 to the quotient $4+1=5=y$, and $3+\frac{14}{1}=17=x$. Or $4+\frac{14}{1}=18=y$, and $3+1=4x$. "And no other case is possible." Dividing by 2, the quotient will be 7; $y=11$ and $x=5$. And by another method y will be found $=6$ and $x=10$ *.

To find x and y so that $10x+14y-58=2xy$. After reducing the equation to $5x+7y-29=xy$. By the rule above given, assume divisors of $5\times7-29$; 1 being the divisor, 6 is the quotient.

$$5+1=6=y \text{ and } 7+6=13=x,$$
$$\text{or } 5+6=11=y \qquad 7+1=8=x,$$
$$\text{or } 5-1=4=y \qquad 7-1=6=x.$$

2 being the divisor, 3 is the quotient.

$$y=8, \qquad y=7, \qquad y=3,$$
$$x=9, \qquad x=10, \qquad x=4;$$

and no others are possible. 3 being the divisor 2 is the quotient, and the quantities are as above. It is added that these two examples may be proved by geometrical figures as well as numbers.

* In Mr. Burrow's copy there is another example which is wanting in mine. It is as above.

THE END.

Mr. Davis's Notes.

I HERE put together all I have been able to make out of Mr. Davis's notes of the Bija Ganita. What I have extracted literally is marked by inverted commas; the rest is either abstract, or my own remarks or explanations. I have preserved the divisions of the Persian translation for the convenience of arrangement and for easy reference. Mr. Davis's letter to me, authenticating these notes, is annexed.

Chapter 1st of Introduction.

THE manner in which the negative sign is expressed, is illustrated in the notes by the addition and subtraction of simple quantities, thus: " Addition.—When " both affirmative or both negative, &c. When contrary signs, the difference " is the sum.

$$\begin{array}{cccc} \dot{3} & 3 & 3 & \dot{3} \\ \dot{4} & 4 & \dot{4} & 4 \\ \hline \dot{7} & 7 & \dot{1} & 1 \\ \hline \end{array}$$

" Subtraction.

$$\begin{array}{cccc} 3 & \dot{3} & 3 & \dot{3} \\ 2 & \dot{2} & \dot{2} & 2 \\ \hline 1 & \dot{1} & 5 & \dot{5} \\ \hline \end{array}$$

" Multiplication.

" When both are affirmative or both negative the product is affirmative.

$$2 \times 3 = 6,\ \dot{2} \times \dot{3} = 6,\ 2 \times \dot{3} = \dot{6},\ \dot{2} \times 3 = \dot{6}.$$

" Why is the product of two affirmative or two negative quantities always " affirmative? The first is evident. With regard to the second it may be ex- " plained thus: Whether one quantity be multiplied by the other entire, or in " parts, the product will always be the same, thus:

$$\begin{array}{l} \text{“ } 135 \times 12 = 1620 \\ \text{“ } 135 \times 8 = 1080 \\ \text{“ } 135 \times 4 = 540 \\ \hline \phantom{\text{“ } 135 \times 12 = }1620 \end{array}$$

" Then, let 135 be $\times$ by $\dot{4}$, but $12 - \dot{4} = 16$ and $135 \times \dot{4} = 540$; $135 \times 16 = 2160$, and $540 + 2160 = 2700$, which is absurd: but $\dot{540} + 2160 = 1620$."

Mr. Davis remarks to me that there are here evidently some errors and some omissions, and he thinks that the meaning of the last part of the passage must have been to this effect: 12 may be composed of 16 added to $\dot{4}$. Let 135 be multiplied by 12, so composed

$$\begin{array}{l} 135 \times 16 = 2160 \\ 135 \times \dot{4} = 540 \\ \hline 135 \times 12 = 2700 \end{array} \text{ This is absurd: but } \begin{array}{l} 135 \times 16 = 2160 \\ 15 \times \dot{4} = \dot{540} \\ \hline 135 \times 12 = 1620 \end{array} \text{ which is}$$

right. Thus too $\dot{4}$ may be taken as formed by $12 + \dot{16} = \dot{4}$, and if

$$\begin{array}{l} \dot{135} \times \dot{16} = \dot{2160} \\ \dot{135} \times 12 = \dot{1620} \\ \hline \dot{135} \times \dot{4} = 3780 \end{array} \text{ which is absurd: but } \begin{array}{l} \dot{135} \times \dot{16} = 2160 \\ 135 \times 12 = \dot{1620} \\ \hline \dot{135} \times \dot{4} = 540 \end{array} \text{ which is right.}$$

Perhaps something like the following might have been intended:

$-135 \times -12 = 1620$ either $+$ or $-$; $\left.\begin{array}{l} -135 \times -8 \\ -135 \times -4 \end{array}\right\} = 1620$ either $+$ or $-$; now $4 - 12 = -8$; and $8 - 12 = -4$; therefore the sum of $\left.\begin{array}{l} -135 \times (4 - 12) \\ -135 \times (8 - 12) \end{array}\right\}$ must be $= -135 \times -12$,

$-135\times(4-12)=-\ 540+$ or -1620
$-135\times(8-12)=-1080+$ or -1620

product -1620 $\quad -3240=-4860$ if $-\times-$ gives $-$; but
$-1620+3240=+1620$ if $-\times-$ gives $+$; therefore $-135\times-12=+1620$.

Chapter 3.

" OF QUANTITIES UNKNOWN, BUT EXPRESSED BY LETTERS."

" Jabut tabut . . . . . . 1st . . या
" Kaluk . . . . 2d . . का
" Neeluk . . . . 3d . . नी
" Peet . . . . 4th . पी
" Loheet . . . . 5th . लो
&c.
" Commentary adds Hurretaka . . . 1
" Chitraka 2
&c.

" These are styled abekt or unknown.

" These may be added to themselves, subtracted, &c. but cannot be added " to, &c. known quantities in the manner explained, or to unlike quantities of " any kind. The square of या cannot be added to या, but the addition may be " expressed thus या 1 add to या या; the reason is, because to add 5 signs " to 2 degrees we cannot say 5 added to 2 is equal to seven, for this would be " absurd, we therefore write the sum $5^s\ 2^o$. But when the unknown quantity is " discovered it may then be added to the known, into one simple quantity.

" The unknown quantities are usually written first, and the highest powers of " them before the lower..

" या व2 | या3 | 3. This is $2x^2 + 3x + 3$.

Also
" The multiplication of unknown quantities.

" To multiply या2 | into 2 | we have या4.

या by या gives its square or या व, and this multiplied by या, gives या घ, &c.

Also this example of multiplication.

" या3	या5	लो$\dot{1}$	या व15	या$\dot{3}$	
" लो2	या5	लो$\dot{1}$	या10	लो$\dot{2}$	
			या व15	या7	लो$\dot{2}$

which is the product of $(5x - 1) \times (3x + 2)$.

Chapter 4.

" OF THE CARNI OR SURD QUANTITIES."

" Example of two numbers, 2 and 8.
" $2 + 8 = 10$, the mahti carni.
" $2 \times 8 = 16$; its root is 4, and $4 \times 2 = 8$ the laghoo carni.

" The mahti carni 10
" Laghoo carni added . . 8

18, the sum of these carnis. This 18 is the square of " the sum of their roots."

And there is another example with the numbers 4 and 9, and the following theorem, "2)8(4, its root is 2,

$$\begin{array}{cc} 2 & 2 \\ +\,1 & -\,1 \\ \hline 3 & 1 \end{array}$$

"3 × 3 = 9   9 × 2 = 18 sum.
"1 × 1 = 1   1 × 2 = 2 difference."

Also this: "The carni 18 is found; its root is the sum of the roots of the two "given numbers; but if there be two roots there must be two squares, the "difference is the square of the difference between these squares."

And the following examples in multiplication: "To multiply the square roots "of 2, 8, and 3, by the square root of 3 and the integral number 5.

"These are surds, therefore take the square of the sum of the square roots of 2 and 8, and multiply by the square of 5.

"Square of sum of square roots of 2 and 8 is 18.

18	25, 3	450, 54	
3	25, 3	75, 9	root of 9 is 3 roop.

Sqrs. 450   Sqrs. 54   Sqrs. 75 — roop 3.

"Example second.

	Roop.	Carni.	Carni.
"Multipliers	$\dot{5}$,	3,	12.

" $\dot{5}$	$\dot{25}$	25, 3	625, $\dot{75}$	$\dot{25}$ roop	$\dot{25}$ roop	675
" 3 } 12 }	27	25, 3	675, 81	9 roop	9 roop	$\dot{75}$
					$\dot{16}$	300

"The product therefore is $\dot{16}$ roop, 300 carni."

The square of a negative quantity being made negative is here taken notice of as in the Persian Translation: In division the following rule is mentioned.

"The carni divisor: reverse of each term, its sign, and multiply both divisor "and dividend."

Carni which here means surd, means also the hypothenuse of a right-angled triangle.

Chapter 5.

" WHAT is that number by which when 221 is multiplied and 65 added to the " product, and that product divided by 195, nothing will remain.

" The dividend *bhady*, divisor *hur* or *bhujuk*, the number added or subtracted " is called *chepuk*. The bhady is here 221, the bhujuk 195; when divided the " quotient is 1, this is disregarded; the *seke* or remainder is 26, by which 195 " divided the quotient is 7 disregarded, the remainder is 13, by which divide " 221, the quotient is 17, the remainder is 0. The quotient 17 is the true or " *dirl-bhady*.

" Then 195 divided by 13, the quotient is 15; the remainder 0. This quotient " is named *dirl-bhujuk*.

" Then divide 65 by 13, the quotient is 5; the remainder 0; the quotient is " the *dirl-chepuk*.

" They are now reduced to the smallest numbers.

" 17 dirl-bhady.
" 15 dirl-bhujuk.
" 5 dirl-chepuk.

The quotients are found and arranged as in the rule with 5 and 0 below,

" 1
thus: 7
5
0 this is called *bullee*; the cipher is called *unte* or the latter; the next (5) " is called *upantea*. Multiply this by its next number (7) and add the next below " 5, this being 0, the product will be 35. Multiply this by the uppermost number " (1) and add the next below (5) the amount is 40."

Then 40 and 35 are directed to be divided by the dirl-bhady and bhujuk.

```
17) 40 (2
    34
    --
     6 this is called lubd.
15) 35 (2
    30
    --
     5 this is called goonuk, and it is the number sought.
```

$\frac{221 \times 5 + 65}{195} = 6$, and directions are given for finding new values of x and y, (supposing $\frac{ax + c}{b} = y$) by adding a (in its reduced state) and its multiples to the value of y; and b and its multiples to the value of x.

The next question in the notes is also the same as that in the Persian.

"Bhady 100, bhujuk 63, and chepuk 90.

"OPERATION.

"These numbers cannot be all reduced to lower proportionals.

"100 divided by 63, the quotient is 1, the remainder 37; by this remainder "divide 63, the quotient is 1, the remainder is 26; by this divide 37, the quotient "is 1, the remainder 11. Divide again; quotient 2, remainder 4. Divide "again; quotient 2, remainder 3. Divide again; quotient 1, remainder 1; this re- "mainder 1 is disregarded. The several quotients write down thus:

```
 1
--
 1
--
 1
--
 2
--
 2
--
 1
--
90 the chepuk.
--
 0
```

"Multiply and add from the bottom as in the former example, $90\times1+0=90$,
"$90\times2+90=270$, $270\times2+90=630$, $630\times1+270=900$, $900\times1+630=1530$,
"$1530\times1+900=2430$.

"The two last are the numbers sought; then

"100)2430(24 this is disregarded.
200
———
430
400
———
30 Seke or remainder is the lubd.

"63)1534(24
126
———
270
252
———
18 this is the goonuk."

$$\frac{100\times18+90}{63}=30.$$

The method of reducing the bhady and chepuk is noticed, and the values of $x=171$ and $y=27$, being first found the true values are found, thus:

63)171(2 and 10)27(2
126   20
———   ———
45   7

$$63-45=x \text{ and } (10-7)\times10=y.$$

The several methods of proceeding: first, by reducing the bhady and chepuk; second, by reducing the bhujuk and chepuk; third, by reducing the bhady and chepuk; and then the reduced chepuk and the bhujuk are also mentioned.

The following explanation of these reductions is given:

"The bhady 27, bhujuk 15;
" these are divided each by 3 . . . . 9 and 5.
" Write 27 in two divisions . . . . . 9 and 18
" these again divided by 3 . . . . . 3 and 6
" these two add $3+6=9$; thus the parts added, how many so ever are, always
" equal to the whole, thus therefore they are reduced to save trouble, and there-
" fore all these numbers are so reduced; but the goonuk is as yet unknown. Let

"it be supposed to be 5, by which multiply the parts of the bhady 9 and 18; "$9\times5=45$, $18\times5=90$, which added are 135, and the bhady $27\times5=$ "the same 135; this divided in two parts, 60 and 75, and added again, are 135. "The lowest terms of 27 and 15 above, are 9 and 5; the common measure 3, "multiplied by 5, $3\times5=15$ and $9\times15=135$.

"Thus too the chepuk must be reduced, and when they are all reduced to the "lowest, the lubd and goonuk will be true; and if their numbers are not reduced "to their lowest terms, the work will be the greater."

The principle on which the chepuk is reduced is explained thus:

"OF THE CHEPUK."

"The bhady 221, bhujuk 195, chepuk 65; the goonuk was found 5, lubd 6.

$221\times5=1105$
195)1105(5 lubd.
975
———
130 seke, which deduct from the bhujuk $195-130=65$ equal "to the chepuk, which divide by the bhujuk 195)195(1. The lubd is 5, to "which add 1; $6=$ the original lubd."

In another example the bhady $=60$, bhujuk $=13$, and chepuk $=16$ or -16. By the bullee are found the numbers 80 and 368; then $368-60\times6=8$ the lubd, and $80-13\times6=2$ the goonuk; $60-8=52$ the lubd corrected, and $13-2=11$ the goonuk corrected. $\frac{60\times11+16}{13}=52$, and $\frac{60\times2-16}{13}=8$.

"Note in the text: The product by the two uppermost terms of the bullee, "when divided by the bhady and bhujuk respectively, have hitherto always "quoted the same number, as in the last example 6 the quotient, and the like "also in the foregoing examples, but when it happens otherwise, as in the fol- "lowing: When the bhady is 5, the bhujuk 3, the chepuk 23 affirmative or "negative, what will be found the goonuk?

3)5(1
3
—
2)3(1
2
—
1 seke disregarded

1
—
1
—
23
—
0
Bullee.

$23\times1=23,+0=23$
$23\times1=23,+23=46$

5)46(9
45
—
1

3)23(7
21
—
2 goonuk

"The two quotients being different numbers they must be taken the same; "thus instead of 9, take the quotient 7.

$$\begin{array}{l} 5)46(7 \\ \ \ 35 \\ \hline \ \ 11 \end{array}$$

"therefore the goon is 2, the lubd 11. $\frac{5 \times 2 + 23}{3} = 11$.

"Next, when the chepuk is negative, or to be deducted, the rule directs to "subtract the lubd from the bhady, but here it cannot be done: the rule is "reversed, thus $11-5=6$, which is the lubd for the negative chepuk; next for "the goon of the rhin chepuk $3-2=1$; therefore the goon and lubd for the "rhin chepuk are 1 and 2; $5 \times 1=5$; but from this the rhin chepuk cannot be "taken; therefore take it from the chepuk $23-5=18$.

"$3)18(6$ the lubd."

$$\begin{array}{l} \ \ 18 \\ \hline \ \ \ 0 \end{array}$$

Other cases are mentioned for the negative chepuk, and for the chepuk reduced, and for new values of the goon and lubd.

The examples $\frac{5x + 0}{13}$ and $\frac{5x + 65}{13}$, which are in the Persian translation, are also stated here, but no abstract of the work is given, only the lubd is said to be 5 and the goonuk 0, which applies to the last of the two only.

"The seke in bekullas is termed sood, meaning that it is the chepuk; the "bhady, let it be 60. The coodin or urgun is the bhujuk, from which the lubd "will be found in bekullas, and the goon will be the seke of the cullas, which "must be taken as the chepuk; making the bhady again 60, the bhujuk will be "the urgun, the lubd of this will be in cullas, the seke is the seke of the ansas, "which seke must be taken as the chepuk; the bhady being taken 30, the "bhujuk is still the urgun, the lubd is in ansas, the seke is the seke of the signs,

" which seke take as the chepuk; making the bhady 12, the bhujuk will be still " the coodin, the lubd here will be signs, the seke is the seke of bhaganas, " revolutions, which seke must be taken as the chepuk; the lubd will here be " in bhaganas, the seke the urgun."

Example. " Let the calp coodin or urgun be 19, the bhaganas 9, the " urgun 13."

" Then by proportion if 19 gives 9, what will 13 give?" This is found to be 6 rev. 1 sign, 26°, 50′, 31″, with a fraction of 11; then from $\frac{60x - 11}{19} = y$, x and y are found $x = 10$, $y = 31$; then from $\frac{60x' - 10}{19} = y'$, $y' = 50$ and $x' = 16$, from $\frac{30x'' - 16}{19} = y''$, $y'' = 26$, $x'' = 17$, from $\frac{12x''' - 17}{19} = y'''$, $y''' = 1$, $x''' = 3$ from $\frac{9x'''' - 3}{19} = y''''$, $y'''' = 6$ and $x'''' = 13$, which is the urgun.

In another Example. Seke bekullas = 11″, bhaganas = 49, calp coodin or urgun = 149, Jeist urgun = 97. The quantity is found by the rule to be = 23 rev. 10 signs, 18°, 23′, 31″, the remainder 11.

" The addy month 1, is the bhady; the coodin 195, the bhujuk; the seke of " the addy month 95, is the chepuk.

" 195)1(0
1 seke disregarded

0
95 bullee.
0

" $0 \times 95 + 0 = 0$

Raas $\frac{0}{95}$

" 1)0(0
0 lubd

195)95(0
95 goonuk.

" $95 \times 1 - 95 = 0$

195)0(0
0

"The che tits 26 is the bhady; coodin 225, is the bhujuk; abum seke 220, "chepuk.

"225)26(0
—
26)225(8
208
—
17)26(1
17
—
9)17(1
9
—
8)9(1
8
—
1 disregarded.

0
—
8
—
1
—
1
—
1
—
220
—
0

Raas 660
—
5720

26)660(25
—
10 seke the lubd,

225)5720(25
—
95 seke the goonuk.

$$\frac{26 \times 95 - 220}{225} = 10$$

"Hence the chandra days are 95."

The last rule of this chapter is taken notice of as follows:

"OF THE SANSTIST COOTUK."

"By what number may 5 be multiplied and divided by 63, the remainder will "be 7; and that number so found, when multiplied by 10 and divided by 63, "the remainder will be 14.

"The two goonuks are 5 and 10, the sum is the bhady; the two sekes are "7 and 14, the sum is the chepuk; the bhujuk in both is the same or 63."

The question is solved as before; it ends "Thus, however numerous be "the goonuks given, let them all be added for the bhady; and the same with "respect to the given sekes for the chepuk; the bhujuk will be always the "same."

Chapter 6.

" THE CHACRA BALA."

" THE multiplication of the square is a chacra bala. There are six cases: " The first quantity assumed is called *hursua* (the smaller); its square must be " multiplied by the *pracrit*, and then must be added the *chepuk*; that is such a " chepuk as will by addition produce a square, and this chepuk may require to be " affirmative or negative, which must be ascertained. The root of this square is " the *jeist*: these three, the canist or hursua, jeist, and chepuk must be noted " down and again written down."

The distinctions of *samans babna* and *anter babna* are given as follows:

" OF THE SAMANS BABNA."

" When the jeist and canist are multiplied into each other (budjra beas) " the sum is the hursa or canist. It is called *budjra beas* from its being a tri- " angular multiplication; the upper, or jeist, or greater, being multiplied by the " lower, smaller, the canist; and the canist multiplied by the greater or jeist; " the two products added is the hurs.

" The two canists multiplied together, and multiplied again by the pracrit, " then the product of the two jeists—added altogether, produces the root of the " jeist; the product of the two chepuks then becomes the chepuk."

The anter babna is described thus: " The difference between the two products " or budjra beas, produces hursa or canist. The product of the canists multiply " by the pracrit, and the difference between (*this and*) the product of the two " jeists is the root of the jeist, and the product of the two chepuks is the " chepuk."

The rest of this is very imperfect, but the cases of $\beta\beta = \text{B}p^2$ and $\beta\beta = \frac{\text{B}}{p^2}$, and the rule $\text{A}\left(\frac{2r}{r^2 - \text{A}}\right)^2 + 1 = \square$, are plainly alluded to. (See notes on the Persian translation.) "Thus" (it is added) "the root of the canist and jeist may be in a "variety of cases found."

After this there are examples the same as in the Persian translation, and worked the same way as far as the "Operation of Circulation;" and, after the examples. "Hence, how various soever the Ist, from the somans babna and anter babna may "be produced canist, jeist, and chepe; and hence it is called the chacra bala."

I find no abstract of the rule for the "operation of circulation," but there is the first example, viz. $67x^2 + 1 = \square$, as follows: "Roop 1 is the canist, $\dot{3}$ is "the chepe; then the pracrit 67, canist 1, jeist 8. Hurs 1 is the bhady, chepe is "the bhujuk, jeist 8 is the chepuk; then by the cootuk gunnit

"Bha. 1, che 8,

"Hur $\dot{3}$; hence the goonuk 1.

"then the square of 1 is 1, $67 - 1 = 66$, but this is not the smallest; then "$\dot{3}+\dot{3}=6$, $6+1=7$; its square 49, deduct from pracrit $67-49=18$; $\dot{3})18(\dot{6}$; "but the negative must be made affirmative 6; and $5\times5=25$, and $25\times67=$ "1675, and $1675+6=1681$ its root 41; then by the cootuk gunnit

"Bha 5, che 41,

"Hur 6;

"then $5\times5=25$ and $61-25=42$, $\dot{6})42(\dot{7}$; the lubd is the canist 11; $11\times11=$ "121, $121\times67=8107$; chepe is $\dot{7}$, $8107+\dot{7}=8100$ its root is 90, which is the "jeist; then by the cootuk

"Canist is bhady 11, che 90,

"Hur $\dot{7}$.

"Here the goon is 2, che $\dot{7}$; $7+2=9$ the second goonuk; its square is 81 "$81-67=14$; $7)14(2$ the other chepe."

"The canist 27. This is made jeist 221.

"Ca. 27, 221 jeist, che 2.

"Ca. 27, 221 jeist, che 2.

"Ca. 11934, jeist 97684, che 4.

"Ca. 5967, jeist 48842, che 1.

"The square ca. 35605089, which multiply by 67, and 1 added, the sum will "be 2385540964, and its root is 48842."

BOOK 1.

"THE unknown quantities, &c. must be clearly stated, and then the equation "must be reduced in the manner hereafter shewn by ×, by ÷, by the rule of "proportion, by progression, ratios, by ◺ ; still maintaining the equality. "When they are otherwise, add the difference; then *sodana* the quantities; the "same with respect to roots. In the other side of the equation the roop must be "sodanad with the roop. When there are surds they must be sodanad with "surds; then by the remainder of the unknown quantities division, the roop "must be divided; the quotient is the quantity sought, now become *visible*."

"Then the quantity so found must be utapanad, in order to resolve the "question."

It will be remarked that the Persian translation has "*the figure of the bride*," for that expression which is represented by ◺ in the above abstract. Mr. Davis tells me that the original had nothing like a reference to Euclid, and that this part related simply to the proportions of right-angled triangles.

There follow abstracts of the seven first questions of this book, with their solutions, which are the same as those in the Persian translation.

The first part of the first example is: "One man had 6 horses and 300 pieces of "silver, and the other had 10 horses, and owed 100 pieces of silver; their pro-"perty was equal. *Quære*, the value of each horse, and the amount of the pro-"perty of each person. Here the unknown quantity is the price of one horse."

"Ja 6, roo 300
"Ja 6, roo $\dot{1}00$ these are equal.

"Ja 6, roo 300
"Ja 10, roo $\dot{1}00$. Sodan, that is transpose.

"Ja 6 + 300 = Ja 10 — 100
"Ja 4 = 400
"Ja = 100

The third example, where the Persian translator has introduced the names Zeid and Omar, is in Mr. Davis's notes thus:

" One man said to another, if you give me 100 pieces of silver I shall have " twice as many as you; the other said give me 10 pieces and I shall have six " times as many as you. *Quære,* the number each had.

" Ja 2 roo 100
" Ja 1 roo 100
" Ja 12 roo 660
" Ja 1 roo 110
" Diff. Ja 11 roo 770
" Ja roo 70

BOOK 2.

" THE square root of the sum of the squares of the bhoje and cote is the carna. " Explain the reason of this truth.

" The carna is ka ja; the figure thus, 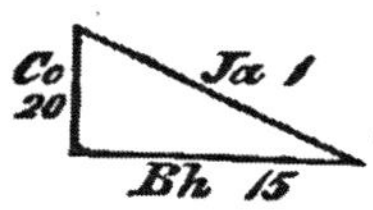

. Divide this by a perpen- " dicular 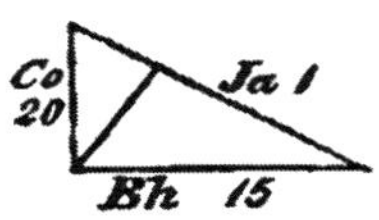

; these are equal triangles. The bhoje is abada or given. " The lumb or perpendicular is the cote, 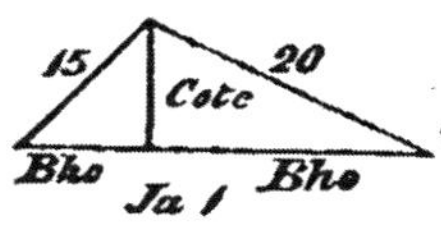

. In the latter the cote " is a carna, the lumb perpendicular is the bhoje, the cote is the carna; they are " similar triangles, When the bhoje, now carna, gives the lumb for the cote, " then cote for carna how much? Thus by proportion the cote is found."
Also
" As bhoje 15 is to carna, then from this carna 15 what bhoje?

"Therefore 15 × 15, and divide by Ja 1, and the small bhoje is found = $\frac{225}{Ja\ 1}$. Again.

"As cote 20, to the carna, so is the carna 20. What cote?"

This is found = $\frac{400}{Ja\ 1}$, and this added to $\frac{225}{Ja\ 1} = \frac{625}{Ja\ 1}$ is the carna; whence 25 = Ja 1.

"Then from the bhoje to find the perpendicular.

"The bhoje 15, its square 225; bhoje abada = 9, its square 81; the differ-"ence is 144; its root is the lumb 12.

"So, the cote 20, its square 400; cote abada 16, its square 256; difference "of squares 144; its root the lumb is 12." Again,

Another way.

"Carna ja 1; then half the rectangle of the bhoje and cote is equal to the "area = 150; therefore the area of the square formed upon the carna in this "manner will be equal to four times the above added to the contained square, "which square is equal to the rectangle of the difference between the bhoje and "cote, which is 5 × 5 = 25. The rectangle of the bhoje and cote is 15 × 20 "=300; and 300×2=600 (or $\frac{300}{2}$ × 4); 600 + 25 = 625, which is equal to "the area of the whole square drawn upon the carna, and therefore the square "root of this is equal to the carna = 25. If this comes not out an integral "number, then the carna is imperfect or a surd root.

"The sum of the squares of the bhoje and cote, and the square of the sum of "the bhoje and cote, the difference of these is equal to twice their rectangles; "therefore (theorem) the square root of the squares of the bhoje and cote is equal "to the carna. To illustrate this, view the figure."

Here a figure is given which requires explanation to make it intelligible.

"In that figure where 3 deducted from the bhoje, and the square root made of "the remainder, and one deducted from the square root, and where the remainder "is equal to the difference between the cote and carna. Required the bhoje, cote, "and carna.

"OPERATION."

"Let the assumed number be 2, to which add 1, its square is made = 9; to this "add 3, whence the bhoje is 12; its square is 144, and this by the foregoing is "equal to the difference between the squares of the cote and carna; and the sum "of the cote and carna multiplied by their difference is equal to this."

Then follows something which I cannot make out, but it appears to be an illustration of the rule, that the difference of two squares is equal to a rectangle under the sum and difference of their sides, probably the same as that in the Persian translation. The end of it is,

"Thus the square of 5 is 25, and the difference between 5 and 7, sides of the "square, is 2; the sum of those sides is 12, which multiplied together is 24; "therefore equal to this is the remainder, when from the square of 7 is deducted "the square of 5.

"The difference between the squares of these is known, and thence the "cote and carna are discovered thus: This difference of squares divide by the "difference of the cote and carna, or difference of roots, as in the Pati Ganita, "$\frac{144}{2} = 72$, and this is the sum of the two quantities sought, as is taught in the "Pati Ganita, but their difference is 2; therefore deduct 2 from the sum, the "remainder is 70, and half of this is the first quantity sought. Again, add 2 to "72, the sum is 74; its half is 37 the other quantity; therefore the cote is 35, "the carna 37.

"When the proposed difference is 1, the numbers are found 7, 24, 25; multi-"ply these by 4, the numbers will be 28, 96, 100.

Then follows a note of the rule, that the difference of the sum of the squares of two numbers, and the square of their sum, is equal to twice the rectangle of the two numbers, and this example as in the Persian translation.

"The two numbers are 3 and 5; the sum of squares $9 + 25 = 34$; the sum "8, its square 64; the difference is $64 - 34 = 30$; then $5 \times 3 = 15$, $15 \times 2 = 30$, "equal to the above. But when the sides are not known, but the difference of "their squares, 16 then divide by 2, *(viz. by the difference of the numbers)* "$\frac{16}{2} = 8$; this is their sum, and deduct their difference $8 - 2 = 6$, half this is "one number, and $8 + 2 = 10$, and $\frac{10}{2} = 5$, the other number."

The next is,

"In the figure where the sum of bhoje, cote, carna is 40, and the product of "bhoje and cote 120. What is the bhoje, cote, carna?

"Multiply the product 120 by 2=240, this will be equal to the difference between "the square of the sum of the bhoje and cote and the carnas square. The sum "of the squares of the bhoje and cote equal to square of the carna; therefore the "product of the bhoje and cote × by 2 is equal to the difference between the "rectangle and cote (the square) of the sum of the bhoje, and the square of the "carna.

"Divide this number 240 by the sum of the bhoje, cote, and carna 40, $\frac{240}{40}=6$, "which is equal to the difference between the carna and the sum of bhoje and "cote. Hence $\frac{40-6}{2} = 17$ the carna; 23 sum of bhoje and cote, squared is "529. Multiply the rectangle of bhoje and cote 120 by 4 = 480, the remainder "49, and its root 7; this is the difference of bhoje and cote; deduct this from "their sum 23; 23 − 7 = 16, its half $\frac{16}{2} = 8$ is the bhoje; 23 + 7 = 30, its "half, is the cote 15."

The next is,

"Where the sum of bhoje, cote, carna is 56, and their product 4200, what "are the bhoje, cote, carna?

"Ja 1, ja, bha 1. The sum of bhoje, cote, carna.

"Carna ja 1; ja $\dot{1}$, roo 56; these three multiplied, 4200.

"The rectangle of bhoje and cote $\frac{\text{roo } 4200}{\text{ja } 1}$ equal to sum of squares of bhoje "and cote is ja bha $\dot{1}$, sum of bhoje and cote ja $\dot{1}$, roo 56; the square ja bha 1, "$\dot{\text{ja}}$ 112, roo 3136; the difference between them is equal to $\frac{8400}{\text{ja } 1}$;

$$\text{"therefore } \frac{\dfrac{\dot{\text{Ja}}\ 112 \quad \text{roo } 3136}{\text{Ja} \quad 0 \quad \text{roo } 8400}}{\dot{\text{ja}}\ 1}$$

"divide both by 112; reduce both sides, and it will be

$$\frac{\text{Ja}\ \dot{1}}{\text{Ja}\ 0}\ \frac{\text{roo}\ 28}{\frac{\text{roo}\ 75}{\text{Ja}\ 1}}$$

Reduce the fractions.

$$\frac{\text{"Ja bha}\ \dot{1},\ \ \text{ja}\ 28,\ \ \text{roo}\ 0}{\text{"Ja bha}\ 0,\ \ \text{ja}\ 0,\ \ \text{roo}\ 75}$$

"Multiply by $\dot{4}$, and add the square of 28.

$$\frac{\text{"Ja bha}\ 4,}{\text{"Ja bha}\ 0,}\ \ \frac{\text{Ja}\ \dot{1}12,}{\text{Ja}\ 0}\ \ \frac{\text{roo}\ 300}{\text{roo}\ 484}\ (\textit{should be}\ 784)$$

"The square root $\frac{\text{ja}\ 2}{\text{ja}\ 0}\ \frac{\text{roo}\ \dot{2}8}{\text{roo}\ 22}$; then add, $\frac{50}{\text{ja}\ 2}$; divide by $2 = 25$, which is "the jabut, and therefore carna.

"Then for the bhoje cote. The three multiplied are 4200. Divide by carna "$\frac{4200}{25} = 168 =$ bhoje × by cote. The sum of bhoje and cote $= 56 - 25 = 31$, "and $168 \times 4 = 672$. The square of $31 = 961$," (the difference) "289, its square "root is the difference of bhoje and cote $= 17$; deduct this, $31 - 17 = 14$; its "half 7, which is the bhoje; and $31 + 17 = 48$; its half 24 is the cote."

The lines above have been carelessly drawn. The true Hindoo method of writing the equation $-x + 28 = \frac{75}{x}$ I understand to be this,

$$\frac{\text{ja}\ \dot{1}\ |\ \text{roo}\ 28,}{\text{Ja}\ 0\ \ \frac{\text{Roo}\ 75}{\text{Ja}\ \ 1}}$$

and that of $-x^2 + 28x = 75$ this,

$$\frac{\text{Ja}\ \dot{\text{b}}\text{ha}\ 1\ |\ \text{ja}\ 28\ |\ \text{roo}\ 0}{\text{Ja bha}\ 0\ |\ \text{ja}\ 0\ |\ \text{roo}\ 75}$$

Books 3, 4, and 5.

I FIND among Mr. Davis's notes a small part only of the beginning of the 3d book, which consists of rules for the application of the cootuk to questions where there are more unknown quantities than conditions. I find also some notes which evidently relate to the first example of this book, but nothing distinct can be made out.

There are no notes relating to the 4th book.

Of the 5th book only this:

"When there are two or more quantities multiplied, the 1st quantity must be "discarded—then"....There is also an abstract of the first example, the same as that in the Persian translation.

Extracts from Mr. Davis's Notes, taken from a modern Hindoo Treatise on Astronomy.

"By the method of the Jeisht and Canist from two jyas* being found, others "may be computed by those who understand the nature of the circle (the bow

* *Jya* or *jaw*; sine.—The modern Europeans acquired their knowledge of the *sine* from the Arabians; and it is obvious that they used the term sinus only, because the word *jeeb* (جيب), by which the Arabians called the line in question, is translated *sinus indusii.* The radical meaning of (جيب) is to cut, and it denotes the bosom of a garment only, because the garment is cut there to make a pocket; accordingly we find that جيب

" and arrow), and thus, by the addition of surds, may the sum and the
" difference of the arc and its sine be computed whether that arc be 90 degrees,
" more or less.

---

does not mean bosom, but that among the Arabians it signifies that part of their dress where the pocket is usually placed, and in some languages which abound in Arabic words, as the Persian and the Hindoostanee, it is the common term, not only for a pocket in the bosom, but for any pocket wherever it may be. In all Arabic dictionaries this word is explained as above, and in some, though not in all, (it is not in the Kushfool Loghat) the line we call *sine* is given as a second meaning.

The Arabs call the arc *koas* (قوس), which signifies *a bow*; the cord *wutr* (وتر), which is the *bow-string*; and the versed sine *suhum* (سهم), which is the *arrow*. But the sine they express by a word which has no connexion whatever with the *bow*.

The Mathematical history of the Arabians is not known enough for us to speak positively about the first use of sines among them, but there seems to be reason to suspect that they had it from a foreign source, probably from the Indians.

The Sanscrit word for the chord is *jaw*, or more properly *jya* and *jiva*. (For these terms see Mr. Davis's paper in the second volume of the Asiatic Researches; the literal explanation of the words has been given me by Mr. Wilkins,) and the sine is called *jya ardhi*, or half cord; but commonly the Hindoos, for brevity, use *jya* for the sine. They also apply the word in composition as we do; thus, they call the cosine *cotijya*, meaning the *sine*, the side of a right-angled triangle; the sine (or right sine) *bhojjya*, meaning the *sine*, the base of a right-angled triangle, and *cramajya* the *sine* moved; the versed sine they call *ootcramajya*, or the *sine* moved upwards; the radius they call *tridjya*, or the *sine* of three, (meaning probably three signs.) In their term for the diameter *jyapinda*, or whole *jya*, the word is used in its proper acceptation for chord, and not for *jya ardhi*, or sine.

It seems as if جيب and *jya* were originally the same word. Mr. Wilkins (the best authority) assures me that *jya*, in the feminine *jiva*, is undoubtedly pure Sanscrit, that it is found in the best and oldest dictionaries, and that its meaning is a *bow-string*.

The Arabians in adapting a term to the idea of chord, had reference to the thing which it resembled, and called it وتر or the *bow-string*; but having so applied this term, they had to seek another for *sine*; then they would naturally refer to the name of the thing, and call it by some word in their own language, which nearly resembled that under which it was originally known to them. This mode of giving a separate designation to the sine was evidently more convenient than that of the Hindoos, so I conjecture that جيب for sine is no other than the Sanscrit word *jya* or *jiva*.

It is remarkable that the Sanscrit terms for the sides of a right-angled triangle have reference to a *bow*: they seem to be named from the angular points which are formed by the end of the bow, the arm which holds it, and the ear to which the string is drawn; thus the side is called *coti*, or *end of the bow*; the base *bhoj*, or the arm; and the hypothenuse *carna*, or the *ear*. Some further explanation however is desirable to shew why *bhojjya* is the term for the sine, and not (as it should be by analogy) the cosine, and *cotijya* the cosine instead of the sine.

The Hindoos have a word for the versed sine, *sur*, which signifies arrow, answering exactly to the Arabic سهم.

"Multiply the jaw of one of two arcs by the cotejaw of the other arc, divide "the product by the tridjaw, add the two quotients and also subtract them; the "sum is equal to the jaw of the two arcs, the other is the jaw of the difference between the two arcs.

"Again, multiply the two bojejaws together, and likewise the two cotejaws "together; divide by the tridjaw. Note the sum and the difference. The sum "is the cotejaw of the sum of the two arcs, the difference is the cotejaw of the "difference of the two arcs.

"In this manner Bhascara computed the sines in his Siromony, and others "have given other methods of their own for computing the same.

The author of the Marichi observes, "that the author of the Siromoni derived "his method of computing his sines by the jeisht and canist, and diagonally multi-"plied (ba jera beas), the jeisht and canist being the cotejaw and the bojejaw; "hence he found the sines of the sum and difference of two arcs, the third "canist being those quantities. He did not use the terms jeisht and canist, but "in their room bojejaw and cotejaw. I shall therefore explain how they "were used.

"The bojejaw = canist (small).

"Cotejaw = jeisht (larger).

"(The theorem then is what square multiplied by 8, and 1 added, will produce "a square).

"Multiply the given number (8) by the square of the canist, and add the "chepuk, the sum must be a square.

"The bojejaw square deducted from the tridjaw square, leaves the cotejaw "square, therefore the bojejaw square is made negative, and the tridjaw square "added to a negative being a subtraction, the tridjaw square is made the chepuk.

"The canist square, which is the bojejaw square, being multiplied by a negative "becomes a negative product, therefore the quantity is expressed by 1 roop "negative.

"Then the bojejaw square multiplied by 1 roop negative, and added to the "tridjaw, its square is the cotejaw.

"Hence the bojejaw and cotejaw in the theorem by Bhascara, represent the "canist and jeisht, and 1 roop negative is the multiplier, and the chepuk is the "square of the tridjaw, and the equation will stand as follows:

"Canist 1st. jaw 1 : jeisht 1st. cotejaw 1 : chepuk, tridjaw square 1,
"Canist 2d. jaw 1 : jeisht 2d. cotejaw 1 : chepuk, tridjaw square 1.

" These multiplied diagonally produce

" 1st jaw 1. 2d cotejaw 1.

" 2d jaw 1. 1st cotejaw 1.

" These added produce the first canist, viz.

" 1st jaw + 2 cotejaw.

" 2d jaw + 1 cotejaw,

" which is the sum (or joge) and the difference.

" 1st jaw — 2 cotejaw.

" 2d jaw — 1 cotejaw.

" Thus from the sum and difference are produced two canists, and the square of " the tridjaw squared is the chepuk; but the chepuk wanted being only the " square of the tridjaw, then as the Bija Ganita directs divide by such a number " as will quote the given chepuk.

" Therefore the tridjaw being the ist, or assumed, or given quantity, divide " the canist by it, the quotient will be the tridjaw square, and hence the theorem " in Bhascara for the bojejaw.

" And in like manner the cotejaws are found ; but Bhascara did not give this " theorem for the cotejaws, because it was more troublesome. He therefore gave " a shorter rule. But since the cotejaw square is equal to the bojejaw square " deducted from the tridjaw, therefore the same rule may be applied to the " cotejaw, by making the cotejaw the canist, and the bojejaw jeisht; then by the " foregoing rule the cotejaw of the sum or difference of the arcs may be found".

Second Extract.

"Sloca. The munis determined the equations of the planets centres for the "use of mortals, and this can be effected only by computations of the sines of "arcs. I shall explain and demonstrate their construction and use.

"2. And for this purpose begin with squares and extractions of roots, for the "satisfaction of intelligent persons of ready comprehension.

"3. The square is explained by the ancients to be the product of a number "multiplied by itself. (He goes on to show how squares are found and roots "extracted as in the Lilavati).

"6. Square numbers may be stated infinitely. The roots may be as above "extracted, but there are numbers whose roots are irrational. (Surds.)

"7. The ancients have shewn how to approximate to the roots of such "numbers as follows: Take a greater number than that whose root is wanted; "and by its square multiply the given number, when that given number is an "integer. Extract the root of the product, divide this root by the assumed "number, and the quotient will approximate to the root required. If the given "number be a fraction, multiply and extract as before. To approximate the "nearer the munis assumed a large number, but the approximation may be made "by assuming a small number."

And after a blank.
"In like manner surds are managed in the *abekt* or symbolical letters, "(Algebra) expressing unknown quantities."

Again, after a blank.
"Some have pretended to have found the root of a surd, and that this might

"be effected by the Cutuca Ganita, attend and learn whether or not this could "have been possible. I shall relate what Bhascara and others have omitted to "explain. A root is of two kinds; one a line, the other a number. And the "root of a square formed by a line expressing 5, may be found, though the root "of 5 cannot be numerically expressed; but the numbers 1, 4, 9, &c. may be "expressed both ways. 2, 3, 5, &c. are surds, and can have their roots expressed "only by lines. (He goes on to shew the impossibility of finding the root of a "surd, though it should be eternally pursued through fractional quantities.)

"The root of a surd may be shewn *geometrically.*"

I Have copied these two extracts exactly as I found them; there appear to be one or two errors which it may be as well to mention. In the first extract the latter part of the first sentence should, perhaps, run thus: "By the addition of "the jeisht and canist may the sines of the sum and difference of arcs be "computed," &c.

I observe that where jeisht and canist first occurred in these notes Mr. Davis translated it originally "arithmetic of surds," and afterwards corrected it; probably from oversight it was not corrected in the second place,

The value of the cosine of the sum of two arcs is given instead of that of the difference and *vice versa.*

There is an error also in writing the sum and the difference of the cross products.

I know nothing of the author of the Marichi. Possibly he might have observed that the jeisht and canist rule corresponded with the formulæ for the sines and cosines, and the latter were not derived from the former by Bhascara, but invented at a later period, or introduced among the Hindoos from foreign sources. Probably however the application and the formulæ are both of Indian origin.

As for the second extract the rule for approximating to the square root is the same as that given by Recorde, in his "Whetstone of Wit," which was published in 1557; and by his contemporary Buckley; (for an account of whose method see Wallis's Algebra, p. 32. English edition.) I have before stated, that this rule is also in the Lilavati. I mentioned it generally then only because of its connexion with a trigonometrical proposition. The following is a literal translation of the rule, as given by Fyzee: "Take the squares of the base and "side, and add them together; then multiply by the denominator and write it "down. Then assume a large number and take its square. Then multiply it "by that which was written down. Take the square root of the result and call "it the dividend. Then multiply that denominator by that assumed number, "and call it the divisor. Divide the dividend by the divisor, the quotient is the "hypothenuse." This is not delivered with perfect accuracy, the true meaning however is plain. If the assumed multiplier is decimal the method gives the common approximation in decimal fractions. The writer denies that the root of a surd can be found by the cootuk, but he speaks of it as a subject to which the cootuk was said to have been applied. It is very improbable that such a thing as this should have found its way from Europe to India, and it is very probable that many things of this sort were to be had from Hindoo sources.

Explanation of Sanscrit Words used in Mr. Davis's Notes.

BIJA GANITA—Algebra—Literally seed counting.

Pati Ganita—Arithmetic—Ganita seems to be used as we use arithmetic. Thus as we have arithmetic of integers, arithmetic of surds, decimal arithmetic, &c. the Indians have bija ganita, pati ganita, cutuca ganita, &c.

Jabut Tabut—The unknown quantity, as we use x—Literally *as far, so far.* It is not clear how this comes to be so used. It would be more conformable to the rest of Hindoo notation, if the word pandu (white) were applied; the first letter of pandu is very like that of jabut, and they might easily be confounded.

Kaluk, neeluk, &c.—Unknown quantities—Literally the colours black, blue, &c.

Abekt—Unknown,

Carni, surd—Hypothenuse—Literally ear.

Mahti and laghoo—Greater and less.

Roop—Known quantity—Literally form, appearance.

Bhady—Dividend.

Hur—Divisor.

Bhujuk—Divisor.

Seke—Remainder.

Dirl—Reduced.

Chepuk or *chepe*—Augment.

Bullee—Chain or series.

Unte—Last.

Upantea—Last but one.

Lubd—Quotient.

Goonuk or *Goon*—Multiplicand.

Rhin—Minus—Literally decrease.

Coodin—An astronomical period.

Urgan—Number of days elapsed.

Bekullas—Seconds.

Cullas—Minutes.

Ansas—Degrees.

Bhaganas.—Revolutions.
Calp—The great period.
Raas—Literally a heap, a sum total, a constellation.
Cootuk—The principle on which problems of this form $\frac{ax + c}{b} = y$ are solved.
Sanstist—Ditto of $\frac{ax}{b} = y + c$ and $\frac{dx}{b} = z + e$.
Chacra-bala—Ditto of $ax^2 + b = y^2$—Literally strength.
Hursua, hurs, hursa—x in the above form—Literally small.
Pracrit—a in Ditto—Literally principal.
Jeist or *Jeisht*—y in Ditto—Literally greatest.
Canist—x in Ditto—Literally least.
Samans babna—If $\text{A}x'^2 + \beta = y'^2$ and $\text{A}f^2 + \beta = g^2$, then the rule $x'' = x'g + y'f$ is called samans babna—Literally contemplation of equal degrees.
Anter babna—In the above form, when $x'' = x'g - y'f$, it is called anter babna—Literally contemplation of difference.
Budjra beas—Cross multiplication which produces the above forms—Literally cross diameter.
Cootuk gunnit or *cutuca ganita.*—Cootuk Calculation.
Sodana—Reduce—Literally purify.
Utapana—Brought out.
Bhoje—Base of a right-angled triangle—Literally arm.
Cote—Side of Ditto—Literally end of a bow.
Carna—Hypotheuuse—Literally ear.
Lumb—Perpendicular—Literally length.
Abada—Given.
Ist—Assumed.
Jaw or *Jya*—Sine or chord—Literally bow-string.
Bojejaw—Sine.
Cotejaw—Cosine.
Tridjaw—Radius—Literally sine of three; perhaps meaning of three signs or 90 degrees.
Addy—Intercalary.
Che-tits (Cshaya tithi)—Difference of solar and lunar days.
Abum—? For bhumi savan—solar days.
Chandra—Lunar.

For the literal explanation of these terms, as far as they could be made out, I am obliged to Mr. Wilkins. Most of the words are written here according to their common pronunciation in Bengal.

DEAR STRACHEY,

HAVING just laid my hands on a parcel of papers of notes, containing abstracts and translations from the Bija Ganita, made by me, with the assistance of a Pandit, as long ago as when I was stationed at Bhagulpore *, I send them to you with full liberty to make any use of them. Ever since my removal to Burdwan these papers have lain unnoticed, and might have continued so had it not occurred to me that you are occupied in such researches. There may be trifling inaccuracies in some places, the translations having been made carelessly and never revised; but their authenticity may be depended on, as they were made from the original Sanscrit Bija Ganita, which was procured for me at Benares, by Mr. Duncan. I send also a book of memoranda, containing chiefly trigonometrical extracts from a modern astronomical work in Sanscrit, which I suppose to have been written in Jey Sings time.

I am very sincerely your's,

Portland Place, Jan. 1812. S. DAVIS.

THE END.

---

* About the year 1790.

Some Obſervations on the originality, extent, and importance of the Mathematical ſcience of the Hindoos; *with Extracts from* Perſian *Tranſlations of the* Leelawuttee *and* Beej Gunnit—*By* EDWARD STRACHEY, *of the Bengal Civil Eſtabliſhment.*

THE character which Sir WILLIAM JONES has given of *Perſian* tranſlations from the *Sanſcrit* is enough to deter men from the labour of examining them. To diſcover the full extent of *Hindoo* learning the *Sanſcrit* originals ſhould be ſtudied.

NEVERTHELESS ſome of theſe tranſlations have their value. If examined attentively and without prejudice, they will, on many points, give an inſight into *Hindoo* ſcience without hazard of deception, although they are juſtly open to a general objection of confuſion and inaccuracy.

THE tranſlator ſeldom diſtinguiſhes the text from his own additions, but he ſometimes introduces matter which he muſt have been incapable of ſupplying, if he had not had acceſs to ſome extraordinary means of information, which means I conclude to be the original work he pretends to tranſlate, or ſome other *Hindoo* books of ſcience.

IN works which are avowedly tranſlated from ancient or obſcure authors, but are ſuſpected to abound with interpolations, we cannot pronounce any propoſition to be original, without a previous conſideration of its nature, and of the circumſtances of the tranſlator and the reputed author.

If the propoſition in queſtion is thought to have been invented at a period later than the age of the perſon now ſaid to be the author, and is to be found in books to which the tranſlator undoubtedly had, or poſſibly might have had, acceſs, we may well ſuſpect that it is not genuine.

If, however, it is directly deduced, or deducible from, or in any way intimately connected with unſuſpected matter, we may perhaps be diſpoſed to admit its claim to originality; at all events we ſhall heſitate in pronouncing it ſpurious.

But if the propoſition could not be derived from any of the common ſources of knowledge which were extant in the time of the tranſlator, we muſt neceſſarily ſuppoſe the exiſtence of ſome other ſource: and the diſcovery of a well connected ſeries of ſuch propoſitions, would afford ample proof of the exiſtence of a fund of ſcience, to which the world has not hitherto had acceſs.

Let theſe principles be applied to an examination of the *Perſian* tranſlations of the *Beej Gunnit* and *Leelawuttee*; and many new and curious facts will be aſcertained, illuſtrative of the early hiſtory of Algebra and of the ſtate of Mathematical knowledge among the *Hindoos*.

The *Beej Gunnit* and *Lelawuttee*, were both written by Bhasker Acharij, a famous *Hindoo* mathematician and aſtronomer, who lived about the beginning of the 13th century of the *Chriſtian* era: the former of the two treatiſes is on Algebra with ſome of its application; the latter is on Arithmetic and Algebra, and Menſuration, or Practical Geometry. The *Beej Gunnit* was tranſlated into *Perſian* in 1634 A. C. by Utta Ulla

RUSHEEDEE, (at *Agra* or *Dehli* probably), and the *Leelawuttee* in 1587 A. C. by the celebrated FYZEE.

BEFORE any opinion is formed of the extent to which the tranſlators might have interpolated, a view of the ſources of their knowledge ſhould be taken.

IT is well known that the only *Perſian* ſcience is *Arabian*, and that the *Arabs* had much of their mathematical knowledge from the *Greeks*; It is certain that they had their Arithmetic from the *Indians*, and moſt likely their Algebra was derived from the ſame ſource; but the time and other circumſtances reſpecting the introduction of theſe ſciences among the *Arabs* is unknown *.

As we are not informed of the full extent of *Greek* knowledge among the *Arabs*, nor of the *Greek* and other books, which may have been tranſlated into *Arabic*, and which UTTA ULLA RUSHEEDEE and FYZEE, might have had acceſs to; and as we cannot be certain that they had not the means (through travellers for inſtance) of becoming acquainted with the modern *European* diſcoveries, we muſt ſuppoſe that they might have had the benefit of all the *Greek*, and all the *Arabian*, and all the modern *European* learning, which was known in their time †.

* The firſt account of any *Indian* mathematical ſcience among the *Arabs*, is, I believe, of *Indian* aſtronomy, which was known in the reign of AL MAMOON.

In later times, many *Mohammedans* have had acceſs to the *Hindoo* books: There are accounts of ſeveral in the *Ayeen Ackbery*, and in D'HERBELOT. ABUL FUZL gives a liſt of *Sanſcrit* books, which were tranſlated into *Perſian* in AKBER's time. The *Leelawuttee* is the only mathematical work amongſt them.

† BERNIER, who arrived in *India* in 1655, is ſaid to have tranſlated or explained the philoſophy of GASSENDI and DES CARTES for his patron at the *Mogul's* court, but it is likely that only the metaphyſics of theſe writers are alluded to. BERNIER had a good opportunity of making reſearches into the learning of the *Hindoos*, and he has given ſome account of it; but his information appears to have been very circumſcribed; he was entirely ignorant of the extent of their mathematical ſciences, and knew ſcarcely any thing of their aſtronomy. In the beginning of the eighteenth century, JYE SING had acceſs to the modern *European* aſtronomy and mathematics, and introduced a great deal of them into *India*. (See Mr. HUNTER's paper in the fifth volume of the *Aſiatick* Reſearches,

It is however probable, that, exclusive of what they might have had from the *Hindoos*, Utta Ulla Rusheedee and Fyzee had no means of acquiring science except through *Arabic* books.

From the translation of the *Leelawuttee* should be rejected, as not certainly genuine, all such propositions as were known to the *Greeks* or *Arabs*, or to the modern *Europeans*, till the end of the sixteenth Century; and from the translation of the *Beej Gunnit*, all such as were known till the beginning of the seventeenth century, except such as are intimately connected with others whose originality cannot be doubted.

It is very desireable that some person properly qualified for the task should compare the Algebra of the *Arabs*, and that of the *Greeks* and that of the modern *Europeans* with the *Persian* translations of the *Beej Gunnit* and *Leelawuttee*.*

I have no doubt that the result of the comparison would shew:

That the Algebra of the *Arabs* is quite different from that of Diophantus, and that neither of them could have been taken from the other, though both might have been taken from one common source:

That if the *Arabs* did learn from the *Indians*, (as they probably did) they did not borrow largely from them:

---

* The only known book of *Greek* Algebra, is *Diophantus*.

Of *Arabian* Algebra, no full account, as far as I know, has hitherto been given, but it is certain that the first *European* treatises were taken from it entirely. Many *Arabic* Algebraical works are extant, and well known in *India*; some of them have been translated into *Persian*.

THAT the *Perſian* tranſlations of the *Beej Gunnit* and *Leelawuttee* contain principles, which are ſufficient for the ſolution of any propoſitions in the *Arabian*, or in the *Diophantine* Algebra : *

THAT theſe tranſlations contain propoſitions, which are not to be ſolved on any principles which the *Arabian* or the *Diophantine* Algebra could ſupply :

THAT the *Hindoos* were farther advanced in ſome branches of this

* Perhaps this may be going too far ; it is not eaſy to ſay what principles are neceſſary for the developement of the *Diophantine* Algebra, which is merely a collection of difficult queſtions, ſhewing more ingenuity than mathematical knowledge.

The *Beej Gunnit* will be found to differ much from DIOPHANTUS's work. It contains a great deal of knowledge which the *Greeks* had not ; ſuch as the uſe of an indefinite number of unknown quantities and the uſe of arbitrary marks to expreſs them ; a good arithmetic of SURDS ; a perfect theory of indeterminate problems of the firſt degree ; a very extenſive and general knowledge of thoſe of the ſecond degree ; a knowledge of quadratic equations, &c. The arrangement and manner of the two works will be found as eſſentially different as their ſubſtance. The one conſtitutes a body of ſcience, the other does not. The *Beej Gunnit* is well digeſted and well connected, and is full of general rules, which ſuppoſe great learning ; the rules are illuſtrated by examples, and the ſolutions are performed with ſkill. DIOPHANTUS, though not entirely without method, gives very few general propoſitions, and is chiefly remarkable for the ability with which he makes aſſumptions in view to the ſolution of his queſtions. The former teaches Algebra as a ſcience, by treating it ſyſtematically ; the latter ſharpens the wit, by ſolving a variety of abſtruſe and complicated problems in an ingenious manner. The author of the *Beej Gunnit* goes deeper into his ſubject, and treats it more abſtractedly, and more methodically, though not more acutely, than DIOPHANTUS. The former has every characteriſtic of an aſſiduous and learned compiler ; the latter of a man of genius in the infancy of ſcience. This compariſon however, it muſt be admitted, is made from a view ſomewhat partial and ſuperficial. The *Beej Gunnit* is ſeen through a very defective medium. It may have been improved, or it may have been deteriorated by the tranſlator : and the account here given of DIOPHANTUS, is not the reſult of deep ſtudy of that very difficult author, but of a haſty review of his work, and an examination of a few only of his material propoſitions.

It may be proper to advert to the following point, which may be thought important : " Whether it is " poſſible, or, if poſſible, whether it is probable, that the Algebra of the *Hindoos* is nothing more than a " branch of *Greek* ſcience long loſt, but now reſtored ?" I am perſuaded that it is not : but a good diſcuſſion of this queſtion is neceſſary, before the originality of the *Indian* ſcience can be eſtabliſhed on ſolid grounds.

The intent of this paper is to throw out hints, for inquiry into the mathematical ſciences of the *Hindoos*. I cannot by any means pretend to embrace the ſubject in its full extent ; my opinions therefore will be received with caution ; they are ſubmitted with deference.

ſcience than the modern *Europeans*, with all their improvements, till the middle of the eighteenth century.

ANNEXED, are a few ſpecimens of Arithmetic, Geometry, and Algebra, taken from the tranſlations of the *Beej Gunnit* and *Leelawuttee*.

On Series, with Extracts from the Leelawuttee.

IN the tranſlation of the *Leelawuttee*, is a chapter on combinations, and another on progreſſions, as follows:

COMBINATIONS.

" To find a number from the mixture of different things."

" IF it is required to add different things together, ſo that all the com-
" binations ariſing from their addition may be known, this is the rule:

" FIRST, write them all with one, in order, and below write one
" the laſt oppoſite to the firſt in order. Then divide the firſt term of
" the firſt line, by the number which is oppoſite to it in the ſecond
" line. The quotient will be the number of combinations of that
" thing. Multiply this quotient by the ſecond term of the firſt line,
" and divide the product by the number which is oppoſite to it in the
" ſecond line, the quotient will be the number of combinations of that
" thing; and multiply this quotient by the third term, and divide by
" that which is below it, and add together whatever is obtained below
" each term, the ſum will be the amount of all the combinations of
" theſe things."

OR ſhortly: The rule for combinations of any number of things (n) taken 2 by 2, 3 by 3, 4 by 4, &c. is $\frac{n}{1}\times\frac{n-1}{2}\times\frac{n-2}{3}\times\frac{n-3}{4}$ &c. continued to as many factors as there are things to be combined.

EXAMPLE.

" THE ſix flavoured, called in *Hindee Khut Rus*, contains 1ſt a ſweet, " 2d a ſalt, 3d a ſour, 4th a ſoft, 5th a bitter, 6th a ſharp. I would " know the number of different mixtures which may be had by adding " theſe together. Write them thus

1	2	3	4	5	6
6	5	4	3	2	1

$\frac{6}{1}=6$, $\frac{6\times5}{2}=15$, $\frac{15\times4}{3}=20$, " $\frac{20\times3}{4}=15$, $\frac{15\times2}{5}=6$, $\frac{6\times1}{6}=1$, the ſum is 63. The number of mixtures then " of 6 things is 63."

PROGRESSION.

" OF numbers encreaſing. This may be of ſeveral kinds; Firſt, with " one number, that is, when each number exceeds the preceding by 1. The " way to find any number is; Add 1 to that number, and multiply by " half that number. To find the ſum of the added numbers; Add 2 to " whatever number you ſuppoſe the laſt, and multiply by the ſum of " that number; Divide by 3, the quotient will be the ſum of the added " number, or this number which was ſuppoſed the laſt."

THE rule is illuſtrated by theſe examples. In a ſeries encreaſing from 1, to find the ſum of 4 terms.

$1+2+3+4=\overline{1+4}\times\frac{4}{2}=10$. In the ſame ſeries to find the ſum of 6 terms $\overline{1+6}\times\frac{6}{2}=21$, the ſum of 9 terms $\overline{1+9}\times\frac{9}{2}=45$.

THIS is when the encreaſe is by 1. To find the ſum of the added terms "with 3." $\frac{\overline{2+3} \times \overline{1+2+3}}{3} = 10$ with 4, $\frac{\overline{2+4} \times \overline{1+2+3+4}}{3} = 20$, with 9, $\frac{\overline{2+9} \times \overline{1+2+3+4+5+6+7+8+9}}{3} = 165$.

"IF a perſon gives away at this rate, 1ſt day 1, 2d day 2, 3d day 3, 4th "day 4, and ſo on, encreaſing by 1 to 9 days. According to the 1ſt rule by "the 3d day he will have given 10, by the 4th 20, by the 6th 45, by the 9th "165." Theſe rules are ſhortly $\overline{1+n} \times \frac{n}{2} = s$; where n is the number of terms, and s the ſum of the ſeries 1, 2, 3, 4, 5, &c. and $\frac{(2+n) \times s}{3} = S$ the ſum of the triangulars.

THE next rule is for the ſummation of ſeries of ſquare and cube numbers, applied to the ſeries 1, 4, 9, 16, 25, &c. and 1, 8, 27, 64, 125, &c. The ſum of n terms of the former will be $\frac{\overline{2n+1} \times s}{3}$ and the ſum of n terms of the latter will be s^2. Rules are then given for arithmetical progreſſions, viz. (ſuppoſing a to repreſent the firſt term, m the middle term, z the laſt term, d the common difference) $\overline{n-1} \times d + a = z$, $\frac{z+a}{2} = m$, $m\,n = s$, $\frac{s}{n} - \overline{n-1} \times \frac{d}{2} = a$, $\frac{\frac{s}{n} - a}{\frac{n-1}{2}} = d$ $\frac{\sqrt{\left(a-\frac{d}{2}\right)^2 + 2sd} - a + \frac{d}{2}}{d} = n$.

A RULE for ſumming a geometrical progreſſion comes next.

"A PERSON gave a number the firſt day; the 2d day he added that "number multiplied by itſelf, and ſo on for ſeveral days, adding every "product multiplied by the firſt number. The rule for finding the ſum

" is this; firſt, obſerve whether the number of the time is odd or even: " if it is odd, ſubtract 1 from it, and write it ſomewhere, placing a " mark of multiplication above it. If it is even, place a mark of a ſquare " above it, and halve it till the number of the time is finiſhed: after " that, beginning at the bottom with the number of encreaſe, multiply, " where there is a mark of multiplication, and take the ſquare, where " there is a mark of a ſquare: ſubtract 1 from the product, and divide " what remains by the number of encreaſe leſs 1, and multiply the " quotient by the number of the firſt day: the product will be the ſum " of the progreſſion."

EXAMPLE, where the number of terms is even, 2, 4 &c. to 30 terms — Example, where the number of terms is odd, 2, 6, 18, 54 &c. to 7 terms. In theſe examples the reſult is given without any detail of the application of rule to the caſe. Probably there is ſome error in the rule; it ſhould be $\frac{r^n - 1}{r - 1} \times a = s$. From want of books one cannot in this country have the means of aſcertaining preciſely the time when each particular mathematical rule was invented in *Europe*, but I have no doubt it will appear, that all the rules which are in theſe two chapters were not known in *Europe* till after the ſixteenth century. The formula $\frac{n}{1} \times \frac{n-1}{2} \times \frac{n-2}{3}$ &c. is the ſame as that for finding the coefficients in the binomial theorem, which was in *Europe* firſt taught by BRIGGS about the year 1600. It does not appear whether this uſe of it was known to the *Hindoos*. Mr. REUBEN BURROW publiſhed in the *Aſiatick* Reſearches a queſtion ſolved by the laſt mentioned rule, inferring from it, that the *Hindoos* had the binomial theorem.

PELETARIUS in his Algebra, which was printed in 1558, gave a table of ſquare and cube numbers, remarking, among other properties of theſe numbers*, "that the ſum of any number of the cubes taken from the beginning, always makes a ſquare number, the root of which is the ſum of the roots of the cubes;" which is the ſame thing as the *Leelawuttee* rule.

It does not appear whether the *Hindoos* had any knowledge of figurate numbers further than what is here given.

On the menſuration of the Circle and Sphere, with extracts from the Leelawuttee.

The rules in the *Leelawuttee* for the menſuration of the circle and of the ſphere are theſe:

To find the circumference of a circle, multiply the diameter by 3927, and divide the product by 1250; or multiply the diameter by 22, and divide by 7.

And (ſuppoſing D to be the diameter and C the circumference) $\frac{D \times C}{4} =$ area. $D \times C =$ ſurface of a ſphere. $\frac{D^2 \times C}{6} =$ ſolidity of a ſphere. Other rules given are $\frac{D^2 \times 3927}{5000} =$ area. $\frac{D^2 \times 11}{14} =$ area $\frac{D}{2} + \frac{\frac{D^3}{2}}{21} =$ ſolidity of a ſphere, (v being the verſed ſine, and c the chord of an arch a). $\frac{D - \sqrt{(D+c)(D-c)}}{2} = v$ and $2 \times \sqrt{(D-v)v} = c$, $\frac{4aD(C-a)}{\frac{5C^2}{4} - (C-a)a} = c$ and $\frac{C}{2} - \sqrt{\frac{C^2}{4} - \frac{\frac{5C^2c}{4}}{4D+c}} = a$.

* Quoted from Hutton's Dictionary, Art. Algebra.

Rules for finding the ſides of regular figures inſcribed in a circle*.

3 gon $\frac{D\times 130323}{120000}$

4 gon $\frac{D\times 84853}{120000}$

5 gon $\frac{D\times 70534}{120000}$

6 gon $\frac{D\times 60000}{120000}$

7 gon $\frac{D\times 52055}{120000}$

8 gon $\frac{D\times 45922}{120000}$

9 gon $\frac{D\times 41031}{120000}$

It is to be lamented that the method of deducing theſe rules is not ſtated.

The ratio for that of the circumference of a circle to its diameter 22 : 7 is the ſame as that of Archimedes; that of 3927 : 1250 is, I believe, a nearer approximation than was known in *Europe* before Vieta. This is moſt probably (if not certainly) an *Hindoo* invention, and therefore ſhould give the credit of originality to the other rules which are connected with it.

On Quadratic Equations, with extracts from the Leelawuttee, *the* Beej Gunnit, *and* Diophantus.

In the tranſlation of the *Leelawuttee*, the rule for quadratic equations is, " When the number, by which the root of the number thought of is " multiplied, is given; and, the ſum or difference of the product when " added to, or ſubtracted from, the number thought of, is alſo given; the " rule for finding the number is: Take half the multiplier and ſquare it, " add what remains to it; take its root; add, or ſubtract, half the multi- " plicand to the root, according as the queſtion is of ſubtraction, or addi-

* Some of theſe numbers appear to be wrong.

" tion; take the ſquare of the aggregate, and that will be the number thought of ‡."

A RULE is given, for clearing the higher power of fractional coefficients. Thus:

" To add to the number thought of, or to ſubtract from it, a fraction of
" that number, the rule is: Add, or ſubtract, the fraction from 1; divide
" the multiplier and the remainder by the ſum or the difference, and pro-
" ceed according to the foregoing rule, with the quotients of the multiplier
" and remainder ||."

IN the tranſlation of the *Beej Gunnit*, the rule is;

" THE ſquare of unknown being equal to number, multiply both, or
" divide both, by an aſſumed number, and add a number to the two
" reſults, or ſubtract it from them, that both may be ſquares. For
" one ſide being a ſquare, the other will alſo be a ſquare; for they are
" equal and by the equal increaſe or diminution of two equals,
" two equals will be obtained. Take the roots of both, and, after
" equating, divide the number by the root of the ſquare of un-
" known: the reſult will be what was required."

---

‡ $x \pm a\sqrt{x} = b$, a and b are given, x is required. Rule $\left(\sqrt{\frac{a}{2}^2+b}\mp\frac{a}{2}\right)^2 = x$.

|| If $x \pm \frac{x}{m} \pm a\sqrt{x} = b$:

then, $$\left(\sqrt{\left(\frac{\frac{a}{2}}{1\pm\frac{1}{m}}\right)^2+\frac{b}{1\pm\frac{1}{m}}}\mp\frac{\frac{a}{2}}{1\pm\frac{1}{m}}\right)^2=x$$

AGAIN, " After equating, if the two ſides are not ſquares, the me-" thod of making them ſquares is this: Aſſume the number 4, and mul-" tiply it by the ſquare of the unknown of the firſt ſide, and multiply " both ſides by the product, and in the place of number encreaſe both " ſides by the ſquare of the thing of unknown which is on that ſide. " Both ſides will be ſquares. Take the roots of both and equate them, " and the quantity of unknown will be found *"

THIS rule is not very accurately expreſſed, but there can be no doubt of what is intended by it. The following example will ſerve to illuſtrate the rule, and ſhew the manner in wich the equation is reduced.

" SOME bees were ſitting on a tree; at once, the ſquare root of half " their number flew away; again, eight-ninths of the whole flew away " and two bees remained. How many were there? The method of " bringing it out, is this: From the queſtion it appears that half the ſum " has a root. I therefore ſuppoſe 2 ſquare of unknown; and I take " one unknown, that is the root of half; and $\frac{8}{9}$; and as the queſtioner " mentions, that 2 bees remain; 1 unknown and $\frac{8}{9}$ of two ſquare of " unknown that is $\frac{16}{9}$ of 1 ſquare of unknown, and 2 units is equal to " 2 ſquare of unknown. I perform the operation of equating the frac-" tions in this manner. I multiply both ſides by 9, which is the deno-" minator of a ninth, 16 ſquare of unknown and 9 unknown and 18 " units is equal to 18 ſquare of unknown. I equate them thus:—I ſub-" tract 16 ſquare of unknown of the firſt ſide from 18 ſquare of un-" known of the ſecond ſide. It is 2 ſquare of unknown affirmative,

* Should be, If $a x^2 + b x = c$ multiply both ſides by 4 a, and add b^2; then extract the root and reduce the equation.

" and in like manner I ſubtract 9 unknown of the firſt ſide from cipher
" unknown of the ſecond ſide, 9 unknown negative remains. Then
" I ſubtract cipher the numbers of the ſecond ſide from 18 units of the
" firſt ſide. It is the ſame. The firſt ſide then is 2 ſquare of unknown
" affirmative and 9 unknown negative, and the ſecond ſide is 18 units
" affirmative. In this example there is equality of ſquare of unknown,
" and unknown, to number; that is equality of ſquare and thing to
" number. As the roots of theſe two ſides cannot be found, ſuppoſe
" the number 4, and multiply it by 2 which is the number of the
" ſquare of unknown; it is 8. I multiply both ſides by 8. The firſt
" ſide is 16 ſquare of thing, and 72 unknown negative; and the ſecond
" ſide is 144 units. I then add the ſquare of the number of the un-
" known, which is 81 to the reſult of both ſides. The firſt ſide is 16
" ſquare of unknown, and 72 unknown negative, and 81 units; and
" the ſecond ſide is 225 units. I take the roots of both ſides. The
" root of the firſt ſide is 4 unknown, and 9 units negative; and the root
" of the ſecond ſide is 15 units affirmative. I equate them in this man-
" ner. I ſubtract cipher unknown of the ſecond ſide from 4 unknown
" of the firſt ſide; and 9 units negative of the firſt ſide, from 15 units
" affirmative of the ſecond ſide. The firſt is 4 thing and the ſecond ſide
" is 24 units affirmative. I divide; 6 is the reſult, and this is the
" quantity of the unknown, and 36 is the ſquare of the unknown.
" And as we ſuppoſed 2 ſquare of unknown, we double 36; the whole
" number of bees then was 72."

FARTHER, " When on one ſide is thing and the numbers are negative,
" and on the other ſide the numbers are leſs than the negative numbers on
" the firſt ſide, there are two methods. The firſt is to equate them without
" alteration—The ſecond is, if the numbers of the ſecond ſide are affirma-

" tive, to make them negative; and if negative, to make them affirmative. " Equate them; 2 numbers will be obtained, both of which will pro- " bably anſwer."

FROM this it will appear that in the tranſlations of the *Leelawutte* and *Beej Gunnit*, the knowledge of quadratic equations is carried as far as it was among the *Arabs* and the modern *Europeans* before CARDAN, and no farther. HUTTON* ſays of LUCAS DE BURGO, whoſe book was printed about the end of the 15th century, 'He uſes both the roots or values of 'the unknown quantity, in that caſe of the quadratics which has two 'poſitive roots, but he takes no notice of the negative roots in the other 'two caſes.'

BACHET in his commentary on the 33d queſtion of the 1ſt book of DIOPHANTUS, takes a view of the rules for the ſolution of quadratic equations which were known in his time—And he thinks that DIOPHANTUS had ſimilar rules: He judges ſo, becauſe in the 30th and 33d queſtions of the 1ſt book, DIOPHANTUS has theſe propoſitions, which he gives as the conditions of his queſtions, $(\frac{x+y}{2})^2 - xy = \square$ and $4xy + (x-y)^2 = \square$, and ſays of each of them εςι δε τυτο πλασματικον. BACHET is of opinion, that theſe words indicate that rules for quadratic equations may be deduced from the propoſitions, and he accordingly deduces rules, calling them DIOPHANTUS's method. DIOPHANTUS however had no ſuch method. He always aſſumes his numbers ſo as to avoid quadratic equations: He nowhere ſolves quadratic equations, and therefore it may be preſumed that he did not underſtand them.

IN the 45th queſtion of the 4th book, however, he has a proceſs which

* Mathematical Dictionary, article Algebra.

is very like that of the ſolution of a quadratic equation " *6 N + 12 " minus ſunt quam 2 Q − 6. Adjiciantur quæ deſunt utrimque unitates, " erunt 2 Q majores quam 6 N + 18. In æquatione autem hac expli- " canda, dimidium numerorum in ſe ducimus, et fit 9. Ducimus etiam " quadratos in unitates, et fiunt 36. et addito 9 fiunt 45. cujus latus " non minus eſt 7 adde ſemiſſim numerorum, et divide per quadratos, " fit 1 N minor 5." And, in queſtion 33, book 4, DIOPHANTUS, having the equation $3x + 18 = 5x^2$, proceeds thus: " et non eſt rati- " onalis atqui 5 Q eſt quadratus unitate auctus. Oportet itaque hunc duc- " tum in unitates 18 et adſumentem quadratum ſemiſſis 3 N nimirum $2\frac{1}{4}$ " facere quadratum" &c. (ſee queſtion and BACHET's commentary) but no quadratic equation is ſolved.

IT may be preſumed from what has been ſaid above, that the knowledge which the *Arabians* had of Algebra, as far as regards quadratic equations, was not derived from the *Diophantine* Algebra, but either that it was invented by themſelves, or, which is moſt likely the caſe, that it was had from the *Hindoos*.

On Indeterminate Problems of the 2d Degree, with extracts from Diophantus *and the* Beej Gunnit.

THE 16th Queſtion of the 6th book of DIOPHANTUS is as follows:

" DATIS duobus numeris, ſi aliquo quadrato in unum eorum ducto, et " altero de producto ſubtracto, fiat quadratus: invenietur et alius qua- " dratus major quadrato prius ſumpto, qui hoc idem præſtet. Dentur " duo numeri 3 et 11, et quadrato aliquo, puta à latere 5 ducto in 3 et

* BACHET's tranſlation.

" a producto detracto 11 fiat quadratus à latere 8. oporteat invenire alium " quadratum majorem quàm 25 qui hoc ipsum præstet. Esto latus quadrati 1 N + 5 fit quadratus 1 Q + 10 N + 25—Hujus triplum dempto 11 " fit 3 Q + 30 N + 64 æquale quadrato; sit ejus latus 8 − 2 N et fit N, 62. " Est ergo latus 67 quadratus 4489, qui præstat imperata."

And in the next example, referring to this, he says, by pursuing this method an infinite number of squares may be found.

In the *Beej Gunnit* this problem is solved very generally and scientifically, by the assistance of another, which was in *Europe* first known in the middle of the 17th century, and first applied to questions of this nature by Euler in the middle of the 18th century.

Abstracting from the sign, the *Beej Gunnit* rule for finding new values of $ax^2 + b = y^2$ is: Suppose $af^2 + b = g^2$ a particular case — find m and n so that $an^2 + 1 = m^2$ then $x = ng + mf$ and $y = mg + Anf$.

General methods according to the *Hindoos* for the solution of indeterminate problems of the 1st and 2d degrees will be found in the 5th and 6th chapters of the *Beej Gunnit.*

POSTSCRIPT.

Since writing the above I have had access to *English* translations of the *Leelawuttee* and part of the *Beej Gunnit*; and I have the satisfaction to find that in all the most material points they agree with the *Persian* translations.

III.

On the early History of Algebra.

By EDWARD STRACHEY, Esq.

If it were as generally known as it is certainly true, that there is a fine field for oriental research in the mathematical sciences, and that it is easy of access, the subject would not be so much neglected as it is at present.

Four years ago I printed at *Calcutta*, some observations on the mathematical sciences of the *Hindùs*. In that tract I proved, that an extensive and accurate knowledge of the Algebra of the *Hindùs* might be had, by means of translations, extant in the *Persian* language, of certain *Sanscrit* books. As the *Persian* language is understood by most of the Company's civil servants in *Bengal*, I conceived that a consideration of the fact might induce persons who were competent to such studies, to direct their attention to them. Of the *Bíja Ganita*, or *Hindù* Algebra of Bha'scara Acha'rya, I have sent home a full account, which I suppose must have been published by this time. In that account (derived entirely from a *Persian* translation) it is proved, that the *Hindùs* had made a wonderful progress in some parts of Algebra; that in the indeterminate analysis they were in possession of a degree of knowledge, which was in *Europe*, first communicated to the world by BACHET and FERMAT, in the seventeenth century, and by EULER and DE LA GRANGE, in the eighteenth. It would be very curious to push these inquiries into the *Hindù* indeterminate analysis, as far as possible. They might, perhaps, shew that the *Indians* had a knowledge of continued fractions, and possibly speculations in physics and the higher geometry, that we know nothing of: for the foundation of the indeterminate analysis of the *Hindùs* is directly explicable on the principle of continued fractions. And there are branches of natural philosophy and mathematics, where equations will arise, which can be solved only by the rules of the indeterminate analysis. In the introduction to the *Bíja Ganita*, where the first principles are given, a method is taught of solving problems of the form $Ax^2+b=\square$. This, simply considered, may be thought only a vain speculation on numbers; but, in the body of the *Bíja Ganita*, the rule is applied to the solution of equations. It is true, that these equations arise from questions purely numeral; yet it appears, nevertheless, that the application of the rule was understood. But whatever may be thought of this argument, it is, at all events, interesting, to ascertain the progress which has been made in the sciences, by different nations, in distant times.

A GOOD comparison of any of the mathematical sciences of the *Greeks*, the *Arabs*, and the *Indians*, would be exceedingly valuable; and every information, which will serve to illustrate the subject, is of importance to the early history of science.

WE know but very little of Algebra, in its infancy and first progress.

It was introduced into *Europe*, from *Arabia*, towards the beginning of the thirteenth century; and the work of DIOPHANTUS became known about three hundred years after. From the difference between his Algebra and that of the *European* writers, there was reason to believe that they were not of the same origin.

SOME learned persons thought that DIOPHANTUS was the inventor; but the more received opinion was, that his writings bore internal evidence of the contrary; and that Algebra must have been known long before his time.

IN 1579, BOMBELLI published a treatise of Algebra, in which he says, that he and a lecturer at *Rome*, whom he names, had translated part of DIOPHANTUS, adding, "that they had found that in the said work the "*Indian* authors are often cited; by which they learned that this science "was known among the *Indians* before the *Arabians* had it." (HUTTON'S *Dictionary*.)

DR. HUTTON has adopted the opinion, that the *Arabians* had their Algebra from the *Greeks*. In his dictionary (article Algebra) we find, "the "*Arabians* say, it was invented amongst them, by MAHOMET* BIN-"MU'S'A or son of MOSES, who it seems flourished about the eighth or "ninth century." It may be observed, by the way, that no *Arabian* writer has been cited in support of this. It does not appear on what foundation the assertion stands; I imagine it is taken from WALLIS. The learned *Muslemàns* in *India*, certainly consider the science as having originated among the *Indians*; and the arithmetic, which in their treatises always precedes Algebra, is undoubtedly *Indian*.

* MUH'AMMED-BIN-MU'S'A-UL-KHA'REZMI, according to D'HERBELOT, flourished under the *Khalifa* MAM'UN, and left a set of astronomical tables, which were highly esteemed, before NAS'RUDDIN TU'SI published his.

Dr. Hutton goes on: "It is more probable, however, that Mahomet "was not the inventor, but only a person well skilled in the art; and it "is further probable, that the *Arabians* drew their knowledge of it from "Diophantus or other *Greek* writers; and, according to the testimony "of Abulpharagius, the arithmetic of Diophantus was translated into "*Arabic*, by Mahomet-Bin-Yahya-Baziana." This I suppose is taken from Pococke's translation,* but the word which he has explained by "interpretatus est" is فسّر meaning he commented on, rather than he translated. Surely, this is not sufficient to give rise to a probability, that the *Arabians* derived their Algebra from the *Greeks*. The Algebra of the *Arabians* bears no resemblance to that of Diophantus, the only *Greek* writer on the subject who has ever been heard of. Inquiries have been made, in different parts of *India* and *Persia*, for the supposed translation of Diophantus; but without success. In the five first propositions of the 13th book of Euclid, and in the 10th and 11th propositions of Archimedes' book on spiral lines, and in the 9th proposition of the 2d book of his *Isorropics*, Wallis thought he saw traces of Algebra; and it is to be presumed, that no farther evidence of its existence, among the ancient *Greeks*, is discoverable; for, except the above, I do not know that any authors have been directly quoted, in proof of the argument; although there has been much assertion, in general terms, that the works of certain writers do contain traces of Algebra. If there were any undoubted marks of it, in the writings of the ancients, they could not have escaped the notice of so learned and so indefatigable a scholar as Wallis. What he says on this subject, appears to result from a prejudiced conviction of the antiquity of the science, and not from an unbiased search for truth.

---

* Diophanti librum de Algebra interpretatus est.

If the analysis of the five first propositions of the 13th book of EUCLID were (as is believed) by THEON, they could not well be adduced in proof of the ancient *Greeks* having a knowledge of Algebra; because THEON is supposed to have been nearly contemporary with DIOPHANTUS. He could not have been long before him, if it is true, that his daughter HYPATIA commented on a work of DIOPHANTUS. But, be this as it may, the analysis of the propositions in question is not at all Algebraical. It is the common analysis of the ancient geometers, which is quite different from Algebra; the former being geometrical and the latter arithmetical. WALLIS's reasoning, on the three propositions of ARCHIMEDES, to which he refers, amounts to no more than this. The demonstrations, as they now stand, are difficult; they might have been done by Algebra with ease; therefore, it is probable they were done by Algebra. We know of no *Greek* writer on Algebra, but DIOPHANTUS; neither he, nor any known author, of any age, or of any country, has spoken, directly or indirectly, of any other *Greek* writer on Algebra, in any branch whatever; the *Greek* language has not even a term to designate the science. The instance of DIOPHANTUS's treatise, with some indirect and disputable arguments, drawn, by inference, from works on other subjects than Algebra, is not sufficient. It is unlikely that the ravages of time and the depredations of barbarians should have destoyed all the direct and indisputable proofs. Such causes might account for the deficiency of our information on certain particulars, but will not authorise forced constructions, to argue the existence of a complete science, from its supposed demolition. The general extent of the literature of the *Greeks*, especially in mathematics, is well known; and that they had Algebra, can be established only by clear and positive evidence. For the different arguments which have been used, and the authorities which have been quoted on this question, see on one side WALLIS's Algebra, Chap. 1, 2, 75, &c. with the authors he refers to; and, on the other side, the *French Encyclopedie* Art. *Algebre, Application, Diophante* by D'ALEMBERT, and *Analyse* by DE CASTILLON. See also MONTUCLA. Though BHA'SCARA ACHA'RYA, who is comparatively a modern writer, could not have been one of the authors whom DIOPHANTUS is said to have quoted, it is by no means improbable that some *Alexandrian* merchant, trading to *India*, might have learned a little Algebra from the *Bramins*, and instructed some of his countrymen; or DIOPHANTUS might have learned from *Indians* at *Alexandria*. If there is doubt of the *Diophantine* Algebra being of *Greek* origin, it is worthy of remark that its author had opportunity of communicating with persons from whom he might have drawn materials for his work, and whom there is evidence of his having actually cited. It is objected that BOMBELLI is the only person who has taken notice of DIOPHANTUS' reference to *Indian* authors, and that no such reference is now to be found in his work. But the authority of BOMBELLI, on this point, cannot be overset, till it is ascertained that the manuscript of the *Vatican*, which he particularizes, does not contain the citations. One would think that BOMBELLI's assertion must have had some foundation, that it is not a mere fabrication. Though it does not appear that any *Sanscrit* works on this science, of greater antiquity than the *Bíja Ganita*, have yet been discovered, we are not to conclude, therefore, that there are none; for the author of the *Bíja Ganita* expressly says, his work is extracted from three copious treatises. These books have not been found; we know nothing of their contents nor their dates. The following was the result of a general comparison of the *Bíja Ganita* with DIOPHANTUS.* "The

---

* From "observations," &c. above referred to.

" *Bíja Ganita* will be found to differ much from DIOPHANTUS' work. " It contains a great deal of knowledge which the *Greeks* had not; such " as the use of an indefinite number of unknown quantities, and the use " of arbitrary marks to express them; a good arithmetic of surds; a " perfect theory of indeterminate problems of the first degree; a very " extensive and general knowledge of those of the second degree; a " knowledge of quadratic equations, &c. The arrangement and man- " ner of the two works will be found as essentially different as their " substance. The one constitutes a body of science, which the other " does not. The *Bíja Ganita* is well digested and well connected, and " is full of general rules which suppose great learning: the rules are " illustrated by examples, and the solutions are performed with skill. " DIOPHANTUS, though not entirely without method, gives very few ge- " neral propositions, and is chiefly remarkable for the ability with which " he makes assumptions in view to the solution of his questions. The " former teaches Algebra as a science, by treating it systematically; the " latter sharpens the wit by solving a variety of abstruse and complicated " problems, in an ingenious manner. The author of the *Bíja Ganita* " goes deeper into his subject, and treats it more methodically, though " not more acutely, than DIOPHANTUS. The former has every charac- " teristic of an assiduous and learned compiler; the latter of a man of " genius in the infancy of science."

THE *Greek* Algebra may be seen in DIOPHANTUS, who is the only *Greek* writer on the subject who has ever been heard of.

THE *Indian* Algebra may be seen in the *Bíja Ganita*, and the *Lílavati* (by the author of the *Bíja Ganita*,) and as the *Persian* translations of these works contain a degree of knowledge, which did not exist in any of the ordinary sources of science, extant in the time of the translators, they may be safely taken as *Indian*, and of ancient origin. To give some idea of the Algebra of the *Arabians*, whereby we may be enabled to judge, whether, on the one hand, it could have been derived from DIOPHANTUS; or, on the other, that of the *Hindùs* could have been taken from them, the work entitled *Khulásat-ul-Hisàb*, may be taken as a specimen; especially because, as will be more particularly stated in another place, there is a part of this book which marks the limits of Algebraical knowledge, in the time of the writer.

WE have seen, that the first *European* Algebraists learnt of the *Arabians*, but no account has been given of the nature, the extent, and the origin of *Arabian* Algebra. No distinct abstract or translation of any *Arabic* book, on the subject, has appeared in print; nor has it been established beyond controversy, who taught the *Arabians*. The *Khulásat-ul-Hisàb* is of considerable repute in *India*; it is thought to be the best treatise on Algebra, and it is almost the only book on the subject, read here. I selected it, because I understood, that as well as the shortest, it was the best treatise that could be procured. Besides general report, I was guided by the authority of MAULAVI ROSHEN ALÌ, an acknowledged good judge of such matters, who assured me that among the learned *Muslemàns* it was considered as a most complete work; and that he knew of no *Arabian* Algebra beyond what it contained. In the *Sulàfat-ul-Âsr*, a book of biography, by NIZ'AM-UL-DÍN-AH'MED, there is this account of BAH'A-UL-DÍN, the author of the *Khulásat-ul-Hisàb*. "He was "born at *Bâlbec*, in the month *D'hi'lhaj*, 953 *Hijrì*, and died at *Isfahàn* "in *Shawàl*, 1031." Mention is made of many writings of BAHA-UL-DÍN on religion, law, grammar, &c. a treatise on astronomy, and one on the astrolabe. In this list of his works, no notice is taken of his great treatise on Algebra, the *Behr-ul-Hisàb,* which is alluded to in the *Khulásat-ul-Hisàb.* MAULAVI ROSHEN ALÌ tells me the commentators say, it is not extant. There is no reason to believe that the *Arabians* ever knew more than appears in BAHA-UL-DÌN's book, for their learning was at its height long before his time.

FROM what has been stated it will appear, that from the *Khulásat-ul-Hisàb,* an adequate conception may be formed of the nature and extent of the Algebraical knowledge of the *Arabians;* and hence I am induced to hope that a short analysis of its contents will not be unacceptable to the society. I deem it necessary here to state, that possessing nothing more than the knowledge of a few words in *Arabic,* I made the translation, from which the following summary is abstracted, from the *vivâ voce* interpretation into *Persian* of MAULAVI ROSHEN ALÌ, who perfectly understood the subject and both languages, and afterwards collated it with a *Persian* translation, which was made about sixty years after BAH'A-UL-DÌN's death, and which ROSHEN ALÌ allowed to be perfectly correct.

THE work, as stated by the author in his preface, consists of an introduction, ten books and a conclusion.

THE introduction contains definitions of arithmetic, of number, which is its object and of various classes of numbers. The author distinctly ascribes to the *Indian* sages the invention of the nine figures, to express the numbers from one to nine.

BOOK 1, comprises the arithmetic of integers. The rules enumerated under this head are *Addition, Duplation, Subtraction, Halving, Multiplication, Division,* and the *Extraction of the Square Root.* The method of proving the operation by throwing out the nines is described under each of these rules. The author gives the following remarkable definitions of multiplication and division, viz. "Multiplication is finding a number "such that the ratio which one of the factors bears to it shall be the "same as that which unity bears to the other factor," and "division is "finding a number which has the same ratio to unity as the dividend has "to the divisor."

For the multiplication of even tens, hundreds, &c. into one another, the author delivers the following rule, which is remarkable in this respect, that it exhibits an application of something resembling the indexes of logarithms.

"Take the numbers as if they were units, and multiply them together "and write down the product. Then add the numbers of the ranks together, (the place of units being one, that of tens, two, &c.) substract "one from the sum and call the remainder the number of the rank of "the product. For example, in multiplying 30 into 40, reckon 12 of the "rank of hundreds; for the sum of the numbers of their ranks is 4, and "three is the number of the rank of hundreds, multiplying 40 into 500, "reckon 20 of the rank of thousands, for the sum of the numbers of the "ranks is 5."

The following contrivances have sufficient singularity to merit particular mention.

I. To multiply numbers between 5 and 10. Call one of the factors tens, and from the result, subtract the product of that factor by the difference of the other factor from ten. For example, to multiply 8 into 9. Subtract from 90 the product of 9 by 2, there remains 72. Or add the factors together, and call the excess above 10, tens. Multiply together the two differences of the factors from 10, and add the product to the former number. For example, to multiply 8 by 7, add to 50 the product of 2 into 3.

II. To multiply units into numbers between units and 20; add the two factors together, call the difference of the sum from 10, tens. From this result, subtract the product of the difference of the simple number from 10 and of the compound number from 10. For example, to multiply 8 by 14. Subtract from 120, the product of 2 into 4.

III. To multiply together numbers between 10 and 20; add the units of one factor to the other factor and call the sum tens: add to this the product of the units into the units. For example to multiply 12 into 13, add 6 to 150.

IV. To multiply numbers between 10 and 20 into compound numbers between 20 and 100; multiply the units of the smaller by the tens of the greater, add the product to the greater number and call the sum tens. Add to it the product of the units in both numbers. For example, to multiply 12 into 26, add 4 to 26 and call 30, tens. Finish the operation, it is 312.

V. To multiply numbers between 20 and 100, where the digits in the place of tens are the same; add the units of one factor to the other and multiply the sum by the tens, call the product tens, and add to it the product of the units multiplied by the units. For example, to multiply 23 by 25, multiply 28 by two. Call the product 56 tens, finish the operation; 575 is obtained.

VI. To multiply numbers between 10 and 100, when the digits in the place of tens are different. Multiply the tens of the smaller number into the larger number; add to the result, the product of the units of the smaller number into the tens of the greater; call the sum tens; add to this the product of the units into the units. For example, to multiply 23 into 34, add 9 to 68, add 12 to 770.

VII. To multiply two unequal numbers, half the sum of which is simple (*Mufrid,*) take the sum of the two and multiply half of it into itself. From this product, subtract the square of half the difference of the two numbers. For example, to multiply 24 by 36. From 900 subtract the square of half the difference of the numbers, that is 36. There remains 864.

For multiplying numbers consisting each of several places of figures, the method described by this author, under the name of *Shabacah* or net work, and illustrated by the following example, may have suggested the idea of Napier's bones.

Multiply 62374 *by* 207.

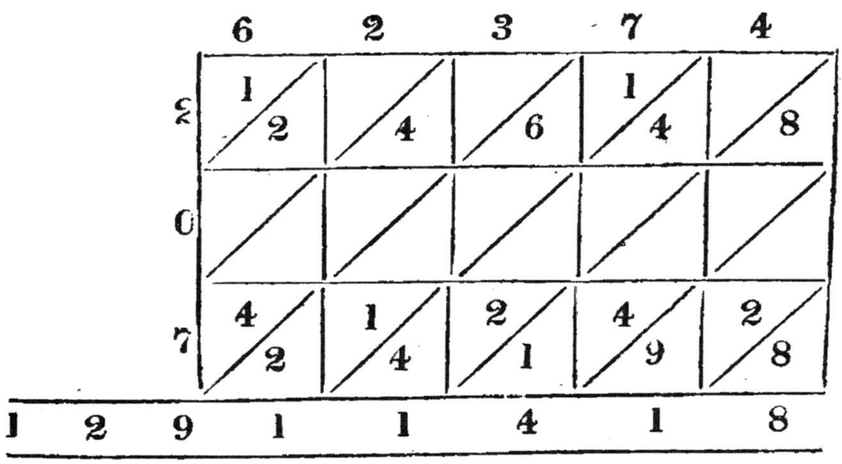

On the other rules, nothing is delivered differing so much from those contained in our common books of arithmetic, as to require specific mention.

Book second, contains the arithmetic of fractions; and book third, the rule of three, or to find an unknown number by four proportionals. Book fourth, delivers the rule of position, or to find an unknown number by assuming one once or twice, and comparing the errors. Book fifth, gives the method of finding an unknown number, by reversing all the steps of the process described in the question.

The sixth book, treats of mensuration. The introduction contains geometrical definitions. Chapter I. treats of the mensuration of rectilinear surfaces. Under this head the two following articles are deserving of notice. I. To find the point in the base of a triangle where it will be cut by a perpendicular, let fall from the opposite angle. Call the greatest side the base; multiply the sum of the two lesser sides by their difference; divide the product by the base, and subtract the quotient from the base; one half the remainder will shew the place on the base, where the perpendicular falls towards the least side.*

---

* Let a be the base, or longest side, b the middle, c the smallest, and x the distance of the perpendicular from the least side. Then

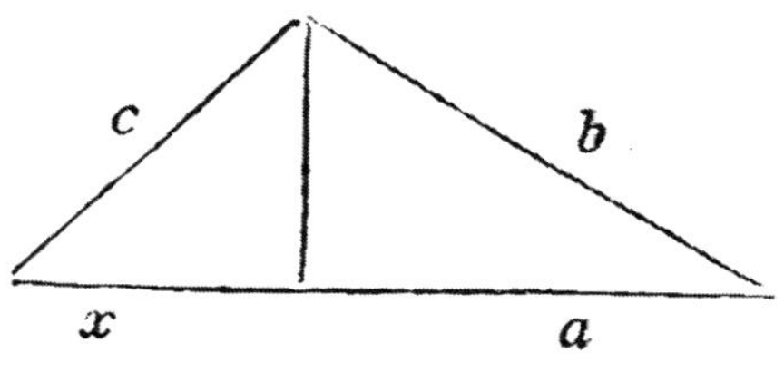

$$b^2 = a^2 + c^2 - 2ax \ (Eucl.\ 13.\ 2.)$$
$$2ax = a^2 + c^2 - b^2$$
$$x = \frac{a}{2} - \frac{b^2 - c^2}{2a}$$

But $b^2 - c^2 = \overline{b+c} \times \overline{b-c}$

2. To find the area of an equilateral triangle. Multiply the square of a quarter of the square of one of the sides by three: the square root of the product is the area required.*

CHAPTER second, treats of the mensuration of curvilinear surfaces. For the circle the rule delivered in many common books of mensuration is given: viz. multiply the square of the diameter by 11, and divide the product by 14.†

CHAPTER third, on the mensuration of solids, contains nothing of singularity sufficient to merit particular notice. This chapter concludes with the following sentence. "The demonstrations of all these rules are "contained in my greater work, entitled *Bahr-ul-Hisàb* (the ocean of "calculation,) may GOD grant me grace to finish it."

BOOK seventh, treats of practical geometry. Chapter first on levelling,

---

$$\text{Therefore } x = \frac{a}{2} - \frac{\overline{b+c} \times \overline{b-c}}{2a}$$

See the geometrical demonstration in the elements of plane trigonometry, annexed to SIMSON's *Euclid*, prop. 7.

* Let a side of the triangle be a and the perpendicular x.

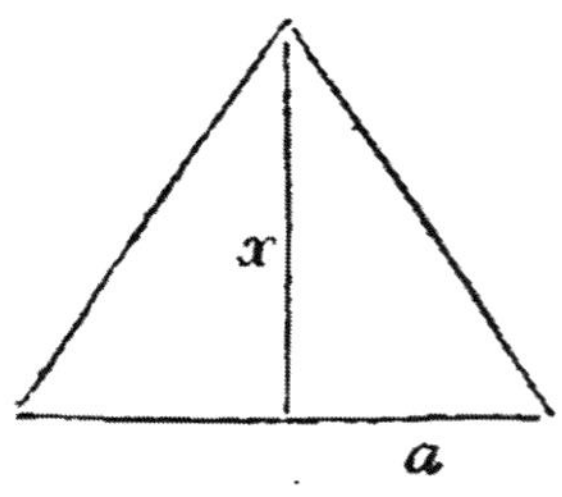

The area is $\frac{ax}{2}$

$$\text{But } x^2 = a^2 - \frac{a^2}{4} = \frac{3a^2}{4}$$

$$x = \sqrt{\frac{3a^2}{4}}$$

$$\frac{ax}{2} = \frac{a}{2}\sqrt{\frac{3a^2}{4}} = \sqrt{\frac{3a^4}{16}}$$

† This is founded on the rough proportion of the diameter, to the circumference as 7 : 22. BHA'SCARA, in the *Lilavati*, assigns 1250 : 3927, which is 1 : 3.1416 and differs only 0.000007 from the most accurate computation hitherto made.

for the purpose of making canals. In this are described the plummet level, and the water level on the same principle with our spirit level.

CHAPTER second, on the mensuration of heights, accessible and inaccessible. Under the former of these heads are delivered the common methods, by bringing the top of a pole whose height is known, in a line between the eye and the top of the height required; by viewing the image of the top in a horizontal mirror; by taking the proportion between a stick of known length, set up perpendicular to the horizon and its shadow; and by taking the length of the shadow of the height when the sun's altitude is 45 degrees. The last method is this, "Place the index of the astro-
" labe at the mark of 45 degrees, and stand at a place from whence the
" height of the object is visible through the sights, and measure from the
" place where you stand to the place where a stone would fall from the
" top; add your own height, and the sum is the quantity required."

FOR the mensuration of inaccessible heights the following rule is delivered, "Observe the top of the object through the sights, and mark on
" what shadow line (division) the lower end of the index falls. Then
" move the index a step forward or backward, and advance or recede
" till you see the top of the object again. Measure the distance between
" your stations, and multiply by 7 if the index is moved a *Dhil-Kadam*,
" and by 12 if it is moved a *Dhil-As bâ*,* according to the shadow lines
" on the Astrolabe. This is the quantity required.

---

* This part of the astrolabe consists of two squares put together laterally; the index of the instrument being at the point of the adjacent angles above. One square has seven, and the other, twelve divisions: the former called *Dhil-i-Kadam*, the latter *Dhil-i-As bâ*. The squares are graduated on the outer sides from the top, and at the bottom from the point of the adjacent angles. The divisions on the upright sides are those lines which CHAUCER, in his treatise on the astrolabe, calls *Umbra-recta;* those on the horizontal he calls *Umbra-versa*.

Chapter third. On measuring the breadth of rivers and the depth of wells. 1st. Stand on the bank of the river, and through the two sights look at the opposite bank; then turn round and look at any thing on the land side, keeping the astrolabe even. The distance from the observer to the object is the same as the breadth of the river. 2d. Place something

---

Chaucer's astrolabe had only one square, *Dhil-i-As'bá*, being divided into twelve parts. The *Umbra-recta* is called *Dhil-Mustawì*, and the *versa*, *Dhil-Máćùs*.

The rule in the text is very inaccurately delivered; for the only case in which it will apply is when at the first station the index coincides with the diagonal of the square, and being afterwards moved one division on the horizontal side, the observer advances towards the object, till the top is again seen through the sights. For let AC be the height required, B the first station, D the second. As the angles at A and B are equal, $AC = BC$. But at the second position $AC : DC :: 7 : 6$. Therefore $AC = 7\,BD$.

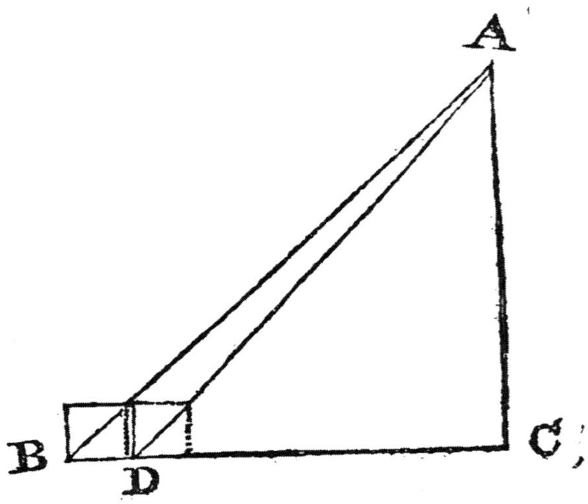

But suppose at the first station B, the index falls on the fourth division, *Dhil-Kadam*, on the vertical side; and that, by retiring from the object to D, it is brought on the third; then it is evident that $BC : AC :: 7 : 4$, and $DC : AC :: 7 : 3$. Therefore $DC = \frac{4\,BC}{3} = 4\,BD$. Consequently $7 : 3 :: 4\,BD : AC = \frac{12\,BD}{7}$.

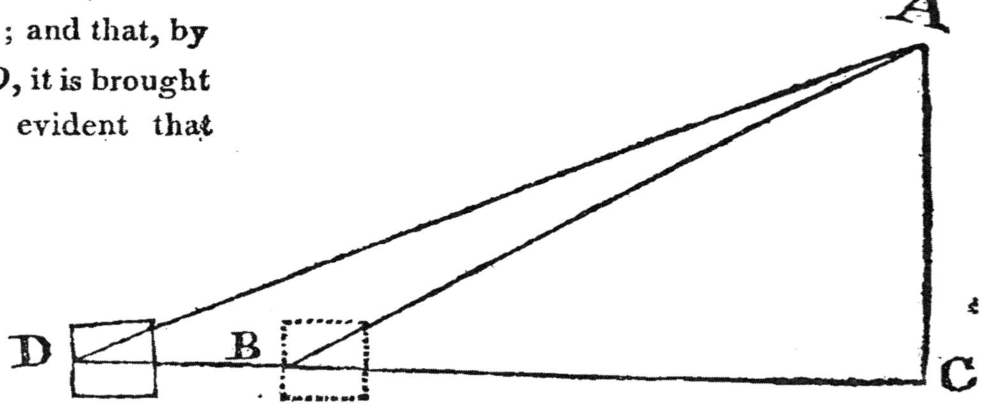

over the well which shall serve for its diameter ; from the center of this diameter drop something heavy and shining till it reach the bottom, and make a mark at the center ; then look at the heavy body through the two sights of the astrolabe, so that the line of vision may cut the diameter. Multiply the distance from the mark on the diameter to the place where the line of vision cuts it, by your own height, and divide the product by the distance from the place where the line is cut to the place where you stand. The quotient is the depth of the well.*

Book eighth. " On finding unknown quantities by Algebra. In this book are two chapters.

" Chapter first. Introductory. Call the unknown quantity *Shai* (thing,) its product into itself *Mál* (possession,) the product of *Mál* into *Shai*, *Cáb* (a die or cube,) of *Shai* into *Cáb*, *Mal-Mál* ; of *Shai* into *Mal-i-Mal*, *Mal-Cáb* ; *Shai* into *Mál-i-Cáb*, *Cáb-i-Cáb* ; and so on, without end. For one *Cáb* write two *Mál*, and from these two *Máls* one becomes *Cáb* ; afterwards both *Máls* become *Cáb*. Thus the seventh power is

---

* The impossibility of attaining accuracy in either of these operations is abundantly obvious. The first depends on the principle, that on a level plain, two places, which with a given height of the observer's eye have the same dip below the horizon must be at equal distances. The second is thus : let the body drop from a to e; and let the observer at $c\,d$ observe it in the line $d\,e$ which cuts $a\,c$ in b. Then $b\,c : c\,d :: a\,b : a\,e = \frac{a\,b \times c\,d}{b\,c}$

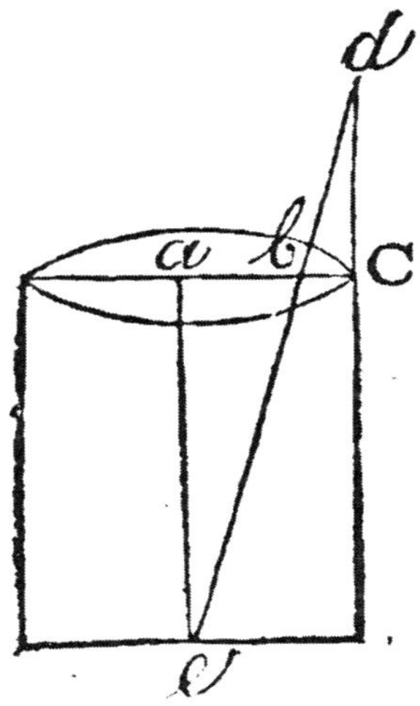

Mál-i-Mál-i-Câb, and the eighth *Mál-i-Câb-i-Câb*, in the ninth *Câb-i-Câb-Câb*, and so on. All these powers are in proportion, either ascending or descending. Thus the ratio of *Mál-i-Mál* to *Câb* is like the ratio of *Câb* to *Mál*, *Mál* to *Shai*, and *Shai* to one, and one to one divided by *Shai*; and one divided by *Shai* to one divided by *Mál*; and one divided by *Mál* to one divided by *Câb*; and one divided by *Câb* to one divided by *Mál-i-Mál*. To multiply one of these powers by another, if they are both on the same side, (viz. of unity) add the exponents of their powers together; the product will have the same denomination as this sum. For example, to multiply *Mál-i-Câb* by *Mál-i-Mál-i-Câb*, the first is the 5th power and the 2d the 7th. The result then is *Câb-i-Câb-i-Câb-i-Câb* or four *Câbs*, which is the 12th power. If the factors are on different sides, the product will be the excess on the side of the greater. The product of one divided by *Mál-i-Mál* into *Mál-i-Câb* is *Shai*; and the product of one divided by *Câb-i-Câb-Câb* into *Câb-i-Mál-i-Mál*, is one divided by *Mál*: and if the factors are at the same distance (from one,) the product is one. The particulars of the methods of division, and extraction of roots and other rules, I have given in my greater book. The rules of Algebra which have been discovered by learned men are six, and they relate to number and *Shai* and *Mál*. The following table will shew the products and quotients of these, which are here given for the sake of brevity.

		Multiplier.						
		$\frac{1}{a^2}$	$\frac{1}{a}$	1	a	a^2		
Dividend.	a^2	1	a	a^2	a^3	a^4	a^2	Multiplicand.
	a	$\frac{1}{a}$	1	a	a^2	a^3	a	
	1	$\frac{1}{a^2}$	$\frac{1}{a}$	1	a	a^2	1	
	$\frac{1}{a}$	$\frac{1}{a^3}$	$\frac{1}{a^2}$	$\frac{1}{a}$	1	a	$\frac{1}{a}$	
	$\frac{1}{a^2}$	$\frac{1}{a^4}$	$\frac{1}{a^3}$	$\frac{1}{a^2}$	$\frac{1}{a}$	1	$\frac{1}{a^2}$	
		a^2	a	1	$\frac{1}{a}$	$\frac{1}{a^2}$		
		Divisor.						

" The use of the table is this : multiply the co-efficient of one of the two quantities by that of the other ; the result is the co-efficient of the product, which is of the denomination contained in the square where the lines from the two factors meet. If on either side there be a substractive (negative) quantity, call the minuend *plus* or affirmative, and the subtrahend *minus* negative. The product of *plus* into *plus* and *minus* into *minus* are both *plus*, and the product of different kinds are *minus*. Multiply the quantities together, and subtract the negative from the affirmative. For example, the product of 10 and one *Shai* into 10 all but one *Shai*, is 100 all but *Mál*. The product of 5 all but *Shai*, by 7 all but *Shai* is 35 and one *Mál* all but 12 *Shai*. Another example. The product of 4 *Mál* and 6 all but 2 *Shai*, into 3 *Shai* all but 5, is 12 *Cáb*, and 28 *Shai* all but 26 *Mál* and 30. In division, find a number which multiplied by the divisor will produce the dividend. Divide the co-efficient of the dividend by that of the divisor, the quotient is the co-efficient of the quantity which is opposite to the dividend and divisor.

"CHAPTER second. On the six rules of Algebra. To find unknown quantities by Algebra depends on acuteness and sagacity; an attentive consideration of the terms of the question, and a successful application of the invention to such things as may serve to bring out what is required. Call the unknown quantity *Shai*, and proceed with it according to the terms of the question, as has been said, till the operation ends with an equation. Let that side where there are negative quantities be made perfect, and let the negative quantity be added to the other side: this is called restoration *(Jebr.)* Let those things which are of the same kind, and equal on both sides, be thrown away: this is opposition *(Mukábalah.)* Equality is either of one species to another, which is of three kinds, called *(Mufridát)* simple; or of one species to two species, which of three kinds, called *(Muktarinát)* compound.

"CASE the first. *Mufridát*. Number is equal to things. Divide the number by the co-efficient of the things, and the unknown quantity will be found. For example; a person admitted that he owed ZAID 1000 and one half of what he owed ÂMER; and that he owed ÂMER 1000 all but one half of what he owed to ZAID. Call ZAID's debt *Shai*. Then ÂMER's debt is 1000, all but half of *Shai*. Then ZAID's is 1500 all but a fourth of *Shai*. This is equal to *Shai*. After *Jebr*, 1500 is equal to one *Shai* and a quarter of *Shai*. So for ZAID is 1200 and for ÂMER 400."

"CASE the second. Multiples of *Shai* equal to multiples of *Mál*. Divide the co-efficient of the things by that of the *Mál*; the quotient is the unknown quantity. Example. Some sons plundered their father's inheritance, which consisted of *Dínárs*. One took 1, another 2, the third 3, and so on increasing by one. The ruling power took back what they had plundered, and divided it among them in equal shares. Then each received 7. How many sons were there, and how many *Dínàrs?* Suppose the number of sons *Shai*, and take the sum of the extremes, that is to say, 1 and *Shai*. Multiply them by half of *Shai*. This is the number of *Dinàrs*. For the product of the sum of any series of numbers in arithmetical progression, is equal to the product of the sum of the two extremes, into half the number of terms. Divide the number of the *Dinàrs* by *Shai*, which is the number of the sons; the quotient, according to the terms of the question, will be seven. Multiply 7 by *Shai*, which is the divisor; 7 *Shai* is the product, which is equal to $\frac{1}{2}$ *Mál* and $\frac{1}{2}$ *Shai*. After *Jebr* and *Múkabalah*, one *Mál* is equal to 13 *Shai*. *Shai* then is 13; and this is the number of the sons. Multiply this by 7. The number of *Dinàrs* will be found 91."

"QUESTIONS of this sort may be solved by position. Thus, suppose the number of sons to be 5; the first error is 4 in defect. Then suppose it to be 9, the second error is 2 in defect. The first *Mahfúdh* is 10 and the second is 36; their difference is 26; the difference of the errors is 2. Another method, which is easy and short, is this. Double the quotient, (the number 7 in the question) subtract one, and the result is the number of sons.

"CASE the third. Number equal to *Mál*. Divide the number by the co-efficient of the *Mál*; the root of the quotient is the unknown quantity. For example. A person admitted that he owed ZAID the greater of two sums of money, the sum of which was 20 and the product 96. Suppose one of them to be 10 and *Shai*, and the other 10 all but *Shai*. The product, which is 100 all but *Mál*, is equal to 96; and after *Jebr* and *Mukábaláh*, one *Mál* is equal to 4, and *Shai* equal to 2. One of the sums then is 8 and the other 12, and 12 is the debt of ZAID.

"FIRST case of *Muktarinàt.* Number equal to *Mál* and *Shai.* Complete the *Mál* to unity if it is deficient, and reduce it to the same if it exceeds, and reduce the numbers and *Shai* in the same ratio, by dividing all by the co-efficient of the *Mál.* Then square one half the co-efficient of the *Shai*, and add this square to the numbers. Subtract from the root of the sum half the co-efficient of the *Shai*, and the unknown will remain. Example. A person admitted that he owed ZAID a sum less than 10, so much that if the square of it was added to its product by $\frac{1}{2}$ what it wants of 10, the sum would be 12. Suppose the number *Shai*, its square is *Mál*; half the remainder from 10 is 5 all but half of *Shai*. The product of *Shai* by this is 5 *Shai* all but $\frac{1}{2}$ of *Mál.* Therefore $\frac{1}{2}$ of *Mál* and 5 *Shai* are equal to 12. One *Mál* and 10 *Shai* are equal to 24. Subtract half the co-efficient of the *Shai* from the root of the sum of the square of $\frac{1}{2}$ the co-efficient of the *Shai* and the numbers. There remains 2, which is the number required.

SECOND case. *Shai* equal to numbers and *Mál.* After completing or rejecting, subtract the numbers from the square of half the co-efficient of the *Shai*, and add the root of the remainder to half the co-efficient of the *Shai*; or subtract the former from the latter; the result is the unknown quantity. Example. What number is that which being multiplied by half of itself and the product increased by 12, the result is five times the original number. Multiply *Shai* by half itself, then half of *Mál* added to 12 is equal to 5 *Shai.* One *Mál* and 24 is equal to 10 *Shai.* Subtract 24 from the square of 5, there remains one, and the root of one is one. The sum or difference of 1 and 5 is the number required.

THIRD Case. *Mál* equal to number and *Shai.* After completion or rejection, add the square of half the co-efficient of the *Shai* to the numbers, and add the root of the sum to half the co-efficient of the *Shai*. This is the unknown quantity. For example. What number is that which being subtracted from its square, and the remainder added to the square, is 10? Subtract *Shai* from *Mál* and go on with the operation, 2 *Mál* all but *Shai* is equal to 10; and after *Jebr* and *Radd*, *Mál* is equal to 5 and $\frac{1}{2}$ of *Shai*. The square of half the coefficient of the *Shai* and 5, is 5 and half an eighth, and its root is $2\frac{1}{4}$. To this add $\frac{1}{4}$, the result is $2\frac{1}{2}$, which is the number required.

Book ninth, contains twelve rules regarding the properties of numbers, viz.

1st. To find the sum of the products of a number multiplied into itself and into all numbers below it: add one to the number, and multiply the sum by the square of the number; half the product is the number required.

2d. To add the odd numbers in their regular order: add one to the last number and take the square of half the sum.

3d. To add even numbers from two upwards: multiply half the last even number by a number greater by one than that half.

4th. To add the squares of the numbers in order: add one to twice the last number, and multiply a third of the sum by the sum of the numbers.

5th. To find the sum of the cubes in succession: take the square of the sum of the numbers.

6th. To find the product of the roots of two numbers: multiply one by the other, and the root of the product is the answer.

7th. To divide the root of one number by that of another: divide one by the other, the root of the quotient is the answer.

8th. To find a perfect number: that is a number which is equal to the sum of its aliquot parts, (EUCLID, book 7, def. 22.) The rule is that delivered by EUCLID, book 9, prop. 36.

9th. To find a square in a given ratio to its root: divide the first number of the ratio by the second; the square of the quotient is the square required.

10th. IF any number is multiplied and divided by another, the product multiplied by the quotient is the square of the first number.

11th. THE difference of two squares is equal to the product of the sum and difference of the roots.

12th. IF two numbers are divided by each other, and the quotients multiplied together, the result is always one.

BOOK tenth, contains nine examples, all of which are capable of solution by simple equations, position, or retracing the steps of the operation, and some of them by simple proportion; so that it is needless to specify them.

THE conclusion, which marks the limits of algebraical knowledge in the age of the writer, I shall give entire, in the author's words. "Conclusion. There are many questions in this science which learned men have to this time in vain attempted to solve; and they have stated some of these questions in their writings, to prove that this science contains difficulties, to silence those who pretend they find nothing in it above their ability, to warn arithmeticians against undertaking to answer every question that may be proposed, and to excite men of genius to attempt their solution. Of these I have selected seven. 1st. To divide 10 into 2 parts, such, that when each part is added to its square root and the sums are multiplied together, the product is equal to a supposed number. 2d. What square number is that which being increased or diminished by 10, the sum and remainder are both square numbers? 3d. A person said he owed ZAID 10 all but the square root of what he owed ÂMER, and that he owed ÂMER 5 all but the square root of what he owed ZAID. 4th. To divide a cube number into two cube numbers. 5th. To divide 10 into two parts, such, that if each is divided by the other, and the two quotients are added together, the sum is equal to one of the parts. 6th. There are three square numbers in continued geometrical proportion, such, that the sum of the three is a square number. 7th. There is a square, such, that when it is increased and diminished by its root and 2, the sum and the difference are squares. Know, reader, that in this treatise I have collected in a small space the most beautiful and best rules of this science, more than were ever collected before in one book. Do not underrate the value of this bride; hide her from the view of those who are unworthy of her, and let her go to the house of him only who aspires to wed her."

IT is seen above that these questions are distinctly said to be beyond the skill of algebraists. They either involve equations of the higher order, or the indeterminate analysis, or are impossible.

IT does not appear that the *Arabians* used algebraic notation or abbreviating symbols; that they had any knowledge of the Diophantine Algebra, or of any but the easiest and elementary parts of the science. We have seen that BAHA'-UL-DÌN ascribes the invention of the numeral figures in the decimal scale to the *Indians*. As the proof commonly given of the *Indains* being the inventors of these figures is only an extract from the preface of a book of *Arabic* poems, it may be as well to mention that all the *Arabic* and *Persian* books of arithmetic ascribe the invention to the *Indians*. The following is an extract from a *Persian* treatise of arithmetic in my possession.

" The *Indain* sages, wishing to express numbers conveniently, invented these nine figures ۱ ۲ ۳ ۴ ۵ ۶ ۷ ۸ ۹. The first figure on the right hand they made stand for units, the second for tens, the third for hundreds, the fourth for thousands. Thus, after the third rank, the next following is units of thousands, the second tens of thousands, the third hundreds of thousands, and so on. Every figure therefore in the first rank is the number of units it expresses; every figure in the second the number of tens which the figure expresses, in the third the number of hundreds, and so on. When in any rank a figure is wanting, write a cipher like a small circle o to preserve the rank. Thus ten is written 10, a hundred 100; five thousand and twenty-five 5025."

Of the *Indian* Algebra in its full extent the *Arabians* seem to have been ignorant; but it is likely they had their Algebra from the same source as their Arithmetic. The *Arabian* and *Persian* treatises on Algebra, like the old *European* ones, begin with the Arithmetic, called in those treatises the Arithmetic of the *Indians*, and have a second part on Algebra; but no notice is taken of the origin of the latter. Most likely their Algebra, being numeral, was considered by the authors as part of Arithmetic.

Though part only of the *Khulásat-ul-Hisàb* is about Algebra, the rest, relating to arithmetic and mensuration, must be thought not wholly unconnected with the subject. It is to be hoped that ere long we shall have either translations from the *Sanscrit* of the *Bíja Ganita* and *Lílawati*, or perfect accounts from the originals; and that other ancient *Hindú* books of Algebra will be found, and made known to the world. But as there is no immediate prospect of these desiderata being realized, the translations into *Persian* will be found well deserving of attention. Only let them be examined without prejudice.

THERE are principles which will safely lead to a distinction of what is interpolated from what is original; and it is the neglect of these principles, and not any fair examination of the translations, that may lead to error.

A DISSERTATION ON THE CONSTRUCTION AND PROPERTIES OF ARCHES.

BY

G. ATWOOD, ESQ. F.R.S.

LONDON:

PRINTED BY W. BULMER AND CO.

CLEVELAND-ROW, ST. JAMES'S.

FOR LUNN, OXFORD-STREET, AND EGERTON, WHITEHALL.

1801.

PREFACE.

An arch being formed (according to the usual modes of construction) by the apposition of wedges, or sections of a wedge-like form, the properties of arches seem to be naturally derived from those of the wedge, on which principle the inquiries in the ensuing Tract are founded.

By considering the subject on this ground, it appears that the theory of arches may be inferred from geometrical construction, depending only on the known properties of the wedge and other elementary laws of mechanics, without having recourse to the more abstruse branches of geometry in explaining this practical subject, to which a more direct and obvious method of inference seems better adapted.

A geometrical construction for adjusting equilibration on these principles, extended to arches of every form, with the various consequences arising from, or connected with it, are the subject of the ensuing pages, in which rules are investigated, in the first place, for establishing the equilibrium of arches on two distinct conditions, namely, either by adjusting the weights of the sections according to the angles which are contained between their sides, supposed to be given quantities: or, secondly, by supposing the weights of the wedges or sections to be given, and investigating what must be the angles contained by their sides, so that the pressures on them, may be an exact counterpoise to the weight of each section, due regard being had to its place in the arch. In the case when the arch is designed to support an horizontal plane or road, on which heavy weights are to be sustained, the intermediate space between the arch and the horizontal road way, ought to be filled up in such a manner, as not only to afford the support required, but also to add to the strength and security of the entire fabric. If this should be effected by columns erected on the arch, and acting on the several sections by their weight in a direction perpendicular to the horizon, rules are given in the following pages for establishing the equilibrium by adjusting the angles of the sections to their several weights, including the weights of the columns superincumbent, so that the pressure on the sides of each section, may be a counterpoise to its weight, taking into account the place it occupies in the arch. But in structures of this description, the columns of masonry which are erected upon the arches of a bridge, as a support to the road way, cannot be expected to act on the sections of an arch according to the exact proportions required, which are assumed as data in the geometrical propositions, for determining the equilibration, as these proportions would probably be altered either by the differences of specific gravity which may occasionally be found in the materials used, or by differences in the cohesive force, which would prevent the columns from settling and pressing on the several parts of the arch with their full weights, such as the theory requires. Perpendicular columns of iron would not be liable to this objection: by adopting supports of this description, the weights of the columns, added to the weight of the road, would press on the interior arch, to be sustained in equilibrio, by adjusting the angles of the sections to the superincumbent weight, according to the rules determined in the pages which follow. But perhaps the space between the interior arch and the road might be more effectually filled up, by other arches terminated by circular arcs, drawn from centres situated in the vertical line which bisects the entire arch, so as to become united in the highest or middle wedge. The sections of these arches may be adjusted, by the rules here given, so as to become distinct arches of equilibration, which when united, will constitute a single arch of equilibration, similar in form to that which is expressed in the plan of an iron bridge, of one arch, which has been proposed to be erected over the river Thames,* as it is represented in the engraving inserted in the Third Report of the Committee of the House of Commons, for the further Improvement of the Port of London.

According to this plan of construction, each part of the edifice would partake of the properties of equilibration, contributing additional strength and security to the whole building.

In the course of this inquiry, exclusive of the general principles which have been here described, sundry other properties are investigated, which, it is presumed, may be of use in the practice of architecture, in the construction of arches of every kind, as well as in explaining some particulars relating to the subject, which have not hitherto been accounted for in a satisfactory manner.

Some propositions of this kind are comprised in six general rules, inserted in page 19, which are expressed in simple terms, and are easily applicable to practical cases.

Supposing an arch to consist of any number of sections or wedges, adjusted to equilibrium; this arch resting on the two abutments, may be considered analagous to a single wedge, the sides of which are inclined at an angle equal to the inclination of the two abutments: the forces therefore which would be necessary to sustain such an arch or wedge when applied perpendicularly to the sides, ought to be equal to the reaction of the pressures on the two abutments; this principle is found on examination to be verified by referring to the tables annexed;† whether the arch consists of sections, without, or with the load of superincumbent weight, and whether the angles of the sections are equal or

* Designed by Messrs. Telford and Douglass.

† Appendix, Tables, I. II. III. IV. V.

unequal : For according to all these tables, the weight of the semiarch is to the pressure on the corresponding abutmént, or the reaction thereof, as the sine of half the angle between the two opposite abutments, is to the radius ; which is a proportion equally applicable to the wedge, and to the arch, when adjusted to equilibrium.

From the second of these rules it appears, that the lateral or horizontal pressure of any arch adjusted to equilibrum depends wholly on the weight and angle between the sides of the highest, or middle section : If therefore the weight and angle of this highest section should continue unaltered, the lateral force or pressure will be invariably the same, however the height, the length, the span, and the weight of the whole arch may be varied. This lateral force is called, in technical language, the *drift* or *shoot* of an arch, and the exact determination of it has been considered as a *desideratum* in the practical construction of arches.

When the dimensions of the sections composing the rectilinear or flat arch appeared to follow from the general construction for determining equilibration, the author was inclined to suspect, from the apparent paradox implied in this inference, that some mistake or misapprehension had taken place, either in the general proposition, or in the deductions from it : but finding from trials on a model of an arch of this description, that the sections formed according to the dimensions stated for the flat arch in page 35 of this Tract, Fig. 15, were supported in equilibrio, without any aid from extraneous force, he was convinced that the properties of equilibration deduced from the principle of the wedge, are no less true when applied to practice, than they are in theory. On inquiry it appears, that this species of arch has been long in use among practical artists; the dimensions of the wedges having been formed according to rules established by custom, but without being referred to any certain principle.

A few observations may be here added, concerning the principles assumed in this Tract, as truths to be allowed. It is supposed, that the constituent parts of an arch are portions of wedges, the sides of which are plane surfaces inclined to each other at an angle. Each wedge is considered as a solid body perfectly hard and unelastic, in respect to any force of pressure which can be applied to crush or alter its figure when forming part of an arch, the equilibrium of which is established by the pressure and gravity of the sections only, independently of the ties or holdings, which are applied for the purpose of preventing the extrusion of the wedges by the force of any occasional weight which may be brought to press on the arch. These fastenings supply in some degree the place of the natural force, by which the parts of solid bodies cohere till they are separated by artificial means. When the weights of the sections are not very great, a defect of equilibrium to a certain extent may subsist, without producing any material change in the figure of the arch, or endangering the security of the fabric. But if heavy massive blocks of stone or iron should be placed together in the form of an arch, without being well adjusted, any considerable defect of equilibrium would cause a stress on the fastenings, which would overbear the weak alliance of cement or the mechanical ties and fastenings, that are applied to prevent the separation of the sections. In other cases, when sections of less weight are used, the cohesion which takes place between the surfaces of blocks of stone, with the aid of cement, and fastenings of various kinds, may impart a considerable degree of strength to edifices; insomuch, that although many arches have been counterpoised according to rules which produce rather a fortuitous arrangement of materials for forming the equilibrium, than an adjustment of it, according to correct principles, the cohesion of the parts have, notwithstanding, preserved them from falling; or from experiencing any considerable change of form. But this power has been sometimes too much relied on, especially by the architects of the twelfth, thirteenth, and the centuries immediately succeeding, who, in particular instances, entertained the bold idea of erecting lofty pillars, subject to a great lateral pressure, without applying any counterpoise. The consequence has been a distortion of figure, too evidently discernible in the pillars which support the domes in most of the old cathedral churches. However great the force of cohesion may be, which connects the parts of buildings, every edifice would be more secure by having all the parts of it duly balanced, independently of cohesion or mechanical fastenings, by which means, that distortion of shape would be prevented which the want of equilibrium in structures, must always have a tendency to create, whether the effects of it should be sufficient to produce a visible change of figure, or should be too small to be discernible by the eye. When arches are not perfectly balanced, and a change of figure ensues, the only security for the preservation of the fabric from entire disunion, is the excess of the cohesive force above the force tending to separate the parts of the building, arising from the want of counterpoise; and as cohesion is a species of force, which cannot be estimated with exactness, where the circumstances of an edifice are such as may weaken this force, or render the effects of it precarious, the more attention is necessary to establish a perfect equipoise between the weights and pressures of the several parts.

A

DISSERTATION

ON THE

CONSTRUCTION OF ARCHES.

As the exterior termination of an arch always exceeds the interior curve (usually called the curve of the arch), the sections or wedges of which it is composed will partake of a similar disproportion, the length of the exterior boundary in each wedge always exceeding that of the interior. A consequence of this wedge-like form is, that the weight of each section by which it endeavours to descend towards the earth, is opposed by the pressure the sides of it sustain from the sections which are adjacent to it. If the pressure should be too small, the wedge will not be supported, but will descend with greater or less obliquity to the horizon, according to its place in the arch. If the pressure should be too great, it will more than counterpoise the weight of the section, and will force it upward. The equilibrium of the entire arch will consequently depend on the exact adjustment of the weight of each section or wedge, to the pressure it sustains, and the angular distance from the vertex. This equilibrium is understood to be established by the mutual pressure and gravity of the sections only, independent of any aid from friction, cohesive cement, or fastenings of any kind.

When an arch is erected, fastenings are necessarily applied, to prevent the extrusion of the wedges by any force of weight which may be occasionally brought to press upon the several parts of the arch. The ensuing geometrical constructions are intended, in the first instance, to adjust the equipoise of the wedges or sections which are disposed according to the direction of any curve line that may be conceived to pass through the extremities of their bases, requiring only, as conditions to be given, the weight of the highest or middle wedge, and the angles contained by the sides of the several wedges or sections. From these *data*, the weight of each section is to be inferred, so that when the whole are put together, they may balance each other in perfect equipoise in every part. Since, according to this construction, the weights of the sections are dependent on the given angles between their sides, the exterior termination of the sections, or the weights superincumbent on them, will usually take some form which cannot be altered, without a change in the conditions given: to effect this change, when requisite, other considerations will be necessary, which are the subject of the latter part of this tract.

For these reasons it appears, that the principle of establishing the equilibrium of an arch, by inferring the weights of the sections from their angles, not requiring a determinate form to the exterior boundary, is best suited to the construction of those arches which are erected either to connect the several parts of an edifice, or for their support and ornament, to which they so eminently contribute in many of those ancient monuments of skill and magnificence, which still remain to be contemplated with delight and admiration.

According to this principle of construction, the architect is not restrained to curves, observing any particular law of curvature, but may adopt any that require mechanical delineation only, for describing the forms of arches he may wish to erect; to this advantage is added, that of having each arch balanced within itself, and the pressure on each part, as well as on the abutments, exactly ascertained. And, as the angles of the sections may be varied at discretion, by properly altering the adjustment of the equilibrium, according to the rules here given, the force of pressure on the abutments may be made to take any direction which best contributes to the strength of the edifice, so far as the limits of those rules will allow.

In addition to the principles which have been the subject of the preceeding observations, the following case is next to be considered. It has been already observed, that when the weights of the sections are inferred from the angles between their sides, the heights of the masses added to the sections, or making a part of them, will be terminated by some line depending on the dimensions of these angles. But arches are often constructed for the purpose of supporting considerable weights, the terminations of which are required to be of particular given forms. In the case of bridges, a wall of masonry is usually erected on the arches, as a support to the road-way, which is always horizontal, or nearly so; the superincumbent weight of this wall, by adding proportionally to the weights of the sections, must require a stronger force of pressure on their sides as a counterpoise to it; this is effected in consequence of two alterations, by which the loaded arc differs from the arc constructed only for supporting its own weight. 1st. The weight of the highest or middle section, being augmented, increases the pressure, and the reaction between the surfaces of all the sections; and to compensate for the different degrees of weight which are superadded to the other sections, the angles contained between their sides, and the pressures upon them, are to be increased in due proportion. For as the angles of the wedges are increased, a given force of pressure acting on their sides, will have the greater effect in supporting the intermediate wedges. The heights of the wall built on the several sections proportional to the weights superincumbent on them, are supposed to be given quantities, so that the upper extremities may terminate in an horizontal, or any other given line: instead therefore of inferring those heights, or weights, from the angles of the sections considered as given, according to the principle of construction, which has been described in the preceding pages, we are to consider the heights of the wall, or weights on the several sections, as given quantities, and to infer from them, what must be the magnitudes of the angles contained by the sides of the sections, so that the weight of each, including the weight superincumbent, may be an exact counterpoise to the pressure on the sides of it. The curve line, which passes through the bases, may be of any form, without affecting the equilibrium established according to these principles. For the counterpoise of gravity and pressure between two or more wedges, is wholly independent of the line which may be drawn through their bases.

If it should be objected that the more nearly an arch approaches to a right line, the less weight it will securely bear, it may be replied, that this insecurity is caused by circumstances which are quite independent of the equilibrium.

If the materials of which an arch is constructed, were perfectly hard and rigid, so as not to be liable to the smallest change in their form, and the abutments were immoveably fixed, an arch, when the sections have been adjusted, although but little deviating from a right line, would be equally secure, in respect to equilibrium, with a semi-circular, or any other arch.

From these general observations, the object of the ensuing tract appears to consist principally in the solutions of two statical problems, which may be briefly expressed in the following terms; 1st, from having given the angles contained by the sides of the wedges which form an arch, together with the weight of the highest or middle section, to infer the weights of the other sections; and conversely, from the weights of each wedge given, together with the angle of the first section, to determine the angles between the sides of the other sections, so as to form an arch perfectly balanced in all its parts.

In the construction of circular arches, the joinings of the sections, or sides of the wedges, are usually directed to the centre of the circle. In the following constructions, the sides of the wedges are directed to any different points; but there is no reason to suppose, that the equilibrium of the arch would be altered, or that the construction would be less secure, from this circumstance.

Considering that an arch supports the weights which press upon it, and preserves its form in consequence of the wedge-like figures of the sections; the principle of its construction and properties seem naturally to be referred to those of the wedge, which principle has been adopted in the ensuing disquisition founded on plain geometry and statics, or the doctrine of equilibrium or equipoise, as established by Gallileo and Newton.

Fig. 1. K C G A, D B G A, D B F E, represent three of the

sections or wedges which form an arch, the lower curve of which passes through the points C, A, B, E, &c.

The wedges are also, for brevity, denoted by the letters B, A, and C respectively.

The highest wedge of the arch is G A D B, which (being here considered isosceles) is terminated on each side by the lines D B, G A inclined to each other at the angle B O A, which is termed, for the sake of distinction, the angle of the wedge or section. The termination of this wedge on the lower side is the line B A, the extremities of which coincide with the curve of the arch, and on the upper part, by the horizontal line D G parallel to B A. If therefore D G is bisected in the point V, a line V O joining the points V and O, will be perpendicular to the horizon. In like manner, the inclination of the sides K C, G A forms the angle of the wedge C, and the inclination of the two sides D B, F E is the angle of the wedge B. In the construction of arches, the angles of the sections are commonly made equal to each other, but in a general investigation of the subject, it will be expedient to consider the angles of the sections of any magnitude, in general, either as quantities given for forming the equilibrium of the arch, by the adjustment of their weights, or as quantities to be inferred, from having the weights of their sections given.

Fig. 1. The wedge A when unimpeded, endeavours by its gravity, to descend in the direction of the line V O, but is prevented from falling by the pressure of the wedges on each side of it, acting in the direction of the lines P Q, K I, perpendicular to the surfaces D B, G A respectively.

By the principles of statics, it is known, that if the force P Q, or its equal K I, should be to half the weight of the wedge, in the same proportion which the line O D bears to V D, that is, in the proportion of radius to the sine of half the angle of the wedge V O D, the weight of the wedge will be exactly counterpoised by these forces; and conversely, if any wedge is sustained in equilibrio by forces applied perpendicularly to the sides, these forces must be to the weight of the wedge in the proportion which has been stated.

It is to be observed, that all pressures are estimated in a direction perpendicular to the surfaces impressed; for if the direction of the pressure should be oblique, it may be resolved into a force perpendicular to the surface, and some other force, which neither increases nor diminishes the pressure.

Fig. 2. If the wedge A when unsupported, should not be at liberty to descend freely in the direction of the vertical line V O, but should be moveable only along the line G A, considered as a fixed abutment,* the force P Q singly applied will sustain it in equilibrio, the reaction of the abutment supplying the necessary counterpoise. For produce P Q (Fig. 2.) till it intersects the line G A in the point X, and in line X P, take M X equal to P Q; the force P Q, considered as applied perpendicular to the surface D B, will have no effect in impelling the wedge toward the point O in the direction D B, or in the opposite direction B D, but the same force M X acting in an oblique direction on the line GA, may be resolved into two forces, M R perpendicular to G A, acting as pressure on it, and the force R X which impells the wedge directly from the point O in the direction of

* To prevent repetitions and unnecessary references, it is to be observed in the following pages, that the lower surface of each section is considered as a fixed abutment, on which the weight of the section, and of all the sections above it, are supported. For this reason, the angle between the lower surface of any section and the vertical line, is termed, for brevity, the angle of the abutment of that section.

the line A G. Through any point A, in the line A G, draw A *a* parallel to the line V O representing in quantity and direction the weight of the wedge A; through the point *a* draw *a* H perpendicular to A G; then will H A represent the force by which the wedge endeavours to descend in the direction of the line G A, considered as a fixed abutment. If then the line H A should be proved equal to the line R X, the contrary directions of these equal forces will balance each other, and the wedge so impelled will remain at rest in equilibrio. The proof that the lines H A and X R are equal is as follows.

By the construction, the line A *a* represents the weight of the wedge A, and the angle H A *a* is equal to the angle V O G, or half the angle of the wedge. And because the line M X is perpendicular to B D, and M R perpendicular to G A, it follows that the inclination of the lines G A, D B is equal to the inclination of the lines M X and M R, or the angle X M R is equal to the angle D O G. By the construction, and the properties of the wedge

$$MX : \tfrac{1}{2} Aa :: \text{radius} : \text{sine of } VOG$$

and

$$RX : MX :: \text{sine } XMR : \text{radius}$$

Joining these ratios

$$RX : \tfrac{1}{2} Aa :: \text{sin. of } XMR : \text{sin. } VOG$$

or because X M R is equal to D O G

$$RX : Aa :: \text{sin. } DOG : 2 \text{ sin. } VOG$$

also by construction $\Big\}$ $Aa : HA :: \text{radius} : \text{cos. } HAa \text{ or } VOG$

Joining these ratios

$$RX : HA : \text{radius} \times \text{sin. } DOG :: 2 \times \text{sin. } VOG \times \text{cos. } VOG.$$

But because the angle D O G is double to the angle V O G, from the principles of trigonometry it follows, that sin. D O G

× radius is equal to 2 sin. V O G × cos. V O G: therefore since the line R X is to the line A H, as sin. D O G × radius, to 2 × sin. G O V × cos. G O V, it follows that the line R X is equal to the line A H.

All the successive sections or wedges which form the arch being by the supposition balanced and sustained by their gravity and mutual pressure, independent of any other force, if the whole of the arch is considered as completed, whatever force P Q (Fig. 1 and 2.), is necessary for sustaining the wedge A G D B in equilibrio will be supplied by the reaction of the wedge adjacent to the surface D B. And in every part of the arch, when perfectly balanced, whatever force of pressure is communicated to any section from that which is contiguous to it, the force of reaction will be precisely equal between the two sections. It appears, therefore, that the equilibrium of the wedges will depend on the due adjustment of their successive weights to the pressures sustained by the sides of the sections. To effect this, the several sections are to be successively balanced; first, the wedge A alone; considering it as moveable along the line G A, as a fixed abutment.

It has been shewn, that if the force (Fig. 1.) P Q is to half the weight of the wedge A, as the line D O is to the line V D, this force P Q acting perpendicularly against the surface D B, and communicating an equal pressure M X obliquely on the line G A will sustain the wedge A from descending along the line G A. In the next place, let the wedge B (Fig. 2.) be adjusted to equipoise conjointly with the wedge A; and let it be required to ascertain the weight of B, in proportion to the weight of A, so that they may continue in equilibrio, when moveable along the fixed abutment K B. (Fig. 2 and Fig. 3.) To effect this, produce M R till it intersects the line K B in the point V, and in the line R M produced, take M N equal to the line H *a*. In V N take V Q equal to R N; and from the point Q draw Q W perpendicular to the line K B produced if necessary, intersecting it in the point W: from any point B in the line K W, take B H equal to W V, and through the point H draw H *z* (indefinite) perpendicular to the line K B. Through B draw B *x* (indefinite) parallel to the line V L O, intersecting the line H *z* in the point *b*; then, the line B *b* will represent by construction the weight of the section B, when the line A *a* denotes the weight of the section A, and the wedges are balanced in equilibrio, although freely moveable in the directions of the lines G A, K B.

For the pressure P Q or M X, which impels the wedge A upward along the line A G with the force R X, is perfectly counterpoised by the force of gravity A H referred to that direction, because it has been proved, that the line R X is equal to A H. If the pressure H *a* or M N* on the line G A, arising from the weight of the section A, be added to the pressure M R, the sum or R N, will be the entire pressure on the surface A G, equal to V Q by construction, or the oblique pressure on the line B K; that is R M + H *a* = R N = Q V; Q V is resolved into two forces, Q W, perpendicular to K B produced, and W V in the direction of that line. The force Q W, acts as pressure on the line B K, and the force W V impels the wedge in a direction contrary to gravity along the line B K. The weight of the section B, is by the construction denoted by the line B *b*, and being resolved into two forces, H B acting in the direction of that line, and H *b* perpendicular to it; the force H *b* acts as pressure, and the force H B is that part of the weight which impels the wedge B to descend in the direction of the line K B. But, by the construction, the line H B, is equal to the line W V,

* The lines H *a* M N, represent the quantity and direction of these pressures, but are not to be understood as determining the point or place where the pressures are applied.

these equal and contrary forces will therefore balance each other: and the wedge so impelled, will remain at rest, so far as regards the direction of the line B K. In respect to the forces Q W, H b, which act in a direction perpendicular to the surface K B, they are perfectly balanced by the reaction of the abutment B K, or the reaction of the wedge C, when the forces in the direction of the line F C have been adjusted to equilibrium.

The result is, that when the weights of the sections A and B, have been adjusted according to the preceding construction, each of the forces both of pressure and gravity is exactly counteracted by an opposite force which is equal to it. (Fig. 3.) The weights of the wedges C and D are adjusted to equilibrium by a similar construction. Produce Q W till it intersects F Z in the point X. In W Q produced, set off Q b equal to H b, and in the line X b take X Y equal to W b; through the point Y draw Y Z perpendicular to F C produced, and from any point C in the line C F, take C H equal to Z X; through H draw the indefinite line H z perpendicular to C F, and through the point C draw the indefinite line C x parallel to V L O; the intercepted line C c will represent the weight of the section C. The weight of the section D is constructed on the same principle, by making the line D H equal to the line F B, and drawing D x parallel to V O, and H z perpendicular to I D, cutting off the line D d, which is the weight of the section D. If the sections D, C, B, A, then adjusted, are placed contiguous, and the opposite semiarch is completed, when the extreme sections D, D, are supported on the two abutments, the whole will remain in equilibrio, although freely moveable in the direction of the lines I D, F C, K B, G A, D C, &c.

These and the remaining weights having been thus adjusted, so as to form an equilibrium, the lines A a, B b, C c, D d, to which they are proportional, might be determined by lineal construction, according to the rules which have been given; but as the correctness of such graphical delineations depends both on the excellence of the instruments employed, and on the skill of the person who uses them, to supply the want of these advantages in any case that may occur, as well as to view the subject under a different form, it may be expedient to express the several weights and pressures which have been hitherto represented geometrically, by analytical and numerical values. From the preceding observations, it has appeared, that the weights and pressures depend in a material degree, on the weight of the highest or middle wedge A, which is bissected by the vertical line V O. (Fig. 1, 2, and 3.) The weight of this section has been denoted by the line A *a* in the construction, and is represented in the analytical values, by the letter w; all other weights being in proportion to it. The initial pressure acting obliquely against the side of the wedge A G, represented by the line P Q = M X, has been found $= \frac{w}{2 \text{ sin. } VOD} = p$; and because the line M X is perpendicular to D C, and M R is perpendicular to G A, it follows that the inclination of the lines D C, G A, is equal to the angle X M R; or if A° is put to represent the angle contained between the sides of the wedge A, it will follow that A° = X M R = A O B.

Since therefore $p = \frac{w}{2 \times \text{sin. } \frac{1}{2} A^\circ} = MX = PQ$, the direct pressure against the surface G A, that is, M R is = M X × cos. A° = $p \times \text{cos. } A^\circ$. And as the additional pressure arising from the weight of the wedge A is = H *a* = A *a* × sin. $\frac{1}{2}$ A° = $w \times \text{sin. } \frac{1}{2} A^\circ$, the entire pressure on the surface G A = $p \times \text{cos. } A^\circ + w \times \text{sin. } \frac{1}{2} A^\circ$; or since $p = \frac{w}{2 \times \text{sin. } \frac{1}{2} A^\circ}$, the entire pressure on G A = M R + H *a* $= \frac{w \times \text{cos. } A^\circ}{2 \times \text{sin. } \frac{1}{2} A^\circ} + w \times \text{sin. } \frac{1}{2} A^\circ = \frac{\text{cos. } A^\circ + 2 \text{ sin.}^2 \frac{1}{2} A^\circ}{2 \text{ sin. } \frac{1}{2} A^\circ} \times w$; or because $2 \text{ sin.}^2 \frac{1}{2} A^\circ$ = the versed sine of the angle A°, it follows that

$M R + H a = V Q = \frac{w}{2 \times \sin. \frac{1}{2} A^\circ} = p$. But, because the line Q V is perpendicular to G A, and Q W is perpendicular to K B, the inclination of the sides K B, G A of the wedge B is equal to the angle V Q W, which may be denoted by B°; and because $Q V = p$, it follows that $Q W = p \times \cos. B^\circ$, and $V W = p \times \sin. B^\circ$; which is equal to the line H B, by the construction. If, therefore, the angle H B *b*, or the angle at which the abutment K B is inclined to the vertical line V O, or B *b* should be represented by V^b, since V W or $B H = p \times \sin. B^\circ$, H *b* will be $= p \times \sin. B^\circ \times \text{tang.} V^b$, and the line B *b* will be $p \times \sin. B^\circ \times \text{secant } V^b \times$ which is the weight of the section B; the pressure on the next section, or C, is Q W + H *b*, which is $= p \times \cos. B^\circ + p \times \sin. B^\circ \times \text{tang.} V^b$: let this be made $= q$; then the weight C *c* of the section C will be found in like manner to be $= q \times \sin. C^\circ \times \sec. V^c$, and the pressure on the next section $D = q \times \cos. C^\circ + q \times \sin. C^\circ \times \text{tang.} V^c$, and so on, according to the order of weights and pressures which are here subjoined.

It is to be observed, that A°, B°, C°, D°, &c. denote the angles of the sections A, B, C, &c. V^a signifies the angle of inclination, to the vertical, of the line G A, on which the section A rests, = to the angle G O V or H A *a*. In like manner V^b is the inclination to the vertical of the line K B, on which the section B rests = to the angle H B *b*: V^c is the inclination to the vertical of the line F C, on which the section C rests, = to the angle H C *c*, and so on. The initial pressure $p = \frac{w}{2 \times \sin. \frac{1}{2} A^\circ}$.

Sections.	Weights of the Sections.	Pressures on the Sections next following.
A	w	$p \times \cos. A^\circ + p \times \sin. A^\circ \times \text{tang.} V^a = p$
B	$p \times \sin. B^\circ \times \sec. V^b$	$p \times \cos. B^\circ + p \times \sin. B^\circ \times \text{tang.} V^b = q$
C	$q \times \sin. C^\circ \times \sec. V^c$	$q \times \cos. C^\circ + q \times \sin. C^\circ \times \text{tang.} V^c = r$
D	$r \times \sin. D^\circ \times \sec. V^d$	$r \times \cos. D^\circ + r \times \sin. D^\circ \times \text{tang.} V^d = s$
E	$s \times \sin. E^\circ \times \sec. V^e$	$s \times \cos. E^\circ + s \times \sin. E^\circ \times \text{tang.} V^e = t$

Or the weights of the sections and pressures on them may be expressed somewhat differently thus: the weights of the successive sections being denoted by the letters *a, b, c, d,* respectively.

Sections.	Weight of the Sections.	Pressures on the Section next following.
A	$a = w$	$p \times \cos. A^\circ + a \times \sin. V^a = p$
B	$b = p \times \sin. B^\circ \times \sec. V^b$	$p \times \cos. B^\circ + b \times \sin. V^b = q$
C	$c = q \times \sin. C^\circ \times \sec. V^c$	$q \times \cos. C^\circ + c \times \sin. V^c = r$
D	$d = r \times \sin. D^\circ \times \sec. V^d$	$r \times \cos. D^\circ + d \times \sin. V^d = s$
E	$e = s \times \sin E^\circ \times \sec. V^e$	$s \times \cos. E^\circ + e \times \sin. V^e = t$

In the following illustration of these analytical values, the angles of the sections are assumed equal to 5° each, and the weight of the first section is put = 1: consequently, the initial pressure or $p = \frac{1}{2 \times \sin. 2^\circ 30'} = 11.46279$ = the pressure on the second section or B: for inferring the weight of the second section, we have $p = 11.46279$, sin. B° = .087156, $V^b = 7^\circ 30'$, and sec. $V^b = 1.008629$; wherefore the weight of B $= p \times \sin. B^\circ \times \sec. V^b = 1.00767$. The pressure on the section next following, or C, $= p \times \cos. B^\circ + p \times \sin. B^\circ \times \text{tang.}\ V^b = 11.550708 = q$, and therefore the weight of C $= q \times \sin. C^\circ \times \sec. V^c = 1.03115$, and the pressure on the next section D $= q \times \cos. C^\circ + q \times \sin. C^\circ \times \text{tang.}\ V^c = 11.72992$; and thenceforward, according to the values entered in the table No. 1.

When any number of sections have been adjusted to their proper weights on each side of the vertical line V O, the whole being supported on the abutments, on the opposite sides, will remain in equilibrio, balanced by the mutual pressure and gravity of the sections only; so that if the contiguous surfaces were made smooth, and oil should be interposed between them, none of the sections would be moved from their respective places.

But if the wedges should be put together without adjustment, the weight of the sections near the abutments, if too great, would raise those which are nearer the vertex, and would themselves descend from their places, in consequence of their overbalance of weight; contrary effects would follow, from giving too small a weight to the lower sections. In either case, they would not retain their places in the arch, unless the fastenings applied in order to prevent them from separating, should be stronger than the force created by the imperfect equilibrium, impelling the sections toward a position different from that which they ought to occupy in the arch.

But a distinction is to be made between the deficiency of equilibrium which is inherent in the original construction, and that which is caused by an excess of weight, which may occasionally be brought to press on an arch.

In the case of occasional weight, such as loads of heavy materials which pass over the arches of a bridge, the stress on the joinings is temporary only; whereas the stress which arises from a want of equilibrium in the construction, acts without intermission, and in a course of time, may produce disturbance in the fastenings, and in the form of the arch itself, which might resist, without injury, a much greater force that acts on the several parts of it during a small interval of time.

When the wedges which form an arch have been adjusted to equilibrium, the whole will be terminated at the extremities by two planes coinciding with the abutments, and the entire arch will in this respect, be similar in form to a single wedge, the sides of which are inclined to each other, at an angle equal to the angle at which the planes of the abutments are inclined. (Fig. 4.) I V C, represents an arch adjusted to equilibrium, and terminated by the curve lines I V C, F B D.

The extremities of the arch are placed on the abutments I F,

C D, which lines when produced, meet in a point O. If the arch be bisected in V, a line joining the points V and O will be perpendicular to the horizon. Let the line K L be drawn perpendicular to the surface I F and M N W perpendicular to C D. The arch acts by its pressure in a direction perpendicular to the abutments, the reaction of which is equal and contrary to the pressure, and in the direction of the lines K L, M N.

From the principles of statics before referred to, it appears, that if forces are applied in the directions K L, M N, perpendicular to the surfaces I F, C D, considered as the sides of a wedge, those forces K L, M N, will sustain the wedge, provided each of them should be to the weight of the semiarch, as radius is to the sine of the semiangle of the wedge, that is as radius to the sine of V O C. If therefore, the abutment should be considered as removed, and two forces or pressures equal to the forces K L, M N, should be substituted instead of them, each being in the proportion that has been stated, the wedge or arch will be sustained in the same manner as it was by the abutments.

The force that sustains the arch or wedge, is the reaction of the abutments, which is exactly equal and contrary to the force of pressure upon either of them, and has been ascertained in the preceding pages, when an arch consisting of any number of sections is adjusted to equilibrium as in the table, No. 1. If, therefore, the forces K L, or M N, be made equal to the pressure on the abutment, determined as above, the following proportion will result:

As the force of pressure on the abutment is to half the weight of the wedge or arch V B C D, so is radius to the sine of the inclination of the abutment to the vertical line, or is as radius to the sine of the angle V O C.

Thus, referring to the order of weights and pressures, stated in page 13, let the semi-arch consist of any number, suppose five sections, including half the first section, or $\frac{1}{2}$ A: then the weight of the semi-arch will be $\frac{1}{2}$ A + B + C + D + E.

The pressure on the abutment which sustains the section E is $= s \times \cos. E^{\circ} + s \times \sin E^{\circ} \times \text{tang}. V^{e} = t$. E° is the angle of E, the fifth wedge $= 5^{\circ}$, and V^{e} is the angle of inclination to the vertical of the abutment on which the section E rests: or $V^{e} = 22^{\circ}. 40'$; then according to the proportion which has been stated, as the sum $\frac{1}{2}$ A + B + C + D + E is to the pressure t, so is the sine of the angle V^{e} to 1, which may be verified by referring to the numerical Table I. according to which, $\frac{1}{2}$ A + B + C + D + E = 4.7436; V^{e} = V O N = 22° 30′; and the pressure on this abutment appears, by the same table, to be = 12.3954: the sine of 22° 30′ = .38268, which being multiplied by the pressure 12.3954, the product is 4.7434, scarcely differing from 4.7436, as entered in the table. In general, let the letter S denote half the weight of an arch, when adjusted to equilibrium: and let Z represent the pressure on the abutment, the inclination of which to the vertical is V^{z}; then $S = Z \times \sin. V^{z}$.

Fig. 4. I F B D C represents an arch of equilibration, which is bisected by the vertical line V O; C D is one of the abutments inclined to the vertical line in the angle V O C: through any point N of the abutment draw the line M W perpendicular to C D, and through N draw the line T Q perpendicular to the horizon. In the line N W set off N E representing the pressure on the abutment C D, and resolve N E into two forces, E A, in the direction parallel to the horizon, and A N perpendicular to it. Then, because the angle A N F is equal to the angle N O V, or the inclination of the abutment to the vertical, denoted by the angle V^{z}, it follows, that the angle N E A is equal to the angle A N F or V O C = V^{z}, from whence the same proportion is derived, which has been otherwise demonstrated before, namely, as N E : N A :: 1 : sin. VOC; that is, the force of pressure on the abutment is to the weight of the semiarch, as radius is to the sine of V^z = N O V. It is observable that the additional weight of wedges, by which the weight of the semiarch is increased, reckoning from the vertex, or highest wedge, always acts in a direction perpendicular to the horizon; but neither increases nor diminishes the horizontal force, which must therefore remain invariably the same, and is represented by the line EA. But the initial force of pressure which has been denoted by the letter p, is not precisely horizontal, being in a direction perpendicular to the surface of the first wedge A, although it is very nearly parallel to the horizon, when the angle of the first section is small, and might be assumed for it as an approximate value: a force which is to the initial pressure, or $p = \frac{w}{2 \times \sin. \frac{1}{2} A^\circ}$, as the cosine* of $\frac{1}{2}$ A° (Fig. 5.) to radius, will approximate still more nearly to the constant force, the direction of which is parallel to the horizon, and is therefore $= \frac{w \times \cos. \frac{1}{2} A^\circ}{2 \times \sin. \frac{1}{2} A^\circ} = \frac{w}{2 \times \text{tang.} \frac{1}{2} A^\circ}$. For the sake of distinction, let this force be represented by $p' = \frac{w}{2 \times \text{tang.} \frac{1}{2} A^\circ}$, to be assumed as an approximate value, which will differ very little from the truth when the angles of the sections are small, and in any case will be sufficiently exact for practical purposes. Then, because E A is denoted by p', N E = Z (Fig. 4.) represents the pressure on the abutment, and N E is the secant of the angle N E A, or V O C, to radius E A, it appears that $Z = p' \times$ secant V^z: by the same construction, A N is the tangent of the angle N E A to radius E A; also A N is the sine of the angle N E A, or V O C, to the radius N E.

* Note in the Appendix.

The following general rules are derived from the proportions, which have been inferred in the preceeding pages:

RULE I. The initial pressure is to the weight of the first section, including the weight superincumbent on it, as radius is to twice the sine of the semiangle of the middle, or highest wedge, or $p = \frac{w}{2 \times \sin. \frac{1}{2} A^{o}}$.

RULE II. The horizontal force, which is nearly the same in every part of the arch, is to the weight of the first section, as radius is to twice the tangent of the semiangle of the first section, or $p' = \frac{w}{2 \times \text{tang.} \frac{1}{2} A^{o}}$.

RULE III. The horizontal or lateral force is to the pressure on the abutment, as radius is to the secant of the inclination of the abutment to the vertical, or $Z = p' \times \sec. V^{x}$.

RULE IV. The horizontal force is to the weight of half the arch as radius is to the tangent of the inclination of the abutment to the vertical, or $S = p' \times \text{tang.}\ V^{x}$.

RULE V. The weight of the semiarch is to the pressure on the abutment, as the sine of the said inclination of the abutment is to radius, or $S = Z \times \sin.\ V^{x}$.

RULE VI. The horizontal force is to the pressure on the abutment as the cosine of the inclination of the abutment is to radius, or $p' = Z \times \cos.\ V^{x}$.

By these rules, the principal properties of the arch of equilibration are expressed in simple terms, and are easily applicable to practical cases.

Rule 3d. The horizontal force, or p', being the weight divided by twice the tangent of the semiangle of the first section, determines the pressure on any abutment of which the inclination to the vertical line is V^{x}; the pressure being $= p' \times$ secant V^{x}.

Rule 4th. The weight of the semiarch, when adjusted to equilibrium, is found by the fourth rule to be $\doteq p' \times$ tang. V^z; or the horizontal pressure increased, or diminished, in the proportion of the tangent of the vertical distance of the abutment to radius. From this property, the reason is evident, which causes so great an augmentation in the weights of the sections, when the semiarch, adjusted to equilibrium, approaches nearly to a quadrant, and which prevents the possibility of effecting this adjustment by direct weight, when the entire arch is a semicircle.

Rule 5th. The fifth rule exemplifies the analogy between the entire arch when adjusted to equilibrium, and the wedge. For let the angle between the abutments be made equal to the angle of the wedge, the weight of which is equal to the weight of the arch; and let Z be either of the equal forces, which being applied perpendicular to the sides of the wedge, sustain it in equilibrio: then by the properties of the wedge, the force Z is to half the weight of the wedge as radius is to the sine of the semiangle of the wedge, which is precisely the property of the arch; substituting the angle between the abutments instead of the angle of the wedge, and the pressure on either abutment instead of the force Z.

Rule 6th. The lateral pressure, or the pressure on the abutment, reduced to an horizontal direction, is nearly the same in all parts of the arc; being to the weight of the first section, as radius is to twice the tangent of the semiangle of the wedge.

The force of pressure on the abutment is therefore at every point resolvable into two forces; one of which is perpendicular to the horizon, and is equal to the weight of the semiarch; and the other is a horizontal or lateral force, which is to the weight of the first section, as radius is to twice the tangent of the semiangle of that section.

These conclusions are the more remarkable from the analogy they bear to the properties of the catenary curve, although they have been deduced from the nature of the wedge, and the principles, of statics only, and without reference to the catenary or other curve, and will be equally true, when applied to the sections of an arch, which are disposed in the form of any curve whatever.

Many cases occur, in the practice of architecture, in which it must be highly useful to form an exact estimate of the magnitude, and direction of pressure, from superincumbent weight, both on account of the danger to be apprehended if such pressure is suffered to act against the parts of an edifice without a suitable counterpoise; and from the consideration, that when the extent of the evil to be provided against is not certainly known, it is probable, that more labour and expense will be employed in making every thing secure, than would have appeared necessary if the pressure to be opposed had been exactly estimated.

The Gothic cathedrals, and other edifices built in a similar style of architecture, which very generally prevailed in this and other countries of Europe, during several centuries, have been constructed on principles to which the preceding observations are not intirely inapplicable.

The striking effects for which these structures are remarkable, seem principally to be derived from the loftiness of the pillars, and arches springing from considerable heights, which could not be securely counterpoised without making great sacrifices of external appearance, and bestowing much labour and expense in imparting sufficient stability to the whole fabric: while, therefore, the eye is gratified by the just proportions and symmetry of design, displayed by the interior of these edifices, with an apparent lightness of structure, scarcely to be thought compatable with the use of such materials, the external building presents the unpleasing contrast of angular buttresses, with their massive weights, which are indispensably necessary for the preservation of the walls, as a counterpoise to the lateral pressure from the ponderous arched roofs.

That the security provided has been perfectly effectual, is evident from the solidity and duration of these buildings; but whether any part of their heavy supports might have been spared, or whether the form of applying them might not have been changed, without diminishing the security of the walls, is a question which would require much practical experience and information to decide. An estimate of the lateral force from arches of this description, may be readily obtained by referring to the rules given in the preceding pages; from which it appears, that the lateral or horizontal force arising from the pressure of any arch is always to the weight of the highest or middle wedge, as radius is to 2 × tangent of the semiangle of the wedge. Some of the highest wedges, in roofs of this description, are said to weigh two ton; the angle of the wedge may be taken (merely to establish a case for illustrating the subject) equal to 3°: the tangent of half this angle, or 1° 30′, is .02618, and the lateral force, or pressure from any part of the arch, will be $\frac{2}{2 \times .02618} = 38.2$ ton, which weight of pressure, acting on walls of great height, must certainly require a very substantial counterpoise for their support; and it is for this purpose, that a buttress is erected against the external walls corresponding to the key-stone of each arch. In this estimate, the arch is supposed to have reference to one plane only; which passes through both the buttresses and the key-stone: but in the case of groined arches, or such as are traversed by other arches crossing them diagonally, on which the same key-stone acts, the lateral pressure in any one plane will be less than has been found according to the preceding estimate.

In the preceding geometrical constructions, the angles of the several sections have been assumed equal to each other, or as given, although of different magnitudes, from which data the weights of the sections have been inferred when they form an arch of equilibration.

Let D C V D, &c. (Fig. 6.) be the curve-line passing through the bases of the sections which form an arch: because the wedges increase as they approach the abutment; the exterior line *a b c d*, &c. will take a form not very dissimilar to that which is represented in the figure, (Fig. 6.): the arch being here adjusted to equilibrium in itself without reference to any extraneous weight or pressure. Although in many cases, it is immaterial what may be the form of the line *a b c*, &c. yet it often happens, that the termination of the sections, or exterior boundary, must of necessity deviate greatly from that which is represented in the figure; particularly in the case of bridges, over which a passage or road-way is required to be made, which is either horizontal, or nearly so. Let E D L D E (Fig. 7.) represent an arch by which an horizontal road, P *a* Q, is supported. For this purpose a wall of masonry is usually erected over the arches; the weight of which must press unequally on the several sections, according to the horizontal breadth and height of the columns, which are super-incumbent on them: through the terminations of the wedges A, B, C, D, &c. (Fig. 7.) draw the lines A *a*, B *b*, C *c*, &c. perpendicular to the horizontal line P Q, and in the lines *a* A, *b* B, *c* C, *d* D, &c. produced, if necessary, take the line *b* B of such a magnitude, that it shall be to the line *a* A in the same proportion, which the weight of the wedge B, with the weight above it, bears to the weight of the wedge A, with the weight above it, and so on; each line *c* C, *d* D, &c. being taken proportional to the weight of the respective wedges, including the weights superincumbent on them. In the next place we are to ascertain from these conditions, together with the angle of the first section or A°, the other angles B°, C°, D°, &c. so that the entire are, when loaded with the weights, denoted by the lines A *a*, B *b*, C *c*, &c. may be equally balanced in all its parts. Admitting that the angle of any section D°, can be ascertained from having given the weight of the section D, and the pressure on it, together with the inclination of the abutment of the preceding section, or the angle of the abutment C to the vertical, it follows as a consequence, that, by the same method of inference, the angles of all the sections will be successively obtained from the angle of the first section, and the initial pressure, which are given quantities in the construction of every arch.

Suppose, therefore, any number of the sections A, B, C, to have been balanced by the requisite adjustments. It is required to determine the angle of the next section or D°, on the following conditions.

1st. That the direct pressure on the abutment F C of the section D, from the preceding sections shall be given, equal to the oblique pressure on the line I F, denoted by the line S B, which is drawn perpendicular to the line F C produced. (Fig. 8.)

2d. That the weight of the section D, including the weight superincumbent on it, shall also be given: let this weight be represented by the line D *d*.

3d. The angle *c* C H being the inclination of the line F C, or the abutment of the preceding section C to the vertical, is also a given quantity.

Referring to figure 3, we observe, that the adjustment of the angle D° depends on the equality of the line H D representing the force arising from gravity, and urging the section to descend along the line I D, and the force B F, which impels it in the opposite direction D I (Fig. 3.) In this case, F B is the sine of the angle * B S F = D° to a radius = B S, and H D is the cosine of the angle H D *d* to a radius = D *d*. Through the point D draw D A parallel to C F; so shall the angle A D *d* be equal to the angle H C *c*, which is given by the conditions: moreover, the angle I D A is the unknown angle of the section D°, which is required to be determined, and the inclination of the line I D to the vertical line D *d*, when constructed, will be equal to the sum of the angles A D *d* + I D A = I D *d*.

B S represents the pressure on the section D (Fig. 8.) From these conditions the angle required D° or I D A, and the inclination of the abutment I D *d* are determined by the following construction: through the point D, which terminates the base of the section D, draw the line D *d* perpendicular to the horizon and equal to the given line which represents the weight of the section D: with the centre D and distance D *d* describe a circle: through the point D draw the line D A parallel to C F, cutting off an arc A *d*, which measures the angle A D *d* equal to the given angle *c* C H. Through the points D and *d*, draw the indefinite lines D Z *d* Y perpendicular to the radius D *d*, and through the point A draw the indefinite line A W parallel to *d* Y. In the line A W set off A N equal to the given line B S, and through the points N and D draw the line D N, intersecting the circle in the point H:

* Because S B, S F are by construction perpendicular to the lines F Z, I F respectively; consequently the inclination of the lines F Z, I F, that is, the angle of the section D°, will be equal to the inclination of the lines S B, S F, or the angle B S F.

from the point A set off an arc AI, equal to the arc GH, and through the points I and D draw the line IDQ. The angle IQF or IDA will be the angle of the section D, which was required to be determined by the construction, and I D d will be the inclination of the abutment D I of the section D to the vertical line D d. The demonstration is as follows: through the point S draw S F perpendicular to I Q, and S B equal to the line denoting the given pressure on the line F I, and perpendicular to F Q; also through G draw GO perpendicular to DG, and through H draw HP perpendicular to DG; also produce DN till it intersects dY in L: produce N A till it intersects Dd in the point F, and through d draw dH perpendicular to DI. It is to be proved that the cosine of the angle I Dd to the radius Dd, is equal to the sine of the angle I D A or G D O to the radius B S, or that the line D H or D K is equal to the line B F.

By the similarity of the triangles P H D, N D F, as P H : D P :: D F : N F; but by the construction $NF = BS + AF$. Wherefore $PH : DP :: DF : BS + AF$, and $PH \times BS + PH \times AF = DF \times DP$, or $PH \times BS = DF \times DP - PH \times AF$: dividing both sides by the radius Dd, $\frac{PH \times BS}{Dd} = \frac{DF \times DP - PH \times AF}{Dd}$.

But because the angle I D A is equal to the angle G D O, $DF \times DP$ is the rectangle under the cosines of the angles ADd, IDA, and $PH \times AF$ is the rectangle under the sines of the said angles: wherefore, by the principles of trigonometry, the difference of those rectangles divided by the radius Dd, that is, $\frac{DF \times DP - PH \times AF}{Dd}$ will be the cosine of the sum of the angles $ADd + ADI$, or the cosine of $IDd = DH$ or DK. But it has been shewn that $\frac{PH \times BS}{Dd} = \frac{DF \times DP - PH \times AF}{Dd}$; therefore

$\frac{PH \times BS}{Dd} = DK$: and by the similar triangles PHD, BSF, as PH : DH or D*d* :: BF : BS; consequently, $BF = \frac{BS \times PH}{Dd}$. But $\frac{BS \times PH}{Dd} = DK$; therefore BF is equal to DK, which was to be proved.

The angle of the section D° will be readily computed from the value of the Fig. 8. tangent $GO = \frac{Dd \times DF}{NF} = \frac{Dd \times DF}{BS + AF} = \frac{DF}{BS + AF}$ to radius $= 1$; or if the given angle $HCc = ADd$ be represented by V^c, we shall have $DF = Dd \times \cos. V^c$, and $AF = Dd \times \sin. V^c$. Wherefore, putting $BS = r$, the tangent in the Tables of the angle $D^\circ = \frac{Dd \times \cos. V^c}{r + Dd \times \sin. V^c}$.

To express the solution of this case generally by analytical values, let the weight of the first section or A be denoted by the letter w; and let the angle of the first section $= A^\circ$. The initial pressure $= p = \frac{w}{2 \times \sin. \frac{1}{2} A^\circ}$, and let the given weights of the successive sections, (Fig. 7.) including the weights superincumbent, be denoted by the letters *a*, *b*, *c*, *d*, &c. respectively, which are represented in the figure by the lines A*a*, B*b*, C*c*, D*d*, &c. the angles of each section, and the pressures on the section next following are as they are stated underneath, for adjusting the arch to equilibration.

Sections.	Weights of the Sections.	Tangents of the Angles of the Sections.	Angular Distances of the Abutments from the vertical Line.	Entire Pressures on the Sections next following.
A	*a*	$\text{tang. } A^\circ = \text{tang. } A^\circ$	$V^a = V^a = \frac{1}{2}A^\circ$	$p \times \cos. A^\circ + a \times \sin. V^a = p$
B	*b*	$\text{tang. } B^\circ = \frac{b \times \cos. V^a}{p + b \times \sin. V^a}$	$V^b = V^a + B^\circ$	$p \times \cos. B^\circ + b \times \sin. V^b = q$
C	*c*	$\text{tang. } C^\circ = \frac{c \times \cos. V^b}{q + c \times \sin. V^b}$	$V^c = V^b + C^\circ$	$q \times \cos. C^\circ + c \times \sin. V^c = r$
D	*d*	$\text{tang. } D^\circ = \frac{d \times \cos. V^c}{r + d \times \sin. V^c}$	$V^d = V^c + D^\circ$	$r \times \cos. D^\circ + d \times \sin. V^d = s$
E	*e*	$\text{tang. } E^\circ = \frac{e \times \cos. V^d}{s + e \times \cos. V^d}$	$V^e = V^d + E^\circ$	$s \times \cos. E^\circ + e \times \sin. V^e = t$

The application of these analytical values will be exemplified by referring to the case of an arch formed by sections, which are disposed according to the figure of any curve, when the columns which are built on the arches, terminate in an horizontal line; the given weights of the sections A, B, C, &c. (including the weights of the columns built upon them), denoted by the lines A a, B b, C c, &c. being as follows.

A a = the weight of the first section, (Fig. 7.) is represented by the number 2; B b = 2.76106, C c = 5.03844, and so on. The weight of the first section, which is denoted by the number 2, may be taken to signify 2 hundred weight, 2 ton, &c. all other weights being in proportion to it; the angle of the first or highest section is 5° = A°, and $w = 2$. The initial pressure or $\frac{w}{2 \times \sin. 2° 30'} = 22.9225 = p$: making $b = 2.76106$, we obtain from the preceding theorem, the tangent of $B° = \frac{b \times \cos. V^a}{p + b \times \sin. V^a}$ = tang. 6° 49′ 31″, wherefore the angle of the section B or B° = 6° 49′ 31″; this added to 2° 30′ will give the inclination of the abutment of the section B to the vertical line = 9° 19′ 31″ = V^b; also since $p = 22.9255$, the pressure on the section $C° = p \times \cos. B° + b \times \sin. V^b = 23.21305 = q$, and thenceforward, according to the successive angles and the pressures on the sections next following, as they are entered in the Table No. II. entitled, A Table shewing the Angles of the Sections, &c. calculated from the given Weights, &c.

The lines a A, b B, c C, representing the given weights of the sections and the weights superincumbent on them, (if the line L a = 2 be subtracted from each) are nearly proportional to the versed sines of the arcs of a circle, increasing by a common difference of 5°; the curve of the arch will therefore be scarcely different from the arch of a circle. The third column of the second Table shews the several angles of the sections, which will create a sufficient force of counterpoise to the weight of the sections, together with the weights of the columns built upon them. It appears by inspecting this Table, that the angles of the sections first increase, reckoning from the highest or middle wedge, till the semiarc is augmented to about 55°; and afterwards decrease; plainly indicating that part of the arch which requires the greatest aid from the increased angles of the sections, as a counterpoise to the weight above them. If therefore the angles of the sections were constructed equal, as they usually are, the form of the arch being circular, and if a wall of solid masonry should be built upon it, terminating in an horizontal line or plane, it is clearly pointed out, what part of the arch would be the most likely to fail, for want of the requisite counterpoise of equilibrium; and although the fastenings should be sufficient to prevent the form of the arch from being immediately altered, the continuance of its constructed figure would depend on the resistance opposed by the fastenings to the stress arising from a defect of equilibrium, which acts incessantly to disunite the sections; a preponderance of this force, to a certain degree, would probably break the arch somewhere between 50° or 60° from the highest or middle section.

In adjusting the equilibrium of an arch, it is observable that the lengths of the bases which form the interior curve, usually termed the curve of the arch, are not among the conditions given, from which the weights or angles of the sections are inferred. A circumstance which renders the solution here given of the problem for adjusting equilibration, very general.

Whatever, therefore, be the figure of the interior curve, the bases of the sections which are disposed in this form, may be of any lengths, provided the weights and angles of the sections are in the proportions which the construction demands: observing only, that if the lengths of the bases should be greatly increased in respect to the depths, although in geometrical strictness, the properties of the wedge would equally subsist, yet when applied to wedges formed of material substance, they would lose the powers and properties of that figure: this shews the necessity of preserving some proportion between the lengths of the bases and depths of the wedges, to be determined by practical experience, rather than by geometrical deduction.

The following constructions and observations will further shew how little the equilibrium of an arch depends on the figure of the curve line by which it is terminated. All the properties of arches being (so far as the preceding constructions and demonstrations may be depended on) the consequences of the weights and pressure of the sections, acting without relation to the figure of any curve, so that arches may be constructed which terminate in a circular, elliptical, or any other curve, retaining the properties of equilibration indifferently in all these cases. To exemplify this principle by a simple case, let all the sections which form any arch be of equal weights, the angle of the first wedge, or A°, being $= 5°$; and let it be required to ascertain the angles of the other sections, so that the pressures may be a counterpoise to their weights in every part. Assuming, therefore, as conditions given, (Fig. 9.) the angle of the first or highest wedge $A° = 5°$, and the weights of the several sections $= 1 = Aa = Bb = Cc = Dd$, &c. we have for the construction of this case the initial pressure $= \frac{1}{2 \times \sin. 2° 30'} = p = MX$, the angle of the abutment A or V^a $= 2° 30'$. From these data the angles* of the sections will be

* If the weighes of the sections A, B, C, D, &c. which are denoted by the lines a, b, c, d, &c. were made equal to 1.0077, 1.0312, 1.0719, &c. as they are stated in the Table

constructed according to the solution in page 27, from which the following results are derived: $\frac{\cos. V^a}{p + \sin. V^a} = \text{tang. } B^\circ = 4^\circ\ 57'\ 40''$, therefore $B^\circ = 4^\circ\ 57'\ 40''$, which being added to $2^\circ\ 30'$, the sum will be equal to the angle H B $b = V^b\ 7^\circ\ 27'\ 40''$. C° is found by the same theorem to be $= 4^\circ\ 51'\ 10''$, and $V^c = 12^\circ\ 18'\ 50''$, and so on, according to the statements in the Table No. 3.

OIVIO (Fig. 10.) is the arc of a circle drawn from the centre O, and bisected by the vertical line V O. P W Q (Fig. 11.) is the arch of a circle drawn from a centre any where in the line V O, produced if necessary; T Y S (Fig. 12.) is the arch of an ellipse, the lesser axis of which coincides with the line V O. W X Z (Fig. 13.) is a catenarian or any other curve which is divided by the vertical line V O into two parts, similar and equal to each other. These three curves form the interior figures of the three arches, the exterior boundaries of which are of any figures which make the semiarches on each side of the vertical line V O similar and equal.

In the next place, the circular arc OIVIO is to be divided into arcs, by which the angles of the sections in the three interior arches are regulated. For this purpose, from the point V on either side thereof, set off an arc V G = $2^\circ\ 30'$; set off also from G the arc G K = $4^\circ\ 58'$, omitting the seconds, as an exactness not necessary: and the subsequent arcs K F, F I, &c. according to the dimensions in the schedule annexed, extracted from the 3d Table, to the nearest minute of a degree.

No. I. The points O, R, Q, P, would all coincide in the point O; if the weights of the sections should be assumed greater than they are stated in the Table No. I, the points R Q P would be situated between the points O and V.

Sections.	Arcs.	Angles. °	′
½ A	V G	2	30
B	G K	4	58
C	K F	4	51
D	F I	4	41
E	I M	4	21
F	M N	4	12
G	N O	3	55
H	O Q	3	39
I	Q R	3	22

The arcs (Fig. 10, et sequent.) V G, G K, K F, &c. having been thus set off, according to the angles of the sections A, B, C, &c. through the points G, K, F, I, in the circular line OIVIO, &c. draw the lines G O, K O, F O, I O, &c. dividing the three arches into sections or wedges A 1, B 1, C 1, &c. A 2, B 2, C 2, and A 3, B 3, C 3, &c. Which wedges, when formed of material substance, will become so many arches of equilibration, if the weights of each section be equal to the weight of the highest or middle wedge A. This construction is not intended to point out any practical mode by which the forms of wedges, that constitute arches of equilibration may be delineated, but merely to shew, by a very simple case, and at one view, how much the curves of arches may be varied, while the properties of equilibrium still remain the same, in a geometrical sense; although in the practical constructions of arches, the greater curvature of an arch allows greater latitude for the unavoidable errors in execution, and for those which are the consequences of the imperfect nature of the materials used in the construction. The figures in which the sections are here disposed have been adopted for the purpose of shewing in what manner the wedges in the several arches A 1, B 1, C 1, &c. A 2, B 2, C 2, &c. are adjusted to equilibrium by means of the division of the external arc, according to the angles inferred from the solution of this case, (page 30) in which the weights of the sections are all equal, producing the angles which are entered in the Table No. III. and in the Schedule, page 32.

Admitting, then, for the sake of establishing a case, that the specific gravity of the sections should be capable of adjustment, so that their weights may be equal, although their magnitudes be different; admitting also, that in increasing or diminishing the volumes of the sections, the angles are continued invariably the same; the lengths of the bases may be lessened or augmented in any proportion that is required, the equilibrium of the section remaining unaltered. Thus, if it should be proposed, that any number of the sections in the arch (Fig. 13.) A 3, B 3, C 3, shall occupy a length denoted by the curve (Fig. 14.) *i v i*, and that the joinings of the sections should intersect the curve in the points *i f k g g k f i*, as represented in the figure.

Through the point *g* draw the line *g* G parallel to G O, and through *k* draw *k* K (Fig. 14.) parallel to K O, and through *f* draw *f* F parallel to F O, and so on: the sections A, B, C, &c. in Fig. 14, admitting their weights to be equal, would form an arch of equilibration: the same consequences will follow if this construction is applied to the rectilinear or flat arch, (Fig. 15.) if it be allowed to use that term, meaning the figure terminated by two arched surfaces when their curvature is diminished to nothing, and coinciding with two plane surfaces parallel to the horizon; such is the rectilinear figure P Q, P Q, Fig. 15. Suppose this figure to be divided into wedges that have the properties of equilibration, by which the force of pressure impelling them upward is counterbalanced by their weight; and suppose the joinings of the wedges are required to pass through the points M, N, O, Q, &c. Through M draw T M parallel to G O, and through N* draw R N parallel to K O and through O draw W O parallel to F O′, &c. If wedges of these forms are disposed on each side of the vertical line V L, the extreme sections being supported by the abutments P Q, P Q; the whole will be sustained in equilibrio, on the condition that the weight of each section is equal to the weight of the section A.

But supposing the wedges to be formed, as is usually the case, of solid substances which are of the same uniform specific gravity, to make their weights equal, the areas of the figures must be adjusted to equality; which requires the solution of the following problem: Having given the angles of any of the wedges as above stated, and having given the area of the wedge $A = \frac{\overline{Tt + Mm} \times VL}{2}$, to ascertain the lengths of the upper surfaces R T, R W, P W, and of the bases M N, N O, O Q, of the wedges B, C, D, &c. So that the areas R N T M, W O R N, P Q W O, may be equal to the area T *t* M *m*, with the condition that the angles of each wedge shall remain unchanged; that is, the lines T M, R N, W O, &c. shall be parallel to the lines G O, K O, F O, I O, &c. respectively: to obtain the lengths of the lines R T, M N, which terminate the wedge B, according to these conditions, make the perpendicular distance $VL = r$, the area $TMtm = A$; cotang. M N R — cotang. L M T = D; then $RT = \frac{2A + r^2 \times D}{2r}$, and $MN = \frac{2A - r^2 \times D}{2r}$.

* Fig. 10.

As an illustration of this theorem, let the angle of the middle wedge A (Fig. 15.) be assumed = 30°: if the weights of all the other sections are equal to that of A, the successive angles as determined by a preceding construction, in page 24, &c. will be as follows, B° = 23° 47′ 38″: and in like manner, the angles C°, D°, and E° are found to be as they are stated in Table IV; the wedges being constructed according to these angles will give the following results: the angle L M T = 90° + V^a = 105°; M N R = 90° + 38° 48′ : = 128° 48′ = 90 + V^b; N O W = 90° + 53° 16′ = 143° 16′ = 90 + V^c, and so on. From hence we obtain the lengths of the lines T R, M N. When the area R N T M is equal to the area T *t* M *m* = A. Let the perpendicular distance V L = *r* = 2 feet; and suppose the radius = 5 feet, then the angle T O *t* being = 30°, T *t* = 2.679492, and M *m* = 1.607695, and the area of the section A = $\overline{2.679492 + 1.607695} \times \frac{2}{2}$ = 4.287187 = A. Cotang. 105° — cotang. 128° 48′ by the Tables = .5360714 = D; wherefore the line T R = $\frac{2A + r^2 D}{2r}$ = 2.679492, and M N = $\frac{2A - r^2 D}{2r}$ = 1.607522.

The dimensions of the sections C, D, &c. are determined from the same rule, and are as underneath.

Sections.	Lengths of the upper Surfaces.	Lengths of the Bases.	Oblique Lines, or Secants.
A	T *t* = 2.679492	M *m* = 1.607695	V L = 2.
B	T R = 2.679665	M N = 1.607522	T M = 2.0705524
C	R W = 2.679548	N O = 1.607639	R N = 2.5662808
D	W P = 2.679077	O P = 1.608110	W O = 3.3439700
E	P X = 2.680363	P Y = 1.606824	P Q = 4.2508096

According to the geometrical construction for adjusting the

equilibrium of an arch by the angles between the sides of the sections or wedges, the architect will be enabled to distribute the mass of materials, whether they consist of stone or iron, of which the arch is intended to consist, among the sections, in any proportion that may best contribute to strengthen and embellish the entire fabric, establishing the equilibrium of the arch at the same time. This principle of construction would be of use, more particularly where circumstances may require that the equilibrium should be adjusted with great exactness. Supposing that according to the plan of the structure, the angles of the sections are equal to each other; if the mass or weight which the adjustment of the equilibrium allots to the sections near the abutments, should be diffused over too great a base; or may be, for other reasons, independent of any consideration of equilibration, judged too weak to support the superincumbent weight with security, this inconvenience would be remedied by adding such a quantity of materials to the weaker sections, as may enable them to support the weights or loads they are required to bear, and afterwards adjusting the angles of these sections, so as to form an arch of equilibration, according to the rules which have been given, (page 27). Or perhaps it might be expedient to arrange, in the first instance, the quantity of materials which ought to be allotted to the several sections of the entire arch, and afterwards to adjust the angle of each section, so as to form the equilibrium: suppose, for instance, the form of the arch be such as is represented in the figure 16: V A B C D, &c. is a circular arc drawn from the centre O and with the radius O V. Let the bases of the sections be terminated by the arcs A B, B C, C D, each of which subtends, at the centre O, an angle of 1°. Through the points

A, B, C, D, &c. draw the indefinite lines A a, B b, C c, perpendicular to the horizon, and suppose the masses or weights allotted to the sections would give a sufficient degree of strength to the entire structure, when the weight of the section contiguous to the abutment is three times the weight of the first section, and the intermediate weights are increased by equal differences, from 1 to 3. If, therefore, the number of sections should be fixed at 49, so as to make the angle of the arch when viewed from the centre O = 49°, the weight of the highest or middle section being assumed equal to unity, the weight of the section B or B b = 1.083333, C c = 1.166666, &c.; and finally the weight of the section next the abutment, or Z = 3; as they are stated in the Table No. V. in the column entitled, Weights of the Sections. Since, therefore, the angle A° is by the supposition = 1°; the initial pressure, or $\frac{1}{2 \times \sin. \frac{1}{2} A^{\circ}} = 57.29649 = p$. And because $V^{a} = 30'$, and b is the line denoting the weight of the section B = 1.083333, according to the rule for determining the angles of the sections, so as to form an arch of equilibration, $\frac{b \times \cos. V^{a}}{p + b \times \sin. V^{a}}$ = the tangent of 1° 34′ 58″ = B°; which angle being added to 30′ or V^{a}, the sum will be = 1° 34′ 50″ = V^{b}, or the inclination of the abutment to the vertical, of the section B; from whence we obtain the entire pressure on the next section $= p \times \cos. B^{\circ} + b \times \sin. V^{b} = 57.31593 = q$, and $\frac{c \times \cos. V^{b}}{q + c \times \sin. V^{b}}$ = tang. 1° 9′ 54″; therefore the angle of the third section C° = 1° 9′ 54″, and so on. The angles of the sections D°, C°, and the corresponding angles of the abutments are entered in Table V. From the angles of the abutments determined by these calculations, the practical delineation of the sections will be extremely easy: having described the arc of a circle with any radius O V, and the several arcs A B, B C, C D, &c. being set off equal to 1°, the positions of the successive abutments which terminate the sections on each side will be found by taking the difference between the inclination of the abutment to the vertical, and the angle subtended by the semi-arc at the centre of the circle, if this difference be put = D, that is, to exemplify for the abutment F Y, if the difference of the angles V P F — V O F, or P F O be made = D; then the line $OP = \frac{\text{sin. } D \times DF}{\text{sin. } VPF}$: consequently the length of the line O P being ascertained, through P and F draw the line P F Y, which will be the position of the abutment on which the section F rests. And a similar construction will determine the positions of all the lines E X, D W, C Q, &c.; when the sections form an arch of equilibration according to the conditions given. By this rule the lines O T, O S, O R, &c. (Fig. 16.) are found, according to the following Table, O V = O F being put = radius = 1000.

Sections.	Distances from the Centre O.	Sections.	Distances from the Centre O.
A	OO = 0	O	= 338.00
B	OT = 52.651	P	= 351.10
C	OS = 90.009	Q	= 363.17
D	OR = 123.22	R	= 374.12
E	OQ = 153.38	S	= 383.21
F	OP = 181.90	T	= 393.25
G	= 207.48	U	= 401.33
H	= 230.95	V	= 408.62
I	= 252.44	W	= 415.13
K	= 273.36	X	= 420.78
L	= 290.93	Y	= 426.15
M	= 307.95	Z	= 429.96
N	= 323.53		

The Tables No. I. II. III. IV. V. subjoined to these pages, have been calculated rigidly from the rules in pages 14 and 27; a column containing the weights of the semiarcs, or the weights of $\frac{1}{2}$ A + B + C + D, &c. has been added to each of the Tables, for the purpose of comparing them with the general rules for approximating to the correct values inserted in page 19. The calculations in the Tables are expressed to five or six places of figures, and the results of the approximate rule 5, which is $S = Z \times \sin. V^2$, coincides with the correct values in the Tables to four or five places, including the integers; the calculations made from the other rules, which include the horizontal force, approximate to the true values the more nearly, as the angles of the sections are smaller; but in any, except very extreme cases, they are sufficiently correct for all practical purposes; which will make the use of these approximations preferable to the troublesome calculations which are required for inferring the correct values from the original rules.

That a judgment may be formed of the errors to which these approximate values are liable, the Table No. VI. is added, containing the comparative results therein stated.

The examples in the Table No. VI. have been taken from the Table No. II. in which the angles are calculated to the nearest second of a degree; and the numbers to be 6 or 7 places of figures: an exactness not necessary, except for the purpose of comparing the results arising from the different rules for computing.

Table No. I.

Shewing the weights of the several sections or wedges which form an arch of equilibration, when the angle of each section is $5°$; and the weight of the highest or middle wedge is assumed = 1. Also shewing the pressures on the lowest surface of each section, considered as an abutment.

The initial pressure $= \frac{w}{2 \times \sin. 2° 30'} = 11.4628 = p$

The lateral or horizontal pressure $= \frac{w}{2 \times \text{tang}. 2° 30'} = 11.4519 = p'$

Sections.	Angles of the Sections.	Angles of Inclination to the vertical Line of the Surface, on which each Section rests.		Weight of each Section.	Pressure on each successive Wedge considered as an Abutment.	Weights of the Semi-arcs, being the successive Sums of the Weights in the 4th Column, deducting from each Sum the Weight of ½ A = ·5.
	°	°	′			
A	5	2	30	1.	11.4628	·5
B	5	7	30	1.0077	11.5507	1.5077
C	5	12	30	1.0312	11.7300	2.5389
D	5	17	30	1.0719	12.0076	3.6108
E	5	22	30	1.1328	12.3954	4.7436
F	5	27	30	1.2180	12.9098	5.9616
G	5	32	30	1.3341	13.5775	7.2957
H	5	37	30	1.4916	14.4346	8.7873
I	5	42	30	1.7064	15.5325	10.4937
K	5	47	30	2.0038	16.9508	12.4975
L	5	52	30	2.4268	18.8116	14.9243
M	5	57	30	3.0515	21.3136	17.9758
N	5	62	30	4.0530	24.8284	22.0288
O	5	67	30	5.6547	29.9582	27.6835
P	5	72	30	8.6830	38.1254	36.3665
Q	5	77	30	15.3661	52.9822	51.7326
R	5	82	30	35.4777	87.9547	87.2103
S	5	87	30	175.7425	263.1952	262.9528

Table No. II.

Shewing the angles of the sections which form an arch of equilibration, calculated from the given weights of the sections, including the weights of the columns built upon them, terminating in a right line parallel to the horizon; the weight of the first section, or A = 2 = w.

The initial pressure $= p = \frac{w}{2 \times \text{sin.} \frac{1}{2} A^{\circ}} = 22.92558$

The horizontal force or pressure* $= p' = \frac{w}{2 \times \text{tang.} \frac{1}{2} A^{\circ}} = 22.903766$

Sections.	Given Weights of the Sections.	Angles of the Sections.			Angles of Inclination to the Vertical of the lower Surfaces of each Section, considered as Abutments.			Total Pressure on the Abutment, or on the Section next following.	Weights of the Semi-arches, being the successive Sums of the Weights in the 2d Column, deducting from each Sum the Weight of ½ A.
		°	′	″	°	′	″		
A	2.00000	5	0	0	2	30	0	22.92558	1.00000
B	2.76106	6	49	31	9	19	31	23.21305	3.76106
C	5.03844	11	41	23	21	0	54	24.53843	8.79950
D	8.81484	16	32	41	37	33	36	28.89592	17.61434
E	14.06148	16	34	7	54	7	43	39.09063	31.67582
F	20.73844	12	15	55	66	23	38	57.19849	52.41426
G	28.79492	7	51	16	74	14	54	84.37357	81.20918
H	38.16960	4	53	24	79	8	18	121.55373	119.37878
I	48.79112	3	6	19	82	14	37	169.71989	168.16990
K	60.57864	2	2	16	84	16	54	229.88977	228.74854

* The invariable horizontal force, or pressure, is called, in the technical phrase, *the drift or shoot of an arch.*

Table No. III.

Containing the angles of the several sections, with the angles between the vertical line and the abutments, calculated from their weights, when they are assumed equal to the weight of the first section, the angle of which is given = 5°; the weight of the first section, or A = 1.

$$\text{The initial pressure} = \frac{w}{2 \times \sin. \frac{1}{2} A^\circ} = 11.46279$$

$$\text{The horizontal force} = \frac{w}{2 \times \text{tang}. \frac{1}{2} A^\circ} = 11.45188$$

Sections.	Angles of the Sections.	Angles of Inclination to the Vertical of the lower Surfaces of each Section, considered as Abutments.	Total Pressure on the Abutment, or on the Section next following.	Weights of the Semiarches.
	° ′ ″	° ′ ″		
A	5 0 0	2 30 0	11.46279	.50000
B	4 57 40	7 27 40	11.54977	1.50000
C	4 51 10	12 18 50	11.72169	2.50000
D	4 40 40	16 59 40	11.97492	3.50000
E	4 27 20	21 27 0	12.30440	4.50000
F	4 12 10	25 39 10	12.70422	5.50000
G	3 55 30	29 34 40	13.16809	6.50000
H	3 38 40	33 13 20	13.68938	7.50000
I	3 21 40	36 35 0	14.26180	8.50000
K	3 5 40	39 40 40	14.87946	9.50000
L	2 50 20	42 31 0	15.53697	10.50000
M	2 36 20	45 7 20	16.22973	11.50000
N	2 23 20	47 30 40	16.95286	12.50000
O	2 11 20	49 42 0	17.70315	13.50000
P	2 0 20	51 42 30	18.47722	14.50000
Q	1 50 40	53 33 10	19.29421	15.50000
R	1 41 40	55 14 50	20.10753	16.50000
S	1 33 30	56 48 20	20.93711	17.50000
T	1 26 30	58 14 50	21.78074	18.50000
U	1 20 0	59 34 50	22.63742	19.50000
V	1 14 0	60 48 50	23.50502	20.50000
W	1 8 50	61 57 40	24.38295	21.50000
X	1 4 0	63 1 40	25.27003	22.50000
Y	0 59 40	64 1 20	26.16520	23.50000
Z	0 55 40	64 57 0	27.06773	24.50000
A	0 52 0	65 49 0	27.97699	25.50000
B	0 48 40	66 37 40	28.91436	26.50000
C	0 45 40	67 23 20	29.83490	27.50000
D	0 43 0	68 6 20	30.76038	28.50000
E	0 40 30	68 46 50	31.69023	29.50000
F	0 38 10	69 25 0	32.62449	30.50000

TABLE No. IV.

Shewing the angles of the sections, and the inclination of the abutments to the vertical line, calculated from the weights of the sections, when the angle of the first section is assumed $= 30°$, and the weight of each section is equal to the weight of the first section $= w = 1$.

The initial pressure $p = \frac{w}{2 \times \sin. \frac{1}{2} A°} = 1.931852$.

The horizontal force $p' = \frac{w}{2 \times \text{tang}. \frac{1}{2} A°} = 1.866025$

Sections.	Angles of the Sections.			Angles of Inclination to the Vertical of the lower Surfaces of each Section, considered as Abutments.			Total Pressure on the Abutments, or on the Section next following.	Weights of the Semi-arches, deducting .5.
	°	′	″	°	′	″		
A	30	0	0	15	0	0	1.931850	.500000
B	23	47	38	38	47	38	2.394167	1.500000
C	14	28	4	53	15	43	3.119616	2.500000
D	8	40	25	61	56	8	3.966357	3.500000
E	5	32	31	67	28	39	4.871542	4.500000
F	3	46	33	71	15	32	5.807912	5.500000
G	2	43	23	73	58	56	6.762509	6.500000
H	2	2	46	76	1	41	7.7286	7.5000
I	1	35	23	77	37	4	8.7024	8.5000
K	1	16	8	78	53	12	9.6815	9.5000
L	1	2	8	79	55	21	10.6645	10.5000
M	0	51	38	80	46	59	11.9504	11.5000

TABLE No. V.

Shewing the angles of 49 sections, forming an arch of equilibrium, calculated from given weights of the sections, when the angle of the first section is 1 degree = A°; and the weight thereof is denoted by unity, the weights of the successive sections increasing by equal differences from 1 to 3, which is the weight of the 25th section of the semiarch Z.

The initial pressure $p = \frac{1}{2 \times \text{sin.} \frac{1}{2} A^\circ} = 57.29649$

The horizontal force $p' = \frac{1}{2 \times \text{tang.} \frac{1}{2} A^\circ} = 57.29432$

Sections.	Weights of the Sections.	Angles of the Sections.	Angles of the Abutments.	Pressure on the Section next following.	Weights of the Semiarches.
		° ′ ″	° ′ ″		
A	1.000000	1 0 0	0 30 0	57.29649	.500000
B	1.083333	1 4 58	1 34 58	57.31593	1.583333
C	1.166666	1 9 54	2 44 51	57.36002	2.750000
D	1.250000	1 14 44	3 59 36	57.43352	4.000000
E	1.333333	1 19 28	5 19 4	57.54176	5.333333
F	1.416666	1 24 3	6 43 8	57.69030	6.750000
G	1.500000	1 28 28	8 11 37	57.88512	8.250000
H	1.583333	1 32 41	9 44 18	58.13190	9.833333
I	1.666666	1 36 35	11 20 53	58.43571	11.500000
K	1.750000	1 40 19	13 1 13	58.80511	13.250000
L	1.833333	1 43 39	14 44 52	59.24522	15.083333
M	1.916666	1 46 38	16 31 30	59.76187	17.000000
N	2.000000	1 49 13	18 20 44	60.36220	19.000000
O	2.083333	1 51 22	20 12 6	61.04895	21.083333
P	2.166666	1 53 4	22 5 10	61.83064	23.250000
Q	2.250000	1 54 18	23 59 29	62.71133	25.500000
R	2.333333	1 55 4	25 54 33	63.69574	27.833333
S	2.416666	1 55 21	27 49 55	64.78815	30.250000
T	2.500000	1 55 11	29 45 7	65.99240	32.750000
U	2.583333	1 54 33	31 39 41	67.31184	35.333333
V	2.666666	1 53 31	33 33 12	68.74902	38.000000
W	2.750000	1 52 4	35 25 17	70.30633	40.750000
X	2.833333	1 50 16	37 15 33	71.98551	43.583333
Y	2.916666	1 48 10	39 3 44	73.78788	46.500000
Z	3.000000	1 45 46	40 49 31	75.71422	49.500000

TABLE No. VI.

For comparing the pressures on the abutments, the weights of the semiarches, and the invariable horizontal or lateral force, calculated from the direct rules in the pages 13 and 27; with the pressures on the abutments, weights on the semiarches, and horizontal forces respectively, deduced by approximation, according to the general rules inserted in page 19.

In this Table, the weight of the highest or middle section is equal to the number 2, and the angle of the said section is $5°$; the weights of the several sections as they are stated in the Table II. By the approximate Rule I, the initial pressure $p = \frac{2}{2 \times \text{sin.} \frac{1}{2} A°} = 22.92558$. By the approximate Rule II, the horizontal force $p' = \frac{2}{2 \times \text{tang. } A°} = 22.90377$. S is the weight of the semiarch, and Z is the pressure on the abutment, the inclination of which to the vertical is $= V^z$.

Sections.	Angles of the Abutments, or V^z.	Rule III. Pressures on the Abutments.			Rule IV. Weights of the Semiarches.		
		Values of the Pressures Z, entered in the Table No. II.	Values of Z by the approximate Rule, $Z = p' \times \text{Sec. } V^z$.	Differences.	Given Weights of the Semiarches, entered in Table II.	Weights by Approximation $S = p' \times \text{Tang. } V^z$.	Differences.
	° ′ ″						
A	2 30 0	22.92558	22.92550	.00008	1.00000	1.	.0
B	9 19 31	23.21305	23.21052	.00253	3.76106	3.76107	.00001
C	21 0 55	24.53843	24.53560	.00283	8.79950	8 79896	.00054
D	37 33 36	28.89592	28.89120	.00472	17.61434	17.61204	.00230
E	54 7 43	39.09063	39.08690	.00373	31.67582	31.67351	.00231
F	66 23 38	57.19849	57.19580	.00269	52.41426	52.40850	.00576
G	74 14 54	84.37537	84.37180	.00357	81.20918	81.20260	.00658
H	79 8 18	121.55373	121.54790	.00583	119.37878	119.36970	.00908
I	82 14 37	169.71989	169.71090	.00899	168.16990	168.15830	.01160
K	84 16 54	229.88977	229.88290	.00687	228.74854	228.73900	.00954

Table No. VI. continued.

Sections.	Rule V. Weights of the Semiarches.			Rule VI. Invariable horizontal Force.		
	Given Weights of the Semiarches, entered in Table II.	Weights by Approximation S = z × Sin. V z.	Differences.	Invariable horizontal Force $= \frac{2}{2 \times \text{Tang. } 2^{\circ} 30'}$	Horizontal Force by Approximation $p = z \times$ Cos. V z.	Differences.
A	1.00000	1.	.00000	22.90377	22.90311	.00066
B	3.76106	3.76147	.00041	22.90377	22.90626	.00249
C	8.79950	8.79990	.00040	22.90377	22.90625	.00248
D	17.61434	17.61473	.00039	22.90377	22.90723	.00346
E	31.67582	31.67647	.00065	22.90377	22.90592	.00215
F	52.41426	52.41092	.00334	22.90377	22.90483	.00106
G	81.20918	81.20665	.00253	22.90377	22.90514	.00137
H	119.37878	119.37512	.00366	22.90377	22.90499	.00122
I	168.16990	168.16712	.00278	22.90377	22.90514	.00137
K	228.74854	228.74630	.00224	22.90377	22.90444	.00067

N. B. The rules for approximating to the weights of the semiarcs, pressures on the abutments, and the invariable horizontal force, when applied to the Tables I. III. IV. and V. will be found to give results for the most part as exact as in the above calculations, which are formed from the Table No. II. The conditions on which this Table is founded being rather more complicated than in the other Tables, it was considered, on this account, to be the most proper test for examining the correctness of the approximate rules.

APPENDIX;

CONTAINING

NOTES AND CORRECTIONS.

Page 2, *Line* 1.

After—"angular distance from the vertex,"—*add* measured by the inclination of the lowest surface to the vertical line.

Page 11, *the three last Lines.*

The weights are supposed to have been adjusted by geometrical proportions, but not mechanically determined with exactness.

Page 12, *Line* 25, *and in several other Places.*

In all the numerical computations of sines, cosines, and other lines drawn in a circle, the radius thereof is assumed equal to unity.

Page 17, *Line* 4.

The semiarch is understood to be that part of any arch which is comprehended between the vertical line and an abutment on either side.

Note, Page 18, *Line* 15.

Fig. 5. Let BOA $= A^\circ$ represent the angle of the highest or middle section, so that the angle VOA shall $= \frac{1}{2} A^\circ$: through any point I in the line OA draw the line KI perpendicular to OA, and supposing the weight of the wedge to be $= w$, let IK $= \frac{w}{2 \times \sin. \frac{1}{2} A^\circ}$, or the initial pressure: resolve IK into two forces, namely, IO parallel, and DK perpendicular, to the horizon. By the similar triangles VOA, IDK, as

H

IK : ID :: radius to the cosine of KID or VOA: it will follow that $ID = \frac{w \times \cos. \frac{1}{2} A^\circ}{2 \times \sin. \frac{1}{2} A^\circ} = \frac{w}{2 \times \text{tang.} \frac{1}{2} A^\circ}$, which is the measure of the invariable force, the direction of which is parallel to the horizon.

Page 26, *Line* 6, *at the word* " Through."

As the point S has not been yet determined by geometrical construction, *instead of*—" through the point S," &c.—*insert* through any point B in the line IQ draw the line BS perpendicular to the line CQ, and equal in length to the given line BS, which represents the pressure on the section D: and through the point S draw the line SF perpendicular to the line FI, and through G, &c.

Page 29, *Line* 6.

After—" till the semiarc is augmented to about 55°"—*add* (estimated by the inclination of the abutment to the vertical line).

ERRATA.

Page 7,	line 18,	*for* the line XP, *read* in the line XP.
—— 9,	—— 20,	*for* Fig. 1, *read* Fig. 1 and 2.
—— 11,	—— 24,	*for* then, *read* thus.
—— 11,	—— 28,	*for* direction, *read* directions.
—— 12,	—— 11,	*for* bissected, *read* bisected.
—— 23,	—— 22,	*for* over, *read* upon.
—— 24,	——	6 et alibi, *for* arc, *read* arch.
—— 29,	——	2 and 9, *for* weight, *read* weights.
—— 30,	—— 12,	*after* terminated *insert* ;
—— 30,	in the note,	*for* weighes, *read* weights.
—— 31,	line 4,	*read* $V^b = 7° 27' 40''$.
—— 32,	—— 5,	*for* 4° 21', *read* 4° 27'.
—— 35,	—— 17,	*for* T'R = 2.679492, *read* 2.679665.
—— 37,	—— 19,	*for* 1° 34' 58", *read* 1° 4' 58".
—— 37,	—— 20,	*for* 1° 34' 50", *read* 1° 34' 58".
—— 38,	—— 10,	*for* DF, *read* OF.

The angles entered in the Tables I. II. III. IV. and V. are expressed to seconds of a degree, in some cases to the nearest ten seconds of a degree. These results will probably be found on examination, in most cases, correct to the degree of exactness here stated. Some errors may be expected to occur in the course of the long and troublesome computations which are required for forming these Tables. On a revisal, the undermentioned errata have been discovered, which the reader is requested to correct, together with any other which his own observation may have pointed out.

Section	Page 39.
C	*for* 90.009, *read* 90.127.
D	*for* 123.22, *read* 124.26.
E	*for* 153.38, *read* 154.03.
K	*for* 273.36, *read* 272.48.
S	*for* 383.21, *read* 384.10.
	Table II. Page 42.
D	*for* 37 33 36, *read* 37 33 35.

Section	Table III. Page 43.
D	*for* 16° 59′ 40″, *read* 16° 59′ 30″.
P	*for* 51 42 30, *read* 51 42 20.
	Table IV. Page 44.
C	*for* 53° 15′ 43″, *read* 53° 15′ 42″.
M	*for* 11.9504, *read* 11.6504.
	Table V Page 45.
C	*for* 2° 44′ 51″, *read* 2° 44′ 52″.
D	*for* 3 59 36, *read* 3 59 35.

The angles opposite the sections F, G, K, &c. are affected by similar errors of 1″, which will appear by adding the angle of any section to the angle of the abutment preceding. The sum ought to be the angle of the abutment of the section.

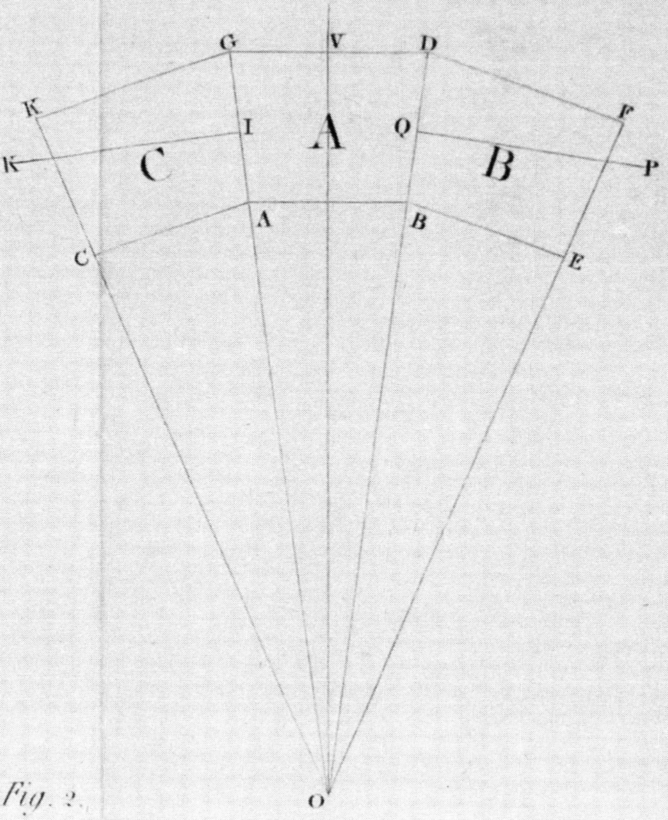

Fig. 1.

Fig. 2.

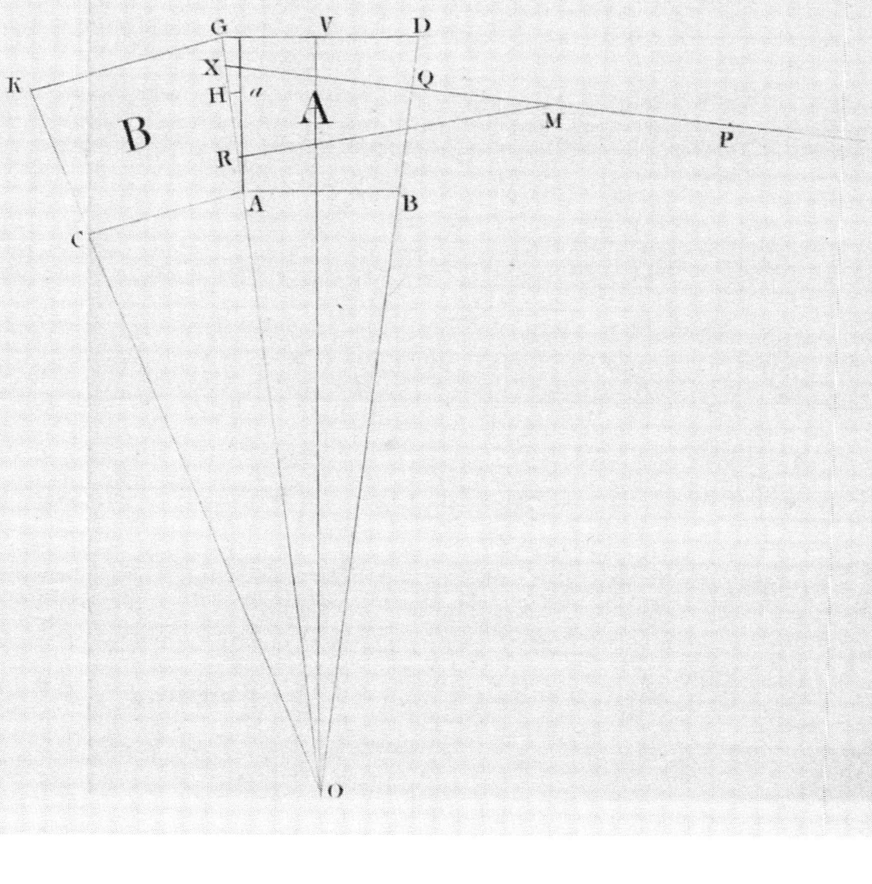

Fig. 3

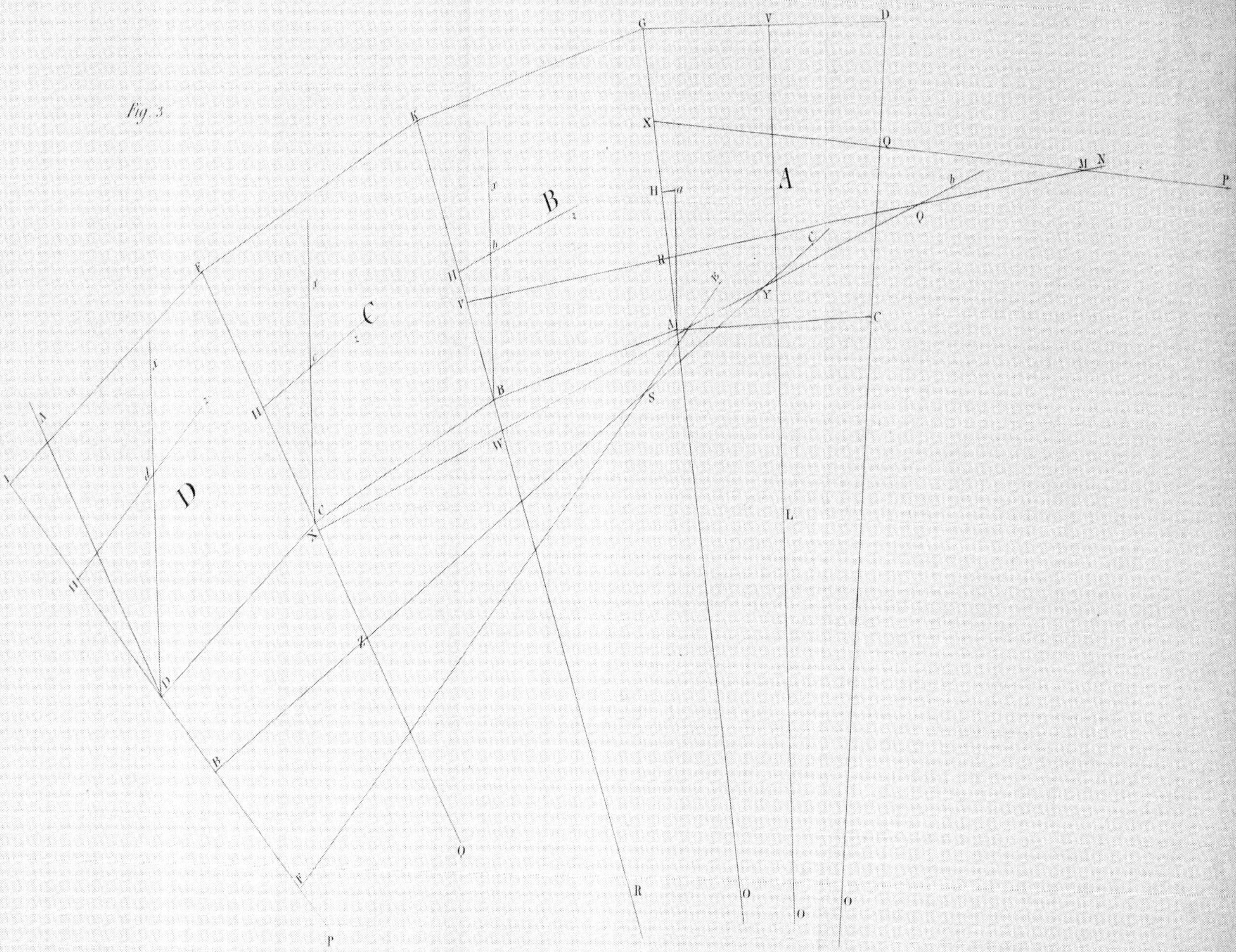

Fig. 4.

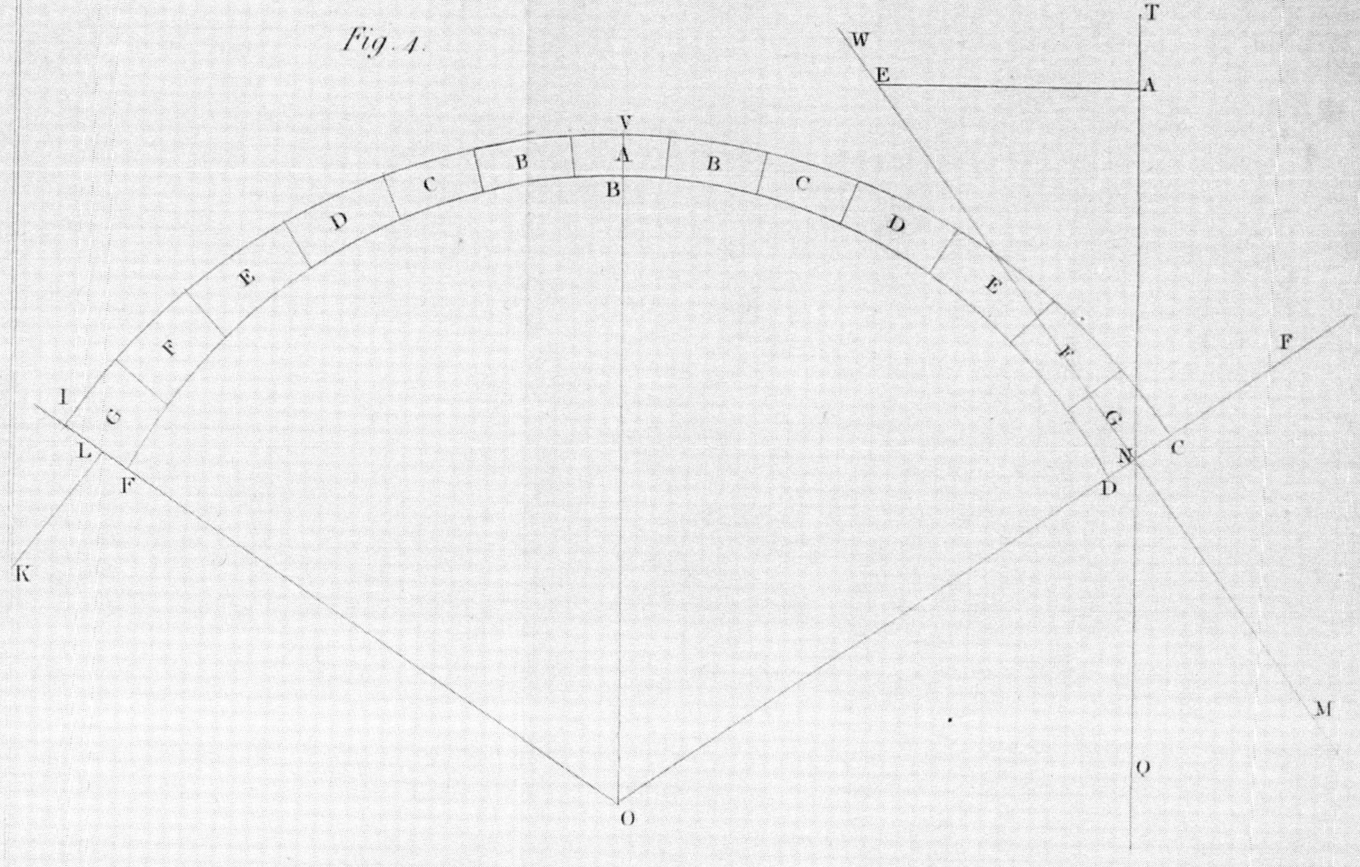

Fig. 5.

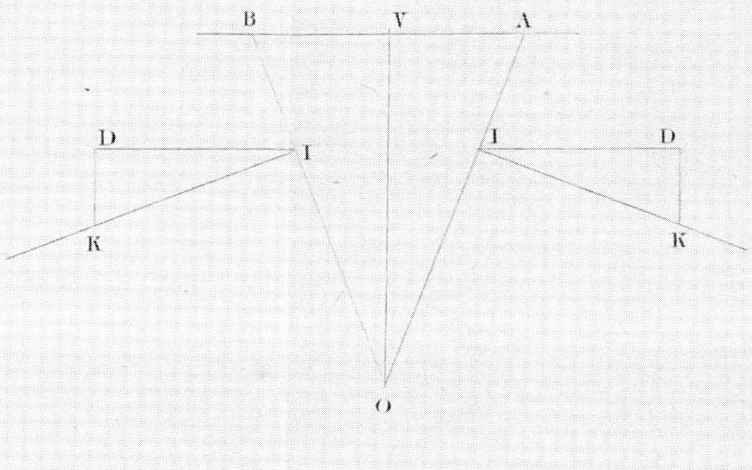

Fig. 6.

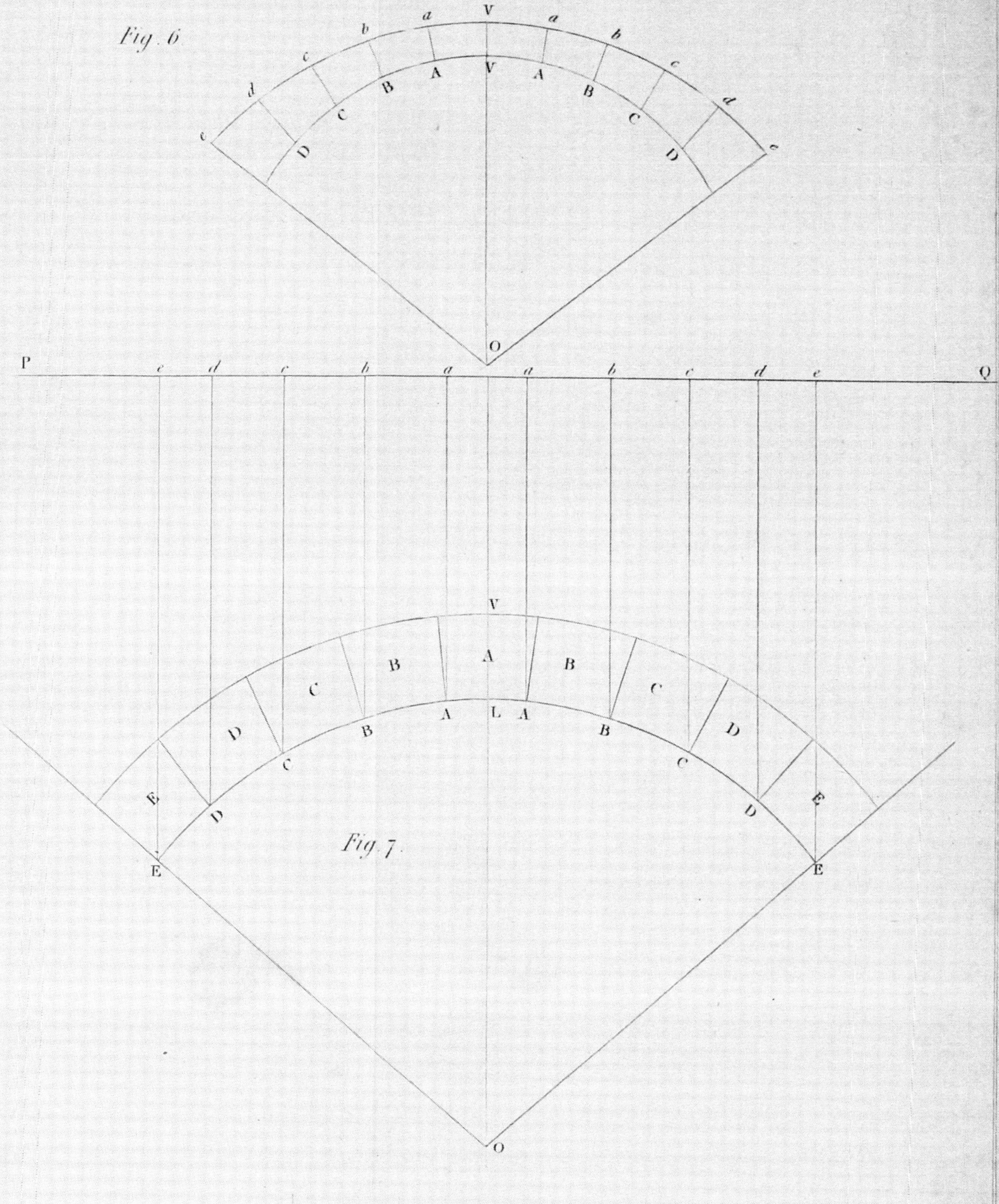

Fig. 7.

Fig. 8.

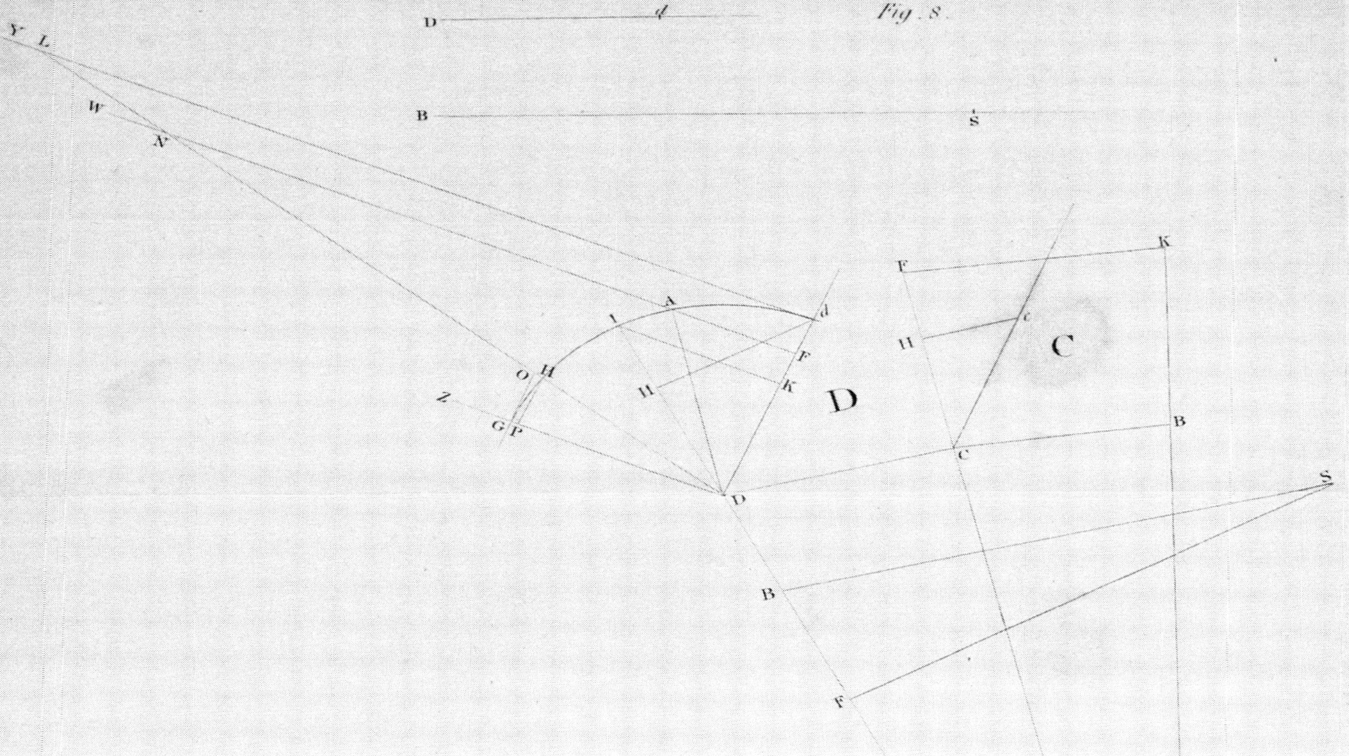

Fig. 9.

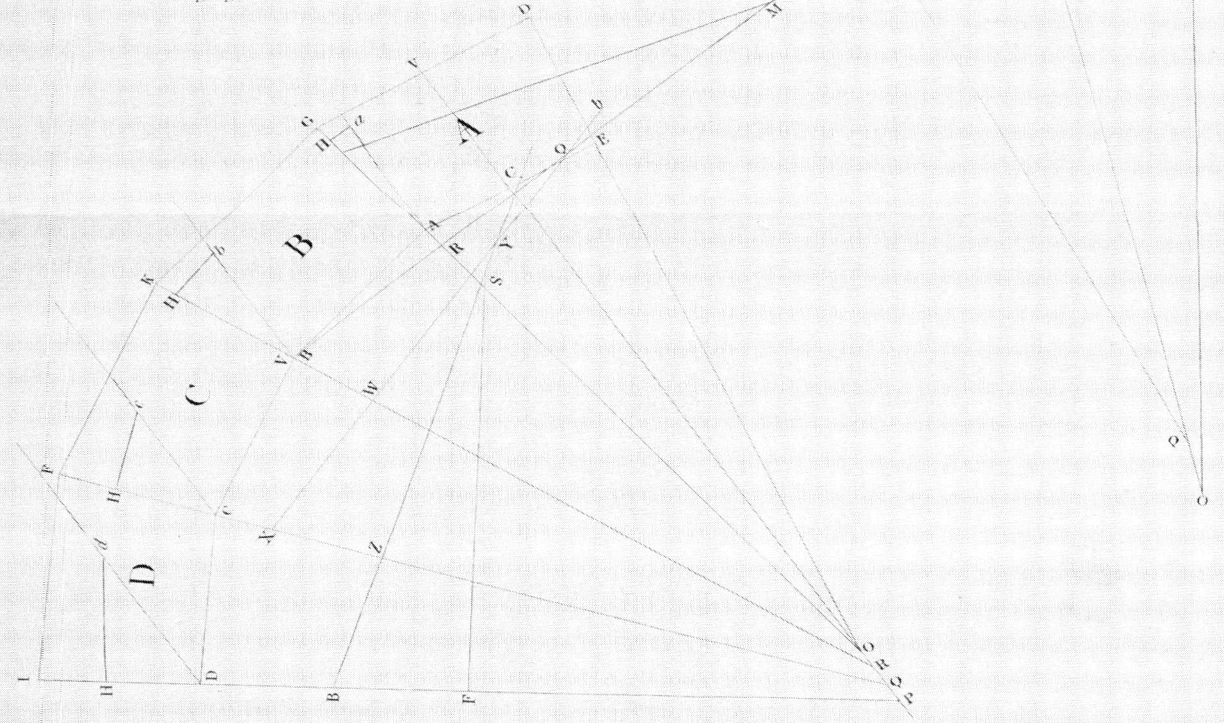

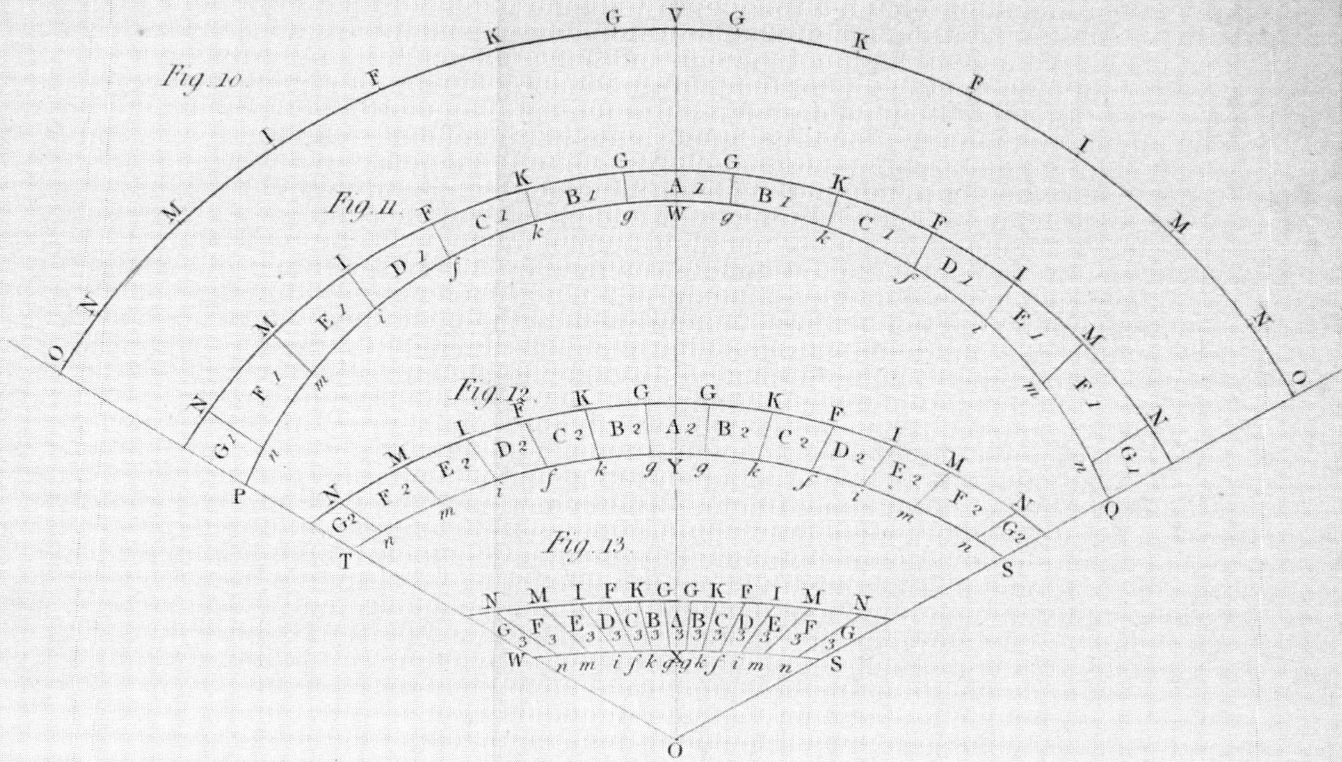
Fig. 10.
O N M I F K G V G K F I M N O
Fig. 11.
K G A 1 G K
F C 1 B 1 B 1 C 1 F
I D 1 W D 1 I
M E 1 k g g k E 1 M
N F 1 f f F 1 N
G 1 i i G 1
m m
n n
P Q
Fig. 12.
F K G G K F
I D 2 C 2 B 2 A 2 B 2 C 2 D 2 I
M E 2 f k g Y g k f E 2 M
N F 2 i i F 2 N
G 2 m m G 2
n n
T S
Fig. 13.
N M I F K G G K F I M N
G 3 F 3 E 3 D 3 C 3 B 3 A 3 B 3 C 3 D 3 E 3 F 3 G 3
W n m i f k g g k f i m n S
O

Fig. 14.

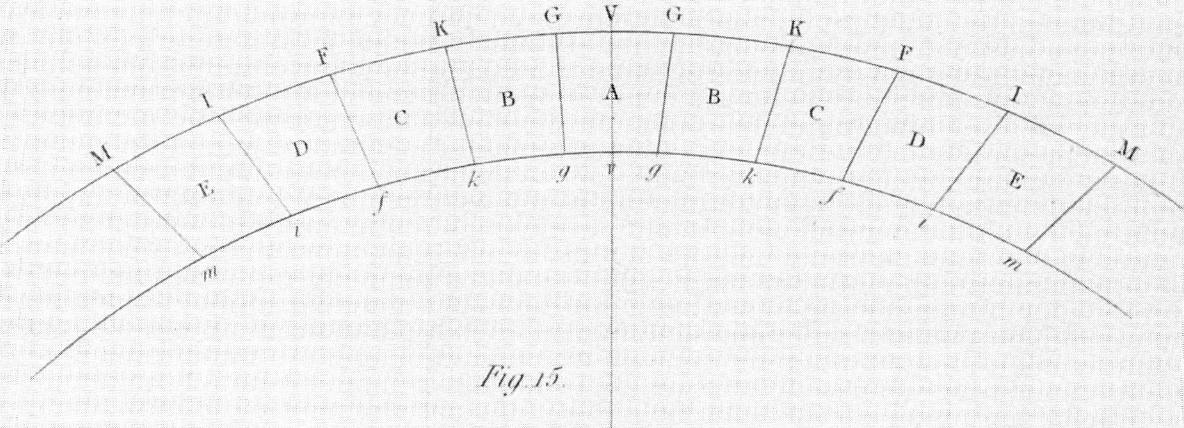
K G V G K
F F
I B A B I
M C C M
D D
E E
k g v g k
f f
i i
m m

Fig. 15.

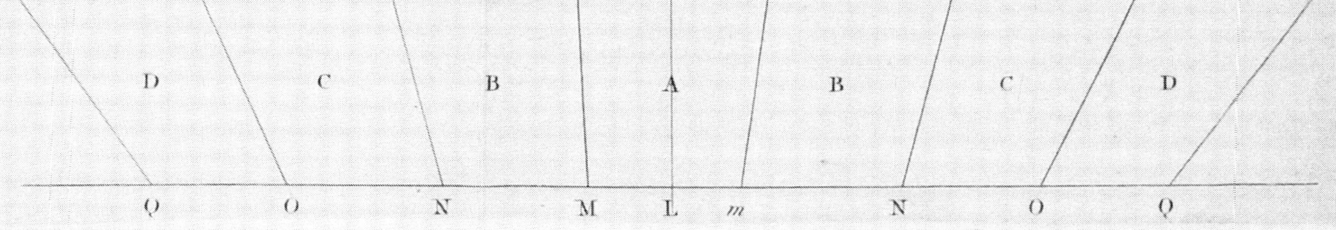
P W R T V t R W P
D C B A B C D
Q O N M L m N O Q

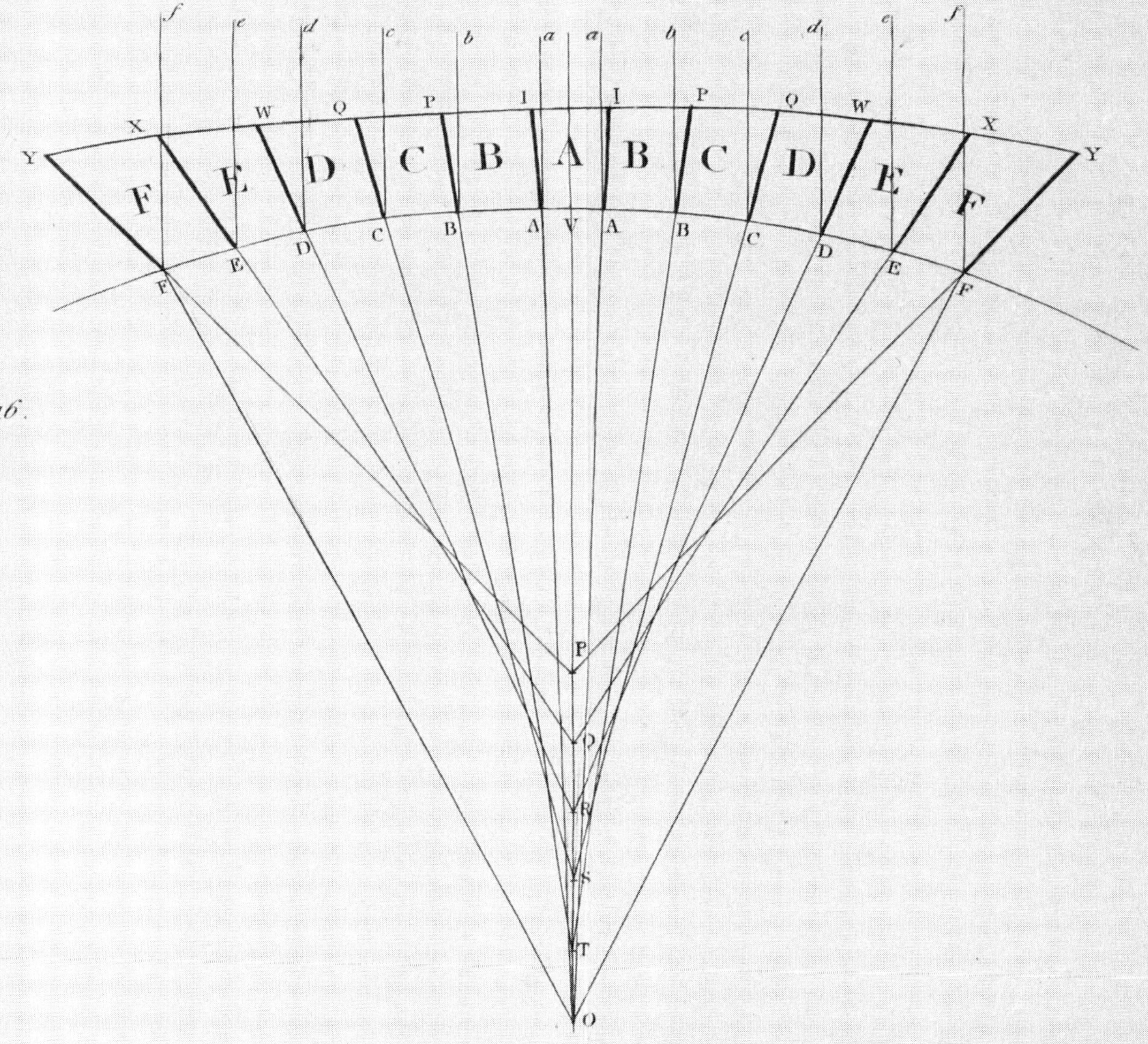

f e d c b a a b c d e f
X W Q P I I P Q W X
Y Y
F E D C B A B C D E F
F E D C B A V A B C D E F
P
Q
R
S
T
O

Fig. 16.

A

SUPPLEMENT TO A TRACT,

ENTITLED

A TREATISE ON THE CONSTRUCTION AND PROPERTIES OF ARCHES,

PUBLISHED IN THE YEAR 1801;

AND CONTAINING

PROPOSITIONS FOR DETERMINING THE WEIGHTS OF THE SEVERAL SECTIONS WHICH CONSTITUTE AN ARCH,

INFERRED FROM THE ANGLES.

ALSO CONTAINING A

DEMONSTRATION OF THE ANGLES OF THE SEVERAL SECTIONS, WHEN THEY ARE INFERRED FROM THE WEIGHTS THEREOF.

TO WHICH IS ADDED,

A DESCRIPTION OF ORIGINAL EXPERIMENTS TO VERIFY AND ILLUSTRATE THE PRINCIPLES IN THIS TREATISE.

WITH

OCCASIONAL REMARKS ON THE CONSTRUCTION OF AN IRON BRIDGE OF ONE ARCH, PROPOSED TO BE ERECTED OVER THE RIVER THAMES AT LONDON.

PART II.

BY THE AUTHOR OF THE FIRST PART.

LONDON:

PRINTED BY W. BULMER AND CO. CLEVELAND-ROW;

SOLD BY T. EGERTON, WHITEHALL; AND J. TAYLOR, AT THE ARCHITECTURAL LIBRARY, 59, HOLBORN.

1804.

PREFACE.

A PLAN for constructing an Iron Bridge of one arch, to be erected over the River Thames, designed by Messrs. Telford and Douglass, and proposed to the Committee of the House of Commons for the further Improvement of the Port of London, has excited considerable attention, both from the novelty and magnitude of the design, and the evident advantages to navigation which would attend such a structure; yet as some doubts arose respecting the practicability of erecting such an edifice, and the prudence of attempting it, the Committee judged it necessary for their own information, as well as to furnish the House with some grounds by which an opinion might be formed, to propose the following Queries, which were therefore transmitted, together with the engraved designs of Messrs. Telford and Douglass, and the explanatory drawings annexed, to such persons as were supposed to be most capable of affording them information.

The following are the Queries that were drawn up and transmitted to the Persons whose Names are undermentioned. (See Page vi.)

QUERIES.

I. What parts of the arch are to be considered as wedges, which act on each other by gravity and pressure, and what part merely as weight, acting by its gravity only, similar to the walls and other loading commonly erected on the arches of stone bridges; or does the whole act as one frame of iron, which cannot be destroyed but by crushing its parts?

Query II. Whether the strength of the arch is affected, and in what manner, by the proposed increase of its width towards the two extremities or abutments, when considered both vertically and horizontally; and if so, what form should the bridge gradually acquire?

III. In what proportion should the weight be distributed, from the centre to the abutments, to make the arch uniformly strong?

IV. What pressure will each part of the bridge receive, supposing it divided into any given number of equal sections, the weight of the middle section being known; and on what part, and with what force, will the whole act upon the abutments?

V. What additional weight will the whole bridge sustain, and what will be the effect of a given weight placed on any of the fore-mentioned sections?

VI. Supposing the bridge executed in the best manner, what horizontal force will it require, when applied to any particular part, to overturn it, or press it out of the vertical position?

VII. Supposing the span of the arch to remain the same, and to spring ten feet lower, what additional strength would it give to the bridge; or, making the strength the same, what saving may be made in the materials; or, if instead of a circular arch, as in the Print and Drawings, the bridge should be made in the form of an elliptical arch, what would be the difference in effect as to strength, duration, and expense?

VIII. Is it necessary or adviseable to have a model made of the proposed bridge, or any part of it, of cast iron; if so, what are the objects to which the experiments should be directed, to the equilibration only, or to the cohesion of the several parts, or to both united, as they will occur in the iron work of the intended bridge?

IX. Of what size ought this model to be made, and in what relative proportion will experiments on the model bear to the bridge when executed?

X. By what means may ships be best directed in the middle stream, or prevented from driving to the side, and striking the arch; and what is the probable consequence of such a stroke?

XI. The weight and lateral pressure of the bridge being given, can abutments be made in the proposed situation, for London Bridge to resist that pressure?

Query XII. The weight of the whole iron work being given, can a centre or scaffolding be erected over the river, sufficient to carry the arch, without obstructing those vessels which at present navigate that part?

XIII. Whether would it be most adviseable to make the bridge of cast and wrought iron combined, or of cast iron only; and if of the latter, whether of the hard and white metal, or of soft grey metal, or of gun metal?

XIV. Of what dimensions ought the several members of the iron work to be made, to give the bridge sufficient strength?

XV. Can frames of iron be made sufficiently correct to compose an arch of the form and dimensions as shewn in the Drawings No. 1 and 2, so as to take an equal bearing in one frame, the several parts being connected by diagonal braces, and joined by iron cement, or other substance? N. B. The Plate XXIV. in the Supplement to the Third Report, is considered as No. 1.

XVI. Instead of casting the ribs in frames of considerable length and breadth, as shewn in the Drawings No. 1 and 2, would it be more adviseable to cast each member of the ribs in separate pieces of considerable length, connecting them together with diagonal braces, both horizontally and vertically, as in No. 3.?

XVII. Can an iron cement be made that will become hard and durable; or could liquid iron be poured into the joints?

XVIII. Would lead be better to use in the whole, or any part, of the joints?

XIX. Can any improvements be made upon the Plans, so as to render the bridge more substantial and durable, and less expensive; if so, what are those improvements?

XX. Upon considering the whole circumstance of the case, agreeably to the Resolutions of the Select Committee, as stated at the conclusion of their Third Report,* is it your opinion, that an arch of 600 feet span,

* The Resolutions here referred to are as follow:

That it is the opinion of this Committee, that it is essential to the improvement and accommodation of the Port of London, that London Bridge should be rebuilt, on such a construction as to permit a free passage, at all times of the tide, for ships as expressed in the Drawings produced by Messrs. Telford and Douglass, on the same plane, with any improvements you may be so good as to point out, is practicable and adviseable, and capable of being rendered a durable edifice?

Query XXI. Does the Estimate communicated herewith, according to your judgment, greatly exceed, or fall short of, the probable expence of executing the Plan proposed, specifying the general grounds of your opinion?

After paying every attention to the subject which the importance of it demanded, it appeared for many reasons absolutely necessary, for furnishing satisfactory answers to the above Queries, to investigate the properties of arches from their first principles. The substance of these properties is comprised in a Tract, entitled a Dissertation on the Construction and Properties of Arches, published in the year 1801, and continued in the present Treatise, now offered to the Public as a Supplement to the former Tract. The

of such a tonnage, at least, as the depth of the river would admit at present, between London Bridge and Blackfriars Bridge.

That it is the opinion of this Committee, that an iron bridge, having its centre arch not less than 65 feet high in the clear above high-water mark, will answer the intended purposes, with the greatest convenience, and at the least expense.

That it is the opinion of this Committee, that the most convenient situation for the new bridge will be immediately above St. Saviour's Church, and upon a line leading from thence to the Royal Exchange.*

ANSWERS BY

1. Dr. Maskelyne,
2. Professor Robertson,
3. Professor Playfair,
4. Professor Robeson,
5. Dr. Milner,
6. Dr. Hutton,
7. Mr. Atwood,
8. Colonel Twiss,
9. Mr. Jessop,
10. Mr. Rennie,
11. M. Watt,
12. Mr. Southern,
13. Mr. Reynolds,
14. Mr. Wilkinson,
15. Mr. Bage,
16. General Bentham,
17. Mr. Wilson.

* See the Report from the Select Committee upon the Improvement of the Port of London.

reader will perceive that most of the propositions in these Dissertations are entirely new, and that they have been verified and confirmed, by new and satisfactory experiments, on Models constructed in brass by Mr. Berge of Piccadilly, whose skill and exactness in executing works of this sort are well known to the Public. Considering the importance of the subject, and the diversity of opinions which has prevailed respecting the construction of arches, and the principles, on which they are founded, it seems requisite, that the final determination of the plan for erecting the bridge of one arch in question, should be subjected to a rigorous examination, in order to discover if any, and what, errors might be found in them. The best means of effecting this appears to be by a publication, in which the propositions recommended for adoption being fairly stated, every person, who is of a different opinion, may have an opportunity of explaining his ideas on the subject, and of suggesting any different modes of construction, that are judged to be less liable to objection. To persons interested in these inquiries, it may be satisfactory to be informed, that the properties of arches, which are comprised in this latter Tract, have been found, on a careful and minute examination, and comparison, in no instance inconsistent with those, which are the subject of investigation in Part the First, but rather appear to strengthen and confirm the theory before published, allowing for the differences in the initial force or pressure, expressed in page 2, and in Figs. 1 and 2, inserted in this Tract, representing the different dispositions of the key-stones, from whence conclusions arise very different from each other, although all of them are strictly consistent with the laws of geometry and statics. It is particularly observable, that the deductions of the weights and pressures arising from a supposition of a single key-stone, do not exhibit conclusions more secure from disunion. The effects therefore of similar or other impediments, such as may be supposed to take place in the construction of real bridges, will have a much greater effect when they consist of iron braces and fastenings of various kinds; by which all efforts to disunite the sections are immediately counteracted.

The effects of this will be not only to prevent the separation of the sections by any casual force, tending to disunite them, but will likewise secure the edifice from the more silent, but not less destructive assaults of time: for when the sections of an arch are not duly balanced, every heavy weight which passes over the road-way, even the motion of a lighter carriage, must create a tendency to separate the sections by degrees, and at length entirely to disunite them; an evil to be remedied only by a requisite equilibration of parts of the bridge.

On a review of the whole, whether the subject is considered theoretically, as depending on the laws of motion, or practically, on the construction of models erected in strict conformity to the theory, it would seem difficult to suppose, that any principle for erecting a bridge of one arch would be adopted, that is very different from those, that have been the subject of the preceding pages: nevertheless, as the most specious theories have been known to fail, when applied to practice, in consequence of very minute alterations in the conditions; and as it is scarcely possible to frame experiments adequate to the magnitude of the intended structure, the Author of this Treatise thinks it incumbent upon him to state freely the doubts which remain upon his mind, respecting the construction of the bridge intended; suggesting, at the same time, such ideas, as have occurred to him, which probably may contribute to remove or to explain those doubts; particularly by causing an arch to be erected, the span of which is from 20 to 50 feet, the expense of which would be of little moment in the case of its success; and, on a supposition, that the experiment should fail, the important consequences that would probably arise from the observation of such a fact would, in the opinion of many persons, amply compensate for its failure. A doubt occurred during the construction of the flat arch,* whether the angles at the summit were most conveniently fixed at 2° 38′ 0″, or whether those angles should not subtend 5°, 10°, 15°, or any other angles, which might better contribute to the strength and stability of the entire structure. Since the materials, of which the Models are formed, are of a soft and elastic nature, which yields in some degree to the force of pressure; this circumstance, joined to that of making the angle subtended at the centre of the circle no greater than 2° 38′ 0″, prevents these sections from having much hold on the contiguous sections above them, and creates some difficulty and attention in adjusting the Model No. 2, to an horizontal plane, suggesting the necessity of forming the angles of the first or highest sections at 5°, or some greater angle, by which the holdings would be more effectually secured; but it is to be remembered, that this source of imperfection could not exist if the sections were made of materials perfectly hard and unelastic; and the Model having been constructed as an experiment, it seems proper that the angles of the first sections should be formed on the smallest allowable dimensions, in order to observe more distinctly the advantages which would arise from making the angles larger in any subsequent experiment, if any should be approved of, previously to a final determination of the plan to be adopted for erecting the iron bridge. It is to be

* The Model No. 2, so called to distinguish it from the Model No. 1, in the form of a semicircular arch.

observed, that no imperfection of the kind which is here spoken of, takes place in the Model of the arch No. 2, after it has been carefully erected: but a larger angle seems to be preferable for the angles of the first sections, from the difficulty which subsists, at present, in adjusting the Model of the arch No. 2, to the true horizontal plane, so much exceeding the trouble and attention in adjusting the Model No. 1.

Many thanks and acknowledgments are due to Mr. Telford and several other engineers, who have had the goodness to favour the Author with their able advice and assistance, in answering such questions as he had occasion to propose to them, respecting the original plan of this Treatise, and subsequently concerning the practical experiments, accounts of which are contained in it.

G. A.

London,
29th November, 1803.

A

DISSERTATION

ON THE

CONSTRUCTION AND PROPERTIES OF ARCHES.

PART II.

THE sections or portions of wedges which constitute an arch may be disposed according to two several methods of construction, which are represented by Fig. 1 and Fig. 2. In Fig. 1 the highest section, or key-stone, is bissected by the vertical plane VO, which divides the entire arch into two parts, similar and equal to each other. In Fig. 2, *two* highest sections A, A, similar and equal to each other, are placed contiguous and in contact with the vertical line VO. The former plan of construction has been before the subject of investigation, in a tract on arches, and published in the year 1801. It remains to consider the properties which result from disposing the sections according to the last-mentioned plan in Fig. 2.

The first material circumstance which occurs is the difference in the direction of the initial pressure, which in the former case, Fig. 1, was inclined to the horizon in the direction EQ perpendicular to AB; whereas, according to the latter disposition, Fig. 2, of the key-stone, the initial pressure is parallel to the horizon in the direction QR. In any arch of equilibration in which two equal and similar sections occupy the summit of the arch, the initial force or pressure is parallel to the horizon, and is to the weight of the first section as radius is to the tangent of the angle of that section.

For let the two highest equal sections, A, A, be represented by Fig. 3, when they form a portion of an arch of this description; let $Vv\,Ta$ represent one of these equal highest sections. Through any point Q, of the line VO, draw QP perpendicular to the line TO, QR parallel, and PR perpendicular, to the horizon; then will the three forces, by which the wedge A is supported in equilibrio, be represented in quantity and direction, by the lines QP, QR, and PR; of which, QP denotes the pressure between the surface TO and the surface of the section B, which is contiguous to it. QR is the force which acts in a direction parallel to the horizon, and is counterbalanced by the reaction of the other section A, similar and equal to the former: and PR measures the weight of the section A. Because PQR is a right-angled triangle, the following proportion will be derived from it: as the horizontal force QR is to the weight of the section A, or PR, so is radius or QR to PR. The tangent of the angle PQR = VOT, which being equal to the angle contained by the sides Vv, aT of the wedge A, may be denoted by A°: finally, if the weight of the section A be put equal to w, we shall have the horizontal force at the summit of the arch $= \frac{w}{\text{tang } A^{\circ}} = w \times \text{cotang. } A^{\circ}$, radius being = 1; from this determination the following construction is derived: having given the several angles of the sections A°, B°, C°, D°, together with the weight of the first section A, to ascertain by geometrical construction, the weights of the successive sections B, C, D, &c. when the arch is balanced in equilibrio. AΔ, AB, BC, CD, &c.

represent the bases of the sections in Fig. 4: through the points A, B, C, D, &c. draw the indefinite lines A *a*, B *b*, C *c*, D *d*, &c. perpendicular to the horizon; through any point X, in the line AF, draw the indefinite line XZ parallel to the horizon; let A *a* denote the weight of the section A; and through the point *a* draw *a z*, at right angles to AF; and in the line XZ take a part XM, which shall be to the line A *a* as radius is to the tangent of the angle VOF or A°; so shall XM represent, in quantity and direction, the pressure between the first section A and the vertical plane VO; or, when both semiarches are completed, the line XM will represent the pressure between the contiguous vertical surfaces of the two highest sections A, A. Through the point M draw MRV perpendicular to OF; and in this line produced, take MN = to *z a*; and make QV = to RN, which will be to radius, as radius is to the sine of VOA or A°. For because the line XM is to A *a* as radius is to the tangent of VOA or A°; if the sin. of A° be put = *s*, and the cos. A° = *c* to radius 1, this will give RM = $\frac{Aa \times c^2}{s}$; and because MN = *z a* = A *a* × *s*, and RM = $\frac{Aa \times c^2}{s}$; RM + MN or RN = $\frac{Aa \times \overline{s^2 + c^2}}{s}$ = VQ = $\frac{Aa}{s}$, which quantity is to radius, as radius is to the sin. of VOA or A°: and VQ or RN = $\frac{Aa}{s}$ is the measure of the entire pressure on the abutment OF.

To construct the weight of the section B, and the pressure on the next abutment OG, through the point Q, draw KT perpendicular to GS, and from any point B, in the line BG, set off B*z* = to VS: through the point *z* draw *zb* perpendicular to G *b* cutting off B*b*, which will be equal to the measure of the weight of the section B; from the point Q in the line KT produced set off QT = to

zb: also in the line KT, make KΣ = to ST, then KΣ or ST is the measure of the pressure on the abutment OG of the section C. On the same principles, the weights of the sections C and D, as well as of the sections following, are geometrically constructed, Cz being set off = WK, and Dz = to ΠI; from this construction, when completed, the general expressions for the weights of the sections are inferred, which are inserted in the 13th and 14th pages in the former tract, except that the initial pressure, arising from a different disposition of the key-stone, represented in Figs. 1 and 2, in consequence of which the initial pressure is $p' = w \times$ cotang. A°, instead of $p = \frac{w}{2 \times \sin. \frac{1}{2} A^\circ}$ in the former tract.

In this manner the weights of the several sections and pressures on the abutments, are found to be as underneath.

Sections.	Weights of the sections on the vertical abutments.	Pressures.
		$p' = w \times$ cotang. A°
	A = w	$p = p' \times$ cos. A° + $p' \times$ sin. A° × tang. V^a
	B = $p \times$ sin. B° × sec. V^b	$q = p \times$ cos. B° + $p \times$ sin. B° × tang. V^b
	C = $q \times$ sin. C° × sec. V^c	$r = q \times$ cos. C° + $q \times$ sin. C° × tang. V^c
	D = $r \times$ sin. D° × sec. V^d	$s = r \times$ cos. D° + $r \times$ sin. D° × tang. V^d
	E = $s \times$ sin. E° × sec. V^e	$t = s \times$ cos. E° + $s \times$ sin. E° × tang. V^e

When the angles of these sections are equal to each other, and consequently A° = B° = C° = D°; &c. in this case, the angles of the abutments will be as follows, V^a = A°, V^b = 2A°, V^c = 3A°, and so on.

On these conditions, the weight of each individual section, as well as the pressures on the corresponding abutments, and the weights of the semiarches, may be inferred by the elementary rules of trigonometry, from the general expressions above inserted.

Weights of the sections, and the pressures on the corresponding abutments, when the angles of the sections are equal each, and $=$ to A°, sin. of each angle $= s$, cos. $= c$, radius $= 1$.

Weights of the sections.	Pressures on the lowest surface of each section.	
	$p' = \frac{c}{s}$ - - -	$=$ cotang. A°
$A = 1$	$p = \frac{c}{s} \times \frac{1}{c}$ . .	$=$ cotang. A $\times$ sec. A
$B = \frac{1}{2c^2 - 1}$	$q = \frac{c}{s} \times \frac{1}{2c^2 - 1}$ . . .	$=$ cotang. A $\times$ sec. 2A
$C = \frac{1}{2c^2 - 1 \times 4c^2 - 3}$ . .	$r = \frac{c}{s} \times \frac{1}{4c^3 - 3c}$	$=$ cotang. A $\times$ sec. 3A
$D = \frac{1}{4c^2 - 3 \times 8c^4 - 8c^2 + 1}$	$s = \frac{c}{s} \times \frac{1}{8c^4 - 8c^2 + 1}$	$=$ cotang. A $\times$ sec. 4A
$E = \frac{1}{16c^4 - 20c^2 + 5 \times 8c^4 - 8c^2 + 1}$	$t = \frac{c}{s} \times \frac{1}{16c^5 - 20c^3 + 5c}$	$=$ cotang. A $\times$ sec. 5A

Sums of the weights of the sections, or weights of the semi-arches, when the angles of the sections are equal to each other, and $=$ to A°, sin. A° $= s$, cos. A° $= c$, radius $= 1$.

Sums of the weights.		
$A = 1$	1 . .	$=$ cotang. A $\times$ tang. A
$A + B$	$= \frac{2c^2}{2c^2 - 1}$	$=$ cotang. A $\times$ tang. 2A
$A + B + C$	$= \frac{4c^2 - 1}{4c^2 - 3}$	$=$ cotang. A $\times$ tang. 3A
$A + B + C + D$.	$= \frac{8c^4 - 4c^2}{8c^4 - 8c^2 + 1}$	$=$ cotang. A $\times$ tang. 4A
$A + B + C + D + E$	$= \frac{16c^4 - 12c^2 + 1}{16c^4 - 20c^2 + 5}$	$=$ cotang. A $\times$ tang. 5A.

When the angles of the sections, instead of being equal to each other, are of any given magnitude, the general demonstration of the weights of the sections, when adjusted to equilibration, and the corresponding pressures on the abutments, will require further examination of the principles on which the construction is formed; with the aid of such geometrical propositions as are applicable to the subject.

To consider, first, the pressures on the successive abutments which are, according to the construction, OV, OF, OG, OH, &c. it is to be proved, that the pressure on the vertical abutment OV = cotang. A°: the pressure on the abutment OF = cotang. A° × sec. A; the pressure on OG = cotang. A° × sec. $\overline{A° + B°}$; and the pressure on OH = cotang. A° × sec. $\overline{A° + B° + C°}$, and so on, according to the same law of progression; radius being = 1, the weight of the first section being also assumed = 1; if the weight of the first section should be any other quantity *w*, the pressures inferred must be multiplied by *w*.

The vertical line OV being parallel to the several lines A*a*, B*b*, C*c*, D*d*, &c. it appears that the angle *z*A*a* = FOV = A°, also *z*B*b* = GOV = A° + B°, *z*C*c* = HOV = A° + B° + C°, *z*D*d* = A° + B° + C° + D°, likewise the angle XMV = A°, VQK = B°, KΣI = C°, INΠ = D°, &c.

From these data the following determinations are obtained; the entire pressure QV on the abutment OF, consists of two parts, namely, RM = the wedge pressure; secondly, MN = *za*, which is that part of weight of the section A resting on the abutment FA, which is to the whole weight as *za* is to A*a*, or as the sine of the angle A° is to radius: the entire pressure therefore upon OF = RM + MN: but MR = MX × cos. A, and MN = *za* × tang. A to radius *z*A = sin. A: the pressure, therefore, on the line OF $= \frac{Aa \times \cos.^2 A}{\sin. A} + Aa \times \sin. A = \frac{Aa \times \overline{\cos.^2 A + \sin.^2 A}}{\sin. A}$ $= \frac{Aa}{\sin. A}$: but $\frac{Aa}{\sin. A}$ = cotang. A × sec. A; we have therefore arrived at the following determination: the entire pressure on the abutment OF = cotang. A° × sec. A, when the weight of the first section is assumed = 1.

The pressure on the abutment OG, that is ΣK, is to be proved $=$ cotang. A $\times$ sec. $\overline{A^\circ + B^\circ}$.

The pressure QV on the abutment preceding, or OF, has been shewn $=$ cotang. A° $\times$ sec. A; but as the angle VQK $=$ B°, it follows that QS $=$ cotang. A° $\times$ sec. A° $\times$ cos. B°, and VS $=$ cotang. A $\times$ sec. A° $\times$ sin. B°; but by the construction VS $=$ Bz: therefore Bz $=$ cotang. A° $\times$ sec. A° $\times$ sin. B°: and because the angle zBb $=$ A° $+$ B°, zb is to Bz (cotang. A° $\times$ sec. A° $\times$ sin. B°) as tang. A° $+$ B° is to radius: the result is, that zb $=$ cotang. A $\times$ sec. A $\times$ sin. B $\times$ tang. $\overline{A^\circ + B^\circ}$: and since SQ $=$ cotang. A° $\times$ sec. A $\times$ cos. B°; it follows that the entire pressure on OG $=$ SQ $+$ QT $=$ KQ $=$ cotang. A° $\times$ sec. A° $\times$ cos. B° $+$ cotang. A $\times$ sec. A° $\times$ sin. B° $\times$ tang. $\overline{A^\circ + B^\circ}$. The subsequent geometrical proposition will verify this construction, and prove at the same time, the relation, in general, of the successive secants of the angles which are proportional to the entire pressures on the successive corresponding abutments.

Given any angle of an abutment A°, and the angle of the section B° next following, it is to be proved that sec. A° is to sec. $\overline{A + B}$ as 1 is to cos. B $+$ sin. B $\times$ tang. $\overline{A + B}$. That is, from the conditions given,

$$\text{Sec. } A^\circ \times \cos. B + \sec. A^\circ \times \sin. B^\circ \times \text{tang. } \overline{A^\circ + B^\circ} = \sec. \overline{A + B}$$

From the elements of trigonometry, cos. B $+$ sin. B $\times$ tang. $\overline{A + B} = \cos. B + \sin. B \times \frac{\sin. \overline{A+B}}{\cos. \overline{A+B}} = \frac{\cos. \overline{A+B} \times \cos. B + \sin. B \times \sin. \overline{A+B}}{\cos. \overline{A+B}}$ $= \frac{\cos. \overline{A+B-B}}{\cos. \overline{A+B}} = \frac{\cos. A}{\cos. \overline{A+B}}$: therefore cos. B $+$ sin. B $\times$ tang. $\overline{A+B}$ $= \frac{\cos. A}{\cos. \overline{A+B}}$: multiply both sides by sec. A, the result will be: sec. A $\times$ cos. B $+$ sec. A $\times$ sin. B $\times$ tang. $\overline{A+B} = \frac{\cos. A \times \sec. A}{\cos. \overline{A+B}} = \sec. \overline{A+B}$.

This proposition may be extended to ascertain, generally, the proportion of the successive secants in an arch of equilibration, by supposing an angle of an abutment M° to consist of the angles of several sections, such as A°, B°, C°, D°, E° = M°, if an additional section F° is next in order after E°; so that the whole arch may consist of sections, the sum of the angles of which = M° + F°, then it is to be proved that the secant of M°, is to the secant of M° + F°, as 1 to cos. F + sin. F° × tang. $\overline{\text{M}^\circ + \text{F}^\circ}$, or sec. M° × cos. M° + sec. M° × sin. F° × tang. $\overline{\text{M}^\circ + \text{F}^\circ}$ = sec. $\overline{\text{M}^\circ + \text{F}^\circ}$.

By the elements of trigonometry, cos. F + sin. F × tang. $\overline{\text{M} + \text{F}}$ $= \text{cos. F} + \text{sin. F} \times \frac{\text{sin. } \overline{\text{M} + \text{F}}}{\text{cos. } \overline{\text{M} + \text{F}}} = \frac{\text{cos. F} \times \text{cos. } \overline{\text{M} + \text{F}} + \text{sin. F} \times \text{sin. } \overline{\text{M} + \text{F}}}{\text{cos. } \overline{\text{M} + \text{F}}}$

or cos. F + sin. F × tang. $\overline{\text{M} + \text{F}} = \frac{\text{cos. } \overline{\text{M} + \text{F} - \text{F}}}{\text{cos. } \overline{\text{M} + \text{F}}} = \frac{\text{cos. M}}{\text{cos. M} + \text{F}}$.

Multiply both sides of the equation by sec. M, the result will be sec. M × cos. F + sec. M × sin. F × tang. $\overline{\text{M} + \text{F}} = \frac{\text{sec. M} \times \text{cos. M}}{\text{cos. M} + \text{F}}$ = sec. M + F.

Thus the relation of the successive secants of the angles between the vertical line and the lowest surface of each section in any arch of equilibration is demonstrated, in general, and the measure of the pressures on the abutments proved to be equal to the weight of the first or highest section × cotang. A° × sec. of the angle of that abutment: and, in general, any sec. of an angle of an abutment is shewn to be to the sec. of the angle of an abutment next following, in the proportion as 1 is to cos. of the angle of the section + sin. of the same angle × tang. of the sum of the angles from the summit of the arch to the abutment.

The ensuing geometrical proposition is intended to investigate the weights of the individual sections in an arch of equilibration:

also to infer the sums of the weights of the sections which form the respective semiarches. A, B, C, D, Fig. 6. is a circular arc drawn from the centre O and with the distance OA. The arc AB $=$ A°, AC $=$ B°, AD $=$ C°; AG is drawn a tangent to the circle at the point A; through the centre O and the points B, C, D draw the lines OBE, OCF, ODG: then the line AE will be a tangent to the arc AB, AF will be a tangent to the arc AC, and AG will be a tangent to the arc AD; through the points B, C, D draw the lines BH, CI, DK perpendicular to the line OA; then will BH be the sin. and OH the cos. of the arc AB $=$ A°, CI and OI the sin. and cos. of the arc AC $=$ B° and DK $=$ the sin. and OK the cos. of the arc AD $=$ C° through C draw CM perpendicular to OE, so shall CM be the sin. of the arc CB.

The following proposition is to be proved: the difference of the tangents of the arcs AC and AB, or the line FE, is to the line CM, or the sine of the difference of the same arcs, so is 1 to the rectangle under the cosines of AB and AC, or OH $\times$ OI: the demonstration follows, radius being $= 1$; the tangent of the arc AB $= \frac{\text{sin. AB}}{\text{cos. AB}}$, and tang. of the arc AC $= \frac{\text{sin. AC}}{\text{cos. AC}}$; therefore the difference of the tang. of AB and AC $= \frac{\text{sin AC}}{\text{cos. AC}} - \frac{\text{sin. AB}}{\text{cos. AB}} = \frac{\text{sin. AC} \times \text{cos. AB} - \text{sin. AB} \times \text{cos. AC}}{\text{cos. AB} \times \text{cos. AC}}$; but the sin. of AC $\times$ cos. AB — sin. AB $\times$ cos. AC $=$ sin. $\overline{\text{AC} - \text{AB}}$ $=$ the sin. of the difference of the same arcs $=$ CM; therefore the difference of the tangents EF $= \frac{\text{CM}}{\text{cos. AB} \times \text{cos. AC}}$; which equation being resolved into an analogy, becomes the following proportion: as the difference of the tangents FE is to the sine of the difference of the arcs sin. $\overline{\text{AC} - \text{AB}}$, so is radius 1 to the rectangle under the cosines OI and OH, which is the proposition to be proved.

Since it has been shewn in the pages preceding, that the pressure on each abutment is $w \times$ cotang. A° × sec. of the angle of that abutment, the pressures on the several sections will be expressed as follows:

Pressure on the vertical abutment VO $= w \times$ cotang. A° $= w \times p'$ sec. V°.

Pressures on the lowest surface of each section.

A	$p = w \times$ cotang. A° × sec. V^a
B	$q = w \times$ cotang. A° × sec. V^b
C	$r = w \times$ cotang. A° × sec. V^c
D	$s = w \times$ cotang. A° × sec. V^d
	&c. &c.

Let CB be an arc which measures the angle of any section, so that OF may represent the secant of the angle AOF, and OE = the secant of the angle of the abutment AOE: the difference of the tangents FE $= \frac{\text{CM}}{\text{cos. AB} \times \text{cos. AC}} =$ sin. B° × sec. of the angle AOB, × sec. of the angle AOC, or, according to the notation which has been adopted, the difference of the tangents FE = sin. B° × sec. of V^a × sec. V^b, radius being = 1.

The weight of the section B, by page 6, $= p \times$ sin. B° × sec. V^b, but by the table in page above inserted, $p = w \times$ cotang. A° × sec. wherefore the weight of the section B $= w \times$ cotang. A° × sin. B° × sec. V^a × sec. V^b: on the same principles the weights of the several sections will be expressed as underneath.

Sections.	Weights.
A	$= w \times$ cotang. A° × sin. A° × sec. V° × sec. V^a
B	$= w \times$ cotang. A° × sin. B° × sec. V^a × sec. V^b
C	$= w \times$ cotang. A° × sin. C° × sec. V^b × sec. V^c
D	$= w \times$ cotang. A° × sin. D° × sec. V^c × sec. V^d
E	$= w \times$ cotang. A° × sin. E° × sec. V^d × sec. V^e
F	$= w \times$ cotang. A° × sin. F° × sec. V^e × sec. V^f
	&c. &c.

Because the lines Fig. 7. AE, EF, FG represent the weights of the several sections AB, BC, CD, the sum of those lines, or AG, will denote the sum of the weights of the sections A + B + C. And in general, if the angle of an abutment in an arch of equilibration should $= V^z$, and the angle of the first section $= A^\circ$, and its weight $= w$, the sum of the weights of the sections when adjusted, will $= w \times$ cotang. $A^\circ \times$ tang. V^z.

On this principle the weights of the sums of the successive sections, or the weights of the semiarches, will be as they are stated underneath.

	Sums of the weights of the sections, or weights of the semiarches.
A	$= w \times$ cotang. $A^\circ \times$ tang. $V^a = w \times$ cotang. $A^\circ \times$ tang. A
A + B . . .	$= w \times$ cotang. $A^\circ \times$ tang. $V^b = w \times$ cotang. $A^\circ \times$ tang. $\overline{A + B}$
A + B + C .	$= w \times$ cotang. $A^\circ \times$ tang. $V^c = w \times$ cotang. $A^\circ \times$ tang. $\overline{A + B + C}$
A + B + C + D	$= w \times$ cotang. $A^\circ \times$ tang. $V^d = w \times$ cotang. $A^\circ \times$ tang. $\overline{A + B + C + D}$
	&c. &c. &c.

The method of fluxions affords an additional confirmation of this proposition: suppose an arch adjusted to equilibrium to be composed of innumerable sections, the angles of which are evanescent; to ascertain the weight of the sum of these evanescent sections included within a given angle from the summit of the arch to the lowest abutment V^c; since the angles of the sections are evanescent, the quantity $V^c = V^d$: and for the same reason, the sin. of the angle D° will ultimately $= \dot{D}$. Wherefore, the evanescent weight of the section $D = r \times$ sin. $\dot{D} \times$ sec. $V^c = r \times \dot{D} \times$ sec. V^c. Let the tangent of the angle $V^c = x$ to radius 1; then the sec. of $V^c = \sqrt{1 + x^2}$; and because $V^c = V^d$, it follows that $V^c \times V^d = \overline{1 + x^2}$: the weight therefore of the evanescent section $D = w \times$ cotang. $A^\circ \times \dot{D} \times \overline{1 + x^2}$;

which is the fluxion of the weight of the arch equal to the fluxion of the angle D° sec.^{2} $V^c \times w \times$ cotang. A°.

But the fluxion of an arc $\times$ into the square of its secant is known to be equal to the fluxion of the tangent of the same arc, when both quantities vanish together: therefore the integral or fluent, that is, the weight of the arch, will be equal to the tangent of the arc $\times$ into constant quantities; that is, the sum of the evanescent sections, or the weight of the entire arch, from the summit to the abutment $= w \times$ cotang. A $\times$ tang. V^c.

On the Model, No. 1, *for veryfying the Construction of an Arch, in which the Weights of the Sections* A, B, C, D, *&c. are inferred from the Angles given in the present Case* $= 5^\circ$ *each.*

Although the various properties of arches described in the preceding pages, respecting the weights and dimensions of the wedges, and their pressures against the abutments, require no further demonstration than what has been given in the preceding pages; yet, as it has been remarked, that philosophical truths, although demonstrable in theory, have often been found to fail when applied to practice; in order to remove every doubt of this sort, concerning the theory of arches, which is the subject of the preceding and present Dissertation, a model of an arch was constructed according to the conditions in Table I. in which the angle of each section $= 5^\circ$, the weight of the first section $= 1$, the weights of all other sections being in proportion to unity. This arch, like most arches which were erected previously to the 16th century, consists of two semiarches, similar and equal and resting against each other, in the middle of the curve, as described in figure 2: the summit of the arch is occupied by two equal wedges A, A, resting against each other when coincident with the vertical plane VO; according to the construction of this proposition, the weight of the wedge A being assumed = 1, the weight of B appears to be 1.01542, and the weight of the wedge C = 1.04724. These weights being applied in the form of truncated wedges, supported upon immoveable abutments, sustain each other in exact equilibrium, although retained in their places by their weights and pressures only, and independently of any ties and fastenings which are usually applied in the case when the structure is intended for the purpose of sustaining superincumbent loads. The pressure between the two first sections in a direction parallel to the horizon $= p' =$ 11.24300, the pressure against the lowest surface of the first section $= p$ = 11.47371: the pressure on the lowest surface of the second section, or B $= q =$ 11.60638: on the lowest surface of C, the pressure is $= r =$ 11.83327. The intention of this model is not only to verify the properties of equilibrium of these wedges, acting on each other, but also to examine and prove the several pressures on the lowest surface of the sections to be in their due proportions, according to the theory here demonstrated. And it ought to be remembered that these pressures being perpendicular to the surfaces impressed, the reaction is precisely equal and contrary; for this reason, each of the surfaces subject to this pressure will have the effect of an abutment immoveably fixed.

The most satisfactory proof that the pressure on any abutment has been rightly assigned is, by removing the abutment and by applying the said force in a contrary direction; the equilibrium that is produced between forces acting under these circumstances, it is a sufficient proof that the reaction of the abutment is precisely equal to the force impressed upon it in a contrary direction.

After the weights of the several wedges in an arch of equilibration have been determined, in proportion to the weight of the first wedge A assumed to be = 1, some difficulty occurs in forming each wedge of proper dimensions, so that their weights shall be correspondent to the conditions required. A wedge being a solid body consisting of length, breadth, and thickness, of which one dimension, namely, the thickness, or depth, remains always the same; the weight of any wedge will be measured by the area or plane surface in each section, which is parallel to the arch; that is, if the thickness or depth of any section K (Fig. 7.) be put = $1\frac{1}{2}$, the solid contents of the section K will be measured by the area KttS multiplied into $1\frac{1}{2}$; put the angle SOT = 5°, the sin. of 2° 30′ 0″ = s, cos. 2° 30′ 0″ = c; also let Ot = x; then we find, by the principles of trigonometry, that the area Ott = $x^2 sc$, and the area OTS = $r^2 sc$, and the area TttS = $x^2 sc - r^2 sc$. Let the area corresponding to the weight of the section proposed = k, so that $x^2 - r^2 sc = k$; and $x^2 = \frac{k + r^2 sc}{sc}$: wherefore $x = \sqrt{\frac{k + r^2 sc}{sc}}$; and T$t$ or St, the slant height of the section K $= \sqrt{\frac{k + r^2 sc}{sc}} - r$. This being determined, the breadth of the section $tt = 2s \times ot = 2sx$, making therefore the radius OV = 11.46281, with the centre O, and the distance OV = 11.46281, describe the circular arc VABC; and in this arc from V set off the several chords VA, AB, BC, &c. = 1 inch, in consequence of which the angles VOA = AOB = BOC, &c. &c. will be 5° each. The slant height and the breadth of each section will be computed by the preceding rules.

On the Model, No. 2, *for illustrating and verifying the Principles of the Arch, when the Angle of each Section, after the first Section* A°, *are inferred according to the Rule in Page 27 of former Tract, from the Weights of the other Sections.*

In the propositions which have preceded, the several angles of the sections A°, B°, C°, D°, &c. have been considered as given quantities, from which the weights of the corresponding wedges have been inferred, both by geometrical construction and by calculation, when they form an arch of equilibration. The next inquiry is to investigate the magnitudes of the angles from having given the weights of the several sections; but as the construction and demonstration would not in the least differ from that which has already appeared in page 27 of the former Tract on Arches, it may be sufficient in the present instance to refer to the former Tract, both for explaining the principles of the construction and the demonstration, inserting in this place only the result, which is comprised in the following rule.

Having given A° the angle of the first section, and the weight $b = 1.25$ of the section B next following, together with the angle at which the lower surface of A is inclined to the vertical, called the angle of the abutment of the section A, or V^a, and the pressure on it $= p$, to ascertain the magnitude of the angle B°, in an arch adjusted to equilibrium: in the proposition referred to it is proved, that on the conditions stated, tang. $B° = \frac{b \times \text{cos. } V^a}{p + b \times \text{sin. } V^a}$ radius being $= 1$.

The model constructed to verify the principles of equilibration, consists of a circular arc drawn to a radius $= 21.7598$ inches. VA, AB, BC, &c. are chords $= 1$ inch each, and subtend at the centre of the circle angles of 2° 38′ 0″: as the angle of the first section A° = 2° 38′ 0″, the angle of the abutment, or the angle contained between the vertical and the lowest surface of the section A = V^a = 2° 38′ 0″: the pressure on the lowest surface of A° = $p = \frac{1}{\text{sin. A}}$ = 21.765553, and according to the rule inserted in page 12, tang. B° = $\frac{1.25 \times \text{cos. } 2° 38' 0''}{p + 1.25 \times \text{sin. } 2° 38' 0''}$ = 3° 16′ 29″. Wherefore the angle of the abutment contained between the lowest surface of B and the vertical line = A° + B° = 2° 38′ 0″ + 3° 16′ 29″ = 5° 54′ 29″ = V^b. By the same rule, the angles of the successive sections C°, D°, E°, &c. &c. and the angles of the abutments corresponding, are computed as they are stated in the columns annexed, in page 17.

Let the arch to be constructed be supposed such as requires for its strength and security, that the weight or mass of matter contained in the lowest section R, shall be five times the weight of the first or highest section A, and let the arch consist of thirty-four sections, seventeen on each side of the vertical plane: on these conditions, the weight of the successive sections will be as follows: A = 1, B = 1.25, C = 1.50, D = 1.75, E = 2.00, F = 2.25, &c. as stated in Table IX: by assuming these weights for computing the several angles B°, C°, D°, &c. according to rule in page 12, they are found to be as in the ensuing columns, and the successive sums of the angles are the angles of the corresponding abutments. By considering the drawing of this model, it is found to contain the conditions necessary for calculating the areas required for estimating the weights of the voussoirs. For the inclination of each abutment to the abutment next following, is equal to the angle of the section which rests on the abutment; thus, the inclination of the lines I*i*, H*i*, is equal to the angle of the section I = H*i*I; also the inclination of the lines H*b*, G*b*, forms the angle of the section H = H*b*G, and so on.

MODEL No. 2.

Dimensions of an Arch of Equilibration: the Angle of the first Section, or A° = 2° 38′ 0″, and the Angles of the other Sections, and the Angles of the Abutments, are as follow:

Angles of the Sections.	°	′	″	Angles of the Abutments.	°	′	″
A° =	2	38	0	V^a =	2	38	0
B° =	3	16	29	V^b =	5	54	29
C° =	3	52	39	V^c =	9	47	8
D° =	4	24	36	V^d =	14	11	44
E° =	4	50	9	V^e =	19	1	53
F° =	5	7	16	V^f =	24	9	9
G° =	5	14	41	V^g =	29	23	50
H° =	5	12	14	V^h =	34	36	4
I° =	5	1	8	V^i =	39	37	12
K° =	4	43	23	V^k =	44	20	35
L° =	4	21	27	V^l =	48	42	2
M° =	3	57	33	V^m =	52	39	35
N° =	3	33	26	V^n =	56	13	1
O° =	3	10	21	V^o =	59	23	22
P° =	2	49	0	V^p =	62	12	22
Q° =	2	29	42	V^q =	64	42	4
R° =	2	12	31	V^r =	66	54	35

Geometrical Construction for drawing the Abutments, in the Model for illustrating Equilibrium of Arches, when the Magnitudes of the Angles are inferred from the Weights of the several Sections.

VABC, &c. represents the portion of a circular arc, which is drawn from the centre O, with the distance OV: VIO (Fig. 8.) is a line drawn perpendicular to the horizon, dividing the entire arch into two parts, similar and equal to each other: the radius OV = 21.7598 inches ∴ from the point V, set off the chord VA = 1 inch, and the chords AB, BC, CD = 1 inch each; the angle of the first section will therefore be = 2° 38′ 0″: for as one half : 1 :: the sin. of $\frac{1}{2}$ A°, or sin. 1° 19′, to radius, which is, consequently, = 21.7598 inches: the semiarch VR consists of seventeen sections, the weights of which increase from 1 to 5, which is the weight of the lowest or last section; and from these conditions it is inferred, by the rule in page 15, that A° = 2° 38′ 0″, B° = 3° 16′ 29″, C° = 3° 52′ 39″, &c. the successive sums of these angles, or the angles of the abutments, A° = 2° 38′ 0″ = V^a, A° + B° = 5° 54′ 29″ = V^b, A + B + C = 9° 47′ 8″ = V^c, &c. as stated in Table IX.

The direction of the line must next be ascertained, determining the position of the abutment on which either of the sections, for instance the section I, is sustained: from the point O draw the line OI: it is first to be observed, that the angle contained between the line I and VO, or the angle V I I = 39° 37′ 12″, according to the Table IX. and the angle VOI = 2° 38′ 0″ × by 9 = 23° 42′ 0″: make therefore the following proportion: as the sine of 39° 37′ 12″, is to the sine of VII — VOI = 15° 55′ 12″, so is radius OV, or 21.7598 inches to OI = 9.3597 inches; this being determined, if a line *i* I *t* is drawn through the point I, the line so drawn will coincide with the abutment on which the lowest surface of the section I is sustained; and by the same principle the directions of all the abutments are practically determined. Also it appears that the successive abutments I*i*, H*i*, include between them the angle H*i*I, which is therefore equal to the angle of the section I; therefore to find the solid contents measured by the area of the section I, the triangle *iss*, being made isosceles the area iss will be $= \frac{is^2 \times \text{sin.}\, sis}{2}$;* from which if the area IiH be subtracted, the remaining sum will be equal the area of the section I: put either of the lines $is = x$, then by the proposition which has been above mentioned, the area $iss = \frac{\overline{is}^2 \times \text{sin.}\, sis}{2}$, and by the same proposition, the area $HiI = \frac{iH \times iI \times \text{sin.}\, HiI^o}{2}$; consequently, is being put $= x$, we shall have $\frac{x^2 \times \text{sin.}\, I^o}{2} - Hi \times Ii \times \frac{\text{sin.}\, I^o}{2} = \text{I}$, it appears that $x^2 = †\frac{2\text{I} + bI \times bH \times \text{sin.}\, I^o}{\text{sin.}\, I^o}$, and consequently $x = \sqrt{\frac{2\text{I} + bI \times bH \times \text{sin.}\, I^o}{\text{sin.}\, I^o}}$: by the same rule the weights and dimensions of all the sections K, L, M, &c. are determined.

By the principles stated in the preceding pages, the weight of either of the highest sections in any course of voussoirs, together with the angle of the said section, regulates the magnitude of the horizontal thrust or shoot, and the perpendicular pressure on the ultimate or lowest abutment and the direct pressure against the lowest surface of any abutment will depend on the cotang. of the angle of the highest section and the sec. of the angle of the abutment jointly.

PROPOSITION.

* The area contained in a right-lined triangle ABC, Fig. 10, is equal to the rectangle under any two sides $\times \frac{1}{2}$ the sine of the included angle.

Let the triangle be ABC; AB and AC the given sides, including the angle BAC, between them.

Through either of the angles B draw BD perpendicular to the opposite base AC: by the elementary principles of geometry it appears, that the area of the triangle ABC = the rectangle under the base AC, and half the perpendicular height BD, or $\frac{AC \times BD}{2}$. But when BA is made radius, BD is the sine of the angle BAC: consequently, the line $BD = \frac{BA \times \text{sin.}\, A^o}{2}$; and the area $ABC = AC \times AB \times \frac{\text{sin.}\, CAB}{2} = \frac{AC \times AB\ \text{sin.}\, A^o}{2}$, which is the proposition to be proved.

† I, here, means the weight of the section I.

In consequence of these properties, since each course of voussoirs stands alone, independent of all the voussoirs above and beneath, the strength of an arch will be much augmented by the degree of support afforded to the voussoirs situated in the course immediately above, as well as to those underneath, which may be connected with the former.

Moreover, the inconvenience is avoided which obviously belongs to the principles, that are sometimes adopted for explaining the nature of an arch, by which the whole pressure on the abutment is united in a horizontal line, contiguous to the impost; whereas the magnitude of the horizontal shoot, and the perpendicular pressure on the ultimate or lowest abutment has appeared by the preceding propositions to be proportioned to the weight of the highest section in the semiarch, and to the sec. of the angle of the abutment jointly; and consequently, the pressure on the different points of the abutment may be regulated according to any proportion that is required.

Whatever, therefore, be the form intended to be given to the structure supporting the road-way, and the weight superincumbent on an arch, no part of the edifice need to be encumbered by superfluous weight; on the contrary, such a structure, consisting of the main arch and the building erected on it, is consolidated by the principle of equilibrium, into one mass, in which every ounce of matter contributes to support itself, and the whole building.

The equilibration of arches being established by theory, and confirmed by experiment, it becomes a further object of experiment to ascertain, amongst the varieties of which the constructions of arches is capable, what mode of construction will be most advantageous, in respect to firmness and stability, when applied to any given case in practice. A simultaneous effort of pressure combined with weight, by which the wedges are pressed from the external towards the internal parts of an arch, being the true principle of equilibration, the wedges by their form endeavour to occupy a smaller space in proportion as they approach more nearly to the internal parts of the curve. It has appeared by the observations in page 29, Part I. that the bases of the sections may be of any lengths, in an arch of equilibration, provided their weights and angles of the wedges be in the proportions which the construction demands, observing only that if the lengths of the bases should be greatly increased, in respect to the depths, although, in geometrical strictness, the properties of the wedge would equally subsist, yet when applied to wedges formed of material substance, they would lose the powers and properties of that figure; this shews the necessity of preserving some proportion between the lengths of the bases and depths of the wedges, to be determined by practical experience rather than by geometrical deduction.

With this view, a further reference to experiment would be of use, to ascertain the heights of the sections or voussoirs, when the lengths of the bases are given, also when the angles B°, C°, D°, &c. are inferred from the weights of the sections considered as given quantities, to ascertain the alterations in the angles B°, C°, D°, &c. from the summit of the arch, which would be the consequence of varying the angle of the first section A°, so as to preserve the equilibrium of the arch unaltered: by referring to Table VI. we observe, that when the weights of the sections are equal to each other, or A = B = C = D, &c. and the angle of the first section = 5°; then to form an arch of equilibration, the angle of the second section, or B° must = 4° 55′ 30″, the angle of the third section C° = 4° 46′ 53″, &c. And it becomes an object of experimental examination how far the stability and firmness of an arch will be affected by any alterations of this kind, and to judge whether in disposing a given weight or mass of matter (iron for instance) in the form of an arch, any advantage would be the consequence of constructing the sections so that the first section will subtend an angle of 1°, 2°, 3°, 5°, or any other angle at the centre of the arch, all other circumstances being taken into account. When the angle of the first section = 5°, and the weights of the successive sections = 1, the angles of the abutments will be severally $V^a = 5° 0' 0''$, $V^b = 9° 55' 30''$, $V^c = 14° 42' 23''$, and so on, as stated in Table VI. By referring likewise to Table VIII. we find the angle of the first section assumed = 1°, and the weight of each of the subsequent sections being = 1, the angles of B°, C°, &c. are severally B° = 1° 4′ 57″, C° = 1° 9′ 51″, D° = 1° 14′ 39″; consequently, the angles of the abutments will be as follows: $V^a = 1°$, $V^b = 2° 4' 57''$, $V^c = 3° 14' 48''$, $V^d = 4° 29' 28''$, &c. which give the dimensions of the sections when they form an arch of equilibration.

It has been frequently observed, by writers on the subject of arches, that a thin and flexible chain, when it hangs freely and at rest, disposes itself in a form which coincides, when inverted, with the form of the strongest arch. But this proposition is without proof, and seems to rest on some fancied analogies arising from the properties of the catenary curve, rather than on the laws of geometry and statics, which are the bases of the deductions in the two Dissertations on Arches, contained in the preceding pages; if it should be proved that an arch built in the form of a catenary or other specific curve, acquires, in consequence of this form, a superior degree of strength and stability, such proof would supercede the application of the properties demonstrated in these Dissertations.

Concerning the relative Positions of the Centres of the Abutments and the Centre of the Circle.*

When the angle of an abutment is greater than the corresponding angle at the centre of the circle; in this case, the centre of the abutment falls above the centre of the circle, as in Fig. 9. When the angle of the abutment is less than the angle at the centre of the circle, the centre of the abutment falls beneath the centre of the circle, as represented in Fig. 9. When the angle of the abutment is equal to the angle at the centre, this case will coincide with that which is stated in pages 4 and 5 preceding, in which $V^a = A°$, $V^b = 2\,A°$, $V^c = 3\,A°$, &c. $V^b = A°$, $V^l = 2\,A°$, $V^b = A°$, &c. &c. and consequently the centre of the abutment coincides with the centre of the circle.†

Further Observations on the Courses of Voussoirs.

A, B, C, D, E, &c. terminating the letter F, denote the sections which form the first course of voussoirs in a semiarch of equilibration, of which A° is the first, or one of the highest, sections: if the weight of the section A be $= w$, and the angle of the abutment VOF $= V^c$. then it has appeared, by the preceding pages, that the pressure against the lowest or ultimate abutment $= w \times$ cotang. A $\times$ sec. V^c. 2dly. Let B° be the angle of the first section in the next course of voussoirs, terminated on each end by the letter L, and let y be the weight of the first section, the

* The point in which any abutment intersects the vertical line is called, in these pages, the centre of that abutment.

† Let VO be a line drawn through V, the middle point of the arch passing through the centre of the circle O; on this arc the angles of the sections and the angles of the abutments are measured: p, the point where any abutment, for instance I, continued intersects the vertical vO, is called the centre of the abutment.

pressure on the last or ultimate abutment $= x \times$ cotang. B $\times$ sec. V^c. Moreover, let z be the weight of the first section C, in the third course of voussoirs, which is terminated by the letter P. It follows that the proportions of pressure on the ultimate abutment denoted by the letters F, L, P, will be $w \times$ cotang. $A^\circ \times$ sec. $V^c + x \times$ cotang. $B^\circ \times$ sec. V^c, and $y \times$ cotang. $C^\circ \times$ sec. V^c respectively, and according to these quantities, the respective pressures on the several parts of the abutment, will be regulated according to any law that may be required.*

The principles of arches having been established according to the preceding theory, and confirmed by experiment, described in the experiments No. 1 and 2; in the first of these, the angles of each section are constructed $= 5^\circ$, and the weight of the section A having been assumed $= 1$, the weights of the sections B°, C°, D°, &c. are inferred as stated in Table I. from the angles B°, C°, D°, &c. considered as given quantities. In No. 2, the angle of the first section is assumed $= 2^\circ\ 38'\ 0''$. The remaining angles are inferred from the given weights by the rule in page 15, $A = 1.00$, $B = 1.25$, $C = 1.50$, &c. to $Z = 5$, which is the weight of the lowest or ultimate section. It has appeared in page 29, in the former Tract, that whatever be the figure of the interior curve corresponding in an arch of equilibration, the bases of the sections which are disposed in this form may be of any lengths, provided the weights and the angles of the sections are in the proportions which the construction demands.

CORRECTION OF THE ENGRAVING FIG. 6.

* That the engraving of the Figure 5 may correspond with the text, the summit of the first course of voussoirs ought to be marked A, the first section of the second course should be marked B, and of the third the first section = C, and so on; this will make the text correspondent with the Figure 6.

A further reference to experiment would be of use in practical cases, to ascertain how far the strength and stability of an arch would be affected by altering the proportion between the lengths of the voussoirs and the heights thereof; for instance, when the lengths of the wedges are given to ascertain the alterations in the stability of the arch when the depths or heights of the sections are three, four, or five times the length. Let the following case be also proposed; the entire weight of an arch being supposed known, what part of this entire weight must the first section consist of, so as to impart the greatest degree of strength to the structure; also to decide whether the angle of the first section ought to be made 1°, 5°, 10°, &c. or of what ever magnitude would contribute to the same end. To these may be added the following cases to be discussed; when the angles of the several sections are inferred from the weights thereof, to investigate what must be the proportion of the said weights, so as to make the arch uniformly strong throughout.

FURTHER CONSIDERATIONS CONCERNING THE CONSTRUCTION OF THE MODELS No. 1 AND No. 2.

Dimensions of a Model No. 1, *of an Arch of Equilibration. Radius* = OV = 11.46281, *the Angle of each Section* = 5°, *the Chord of each Arch* = 5° = 1 *Inch.* (Fig. 7.)

The first section is a brass solid, the base of which = KV = 1 inch, and the sides V*v*, K*k*, or the slant height of the section A = .961, and the depth or thickness of each section = 1½ inch, the breadth of A or *vk* = 1.084.

The weights of the sections, as they are calculated according to Table No. I, the first section being assumed as unity.

Rule for making the brass voussoirs equal to the weights which are expressed in Table No. I. Let the sine $= 2° 30' 0'' = s$, the cosine c when radius $= 1$; then making the radius $= r$, the area of the triangle $vOk = r^2 \times sc$, and the area $VOK = \overline{VO}^2 sc$; from whence Vv, or the slant height of the section A, when the weight $= 1$, is found to be $\sqrt{\frac{1 + r^2 sc}{sc}} - OV = .961$, the breadth $vk = 2s \times Ov = 1.084 = Vk$. Thus, by the same rule, the slant height of the section B $= \sqrt{\frac{B + r^2 sc}{sc}} - r = .9749$, and the breadth $ll = 1.084$, in all the sections entered in Table I. are calculated.

Model, No. I.

Sections.	Weights of the sections as they are calculated in Table No. 1. in the Tract on Arches.	Slant height of the sections.	Breadth of the sections.	Weights of the sections when made of brass, specifically heavier than water, in proportion 8 to 1: in ounces avoirdupois.	Weights of the sections when made of brass, in lbs. avoirdupois.	Sums of the weights in lbs. avoirdupois.
A	= 1.00000	Kk = .961	*vk* = 1.084	A = 6.9444	0.43403	0.43403
B	= 1.01542	L*l* = .974	*ll* = 1.085	B = 7.0515	0.44072	0.87475
C	= 1.04724	M*m* = 1.004	*mm* = 1.087	C = 7.2725	0.45453	1.32928
D	= 1.09752	N*n* = 1.050	*nn* = 1.092	D = 7.6215	0.47535	1.80564
E	= 1.16972	O*o* = 1.116	*oo* = 1.097	E = 8.1230	0.50769	2.31333
F	= 1.26922	P*p* = 1.207	*pp* = 1.105	F = 8.8140	0.55087	2.86421
G	= 1.40427	Q*q* = 1.329	*qq* = 1.116	G = 9.7518	0.60949	3.47370
H	= 1.58754	R*r* = 1.492	*rr* = 1.130	H = 11.024	0.69903	4.16274
I	= 1.83910	S*s* = 1.713	*ss* = 1.149	I = 12.771	0.79822	4.96096
K	= 2.19175	T*t* = 2.016	*tt* = 1.176	K = 15.220	0.95128	5.91224
L	= 2.70196	V*v* = 2.444	*vv* = 1.213	L = 18.764	1.17419	7.08643
M	= 3.47366	U*u* = 3.067	*uu* = 1.264	M = 24.122	1.50619	8.59263
N	= 4.71440	W*w* = 4.098	*ww* = 1.357	N = 32.738	2.04618	10.63882
O	= 6.89199	X*x* = 5 553	*xx* = 1.484	O = 47.860	2.99130	13.63012
P	= 11.25371	Y*y* = 8.279	*yy* = 1.722	P = 78.150	4.88443	18.51455
Q	= 22.16552	Z*z* = 13.836	*zz* = 2.207	Q = 153.92	9 62045	28.13500
R	= 65.8171	A*a* = 29.056	*aa* = 3.534	R = 456.96	28.57000	56.70500

On the Construction of the Model No. 2, *in an Arch of Equilibration, in which the Angles of the several Sections are inferred from the Weights thereof, according to the Rule in Page* 15.

In this model the arc A, B, C, &c. is a portion of an arc of a circle: the first section A subtends an angle at the centre of the circle A° = 2° 38′ 0″, the chord of which = 1 inch = to the chord of BC, CD, DE, &c. radius = OV = 21.7598 inches: the weight of the first section being assumed = 1, the weights of the sections B, C, D, &c. are considered as proportional to the weight of the first section when it is = 1; if the weight of the seventeenth section or R = 5, the weights of the intermediate sections will be B = 1.25, C = 1.50, D = 1.75, &c. as stated in Table IX: and since A° the angle of the first section = 2° 38′ 0″, by applying the rule demonstrated in page 27 in former Dissertation, and referred to in page 15 of this Tract, the angles of the several sections are found to be A° = 2° 38′ 0″, B° = 3° 16′ 29″, C° = 3° 52′ 39″, and the corresponding angles of the abutments, or successive sums of the angles of the sections, are 2° 38′ 0″ + 3° 16′ 29″ = 5° 54′ 29″ = V^b. Moreover, A° + B° + C° = 9° 47′ 8″ = V^c, and thenceforward according to the same law of progression. The next object of inquiry is, to ascertain from what point I in the line OV the line OII must be drawn, so as to coincide with the lowest surface of the section I, when inclined to the vertical at the given angle VII. The angle subtended by the semiarch VI at the centre O is measured by the angle IOI, and the difference of these angles, or VII — IOI = IIO. The radius IO being denoted by the same letters which distinguish the line IO, the different meaning will be determined by the context. From the principles of trigonometry, the following proportion is inferred; as IO : OI :: the sin. of IIO to the sin. of OII or VII; consequently, the line IO $= \frac{OV \times \text{sin. OII}}{VII}$. As an example, let it be required to ascertain the inclination of the abutment to the vertical, on which the section I is sustained when it forms a portion of an arch of equilibration, and the angle of the abutment VII $= 39° 37' 12''$: the angle VIO subtended by the semiarch VI at the centre of the circle $= 23° 42' 0''$, which being subtracted from the angle of the abutment $39° 37' 12''$, leaves the angle IOI $= 15° 55' 12$, and the distance required from the centre, OI $=$ OV $\times \frac{\text{sin. OII}}{\text{sin. VII}}$, or because OV $= 21.7598$ inches, OI $= 9.35978$ inches; making, therefore, the line OI $= 9.35978$ inches, through the points II draw the line I, I, *t*, which will be the position of the abutment on which the section I rests, the angle of which, $V^i =$ VII, is the inclination of the abutment V^i to the vertical: for the same reason VHH $=$ the angle of the abutment $V^b =$ VHH, the difference of these two angles VII $-$ VHH $=$ G*b*H, or the angle of the section H°: making, therefore, the line G*b* $= a$, H*b* $= b$, the properties of trigonometry give the area of the triangle G*b*H $= ab \times \frac{\text{sin. H}}{2}$; on the same principle, the area of the triangle H*i*I $=$ H*i*I $=$ H*i* $\times$ I*i* $\times \frac{\text{sin. H}^{\circ}}{2}$; and thus the areas of all the triangles will be measured, from having given the sides of the triangles and the angles included between them. The sides of the triangles may be measured by a scale of equal parts, as stated in Table I. and in this manner the sides of all the triangles were correctly measured by Mr. Berge, so as not to err from the truth by more than an unit in the fourth decimal place. This measurement was essential for computing the distance of the vertex from the base, so as to form the dimensions of the brass wedges, correctly and independently of their weights, in each triangle. For instance, *r*Q being put $= a$ and *r*R $= b$, this will give the area of the triangle

$rQR = ab \times \frac{\sin. R^\circ}{2}$; and if the triangle *raa* is made isosceles, or $ra = x$, the area of the triangle $Raa = \frac{x^2 \times \sin. R^\circ}{2}$ — the area $\frac{b \times a \times \sin. R^\circ}{\sin. R^\circ}$; or if the difference of the areas is put $= w$, the result will be $\frac{x^2 \times \sin. R^\circ}{2}$ — the area $\frac{b \times a \times \sin. R^\circ}{2} = w$, or $x = ra$ $= \sqrt{\frac{2w + \text{the area } a \times b \times \sin. R^\circ}{\sin. R^\circ}}$; wherefore $Qa = \sqrt{\frac{2w + a \times b \times \sin. R^\circ}{\sin. R^\circ}}$ $= 28.5777 - rQ$ and $Ra = \sqrt{\frac{2w + a \times b \times \sin. R^\circ}{\sin. R^\circ}} - rR$.

Thus, by actual measurement, $a = 23.9248$ inches, and $b =$ 24.3056, and the area $ab \times \frac{\sin. R^\circ}{2} = 10.73670 = \sqrt{\frac{2w + a \times b \times \sin. R^\circ}{\sin. R^\circ}}$ $- Qr$, and $Ra = \sqrt{\frac{2w + a \times b \times \sin. R^\circ}{\sin. R^\circ}} - rR$: the area *raa* $= \frac{x^2 \times \sin. R^\circ}{2} = 15.73670$, or the area $raa = 15.73670$; the result is, that the area $aaRQ = aa - rQR = 5$ square inches: and since every square inch of area is occupied by a weight of a section $= 6.9444$ oz. avoirdupois, we arrive at the following conclusion, that the weight of the section $R = 5 \times 6.9444 = 34.7222$ oz. avoirdupois. Because $\sqrt{\frac{2w + a \times b \times \sin. R^\circ}{\sin. R^\circ}} = ra = 28.57770$, this determines both the greater and lesser sides of the section **R**; namely, the greater side being $= ra - rQ = 4.6529$; and the lesser side being $= ra - rR = 4.2721$ inches; in this way, the Table is formed, shewing the greater and lesser sides of the several sections.

According to this mode, the dimensions of all the brass wedges were formed; the investigation of the angles of the wedges from the weight thereof is the subject of investigation in page 27 of the First Part of the Tract, entitled a Dissertation on the Construction and Properties of Arches; and it appears that if the angle of the first section is given $= A^\circ$, together with the weight thereof $= a$, assumed to be = 1, the weights of the other section B = b = 1.25, the weight of C = c = 1.50, of D = d = 1.75, &c. The principle of equilibrium is established, by making the tang. of the angle B° = $\frac{a \times \cos. A^\circ}{p + a \times \sin. A^\circ}$, also the tang. of the angle C° = $\frac{b \times \cos. B^\circ}{q + b \times \sin. B^\circ}$, as they are stated in Table IX. which contains the conditions, founded on supposing that the strength and security of the arch are such as require that whatever weight should be contained in the first section, the weight of the seventeenth section R shall be five times as great: making, therefore, the weight of A = 1, the weight of B = 1.25, and C = 1.50, and the weight of the seventeenth section or R = 5, &c. Thus the angle of the first section A° being assumed = 2° 38′ 0″, and the initial pressure on the lowest surface of A = p = 21.76555, and the weight of the first section = a = 1: from these data the following results are obtained: $\frac{a \times \cos. V^o}{p + a \times \sin. V^o}$ = 2° 38′ 0″ tang. B° = $\frac{b \times \cos. V^a}{p + b \times \sin. V^a}$ = 3° 16′ 29″ tang. C° = $\frac{c \times \cos. V^b}{q + c \times \sin. V^b}$ = 3° 52′ 39″, &c. &c. according to the statement in Table IX.

The Dimensions of the Sections, according to the Rule in Page 29.

	Lesser Sides.	Greater Sides.		Lesser Sides.	Greater Sides.
A	= 0.97827	0.97827	K	= 2.73754	3.12824
B	= 1.20676	1.21126	L	= 3.14849	3.47069
C	= 1.41568	1.44928	M	= 3.36800	3.71700
D	= 1.61833	1.66693	N	= 3.64620	4.01460
E	= 1.81718	1.90118	O	= 3.87463	4.25476
F	= 2.00676	2.13656	P	= 4.16762	4.55142
G	= 2.20080	2.36920	Q	= 4.43768	4.82038
H	= 2.42850	2.63910	R	= 4 27210	4.65290
I	= 2.62584	2.88134			

Model, No. II.

Table I. Lines measured by Mr. Berge, on a brass plate, being the distances as undermentioned.				Sections	II. Breadth of the sections.		III. Areas of the greater triangles.		IV. Areas of the lesser triangles.	
OV	= 21.7598	OA	= 21.7598	A	*vk*	= 1.0449	O*vk*	= 11.8770	OVA	= 10 8770
*b*A	= 17.4925	*b*B	= 17.4970	B	*ll*	= 1.0689	*bll*	= 9.9918	*b*AB	= 8.7418
*c*B	= 14.8136	*c*C	= 14.8372	C	*mm*	= 1.1010	*cmm*	= 8.9315	*c*BC	= 7.4315
*d*C	= 13.0092	*d*D	= 13.0578	D	*nn*	= 1.0997	*dnn*	= 8.2809	*d*CD	= 6.5309
*e*D	= 11.7886	*e*E	= 11.8726	E	*oo*	= 1.1550	*eoo*	= 7.8994	*e*DE	= 5.8994
*f*E	= 11.0657	*f*F	= 11.1955	F	*pp*	= 1.1796	*fpp*	= 7.7791	*f*EF	= 5.5291
*g*F	= 10.7424	*g*G	= 10.9108	G	*qq*	= 1.2007	*gqq*	= 7.8569	*g*FG	= 5 3569
*b*G	= 10.5917	*b*H	= 10.8023	H	*rr*	= 1.2012	*brr*	= 7.9387	*b*GH	= 5.1887
*i*H	= 10.9460	*i*I	= 11.2015	I	*ss*	= 1.2118	*iss*	= 8.3632	*i*HI	= 5.3632
*k*I	= 11.0478	*k*K	= 11.9385	K	*tt*	= 1.1898	*ktt*	= 8.9881	*k*IK	= 5.7381
*l*K	= 12.0988	*l*L	= 12.4210	L	*vv*	= 1.1838	*lvv*	= 9.2090	*l*KL	= 5.7090
*m*L	= 13.3775	*m*M	= 13.7265	M	*uu*	= 1.1814	*muu*	= 10.0883	*m*LM	= 6.3383
*n*M	= 14.7270	*n*N	= 15.0954	N	*ww*	= 1.1961	*nww*	= 10.8966	*n*MN	= 6.8966
*o*N	= 16.6688	*o*O	= 17.0472	O	*xx*	= 1.1584	*oxx*	= 12.1119	*o*NO	= 7.8619
*p*O	= 18.6297	*p*P	= 19.0135	P	*yy*	= 1.1135	*pyy*	= 13.2031	*p*OP	= 8.7031
*q*P	= 21.0620	*q*Q	= 21.4447	Q	*zz*	= 1.1269	*qzz*	= 14.5810	*q*PQ	= 9.8310
*r*Q	= 23.9248	*r*R	= 24.3056	R	*aa*	= 1.1014	*raa*	= 15.7367	*r*QR	= 10.7367

Model, No. II.

V. Differences between the greater and lesser triangles.	Sections.	Given weights of the sections.	VI. Pressures on the lowest surface of each section.	VII. Angles of the sections.	°	′	″	VIII. Angles of the abutments.	°	′	″	IX. Distances of the vertex from the base of each triangle Ovk.
1.0000	A = a	= 1.00	p = 21.76555	A° =	2	38	0	V^a =	2	38	0	Ok = 22.73807
1.2500	B = b	= 1.25	q = 21.8586[illegible]	B° =	3	16	29	V^b =	5	54	29	bl = 18.70376
1.5000	C = c	= 1.50	r = 22.06356	C° =	3	52	39	V^c =	9	47	8	cm = 16.25288
1.7500	D = d	= 1.75	s = 22.42739	D° =	4	24	36	V^d =	14	11	44	dn = 14.67613
2.0000	E = e	= 2.00	t = 22.99972	E° =	4	50	9	V^e =	19	1	53	eo = 13.68978
2.2500	F = f	= 2.25	v = 23.82853	F° =	5	7	16	V^f =	24	9	9	fp = 13.20226
2.5000	G = g	= 2.50	u = 24.95590	G° =	5	14	41	V^g =	29	23	50	gq = 13.11160
2.7500	H = h	= 2.75	w = 26.41465	H° =	5	12	14	V^h =	34	36	4	hr = 13.23080
3.0000	I = i	= 3.00	x = 28.22645	I° =	5	1	8	V^i =	39	37	12	is = 13.82734
3.2500	K = k	= 3.25	y = 30.40220	K° =	4	43	23	V^k =	44	20	35	kt = 14.77604
3.5000	L = l	= 3.50	z = 32.94376	L° =	4	21	27	V^l =	48	42	2	lv = 15.56949
3.7500	M = m	= 3.75	a = 35.84656	M° =	3	57	33	V^m =	52	39	35	mu = 17.09450
4.0000	N = n	= 4.00	b = 39.10209	N° =	3	33	26	V^n =	56	13	1	nw = 18.74160
4.2500	O = o	= 4.25	c = 42.69992	O° =	3	10	21	V^o =	59	23	22	ox = 20.92166
4.5000	P = p	= 4.50	d = 46.62917	P° =	2	49	0	V^p =	62	12	22	py = 23.18112
4.7500	Q = q	= 4.75	e = 50.87939	Q° =	2	29	42	V^q =	64	42	4	qz = 25.88238
5.0000	R = r	= 5.00	f = 55.44104	R° =	2	12	31	V^r =	66	54	35	ra = 28.57770

From the preceding observations, the following practical rules may be inferred for deducing, in general, the weights of the sections, the pressures on the lowest surfaces thereof, and the weights of the semiarches, from the conditions on which they depend: to give a few examples of each rule, are applied to the Tables subjoined to this Treatise: it appears from page 10, that the weight of any section is equal the product formed by multiplying the weight of the first section, (assumed $= w$) into the cotang. of the first section, × into the sine of the angle of the given section × secant of the angle of the abutment of the preceding section, × secant of the angle of the abutment of the section given: in this manner the weight of the section R in Table No. I. may be found: for w being $= 1$, and the angle of the first section $= 5°$, the cotang. of $5° = 11.430052$, and the angle of the section R $= 5°$, sin. $5° = .0871557$: the angle of the abutment of the section preceding $= V^q = 80°$, and the angle of the abutment of the section given $V^r = 85°$: the result is, that the weight of the section R $= 11.430052 \times .0871557 \times 5.7587705 \times 11.473713 = 65.8171$. By page 10 it also appears, that the pressure upon the lowest surface of any section R is equal to the product which arises from multiplying the weight of the first section × cotang. of the angle of the first section × by the secant of the angle of the abutment of the given section, which makes the pressure on the lowest surface of the section R $= 11.430052 \times 11.473713 = 131.1450$, agreeing with the number entered opposite to the section in the column entitled entire pressures.

Lastly, the sum of the weight of the sections is found to be cotang. $A° = 11.430052 \times$ tang. $85° = 130.6401$, when the weight of the first section is $= 1$, agreeing with the number entered in Table No. I. opposite Sr. By similar rules applied to the several

Tables II, III, IV, V, &c. the results will be found to correspond with those entered in the respective Tables.

In the Table No. IV. the angles of the sections are taken indiscriminately and at hazard; but the rules which have been exemplified above, in the former cases, will be no less applicable to the computation of the numbers in all the Tables. In the Table No. IV. the angle of the section O = 12°, the weight of the section O = 281.4682; to compare this with the rule; the weight ought to be = w × cotang. 5 × sin. 12° × sec. 76 × sec. 88° = 281.4682, as above stated: also by the rule in page 10, the pressure on the lowest surface of O = w × cotang. 5° × sec. 88° = 327.5108, corresponding with the pressure, as stated in Table IV. Also in this Table the angle of the section P = 1°, and the angle of the abutment V^p = 89°, the angle of the abutment of the section O or V^o = 88°, the other notation remaining as before, the weight of the section P = 327.5107, and the pressure on the lowest surface of P = 654.9206, the weight of the semiarch = w × cotang. 5° × tang. 89 = 654.8220, as entered in Table IV. The computations founded on these rules produce results in no case less correct than in the former instances.

In No. VIII. the angle of the first section = 1°, and the angle of the section R^o = 1° 54′ 18″.421; the angle of the abutment of the same section (R) = 26° 18′ 54″.747: from these data, the rule above mentioned gives the weight of the section R = w × cotang. 1° × sin. 1° 54′ 18″.421 × sec. 24° 24′ 36″.316 × sec. 26° 18′ 54″.747 = 2.33333, which is the correct weight of the section R, as entered in Table VIII. To find the weight of the section R in Table IX. according to this rule, the weight of the section R = cotang. 2° 38′ 0″ × sin. 2° 12′ 31″ × sec. 64° 42′ 4″ × sec. 66° 54′ 35″ = 5.00000, as entered in Table IX.

It is needless to multiply examples to the computation of these Tables, the numbers in all cases being equally correct with those in the preceding instances, by which the rules for computing the Tables have been abundantly verified.

Experiment for determining the horizontal Pressure in Model No. 1.

In considering the circular arch as completed, it is difficult, at first view, to ascertain the magnitude of pressure sustained by any of the surfaces on which the sections are supported. Both the theorists and practical architects have differed considerably concerning this point. From the preceding demonstrations, and the ensuing experiment, it appears, that the magnitude of pressure sustained by the vertical plane is to the weight of the first section as the cotang. of 5° is to radius; and the weight of the first section, or w, having been found = .43403 parts of an avoirdupois lb. and the cotang. of 5° being = 11.430052; the result is, that the horizontal force or pressure = .43403 × 11.430052 = 4.961 lbs. avoirdupois, differing very little from 5 lbs. which, in this experiment, counterbalances the horizontal pressure.

A second Experiment on the Model No. 1.

If the brass collar is placed round the section C, so that the line *cd* may pass over the fixed pulley in the direction *cd*, the equilibrium weight in this case being = w × cotang. 5° sec. 15°, or .43403 × 11.430052 = 5.1360 lbs. avoirdupois, being suspended at the extremity of the line, keeps the whole in equilibrio.

Horizontal Force, by Experiment on Model No. 2.

In this experiment all the sections on one side of the vertical line or plane being taken away, and a force = 11 lbs. weight is suspended at the extremity of the line *c d* passing over the pulley

x, in a direction parallel to the horizon; after the Model and centre arch have been adjusted, as in the last experiment, when the centre arch is taken away, the remaining sections will be sustained in equilibrio.

A second Experiment on the Model No. 2.

The brass collar being placed round the section C, and a weight of $12\frac{1}{2}$ lbs. is applied to act on the lowest surface of the section C, when the brass central arch is removed, all the sections in the remaining half of the arch wil be sustained, without further dependance on the brass central arch.

On the Experiments for illustrating the Propositions concerning the Pressures on the lowest Surface of each Section, and against the vertical Surface, in an Arch of Equilibration.

In the Model No. 1, the angle of the first section $A° = 5°$, and it appears from the preceding propositions, that in this case, the horizontal force or shoot, as it is called, $= w \times$ cotang. $5°$, in which expression w is equal the weight of $1\frac{1}{2}$ cubic inches of brass, the specific gravity of brass is to that of water in the proportion of about 8 to 1, and the weight of a cubic inch of water is very nearly $= .57870$ ounces avoirdupois;* it will follow, that the weight of a cubic inch and half of brass will be $.57870 \times 1\frac{1}{2} \times 8 = 6.9444$ ounces, or 0.43402 parts of a pound avoirdupois.—If all the sections on one side of the arch are removed, and a force in a horizontal direction is applied, that is in a direction perpendicular to the vertical surface of the first section, the whole will be kept

* By a decisive experiment of Mr. Cotes it appeared, that the weight of a cubic foot of pure rain water was exactly 1000 ounces avoirdupois; therefore, since the magnitude of a cubic foot $= 1728$ cubic inches, the weight of a cubic inch of rain water $= \frac{1000}{1728} = .57870$ ounces avoirdupois.—Cotes's Hydrostatics, p. 43.

in equilibrio by a force of 5 pounds avoirdupois, consisting of the equilibrium weight, which is 4.961 added to a friction weight, amounting to 0.039, being a weight exactly sufficient to counteract the effects of friction, cohesion, and tenacity.

Experiment for determining the horizontal Force or Pressure in the Model No. 2, *in which the Weight of the first Section* = .43403 *Parts of an avoirdupois lb. and the Angle of the first Section* = 2° 38′.

If half the number of sections on one side of the arch in Model No. 2. are removed, and a force of 11 pounds weight, acting in a direction parallel to the horizon, is applied to sustain the other half of the arch, the whole will be kept in equilibrio by a weight of 9.437 added to a weight of 1.563, making altogether the weight of 11 pounds avoirdupois.

On the general Proportion of the Pressures on the lowest Surface of each Section in the Model No. 1, *expressed in general by* $w \times$ *Cotang.* A° × *Sec.* V^c.

In the case of the pressure on the section C = w × cotang. A° × sec. V^c: here w = 0.43402 pounds; the angle of the abutment = 15°, the secant of which = 1.0352762, and the cotang. of 5° being = 11.430052, the pressure on the lowest surface of the section C = 5.1359, the equilibrium weight, when all the sections below the section C are removed, in the Model No. 1, and the weight of $5\frac{1}{2}$ pounds is applied against the lower surface of C, the friction weight being = 0.3641, when the brass central arch is removed, the whole will be sustained in equilibrio.

Similar Experiment upon the Model No. 2

The weight of w, that is, the weight of the first section in Model No. 2, is the same with the weight of w in Model No 1;

that is, $w = 6.9444$ ounces, $= 0.43402$ pounds avoirdupois; which is the weight of $1\frac{1}{2}$ cubic inch of brass; and, by the rule in page 10, the pressure on the lowest surface of C $= w \times$ cotang. $2° 38' 0'' \times$ sec. $V^c = 9.5762$.* If, therefore, all the sections below C are removed, and a weight of $12\frac{1}{2}$ pounds is applied against the lowest surface of C, when the centre brass arch is taken away, the remaining arch will be sustained in equilibrio.

By a similar experiment, the proper weight $= w \times$ cotang. A° $\times$ sec. V^z applied in a direction against the lower surface of any other section Z, or perpendicular to it, would have the effect of sustaining it in equilibrio.

It has been remarked, in the First Part of this Tract, (page 5.) that if the materials of which an arch is constructed were perfectly hard and rigid, so as not to be liable to any change in their form, and the abutments were removably fixed; an arch, when the sections have been adjusted to equilibration, although little deviating from a right line, would be equally secure, in respect to equilibrium, with a semicircular or any other arch. This observation applies in some degree to the construction of a rectilinear or flat arch, according to a method employed by engineers, for transmitting water through the cavities of the several sections, each of which, when filled with water, will be nearly of the same weight; and for this reason it would be expedient to adopt the plan of construction which is numerically represented in Table VI. or one of the various other plans, in each of which the weights of each section are assumed $= 1$.

Construction of a Rectilinear Arch. Fig. 11.

COC represents a horizontal line, in which the lines OA, AB, BC, &c. are set off at equal distances from each other. From the

* $w = .434027$ cotang. $2° 38' 0'' = 21.742569$ sec. $V^c = 1.014763$ $w \times$ cotang. A° $\times$ $9° 47' 8'' = 9.5762$.

point O, considered as a centre, draw Oa inclined to the line OV, at an angle of 5°: through the point O likewise draw Ob, inclined to OV, at the angle 9° 55′ 30″; also through the point O draw Oc inclined to OV, at an angle = 14° 42′ 23″; and draw through the point Aa parallel to Oa, through B draw Bb parallel to Ob; likewise through C draw Cc parallel to Oc, &c. these lines, representing thin metallic plates, of which the angles are 5°, 4°, 55′ 30″, 4° 46′ 53, &c. respectively; and the sections OV, Aa, Bb, Cc, &c. being formed of dimensions similar and equal to the sections on the other side; that is, VO, aa, forming an angle of 5°; Aa, Bb, 4° 55′ 30″; and Bb, Cc, an angle of 4° 46′ 53″, &c. the whole will constitute a rectilinear arch of equilibration, supporting itself in equilibrio by the help of small assistance from beneath, and admitting the water to pass freely through the cavities of the sections.

The geometrical figures were drawn to a scale equal to the original Model; that is, the radius of Fig. 7. was 11,46281 inches, and the radius of the Model No. 2. = 21.7598 inches; the engraving of these drawings are in proportion to those numbers; that is, Fig. 7. and in the Fig. 8. in the proportion of 1 to 3. It may be added, that the Figure 9. was drawn to a radius = 10 inches, which is engraved in proportion of $\frac{1}{2}$, or to a radius = 5 inches.

The radius = OV (Fig. 8.) in the original drawing is = 21.7598 inches, and OQ is, by Table X. = 9.2368, the difference of these quantities will be 12.5230 in the original drawing, or in the engraved plate, equal to one-third part, which makes the line Vq equal one-third of the tang. of the angle of the abutment, to a radius 12.5230 = 8.831, scarcely differing from the figure in the engraved plate.

Fig. 9. is drawn to a radius of 10 inches, OV in the engraved plate = 5 inches; which makes the line Ok = OV $\frac{\text{sin. } 8^\circ 49' 9''}{\text{sin. } 41^\circ 10' 51''}$ = 1.1642 whence the line Vk is equal to the tang. of 41° 10′ 51″, when the radius 6.1642 = 5.3926, which is nearly the length in inches of the line Vk in the engraved plate.

On the Use of Logarithms, applied to the Computation of the subjoined Tables.

Logarithms are useful in making computations on mathematical subjects, particularly those that require the multiplication or division of quantities, by which the troublesome operations of multiplication and division are performed by corresponding additions and subtractions of logarithms only. By the preceding propositions it appears, that the quantity most frequently occurring in these computations is the weight of the first section, represented by w, and the cotang. of the angle of the first section. In the Table No. I. (Model No. 1.) Fig. 11, the angle of the first section A° = 5°, and in Table No. IX. Model No. 2, Fig. 13, the angle of the first section A° = 2° 38′ 0″; in the two Models which have been described, the weights of the first section in each Model are equal, each being the weight of a cubic inch and half of brass; the specific gravity of brass is to that of rain water in a proportion not very different from that of 8 to 1; sometimes a little exceeding, or sometimes a falling short of that proportion; on an average, therefore, the specific gravity of brass may be taken to that of water as 8 to 1: a cubic foot is equal in capacity 1728 cubic inches, and as a cubic foot of rain water has been found by experiment to weigh 1000 ounces avoirdupois almost exactly, it is evident, that the weight of a cubic inch of brass, of average specific gravity, weighs nearly

8 × .57870 = 4.62960 ounces, therefore $1\frac{1}{2}$ cubic inch of brass, weighs 6.9444 ounces, = .434027 parts of an avoirdupois pound = w;* the logarithm of which, or L. w = 9.6375176.

One of the most troublesome operations in the computation of the Tables subjoined, is to ascertain the weight of a single section, from having given the conditions on which the weight depends, which are as follows: The weight of one of the first or highest sections of the semiarch; the angle of the given section, with the angle of the abutment thereof, together with the angle of the abutment of the section preceding: to exemplify this rule, let it be proposed to find the weight of the section P in an arch of equilibration, in Table No. I. the first section of which = 5°, the angle of the section given = 5°, the angle of the abutment of V^p = 75°, the angle of the abutment preceding or V^o = 70°.

Computation for the weight in avoirdupois lbs.		Computation for L. w.	
Log. w -	= 9.6375176	Log. $\frac{1000}{1728}$	= 9.7624563
L. cotang. 5°	= 1.0580482	L. $\frac{8}{16}$	= 9.6989700
L. sin. 5°	= 8.9402960	L. $\frac{3}{2}$	= 0.1760913
L. sec. 75°	= 0.5870038		
L. sec. 70°	= 0.4659483	L. w	= 9.6375176
L. weight of P	= 0.6888139		
Weight of P	= 4.8844 lbs. avoirdupois.		

* In the Model No. 1. the dimensions of the first section of the semiarch are as follow: the base = 1 inch, the slant heighton either side = .961, and the breadth = 1.084; which makes the area of the first section parallel to the plane of the arch = 1 square inch; this multiplied into the depth or thickness, makes the solid contents of the first section = 1 × 1 × $1\frac{1}{2}$, which is a cubic inch and half a cubic inch.

In Model No. 2. the dimensions in the first section of the semiarch: the base, or the chord of 2° 38′ 0″, to a radius of 21.7598 = 1 inch, the slant height are as follows: the area of the first section parallel to the plane of the arch = 1 square inch; this multiplied into the deprh or thickness, which is $1\frac{1}{2}$ inches, the solid contents of the first section becomes = 1 × 1 × $1\frac{1}{2}$, or the solid contents of the first section = $1\frac{1}{2}$ cubic inches = .9782, and the breadth = 1.0449, which makes the solid contents of the section = $1\frac{1}{2}$ cubic inches, the weight of which = 4.3027 parts of an avoirdupois pound.

By this means, another method of computing the weight of any section P is obtained, by putting the sum of the weights of all the sections from the summit to the section P; that is, the sum of all the weights from A° to P° = *Sp*, and the sum of the weights of all the sections from A to O = *So*, the weight of the section P will be = *Sp* — *So*, for the rule in page 10,

Computation for *Sp*.			Computation for *So*.		
Log. *w*	-	= 9.6375176	Log. *w*	-	= 9.6375176
L. cotang.	5°	= 1.0580482	L. cotang.	5°	= 1.0580482
L. tang.	75°	= 0.5719475	L. tang.	70°	= 0.4389341
L. *Sp* = 1.2675133 *Sp* = 18.514			L. *So* = 1.1344999 *So* = 13.630		

Sp = 18.514
So = 13.630

Sp — *So* = weight of the section P = 4.884, as before determined.

The computations of the dimensions (Fig. 7) of the brass sections in the Model No. 1. are much facilitated by the use of logarithms, particularly in finding the slant height O*t* from the centre O of any section (K,) and the height of the section itself, or S*t* = T*t*.

Computation of the slant Height OT *of the Section* K.

It is first necessary to ascertain the area of the surface OST comprehended between the radii OS, OT, and the chord ST.

Since the radius OS = 11.46281 and the angle SOT = 5°, half SOT = 2° 30′ 0″, the

Sin. of 2° 30′ 0″ or s = 8.6396796	Log. r = 1.0592910
Cos. 2 30 0 or c = 9.9995865	2
L. sc = 8.6392661	L. r^2 = 2.1185820
L. $\frac{1}{sc}$ = 1.3607339	L. sc = 8.6392661

Log. of the area OST, or L. $sc \times r^2$ = 0.7578481

$$\text{The area OST} = 5.72595$$
$$\text{The weight K} = 2.19175$$
$$K + r^2 sc = 7.91770$$
$$\text{L. } \overline{K + r^2 sc} = 0.8985990$$
$$\text{L. } \frac{1}{sc} = 1.3607339$$
$$\text{L. } \frac{K + r^2 sc}{sc} = 2.2593329$$
$$\text{L. } \sqrt{\frac{K + r^2 sc}{sc}} = 1.1296664$$
$$Ot = 13.47928$$
$$\text{Radius OS, or} = r = 11.46281$$
$$\text{Height of the section K} = tt = 2.01647$$

Similar Computation for the Section L.

$$\text{L. } r^2 = 2.1185820$$
$$\text{L. } sc = 8.6392661$$
$$\text{Log. of the area OTV} = 0.7578481$$
$$\text{area OTV} = 5.72595$$
$$L = 2.70196$$
$$L + r^2 sc = 8.42791$$
$$\text{L. } \overline{L + r^2 sc} = 0.9257199$$
$$\text{L. } \frac{1}{sc} = 1.3607339$$
$$\text{L. } \frac{L + r^2 sc}{L\, sc} = 2.2864538$$
$$\text{L. } \sqrt{\frac{L + r^2 sc}{sc}} = 1.1432269$$
$$Ov = 13.90679$$
$$r = 11.46281$$
$$\text{Height of the section L} = vv = 2.44398$$

For the Section M.

$$\text{L. } r^2 = 2.1185820$$
$$\text{L. } sc = 8.6392661$$

$$\text{Log. of the area OVU} = 0.7578481$$
$$\text{area OVU} = 5.72595$$
$$\text{M} = 3.47366$$

$$\text{M} + r^2\, sc = 9.19961$$
$$\text{L. } \overline{\text{M} + r^2\, sc} = 0.9637694$$
$$\text{L. } \frac{1}{sc} = 1.3607339$$

$$\text{L. } \frac{\text{M} + r^2\, sc}{sc} = 2.3245033$$
$$\text{L. } \sqrt{\frac{\text{M} + r^2\, sc}{sc}} = 1.1622516$$
$$\text{O}u = 14.52953$$
$$r = 11.46281$$

$$\text{Height of the section M} = uu = 3.06672$$

Computation of $\sqrt{\frac{2\,w + a\,b \times \sin. \text{L}^\circ}{\sin. \text{L}^\circ}}$.

$$\text{L. } a = 1.0827423$$
$$\text{L. } b = 1.0941566$$
$$\text{L. sin. L}^\circ = 8.8806960$$

$$\text{L. } a\,b \times \sin. \text{L}^\circ = 1.0575949$$
$$a\,b \times \sin. \text{L}^\circ = 11.41812$$
$$2\,w = 7.$$

$$\text{L. } 2\,w + a\,b \times \sin. \text{L}^\circ = 18.41812$$

$$L.\ \overline{2w + ab} \times \sin. L^\circ = 1.2652453$$
$$L.\ \sin. L^\circ = 8.8806960$$

$$L.\ \frac{\overline{2w + ab} \times \sin. L^\circ}{\sin. L^\circ} = 2.3845493$$
$$L.\ \sqrt{\frac{\overline{2w + ab} \times \sin. L^\circ}{\sin. L^\circ}} = 1.1922746$$
$$\sqrt{\frac{\overline{2w + ab} \times \sin. L^\circ}{\sin. L^\circ}} = 15.56949$$

See page 19 and page 29, in which the computation is inserted of the quantity $w = \sqrt{\frac{\overline{2w + ab} \times \sin. R^\circ}{\sin. R^\circ}}$.

Computation for M°.

$$L.\ a = 1.1263101$$
$$L.\ b = 1.1375598$$
$$L.\ \sin. M^\circ = 8.8391355$$

$$L.\ ab \times \sin. M^\circ = 1.1030054$$
$$ab \times \sin. M^\circ = 12.67667$$
$$2w = 7.5$$

$$2w + ab \times \sin. M^\circ = 20.17667$$
$$L.\ \overline{2w + ab} \times \sin. M^\circ = 1.3048496$$
$$L.\ \sin. M^\circ = 8.8391355$$

$$L.\ \frac{\overline{2w + ab} \times \sin. M^\circ}{\sin. M^\circ} = 2.4657141$$
$$L.\ \sqrt{\frac{\overline{2w + ab} \times \sin. M^\circ}{\sin. M^\circ}} = 1.2328570$$
$$\sqrt{\frac{\overline{2w + ab} \times \sin. M^\circ}{\sin. M^\circ}} = 17.0945$$

Breadth of the Section L.

Log. slant height from the centre = 1.1922561
L. 2 = 0.3010300
L. sin. $\frac{1}{2}$ L° = 8.5799524

Log. breadth of L° = 0.0732385
Breadth of L° = 1.1836
Breadth of L in the drawing = 1.1838

2 error.

Breadth of M.

Log. slant height from the centre = 1.2328570
L. 2 = 0.3010300
L. sin. $\frac{1}{2}$ M° = 8.5385170

L. breadth of M° = 0.0724040
Breadth of M° = 1.1814
Breadth of M by the drawing = 1.1814

Explanatory Notes on the Propositions in Pages 13 *and* 14 *in the First Part of this Tract, in which* A° = 5°, B° = 5°, = C° = D°, *&c. according to the Explanation in Page* 12. *The initial Pressure* $= \frac{1}{2 \times \sin. \frac{1}{2} A°}$, *or putting* $w = 1$, *the initial Pressure or* $p = \frac{1}{2} \times$ *cosecant* 2° 30′ 0″.

L. p = 1.0592904
L. cos. A° = 9.9983442

L. p × cos. A° = 1.0576346
p × cos. A° = 11.41917
V^a × sin. 2° 30′ 0″ = .04362

11.46279 = p

L. p = 1.0592904
L. sin. A° = 8.9402960
L. tang. 2° 30′ 0″ = 8.6400931

L. p × sin. A° × tang. 2° 30′ 0″ = 8.6396795
p × sin. A° × tang. 2 30 0 = .04362

It appears from this computation that p × sin. A° × tang. V^a is equal a × sin. V^a, when the weight of the first section, or $a = 1$.

The Weight and Pressure on the lowest Surface of the Section B.

$$\text{L}.p = 1.0592904$$
$$\text{L. cos. B}^\circ = 9.9983442$$

$$\text{L}.p \times \text{cos. B}^\circ = 1.0576346$$
$$p \times \text{cos. B}^\circ = 11.41917$$
$$b \times \text{sin. V}^b = .13153$$

$$11.55070 = q$$
$$\text{L}.p = 1.0592904$$
$$\text{L. sin. B}^\circ = 8.9402960$$
$$\text{L. sec. V}^b = 0.0037314$$

$$\text{L}.p \times \text{sin.B}^\circ \times \text{sec.V}^b = 0.0033178$$
$$p \times \text{sin.B}^\circ \times \text{sec.V}^b = 1.0076$$

$$\text{L}.p = 1.0592904$$
$$\text{L. sin. B}^\circ = 8.9402960$$
$$\text{L. tang. V}^b = 9.1194291$$

$$\text{L}.p \times \text{sin. B}^\circ \times \text{tang.V}^b = 9.1190155$$
$$p \times \text{sin. B}^\circ \times \text{tang.V}^b = .13153$$
$$p \times \text{cos. B}^\circ = 11.41917$$

$$p \times \text{cos. B}^\circ + p \times \text{sin. B}^\circ \times \text{tang.V}^b = 11.55070$$

ERRATA.

Page 5, line 5, *for* cotang. A × sec. A, *read* cotang. A° × sec. A°.
—— 6, — 19, *for* that part of weight, *read* that part of the weight.
—— 10, — 20, *for* $p = w \times$ cotang. A° × sec. *read* $w \times$ cotang. A° × sec. V^b.
—— 14, — 12, *for* area K*ts*, *read* T*tts*.
—— 14, — 17, *for* $x^2 - r^2 sc = k$, *read* $x^2 sc - r^2 sc = k$.
—— 23, — 5, *for* Fig. 9, *read* Fig. 8.
—— 24, — 1, *for* x × cotang. B, *read* y × cotang. B.
—— 24, — 5, *for* x × cotang. B°, *read* z × cotang. B°.
—— 24, — 16, *for* in No. 2, *read* in the Model No. 2.
—— 28, — 9, *for* OI, *read* OV.
—— 28, — 12, *for* the point II, *read* through the points II.
In Table No. IV. in the weight of the section I, *insert* 0.654983.
In Table No. X. *for* OV^2, *read* OV taken at 21.7598.

Table No. I.

Shewing the weights of the several sections or wedges which form an arch of equilibration, when the angle of each section is 5°; and the weight of the highest wedge is assumed = 1. Also shewing the pressures on the lowest surface of each section, considered as an abutment.

The weights of the two first sections A in each semiarch = 1. The lateral or horizontal pressure = p' = 11.430052, Sd = the sum of the four successive weights = A + B + C + D, &c. &c.

Sections.	Angles of Sections.	Angles of the Abutments.		Weights of each Section.	Weights of the Semiarches.	Entire Pressures on the lowest Surface of each Section.
A	5°	V^a	5°	1.00000	Sa = 1.000000	11.47371 = p
B	5	V^b	10	1.01542	Sb = 2.015426	11.60638 = q
C	5	V^c	15	1.04724	Sc = 3.062673	11 83327 = r
D	5	V^d	20	1.09752	Sd = 4.160196	12.16360 = s
E	5	V^e	25	1.16972	Se = 5.329920	12.61165 = t
F	5	V^f	30	1.26922	Sf = 6.599144	13.19829 = v
G	5	V^g	35	1.40427	Sg = 8.003420	13.95351 = u
H	5	V^h	40	1.58754	Sh = 9.590960	14.92087 = w
I	5	V^i	45	1.83910	Si = 11.43006	16.16453 = x
K	5	V^k	50	2.19175	Sk = 13.62181	17.78200 = y
L	5	V^l	55	2.70196	Sl = 16.32377	19.92768 = z
M	5	V^m	60	3.47366	Sm = 19 79743	22.86010 = a
N	5	V^n	65	4.71440	Sn = 24.51183	27.04880 = b
O	5	V^o	70	6.89199	So = 31.40382	33 41923 = c
P	5	V^p	75	11.2537	Sp = 42.65753	44.16234 = d
Q	5	V^q	80	22.1655	Sq = 64.82305	65 82304 = e
R	5	V^r	85	65.8171	Sr = 130.6401	131.1450 = f

TABLE No. II.

In which the angles of the sections are inferred from the given weights thereof, by the rule demonstrated in page 27 of the First Part of this Tract, and proportional to the versed sines of a circle terminated by a horizontal line. The angle of the first section $A^\circ = 5^\circ$, and the initial pressure parallel to the horizon = 11.43005; a the pressure on the lowest surface of the first section = 11.4371.

Sections.	Weights of the sections.	Tang. of the angles of the sections.	Angles of the sections.	Angles of the abutments.	Pressures on the lowest surface of each section.
					Cotang. $A^\circ =$ 11.43005 $= p'$
A $a =$	1.00000	$\frac{a \times \cos. V^o}{p' + a \times \sin. V^o} = \text{tang. } A^\circ$	5° 0′ 0″	$V^a =$ 5° 0′ 0″	$p =$ 11.47371
B $b =$	1.38053	$\frac{b \times \cos. V^a}{p + b \times \sin. V^a} = \text{tang. } B^\circ$	6° 45′ 53″	$V^b =$ 11° 45′ 53″	$q =$ 11.67533
C $c =$	2.51922	$\frac{c \times \cos. V^b}{q + c \times \sin. V^b} = \text{tang. } C^\circ$	11° 26′ 19″	$V^c =$ 23° 12′ 12″	$r =$ 12.43599
D $d =$	4.40742	$\frac{d \times \cos. V^c}{r + d \times \sin. V^c} = \text{tang. } D^\circ$	15° 57′ 5″	$V^d =$ 39° 9′ 17″	$s =$ 14.74004
E $e =$	7.03074	$\frac{e \times \cos. V^d}{s + e \times \sin. V^d} = \text{tang. } E^\circ$	15° 52′ 6″	$V^e =$ 55° 1′ 23″	$t =$ 19.93919
F $f =$	10.36922	$\frac{f \times \cos. V^e}{t + f \times \sin. V^e} = \text{tang. } F^\circ$	11° 48′ 25″	$V^f =$ 66° 49′ 48″	$v =$ 29.05015
G $g =$	14.39746	$\frac{g \times \cos. V^f}{v + g \times \sin. V^f} = \text{tang. } G^\circ$	7° 37′ 48″	$V^g =$ 74° 27′ 36″	$u =$ 42.66403
H $h =$	19.80480	$\frac{h \times \cos. V^g}{u + h \times \sin. V^g} = \text{tang. } H^\circ$	4° 47′ 14″	$V^h =$ 79° 14′ 50″	$w =$ 61.26446
I $i =$	24.39556	$\frac{i \times \cos. V^h}{w + i \times \sin. V^h} = \text{tang. } I^\circ$	3° 3′ 24″	$V^i =$ 82° 18′ 14″	$x =$ 85.35309
K $k =$	30.28932	$\frac{k \times \cos. V^i}{x + k \times \sin. V^i} = \text{tang. } K^\circ$	2° 1′ 5″	$V^k =$ 84° 19′ 19″	$y =$ 115.44084

Table No. III.

In which the angles of the sections are 1°, 2°, 3°, &c. making the angles of the abutments 1°, 3°, 6°, 10°, for inferring the weights of the successive sections and the sums thereof, with the pressures on the lowest surface of each section, as computed from the general rules in page 15, as they are inserted in the 5th, 6th, and 7th columns of this Table.

	Angles of the sections.	Angles between the lowest surface of each section and the vertical, or angles of the abutments		Weights of the successive sections.	Weights of the successive semiarches.	Pressures on the abutments.
A	1°	V^a	1°	1.000000	1.00000	$p = 57.29869$
B	2	V^b	3	2.002440	3.00244	$q = 57.36859$
C	3	V^c	6	3.018978	6.02141	$r = 57.60538$
D	4	V^d	10	4.080347	10.10176	$s = 58.17374$
E	5	V^e	15	5.249031	15.35079	$t = 59.31090$
F	6	V^f	21	6.640753	21.99154	$v = 61.36580$
G	7	V^g	28	8.470050	30.46159	$u = 64.88482$
H	8	V^h	36	11.16197	41.62356	$w = 70.81421$
I	9	V^i	45	15.66635	57.28991	$x = 81.02014$
K	10	V^k	55	24.52854	81.81845	$y = 99.88185$
L	11	V^l	66	46.85674	128.6751	$z = 140.8525$
M	12	V^m	78	140.8525	269.5276	$a = 275.5490$

TABLE No. IV.

In this Table the angle of the first section $A^\circ = 5^\circ$, and the angles B°, C°, D°, &c. are assumed of any given magnitude, taken at hazard $= 6^\circ, 8^\circ, 12^\circ$, &c. making the angles of the abutments $= 5^\circ, 11^\circ, 19^\circ, 31^\circ$, and $p = 11.4737$, &c. The initial pressure $p' = 11{,}43005$.

Sections.	Angles of the sections	Angles contained between the lower surface of each section and the vertical line.	Weights of the sections.	Weights of the semi-arches, found by calculating from the values inserted in page 14 of the Dissertation on Arches.	Entire pressures on the lower surface of each section, considered as an abutment, found by calculations from the values for the pressures inserted in page 14 of the Dissertation on Arches.
A	5°	$V^a = 5^\circ$	$a = 1.000000$	1.00000	$11.47371 = p$
B	6	$V^b = 11$	$b = 1.221776$	2.22177	$11.64392 = q$
C	8	$V^c = 19$	$c = 1.713895$	3.93567	$12.08864 = r$
D	12	$V^d = 31$	$d = 2.932180$	6.86785	$13.33465 = s$
E	10	$V^e = 41$	$e = 3.068117$	9.93596	$15.14492 = t$
F	9	$V^f = 50$	$f = 3.685800$	13.62176	$17.78193 = v$
G	4	$V^g = 54$	$g = 2.110300$	15.73206	$19.44585 = u$
H	2	$V^h = 56$	$h = 1.213626$	16.94569	$20.44014 = w$
I	1	$V^i = 57$	$i = .654983$	17.60067	$20.98633 = x$
K	7	$V^k = 64$	$k = 5.834303$	23.43498	$26.07373 = y$
L	4	$V^l = 68$	$l = 4.855258$	28.29023	$30.51193 = z$
M	3	$V^m = 71$	$m = 4.904875$	33.19511	$35.10776 = a$
N	5	$V^n = 76$	$n = 12.64806$	45.84317	$47.24652 = b$
O	12	$V^o = 88$	$o = 281.4682$	327.3113	$327.5108 = c$
P	1	$V^p = 89$	$p = 327.5107$	654.8220	$654.9206 = d$

Table V.

Shewing the angles of the wedges in an arch of equilibration, in which the weights of the several sections are $= 1$, the angle of the first section $= 15^\circ$; the initial pressure parallel to the horizon $p' = 3.73205$, and the pressure on the lowest surface of the first section $= p = 3.86370$.

Sections.		Weights of the sections.	Tang. of the angles of the sections.	Angles of the sections.	Angles of the abutments.	Pressures on the lowest surface of each section.
A	$a =$	1	$\frac{a \times \cos. V^o}{p' + a \times \sin. V^o} = \text{tang. } A^\circ =$	$15^\circ\ 0'\ 0''$	$V^a = 15^\circ\ 0'\ 0''$	Cosec. $A = p = 3.86370$
B	$b =$	1	$\frac{b \times \cos. V^a}{p + b \times \sin. V^a} = \text{tang. } B^\circ =$	$13^\circ\ 11'\ 12''$	$V^b = 28^\circ\ 11'\ 12''$	$4.234170 = q$
C	$c =$	1	$\frac{c \times \cos. V^b}{q + c \times \sin. V^d} = \text{tang. } C^\circ =$	$10^\circ\ 36'\ 25''$	$V^c = 38^\circ\ 47'\ 37''$	$4.788337 = r$
D	$d =$	1	$\frac{d \times \cos. V^c}{r + d \times \sin. V^d} = \text{tang. } D^\circ =$	$8^\circ\ 11'\ 27''$	$V^d = 46^\circ\ 59'\ 4''$	$5.470659 = s$
E	$e =$	1	$\frac{e \times \cos. V^d}{s + e \times \sin. V^e} = \text{tang. } E^\circ =$	$6^\circ\ 16'\ 38''$	$V^e = 53^\circ\ 15'\ 42''$	$6.239237 = t$
F	$f =$	1	$\frac{f \times \cos V^e}{t + f \times \sin. V^f} = \text{tang. } F^\circ =$	$4^\circ\ 51'\ 22''$	$V^f = 58^\circ\ 7'\ 4''$	$7.065979 = v$
G	$g =$	1	$\frac{g \times \cos. V^f}{v + g \times \sin. V^g} = \text{tang. } G^\circ =$	$3^\circ\ 49'\ 3''$	$V^g = 61^\circ\ 56'\ 7''$	$7.932716 = u$
H	$h =$	1	$\frac{h \times \cos. V^h}{u + h \times \sin. V^h} = \text{tang. } H^\circ =$	$3^\circ\ 3'\ 18''$	$V^h = 64^\circ\ 59'\ 25''$	$8.827677 = w$
I	$i =$	1	$\frac{i \times \cos. V^i}{w + i \times \sin. V^i} = \text{tang. } I^\circ =$	$2^\circ\ 29'\ 53''$	$V^i = 67^\circ\ 28'\ 18''$	$9.743980 = x$

Table No. VI.

Shewing the angles of the several sections, in which the weight of each of the sections = 1, and the angle of the two highest sections = A°; in each semiarch = 5°, the initial horizontal pressure = cotang. 5° = 11.43005; and therefore the pressure on the lowest surface of the first section = cosec. 5° = 11.47371.

Sections.		Weights of the sections.	Tang. of the angles of the sections.	Angles of the sections.	Angles of the abutments.	Pressures on the lowest surface of each section.
A	$a =$	1	$\frac{a \times \cos. V^{o}}{p' + a \times \sin. V^{o}} = \text{tang. } A^{\circ} =$	5° 0′ 0″	$V^{a} =$ 5° 0′ 0″	$p =$ 11.47371
B	$b =$	1	$\frac{b \times \cos. V^{a}}{p + b \times \sin. V^{a}} = \text{tang. } B^{\circ} =$	4° 55′ 30″	$V^{b} =$ 9° 55′ 30″	$q =$ 11.60380
C	$c =$	1	$\frac{c \times \cos. V^{b}}{q + c \times \sin. V^{b}} = \text{tang. } C^{\circ} =$	4° 46′ 53″	$V^{c} =$ 14° 42′ 23″	$r =$ 11.81728
D	$d =$	1	$\frac{d \times \cos. V^{c}}{r + d \times \sin. V^{c}} = \text{tang. } D^{\circ} =$	4° 34′ 52″	$V^{d} =$ 19° 17′ 15″	$s =$ 12.10992
E	$e =$	1	$\frac{e \times \cos. V^{d}}{s + e \times \sin. V^{d}} = \text{tang. } E^{\circ} =$	4° 20′ 20″	$V^{e} =$ 23° 37′ 35″	$t =$ 12.47598
F	$f =$	1	$\frac{f \times \cos. V^{e}}{t + f \times \sin. V^{e}} = \text{tang. } F^{\circ} =$	4° 4′ 11″	$V^{f} =$ 27° 41′ 46″	$v =$ 12.90929
G	$g =$	1	$\frac{g \times \cos. V^{f}}{v + g \times \sin. V^{f}} = \text{tang. } G^{\circ} =$	3° 47′ 16″	$V^{g} =$ 31° 29′ 2″	$u =$ 13 40333
H	$h =$	1	$\frac{h \times \cos. V^{g}}{u + h \times \sin. V^{g}} = \text{tang. } H^{\circ} =$	3° 30′ 15″	$V^{h} =$ 34° 59′ 17″	$w =$ 13.95167
I	$i =$	1	$\frac{i \times \cos. V^{h}}{w + i \times \sin. V^{h}} = \text{tang. } I^{\circ} =$	3° 13′ 42″	$V^{i} =$ 38° 12′ 59″	$x =$ 14 54815
K	$k =$	1	$\frac{k \times \cos. V^{i}}{x + k \times \sin. V^{i}} = \text{tang. } K^{\circ} =$	2° 57′ 52″	$V^{k} =$ 41° 10′ 51″	$y =$ 15.18711
L	$l =$	1	$\frac{l \times \cos. V^{k}}{y + l \times \sin. V^{k}} = \text{tang. } L^{\circ} =$	2° 43′ 10″	$V^{l} =$ 43° 54′ 1″	$z =$ 15.86340

Table No. VII.

Containing the weights in an arch of equilibration, in which the angles of each section are = 2° 30′ 0″, the pressure on the lowest surface of each section; the initial pressure parallel to the horizon = cotang. 2° 30′ = 22.90376 = p'; and the pressure on lowest surface of the first section = cosec. 2° 30′ = 22.92558.

Sections	Angles of the sections.		Angles of the abutments.			Weights of the sections.	Sums of the weights of the sections.	Pressures on the lowest surface of each section.
	°	′		°	′			
A	2	30	$V^a =$	2	30	1.00000	$Sa =$ 1.000000	22.92558 = p
B	2	30	$V^b =$	5	0	1.00382	$Sb =$ 2.003820	22.99125 = q
C	2	30	$V^c =$	7	30	1.01151	$Sc =$ 3.015331	23.10140 = r
D	2	30	$V^d =$	10	0	1.02322	$Sd =$ 4.038552	23.25714 = s
E	2	30	$V^e =$	12	30	1.03909	$Se =$ 5.077642	23.45986 = t
F	2	30	$V^f =$	15	0	1.05940	$Sf =$ 6.137047	23.71172 = v
G	2	30	$V^g =$	17	30	1.09448	$Sg =$ 7.221530	24.01526 = u
H	2	30	$V^h =$	20	0	1.11476	$Sh =$ 8.336290	24.37368 = w
I	2	30	$V^i =$	22	30	1.15076	$Si =$ 9.487050	24.79086 = x
K	2	30	$V^k =$	25	0	1.19315	$Sk =$ 10.68020	25.27151 = y
L	2	30	$V^l =$	27	30	1.24374	$Sl =$ 11.92394	25.82129 = z
M	2	30	$V^m =$	30	0	1.29956	$Sm =$ 13.22350	26.44699 = a
N	2	30	$V^n =$	32	30	1.36780	$Sn =$ 14.59130	27.15674 = b
O	2	30	$V^o =$	35	0	1.44608	$So =$ 16.03738	27.96033 = c
P	2	30	$V^p =$	37	30	1.53730	$Sp =$ 17.57468	28.86956 = d
Q	2	30	$V^q =$	40	0	1.64386	$Sq =$ 19.21854	29.89874 = e
R	2	30	$V^r =$	42	30	1.76889	$Sr =$ 20.98743	31.06533 = f
S	2	30	$V^s =$	45	0	1.91634	$Ss =$ 22.90377	32.39081 = g
T	2	30	$V^t =$	47	30	2.09130	$St =$ 24.99507	33.90187 = h
V	2	30	$V^v =$	50	0	2.30058	$Sv =$ 27.29565	35.63193 = i
U	2	30	$V^u =$	52	30	2.55312	$Su =$ 29.84877	37.62355 = k
W	2	30	$V^w =$	55	0	2.85112	$Sw =$ 32.70989	39.93149 = l
X	2	30	$V^x =$	57	30	3.25182	$Sx =$ 35.95171	42.62755 = m
Y	2	30	$V^y =$	60	0	3.71877	$Sy =$ 39.67048	45.80753 = n
Z	2	30	$V^z =$	62	30	4.32724	$Sz =$ 43.99772	49.60224 = o
A	2	30	$V^a =$	65	0	5.11958	$Sa =$ 49.11730	54.19492 = p
B	2	30	$V^b =$	67	30	6.17727	$Sb =$ 55.29457	59.85041 = q
C	2	30	$V^c =$	70	0	7.63300	$Sc =$ 62.92757	66.96511 = r
D	2	30	$V^d =$	72	30	9.71389	$Sd =$ 72.64146	74.11813 = s
E	2	30	$V^e =$	75	0	12.83654	$Se =$ 85.47800	88.49336 = t

TABLE No. VIII.

Shewing the angles of fifty sections, forming an arch of equilibration, calculated from given weights of the sections when the angle of the first section is one degree $= A^\circ$; and the weight thereof is denoted by unity; the weights of the successive sections encreasing by equal differences from 1 to 3, which is the weight of the twenty-fifth section $= Z$ in each semiarch. The initial pressure parallel to the horizon $p' =$ cotang. $A^\circ = 57.28996$: the pressure on the lowest surface of the first section is $= p = 57.29868 =$ cosecant A°.

Sections.		Weights of the sections.	Tang. of the angles of the sections.	Angles of the sections.	Angles of the abutments.	Pressures on the lowest surface of each section.
A	$a =$	1.000000	$\frac{a \times \cos. V^o}{p' + a \times \sin. V^o} = \text{tang. } A^\circ =$	$1^\circ\ 0'\ 0''$	$V^a = 1^\circ\ 0'\ 0''$	$p = 57.29868$
B	$b =$	1.083333	$\frac{b \times \cos. V^a}{p + b \times \sin. V^a} = \text{tang. } B^\circ =$	$1^\circ\ 4'\ 57'',457$	$V^b = 2^\circ\ 4'\ 57'',457$	$q = 57.32782$
C	$c =$	1.166666	$\frac{c \times \cos. V^b}{q + c \times \sin. V^b} = \text{tang. } C^\circ =$	$1^\circ\ 9'\ 51'',204$	$V^c = 3^\circ\ 14'\ 48'',661$	$r = 57.38205$
D	$d =$	1.250000	$\frac{d \times \cos. V^c}{r + d \times \sin. V^c} = \text{tang. } D^\circ =$	$1^\circ\ 14'\ 39'',795$	$V^d = 4^\circ\ 29'\ 28'',456$	$s = 57.46639$
E	$e =$	1.333333	$\frac{e \times \cos. V^d}{s + e \times \sin. V^d} = \text{tang. } E^\circ =$	$1^\circ\ 19'\ 21'',558$	$V^e = 5^\circ\ 48'\ 50'',014$	$t = 57.58614$
F	$f =$	1.416666	$\frac{f \times \cos. V^e}{t + f \times \sin. V^e} = \text{tang. } F^\circ =$	$1^\circ\ 23'\ 54'',634$	$V^f = 7^\circ\ 12'\ 44'',648$	$v = 57.74684$
G	$g =$	1.500000	$\frac{g \times \cos. V^f}{v + g \times \sin. V^f} = \text{tang. } G^\circ =$	$1^\circ\ 28'\ 16'',987$	$V^g = 8^\circ\ 41^\circ\ 1'',638$	$u = 57.95427$
H	$b =$	1.583333	$\frac{h \times \cos. V^g}{u + h \times \sin. V^g} = \text{tang. } H^\circ =$	$1^\circ\ 32'\ 26'',417$	$V^h = 10^\circ\ 13'\ 28'',055$	$w = 58.21435$
I	$i =$	1.666666	$\frac{i \times \cos. V^h}{w + i \times \sin. V^h} = \text{tang. } I^\circ =$	$1^\circ\ 36'\ 20'',646$	$V^i = 11^\circ\ 49'\ 48'',701$	$x = 58.53326$
K	$k =$	1.750000	$\frac{k \times \cos. V^i}{x + k \times \sin V^i} = \text{tang. } K^\circ =$	$1^\circ\ 39'\ 57'',365$	$V^k = 13^\circ\ 29'\ 46'',066$	$y = 58.91692$
L	$l =$	1.833333	$\frac{l \times \cos. V^k}{y + l \times \sin. V^k} = \text{tang. } L^\circ =$	$1^\circ\ 43'\ 14'',297$	$V^l = 15^\circ\ 13'\ 0'',363$	$z = 59.37154$
M	$m =$	1.916666	$\frac{m \times \cos. V^l}{z + m \times \cos. V^l} = \text{tang. } M^\circ =$	$1^\circ\ 46'\ 9'',294$	$V^m = 16^\circ\ 59'\ 9'',667$	$a = 59.90315$
N	$n =$	2.000000	$\frac{n \times \cos. V^m}{a + n \times \sin. V^m} = \text{tang. } N^\circ =$	$1^\circ\ 48'\ 40'',404$	$V^n = 18^\circ\ 47'\ 50'',071$	$b = 60.51760$
O	$o =$	2.083333	$\frac{o \times \cos. V^n}{b + o \times \sin. V^n} = \text{tang. } O^\circ =$	$1^\circ\ 50'\ 45'',954$	$V^o = 20^\circ\ 38'\ 36'',071$	$c = 61.22067$
P	$p =$	2.166666	$\frac{p \times \cos\ V^o}{c + p \times \sin. V^o} = \text{tang. } P^\circ =$	$1^\circ\ 52'\ 24'',611$	$V^p = 22^\circ\ 31'\ 0'',715$	$d = 62.01767$
Q	$q =$	2.250000	$\frac{q \times \cos. V^p}{d + q \times \sin. V^p} = \text{tang. } Q^\circ =$	$1^\circ\ 53'\ 35'',611$	$V^q = 24^\circ\ 24'\ 36'',326$	$e = 62.91365$
R	$r =$	2.333333	$\frac{r \times \cos. V^q}{e + r \times \sin. V^q} = \text{tang. } R^\circ =$	$1^\circ\ 54'\ 18'',421$	$V^r = 26^\circ\ 18'\ 54'',747$	$f = 63.91325$
S	$s =$	2.416666	$\frac{s \times \cos. V^r}{f + s \times \sin. V^r} = \text{tang. } S^\circ =$	$1^\circ\ 54'\ 33'',186$	$V^s = 28^\circ\ 13'\ 27'',933$	$g = 65.02070$
T	$t =$	2.500000	$\frac{t \times \cos. V^s}{g + t \times \sin. V^s} = \text{tang. } T^\circ =$	$1^\circ\ 54'\ 20'',477$	$V^t = 30^\circ\ 7'\ 48'',410$	$b = 66.23967$
U	$u =$	2.583333	$\frac{u \times \cos. V^t}{h + u \times \sin. V^t} = \text{tang. } U^\circ =$	$1^\circ\ 53'\ 41'',334$	$V^u = 32^\circ\ 1'\ 29'',744$	$i = 67.57337$
V	$v =$	2.666666	$\frac{v \times \cos. V^u}{i + v \times \sin. V^u} = \text{tang. } V^\circ =$	$1^\circ\ 52'\ 37'',272$	$V^v = 33^\circ\ 54'\ 7'',016$	$k = 69.02449$
W	$w =$	2.750000	$\frac{w \times \cos. V^v}{k + w + \sin. V^v} = \text{tang. } W^\circ =$	$1^\circ\ 51'\ 10'',121$	$V^w = 34^\circ\ 45'\ 17'',137$	$l = 70.59525$
X	$x =$	2.833333	$\frac{x \times \cos. V^w}{l + x \times \sin. V^w} = \text{tang. } X^\circ =$	$1^\circ\ 49'\ 22'',000$	$V^x = 37^\circ\ 34'\ 39'',137$	$m = 72.28737$
Y	$y =$	2.916666	$\frac{y \times \cos. V^x}{m + y \times \sin. V^x} = \text{tang. } Y^\circ =$	$1^\circ\ 47'\ 15'',273$	$V^y = 39^\circ\ 21'\ 54'',410$	$n = 74.10210$
Z	$z =$	3.000000	$\frac{z \times \cos. V^y}{\bullet + z \times \sin. V^y} = \text{tang. } Z^\circ =$	$1^\circ\ 44'\ 52'',429$	$V^z = 41^\circ\ 6'\ 46'',839$	$o = 76.04024$

Table No. IX.

Containing the angles of thirty-four sections or wedges, constituting the model of an arch, No. 2, the weights of which increase regularly in each semiarch, from 1, which is assumed as the weight of the first section, to 5, which is the weight of the lowest or seventeenth section from the summit: the angle of the first section A° = 2° 38′ 0″, and B, C, D, &c. are inferred by the rule in page 15, from the weights of the said sections. The initial pressure parallel to the horizon = cotang. 2° 38′ = 21.7425 = p': the pressure upon the lowest surface of the section A, cosecant A° = 21.76555 = p.

Sections.	Weights of the sections.	Tang. of the angles of the sections.	Angles of the sections.	Angles of the abutments.	Pressures on the lowest surface of each section.
A $a =$	1.00	$\frac{a \times \cos. V^o}{p' + a \times \sin. V^a} =$ tang. A° =	2° 38′ 0′,	$V^a =$ 2° 38′ 0″	$p =$ 21.76555
B $b =$	1.25	$\frac{b \times \cos. V^a}{p + b \times \sin. V^a} =$ tang. B° =	3° 16′ 29″	$V^b =$ 5° 54′ 29″	$q =$ 21.85867
C $c =$	1.50	$\frac{c \times \cos. V^b}{q + c \times \sin. V^b} =$ tang. C° =	3° 52′ 39″	$V^c =$ 9° 47′ 8″	$r =$ 22.06356
D $d =$	1.75	$\frac{d \times \cos. V^c}{r + d \times \sin. V^c} =$ tang. D° =	4° 24′ 36″	$V^d =$ 14° 11′ 44″	$s =$ 22.42739
E $e =$	2.00	$\frac{e \times \cos. V^d}{s + e \times \sin. V^d} =$ tang. E° =	4° 50′ 9″	$V^e =$ 19° 1′ 53″	$t =$ 22.99972
F $f =$	2.25	$\frac{f \times \cos. V^e}{t + f \times \sin. V^e} =$ tang. F° =	5° 7′ 16″	$V^f =$ 24° 9′ 9″	$v =$ 23 82853
G $g =$	2.50	$\frac{g \times \cos. V^f}{v + g \times \sin. V^f} =$ tang. G° =	5° 14′ 41″	$V^g =$ 29° 23′ 50″	$u =$ 24.95590
H $h =$	2.75	$\frac{h \times \cos. V^g}{u + h \times \sin. V^g} =$ tang. H° =	5° 12′ 14″	$V^h =$ 34° 36′ 4″	$w =$ 26.41465
I $i =$	3.00	$\frac{i \times \cos. V^h}{w + i \times \sin. V^h} =$ tang. I° =	5° 1′ 8″	$V^i =$ 39° 37′ 12″	$x =$ 28.22645
K $k =$	3.25	$\frac{k \times \cos. V^i}{x + k \times \sin. V^i} =$ tang. K° =	4° 43′ 23″	$V^k =$ 44° 20′ 35″	$y =$ 30.40220
L $l =$	3.50	$\frac{l \times \cos. V^k}{y + l \times \sin. V^k} =$ tang. L° =	4° 21′ 27″	$V^l =$ 48° 42′ 2″	$z =$ 32.94376
M $m =$	3.75	$\frac{m \times \cos. V^l}{z + m \times \sin. V^l} =$ tang. M° =	3° 57′ 33″	$V^m =$ 52° 39′ 35″	$a =$ 35.84656
N $n =$	4.00	$\frac{n \times \cos. V^m}{a + n \times \sin. V^m} =$ tang. N° =	3° 33′ 26″	$V^n =$ 56° 13′ 1″	$b =$ 39.10209
O $o =$	4.25	$\frac{o \times \cos. V^n}{b + o \times \sin. V^n} =$ tang. O° =	3° 10′ 21″	$V^o =$ 59° 23′ 22″	$c =$ 42.69992
P $p =$	4.50	$\frac{p \times \cos. V^o}{c + p \times \sin. V^o} =$ tang. P° =	2° 49′ 0″	$V^p =$ 62° 12′ 22″	$d =$ 46.62917
Q $q =$	4.75	$\frac{q \times \cos. V^p}{q + d \times \sin. V^p} =$ tang. Q° =	2° 29′ 42″	$V^q =$ 64° 42′ 4″	$e =$ 50.87939
R $r =$	5.00	$\frac{r \times \cos. V^q}{r + e \times \sin. V^q} =$ tang. R° =	2° 12′ 31″	$V^r =$ 66° 54′ 35″	$f =$ 55.44104

Table No. X.

Shewing the method of determining the points in the vertical line OV, from which lines being drawn to the several points B, C, D, E, &c. will determine the positions of the abutments on which the said sections are sustained: when the angle of the first section A° is assumed = 2° 38′, and the angles of the sections B°, C°, D°, &c. are inferred from the weights thereof. The distances OA, OB, OC, &c. being negative, shew that the numbers corresponding are to be subtracted from the radius OV.

	A	B	C	D	E	F	G
Angles of the abutments Angles at the centre	2° 38′ 0″ 2° 38′ 0″	5° 54′ 29″ 5° 16′ 0″	9° 47′ 8″ 7° 54′ 0″	14° 11′ 44″ 10° 32′ 0″	19° 1′ 53″ 13° 10′ 0″	24° 9′ 9″ 15° 48′ 0″	29° 23′ 50″ 18° 26′ 0″
Differences of the angles	0° 0′ 0″	0° 38′ 29″	1° 53′ 8″	3° 39′ 44″	5° 51′ 53″	8° 21′ 9′	10° 57′ 50″
Log. radius = 21.7598 inches Log. sin. differences of angles Log. cosec. of the angles of the abutments		1.3376550 8.0189897 0 9874480	1.3376550 8 5172383 0.7696505	1.3376550 8.8053263 0.6104225	1.3376550 9.0093662 0 4866677	1.3376550 9.1621545 0.3880997	1.3376550 9.2791883 0.3090410
Log. distances from the centre Distances from the centre	OA = − 0.0000	0.3740927 OB = − 2.3664	0.6245438 OC = − 4.2125	0.7534038 OD = − 5.6676	0.8336889 OE = − 6.8183	0.8879092 OF = − 7.7252	0.9258843 OG = − 8.4311

	H	I	K	L	M	N
Angles of the abutment Angles at the centre	34° 36′ 4″ 21° 4′ 0″	39° 37′ 12″ 23° 42′ 0″	44° 20′ 35″ 26° 20′ 0″	48° 42′ 2″ 28° 58′ 0″	52° 39′ 35″ 31° 36′ 0″	56° 13′ 1″ 34° 14′ 0″
Differences of the angles	13° 32′ 4″	15° 55′ 12″	18° 0′ 35″	19° 44′ 2″	21° 03′ 35″	21° 59′ 1″
Log. radius Log. sin differences of angles Log. cosec. of the angles of the abutments	1.3376550 9.3692713 0.2457589	1.3376550 9.4382178 0.1953884	1.3376550 9.4892091 0.1554521	1.3376550 9.5284694 0.1242034	1.3376550 9.5555066 0.09[illegible]6070	1.3376550 9.5732678 0.0803211
Log. distances from the centre Distances from the centre	0 9526852 OH = − 8.9677	0.9712612 OI = − 9.3597	0 9824162 OK = − 9.6032	0.9903278 OL = − 9.7797	0.9927686 OM = − 9.8348	0.9012439 ON = − 9.8084

	O	P	Q	R
Angles of the abutments Angles at the centre	59° 23′ 22″ 36° 52′ 0″	62° 12′ 22″ 39° 30′ 0″	64° 42′ 4″ 42° 8′ 0″	66° 54′ 35″ 44° 46′ 0″
Differences of the angles	22° 31′ 22″	22° 42′ 22″	22° 34′ 4″	22° 8′ 35″
Log. radius Log. sin. differences of angles Log. cosec. of the angles of the abutments	1.3376550 9.5832[illegible]62 0.0651743	1.3376550 9.5865923 0.0532380	1.3376550 9.584[illegible]779 0.0437879	1.3376550 9.5762497 0 0362650
Log distances from the centre Distances from the centre	0.9860855 OO = − 9.6847	0.9774853 OP = − 9.4948	0 9655208 OQ = − 9.2368	0.9501697 OR = − 8.9160

Table No. XI.

Shewing the method of determining the points in the line OV, taken = 10 inches; from which, lines being drawn to the several points B, C, D, &c. will determine the position of the abutments on which the said sections are sustained when the angle of the first section A is assumed = 5°, and the angles of the sections B°, C°, D°, &c. are inferred from the weights thereof, assumed = A = B = C = D, &c. = 1, as stated in Table VI.

		A	B	C	D	E	F
Angles at the centre	−	5° 0′ 0″	10° 0′ 0″	15° 0′ 0″	20° 0′ 0″	25° 0′ 0″	30° 0′ 0″
Angles of the abutments	+	5° 0′ 0″	9° 55′ 30″	14° 42′ 23″	19° 17′ 15″	23° 37′ 35″	27° 41′ 46″
Difference of the angles	∓	0° 0′ 0″	0° 4′ 30″	0° 17′ 37″	0° 42′ 45″	1° 22′ 25″	2° 18′ 14″
Log. 10 inches	=	- - -	1.0000000	1.	1.	1.	1.
Log. sin. differences of the angles	=	- - -	7.1169385	7.7096480	8.0946510	8.3796996	8.6042219
Log. cosec. angles of the abutments		- - -	0.7635662	0.5953958	0.4810803	0.3971037	0.3327507
Log. distance from the centre		- - -	8.8805047	9.3050438	9.5757313	9.7768033	9.9369726
Distances from the centre O	=	- - -	OB = ∓ .075946	OC = ∓ .20185	OD = ∓ .37647	OE = ∓ .59814	OF = ∓ .86491
Radius added to the distances from O		- - -	10.075946	10.20185	10.37647	10.59814	10.86491
Log. distances from the centre		- - -	1.00328	1.00868	1.01603	1.02522	1.03602
Log. tang. of the angles of the abutments		- - -	9.24298	9.41907	9.54400	9.64091	9.72009
Log. tang. of the angle of the abutments to radius 10		- - -	0.24626	0.42775	0.56003	0.66613	0.75611
Tang. of the angle of the abutments to radius 10		- - -	Inches ∓ 1.7630	∓ 2.6776	∓ 3.6311	∓ 4.6359	∓ 5.7032

			G	H	I	K	L
Angles at the centre	−	- - -	35° 0′ 0″	40° 0′ 0″	45° 0′ 0″	50° 0′ 0″	55° 0′ 0″
Angles of the abutments	+	- - -	31° 29′ 2″	34° 59′ 17″	38° 12′ 59″	41° 10′ 51″	43° 54′ 1″
Difference of the angles	∓	- - -	3° 30′ 58″	5° 0′ 43″	6° 47′ 1″	8° 49′ 9″	11° 5′ 59″
Log. 10 inches	=	- - -	1.	1.	1.0000000	1.	1.
Log. sin. differences of the angles	=	- - -	8.7876673	8.9413296	9.0723232	9.1855886	9.2834696
Log. cosec. angles of the abutments		- - -	0.2821142	0.2415380	0.2085668	0.1814853	0.1590128
Log. distance from the centre		- - -	0.0697815	0.1828676	0.2808900	0.3670739	0.4424824
Distances from the centre O	=	- - -	OG = ∓ 1.1743	OH = ∓ 1.5235	OI = ∓ 1.9093	OK = ∓ 2.3285	OL = ∓ 2.7700
Radius added to the distances from O		- - -	11.1743	11.5235	11.9093	12.3285	12.7700
Log. distances from the centre		- - -	1.04821	1.06156	1.07587	1.09089	1.10619
Log. tang. of the angles of the abutments		- - -	9.78704	9.84503	9.89618	9.94193	9.98332
Log. tang. of the angle of the abutments to radius 10		- - -	0.83525	0.90659	0.97205	1.03282	1.08951
Tang. of the abutments to radius 10		- - -	Inches ∓ 6.8432	∓ 8.0649	∓ 9.3769	∓ 10.785	∓ 12.289

When the angle of the abutment is greater than the angle at the centre, the upper sign prevails, as in Fig. 8; but when the angle at the abutment is less than the angle of the centre, the lower sign prevails, as in Fig. 9.

Plate I.

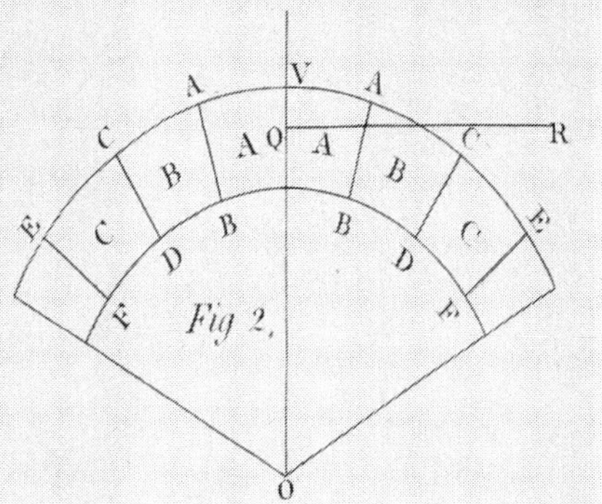

Fig 2.

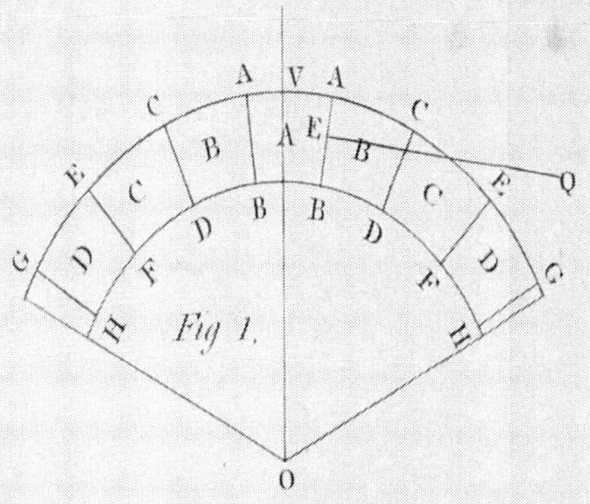

Fig 1.

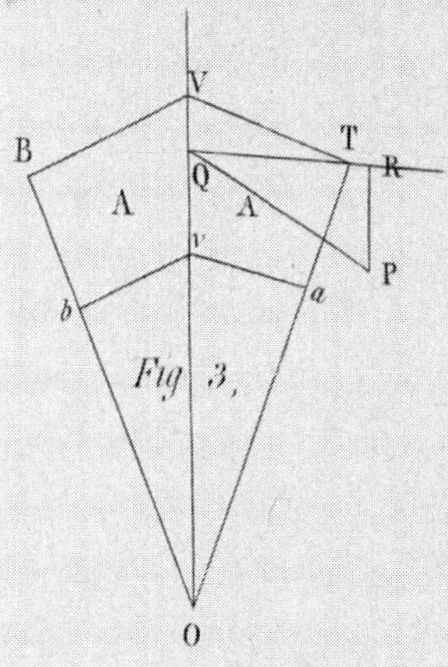

Fig 3.

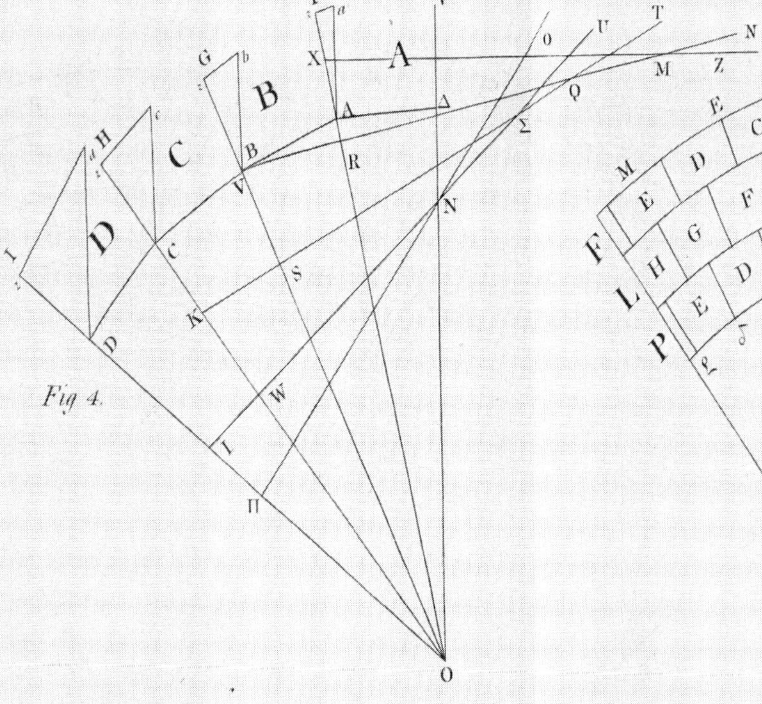

Fig 4.

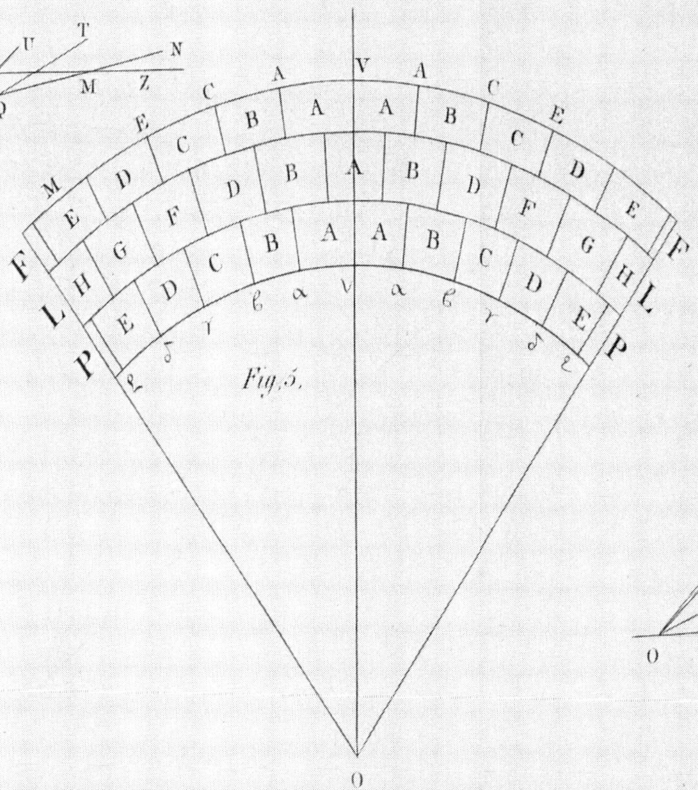

Fig. 5.

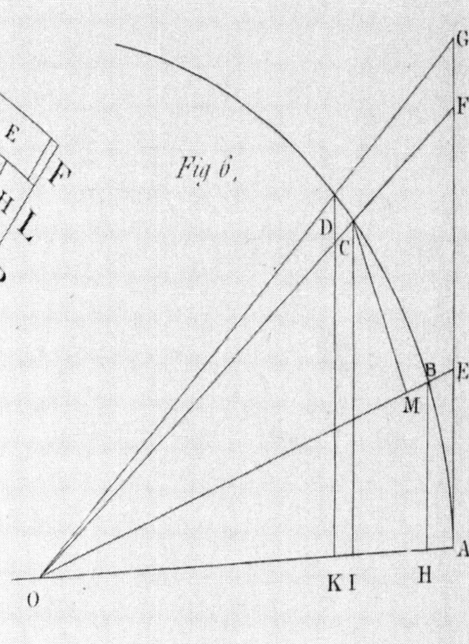

Fig 6.

Plate II.

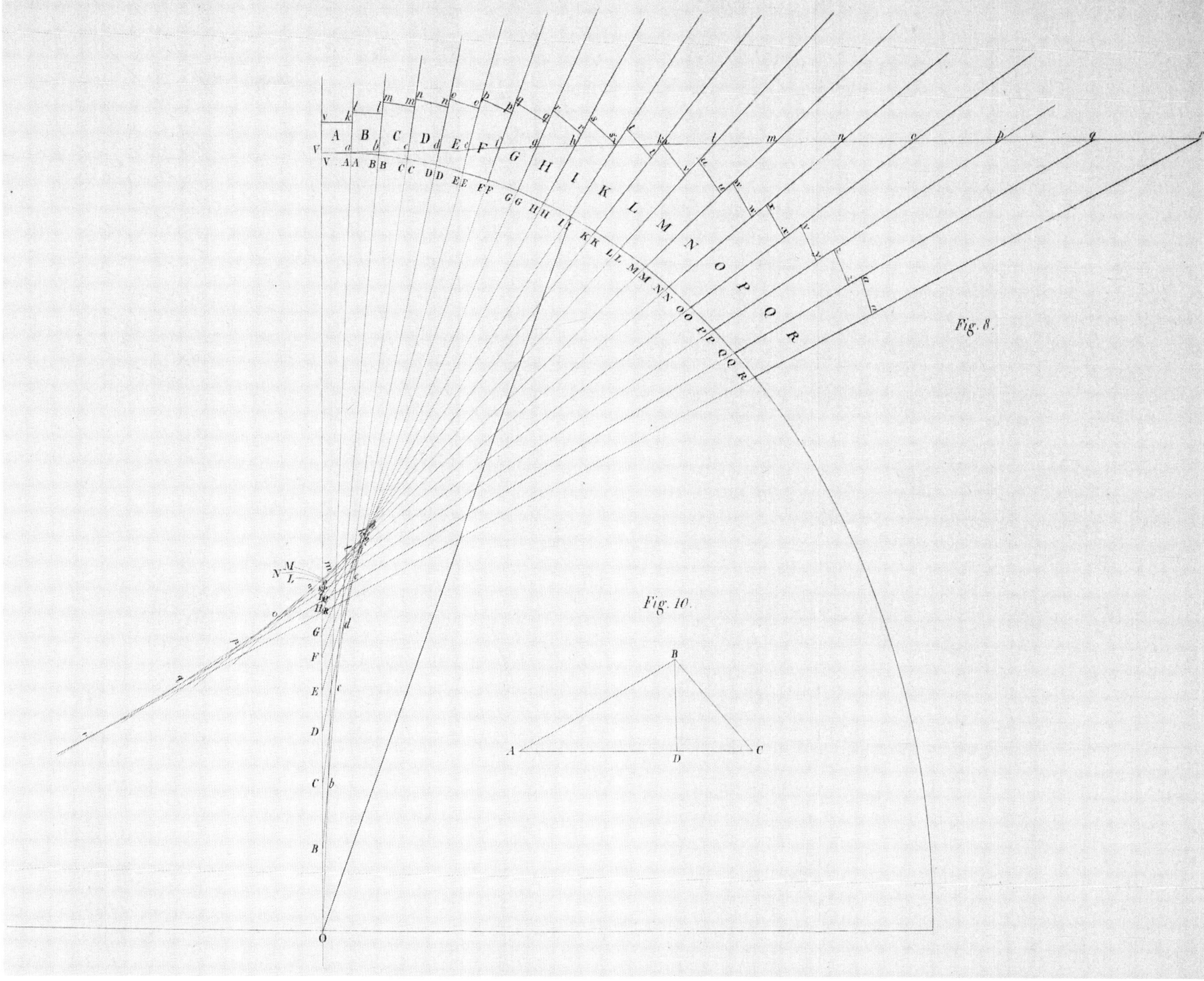

Fig. 8.

Fig. 10.

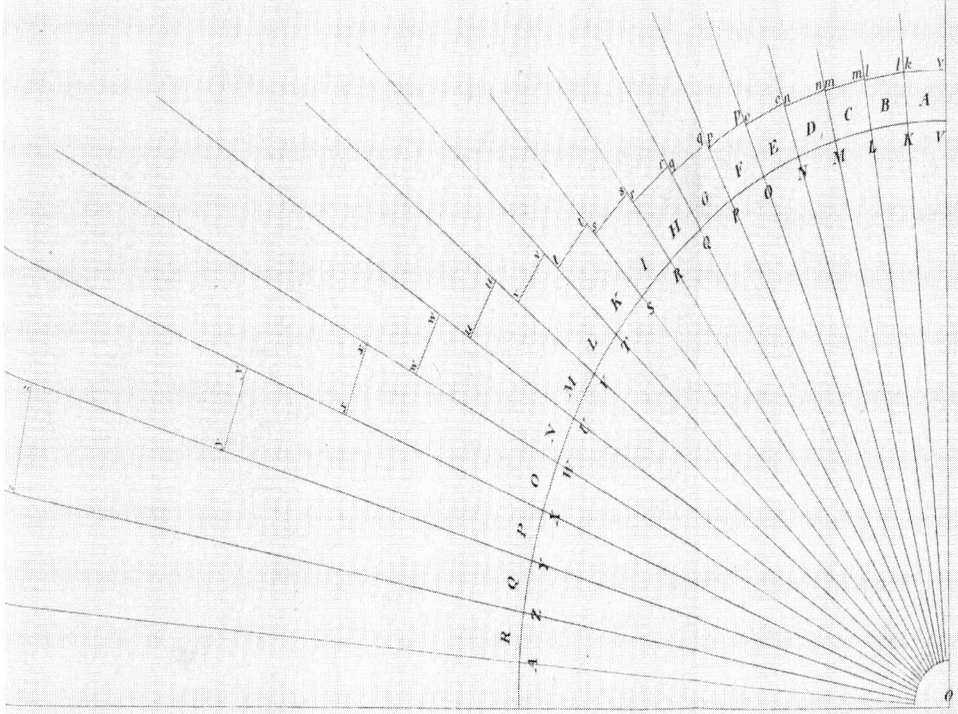

Fig. 7.

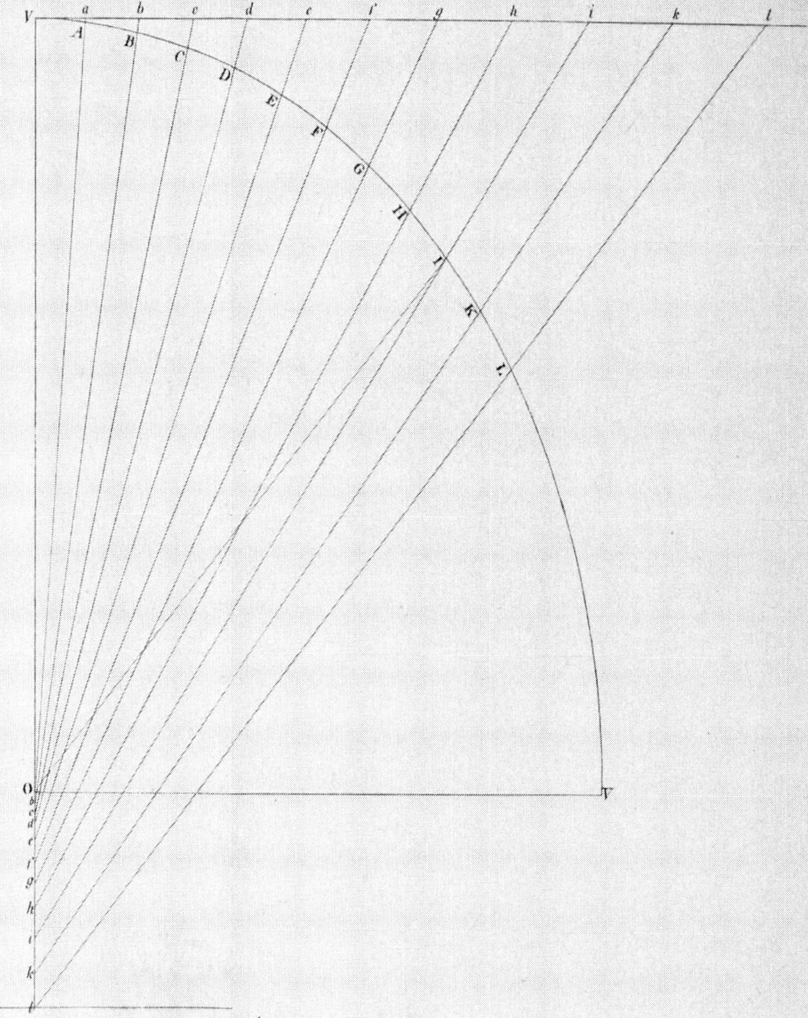

Fig. 9.

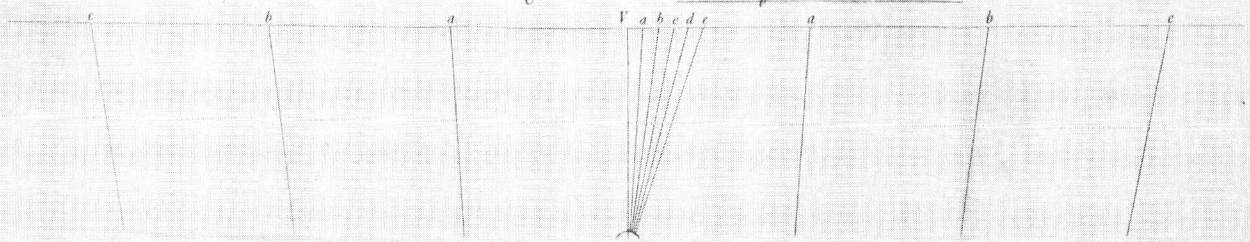

Fig. 11.

Plate IV.

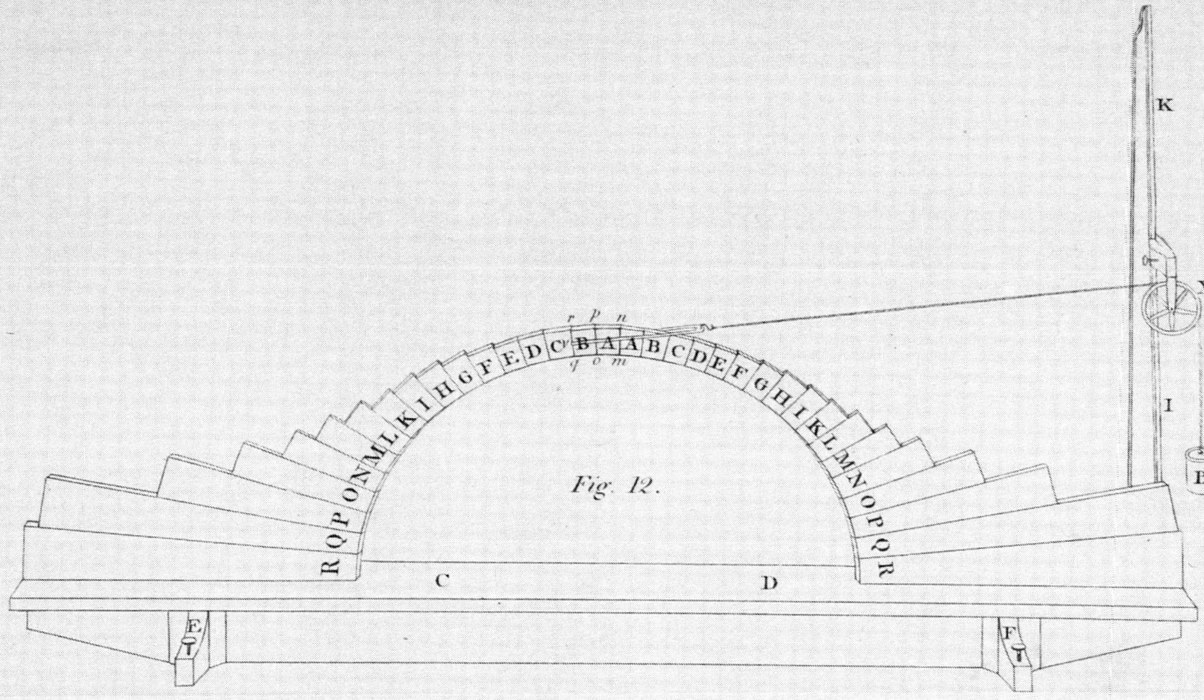

Fig. 12.

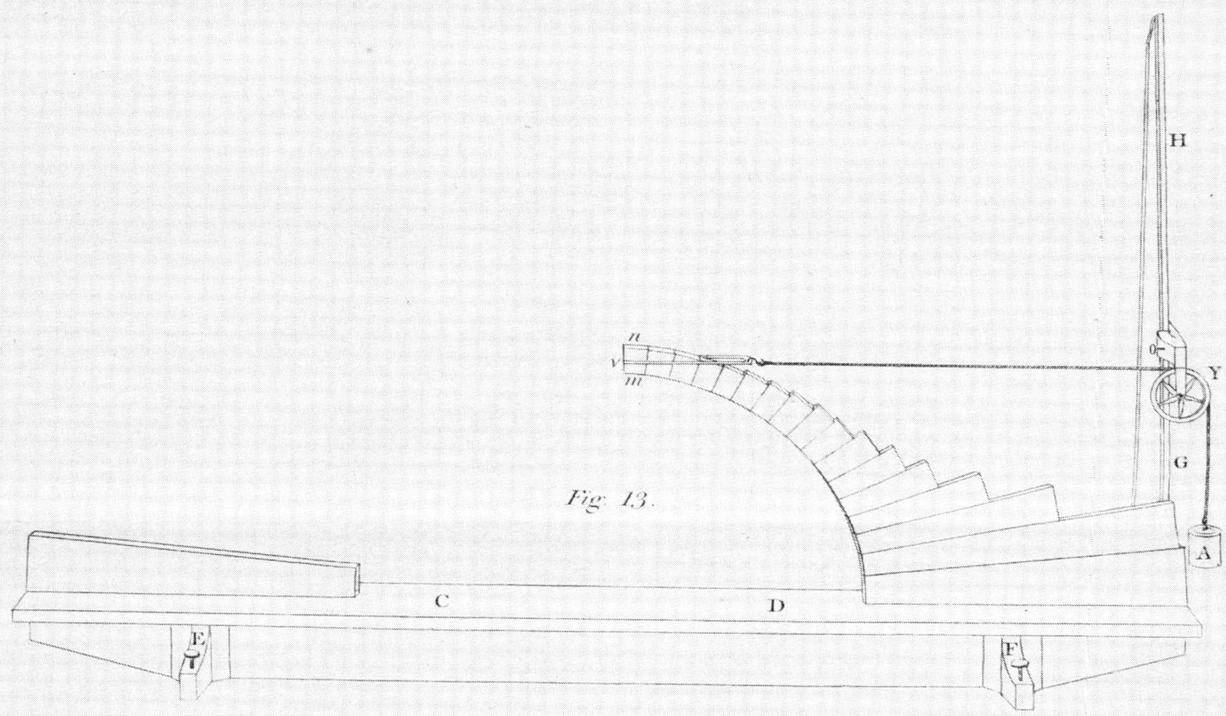

Fig. 13.

Plate V.

Fig. 14.

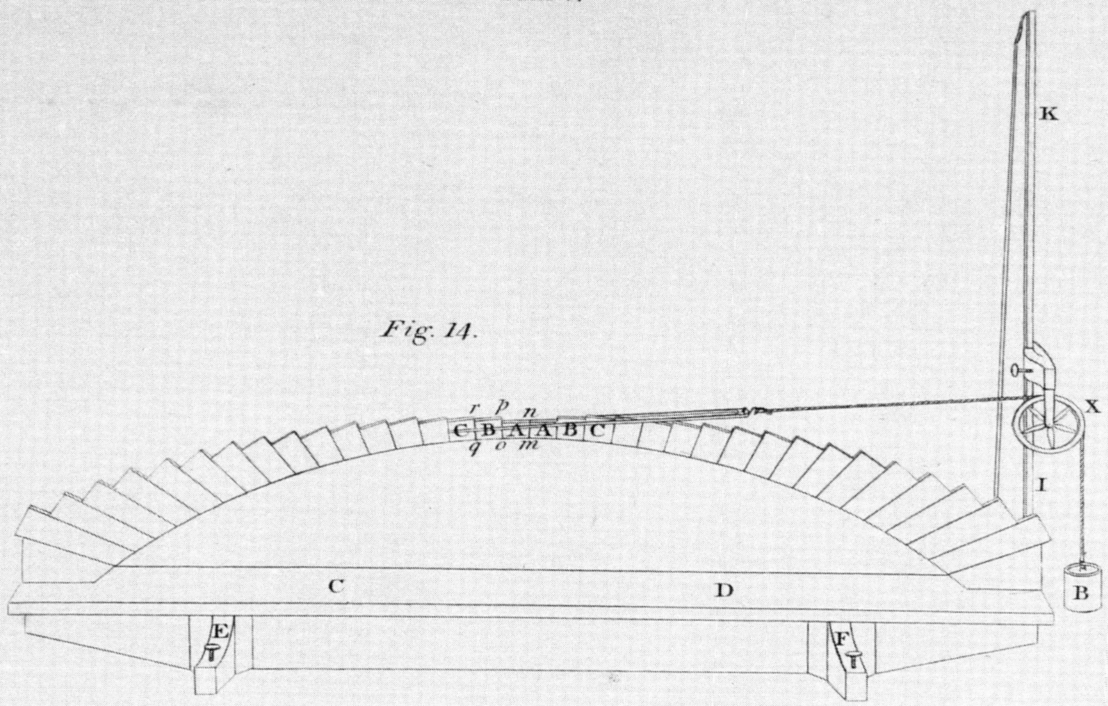

Fig. 15.

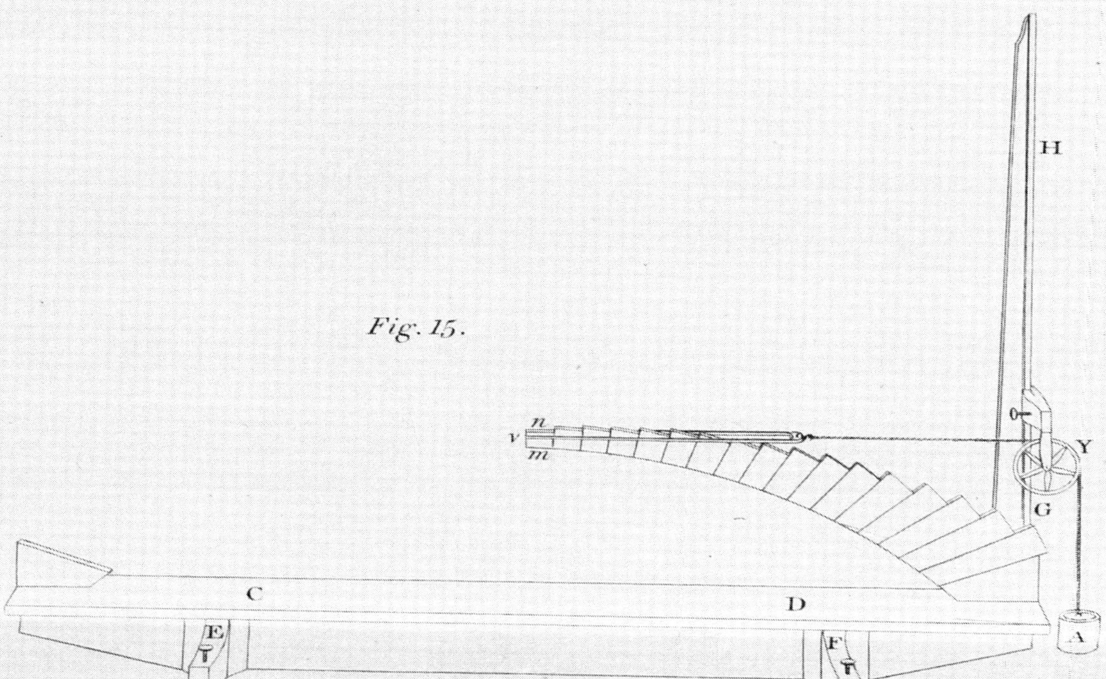

NOUVELLE MÉTHODE

POUR LA RÉSOLUTION

DES ÉQUATIONS NUMÉRIQUES

D'UN DEGRÉ QUELCONQUE.

NOUVELLE MÉTHODE

POUR LA RÉSOLUTION

DES ÉQUATIONS NUMÉRIQUES

D'UN DEGRÉ QUELCONQUE;

D'après laquelle tout le calcul exigé pour cette Résolution se réduit à l'emploi des deux premières règles de l'Arithmétique :

PAR F. D. BUDAN, D. M. P.

« On peut regarder ce point comme le plus important de toute l'Analyse......
» Il conviendroit de donner dans l'Arithmétique, les règles de la Résolution des
» Équations numériques, sauf à renvoyer à l'Algèbre la démonstration de celles
» qui dépendent de la théorie générale des Équations [*Traité de la Résolution*
» *des Equations numériques de tous les degrés*, *par* J. L. LAGRANGE; *Leçons*
» *du même auteur aux Ecoles normales*] ».

A PARIS,

Chez COURCIER, Imprimeur-Libraire pour les Mathématiques, quai des Augustins, n° 57.

ANNÉE 1807.

A L'EMPEREUR ET ROI.

SIRE,

TANDIS que les Muses qui président à la Poésie et à l'Éloquence s'empressent, à l'envi, d'offrir leurs tributs à VOTRE MAJESTÉ, la Muse des Hautes Sciences pourroit-elle demeurer en retard ? Les Sciences et les

Arts doivent surtout l'hommage de leurs découvertes à un Prince qui joint au pouvoir de les protéger, l'avantage d'être, par ses vastes connoissances, un juste appréciateur de leurs progrès.

Vous le savez, SIRE, les inventions dans l'Analyse algébrique sont des phénomènes assez rares. Peut-être aussi VOTRE MAJESTÉ jugera-t-elle que la Méthode que j'ai eu le bonheur de découvrir, n'est pas sans quelque utilité. Quels résultats, en effet, n'a-t-on pas droit d'en attendre dans ces recherches physico-mathématiques, où l'on est conduit à des équations d'un degré tant soit peu élevé, qui jusqu'à ce jour déconcertoient les plus savans calculateurs, et dont la résolution, par la nouvelle Méthode, sera désormais l'ouvrage des arithméticiens les moins versés dans les profondeurs de la Science.

Par ce double motif, j'ose espérer que V. M. daignera me permettre de Lui dédier ce produit d'une longue méditation.

Je suis, avec le plus profond respect,

SIRE,

DE VOTRE MAJESTÉ

Le très-humble, très-obéissant
et très-fidèle Sujet,

F. D. BUDAN, D. M. P.

AVANT-PROPOS.

Cet Ouvrage traite d'une matière sur laquelle se sont exercés les plus célèbres Analystes, depuis Viète jusqu'à M. Lagrange ; c'est-à-dire, depuis le premier âge de l'Algèbre jusqu'à nos jours.

Avant les écrits de M. Lagrange sur la résolution des équations numériques, les travaux multipliés de ses prédécesseurs n'avoient abouti qu'à des méthodes incertaines, et rebutantes dans la pratique. Celle qu'il a publiée est exempte d'incertitude, mais on convient généralement que la pratique en est encore assez rebutante. Elle ne permettroit certainement pas de remplir le vœu de cet illustre Géomètre, qui voudroit qu'on enseignât, dans l'Arithmétique même, les règles de la résolution des équations numériques.

C'est donc pour nous conformer à son desir que nous avons cherché une méthode d'une théorie plus simple, qui fût en même temps sûre et vraiment usuelle, susceptible, en un mot, d'être pratiquée par les commençans eux-mêmes. Cette méthode simple et facile, nous sommes parvenus à la découvrir ; et nous avons ainsi couronné assez heureusement, ce semble, les travaux de deux siècles sur cet objet.

Il a paru convenable de présenter d'abord une histoire abrégée de ces travaux : on pourra, d'après cette notice, juger de l'importance attachée par les plus grands Géomètres, au problême de la résolution des équations numériques.

Nous donnons ensuite un algorithme qui fait trouver, par de simples additions et soustractions, tous les termes des transformées en $(x-1)$, $(x-2)$, etc., d'une équation donnée en x. Cet algorithme a reçu, le 23 mai 1803, l'approbation de la première Classe de l'Institut.

Puis, après avoir rappelé diverses notions fournies par l'Algèbre, concernant les équations numériques, nous exposons successivement les trois parties dont se compose la nouvelle Méthode. Nous faisons voir quels sont les cas dans lesquels la première partie suffit toute seule à la résolution de l'équation; quels sont ceux dans lesquels il faut joindre la seconde à la première; et dans quels cas, enfin, l'on est obligé de recourir à la troisième pour découvrir les limites des racines incommensurables. Cette dernière partie sert aussi à approcher, jusqu'à telle décimale qu'on voudra, de la valeur exacte des racines dont on a déjà des limites.

Cet écrit est terminé par des Notes contenant des détails qui nous ont paru d'une assez grande importance pour nous faire desirer qu'elles soient lues avec la même attention que le corps de l'Ouvrage.

La première partie de notre Méthode a obtenu, le 31 octobre 1803, l'approbation de la première Classe de l'Institut, qui a reconnu, dans ce nouveau procédé, *une Méthode générale, directe et sûre*, pour résoudre une équation numérique, dans les cas où l'on sait que toutes ses racines sont réelles. Des circonstances particulières ont empêché de présenter à cette même Classe la suite de notre travail; mais nous ne craignons pas d'avancer que les deux autres parties complètent l'ouvrage commencé dans la première.

ERRATA.

Page 30, lignes 1, 3, 15 et 16, au lieu de 7, mettez 4.
Ibid., ligne 17, au lieu de 0, mettez 3.
Ibid., ligne 18, au lieu de *est* — 1, mettez *est entre* 0 *et* — 1.
Ibid., avant-dernière et dernière lignes, ... :

au lieu de . . . 1 + 9 + 14 — 1
1 + 12 + 35 + 23,

mettez . . . . . . 1 + 9 + 20 — 1
1 + 12 + 41 + 29.

Page 36, lig. 4 en remontant, au lieu de . . . . *permanence*, mettez *permanences*.
Page 39, lig. 13, au lieu de $+6-12$, mettez $+6x-12$.
Ibid., lig. 19, au lieu de 32, mettez 24.
Page 44, ligne 2, au lieu de -0, mettez $=0$.
Page 45, ligne 4, au lieu de x', mettez $\overset{1}{x'}$.
Ibid., ligne 14, à la fin, au lieu de 1, mettez 8.
Page 46, ligne 2, au lieu de 161000, mettez 160000.
Page 47, ligne 15, au lieu de *n'est pas*, mettez *est*.
Ibid., ligne 3 en remontant, au lieu de $\frac{x'''}{10}$, mettez x'''.
Page 48, ligne 9, au lieu de $\frac{1}{4 \times 10^n}$, mettez $\frac{1}{4 \times 10^{2(n-1)}}$.
Page 54, ligne 7, au lieu de *valeurs*, mettez *racines*.
Page 56, ligne 4, au lieu de *entre et* 1, mettez *entre* zéro *et* 1.
Ibid., ligne 10, après *prendre la somme*, mettez $n^{ième}$.
Page 65, ligne 8, au lieu de $\frac{p}{10}$, mettez $\frac{p'}{10}$.
Ibid., ligne 17, au lieu de p^n, mettez $p^{(n)}$.
Page 66, ligne 2, avant $A_{m-1}x$, mettez $+$.
Page 72, ligne 15, au lieu de x^2, mettez x^3.
Page 84, ligne 6, au lieu de $\frac{p'}{1}$, mettez $\frac{p'}{10}$.

NOUVELLE MÉTHODE

POUR LA RÉSOLUTION

DES ÉQUATIONS NUMÉRIQUES

D'UN DEGRÉ QUELCONQUE.

CHAPITRE PREMIER.

Histoire abrégée des travaux entrepris sur cette matière pendant les deux derniers siècles.

1. Le problême de la Résolution des Équations numériques peut être regardé, suivant l'illustre successeur d'Euler, comme le point le plus important de toute l'Analyse. La raison qu'il en donne est que la solution de tout problême déterminé conduit à une ou plusieurs équations numériques, c'est-à-dire, dont les coefficiens sont donnés en nombres; que tout le calcul qu'on a fait est en pure perte, si l'on n'a pas les moyens de résoudre ces équations; que dès le troisième degré l'expression algébrique des racines est insuffisante pour

faire connoître, dans tous les cas, leur valeur numérique ; qu'à plus forte raison le seroit-elle, si on parvenoit enfin à l'obtenir pour les équations des degrés supérieurs ; et qu'on seroit toujours forcé de recourir à d'autres moyens pour déterminer, en nombres, les valeurs des racines d'une équation donnée ; détermination qui est, en dernier résultat, l'objet de tous les problêmes que le besoin ou la curiosité offrent à résoudre. [*Séances des Ecoles Normales*, tom. 3, p. 463, 476.]

2. Indépendamment d'une autorité aussi grave sur ce point, l'importance de ce problême est assez démontrée par les efforts multipliés d'un grand nombre d'analystes célèbres des XVIIe et XVIIIe siècles, pour obtenir une méthode générale, directe et sûre, propre à faire découvrir toutes les racines réelles d'une équation numérique donnée. Nous allons présenter une légère esquisse des travaux de ces analystes, en prenant pour guide l'illustre auteur déjà cité.

3. Viète qui, le premier, s'occupa de la résolution des équations numériques d'un degré quelconque, y employa des opérations analogues à celles qui servent à extraire les racines des nombres. Harriot, Ougtred, etc., ont essayé de faciliter la pratique de sa méthode. « Mais » la multitude des opérations qu'elle demande, et l'incer» titude du succès dans un grand nombre de cas, l'ont » fait abandonner entièrement, avant la fin du XVIIe siècle ». [*De la Résolution des Equations numériques, par M. Lagrange*, pag. 1.]

4. La méthode de Newton a succédé à celle de Viète. Ce n'est proprement qu'une méthode d'approximation,

qui suppose qu'on connoît déjà la racine cherchée, à une quantité près, moindre que le dixième de cette racine. « Elle ne sert, comme on voit, que pour les » équations numériques qui sont déjà à-peu-près résolues ; » de plus, elle n'est pas toujours sûre ; elle a encore l'in» convénient de ne donner que des valeurs approchées » des racines mêmes qui peuvent être exprimées exacte» ment en nombres, et de laisser en doute si elles sont » commensurables ou non ». [*De la Résolution des Equations numériques*, p. 3.]

5. La méthode que Daniel Bernoulli a déduite de la considération des séries récurrentes, et qu'Euler a exposée dans son Introduction à l'Analyse infinitésimale, n'offre aussi qu'un moyen d'approximation. « Cette méthode » et celle de Newton, quoique fondées sur des principes » différens, reviennent à-peu-près au même, dans le fond, » et donnent des résultats semblables ». [*De la Résolution* etc., p. 152.]

6. Ce fut Hudde qui trouva qu'en multipliant chaque terme d'une équation donnée par l'exposant de l'inconnue, et en égalant le produit total à zéro, on obtient une équation qui renferme les conditions de l'égalité des racines de la proposée. Rolle, de l'Académie des Sciences, découvrit ensuite que les racines de l'équation ainsi formée sont les limites de celles de l'équation proposée. Ce principe est la base de sa méthode des *Cascades*, publiée d'abord sans démonstration, dans son Traité d'Algèbre en 1690. Cette méthode a été ainsi nommée, parcequ'elle fait dépendre la détermination des limites de chacune des racines de l'équation

proposée, de la résolution de différentes équations successives, qui vont toujours en baissant d'un degré. « La longueur des calculs que cette méthode demande, » et l'incertitude qui naît des racines imaginaires, l'ont » fait abandonner depuis longtemps » [*De la Résolution*, etc. p. 166]. Rolle, dans ce même Traité d'Algèbre, assigne pour limite de la plus grande valeur de l'inconnue, le plus grand coefficient négatif de l'équation, augmenté d'une unité ; le coefficient du premier terme étant 1.

7. La méthode de Stirling, pour déterminer le nombre et les limites des racines réelles du troisième et du quatrième degré, a été généralisée depuis par Euler, dans son Traité du Calcul différentiel. « Elle revient dans le » fond à celle de Rolle ». [*De la Résolution* etc., p. 166.]

8. En 1747, le célèbre Fontaine donna, sans démonstration, une nouvelle méthode. *Je la donne*, disoit-il, *pour l'analyse en entier, que l'on cherche si inutilement depuis l'origine de l'Algèbre.* Cette méthode suppose que l'on peut toujours, par la substitution des nombres 1, 2, 3, etc., au lieu de l'inconnue, dans les équations qu'elle emploie, trouver deux nombres qui donnent deux résultats de signes différens : « ce qui n'a » lieu, dit M. Lagrange, qu'autant que ces équations » ont des racines positives, dont la moindre différence » est plus grande que l'unité ; (*ou, pour parler plus » exactement, qu'autant qu'il y a de ces racines qui ne » sont pas comprises, en nombre pair, entre deux nombres » entiers consécutifs*). D'après cette considération, il est » facile de trouver des exemples où la méthode de Fon-

» taine est en défaut ». [*De la Résolution* etc., p. 162.]

9. Ce défaut avoit lieu également dans toute méthode qui emploie les substitutions pour déterminer les limites des racines réelles et inégales d'une équation numérique, lorsque M. Lagrange publia, dans les Mémoires de l'Académie de Berlin pour l'année 1767, un nouveau procédé, le seul jusqu'ici qui ait offert un moyen direct et sûr d'obtenir cette détermination. Son Mémoire contenoit aussi une méthode pour approcher, autant qu'on veut et en employant l'expression la plus simple, de la valeur exacte d'une racine, lorsque l'on connoît le plus grand nombre entier compris dans cette valeur.

Le procédé dû à M. Lagrange, consiste à substituer successivement, à la place de l'inconnue, dans l'équation débarrassée des racines égales qu'elle peut avoir, les termes d'une progression arithmétique $0, D, 2D, 3D$, etc., dont la différence D soit moindre que la plus petite différence des diverses racines de cette équation. La grande difficulté étoit de trouver ce nombre D : le génie fécond de l'illustre géomètre lui fournit trois manières d'y parvenir.

10. La première, qu'il proposa en 1767, exige le calcul de l'équation qui a pour racines les différences entre les racines de l'équation proposée. « Mais, dit » M. Lagrange, pour peu que le degré de l'équation » proposée soit élevé, celui de l'équation des différences » monte si haut, qu'on est effrayé de la longueur du » calcul nécessaire pour trouver la valeur de tous les » termes de cette équation ; puisque le degré de la pro-

» posée étant m, on a $\frac{m(m-1)}{2}$ coefficiens à calculer.
» [*Par exemple, pour une équation du dixième degré,*
» *la transformée seroit du quarante-cinquième*].

» Comme cet inconvénient pouvoit rendre la mé-
» thode générale presque impraticable dans les degrés
» un peu élevés, je me suis longtemps occupé des
» moyens de l'affranchir de la recherche de l'équation
» des différences, et j'ai reconnu en effet que, sans cal-
» culer entièrement cette équation, on pouvoit néan-
» moins trouver une limite moindre que la plus petite
» de ses racines; ce qui est le but principal du calcul de
» cette même équation». [*De la Résolution* etc., p. 124.]

11. La seconde manière de trouver le nombre D est consignée dans les leçons que l'auteur donna aux Ecoles Normales, en 1795. Elle demande le calcul d'une équation du même degré que la proposée, ayant pour ses racines les différentes valeurs dont est susceptible le coefficient Y de l'avant-dernier terme d'une équation en $(x-a)$; a étant une racine réelle quelconque de la proposée, dont x est l'inconnue. « Mais cette équation
» en Y, dit M. Lagrange, peut encore être fort longue
» à calculer, soit qu'on la déduise de l'élimination, soit
» qu'on veuille la chercher directement par la nature
» même de ses racines». [*De la Résolution* etc., p. 127.]

12. Ce coefficient Y étant une fonction de x, l'auteur a fait depuis réflexion qu'on pouvoit toujours éliminer l'inconnue x du produit du polynome Y, multiplié par un polynome ξ à coefficiens indéterminés, procédant suivant les puissances $m-1$, $m-2$, etc., de x; en

faisant disparoître du produit $Y\xi$, au moyen de la proposée, toutes les puissances de x plus hautes que x^{m-1}, puis égalant à o chacun des multiplicateurs de x, ce qui donne la valeur des coefficiens indéterminés de ξ, et réduit le produit $Y\xi$ à son terme tout connu représenté par K, d'où $Y=\frac{K}{\xi}$. Par suite de ces opérations, les coefficiens de l'équation inverse de celle aux différences, qui étoient divisés par Y, ne sont plus affectés que d'un diviseur indépendant de x, et la recherche de D en devient moins pénible. Ce troisième procédé, publié en 1798, est moins rebutant que les deux autres; néanmoins son auteur reconnoît qu'*il peut entraîner dans des calculs assez longs*. [*De la Résolution* etc., p. 223.]

13. « Le nombre D [*trouvé d'une de ces trois manières*] » pourra être souvent beaucoup plus petit qu'il ne seroit » nécessaire pour faire découvrir toutes les racines; mais, » dit M. Lagrange, il n'y a à cela d'autre inconvénient que » d'augmenter le nombre des substitutions successives à » faire pour x dans la proposée » [*Séances des Ecoles Normales*, tome 3, p. 466]. Cet inconvénient paroît encore assez grave dans la pratique, car il peut, en certains cas, donner lieu à des milliers, et même à un nombre indéfiniment plus grand, d'opérations superflues. Du reste, l'auteur l'a considérablement diminué, en donnant le moyen d'opérer, par de simples additions et soustractions, les substitutions de nombres entiers qui suivent celles des m premiers nombres 1, 2, 3, etc., dans une équation du degré m.

14. Il semble donc que la méthode de la limite de la

plus petite différence des racines, qui d'ailleurs porte l'empreinte du génie de son immortel auteur, ne réponde pas, en tout point, à l'objet qu'il s'est proposé, qui est de « déterminer les premières valeurs à substituer » pour x, desorte que, d'un côté, *on ne fasse pas trop* » *de tâtonnemens inutiles*, et que, de l'autre, on soit » assuré de découvrir, par ce moyen, toutes les racines » réelles de l'équation » [*Séances des Ecoles Normales*, tome 3, p. 477]. Nous ferons voir dans les chapitres suivans qu'on peut, à beaucoup moins de frais et sans recourir à cette longue et pénible recherche de la limite de la moindre différence des racines, se procurer toujours cette assurance.

15. En outre, le desir du célèbre auteur étant que les règles de la résolution des équations numériques soient données dans l'arithmétique, sauf à renvoyer à l'algèbre les démonstrations qui dépendent de cette dernière science, ne peut-on pas dire que ce vœu ne se trouve point rempli par une méthode dont la théorie est trop compliquée, et la pratique trop difficile pour des commençans?

16. Il restoit donc encore à glaner dans ce même champ où M. Lagrange a recueilli une si abondante moisson. Nous avons cherché à réaliser son projet, en découvrant une méthode nouvelle d'une théorie simple et d'une application facile. Nous présentons aux jeunes élèves un aliment de facile digestion, dont peut-être ils nous sauront quelque gré. Nous n'osons nous flatter d'obtenir le même accueil des personnages consommés dans la science: suivant un ancien adage, les mouches ne sont

point la pâture des aigles, *aquila non capit muscas.* On voudra bien cependant observer que les méthodes des anciens, lesquelles supposoient un grand travail, une grande force de tête, ont cédé la place, dans l'enseignement, à des méthodes modernes plus à la portée du vulgaire; nous espérons que cette considération préservera d'un superbe dédain les procédés aussi faciles à pratiquer qu'à concevoir, que nous offrons en ce moment au public.

17. A cette considération il en faut joindre une autre, tirée du besoin que l'on a d'une méthode qui soit praticable et vraiment usuelle pour la résolution des équations numériques, si l'on veut que l'algèbre puisse s'appliquer convenablement aux arts et aux besoins de la société. Nous rappellerons, à ce sujet, ce que disoit l'académicien Rolle, lorsqu'il publia sa méthode des *Cascades.* « Lorsqu'on a envisagé toutes les conditions qui sont nécessaires pour le succès d'une entreprise, on pourroit souvent s'aider de l'algèbre pour y réussir ou pour en connoître l'impossibilité; mais on aime mieux chercher d'autres conditions, ou tenter l'exécution par différens moyens, que d'avoir recours à cette science, et, en cela, on a eu quelque raison : car si l'on veut se servir de l'algèbre dans l'invention d'une machine ou pour quelqu'autre recherche, en n'employant d'ailleurs que les expériences des physiciens et les principes des géomètres, on arrivera à des égalités (*équations*) irrationnelles d'un degré fort élevé, et il est plus difficile d'éviter ces égalités dans cette application, que d'éviter les fractions quand on pratique l'arpentage. Cependant les règles qu'on a données jusqu'ici pour résoudre ces égalités, ne

» sont ni scientifiques ni générales, et il suffit de les éprou-
» ver pour en être rebuté ». On a aujourd'hui, à la vérité, des *règles scientifiques et générales* ; mais quel est celui qui, les ayant essayées, pourra dire qu'elles ne sont pas rebutantes ?

18. Si dans cette esquisse des travaux de deux siècles, concernant la résolution des équations numériques, l'immortel Descartes semble avoir été oublié, c'est que nous nous sommes réservé d'en parler ailleurs. Comment aurions-nous pu oublier sa fameuse règle des variations et des permanences de signes, publiée pour la première fois en 1637, et qui, longtemps négligée, reçoit dans notre méthode une application nouvelle, et, en quelque sorte, une nouvelle existence ?

CHAPITRE II.

PROBLÊME PRÉLIMINAIRE : *Etant donnée une équation numérique en* x *d'un degré quelconque, trouver, par de simples additions et soustractions, les coefficiens de sa transformée en* (x — 1); *et généralement, de sa transformée en* (x — n), n *étant un nombre entier ou décimal.*

19. AVANT que de donner la solution de ce problême, nous expliquerons ce qu'il faut entendre par les sommes premières, secondes, troisièmes, etc., d'une suite de termes.

Lorsqu'une suite de termes quelconques étant donnée, on forme une autre suite *sommatoire* de la première, c'est-à-dire, qui a pour loi que son $n^{ième}$ terme soit la somme des *n* premiers termes de la suite donnée, cela s'appelle prendre les *sommes premières*, ou simplement les sommes de la première suite.

Ce mot *somme* doit s'entendre dans le sens algébrique; il exprime l'excédant de la somme des termes précédés d'un des signes + ou — sur celle des termes précédés du signe contraire.

Prendre ensuite les sommes de ces sommes premières, cela s'appelle prendre les *sommes-secondes* de la suite donnée. De même, les sommes de ces *sommes-secondes* s'appellent les *sommes-troisièmes* de la première suite, et ainsi du reste.

Voici un exemple de ces diverses sommes :

Suite donnée . . . . 1 . . . 1 . . . 1 . . . 1 . . . 1.
Sommes-premières . . . . . 1 . . . 2 . . . 3 . . . 4 . . . 5.
Sommes-secondes . . . . . . 1 . . . 3 . . . 6 . . . 10 . . . 15.
Sommes-troisièmes . . . . . 1 . . . 4 . . . 10 . . . 20 . . . 35,
etc. etc.

Les suites dont on s'est servi dans ce premier exemple, appartiennent à celles des nombres que les Géomètres appellent *nombres figurés*, lesquelles ont généralement pour 1er terme, l'unité ; pour 2e terme, un nombre entier m ; et pour terme $n^{\text{ième}}$, un nombre exprimé par $\frac{m(m+1)\ldots(m+n-2)}{1.2\ldots\ldots\ldots(n-1)}$.

Autre exemple, dans lequel la suite donnée est composée de termes pris arbitrairement, les uns positifs, les autres négatifs :

Suite donnée . . . . 2 + 5 − 3 + 4 − 3 + 0 − 1.
Sommes-premières . . 2 + 7 + 4 + 8 + 5 + 5 + 4.
Sommes-secondes . . . 2 + 9 + 13 + 21 + 26 + 31 + 35.
Sommes-troisièmes . . 2 + 11 + 24 + 45 + 71 + 102 + 137.
etc. etc.

20. Voici maintenant deux propositions d'où résulte la solution demandée. (*Pour leur démonstration, voyez ci-après les* Notes.)

Première proposition. La somme $m^{ième}$ des n premiers termes d'une suite quelconque, égale la somme de ces termes multipliés respectivement, mais en ordre inverse, par les n premiers nombres figurés de l'ordre m, c'est-à-dire, appartenant à la suite dont le second terme est m.

Ainsi la somme $m^{ième}$ des n premiers termes de cette suite.....

$$A_0 + A_1 + A_2 + \ldots\ldots + A_{n-1}$$

est égale à.... $A_{n-1} + mA_{n-2} + \ldots\ldots + \frac{m\ldots.(m+n-2)}{1\ldots..(n-1)} A_0$

Par exemple, la somme-troisième de ces quatre termes $2+5-3+4$ est $(1\times 4-3\times 3+6\times 5+10\times 2)=45$, de même qu'on l'a reconnu plus haut en prenant les sommes et les sommes de sommes.

Seconde proposition. Un polynome quelconque, procédant suivant les puissances entières et positives d'une quantité x, depuis le degré m jusqu'au degré zéro, se transforme en un autre polynome d'égale valeur, procédant suivant les mêmes puissances de $(x-1)$, dont les coefficiens respectifs, à commencer par celui du dernier terme, sont,

1°. La somme-première de tous les coefficiens du polynome donné.

2°. La somme-seconde de tous les coefficiens, hormis le dernier.

3°. La somme-troisième de ces coefficiens, excepté les deux derniers. Et ainsi de suite.

Soit, par exemple, ce polynome

$$2x^3 - 3x^2 + 5x - 3.$$

Coefficiens donnés . . .	$2 - 3 + 5 - 3.$
Sommes-premières . . .	$2 - 1 + 4 + 1.$
Sommes-secondes. . . .	$2 + 1 + 5.$ . .
Sommes-troisièmes . . .	$2 + 3.$ . . . .
Sommes-quatrièmes. . .	$2.$ . . . . . .

Ainsi les coefficiens du polynome en $(x - 1)$ sont....

$$2 + 3 + 5 + 1\ ;$$

et l'on a

$$2(x-1)^3 + 3(x-1)^2 + 5(x-1) + 1 = 2x^3 - 3x^2 + 5x - 3.$$

Cette équation a lieu, quelque valeur qu'on donne à x.

S'il manque dans le polynome proposé quelque puissance de x, il faut la mettre en évidence, en lui donnant zéro pour coefficient.

Soit, par exemple, $x^3 - 7x + 7$.

Coefficiens donnés. . . .	$1 + 0 - 7 + 7.$
Sommes-premières . . .	$1 + 1 - 6 + 1.$
Sommes-secondes	$1 + 2 - 4.$ . .
Sommes-troisièmes . . .	$1 + 3.$ . . . .
Sommes-quatrièmes. . .	$1.$ . . . . . .

On a donc....

$$x^3 - 7x + 7 = (x-1)^3 + 3(x-1)^2 - 4(x-1) + 1.$$

21. Il est évident qu'une équation dont le premier membre est égal à zéro, offre précisément le même cas que le polynome de la proposition précédente. Ainsi l'algorithme par lequel on obtient la transformée en $(x - 1)$ d'une équation donnée en x, consiste dans le

même procédé employé pour la transformation d'un polynome d'une valeur quelconque.

Etant donc donnée l'équation....

$$x^3 - 7x + 7 = 0,$$

les coefficiens de sa transformée en $(x - 1)$ sont....

$$1 + 3 - 4 + 1.$$

Pareillement, pour l'équation....

$$x^3 - 2x - 5 = 0,$$

les coefficiens de sa transformée en $(x - 1)$ sont....

$$1 + 3 + 1 - 6.$$

22. Par le même algorithme, on passera de la transformée en $(x - 1)$ à celle en $(x - 2)$; de celle-ci à la transformée en $(x - 3)$; et ainsi de suite indéfiniment.

On obtiendra donc très-promptement les coefficiens de ces diverses équations.

Coefficiens des équations, dans le 1er exemple du n° 21...

en x	$1 + 0 - 7 \pm 7$
en $(x - 1)$. . .	$1 + 3 - 4 + 1$
en $(x - 2)$. . .	$1 + 6 + 5 + 1$
en $(x - 3)$. . .	$1 + 9 + 20 + 13$
etc.	etc.

Coefficiens des équations, dans le second exemple....

en x	$1 + 0 - 2 - 5$
en $(x - 1)$. . .	$1 + 3 + 1 - 6$
en $(x - 2)$. . .	$1 + 6 + 10 - 1$
en $(x - 3)$. . .	$1 + 9 + 25 + 16$
etc.	etc.

23. Il est aisé d'observer que par ces transformations, on finit par avoir des coefficiens qui sont tous de même signe.

Observons aussi que si l'équation proposée n'est que du troisième degré, on peut obtenir les coefficiens de ses transformées successives par un moyen encore plus rapide que l'algorithme général. Nos lecteurs le devineront sans peine à la simple inspection des coefficiens représentés dans le n° précédent. Dans ce cas, le calcul des transformées s'opère instantanément, sans avoir besoin d'écrire d'autres chiffres que ceux qu'on voit ici.

24. Le même algorithme fournit le moyen d'obtenir les transformées en $(x-10)$, $(x-20)$, $(x-30)$, etc.; celles en $(x-100)$, $(x-200)$, $(x-300)$, etc.; etc.

Il faut, pour cela, substituer dans la proposée une inconnue x' qui soit, respectivement, dix fois, cent fois, etc. moindre que x. Les coefficiens de cette équation en x' s'obtiennent, comme l'on sait, sans calcul, par le placement convenable de la virgule qui indique les décimales.

On se procure ensuite les transformées en $(x'-1)$, $(x'-2)$, $(x'-3)$, etc.; ou, ce qui revient au même, en $\left(\frac{x-10}{10}\right)$, $\left(\frac{x-20}{10}\right)$, $\left(\frac{x-30}{10}\right)$, etc.; ou bien en.... $\left(\frac{x-100}{100}\right)$, $\left(\frac{x-200}{100}\right)$, $\left(\frac{x-300}{100}\right)$, etc.; selon qu'on a fait $x'=\frac{x}{10}$, ou $x'=\frac{x}{100}$, etc.

Il ne s'agit plus que de rendre les inconnues de ces transformées, respectivement, dix ou cent fois, etc. aussi grandes ; ce qui s'opère par le déplacement convenable de la virgule dans leurs coefficiens.

Soit, par exemple, l'équation

$$x^3 - 4x^2 + 3x - 6 = 0,$$

dont on demande les transformées en $(x-10)$, $(x-20)$, etc.

On fera $x = 10x'$; d'où....

$$x'^3 - 0{,}4x'^2 + 0{,}03x' - 0{,}006 = 0.$$

Coefficiens des équations....

en x'........................ $1 - 0{,}4 + \quad 0{,}03 - 0{,}006$

en $\left(\frac{x-10}{10}\right)$ ou $(x'-1)$... $1 + 2{,}6 + \quad 2{,}23 + 0{,}624$

en $\left(\frac{x-20}{10}\right)$ ou $(x'-2)$... $1 + 5{,}6 + 10{,}43 + 6{,}454$

etc. etc.

Et par conséquent on aura, pour les coefficiens des équations....

en $(x-10)$... $1 + 26 + \quad 223 + \quad 624$

en $(x-20)$... $1 + 56 + 1043 + 6454$

etc. etc.

On voit aisément comment, par une marche analogue, on se procureroit les transformées en $(x-\frac{1}{10})$, $(x-\frac{2}{10})$, etc. ; celles en $(x-\frac{1}{100})$, $(x-\frac{2}{100})$, etc. ; etc.

25. Si l'on veut avoir l'équation où l'inconnue de la proposée est diminuée d'un nombre de plusieurs chiffres, par exemple, l'équation en $(x-312)$; on se procurera d'abord l'équation en $(x'-3)$, en faisant $x = 100x'$; et par suite, celle en $(x-300)$, comme il vient d'être indiqué.

Puis on fera $x - 300 = 10x''$; on obtiendra l'équation en $(x''-1)$; et par suite, celle en $(x-310)$. De cette dernière, on passera à celle en $(x-311)$; et de celle-ci à l'équation demandée en $(x-312)$.

Voici, par exemple, la marche qu'il faudroit suivre, si la proposée était....

$$x^3-4x^2+3x-6=0.$$

Soit $x=100x'$; d'où

$$x'^3-0{,}04x'^2+0{,}0003x'-0{,}000006=0.$$

Coefficiens des équations.....

en x' .... $1-0{,}04+0{,}0003-0{,}000006$
en $(x'-1)$... $1+2{,}96+2{,}9203+0{,}960294$
en $(x'-2)$... $1+5{,}96+11{,}8403+7{,}840594$
en $(x'-3)$... $1+8{,}96+26{,}7603+26{,}640894$

Ainsi les coefficiens de l'équation en $(x-300)$ sont....

$$1+896+267603+26640894.$$

Faisant ensuite $x-300=10x''$, on a les coefficiens des équations...

en x'' .... $1+89{,}6+2676{,}03+26640{,}894$
en $(x''-1)$... $1+92{,}6+2858{,}23+29407{,}524$.

Or $x''-1=\frac{x-310}{10}$; il s'ensuit qu'on aura les coefficiens des équations....

en $(x-310)$... $1+926+285823+29407524$
en $(x-311)$... $1+929+287678+29694274$
en $(x-312)$... $1+932+289539+29982882$.

Il est aisé de voir comment on obtiendroit l'équation où l'inconnue de la proposée seroit diminuée d'un nombre décimal de plusieurs chiffres; par exemple, l'équation en $\left(x-\frac{312}{100}\right)$: nous ne nous arrêterons point à ces détails.

26. En considérant le tableau des opérations par lesquelles on passe d'un polynome en x à son équivalent en $(x-1)$ [20], on n'aura pas de peine à reconnoître comment on peut passer réciproquement d'un polynome en $(x-1)$ à son équivalent en x; et parconséquent, de celui en x à son équivalent en $(x+1)$, et ainsi de suite. Dans le premier cas, on a pris des *sommes*; dans le second, on prend des *différences*.

Choisissons pour exemple, le polynome en x du n° 20, dont les coefficiens sont....

$$2-3+5-3;$$

et son équivalent en $(x-1)$, qui a pour coefficiens....

$$2+3+5+1.$$

Pour passer de celui-ci à l'autre, on écrit ses coefficiens et on procède comme il suit :

Coefficiens du polynome en $(x-1)$...		$2+3+5+1$
Suites dans chacune desquelles le $n^{ième}$ terme est la différence du terme qui le précède au terme $n^{ième}$ de la suite supérieure...	1ère...	$2+1+4-3$
	2ième...	$2-1+5$....
	3ième...	$2-3$........
	4ième...	2............

On obtient ainsi les coefficiens du polynome en x, et l'on se procurera de la même manière ceux du polynome en $(x+1)$. En voici le tableau

Coefficiens du polynome en x		$2-3+5-3$
Suites de différences prises suivant la loi qui vient d'être indiquée......................	1ière...	$2-5+10-13$
	2ième...	$2-7+17$....
	3ième...	$2-9$........
	4ième...	2............

Les coefficiens obtenus pour le polynome en $(x+1)$, sont....

$$2-9+17-13;$$

ce qu'il est d'ailleurs aisé de vérifier par le procédé inverse.

27. On a remarqué ci-dessus qu'en opérant les transformations successives en $(x-1)$, $(x-2)$, etc., on parvient à une transformée en $(x-u)$, dont tous les termes sont de même signe. Ici l'on observera que les transformations en $(x+1)$, $(x+2)$, etc. conduisent à une transformée en $(x\pm u')$, dont les termes ne présentent que des *variations* de signe, comme on le remarque dans le polynome en $(x+1)$ du dernier exemple, dont les coefficiens sont alternativement précédés du signe $+$ et du signe $-$. Lorsqu'on est une fois parvenu à ce polynome en $(x+u')$, les transformées ultérieures en $(x+u'+1)$, $(x+u'+2)$, etc. n'offriront aucune *permanence* de signe : cela s'apperçoit par la nature même du procédé.

Les équations du troisième degré sont susceptibles d'une abréviation analogue à celle qui est indiquée au n° 23.

CHAPITRE III.

Diverses notions fournies par l'Algèbre, concernant les équations numériques.

28. On peut toujours transporter dans un même membre tous les termes d'une équation, ensorte qu'elle paroisse sous cette forme :

$$A_0x^m + A_1x^{m-1} + \ldots\ldots + A_{m-1}x^1 + A_mx^0 = 0\,;$$

m étant un nombre entier positif; les coefficiens ayant par eux-mêmes une valeur positive ou négative, et quelques-uns pouvant aussi être nuls. C'est sous cette forme que nous considérerons toujours les équations.

Le but principal qu'on se propose dans la résolution d'une équation déterminée, est de trouver exactement ou par approximation, s'il y a lieu, tous les nombres réels, dont la substitution, à la place de l'inconnue, rend nulle la somme de tous les termes du premier membre. On donne à ces nombres le nom de *racines réelles de l'équation*; elles sont ou positives ou négatives.

29. Le nombre des racines réelles d'une équation ne peut jamais surpasser *m*, c'est-à-dire, le nombre qui en indique le degré; il peut lui être inférieur, ou même être nul. L'excédant de *m* sur le nombre des racines réelles est nécessairement un nombre pair, indicateur du nombre des racines imaginaires qui satisfont à l'équation.

On entend par quantité imaginaire, le symbole d'un résultat d'opération, impossible à obtenir, à raison de son absurdité : par exemple, la racine quarrée d'une quantité négative, telle que $\sqrt{-4}$.

Toute racine ou quantité imaginaire se peut réduire à l'une de ces formes, $\pm A + \sqrt{-B}$, et $\pm A - \sqrt{-B}$, A et B étant des quantités réelles. Si une équation a une de ses racines sous une de ces formes, elle en a nécessairement une sous l'autre ; les racines imaginaires se trouvant ainsi toujours unies par couples.

30. Toute équation qui a pour racine un nombre $\pm n$, est divisible par le facteur $x \mp n$; celle qui a une couple de racines imaginaires, est divisible par le facteur réel du second degré, $x^2 \mp 2Ax + A^2 + B$.

Généralement, une équation du degré m est le produit de m facteurs simples, soit réels, soit imaginaires : le nombre des facteurs simples réels est égal à celui des racines réelles de l'équation.

31. Lorsque, par la substitution d'un nombre n à la place de x, la somme de tous les termes de l'équation est rendue égale à une quantité positive ; et que la substitution d'un autre nombre n' donne au contraire un résultat négatif, on est assuré qu'il y a une ou plusieurs racines en nombre impair, dont la valeur est comprise entre n et n', et réciproquement.

Mais la substitution ne donne point de résultats de signes différens, lorsque les racines comprises entre n et n' sont en nombre pair.

La substitution de quelque nombre que ce soit ne donne que des résultats positifs, lorsque l'équation n'a que des racines imaginaires.

32. Quand on change, dans une équation, le signe des termes du rang pair, ou de ceux du rang impair, les racines de l'équation, après ce changement, sont les mêmes qu'avant, au signe près; c'est-à-dire que les racines négatives deviennent positives, et que les positives deviennent négatives.

Il s'ensuit que pour trouver toutes les racines réelles d'une équation, il suffit de savoir trouver les racines positives.

33. Toute équation de degré impair a, pour le moins, une racine réelle positive, si son dernier terme est négatif; ou une racine réelle négative, si ce terme est positif.

Dans les équations de degré pair, il y a toujours, pour le moins, une racine réelle positive, et une autre négative, si le dernier terme est négatif; mais si ce terme est positif, on n'en peut rien conclure pour la réalité des racines.

34. Le résultat de la substitution d'un nombre $\pm n$, à la place de x, dans une équation donnée, est égal au terme tout connu de sa transformée en $(x \mp n)$. Par conséquent $\pm n$ est une racine de la proposée, lorsque le dernier terme de la transformée en $(x \mp n)$ est égal à zéro. Et généralement, la proposée a autant de racines égales à $\pm n$, qu'il y a, dans cette transformée, de termes consécutifs, à commencer par le dernier, qui égalent zéro.

35. La somme du coefficient du premier terme d'une équation et du plus grand coefficient de signe contraire étant prise sans qu'on ait égard aux signes, et divisée par le premier coefficient, le quotient est plus grand que la plus grande racine positive qui puisse appartenir à l'équa-

tion ; et ce quotient s'appelle une limite de cette plus grande racine.

Si le coefficient du premier terme de l'équation est $+1$, le plus grand coefficient négatif, pris positivement et augmenté de l'unité, est une limite de la plus-grande racine positive.

On a, pour obtenir une limite plus approchée de la plus grande racine positive, divers moyens qu'il est inutile de rappeler ici. Observons seulement qu'on peut souvent y parvenir en faisant $x=10x'$, ou $x=100x'$, etc., l'équation en x' pouvant indiquer une limite de la plus grande valeur de x', qui décuplée, ou centuplée, etc., donne pour x une nouvelle limite beaucoup plus rapprochée.

Exemple....

Equation en x...... $x^4+2x^3+3x^2-451=0$

Equation en $x'=\frac{x}{10}$... $x'^4+0,2x'^3+0,03x'^2-0,0451=0$;

la limite en plus de x' étant 1,0451, celle de x est 10,451 ; et cette dernière est bien plus resserrée que 452, limite indiquée par le plus grand coefficient négatif de l'équation en x. Cette limite plus resserrée peut se reconnoître à la seule vue de la proposée, par une simple opération mentale.

Le terme tout connu de l'équation étant divisé par la somme de ce terme et du plus grand coefficient de signe contraire, prise sans égard pour les signes, le quotient est plus petit que la plus petite racine positive que l'équation puisse avoir ; il en est une limite.

36. L'Algèbre fournit le moyen de préparer une équation, de manière que son premier terme n'ait d'autre

coefficient que l'unité, et que les autres coefficiens soient tous des nombres entiers. Il en résulte que les équations à résoudre peuvent toutes être considérées comme ramenées à cette forme.

L'équation ainsi préparée ne peut avoir pour racines réelles que des nombres entiers ou des nombres fractionnaires irrationnels. En général, ces racines irrationnelles ne sont susceptibles d'être déterminées que par approximation.

37. L'Algèbre donne aussi le moyen de débarrasser une équation des racines égales qu'elle peut avoir, ensorte que les racines multiples n'y subsistent plus que comme racines simples. Ainsi les équations à résoudre peuvent être considérées comme n'ayant que des racines inégales.

38. Une équation ne peut avoir plus de racines réelles positives, qu'il n'y a de variations dans la succession des signes de ses coefficiens; ni plus de racines réelles négatives, qu'il ne s'y trouve de permanences de signes: telle est la fameuse règle de Descartes.

Ainsi, dans le cas où toutes les racines de l'équation sont réelles, il y a précisément autant de racines positives que de variations de signe, et autant de racines négatives que de permanences.

Quand un des coefficiens de l'équation est zéro, et que les coefficiens du terme précédent et du suivant sont de même signe, l'équation a nécessairement des racines imaginaires.

On peut reconnoître si une équation a toutes ses racines réelles ou non, au moyen de l'équation dont les racines sont les quarrés des différences des racines de la proposée. Dans le premier cas, cette équation aux quarrés des différences n'a que des variations de signe ; tandis qu'elle a nécessairement des permanences, si la proposée a des racines imaginaires. Mais le calcul des coefficiens de cette équation est en général tellement pénible, qu'on n'est guères tenté d'employer ce moyen.

39. On peut déduire de la règle de Descartes, les deux propositions suivantes :

1°. Une équation en x, dont toutes les racines sont réelles, a autant de racines comprises entre zéro et p, qu'il y a de permanences de signe dans la transformée en $(x-p)$, de plus que dans l'équation en x.

2°. Une équation de cette espèce ne peut avoir, soit une, soit deux, soit n racines comprises entre zéro et p, si sa transformée en $(x-p)$ n'a pas, respectivement, une, ou deux, ou n permanences de signe, de plus que l'équation en x.

Nous avons même de fortes raisons de croire que la seconde proposition est applicable à une équation quelconque.

CHAPITRE IV.

Exposition de la nouvelle Méthode. Première Partie. Cas où l'on n'a besoin que de cette partie de la Méthode.

40. Nous allons maintenant exposer successivement les divers procédés qui constituent notre Méthode, en renvoyant aux nos du chapitre précédent, où sont contenus les principes qui servent de base aux résultats que l'on obtient par ces procédés. Pour concevoir le rapport des uns aux autres, il suffit au lecteur qui ne seroit point assez avancé dans l'Algèbre, de tenir les principes pour démontrés, sans chercher à en connoître la démonstration; et s'il ne veut que posséder le *mécanisme* de la Méthode, il n'a besoin que de savoir opérer les transformations, conformément à l'algorithme du second chapitre.

41. Etant donc donnée une équation en x du degré m, on se procurera ses transformées successives en $(x-1)$, $(x-2)$, $(x-3)$, et ainsi de suite, jusqu'à ce qu'on parvienne à une transformée en $(x-u)$, dont les coefficiens soient tous de même signe.

Cette dernière transformée ne pouvant point avoir de racine positive, le nombre entier u est une limite de la plus grande valeur positive de l'inconnue.

S'il arrive que la proposée elle-même n'offre que des permanences de signe, il ne reste à chercher que les racines négatives qu'elle peut avoir, et on procédera comme il sera dit plus bas [44].

42. Lorsque le dernier coefficient d'une équation qui a pour inconnue $(x-p)$, est égal à zéro, l'équation en x a une racine égale au nombre p; et plus généralement, si n coefficiens consécutifs de la transformée, à compter du dernier, sont égaux chacun à zéro, la proposée a n racines égales, chacune, à p [34]. Par cette circonstance, l'équation en $(x-p)$ se trouve abaissée de n degrés.

A raison de cet abaissement, il peut y avoir quelque avantage à ne débarrasser l'équation de ses racines égales, qu'après avoir opéré les transformations du n° 41.

43. Lorsque le dernier coefficient d'une équation en $(x-p)$ est de signe contraire à celui de la transformée en $(x-p-1)$, la proposée a une ou plusieurs racines en nombre impair, dont la valeur est comprise entre p et $p+1$. Car les coefficiens dont il s'agit, expriment précisément les résultats que donne la proposée, quand on y met successivement p et $p+1$ à la place de x [31].

44. Les racines négatives de la proposée étant, au signe près, égales aux racines positives qu'auroit cette équation si les signes de ses termes pairs étoient tous changés, on fera ce changement, puis on opérera comme ci-dessus [41], et on obtiendra des résultats analogues.

45. Par cette première partie de la Méthode, on trouve,

en certains cas, toutes les racines réelles de l'équation, soit exactement, soit approximativement, à moins d'une unité près.

Un premier cas est celui où la proposée n'a ni racines imaginaires, ni plusieurs racines réelles comprises entre deux nombres entiers p et $p+1$.

Un second cas est celui où l'on sait d'avance que toutes les racines de la proposée sont réelles, encore que parmi ces racines, il y en ait d'incommensurables comprises, en tel nombre que ce soit, entre deux nombres entiers consécutifs.

Un troisième cas a lieu, lorsqu'on sait que l'équation n'a qu'une racine réelle, positive ou négative, ou bien qu'elle en a deux, l'une positive, et l'autre négative, ainsi qu'il arrive dans des équations de cette forme, $x^m \mp A = 0$.

46. *Premier exemple.* Soit l'équation....

$$x^4 - 10x^3 + 36x^2 - 54x + 27 = 0.$$

Coefficiens des équations....

en x	1	-10	$+36$	-54	$+27$
en $(x-1)$...	1	-6	$+12$	-8	$+0$
en $(x-2)$...	1	-3	$+3$	-1	
en $(x-3)$...	1	$+0$	$+0$	$0.$	

Les racines de cette équation sont donc 1 et 3; cette dernière racine est triple [42], c'est-à-dire que la proposée est divisible par $(x-3)^3$.

Second exemple.... $x^3 - 5x^2 + x + 7 = 0$.

Coefficiens des équations.....

en x........	1	$-$ 5	$+$ 1	$+$ 7
en $(x-1)$...	1	$-$ 2	$-$ 6	$+$ 1
en $(x-2)$...	1	$+$ 1	$-$ 7	$-$ 6
en $(x-3)$...	1	$+$ 4	$-$ 2	$-$ 11
en $(x-4)$...	1	$+$ 7	$+$ 9	$-$ 8
en $(x-5)$...	1	$+$ 10	$+$ 26	$+$ 9.

La proposée a donc deux racines positives incommensurables, dont les valeurs sont respectivement comprises entre 1 et 2, et entre 4 et 5. Pour avoir ensuite la racine négative, on change les signes des termes de rang pair dans la proposée [44], et l'on a....

$$\mathrm{x}^3 + 5\mathrm{x}^2 + \mathrm{x} - 7 = 0.$$

Coefficiens des équations.....

en $\mathrm{x} = -x$ ..	1	$+$ 5	$+$ 1	$-$ 7
en $(\mathrm{x}-1)$...	1	$+$ 8	$+$ 14	$+$ 0.

Donc la racine négative de la proposée est -1.

Troisième exemple.... $x^3 - 7x + 7 = 0$.

Coefficiens des équations....

en x.........	1	$+$ 0	$-$ 7	$+$ 7
en $(x-1)$...	1	$+$ 3	$-$ 4	$+$ 1
en $(x-2)$...	1	$+$ 6	$+$ 5	$+$ 1.

Coefficiens des équations....

en $\mathrm{x} = -x$...	1	$-$ 0	$-$ 7	$-$ 7
en $(\mathrm{x}-1)$...	1	$+$ 3	$-$ 4	$-$ 13
en $(\mathrm{x}-2)$...	1	$+$ 6	$+$ 5	$-$ 13
en $(\mathrm{x}-3)$...	1	$+$ 9	$+$ 14	$-$ 1
en $(\mathrm{x}-4)$...	1	$+$ 12	$+$ 35	$+$ 23.

L'équation proposée étant de celles qu'on sait avoir toutes ses racines réelles, il en résulte que non-seulement elle a une racine négative dont la valeur est entre — 3 et — 4 [43], mais aussi qu'elle a deux autres racines positives comprise entre 1 et 2, parceque la transformée en $(x-2)$ a deux permanences de signe de plus que celle en $(x-1)$ [39]. Telle est, dans ce cas, la conséquence de la règle de Descartes.

Quatrième exemple.... $x^3 - 1745 = 0$.

Coefficiens des équations....

en x..........	$1+$	$0+$	$0-$	1745
en $(x-1)$...	$1+$	$3+$	$3-$	1744
en $(x-2)$...	$1+$	$6+$	$12-$	1737
en $(x-3)$...	$1+$	$9+$	$27-$	1718
en $(x-4)$...	$1+$	$12+$	$48-$	1681
en $(x-5)$...	$1+$	$15+$	$75-$	1620
en $(x-6)$...	$1+$	$18+$	$108-$	1529
en $(x-7)$...	$1+$	$21+$	$147-$	1402
en $(x-8)$...	$1+$	$24+$	$192-$	1233
en $(x-9)$...	$1+$	$27+$	$243-$	1016
en $(x-10)$...	$1+$	$30+$	$300-$	745
en $(x-11)$...	$1+$	$33+$	$363-$	414
en $(x-12)$...	$1+$	$36+$	$432-$	17
en $(x-13)$...	$1+$	$39+$	$507+$	452.

Donc la racine de l'équation est entre 12 et 13.

47. Nous avons suivi dans ce dernier exemple, la marche la plus longue; car il est aisé de voir que x devant être un nombre entier, exprimé par deux chiffres,

on pouvoit d'abord se procurer les transformées en $(x-10)$, $(x-20)$, etc., par le procédé indiqué plus haut [24], en faisant d'abord $x=10x'$, ce qui changeoit l'équation en..... $x'^3-1{,}745=0$.

Coefficiens des équations....

$$\begin{array}{ll} \text{en } x' \ldots\ldots\ldots\ldots\ldots\ldots\ldots & 1+0+\ 0-1{,}745 \\ \text{en } \left(\frac{x-10}{10}\right) \text{ ou } (x'-1)\ldots & 1+3+\ 3-0{,}745 \\ \text{en } \left(\frac{x-20}{10}\right) \text{ ou } (x'-2)\ldots & 1+6+12+6{,}255 \end{array}$$

Et par conséquent....

$$\begin{array}{ll} \text{en } (x-10)\ldots & 1+30+\ 300-745 \\ \text{en } (x-20)\ldots & 1+60+1200+6255. \end{array}$$

Donc la racine est entre 10 et 20. Il ne reste qu'à se procurer les transformées successives après celle en $(x-10)$, jusqu'à celle en $(x-19)$ tout au plus.

Coefficiens des équations....

$$\begin{array}{ll} \text{en } (x-10)\ldots & 1+30+300-745 \\ \text{en } (x-11)\ldots & 1+33+363-414 \\ \text{en } (x-12)\ldots & 1+36+432-\ \ 17 \\ \text{en } (x-13)\ldots & 1+39+507+452. \end{array}$$

Et l'on conclura, comme plus haut, que la racine 3ième ou cubique de 1745 est entre 12 et 13.

La nouvelle Méthode offre donc un moyen d'extraire, par des additions et soustractions, la racine $m^{ième}$, exacte ou approchée, d'un nombre quelconque. Si l'on veut comparer cette méthode avec les anciens procédés, nous laissons à juger lequel des deux moyens mérite la préférence.

48. Le procédé que nous avons employé dans le n° précédent, n'est pas applicable seulement aux équations à deux termes; on peut aussi l'employer dans une équation quelconque, toutes les fois qu'on aura sujet de penser, d'après l'examen des coefficiens de la proposée, que le plus grand nombre entier, faisant partie de la plus grande racine positive, peut être exprimé par plusieurs chiffres. Dans ce cas, il pourra être plus convenable de faire $x = 10x'$, ou $x = 100x'$, etc., et de se procurer d'abord les transformées en $(x - 10)$, $(x - 20)$, etc.; ou en $(x - 100)$, $(x - 200)$, etc, etc.; ou bien encore, de résoudre l'équation en x', à l'aide des transformées successives en $(x' - 1)$, $(x' - 2)$, etc.; puis d'en déduire les valeurs de x.

Ces remarques détruiront sans doute cette objection que l'irréflexion pourroit opposer à notre Méthode; savoir: « que si les racines étoient exprimées en nombres » un peu grands, la Méthode seroit impraticable » par sa longueur, et qu'on auroit beaucoup plus tôt » fait de chercher les mêmes choses par les méthodes » ordinaires ».

On peut se rassurer contre cette prétendue longueur, puisque le nombre des transformées successives exigées par cette Méthode, si faciles d'ailleurs à obtenir par notre Algorithme, est égal au nombre des chiffres qu'on veut avoir à la racine, plus la somme de ces mêmes chiffres considérés comme n'exprimant chacun que des unités simples. Par exemple , pour avoir le nombre 812, le nombre des transformées seroit $3 + 8 + 1 + 2 = 14$.

49. Veut-on maintenant avoir , dans les cas précédens, des racines plus approchées , à telle unité décimale près qu'il plaira, on peut employer la méthode d'approximation qui sera exposée ci-après, au Chapitre VI.

CHAPITRE V.

Suite de l'exposition de la nouvelle Méthode. Seconde Partie. Cas où cette Partie, jointe à la première, suffit pour faire découvrir les limites de toutes les racines réelles d'une équation.

50. LES cas mentionnés dans le chapitre précédent ne sont pas les plus nombreux. Tantôt l'équation à résoudre n'a que des racines imaginaires; tantôt ses racines sont toutes réelles, mais on l'ignore, et plusieurs d'entr'elles ayant pour limites les mêmes nombres entiers p et $p+1$, on ne peut les découvrir toutes par les seules transformées en $(x-1)$, $(x-2)$, etc.; d'autres fois quelques-unes des racines sont réelles, et d'autres sont imaginaires, sans qu'on le sache ou qu'on soit instruit du nombre des unes ou des autres. Dans ces diverses circonstances, on aura recours à des transformées *collatérales*, en la manière qui va être expliquée.

51. Il faut d'abord observer que la résolution des équations se réduisant à la recherche des racines positives [32], cette recherche elle-même se réduit à celle des racines positives qu'une équation quelconque peut avoir au-dessous de l'unité. Ceci est une conséquence des transformations successives; car il est évident que pour connoître toutes les racines positives de l'équation en x, il suffit de connoître respectivement les racines positives inférieures à l'unité, 1°. de la proposée; 2°. de sa transformée

en $(x - 1)$; 3°. de celle en $(x - 2)$; et ainsi de suite, jusqu'à la dernière transformée qui conserve quelque variation de signe. On voit en effet que pour découvrir les racines que la proposée peut avoir entre p et $p + 1$, il ne s'agit que de trouver dans l'équation en $(x - p)$, les valeurs de l'inconnue $(x - p)$ comprises entre o et 1. Tel est donc le problême dont il faut obtenir généralement la solution : Etant donnée une équation qui n'a point de racines égales, s'assurer si elle a, ou si elle n'a pas des racines comprises entre o et 1.

52. Lorsqu'on ignore si l'équation proposée a toutes ses racines réelles, l'examen de la succession des signes ne fournit plus un indice certain de l'existence des racines qui peuvent être comprises entre p et $p + 1$. Si l'équation en $(x - p - 1)$ a des permanences de signe de plus que l'équation en $(x - p)$, le signe du dernier terme dans chacune de ces équations étant le même, on peut seulement soupçonner qu'il y a des valeurs de $(x - p)$ entre zéro et un, et parconséquent des valeurs de x entre p et $p + 1$; mais ce soupçon reste à vérifier.

D'une autre part, si la seconde proposition mentionnée au n° 39 étoit admise comme principe général pour une équation quelconque, ce principe fourniroit un motif constant d'exclusion contre toute valeur qu'on voudroit attribuer à $(x - p)$ entre zéro et un, toutes les fois que l'équation en $(x - p - 1)$, n'a pas plus de permanence de signe que l'équation en $(x - p)$. Dès lors on détermineroit sur le champ, au moyen des exclusions qu'on seroit autorisé à prononcer, les seuls nombres entiers parmi lesquels on doive chercher ceux qui sont, à moins d'une unité près, les racines de l'équation proposée. Comme nous n'apporterons point ici de preuves de la généralité de ce principe, nous allons recourir à un autre motif de rejet.

53. Soit, par exemple, cette équation....

$$x^3 - 4x^2 + 3x - 6 = 0;$$

l'équation inverse en z ou $\frac{1}{x}$ est, comme l'on sait, celle dont les coefficiens sont les mêmes que ceux de l'équation en x, mais en ordre inverse....

$$6z^3 - 3z^2 + 4z - 1 = 0.$$

La transformée en $(z - 1)$ est....

$$6(z-1)^3 + 15(z-1)^2 + 16(z-1) + 6 = 0.$$

Cette transformée n'ayant que des permanences de signes, offre un indice ou *criterium* certain de l'absence de toute racine réelle entre zéro et un, dans l'équation en x. *Généralement l'équation en* x *ne peut avoir plus de racines entre* 0 *et* 1, *que la transformée en* $(z - 1)$ *ou* $\left(\frac{1}{x} - 1\right)$ *n'a de variations de signe.*

Et si l'équation en $(z - 1)$ a son dernier terme négatif, celle en x a, pour le moins, une racine réelle entre zéro et un.

54. Appliquons ce *criterium* à l'équation....

$$x^3 - 2x - 5 = 0,$$

et faisons $\frac{1}{x} = z$, $\frac{1}{x-1} = z_1$, $\frac{1}{x-2} = z_2$, et ainsi de suite.

Coefficiens des équations....

en x.........$1+0-2-5$....en $(z-1)$....$5+17+17+6$
en $(x-1)$....$1+3+1-6$....en (z_1-1)....$6+17+13+1$
en $(x-2)$....$1+6+10-1$....en (z_2-1)....$1-7-23-16$
en $(x-3)$....$1+9+25+16$.

Et pour la recherche des racines négatives, soit $x=-\mathrm{x}$, $\frac{1}{\mathrm{x}}=\mathrm{z}$, etc.

Coefficiens des équations....

en x..........$1-0-2+5$....en $(\mathrm{z}-1)$....$5+13+11+4$
en $(\mathrm{x}-1)$....$1+3+1+4$.

Ces transformations collatérales suffisent, comme l'on voit, pour la résolution approximative de l'équation, à moins d'une unité près ; elles donnent l'exclusion à tout nombre négatif; et elles excluent en même temps tout nombre positif, excepté le nombre 2, lequel est admis pour le plus grand nombre entier compris dans la racine, par le double motif que le dernier terme de l'équation en $(x-3)$ est de signe contraire à celui de l'équation en $(x-2)$, et que le dernier terme de l'équation collatérale en (z_2-1) est négatif : ces deux motifs coincident toujours ensemble.

55. Ces transformations suffisent aussi pour déterminer, à moins d'une unité près, les racines réelles d'une équation, toutes les fois qu'à chaque couple d'équations en $(x-p)$ et $(x-p-1)$, dont les derniers termes respectifs sont de même signe, correspond une équation collatérale en (z_p-1) qui n'a que des permanences de signe.

Exemple.... $x^4 - 12x^3 + 58x^2 - 132x + 121 = 0$.

Coefficiens des équations...

en x... ....1—12+58—132+121...en (z—1)..121+352+388+192+36
en (x—1)...1— 8+28— 48+ 36...en (z_1—1).. 36+ 96+100+ 48+ 9
en (x—2)...1— 4+10— 12+ 9...en (z_2—1).. 9+ 24+ 28+ 16+ 4
en (x—3)...1+ 0+ 4+ 0+ 4...en (z_3—1).. 4+ 16+ 28+ 24+ 9
en (x—4)...1+ 4+10+ 12+ 9.

Les transformées collatérales donnant ici l'exclusion à tout nombre positif, et la proposée n'ayant point de permanence de signe, parconséquent point de racine négative, il s'ensuit que toutes ses racines sont imaginaires.

Autre exemple.... $x^4 - 5x^3 + 5x^2 + 6 - 12 = 0$.

Coefficiens des équations....

en x.........1— 5+ 5+ 6—12....en (z—1)....12+42+49+25+ 5
en (x—1)....1— 1— 4+ 5— 5....en (z_1—1).... 5+15+19+14+ 4
en (x—2)....1+ 3— 2— 2— 4....en (z_2—1).... 4+18+32+23+ 4
en (x—3)....1+ 7+13+ 7— 4....en (z_3—1).... 4+ 9—11—38—24
en (x—4)....1+11+40+58+32.

Puis on fait $x = -\text{x}$, $\frac{1}{\text{x}} = \text{z}$, etc.

Coefficiens des équations....

en x........1+ 5+ 5— 6—12.....en (z—1)...12+54+85+ 51+ 7
en (x—1)...1+ 9+26+ 23— 7.....en (z_1—1)... 7+ 5—53—102—52
en (x—2)...1+13+59+106+52.

D'après les transformées collatérales, on reconnoît que les seules racines réelles de l'équation sont 3 et —1, à moins d'une unité près.

56. L'uniformité des signes dans l'équation en (z_p—1) ne permettant pas d'attribuer aucune valeur à ($x - p$) entre 0 et 1, on peut demander si la proposition inverse est également vraie; c'est-à-dire, si cette uniformité a toujours lieu, lorsque $x - p$ n'a aucune valeur positive

inférieure à l'unité. Si cela étoit, on voit que l'emploi des transformations collatérales ne fourniroit pas seulement un motif certain d'exclusion contre des nombres qui n'appartiennent pas aux racines de l'équation proposée, mais qu'il feroit aussi connoître avec certitude les nombres entiers qui sont, à moins d'une unité près, des racines de cette équation.

57. Pour obtenir la réponse à cette demande, il faut considérer que si $x-p$ n'a pas de valeur entre zéro et un, alors l'équation en z_p ou $\frac{1}{x-p}$ n'ayant pas de valeur supérieure à l'unité, la transformée en (z_p-1) ne peut avoir pour racines réelles que des racines négatives. Donc tous les facteurs réels simples que cette transformée peut avoir, sont de la forme z_p-1+A; et si ces facteurs ne sont associés qu'à des facteurs du second degré de la forme $(z_p-1)^2+P(z_p-1)+Q$, (A, P et Q étant positifs par eux-mêmes), il est évident que la transformée en (z_p-1) n'a pour lors aucune variation de signe. Or cette forme des facteurs du second degré a toujours lieu dans la transformée, à l'exception d'un seul cas, savoir, celui où l'équation en $(x-p)$ a une ou plusieurs couples de racines imaginaires de la forme $+f\pm\sqrt{-\varphi}$; ensorte que f et φ étant l'un et l'autre moindres que l'unité, on ait $\varphi<f(1-f)$, et parconséquent $\varphi<\frac{1}{4}$.

En effet lorsque

$$x-p=f\pm\sqrt{-\varphi},\ z_p=\frac{1}{f\pm\sqrt{-\varphi}}=\frac{f\mp\sqrt{-\varphi}}{f^2+\varphi};$$

et $$z_p-1=\frac{f}{f^2+\varphi}-1\mp\frac{\sqrt{-\varphi}}{f^2+\varphi},$$

la partie réelle $\frac{f}{f^2+\varphi}$ — 1 ne peut être positive, à moins que le dénominateur $f^2+\varphi$ ne soit plus petit que f; ce qui n'a lieu qu'autant que f et φ sont des fractions, et qu'on a $\varphi < f - f^2$, ou $\varphi < f(1-f)$; d'où il suit que φ est alors moindre que $\frac{1}{4}$ ou 0,25; vu que $\frac{1}{4}$ est, comme on sait, le plus grand produit que puisse donner une fraction multipliée par son complément à l'unité.

Ce cas est le seul qui, introduisant dans la transformée en $(z,-1)$ des facteurs de la forme $(z,-1)^2 - P(z,-1) + Q$, pourroit y donner lieu à des variations de signe, et laisser subsister la présomption de l'existence des racines entre zéro et un dans l'équation en $(x-p)$.

58. Ce cas d'exception s'évanouira nécessairement par l'effet des opérations ultérieures de notre Méthode, comme on va le voir dans le chapitre suivant. Mais il suit dès à présent, du numéro précédent, que la seconde partie de cette Méthode fait connoître avec certitude, tantôt l'absence de toute racine réelle dans l'équation en $(x-p)$ entre 0 et 1; tantôt l'alternative de l'existence de plusieurs racines entre zéro et 1, ou de celle d'une couple, au moins, de racines imaginaires, dont la partie réelle est une fraction proprement dite, tandis que la quantité précédée du signe — sous le signe radical, est moindre que $\frac{1}{4}$ ou 0,25, et même que le produit de la partie réelle par son complément à l'unité.

CHAPITRE VI.

Fin de l'exposition de la nouvelle Méthode. Troisième Partie.

59. LORSQU'ON sait avec certitude que la proposée a une ou plusieurs racines comprises entre p et $p+1$, il reste à trouver une valeur exacte de ces racines jusqu'au $n^{ième}$ chiffre décimal; et quand on a lieu seulement de présumer leur existence, il reste à opérer la vérification de ces racines douteuses. Un même procédé va remplir ce double objet; c'est-à-dire que la méthode d'approximation pour les racines déjà connues, sera en même temps une méthode de vérification et d'approximation pour celles qui ne sont que soupçonnées.

60. Soit qu'on ait la certitude que l'équation en $(x-p)$ a quelque racine comprise entre 0 et 1, soit qu'on se trouve seulement autorisé à le soupçonner, on fait $10(x-p)=x'$. Autant $x-p$ a de valeurs entre zéro et un, autant x' en doit avoir entre zéro et dix. Il faut donc, au moyen des transformées en $(x'-1)$, $(x'-2)$, etc., jusqu'à celles en $(x'-10)$ tout au plus, chercher les racines que l'équation en x' a ou peut avoir entre 0 et 10.

On se comporte dans cette recherche comme dans celle des racines de l'équation en x; et l'on parvient de cette manière, soit à trouver la première décimale des racines dont la partie exprimée en nombre entier p est déjà connue; soit à reconnoître et à vérifier, à moins d'un dixième près, l'existence des racines comprises entre p et $(p+1)$, qui jusques-là étoit douteuse, et qui cesse de l'être, parce-que ces mêmes racines ne se trouvent point comprises ensemble entre $\left(p+\frac{p'}{10}\right)$ et $\left(p+\frac{p'+1}{10}\right)$, les différences de ces racines entr'elles pouvant d'ailleurs être indéfiniment moindres que $\frac{1}{10}$; soit encore à détruire la présomption occasionnée par des racines imaginaires $f\pm\sqrt{-\varphi}$, dans le cas où le *criterium* ou moyen d'exclusion mentionné dans la seconde Partie [53], s'est trouvé en défaut [57].

61. On parvient, disons-nous, à détruire ce soupçon à l'aide des équations en $(x'-p')$ et en $(z'_{p'}-1)$, toutes les fois au moins que le centuple de la fraction φ est égal ou supérieur à $\frac{1}{4}$; ou, ce qui revient au même, toutes les fois qu'on n'a pas $\varphi<\frac{1}{400}$, ou bien $\varphi<0{,}0025$.

Pour s'assurer de ceci, il ne faut que faire attention à l'équation $10(x-p)=x'$. Lorsqu'une valeur imaginaire de $(x-p)$ est $f\pm\sqrt{-\varphi}$, la valeur correspondante de x', est $10f\pm\sqrt{-100\varphi}$, et celle de $(x'-p')$ est...... $(10f-p')\pm\sqrt{-100\varphi}$, ou bien $f'\pm\sqrt{-100\varphi}$, si l'on fait $10f-p'=f'$. On raisonnera donc pour l'équation en $(z'_{p'}-1)$, comme on a fait ci-dessus pour celle en (z_p-1) [58].

62. Ce qui précède va s'éclaircir par l'exemple suivant.

Soit à résoudre l'équation....

$$X^3 - 51X^2 + 761X - 2655 = 0;$$

ou bien, X étant égalé à $10x$, soit proposée cette autre équation....

$$x^3 - 5{,}1x^2 + 7{,}61x - 2{,}655 = 0.$$

L'équation n'ayant point de permanence de signe, n'a point de racine réelle négative.

Coefficiens des équations....

en x.........1—5,1+7,61—2,655...en $(z-1)$...2,655+0,355—2,155—0,855
en $(x-1)$...1—2,1+0,41+0,855...en (z_1-1)...0,855+2,975+1,285+0,165
en $(x-2)$...1+0,9—0,79+0,165...en (z_2-1)...0,165—0,295—0,185+1,275
en $(x-3)$...1+3,9+4,01+1,275.

Donc zéro est admis comme racine approchée, à moins d'une unité près; le nombre 1 est exclus; le nombre 2 est à vérifier.

Pour l'approximation de la racine admise, soit $10x = x'$, $\frac{1}{x'} = z'$, etc.

Coefficiens des équations....

en x'.........1	— 51	+ 761	— 2655
en $(x'-1)$....1	— 48	+ 662	— 1944
en $(x'-2)$....1	— 45	+ 569	— 1329
en $(x'-3)$....1	— 42	+ 482	— 804
en $(x'-4)$....1	— 39	+ 401	— 363
en $(x'-5)$....1	— 36	+ 326	+ 0.

Donc $x' = 5$; d'où $x = 0{,}5$.

N. B. On voit que les équations collatérales en $(z'-1)$, (z'_1-1), etc. sont inutiles dans cette circonstance, parceque la transformée en $(z-1)$ n'ayant qu'une variation de signe, il s'ensuit que x' ne peut avoir qu'une seule valeur entre 0 et 10, x n'en pouvant avoir qu'une entre zéro et un [53].

Pour la vérification des racines douteuses, soit.....
$10(x-2)=\overset{1}{x}'$, $\frac{1}{\overset{1}{x}'}=\overset{1}{z}'$, etc.

Coefficiens des équations....

en x'..........1+ 9—79+165.....en $(\overset{1}{z}'-1)$....165+416+346+96
en $(\overset{1}{x}'-1)$....1+12—58+ 96.....en $(\overset{11}{z}'_1-1)$.... 96+230+184+51
en $(\overset{1}{x}'-2)$....1+15—31+ 51.....en $(\overset{1}{z}'_2-1)$.... 51+122+106+36
en $(\overset{1}{x}'-3)$....1+18+ 2+ 36.

Donc $\overset{1}{x}'$ n'a pas de valeur réelle positive; donc 2 est exclus, et l'équation est résolue.

63. *Autre exemple....* $x^5-3x^4-3x^3+7x^2+8x+2=0$.

Coefficiens des équations....

en x..........1— 3— 3+ 7+ 8+ 2...en $(z-1)$... 2+18+ 59+ 86+54+12
en $(x-1)$...1+ 2— 5—10+ 6+12...en (z_1-1)...12+66+134+121+46+ 6
en $(x-2)$...1+ 7+13— 3—16+ 6...en (z_2-1)... 6+14— 7— 32—10+ 1
en $(x-3)$...1+12+51+88+50+ 8.

Coefficiens des équations....

en $x=-x$...1+3— 3— 7+8—2...en $(z-1)$...2+2—5—4+2+0
en $(x-1)$....1+8+19+12+2+0.

Donc une des valeurs de x est -1, et les transformées collatérales ne permettent de soupçonner d'autres racines réelles qu'entre 2 et 3 et entre 0 et -1.

Pour la vérification des racines douteuses positives, soit $10(x-2)=x'$, ou $x=2+\frac{x'}{10}$. On obtient l'équation en x' par une addition convenable de zéros dans les coefficiens de l'équation en $(x-2)$.

Coefficiens des équations....

en x'.........	1	$+\ 70$	$+1300$	$-\ 3000$	-161000	$+600000$
en $(x'-1)$....	1	$+\ 75$	$+1590$	$+\ 1330$	-161815	$+438371$
en $(x'-2)$....	1	$+\ 80$	$+1900$	$+\ 6560$	-154080	$+279552$
en $(x'-3)$....	1	$+\ 85$	$+2230$	$+12750$	-134935	$+134013$
en $(x'-4)$....	1	$+\ 90$	$+2580$	$+19960$	-102400	$+\ 14145$
en $(x'-5)$....	1	$+\ 95$	$+2950$	$+28250$	$-\ 54375$	$-\ 65625$
en $(x'-6)$....	1	$+100$	$+3340$	$+37680$	$+\ 11360$	$-\ 88704$
en $(x'-7)$....	1	$+105$	$+3750$	$+48310$	$+\ 97145$	$-\ 36223$
en $(x'-8)$....	1	$+110$	$+4180$	$+60200$	$+205440$	$+113088.$

Donc x' a deux valeurs, l'une entre 4 et 5, l'autre entre 7 et 8 ; et parconséquent les racines positives de x sont, à moins d'un dixième près, 2,4 et 2,7.

N. B. L'équation en $(z_{2}-1)$ ou $\left(\frac{1}{x-2}-1\right)$ n'ayant que deux variations de signe, ne peut avoir que deux racines positives [53], et parconséquent $(x-2)$ ne peut avoir plus de deux valeurs entre o et 1, ni x' plus de deux valeurs entre o et 10 : les transformées successives faisant ici connaître ces deux valeurs, il est inutile de calculer les collatérales.

Pour la vérification des racines négatives qui peuvent être comprises entre o et 1, on fera $10\,x = x'$, et par les transformées successives en $(x'-1)$, $(x'-2)$, etc., on trouvera deux valeurs pour x', comprises respectivement entre 4 et 5, et entre 7 et 8. D'où il suit que les racines négatives de x sont $-0{,}4$ et $-0{,}7$, à moins d'un dixième près.

64. Les équations en $(x'-p')$ et en $(z'_{p'}-1)$ peuvent n'être pas suffisantes pour déterminer l'admission ou le rejet de la totalité des racines douteuses. Alors on a recours aux équations en $(x''-p'')$ et en $(z''_{p''}-1)$, qu'on obtient

en faisant $10(x'-p')=x''$, $\frac{1}{x''-p''}=z''_{p''}$, et en procédant comme on a fait ci-dessus pour les équations en $(x'-p')$ et en $(z'_{p'}-1)$.

Par ce moyen on approche, jusqu'à la seconde décimale inclusivement, des racines dont l'existence est déjà reconnue, en même temps que l'on découvre les racines réelles jusques-là douteuses, qui étant comprises entre $\left(p+\frac{p'}{10}\right)$ et $\left(p+\frac{p'+1}{10}\right)$, n'ont point pour communes limites $\left(p+\frac{p'}{10}+\frac{p''}{100}\right)$ et $\left(p+\frac{p'}{10}+\frac{p''+1}{100}\right)$, les différences de ces racines entr'elles pouvant d'ailleurs être indéfiniment moindres que $\frac{1}{100}$.

On détruit aussi, par ce même moyen, le soupçon qui auroit été maintenu dans l'équation en $(x'-p')$ par les imaginaires $f'\pm\sqrt{-100\,\varphi}$, toutes les fois, pour le moins, que $10000\,\varphi$ n'est pas égal ou supérieur à $\frac{1}{4}$; ou, ce qui revient au même, toutes les fois qu'on n'a point $\varphi<\frac{1}{40000}$, ou bien $\varphi<0{,}000025$. Les raisonnemens sont ici les mêmes qu'aux numéros 58 et 61.

65. S'il reste encore à vérifier des racines présumées, ou si l'on veut pousser l'exactitude des racines découvertes jusqu'à la troisième décimale inclusivement, on voit comment la vérification et l'approximation se continueront par les équations en $(x'''-p''')$ et en $(z'''_{p'''}-1)$ qu'on obtient en faisant $10(x''-p'')=\frac{x'''}{10}$, et $\frac{1}{x'''-p'''}=z'''_{p'''}$.

66. En procédant de la sorte, au moyen des équations en $(x^{\text{iv}}-p^{\text{iv}})$, en $(x^{\text{v}}-p^{\text{v}})$, etc. etc., s'il y a lieu, on finit

par déterminer quelles sont, parmi les racines présumées de l'équation proposée en x, celles qui doivent être admises et celles que l'on doit exclure. Généralement, on n'est dans le cas de recourir à l'équation en $(x^{(n)} - p^{(n)})$, qu'autant qu'on veut avoir des racines exactes jusqu'à la décimale $n^{ième}$ inclusivement, ou que la proposée a des racines imaginaires dont la partie réelle n'est pas un nombre entier, et dont la partie précédée du signe — sous le signe $\sqrt{\ }$, est moindre que $\frac{1}{4 \times 10^n}$; encore, dans la seconde circonstance, ce recours n'est-il pas toujours nécessaire.

Nous sommes donc arrivés, par notre Méthode, au but que nous nous sommes proposé, qui est de trouver exactement, jusqu'à telle décimale qu'on voudra, les seules valeurs réelles qui puissent être assignées à l'inconnue d'une équation numérique d'un degré quelconque; et nous y sommes parvenus par le seul emploi des deux premières règles de l'Arithmétique. La pratique étant la pierre de touche de la commodité des diverses méthodes, nous desirons que nos Lecteurs s'exercent à résoudre les mêmes équations numériques par la nôtre et par celles qui l'ont précédée; qu'ils résolvent, par exemple, l'équation du cinquième degré du n° 63, et celles du quatrième degré du n° 55.

NOTES.

Sur le CHAPITRE Ier.

(A) Nous avons dit, au sujet du procédé que M. Lagrange a proposé pour corriger la méthode des substitutions successives, qu'il pouvoit donner lieu, en certains cas, à des milliers, et même à un nombre indéfiniment plus grand, d'opérations superflues. Soit, par exemple, une équation du quatrième degré ayant une de ses racines entre 0 et 1; une autre racine entre 1 et 2; une troisième égale à 4, moins un demi-millionième; et, pour dernière racine, 4, plus un demi-millionième (on prend ici, pour plus grande commodité, une fraction rationnelle). Dans ce cas, la limite de la plus petite différence des racines sera moindre qu'un millionième. Donc si l'on fait $D < \frac{1}{1000000}$ dans la progression arithmétique 0, D, 2D, 3D, etc., le nombre des termes à substituer devra s'élever à plus de quatre millions; tandis que cette même équation peut se résoudre par la seule substitution des nombres 0, 1, 2, 3, 4 et 5. Cette extrême multiplicité de substitutions est donc un *luxe* infiniment onéreux; et l'on auroit, généralement, plus tôt fait d'employer successivement, pour les substitutions, au lieu de la série 0, D, 2D, 3D, etc., la série des unités simples; puis, en cas d'insuffisance, celle des dixièmes; puis encore celle des centièmes, et ainsi de suite.

Ce parti seroit préférable, lors même qu'on seroit tenu, en l'adoptant, d'opérer la substitution des nombres de chaque série compris entre chaque terme de la série précédente et le terme suivant, c'est-à-dire, de substituer les dixièmes compris entre 0 et 1, entre 1 et 2, entre 3 et 4, et ainsi de suite sans exception, etc. A plus forte raison, ce mode de substitution doit-il être préféré lorsqu'on a trouvé le moyen de se dispenser de la plupart de ces intercalations ou substitutions intermédiaires, ainsi que cela se rencontre dans notre Méthode.

Par le même motif, dans une équation dont la plus grande racine paroîtroit susceptible de renfermer dans sa valeur des dixaines, ou des centaines, etc., on devroit employer, pour les premières substitutions, la série des dixaines, ou celle des centaines, etc. Les termes de chacune des progressions arithmétiques qu'il conviendroit d'employer successivement, peuvent être représentés d'une manière générale par 0, 10^n, 2.10^n, 3.10^n, etc.; n étant un nombre entier positif, ou zéro, ou un nombre entier négatif. On doit commencer par la substitution des termes de la progression dont la différence 10^n est la puissance de 10 immédiatement inférieure à la limite de la plus grande racine positive. Si cette limite, par exemple, étoit comprise entre cent et mille, la différence de la première progression à employer seroit 10^2. La dernière progression à laquelle on puisse être dans le cas de recourir, est celle dont la différence est la puissance de 10 immédiatement inférieure à D; mais on pourra souvent, ainsi que nous l'avons fait observer, se trouver dispensé d'en venir à cette progression, et même à plusieurs de celles dont l'emploi doit précéder le sien. L'exemple allégué au commencement de cette note en est une preuve sensible. Quoique les puissances de tout autre nombre que 10 pûssent être prises pour les différences respectives de ces progressions, ce dernier nombre doit, en général, être adopté de préférence, à cause de la facilité des calculs, qui résulte de ce qu'il est la base du systême de numération usité.

Si les quatre premières racines d'une équation proposée, du sixième degré, étoient des imaginaires dont la partie réelle fût un nombre entier positif moindre que 3, les deux dernières racines restant les mêmes que ci-dessus, c'est-à-dire, $4 - \frac{1}{2000000}$ et $4 + \frac{1}{2000000}$; alors les quatre millions, et plus, de substitutions à opérer, seroient rigoureusement nécessaires pour la résolution de l'équation, selon la méthode de M. Lagrange; et cette dure nécessité est encore un inconvénient extrêmement grave. Pour résoudre une semblable équation, à moins d'une unité près, suivant la nouvelle méthode, il ne faut que quelques minutes.

(B) En parlant du fameux théorême de Descartes, l'illustre Auteur du Traité de la Résolution des Equations numériques y rappelle que les Anglois attribuent cette règle à leur compatriote Harriot. Il est vrai que Descartes, de son vivant même, fut accusé, par les Anglois, de cette espèce de plagiat, comme ils ont formé depuis une semblable imputation contre Leibnitz. Mais en rappelant cette accusation surannée, qui n'a point empêché que le théorême dont il s'agit n'ait été constamment appelé *la Règle de Descartes*, il est juste aussi d'observer qu'elle a été detruite par plusieurs Auteurs du dix-septième siècle. Le P. Prestet, dans ses Elémens imprimés en 1689, provoque, à ce sujet, la comparaison des écrits d'Harriot avec ceux de Descartes. « Lorsque M. Wallis, dit-il, un peu trop » jaloux de la gloire que la France s'est acquisé dans les » Mathémathiques, vient renouveler cette accusation ridicule, » on est en droit de ne le point croire, puisqu'il parle sans » preuves. M. Hudde, hollandois, qui n'est point suspect, puis- » qu'il n'avoit aucun intérêt à soutenir l'honneur des auteurs » françois, est bien plus équitable dans le jugement qu'il porte » de M. Descartes ».

Sur le CHAPITRE II.

(C) Les deux propositions, dont dépend l'Algorithme du chapitre second, nous avoient paru nouvelles. Mais nous ne devons pas taire que M. Legendre, dans son rapport sur une partie de notre travail, en a jugé autrement. Suivant lui, « ces » deux théorêmes que l'Auteur regarde comme nouveaux, ne » sont que *l'énoncé de propriétés déjà connues*, relatives à » la sommation des suites, et ce qui lui appartient se réduit » à l'Algorithme propre à opérer les transformations ».

Si l'on considère que le second de ces théorêmes et l'Algorithme ne sont qu'une seule et même chose, on aura sans doute quelque peine à comprendre que l'un appartienne à l'Auteur, si l'autre ne lui appartient pas. Peut-être le Rapporteur se seroit-il exprimé avec plus de justesse et de *justice*, s'il eût dit que ces deux propositions, jusqu'ici inconnues, sont des conséquences si faciles à déduire des principes déjà reçus, qu'il peut paroître étonnant qu'on ne s'en soit pas avisé plus tôt. Peut-être, du moins, auroit-il mieux valu que M. Legendre, en niant la nouveauté de ces propositions, ne se fût pas borné à cette simple négation, et qu'il eût bien voulu indiquer en quel ouvrage, élémentaire ou non, elles se trouvent consignées. Quoi qu'il en soit, d'après l'imposante autorité du savant Rapporteur, on conçoit qu'il est inutile de s'arrêter ici à prouver *des propriétés connues*.

(D) L'Algorithme indiqué au n° 26, pourroit être employé à la recherche directe des racines négatives; mais il nous a paru plus simple et plus commode de ramener cette recherche, comme on a coutume de faire, à celle des racines positives et d'employer, à cet effet, notre Algorithme ordinaire.

(E) L'Algorithme du second chapitre, en perdant un peu de sa simplicité, peut s'étendre au calcul de la transformée en $\left(x - \frac{n}{d}\right)$, d n'étant plus seulement une puissance de 10, mais un nombre entier quelconque. Il faut, pour cela, faire $x = \frac{x'}{d}$, et, pour avoir les coefficiens de l'équation en x', multiplier respectivement ceux de l'équation en x, à compter de celui de x^m, par d^0, d^1, d^2,... d^m. Ensuite, par de simples additions et soustractions, on se procure [n°s 22, 24, 25] la transformée en $x' - n$, dont les coefficiens, à compter de celui de la plus haute puissance, respectivement divisés par d^0, d^1, d^2,... d^m, deviennent ceux de l'équation en $\left(x - \frac{n}{d}\right)$. Par ce procédé, le nombre des multiplications et divisions est diminué, autant qu'il se peut.

Sur le CHAPITRE III.

(F) ON a vu [n° 35] comment on peut déterminer une limite, en moins, de la plus petite valeur positive, et une limite, en plus, de la plus grande valeur que puisse avoir l'inconnue d'une équation. Mais il est une remarque qui n'a pas encore été faite, c'est qu'on peut déterminer deux limites semblables pour les valeurs réelles qu'une équation peut avoir entre zéro et un; et voici comment.

Pour obtenir une limite moindre que la plus petite racine, on use du même procédé qu'au n° 35; c'est-à-dire, on prend le quotient du dernier terme divisé par la somme de ce même terme et du plus grand coefficient précédé d'un signe contraire : ce quotient donne nécessairement une fraction pour limite de la plus petite racine positive.

La limite de la plus grande racine qui puisse être comprise entre zéro et un, se découvre à l'aide de la transformée en $(x-1)$, après qu'on a changé les signes de ses coefficiens de rang pair : le plus grand coefficient de cette équation, ainsi modifiée, de signe contraire à celui de son dernier terme, étant divisé par la somme de ce coefficient et du dernier terme, le quotient est une fraction dont la valeur surpasse celle de la plus grande racine que la proposée en x puisse avoir entre 0 et 1. Cette fraction est le complément, à l'unité, de celle qui exprime la limite de la racine la plus voisine de zéro, que l'équation en $(x-1)$ puisse avoir entre 0 et -1. Avec un peu de réflexion, on apperçoit aisément la raison de ceci.

On jugera, par la suite de ces Notes, de quelle importance peut être cette remarque.

Sur le CHAPITRE IV.

(G) PARMI les cas susceptibles d'être résolus par la première partie de la nouvelle Méthode, on a compté celui où la proposée n'a ni racines imaginaires, ni plusieurs racines réelles comprises entre deux nombres entiers p et $p+1$. Il peut néanmoins se présenter alors une difficulté, provenant de la présence des racines commensurables dans l'équation : en voici un exemple avec le moyen d'y obvier. Soit l'équation...

$$x^3+x^2-3x+1=0;$$

on a les coefficiens des équations....

$$\begin{array}{ll} \text{en } x \ldots\ldots\ldots\ldots\ldots & 1+1-3+1 \\ \text{en } (x-1) \ldots\ldots\ldots & 1+4+2+0. \end{array}$$

Dans cette circonstance où la proposée a l'unité pour racine, il se pourroit qu'il y eût une autre racine entre zéro et un, dont l'existence ne seroit point manifestée par le dernier terme. Si cette racine existe en effet, on s'en assurera en prenant la somme des trois premiers termes de la proposée $1+1-3$, laquelle somme égalant -1, est de signe contraire au troisième terme $+2$, de la transformée en $(x-1)$, et par conséquent, atteste l'existence d'une racine entre 0 et 1.

La raison de ceci est que, dans ce cas, l'équation du deuxième degré qui résulte de la division de la proposée par $x-1$, a pour ses coefficiens respectifs les sommes-premières des coefficiens de la proposée, à commencer du premier jusqu'au troisième. Ces sommes étant 1, 2, -1, l'équation du second degré est....

$$x^2+2x-1=0,$$

dont la transformée en $(x-1)$ est....

$$(x-1)^2+4(x-1)+2=0.$$

Cette opération seroit inutile, si l'on savait d'avance que la proposée n'a point de racines imaginaires, la simple comparaison des signes de cette équation avec ceux de sa transformée étant alors suffisante pour manifester l'existence de la racine entre et 1.

Quoique l'exemple employé dans cette note, soit celui d'une équation en x du troisième degré, dont la transformée en $(x-1)$ n'a que son dernier terme égal à zéro, le procédé est général. La proposée étant du degré m, et sa transformée en $(x-1)$ ayant ses n derniers termes égaux, chacun, à zéro, il faut alors prendre la somme des $m+1-n$ premiers coefficiens de l'équation proposée; cette somme est la valeur du dernier terme de l'équation en x du degré $(m-n)$, qui est le même degré auquel la transformée en $(x-1)$ se trouve abaissée par l'égalité à zéro de ses n derniers termes.

(H) Nous n'aurions peut-être pas dû faire mention, au n° 48, de l'objection opposée à la nouvelle Méthode; mais nous savons que cette objection a été faite dans les propres termes que nous avons rapportés; et dès lors il a bien fallu en montrer la frivolité. Quelles sont d'ailleurs ces Méthodes ordinaires qu'on puisse dire *plus expéditives*, et en même temps *aussi sûres*, *aussi générales* que la nôtre ?

Sur le CHAPITRE V.

(I) OUTRE le *criterium* que nous avons fait connoître [n° 53], il en existe plusieurs autres qui, sans avoir tous les avantages du premier, peuvent souvent en tenir lieu. Un second *criterium* consiste dans ce corollaire aussi important par son utilité que facile à déduire de la remarque que nous avons consignée dans la note (F) :

Une équation n'a point de racine entre zéro et un, lorsque la limite, en moins, de sa plus petite racine, est égale ou supérieure à la limite, en plus, de la plus grande racine qu'elle puisse avoir entre o *et* 1.

Soit, pour exemple, la même équation du n° 53...;

$$x^3 - 4x^2 + 3x - 6 = 0.$$

Coefficiens des équations....

en x............1 — 4 + 3 — 6
en $(x - 1)$.....1 — 1 — 2 — 6.

Ici la plus petite valeur que x puisse avoir entre 0 et 1, doit être supérieure à $\frac{6}{9}$ ou $\frac{2}{3}$; et la plus grande doit être au-dessous de $\frac{2}{8}$ ou $\frac{1}{4}$; la contradiction qui se rencontre entre ces deux conditions fait voir l'impossibilité qu'il y ait des valeurs positives de x au-dessous de l'unité.

(K) A l'aide du *criterium* que nous avons indiqué dans la note précédente, on peut souvent résoudre une équation numérique, sans avoir besoin de recourir aux transformées collatérales.

Prenons pour exemple la même équation....

$$x^3 - 4x^2 + 3x - 6 = 0.$$

Coefficiens des équations....

en x.........$1 - 4 + 3 - 6$
en $(x - 1)$....$1 - 1 - 2 - 6$
en $(x - 2)$....$1 + 2 - 1 - 8$
en $(x - 3)$....$1 + 5 + 6 - 6$
en $(x - 4)$....$1 + 8 + 19 + 6$.

On a déjà vu que x ne peut avoir de valeur entre 0 et 1.

La plus petite racine de l'équation en $(x - 1)$ doit surpasser $\frac{6}{7}$, et la plus grande racine positive, inférieure à 1, que cette équation puisse avoir, doit être au-dessous de $\frac{2}{10}$ ou $\frac{1}{5}$. La contradiction est évidente. Donc l'équation en $(x - 1)$ n'a point de racine positive entre 0 et 1 ; et par conséquent, celle en x n'en a point entre 1 et 2.

De même, les fractions qu'on voudroit admettre comme racines de l'équation en $(x - 2)$, devroient être en même temps au-dessus de $\frac{8}{10}$ ou $\frac{4}{5}$, et au-dessous de $\frac{5}{11}$, conditions incompatibles. Donc l'équation en $(x - 2)$ n'a pas de racine entre 0 et 1 ; et par conséquent celle en x n'en a point entre 2 et 3.

L'équation en $(x - 3)$ n'a qu'une racine positive qui est manifestée entre 0 et 1 ; par conséquent x a une valeur positive entre 3 et 4. Et la proposée n'a pas d'autre racine réelle, vu que n'ayant point de permanence de signe, elle n'a point de racine négative, et que l'absence des variations de signe dans la transformée en $(x - 4)$ établit le nombre 4 pour limite de la plus grande racine positive de la proposée.

(L) Un troisième *criterium* s'offre encore à nous : *Une équation n'a point de racine entre zéro et un, lorsque la suite formée par les sommes-premières de ses coefficiens pris à rebours, ne présente point de variation de signe.* Cette proposition est une conséquence de notre Algorithme [n° 20]; car il est évident que l'absence des variations de signe dans cette suite, entraîne cette même absence dans la transformée collatérale.

Ainsi dans la même équation qui vient de nous servir d'exemple, les coefficiens pris à rebours étant....

$$-6+3-4+1,$$

les sommes-premières sont... $-6-3-7-6$;

d'où il suit que l'équation en x n'a point de racine entre o et 1.

Ce *criterium* s'applique pareillement aux deux transformées de cette équation en $(x-1)$ et en $(x-2)$. L'opération qu'il exige peut souvent se faire mentalement, et même d'un coup-d'œil, comme cela se trouve dans le cas pris pour exemple; ce qui rend ce *criterium* très-commode.

(M) Il est encore d'autres circonstances où l'on peut se dispenser de calculer les transformées collatérales.

Lorsque les transformées successives en $(x-1)$, $(x-2)$, etc. ont fait découvrir autant de racines positives que la proposée a de variations de signe, on voit que les collatérales en $(z-1)$, (z_1-1), (z_2-1), etc. deviennent inutiles. C'est donc surabondamment que ces dernières ont été employées au n° 54, dans la recherche des racines positives de l'équation....... $x^3-2x-5=0$; et au n° 55, dans celle des racines négatives de l'équation $x^4-5x^3+5x^2+6x-12=0$.

Dans la première équation de ce même n° 55, la seule règle de Descartes rendoit inutiles toutes les transformées collatérales, à l'exception de celle en (z_2-1). Il suffit, pour s'en convaincre, de jeter les yeux sur les signes des coefficiens de cette équation et de ses transformées successives. On en peut dire autant par rapport à l'équation en x du n° 62, et à ses transformées successives. En général, il ne faut point perdre de vue cette règle de Descartes, dont les applications se présentent fréquemment dans la nouvelle Méthode.

Lorsqu'on est parvenu à découvrir $m-2$ racines réelles d'une équation du degré m, on ne peut supposer que les deux restantes aient des valeurs réelles comprises entre deux nombres entiers p et $p+1$, si l'équation en $(x-p-1)$ n'a pas au moins deux permanences de signe de plus que celle en $(x-p)$. Ainsi dans l'équation du n° 46, $x^3-7x+7=0$, lors même qu'on ignoreroit que toutes ses racines sont réelles, la seule vue des transformées successives apprendroit qu'il ne faut chercher les deux racines positives de la proposée qu'entre 1 et 2.

(N) Le *criterium* qui est indiqué au n° 53, et que l'on doit considérer comme le plus important, peut être généralisé ainsi : *une équation en* x *ne peut avoir plus de racines comprises entre zéro et* u, *qu'il n'y a de variations de signe dans l'équation en* $\left(\mathrm{z}-\frac{1}{\mathrm{u}}\right)$; u *représentant une valeur positive quelconque, et* z *égalant* $\frac{1}{\mathrm{x}}$.

Sur quoi, il faut observer qu'en faisant $z'=uz$, on a les mêmes variations de signe dans l'équation en $(z'-1)$ ou $\left(\frac{u}{x}-1\right)$ que dans celle en $\left(z-\frac{1}{u}\right)$ ou $\left(\frac{1}{x}-\frac{1}{u}\right)$; ensorte qu'il suffit, sous ce rapport, d'obtenir la première.

Ainsi la proposée en x n'aura point de racine entre zéro et u, lorsque la transformée en $(z'-1)$ ou $\left(\frac{u}{x}-1\right)$ n'aura que des permanences de signe.

Cette uniformité des signes de la transformée aura constamment lieu, lorsqu'il n'y a aucune valeur de x entre o et u, si ce n'est quand la proposée a une ou plusieurs couples de racines imaginaires de la forme $f\pm\sqrt{-\varphi}$, f ayant une valeur positive moindre que celle de u, et φ étant moindre que $f(u-f)$, et par conséquent moindre que $\frac{u^2}{4}$. Ce cas d'exception est le seul qui puisse produire quelque variation de signe dans la transformée en ($z'-1$); encore n'en est-ce pas un effet nécessaire.

Dans ce cas, si $u=1$, f est une fraction, et φ est $<\frac{1}{4}$.

Si $u=10$, f est entre 0 et 10, et φ est $<\frac{10^2}{4}$ ou 25.

Si $u=100$, f est entre 0 et 100, et φ est $<\frac{100^2}{4}$ ou 2500.

Et généralement, si $u=10^n$, f est entre 0 et 10^n, et φ est $<\frac{10^{2n}}{4}$ ou $25.10^{2(n-1)}$. Ceci a également lieu lorsque l'exposant n est négatif.

Ces résultats se lient avec ceux des n°s 57, 61, 64; et ce *criterium*, ainsi généralisé, se démontre d'une manière analogue à celle du n° 57 : z' ou $\frac{u}{x}$ est ici $\frac{u}{f\pm\sqrt{-\varphi}}$ ou $\frac{uf\mp\sqrt{-u^2\varphi}}{f^2+\varphi}$; ainsi la partie réelle de $z'-1$ est $\frac{f(u-f)-\varphi}{f^2+\varphi}$; quantité qui ne peut être >0 qu'autant que le nombre f est positif et plus petit que u, et que φ est $<f(u-f)$.

(O) Appliquons ceci à l'équation....

$$x^4-12x^3+58x^2-132x+121=0.$$

Cette équation est la même qui a été résolue au n° 55, à l'aide de ses transformées successives en $(x-1)$, etc., et des transformées collatérales en $(z-1)$, (z_1-1), etc. Il est aisé de reconnoître [55] que ses racines positives, si elle en a, sont moindres que 3.

Les coefficiens de l'équation inverse en z ou $\frac{1}{x}$ étant...

$$121-132+58-12+1;$$

ceux de l'équation en $z'=3z$ sont...

$$121-3.132+3^2.58-3^3.12+3^4;$$

ou bien $\quad 121-396+522-324+81.$

Les coefficiens de l'équation en $(z'-1)$, calculés par l'Algorithme, sont......

$$121+88+60+16+4.$$

Donc la proposée n'a point de racine positive moindre que 3; et comme elle n'en peut avoir qui soit égale ou supérieure à ce nombre, et que l'absence des permanences en exclut toute racine négative, il s'ensuit que l'équation en x n'a point de racines réelles.

L'application de ce *criterium* n'a pas le même résultat dans l'équation suivante....

$$x^3-2,1x^2+0,41x+0,855=0,$$

équation dont la plus grande racine positive, s'il y en a, est <4.

Les coefficiens de l'équation en $z'=4z=\frac{4}{x}$, sont....

$$0,855+4\times0,41-16\times2,1+64,$$

ou bien... $0,855+1,64-33,6+64.$

Ceux de l'équation en $(z'-1)$ sont....

$$0,855+4,205-27,755+32,895.$$

Donc la proposée en x a, soit une couple de racines positives, soit une couple de racines imaginaires dont la partie réelle est entre 0 et 4, et dont la partie précédée du signe $-$ sous le signe $\sqrt{\ }$ est $<\frac{4^2}{4}$ ou <4.

Si l'on fait attention que les coefficiens de cette proposée sont les mêmes que ceux de la transformée en $(x-1)$ du n° 62, on appercevra aisément que c'est un cas d'exception semblable à celui que présente l'équation en x résolue dans ce numéro.

(P) Le problême de la résolution des équations numériques étant réduit par la nouvelle méthode à la recherche des racines d'une équation comprises entre zéro et un, il est avantageux de multiplier les moyens de reconnoître l'absence de toute racine réelle entre ces deux limites : en voici donc un quatrième.

On prendra la somme des coefficiens de signe contraire à celui du dernier terme; si elle n'est pas plus grande que ce terme, on en conclura évidemment que l'équation n'a pour racine aucune valeur entre o et 1.

Ce moyen si simple, appliqué successivement aux diverses transformées, suffit quelquefois à la résolution d'une équation. Reprenons l'exemple déjà employé....

$$x^3 - 4x^2 + 3x - 6 = 0$$

Coefficiens des équations....

en x..........	$1 - 4 + 3 - 6$
en $(x - 1)$...	$1 - 1 - 2 - 6$
en $(x - 2)$...	$1 + 2 - 1 - 8$
en $(x - 3)$...	$1 + 5 + 6 - 6$
en $(x - 4)$...	$1 + 8 + 19 + 6$

Au premier coup-d'œil jeté sur les coefficiens, on reconnoît à l'aide de ce quatrième *criterium*, que la proposée n'a point de racine réelle entre o et 3; et par la règle de Descartes, on voit que la proposée n'a qu'une racine réelle, comprise entre 3 et 4. Cette seule règle, d'ailleurs, suffisoit pour indiquer l'absence de toute racine réelle entre 1 et 3.

(Q) Si l'essai du moyen précédent n'a pas suffi, on peut aussi prendre la limite, en plus, des valeurs positives que l'équation peut avoir pour racines entre o et 1, en la manière indiquée par la note (F), substituer cette limite à la place de l'inconnue dans les termes de signe contraire à celui du dernier terme, et prendre la somme des termes où la substitution a été faite. Pour que l'inconnue puisse avoir quelque valeur entre o et 1, il faut évidemment que cette somme surpasse la valeur du dernier terme. Ce moyen est d'une application assez facile, quand la limite dont il s'agit est une fraction dont les deux termes n'ont, chacun, qu'un seul chiffre; et il est souvent aisé de s'en procurer une semblable.

(R) Si l'on fait $-(x-1)=\xi$, et par conséquent $-x=\xi-1$, après le changement des signes des termes de rang pair dans les équations en $(x-1)$ et en x, on aura deux équations en ξ et $(\xi-1)$, auxquelles on pourra appliquer les mêmes moyens indiqués dans les notes précédentes, pour manifester l'absence des racines réelles entre zéro et un dans l'équation en ξ, et par conséquent dans celle en x.

(S) Ces divers moyens tendant à diminuer beaucoup le nombre des opérations, ne doivent pas être négligés dans l'usage de la nouvelle Méthode. Néanmoins il pourra paroître convenable de ne point embarrasser les commençans par trop de détails, et de les exercer d'abord à résoudre les équations par les seuls procédés indiqués dans le corps de l'ouvrage.

(T) Un *criterium* d'une plus grande importance est celui qui résultera de la seconde proposition du n° 39, si on l'admet en principe général pour une équation quelconque. « Il arrive » quelquefois dans ces matières, dit Fontenelle, que l'on trouve » de bonnes méthodes, et qu'il n'est pas aisé d'en trouver une » démonstration assez précise ou assez claire. On voit la route » qu'il faut tenir, on voit que l'on arrivera, on arrive tou- » jours ; mais à toute rigueur, on pourroit douter, et on ne » forceroit pas un incrédule, triomphe indispensable pour les » Mathématiques ». Et cependant la règle même de Descartes, la théorie des parallèles, et plusieurs autres vérités mathématiques, ont été généralement admises long-temps avant qu'elles aient été rigoureusement démontrées.

Sur le CHAPITRE VI.

(U) D'APRÈS les équations.....

$10(x-p)=x'$, $10(x'-p')=x''$, ... $10(x^{(n-1)}-p^{(n-1)})=x^{(n)}$;

on reconnoît aisément que

$$x^{(n)}-p^{(n)}=10^n\left(x-p-\frac{p'}{10}-\frac{p''}{100}-\ldots\ldots-\frac{p^{(n)}}{10^n}\right).$$

Il est donc facile de passer, respectivement, des équations en $(x'-p')$, $(x''-p'')$, $(x'''-p''')$, etc. aux équations en $\left(x-p-\frac{p}{10}\right)$, $\left(x-p-\frac{p'}{10}-\frac{p''}{100}\right)$, $\left(x-p-\frac{p'}{10}-\frac{p''}{100}-\frac{p'''}{1000}\right)$, etc.

Généralement, les coefficiens de l'équation en $(x^{(n)}-p^{(n)})$ du degré m, divisés respectivement, à compter de celui de la plus haute puissance, par $(10^n)^0$, $(10^n)^1$, ...$(10^n)^m$, deviennent les coefficiens de l'équation en $\left(x-p-\frac{p'}{10}-\ldots\ldots-\frac{p^{(n)}}{10^n}\right)$.

Ainsi le terme tout connu de cette dernière équation est égal au terme tout connu de celle en $(x^{(n)}-p^{(n)})$, divisé par 10^{nm}. Par conséquent, le dernier terme d'une transformée en $(x^{(n)}-p^{(n)})$, divisé par 10^{nm}, est égal au résultat que donne le nombre $\left(p+\frac{p'}{10}+\ldots+\frac{p^n}{10^n}\right)$ substitué à x dans l'équation proposée.

(a) Il résulte de ce qui précède que les transformées en $(x-p)$, $(x'-p')$, etc., sans autre opération ultérieure de calcul que le placement convenable de la virgule indicative des décimales, donnent arithmétiquement les valeurs de l'ordonnée y, correspondant aux valeurs entières et décimales de l'abscisse x, dans la courbe qui a pour équation....

$$A_0x^m + A_1x^{m-1} + \ldots\ldots A_{m-1}x^1 + A_mx^0 = y.$$

On ne s'arrêtera point ici à montrer comment la considération de ces valeurs numériques de y peuvent contribuer à la résolution d'une équation numérique.

(b) Une autre conséquence est que les coefficiens de l'équation en $(x^{(n)} - 10)$, respectivement divisés par $10^0, 10^1, 10^2, \ldots 10^m$, deviennent ceux de l'équation en $(x^{(n-1)} - p^{(n-1)} - 1)$; c'est-à-dire, l'équation en $(x' - 10)$, ainsi modifiée, devient celle en $(x - p - 1)$; l'équation en $(x'' - 10)$ devient pareillement celle en $(x' - p' - 1)$, et ainsi de suite. Cela se prouve généralement par l'équation $10(x^{(n-1)} - p^{(n-1)}) = x^{(n)}$; d'où...... $x^{(n)} - 10 = 10(x^{(n-1)} - p^{(n-1)} - 1)$.

Or cette conséquence mérite quelque attention, en ce qu'elle fournit au calculateur un *contrôle*, ou, comme on s'exprime en Arithmétique, une *preuve* de la justesse des calculs relatifs aux transformées successives. Et par cette raison, lorsqu'on attache quelque importance à éviter les erreurs, et que les mêmes opérations ne se font point concurremment par deux calculateurs qui se servent mutuellement de contrôle, il convient de continuer les transformations jusqu'à celle en $(x^{(n)} - 10)$, quoique, sans ce motif, on fût souvent dans le cas de s'arrêter plus tôt.

Prenons pour exemple l'équation du cinquième degré du n° 63. On a pour les coefficiens de ses transformées....

en $(x - 2)$.....$1 + 7 + 13 - 3 - 16 + 6$.
en $(x - 3)$.....$1 + 12 + 51 + 88 + 50 + 8$.

On s'est trouvé dans le cas de faire $10(x - 2) = x'$, et de calculer les équations en $(x' - 1)$, $(x' - 2)$, etc., jusqu'à celle en $(x' - 8)$; mais pour s'assurer qu'il n'y a point d'erreur de calcul dans ces transformations, il faut les continuer jusqu'à l'équation en $(x' - 10)$.

Coefficiens des transformées.....

en $(x'-8)$....$1+110+4180+60200+205440+113088$
en $(x'-9)$....$1+115+4630+73410+338825+583019$
en $(x'-10)$....$1+120+5100+88000+500000+800000$.

Les coefficiens de la transformée en $(x'-10)$ respectivement divisés par 10^0, 10^1, 10^2, ...10^5, deviennent

$$1+12+51+88+50+8;$$

ils se réduisent, comme cela devoit être, à ceux de la transformée en $(x-3)$.

(V). On a vu, dans le Chapitre VI, comment une même méthode nous sert à approcher davantage d'une racine déjà manifestée, à moins d'une unité près entière ou décimale, et à opérer simultanément la vérification et l'approximation des racines qui restent encore à déterminer. Cette unité de méthode a été prescrite par la nature même de la chose, dans le dernier cas; et il a paru convenable de la conserver dans le premier, autant pour ne pas déroger à la simplicité des moyens, que pour ne point multiplier les méthodes sans nécessité, et pour conserver dans tous les calculs l'espèce de *preuve* ou de *contrôle* mentionné dans la note précédente.

Voici néanmoins un nouveau procédé d'approximation que nous proposons pour le premier cas, c'est-à-dire pour celui où, à l'aide de deux transformées successives en $(\xi-\pi)$ et $(\xi-\pi-1)$, et en cas de besoin, de la collatérale en $(\zeta_\pi-1)$, on a reconnu l'existence d'une seule racine comprise entre 0 et 1, pour l'équation en $(\xi-\pi)$, et par conséquent d'une seule comprise entre π et $\pi+1$, pour l'équation en ξ.

(a) Soit $\xi=\pi+\xi_1$, ou $\xi-\pi=\xi_1$; soient respectivement π_1 et Π_1 les limites, en moins et en plus, de la valeur de ξ_1 comprise entre 0 et 1, déterminées conformément à ce qui a été dit plus haut [note (F)]. On peut prendre, ou π_1, ou Π_1 pour deuxième valeur approchée de ξ_1, les premières étant zéro et un; et par conséquent $\pi + \pi_1$, ou $\pi + \Pi_1$, pour deuxième valeur approchée de ξ.

Supposons d'abord qu'on veuille approcher de la racine par des valeurs de plus en plus convergentes, qui soient toujours inférieures à la valeur exacte.

On fera $\xi_1 = \pi_1 + \xi_2$, ou $\xi_1 - \pi_1 = \xi_2$; on passera de l'équation en ξ_1 à celle en ξ_2 [*voyez* la note (E)], et l'on déterminera la limite, en moins, de la valeur de ξ_2 comprise entre o et 1. Cette limite étant représentée par π_2, la troisième valeur approchée de ξ sera $\pi + \pi_1 + \pi_2$.

On se procurera ainsi successivement les équations en ξ_3, ξ_4, ... ξ_ν; et l'on aura $\pi + \pi_1 + \pi_2 + \ldots + \pi_\nu$ pour la $(\nu+1)^{ième}$ valeur approchée de ξ.

Supposons maintenant qu'on veuille approcher de la racine par des valeurs de plus en plus convergentes, mais toujours supérieures à la valeur exacte de ξ.

On passera de l'équation en ξ_1 à celle en $(\xi_1 - \Pi_1)$; puis faisant $\xi_1 = \Pi_1 - \Xi$, ou $\Xi = -(\xi_1 - \Pi_1)$, on obtiendra l'équation en Ξ, en changeant les signes des termes de rang pair dans l'équation en $(\xi_1 - \Pi_1)$. Il ne restera plus qu'à obtenir des valeurs de plus en plus convergentes, mais toujours inférieures à Ξ; de sorte que la valeur de plus en plus approchée de $(\Pi_1 - \Xi)$ ou ξ_1, et par conséquent celle de ξ ou $\pi + \xi_1$, demeureront toujours plus grandes que la valeur exacte. Ces approximations vers la valeur de Ξ se feront de la même manière que dans la première supposition.

(b) Prenons pour exemple cette équation que nous avons déjà résolue [54], à moins d'une unité près....

$$x^3 - 2x - 5 = 0.$$

On a trouvé pour les coefficiens de ses transformées....

$$\text{en } (x-2)\ldots\ldots 1+6+10-1$$
$$\text{en } (x-3)\ldots\ldots 1+9+25+16.$$

Il résulte de ces transformées que l'équation en $(x-2)$ a une racine comprise entre 0 et 1, dont les premières valeurs approchées, l'une en moins, l'autre en plus, sont, respectivement, 0 et 1. Mais, en outre, ces deux transformées fournissent immédiatement les secondes valeurs approchées de cette racine, qui sont $\frac{1}{1+10}$ ou $\frac{1}{11}$ pour la valeur en moins, et $\frac{25}{25+16}$ ou $\frac{25}{41}$ pour la valeur en plus. [*Voyez* la note (F).]

On voit donc, en se bornant aux valeurs approchées en moins, que les deux premières sont, pour la proposée....

$$2 \text{ et } 2+\frac{1}{11}, \text{ ou } \frac{23}{11}; \text{ ou bien } 2{,}0909090909\ldots\ldots$$

On reconnoîtra ci-après que cette dernière valeur est exacte dans ses deux premières décimales.

Il faut maintenant, en faisant $x-2=\xi_1$, passer de l'équation en ξ_1 à celle en ξ_2 ou $\left(\xi_1-\frac{1}{11}\right)$. On peut employer à cet effet l'Algorithme modifié [note (E)], de la manière suivante.

Soit $11\xi_1=\xi'_1$: on a pour les coefficiens des équations....

$$\text{en } \xi'_1\ldots\ldots\ldots\ldots 1+6.11+10.11^2-1.11^3$$
$$\text{ou}\ldots\ldots\ldots\ldots\ldots 1+66\quad+1210\quad-1331$$
$$\text{en } (\xi'_1-1)\ldots\ldots 1+69\quad+1345\quad-54.$$

Substituant à ξ'_1-1 sa valeur $11\xi_1-1$, ou $11\left(\xi_1-\frac{1}{11}\right)$, et faisant $\xi_1-\frac{1}{11}=\xi_2$, on a pour les coefficiens de l'équation....

$$\text{en } \xi_2\ldots\ldots 11^3\quad+69.11^2+1345.11-54.$$
$$\text{ou}\ldots\ldots\ldots 1331+8349\quad+14795\quad-54.$$

La limite, en moins, de ξ_2 est $\frac{54}{54+14795}$ ou $\frac{54}{14849}=\frac{1}{274+\frac{53}{54}}$; limite à laquelle on peut substituer, pour plus de simplicité, $\frac{1}{275}=\frac{1}{11.25}=0,0036363636\ldots\ldots$

Ainsi la troisième valeur approchée de x est...

$$2+\frac{1}{11}+\frac{1}{11.25}, \text{ ou } \frac{576}{275}; \text{ ou bien } 2,0945454545\ldots.$$

Nous ferons voir que cette valeur est exacte jusqu'à la quatrième décimale inclusivement.

On passe ensuite, de la même manière, de l'équation en ξ_2 à celle en ξ_3 ou $\left(\xi_2-\frac{1}{11.25}\right)$. Faisant $11.25\xi_2=\xi'_2$, et substituant dans l'équation en ξ_2, on a pour les coefficiens des équations...

en ξ'_2............ $1+69.25+1345.25^2-54.25^3$

ou............... $1+1725\quad+840625\quad-843750$

en (ξ'_2-1).... $1+1728\quad+844078\quad-1399.$

Substituant à ξ'_2-1 sa valeur $11.25\xi_2-1$, ou $11.25\left(\xi_2-\frac{1}{11.25}\right)$, et faisant $\xi_2-\frac{1}{11.25}=\xi_3$, on a pour les coefficiens de l'équation.....

en ξ_3.... $11^3.25^3+1728.11^2.25^2+844078.11.25-1399$,

ou....... $20796875+13763750\quad+232121450\quad-1399.$

La limite, en moins, de ξ_3 est....

$$\frac{1399}{1399+232121450}, \text{ ou } \frac{1399}{232122849}; \text{ ou bien } \frac{1}{165920\frac{769}{1399}}.$$

Mais on peut, pour simplifier, lui substituer....

$$\frac{1}{165925}=\frac{1}{25.6637}.$$

Ainsi la quatrième valeur de x, approchée en moins, est....

$$2+\frac{1}{11}+\frac{1}{275}+\frac{1}{165925},$$

ou........2,09454545454...+0,00000060268 19...,

ou bien....2,0945514813 64....,

et cette dernière valeur est exacte jusqu'à la neuvième décimale inclusivement, comme on le verra plus bas.

(c) Les valeurs approchées de cette même racine, calculées par Newton, suivant le procédé qui lui appartient, sont....

2....2,1....2,0946....2,09455147....

M. Lagrange a aussi calculé, suivant son procédé, les valeurs approchées de cette racine, en fractions continues, alternativement plus petites et plus grandes que x. Les résultats sont....

$$\frac{2}{1},\ \frac{21}{10},\ \frac{23}{11},\ \frac{44}{21},\ \frac{111}{53},\ \frac{155}{74},\ \frac{576}{275},\ \frac{731}{349},\ \frac{1307}{624},\ \frac{16415}{7837},\ \text{etc.}$$

La dixième de ces valeurs, $\frac{16415}{7837}$, qui est approchée en plus, étant réduite en décimales, devient 2,0945514865.

Les valeurs approchées en moins, trouvées suivant le nouveau procédé que nous indiquons dans cette note, étant....

$$2\ldots 2+\frac{1}{11} \text{ ou } \frac{23}{11}\ldots 2+\frac{1}{11}+\frac{1}{275} \text{ ou } \frac{576}{275}\ldots 2+\frac{1}{11}+\frac{1}{275}+\frac{1}{165925};$$

ou bien 2,09090909.....2,09454545.......2,0945514813 64...,

on voit que ce procédé a donné des résultats un peu plus exacts que celui de Newton, et qu'il les a donnés plus promptement qu'on ne les obtient par le procédé de M. Lagrange.

En outre, ce procédé est général et sûr, et la méthode de Newton n'a pas ces avantages. « En général, l'usage de cette » méthode n'est sûr, dit M. Lagrange, que lorsque la valeur » approchée est à la fois ou plus grande ou plus petite que

» chacune des racines réelles de l'équation, et que chacune des » parties réelles des racines imaginaires; et par conséquent, cette » méthode ne peut être employée sans scrupule que pour trouver » la plus grande ou la plus petite racine d'une équation qui » n'a que des racines réelles ou qui en a d'imaginaires, mais » dont les parties réelles sont moindres que la plus grande » racine réelle, ou plus grande que la plus petite de ces » racines..... en regardant, comme on le doit, les quan- » tités négatives comme plus petites que les positives, et les » plus grandes négatives comme plus petites que les moins » grandes. (*De la Résolution des Equations numériques*, » *page* 141.) »

Si l'on emploie, au lieu du procédé de Newton, la méthode d'approximation tirée des séries récurrentes, on trouve, pour les valeurs approchées de x, dans l'équation $x^2 - 2x - 5 = 0$....

2,089....2,09467....2,094549....2,0945515...etc.

On ne pourroit, ainsi que l'a prouvé M. Lagrange, employer généralement cette méthode d'approximation pour chacune des racines réelles d'une équation quelconque, qu'autant que l'on connoîtroit d'avance une valeur approchée de cette racine, telle que la différence entre cette valeur et la vraie valeur de la racine fût moindre en quantité, c'est-à-dire, abstraction faite des signes, que la différence entre la même valeur et chacune des autres racines, et en même temps moindre que la racine quarrée de chacun des produits des racines imaginaires correspondantes, s'il y en a, diminuées de la même valeur. Autrement, cette méthode ne sert qu'à trouver la plus grande et la plus petite des racines réelles; encore faut-il que le quarré de la plus grande ou de la plus petite racine cherchée soit en même temps plus petit que chacun des produits réels des racines imaginaires correspondantes, et qu'on ait quelque moyen de s'en assurer. [*De la Résolution* etc., pag. 147, 151].

(d) Nous avons indiqué plus haut comment on pourroit se procurer une suite de valeurs approchées de l'inconnue, convergentes en plus. Mais pour éviter des calculs inutiles, on peut, au moyen de quelques opérations ajoutées à celles qui ont donné les équations en ξ_1, ξ_2, ξ_3, ... ξ_ν, obtenir une limite, en plus, de ξ_ν, et par conséquent de toutes les valeurs approchées de ξ, depuis la première jusqu'à la $\nu^{ième}$. Nous prendrons d'abord un exemple particulier, et nous traiterons ensuite ce sujet d'une manière générale.

Dans l'exemple qui nous a servi, on a trouvé $\frac{1}{165925}$ ou $\frac{1}{25.6637}$, pour la valeur de π_3, c'est-à-dire, de la limite, en moins, de ξ_3. Faisant donc $\xi_3 = \frac{1}{25.6637}\xi'_3$, et calculant les équations en ξ'_3, $(\xi'_3 - 1)$, $(\xi'_3 - 2)$, on trouve pour les coefficiens des équations....

en $(\xi'_3 - 1)$...$1331 + 1387721049 + 408998623104907 - 12049759756$
en $(\xi'_3 - 2)$...$1331 + 1387723042 + 409001398548998 + 408987961067521$.

Puis on fait $10^3(\xi'_3 - 1) = \xi''_3$; et l'on obtient les coefficiens des équations....

en ξ''_3.........$1331 + 1387721049000 + 408998623104907000000 - 12049759756000000000$
en $(\xi''_3 - 1)$...$1331 + 1387721052993 + 408998625880349101993 + 396948864736628050331$.

Donc la limite, en plus, de ξ''_3 est....

$$\frac{408998\ldots\ldots\ldots\ldots\ldots}{408998\ldots\ldots\ldots\ldots\ldots + 396948\ldots\ldots\ldots\ldots\ldots} \text{ ou } \frac{408998\ldots\ldots\ldots\ldots\ldots}{805897\ldots\ldots\ldots\ldots\ldots}$$

On peut donc faire $\xi''_3 < \frac{409}{805}$; et par conséquent....

$$\xi'_3 < 1 + \frac{409}{805000}; \text{ et } \xi_3 < \frac{1}{165925} + \frac{409}{165925.805000}.$$

D'une autre part, on a $\xi_3 > \frac{1}{165925}$.

Donc, en se tenant à cette dernière valeur, l'erreur est moindre que $\frac{409}{165925.805000}$ ou 0,0000000003062....

Bien plus, dans l'exemple qui nous occupe, il suffit de jeter les yeux sur les coefficiens de l'équation en ξ''_3 pour reconnoître qu'on a

$$\xi''_3 < \frac{1}{10}, \text{ et par conséquent } \xi'_3 < 1 + \frac{1}{10000},$$

$$\text{et} \ldots \xi_3 < \frac{1}{165925} + \frac{1}{1659250000};$$

donc l'erreur est moindre que 0,0000000006026819....

Il suffisoit même de l'équation en $(\xi'_3 - 1)$ pour s'assurer d'un tel résultat, puisqu'à la seule inspection des coefficiens de cette équation, on peut reconnoître que l'on a $\xi'_3 - 1 < \frac{1}{10000}$.

Cette même équation fait voir que $\xi'_3 - 1$ est plus grand que $\frac{1}{41000}$; donc on a

$$\xi'_3 > 1 + \frac{1}{41000}, \text{ et } \xi_3 > \frac{1}{165925} + \frac{1}{165925 . 41000},$$

ou $> 0{,}0000060268 19 \ldots + 0{,}0000000001469 \ldots$

ou bien $> 0{,}000006026 96 \ldots$

On a de l'autre part.....

$$\xi_3 < \frac{1}{165925} + \frac{1}{1659250000},$$

ou $< 0{,}0000060268 19 \ldots + 0{,}0000000006026 \ldots$

ou bien $< 0{,}00000602742 \ldots$

Ici la différence des deux limites est 0,00000000046....

Donc, si l'on prend une des deux limites pour la valeur de ξ_3, l'erreur ne peut avoir lieu qu'à la dixième décimale.

Ainsi la valeur exacte de x, dans l'équation $x^3 - 2x - 5 = 0$, est entre

2,0945514813........et 2,0945514844.....

et même entre...

2,0945514815........et 2,0945514819.....

En prenant le premier de ces nombres, ou l'un des deux derniers, pour la valeur approchée de x, on est assuré que cette valeur est exacte jusqu'à la neuvième décimale, inclusivement, comme nous l'avons annoncé plus haut.

On est également assuré par ce moyen, que les deuxième et troisième valeurs approchées en moins, que nous avons trouvées ci-dessus pour x, sont, respectivement, exactes jusqu'à la seconde et à la quatrième décimale, inclusivement.

La dixième approximation, suivant le procédé de M. Lagrange, a bien donné la huitième décimale exacte, mais l'exactitude de cette décimale n'est pas assurée par le procédé même, vu qu'il indique pour limite de l'erreur, 0,0000000163...; d'où il résulte que la valeur de x est comprise entre....

$$2,0945514702\ldots\ldots\text{ et } 2,0945514865\ldots\ldots$$

et que l'exactitude de la valeur approchée n'est garantie que pour les sept premières décimales.

(e) Voici maintenant comment on peut procéder d'une manière générale.

Soient

$$\xi_{,} = X;\ \pi_{,} = \frac{1}{K};\ \text{et}\ KX = X'.$$

X n'ayant qu'une valeur entre 0 et 1, X′ n'en a qu'une seule entre 0 et K.

On se procurera donc les deux transformées en $(X'-P')$ et $(X'-P'-1)$ dont les termes tout connus sont de signes contraires; P′ étant $< K$.

Ces deux transformées fournissent déjà une double limite, en plus et moins, pour $(X'-P')$, et par conséquent pour X. Mais pour avoir des limites plus resserrées, on fera...... $10^N(X'-P') = X''$; et comme $(X'-P')$ n'a qu'une seule valeur entre 0 et 1, X″ n'en a qu'une seule entre 0 et 10^N.

On se procurera donc les deux transformées en $(X''-P'')$ et $(X''-P''-1)$ dont les termes tout connus sont de signes contraires; P″ étant $< 10^N$.

Ces deux transformées donneront une double limite, en plus et en moins, de $(X''-P'')$, et par conséquent, de X′ et de X.

Soit la limite en moins $=\frac{1}{\mathrm{K}''}$; et la limite en plus $=\frac{1}{K''}$.

On aura $\quad \mathrm{X}''-\mathrm{P}''>\frac{1}{\mathrm{K}''}$, et $<\frac{1}{K''}$;

d'où $\quad \mathrm{X}''>\mathrm{P}''+\frac{1}{\mathrm{K}''}$, et $<\mathrm{P}''+\frac{1}{K''}$;

et $\quad \mathrm{X}'-\mathrm{P}'>\frac{\mathrm{P}''}{10^{\mathrm{N}}}+\frac{1}{10^{\mathrm{N}}\mathrm{K}''}$, et $<\frac{\mathrm{P}''}{10^{\mathrm{N}}}+\frac{1}{10^{\mathrm{N}}K''}$;

d'où X' ou KX $>\mathrm{P}'+\frac{\mathrm{P}''}{10^{\mathrm{N}}}+\frac{1}{10^{\mathrm{N}}\mathrm{K}''}$, et $<\mathrm{P}'+\frac{\mathrm{P}''}{10^{\mathrm{N}}}+\frac{1}{10^{\mathrm{N}}K''}$;

et enfin $\quad \mathrm{X}>\frac{\mathrm{P}'}{\mathrm{K}}+\frac{\mathrm{P}''}{10^{\mathrm{N}}\mathrm{K}}+\frac{1}{10^{\mathrm{N}}\mathrm{K}\mathrm{K}''}\ldots\ldots$

et $\quad \mathrm{X}<\frac{\mathrm{P}'}{\mathrm{K}}+\frac{\mathrm{P}''}{10^{\mathrm{N}}\mathrm{K}}+\frac{1}{10^{\mathrm{N}}\mathrm{K}K''}$.

Si l'on prend pour X une de ces deux limites, l'erreur sera moindre que leur différence, qui est $\frac{1}{10^{\mathrm{N}}\mathrm{K}}\left(\frac{\mathrm{K}''-K''}{\mathrm{K}''K''}\right)$.

Soit $\mathrm{N}'+1$ le nombre de chiffres que renferme le nombre entier K. Il est évident que l'erreur sera $<\frac{1}{10^{\mathrm{N}+\mathrm{N}'}}$; d'où il suit que si on veut obtenir, par ce procédé, une valeur approchée, exacte jusqu'à la $n^{ième}$ décimale au moins, il faut, pour en être généralement sûr, prendre $\mathrm{N}=n-\mathrm{N}'$.

C'est ainsi que dans l'exemple dont on s'est servi, K ou 165925 étant composé de six chiffres, d'où $\mathrm{N}'=5$, on a dû faire $\mathrm{N}=3$, si l'on a prétendu avoir une valeur exacte jusqu'à la huitième décimale.

Dans ce même exemple, P'' s'est trouvé $=0$, et $\mathrm{P}'=1$; ce qui a rendu le calcul très-expéditif. En pareil cas, si l'on s'en tient à $\frac{1}{\mathrm{K}}$ pour la valeur de X approchée en moins, l'erreur est toujours moindre que $\frac{1}{10^{\mathrm{N}}\mathrm{K}K''}$; et par conséquent $<\frac{1}{10^{\mathrm{N}+\mathrm{N}'}}$.

(f) Ce procédé pourroit être étendu à la recherche de plusieurs racines comprises entre deux nombres entiers consécutifs, et l'on tireroit pour lors un assez bon parti du *criterium* que nous avons généralisé dans la note (N). Mais il nous paroît inutile d'entrer dans ces détails. Notre principal objet dans cet Ouvrage, a été de présenter, pour la résolution des équations numériques, une Méthode qui fût praticable, comme *mécaniquement ;* la science du calcul pouvant, de même que les arts, avoir ses *manouvriers*, et en tirer, dans des travaux en grand, de notables avantages. Sous ce rapport, notre Méthode générale sera peut-être préférée au procédé particulier que nous donnons ici, surtout si l'on ne veut avoir des racines exactes que jusqu'à la seconde ou troisième décimale.

(g) L'évaluation des racines en fractions continues, suivant le procédé de M. Lagrange, est particulièrement recommandable, lorsqu'elle fait connoître les facteurs commensurables du second degré dans un polynome qu'on se propose de décomposer en facteurs de ce degré. Mais quand il ne s'agit que de la résolution, proprement dite, d'une équation numérique, ce procédé ne nous paroît pas préférable à l'approximation en nombres décimaux, soit pour la commodité des calculs, soit pour la rapidité de l'approximation. De plus, la méthode de M. Lagrange et la nôtre étant de telle nature qu'on y procède simultanément à la vérification et à l'approximation des racines, il semble que c'est surtout à ces deux Méthodes que l'évaluation des racines en fractions continues ne sauroit être généralement convenable. Par exemple, dans celle de l'illustre Géomètre, si le nombre D, ou la limite de la plus petite différence des racines, étoit un millième, il est évident que chaque racine seroit tout à la fois reconnue et appréciée, à moins d'un millième près. Or il paroît infiniment dur, lorsqu'on a obtenu par des milliers de substitutions, une valeur aussi approchée, d'être forcé de rétrograder jusqu'à la valeur du plus grand nombre entier contenu dans cette racine, pour chercher une nouvelle évaluation en fractions continues.

C'est par un semblable motif, joint à quelques autres, que nous n'avons pas cru devoir adapter ce procédé à notre

Méthode ; et ce motif semble plus décisif encore dans la Méthode de M. Lagrange, qui exige un bien plus grand nombre d'opérations pour la manifestation des premières limites des racines. En effet, lorsque D est, par exemple, un millième, on ne peut, suivant la méthode dont il s'agit, découvrir deux racines moindres que l'unité, telles que 0,920... et 0,921..., qu'au moyen de neuf cent vingt-deux substitutions, tandis que le nombre des transformées exigées pour le même objet dans la nouvelle Méthode, égale seulement 10 + 3 + 2, c'est-à-dire, 15. En un mot, s'il faut découvrir une racine ayant n décimales, la recherche de ces décimales n'exige au plus que $10.n$ transformations, tandis qu'elle peut exiger jusqu'à 10^n substitutions, suivant la progression 0, D, 2D, etc.

(h) La comparaison que nous venons de présenter, concernant le nombre des opérations, dans la nouvelle Méthode des transformées, et dans la Méthode des substitutions successives, telle qu'elle a été perfectionnée par M. Lagrange, a donné lieu à une observation qu'il est bon de rapporter ici, ne fût-ce que pour empêcher qu'elle ne soit désormais reproduite.

« Si la résolution des équations, a-t-on dit, exigeoit » l'emploi d'une pareille Méthode (*celle de M. Lagrange*), » assurément celle de l'Auteur, quoique très-longue, mériteroit » encore la préférence. Mais, pour l'ordinaire, on ne procède » pas ainsi. La Méthode de Newton, qui est la plus usitée, » suppose qu'on connoît, soit par la voie des substitutions, » soit par des constructions géométriques, une première va- » leur de x, qui approche au moins dix fois plus d'une racine » de l'équation que de toute autre racine ; et d'après cette » valeur, on en trouvera facilement une autre dont l'erreur » n'est qu'environ le quarré de la première, savoir $\frac{1}{100}$, si la » première valeur est $\frac{1}{10}$. Une seconde opération qu'on peut » faire par la même formule, réduit l'erreur du centième à

» son quarré, qui est d'environ $\frac{1}{10000}$; et ainsi de suite. D'où » l'on voit que l'approximation continuelle est beaucoup plus » rapide par cette Méthode que par celle que propose l'Auteur. » [*Il s'agit de celle que nous avons exposée au Chapitre VI*].»

Une pareille observation prouve que son Auteur n'a nullement compris l'état de la question. Nous nous sommes proposé de comparer deux Méthodes qui, l'une et l'autre, procèdent simultanément à la vérification et à l'approximation des racines, et qui jouissent, toutes deux, de l'avantage de résoudre généralement et avec certitude, une équation numérique, dans des cas où toutes les Méthodes précédentes échouent, ou n'aboutissent qu'à des résultats faux ou douteux : et l'on vient nous opposer le procédé de Newton, qui n'est pas même une méthode de résolution proprement dite, et qui d'ailleurs, comme nous l'avons dit plus haut d'après M. Lagrange, n'a pas même le mérite d'être généralement sûr ! Ce procédé, fût-il aussi sûr qu'il l'est peu, est évidemment insuffisant pour l'approximation des racines qui, étant par exemple, 8,1...8,2...8,3..., ont une même première valeur connue 8, tandis que, dans notre Méthode, il ne faut que quelques instans pour découvrir la décimale de chacune de ces racines. Et c'est un procédé aussi incertain qu'incomplet qu'on a prétendu opposer à une Méthode générale et sûre !

Encore une fois, nous en appelons à la pratique. Qu'on se donne la peine de résoudre les équations numériques par les diverses Méthodes, et l'on verra qu'abstraction faite du procédé approximatif indiqué dans cette note, notre Méthode générale, même en ne faisant découvrir, qu'un à un, les chiffres de la racine, est encore celle qui, dans son ensemble, se trouve en même temps, la plus sûre et la plus expéditive. Bien plus, dans certains cas, on sera forcé de reconnoître qu'elle est la seule praticable.

Il faut l'avouer, cette observation, que nous avons rapportée *textuellement*, et l'objection citée au n° 48, réunies à quelques autres indices, ont paru provenir d'une disposition d'esprit peu favorable, et nous ont rappelé la pensée de Pascal au sujet de ceux qui inventent. Il faut sans doute, suivant son conseil, que celui qui a rencontré quelques inventions, *ne se pique point* de cet avantage. Quand on considère un objet sous toutes ses faces, avec une attention persévérante, il est difficile qu'il ne se présente pas à l'esprit quelques vues nouvelles; et, ce qui semble réduire à peu de chose cette gloire à laquelle on croit pouvoir prétendre par des inventions scientifiques, c'est que la science même a ses hasards, et que souvent les inventions s'offrent comme fortuitement à l'esprit, à l'instant même où ses recherches le portoient ailleurs. Mais il peut, du moins, être permis à l'auteur d'une découverte utile, de desirer que la communication qu'il en donne, soit accueillie avec quelque bienveillance.

(X) Quoique l'on puisse tirer quelque parti de la nouvelle Méthode pour la détermination des racines imaginaires, nous ne nous arrêterons point à cet objet, qui appartient au problême de la décomposition d'un polynome en facteurs réels du second degré, plutôt qu'à celui de la résolution des équations numériques; l'objet essentiel de cette résolution étant de trouver les valeurs réelles qui peuvent être attribuées à l'inconnue. C'est ce qu'a reconnu M. Lagrange, lorsqu'il a donné des moyens de trouver une limite de la plus petite différence des racines, sans recourir à l'équation aux quarrés de leurs différences.

Cependant l'illustre auteur a cru pouvoir surabondamment se servir de cette équation, qui donne la valeur de la quantité B précédée du signe — sous le radical dans les racines imaginaires, pour déterminer, au moins par approximation, la partie réelle de ces racines. Pour cela on substitue $A + \sqrt{-B}$ à x, dans la proposée, et on en tire deux équations en A, dont l'une a tous ses termes réels, et dont l'autre a tous ses termes multipliés par $\sqrt{-B}$, facteur commun que l'on fait disparoître; ce qui rend les termes de la seconde équation tous réels, parce qu'ils ne dépendent alors, ainsi que ceux de la première, que du quarré de $\sqrt{-B}$, c'est-à-dire, de $-B$.

Ensuite, procédant à la recherche du plus grand commun diviseur de ces deux équations, on s'arrête au reste où A n'est plus qu'au degré n et au-dessous, n étant le nombre des valeurs égales que l'équation au quarré des différences a fournies pour B. Ce reste étant égalé à zéro, on y substitue à B sa valeur exacte ou approchée, et cette équation étant ainsi devenue numérique, on en tire les valeurs réelles de A.

Cette résolution a, comme l'on voit, l'inconvénient d'exiger la formation de l'équation aux quarrés des différences; mais en outre, il semble qu'on puisse douter qu'elle soit *généralement* exacte dans les cas où le plus grand commun diviseur est de plusieurs dimensions. Car la substitution de la valeur approchée de B ne donnant aux coefficiens de l'équation en A qu'une valeur approchée, ne peut-il pas arriver que cette altération, même très-légère, change la nature des racines de l'équation, en substituant des racines imaginaires à des racines réelles, *et vice versâ* ?

Lorsque le reste égalé à zéro est seulement du premier degré, et qu'on a ainsi déterminé la valeur de A en fonction de B, il semble qu'en y donnant à B deux valeurs respectivement approchées en plus et en moins, il en doit provenir deux limites entre lesquelles se trouve la valeur exacte de A. Cependant le résultat même obtenu par M. Lagrange, dans la résolution de l'équation $x^3 - 2x - 5 = 0$, est évidemment fautif. D'après ce résultat, la valeur de A seroit comprise entre $-\frac{15}{16}$ et $-\frac{15}{18}$. [*De la Résolution* etc., pag. 39]. Or on a vu plus haut que la racine positive de l'équation est bien certainement 2,0945...; et son second terme ayant zéro pour coefficient, il s'ensuit avec la même certitude, que A égale la moitié de cette racine positive, précédée du signe $-$; on voit donc que la valeur exacte de A est comprise entre $-1,047\ldots$ et $-1,048\ldots$ Ce résultat n'est nullement d'accord avec le précédent ; ce qui vient apparemment de quelque erreur de calcul.

L'observation que nous avons faite sur le changement possible de la nature des racines d'une équation par une légère altération dans la valeur de ses coefficiens, peut aussi inspirer quelque doute sur la légitimité de la résolution de deux équations à deux inconnues x et y, lorsqu'après l'élimination de x, on obtient pour y une valeur seulement approchée, dont la substitution ne peut produire que des coefficiens d'une valeur approchée pour l'équation en x. La même difficulté se rencontre dans la décomposition d'un polynome en facteurs du second degré.

D'une autre part, il seroit extrêmement fâcheux de ne pouvoir, en aucun cas, se fier aux résultats qu'on obtiendroit d'une équation numérique, propre à résoudre un problême physico-mathématique, lorsqu'on n'a point la valeur rigoureuse de ses coefficiens. Il est donc à desirer que l'on trouve quelque règle certaine qui fasse connoître quelles sont les équations dont les racines ne changent point de nature, malgré l'altération produite dans leurs coefficiens.

(Y) On auroit un grand embarras de moins, si l'on pouvoit découvrir toutes les valeurs réelles de l'inconnue, sans dépouiller l'équation des racines égales qu'elle peut avoir. On a vu que, dans notre Méthode [46], la présence des racines égales commensurables ne forme point un obstacle à la résolution d'une équation; et il est aisé d'appercevoir que la présence des racines égales imaginaires n'en forme pas davantage. Bien plus, lorsqu'on sait d'avance que toutes les racines de l'équation sont réelles, on peut la résoudre, sans qu'elle ait été préalablement dépouillée de ses racines multiples, même de celles qui sont réelles incommensurables. Car une fois qu'on sera parvenu à reconnoître l'existence d'une racine, au moins, entre deux limites qui ne diffèrent que d'une unité décimale de l'ordre que l'on veut, ou qu'exige le problême dont la solution dépend de l'équation à résoudre, il est indifférent, pour la pratique, que la valeur trouvée appartienne à une ou à plusieurs racines, soit absolument égales entr'elles, soit égales seulement jusqu'à tel chiffre demandé. L'essentiel est que l'on connoisse toutes les valeurs réelles qui représentent, jusqu'au degré requis d'exactitude, celles dont l'inconnue de l'équation est susceptible.

D'après cette considération, on pourroit même, dans tous les cas, laisser subsister les racines égales d'une équation numérique, si l'on avoit le moyen de connoître une limite, en moins, de la valeur de φ, c'est-à-dire, de la plus petite valeur que pourroit avoir la partie des racines imaginaires représentées par $A \pm \sqrt{-\varphi}$, précédée du signe — sous le signe $\sqrt{\ }$.

En effet, lorsque l'existence d'une couple de variations dans la collatérale en $(z_{,} - 1)$ a donné lieu de présumer qu'il y a une couple de racines réelles entre o et 1, dans l'équation en $(x - p)$, et qu'on est ensuite parvenu à l'équation en...... $(x^{(n)} - p^{(n)})$ et à sa collatérale, sans que cette présomption soit détruite, on en peut conclure que la présomption se change en certitude, quand on sait d'ailleurs que, si les deux racines qui occasionnent les variations dont il s'agit étoient des imaginaires de la forme $A \pm \sqrt{-\varphi}$, la valeur de φ seroit, d'après sa limite en moins, plus grande que $\frac{1}{4 \times 10^{2n}}$; car, dans ce cas, l'existence de ces racines imaginaires devroit se manifester par l'équation collatérale en $(z^{(n)}_{p^{(n)}} - 1)$, qui n'auroit point de variations de signe, et la présomption de l'existence des racines réelles entre p et $p + 1$ devroit être ainsi détruite [66].

Or il paroît qu'en substituant $\sqrt{-\varphi}$ à l'inconnue de l'équation en $\left(x - p - \frac{p'}{10} \ldots - \frac{p^{(n)}}{10^n}\right)$, on peut déterminer une limite de la plus petite valeur dont φ soit susceptible, la valeur de la partie réelle A étant supposée exister entre...

$$p + \frac{p'}{10} + \ldots + \frac{p^{(n)}}{10^n} \text{ et } p + \frac{p'}{10} + \ldots + \frac{p^{(n)} + 1}{10^n}.$$

L'objection qui résulte de la légère altération des coefficiens, se représente ici, mais moins grave que dans la note précédente. Il semble bien que cette altération, toute légère qu'elle puisse être, suffit pour rendre positif, dans l'équation en φ, tel coefficient, qui eût été négatif, si l'on n'avoit pas pris pour A une valeur simplement égale à $p+\frac{p'}{1}+\ldots+\frac{p^{(n)}}{10^n}$; ou bien, *vice versâ*. Mais cet inconvénient ne paroît devoir conduire qu'à l'obligation de modifier la manière de déterminer la limite, en moins, des racines d'une équation numérique. Cette manière dépend, comme on sait, de celle de trouver la limite, en plus, des racines de l'équation inverse. C'est donc cette dernière détermination qu'il faudra modifier, en prenant le plus grand de tous les coefficiens de cette équation, au lieu du plus grand coefficient de signe contraire à celui de son premier terme. Au surplus, nous n'entendons donner ici qu'un simple apperçu, concernant la possibilité de conserver les racines égales dans la nouvelle Méthode.

(Z) On voit que nous nous sommes frayé une route bien différente de celle qui a été tracée par l'illustre Auteur du *Traité de la Résolution des Equations numériques*. Mais c'est en nous fortifiant par la lecture de ses écrits, que nous avons appris à marcher seuls, et nous nous plaisons à lui rendre ici cet hommage.

Tout en recommandant aux Auteurs de son temps, la lecture assidue des écrits des Grecs......

(Vos exemplaria græca
Nocturnâ versate manu, versate diurnâ),

Horace ne savoit pas mauvais gré aux Ecrivains de Rome de ne pas se traîner servilement sur les pas de leurs Maîtres, et d'oser aussi marcher dans leurs propres voies.....

Nec minimum meruêre decus vestigia græca
Ausi deserere.....

FIN.

TABLE.

NOTES.

FIN DE LA TABLE.

DEMONSTRATIO NOVA ALTERA

THEOREMATIS

OMNEM FVNCTIONEM ALGEBRAICAM RATIONALEM INTEGRAM VNIVS VARIABILIS

IN FACTORES REALES PRIMI VEL SECVNDI GRADVS RESOLVI POSSE

AVCTORE

CAROLO FRIDERICO GAVSS.

GOTTINGAE

APVD HENRICVM DIETERICH.

MDCCCXVI.

DEMONSTRATIO NOVA ALTERA
THEOREMATIS
OMNEM FVNCTIONEM ALGEBRAICAM RATIONALEM INTEGRAM VNIVS VARIABILIS IN FACTORES REALES PRIMI VEL SECVNDI GRADVS RESOLVI POSSE

AVCTORE

CAROLO FRIDERICO GAVSS

SOC. REG. SC. TRADITA DEC. 7. 1815.

I.

Quamquam demonſtratio theorematis de reſolutione functionum algebraicarum integrarum in factores, quam in commentatione ſedecim abhinc annis promulgata tradidi, tum reſpectu rigoris tum ſimplicitatis nihil deſiderandum relinquere videatur, tamen haud ingratum fore geometris ſpero, ſi iterum ad eandem quaeſtionem grauiſſimam reuertar, atque e principiis prorſus diuerſis demonſtrationem alteram haud minus rigoroſam adſtruere coner. Pendet ſcilicet illa demonſtratio prior, partim ſaltem, a conſiderationibus geometricis: contra ea, quam hic exponere aggredior, principiis mere analyticis innixa erit. Methodorum analyticarum, per quas vsque ad illud quidem tempus alii geometrae theorema noſtrum demonſtrare ſuſceperunt, inſigniores loco citato recenſui, et quibus vitiis laborent copioſe expoſui. Quorum gra-

 viſſimum

viſſimum ac vere radicale omnibus illis conatibus; perinde ac recentioribus, qui quidem mihi innotuerunt, commune: quod tamen neutiquam ineuitabile videri in demonſtratione analytica, iam tunc declaraui. Eſto iam penes peritos iudicium, an fides olim data per has nouas curas plene ſit liberata.

2.

Diſquiſitioni principali quaedam praeliminares praemittentur, tum ne quid deeſſe videatur, tum quod ipſa forſan tractatio iis quoque, quae ab aliis iam delibata fuerant, nouam qualemcunque lucem affundere poterit. Ac primo quidem de altiſſimo diuiſore communi duarum functionum algebraicarum integrarum vnius indeterminatae agemus. Vbi praemonendum, hic ſemper tantum de functionibus integris ſermonem eſſe: e qualibus duabus ſi productum conſletur, vtraque huius *diuiſor* vocatur. Diuiſoris *ordo* ex exponente ſummae poteſtatis indeterminatae quam continet diiudicatur, nulla prorſus coëfficientium numericorum ratione habita. Ceterum quae ad diuiſores communes functionum pertinent eo breuius abſoluere licet, quod iis, quae ad diuiſores communes numerorum ſpectant, omnino ſunt analoga.

Propoſitis duabus functionibus Y, Y' indeterminatae x, quarum prior ſit ordinis altioris aut ſaltem non inferioris quam poſterior, formabimus aequationes ſequentes

$$Y = q\,Y' + Y''$$
$$Y' = q'\,Y'' + Y'''$$
$$Y'' = q''\,Y''' + Y^{\text{iv}}$$
etc. vsque ad
$$Y^{(\mu-1)} = q^{(\mu-1)}\,Y^{(\mu)}$$

ea ſcilicet lege, vt primo Y diuidatur ſueto more per Y'; dein Y' per reſiduum primae diuiſionis Y'', quod erit ordinis inferioris quam Y'; tunc rurſus reſiduum primum per ſecundum Y''' et ſic porro,

porro, donec ad diuiſionem absque reſiduo perueniatur, quod tandem neceſſario euenire debere, inde patet, quod ordo functionum Y', Y'', Y''' etc. continuo decreſcit. Quas functiones perinde atque quotientes q, q', q'' etc. eſſe functiones *integras* ipſius x, vix opus eſt monere. His praemiſſis, manifeſtum eſt,

I. regrediendo ab vltima iſtarum aequationum ad primam, functionem $Y^{(\mu)}$ eſſe diuiſorem ſingularum praecedentium, adeoque certo diuiſorem communem propoſitarum Y, Y'.

II. Progrediendo a prima aequatione ad vltimam, elucet, quemlibet diuiſorem communem functionum Y, Y' etiam metiri ſingulas ſequentes, et proin etiam vltimam $Y^{(\mu)}$. Quamobrem functiones Y, Y' habere nequeunt vllum diuiſorem communem altioris ordinis quam $Y^{(\mu)}$, omnisque diuiſor communis eiusdem ordinis vt $Y^{(\mu)}$ erit ad hunc in ratione numeri ad numerum, vnde hic ipſe pro diuiſore communi ſummo erit habendus.

III. Si $Y^{(\mu)}$ eſt ordinis o, i. e. numerus, nulla functio indeterminatae x proprie ſic dicta ipſas Y, Y' metiri poteſt: in hoc itaque caſu dicendum eſt, has functiones diuiſorem communem non habere.

IV. Excerpamus ex aequationibus noſtris penultimam; dein ex hac eliminemus $Y^{(\mu-1)}$ adiumento aequationis antepenultimae; tunc iterum eliminemus $Y^{(\mu-2)}$ adiumento aequationis praecedentis et ſic porro: hoc pacto habebimus

$$\begin{aligned} Y^{(\mu)} &= +\,k\,Y^{(\mu-2)} - Y^{(\mu-1)} \\ &= -\,k'\,Y^{(\mu-3)} + Y^{(\mu-2)} \\ &= +\,k''\,Y^{(\mu-4)} - Y^{(\mu-3)} \\ &= -\,k'''\,Y^{(\mu-5)} + Y^{(\mu-4)} \\ &\text{etc.} \end{aligned}$$

ſi functiones k, k', k'' etc. ex lege ſequente formatas ſupponamu

$$k = 1$$
$$k' = q^{(\mu-2)}$$
$$k'' = q^{(\mu-3)}k' + k$$
$$k''' = q^{(\mu-4)}k'' + k'$$
$$k^{\mathrm{IV}} = q^{(\mu-5)}k''' + k''$$

etc.

Erit itaque

$$\pm k^{(\mu-2)}Y \mp k^{(\mu-1)}Y' = Y^{(\mu)}$$

valentibus ſignis ſuperioribus pro μ pari, inferioribus pro impari. In eo itaque caſu, vbi Y et Y' diuiſorem communem non habent inuenire licet hoc modo duas functiones Z, Z' indeterminatae x tales vt habeatur

$$ZY + Z'Y' = 1.$$

V. Haec propoſitio manifeſto etiam inuerſa valet, puta, ſi ſatisfieri poteſt aequationi

$$ZY + Z'Y' = 1$$

ita, vt Z, Z' ſint functiones integrae indeterminatae x, ipſae Y et Y' certo diuiſorem communem habere nequeunt.

3.

Disquiſitio praeliminaris altera circa transformationem functionum ſymmetricarum verſabitur. Sint a, b, c etc. quantitates indeterminatae, ipſarum multitudo m, deſignemusque per λ' illarum ſummam, per λ'' ſummam productorum e binis, per λ''' ſummam productorum e ternis etc. ita vt ex euolutione producti

$$(x-a)(x-b)(x-c)\ldots.$$

oriatur

$$x^m - \lambda' x^{m-1} + \lambda'' x^{m-2} - \lambda''' x^{m-3} + \text{etc.}$$

Ipſae itaque $\lambda', \lambda'', \lambda'''$ etc. ſunt functiones ſymmetricae indeterminatarum a, b, c etc., i. e. tales, in quibus hae indeterminatae

eodem

eodem modo occurrunt, siue clarius, talis, quae per qualemcunque harum indeterminatarum inter permutationem non mutantur. Manifesto generalius, quaelibet functio integra ipsarum $\lambda', \lambda'', \lambda'''$, etc. (siue has solas indeterminatas implicet, siue adhuc alias ab a, b, c etc. independentes contineat) erit functio symmetrica integra indeterminatarum a, b, c etc.

4.

Theorema inuersum paullo minus obuium. Sit ρ functio symmetrica indeterminatarum a, b, c etc., quae igitur composita erit e certo numero terminorum formae

$$Ma^{\alpha} b^{\beta} c^{\gamma} \ldots.$$

denotantibus α, β, γ etc. integros non negatiuos, atque M coëfficientem vel determinatum vel saltem ab a, b, c etc. non pendentem (si forte aliae adhuc indeterminatae praeter a, b, c etc. functionem ρ ingrediantur). Ante omnia inter singulos hos terminos ordinem certum stabiliemus, ad quem finem primo ipsas indeterminatas a, b, c etc. ordine certo per se quidem prorsus arbitrario disponemus, e. g. ita, vt a primum locum obtineat, b secundum, c tertium etc. Dein e duobus terminis

$$Ma^{\alpha} b^{\beta} c^{\gamma} \ldots. \text{ et } Ma^{\alpha'} b^{\beta'} c^{\gamma'} \ldots.$$

priori ordinem altiorem tribuemus quam posteriori, si fit vel $\alpha > \alpha'$, vel $\alpha = \alpha'$ et $\beta > \beta'$, vel $\alpha = \alpha'$, $\beta = \beta'$ et $\gamma > \gamma'$ vel etc. i. e. si e differentiis $\alpha - \alpha'$, $\beta - \beta'$, $\gamma - \gamma'$ etc. prima, quae non euanescit, positiua euadit. Quocirca quum termini eiusdem ordinis non differant nisi respectu coëfficientis M, adeoque in terminum vnum conflari possint, singulos terminos functionis ρ ad ordines diuersos pertinere supponemus.

Iam obseruamus, si $Ma^{\alpha} b^{\beta} c^{\gamma} \ldots.$ sit ex omnibus terminis functionis ρ is, cui ordo altissimus competat, necessario α esse maiorem, vel saltem non minorem, quam β. Si enim esset $\beta > \alpha$,

$\beta > \alpha$, terminus $Ma^{\beta}b^{\alpha}c^{\gamma}\ldots\ldots$, quem functio ϱ, vtpote symmetrica, quoque inuoluet, foret ordinis altioris quam $Ma^{\alpha}b^{\beta}c^{\gamma}\ldots\ldots$, contra hyp. Simili modo β erit maior vel saltem non minor quam γ; porro γ non minor quam exponens sequens δ etc.: proin singulae differentiae $\alpha-\beta$, $\beta-\gamma$, $\gamma-\delta$ etc. erunt integri non negatiui.

Secundo perpendamus, si e quotcunque functionibus integris indeterminatarum a, b, c etc. productum conflетur, huius terminum altissimum necessario esse ipsum productum e terminis altissimis illorum factorum. Aeque manifestum est, terminos altissimos functionum λ', λ'', λ''' etc. resp. esse a, ab, abc etc. Hinc colligitur, terminum altissimum e producto

$$p = M\lambda'^{\alpha-\beta}\lambda''^{\beta-\gamma}\lambda'''^{\gamma-\delta}\ldots\ldots$$

prodeuntem esse $Ma^{\alpha}b^{\beta}c^{\gamma}\ldots\ldots$; quocirca statuendo $\varrho - p = \varrho'$, terminus altissimus functionis ϱ' certo erit ordinis inferioris quam terminus altissimus functionis ϱ. Manifesto autem p, et proin etiam ϱ, fiunt functiones integrae symmetricae ipsarum a, b, c etc. Quamobrem ϱ' perinde tractata, vt antea ϱ, discerpetur in $p' + \varrho''$, ita vt p' sit productum e potestatibus ipsarum λ', λ'', λ''' etc. in coëfficientem vel determinatum vel saltem ab a, b, c etc. non pendentem, ϱ'' vero functio integra symmetrica ipsarum a, b, c etc. talis, vt ipsius terminus altissimus pertineat ad ordinem inferiorem quam terminus altissimus functionis ϱ'. Eodem modo continuando manifesto tandem ϱ ad formam $p + p' + p'' + p'''$ etc. redacta, i. e in functionem integram ipsarum λ', λ'', λ''' etc. transformata erit.

5.

Theorema in art. praec. demonstratum etiam sequenti modo enunciare possumus: Proposita functione quacunque indeterminatarum a, b, c etc. integra symmetrica ϱ, assignari potest functio integra totidem aliarum indeterminatarum l', l'', l''' etc. talis, quae pe per ſubſtitutiones $l' = \lambda'$, $l'' = \lambda''$, $l''' = \lambda'''$ etc. transeat in ρ. Facile inſuper oſtenditur, *hoc vnico tantum modo fieri poſſe.* Supponamus enim, e duabus functionibus diuerſis indeterminatarum l', l'', l''' etc. puta tum ex r, tum ex r' poſt ſubſtitutiones $l' = \lambda'$, $l'' = \lambda''$, $l''' = \lambda'''$ etc. reſultare eandem functionem ipſarum a, b, c etc. Tunc itaque $r - r'$ erit functio ipſarum l', l'', l''' etc. per ſe non euaneſcens, ſed quae identice deſtruitur poſt illas ſubſtitutiones. Hoc vero abſurdum eſſe, facile perſpiciemus, ſi perpendamus, $r - r'$ neceſſario compoſitam eſſe e certo numero partium formae

$$M l'^{\alpha} l''^{\beta} l'''^{\gamma} \ldots\ldots$$

quarum coëfficientes M non euaneſcant, et quae ſingulae reſpectu exponentium inter ſe diuerſae ſint, adeoque terminos altiſſimos e ſingulis iſtis partibus prodeuntes exhiberi per

$$M a^{\alpha + \beta + \gamma + \text{etc.}} b^{\beta + \gamma + \text{etc.}} c^{\gamma + \text{etc.}} \ldots\ldots$$

et proin ad ordines diuerſos referendos eſſe, ita vt terminus abſolute altiſſimus nullo modo deſtrui poſſit.

Ceterum ipſe calculus pro huiusmodi transformationibus pluribus compendiis inſigniter abbreuiari poſſet, quibus tamen hoc loco non immoramur, quum ad propoſitum noſtrum ſola transformationis poſſibilitas iam ſufficiat.

6.

Conſideremus productum ex $m(m-1)$ factoribus

$$\begin{array}{l} (a-b)\,(a-c)\,(a-d)\,\ldots\ldots \\ \times\,(b-a)\,(b-c)\,(b-d)\,\ldots\ldots \\ \times\,(c-a)\,(c-b)\,(c-d)\,\ldots\ldots \\ \times\,(d-a)\,(d-b)\,(d-c)\,\ldots\ldots \\ \text{etc.} \end{array}$$

quod per π denotabimus, et, quum indeterminatas a, b, c etc. ſymmetrice inuoluat, in formam functionis ipſarum λ', λ'', λ''' etc. redactum ſupponemus. Transeat haec functio in p, ſi loco

 ipſa-

ipſarum λ', λ'', λ''' etc. reſp. ſubſtituuntur l', l'', l''' etc. His ita factis, ipſam p vocabimus *determinantem* functionis

$$y = x^m - l'x^{m-1} + l''x^{m-2} - l'''x^{m-3} + \text{etc.}$$

Ita e. g. pro $m = 2$ habemus

$$p = -l'^2 + 4l''$$

Perinde pro $m = 3$ inuenitur

$$p = -l'^2 l''^2 + 4l'^3 l''' + 4l''^3 - 18l'l''l''' + 27l'''^2$$

Determinans functionis y itaque eſt functio coëfficientium l', l'' l''' etc. talis, quae per ſubſtitutiones $l' = \lambda'$, $l'' = \lambda''$, $l''' = \lambda'''$ etc tranſit in productum ex omnibus differentiis inter binas quantita tum a, b, c etc. In caſu eo, vbi $m = 1$, i. e. vbi vnica tantun indeterminata a habetur, adeoque nullae omnino adſunt differen tiae, ipſum numerum 1 tamquam determinantem functionis y adoptare conueniet.

In ſtabilienda notione determinantis, coëfficientes functioni y tamquam quantitates indeterminatas ſpectare oportuit. Deter minans functionis cum coëfficientibus determinatis

$$Y = x^m - L'x^{m-1} + L''x^{m-2} - L'''x^{m-3} + \text{etc.}$$

erit numerus determinatus P, puta valor functionis p pro $l' = L'$ $l'' = L''$, $l''' = L'''$ etc. Quodſi itaque ſupponimus, Y reſolui poſſ in factores ſimplices

$$Y = (x - A)(x - B)(x - C) \ldots\ldots$$

ſiue Y oriri ex

$$v = (x - a)(x - b)(x - c) \ldots\ldots$$

ſtatuendo $a = A$, $b = B$, $c = C$ etc., adeoque per easdem ſubſtitu tiones λ', λ'', λ''' etc. reſp. fieri L', L'', L''' etc., manifeſto P ae qualis erit producto e factoribus

$$\begin{aligned} & (A - B)(A - C)(A - D) \ldots\ldots \\ \times\; & (B - A)(B - C)(B - D) \ldots\ldots \\ \times\; & (C - A)(C - B)(C - D) \ldots\ldots \\ \times\; & (D - A)(D - B)(D - C) \ldots\ldots \\ & \text{etc.} \end{aligned}$$

Pate

Patet itaque, ſi fiat $P = 0$, inter quantitates A, B, C etc. duas ſaltem aequales reperiri debere; contra, ſi non fuerit $P = 0$, cunctas A, B, C etc. neceſſario inaequales eſſe. Iam obſeruamus, ſi ſtatuamus $\frac{dY}{dx} = Y'$, ſiue

$$Y' = m x^{m-1} - (m-1) L' x^{m-2} + (m-2) L'' x^{m-3} - (m-3) L''' x^{m-4} + \text{etc.},$$

haberi

$$\begin{aligned} Y' = & (x-B)(x-C)(x-D) \ldots\ldots \\ & + (x-A)(x-C)(x-D) \ldots\ldots \\ & + (x-A)(x-B)(x-D) \ldots\ldots \\ & + (x-A)(x-B)(x-C) \ldots\ldots \\ & + \text{etc.} \end{aligned}$$

Si itaque duae quantitatum A, B, C etc. aequales ſunt, e. g. $A = B$, Y' per $x - A$ diuiſibilis erit, ſiue Y et Y' implicabunt diuiſorem communem $x - A$. Vice verſa, ſi Y' cum Y vllum diuiſorem communem habere ſupponitur, neceſſario Y' aliquem factorem ſimplicem ex his $x - A$, $x - B$, $x - C$ etc. implicare debebit, e. g. primum $x - A$, quod manifeſto fieri nequit, niſi A alicui reliquarum B, C, D etc. aequalis fuerit. Ex his omnibus itaque colligimus duo theoremata:

I. Si determinans functionis Y fit $= 0$, certo Y cum Y' diuiſorem communem habet, adeoque, ſi Y et Y' diuiſorem communem non habent, determinans functionis Y nequit eſſe $= 0$.

II. Si determinans functionis Y non eſt $= 0$, certo Y et Y' diuiſorem communem habere nequeunt; vel, ſi Y et Y' diuiſorem communem habent, neceſſario determinans functionis Y eſſe debet $= 0$.

7.

At probe notandum eſt, totam vim huius demonſtrationis ſimpliciſſimae inniti ſuppoſitioni, functionem Y in factores ſimpli-

 ces

ces reſolui poſſe: quae ipſa ſuppoſitio, hocce quidem loco, vbi de demonſtratione generali huius reſolubilitatis agitur, nihil eſſet niſi petitio principii. Et tamen a paralogismis huic prorſus ſimilibus non ſibi cauerunt omnes, qui demonſtrationes analyticas theorematis principalis tentauerunt, cuius ſpecioſae illuſionis originem iam in ipſa disquiſitionis enunciatione animaduertimus, quum omnes in *formam* tantum radicum aequationum inquiſiuerint, dum *exiſtentiam* temere ſuppoſitam demonſtrare oportuiſſet. Sed de tali procedendi modo, qui nimis a rigore et claritate abhorret, ſatis iam in commentatione ſupra citata dictum eſt. Quamobrem iam theoremata art. praec., quorum altero ſaltem ad propoſitum noſtrum non poſſumus carere, ſolidiori fundamento ſuperſtruemus: a ſecundo, tamquam faciliori initium faciemus.

8.

Denotemus per ϱ functionem

$$\frac{\pi\,(x-b)\,(x-c)\,(x-d)\,\ldots\ldots}{(a-b)^2\,(a-c)^2\,(a-d)^2\,\ldots\ldots}$$
$$+\frac{\pi\,(x-a)\,(x-c)\,(x-d)\,\ldots\ldots}{(b-a)^2\,(b-c)^2\,(b-d)^2\,\ldots\ldots}$$
$$+\frac{\pi\,(x-a)\,(x-b)\,(x-d)\,\ldots\ldots}{(c-a)^2\,(c-b)^2\,(c-d)^2\,\ldots\ldots}$$
$$+\frac{\pi\,(x-a)\,(x-b)\,(x-c)\,\ldots\ldots}{(d-a)^2\,(d-b)^2\,(d-c)^2\,\ldots\ldots}$$
$$+\text{ etc.}$$

quae, quoniam π per ſingulos denominatores eſt diuiſibilis, fit functio integra indeterminatarum x, a, b, c etc. Statuamus porro $\frac{\partial v}{\partial x} = v'$, ita vt habeatur

$$\begin{aligned} v' = &(x-b)\,(x-c)\,(x-d)\,\ldots\ldots \\ &+(x-a)\,(x-c)\,(x-d)\,\ldots\ldots \\ &+(x-a)\,(x-b)\,(x-d)\,\ldots\ldots \\ &+(x-a)\,(x-b)\,(x-c)\,\ldots\ldots \\ &+\text{ etc.}\end{aligned}$$

Mani-

Manifesto pro $x=a$, fit $\varrho v'=\pi'$, vnde concludimus, functionem $\pi'-\varrho v'$ indefinite diuisibilem esse per $x-a$, et perinde per $x-b$, $x-c$ etc., nec non per productum v. Statuendo itaque

$$\frac{\pi'-\varrho v'}{v}=\sigma'$$

erit σ functio integra indeterminatarum x, a, b, c etc., et quidem, perinde vt ϱ, symmetrica ratione indeterminatarum a, b, c etc. Erui poterunt itaque functiones duae integrae r, s, indeterminatarum x, l', l'', l''' etc, tales quae per substitutiones $l'=\lambda'$, $l''=\lambda''$, $l'''=\lambda'''$ etc. transeant in ϱ, σ resp. Quodsi itaque analogiam sequentes, functionem

$mx^{m-1}-(m-1)l'x^{m-2}+(m-2)l''x^{m-3}-(m-3)l'''x^{m-4}+$ etc.

i. e. quotientem differentialem $\frac{dy}{dx}$ per y' denotemus, ita vt y' per easdem illas substitutiones transeat in v', patet $p-sy-ry'$ per easdem substitutiones transire in $\pi'-\sigma v-\varrho v'$, i. e. in o, adeoque necessario iam per se identice euanescere debere (art. 5.): habemus proin aequationem identicam

$$p=sy+ry'$$

Hinc si supponamus, ex substitutione $l'=L'$, $l''=L''$, $l'''=L'''$ etc. prodire $r=R$, $s=S$, erit etiam identice

$$P=SY+RY'$$

vbi quum S, R sint functionis integrae ipsius x, P vero quantitas determinata seu numerus, sponte patet, Y et Y' diuisorem communem habere non posse, nisi fuerit $P=0$. Quod est ipsum theorema posterius art. 6.

9.

Demonstrationem theorematis prioris ita absoluemus, vt ostendamus, in casu eo, vbi Y et Y' non habent diuisorem communem, certo fieri non posse $P=0$. Ad hunc finem primo, per praecepta art. 2. erutas ſupponimus duas functiones integras indeterminatae x, puta fx et φx, tales, vt habeatur aequatio identica

$$fx\,.\,Y + \varphi x\,.\,Y' = 1$$

quam hic ita exhibemus:

$$fx\,.\,v + \varphi x\,.\,v' = 1 + fx\,.\,(v - Y) + \varphi x\,.\,\frac{d(v - Y)}{dx}$$

ſiue, quoniam habemus

$$v' = (x-b)(x-c)(x-d)\ldots\ldots + (x-a)\,.\,\frac{d[(x-b)(x-c)(x-d)\ldots\ldots]}{dx}$$

in forma ſequente:

$$\left\{\begin{array}{l} \varphi x\,.\,(x-b)\,(x-c)\,(x-d)\ldots\ldots \\ + \varphi x\,.\,(x-a)\,.\,\dfrac{d[(x-b)(x-c)(x-d)\ldots\ldots]}{dx} \\ + fx\,.\,(x-a)\,(x-b)\,(x-c)\,(x-d)\ldots\ldots \end{array}\right\}$$

$$= 1 + fx\,.\,(v - Y) + \varphi x\,.\,\frac{d(v - Y)}{dx}$$

Exprimamus breuitatis cauſſa

$$fx\,.\,(y - Y) + \varphi x\,.\,\frac{d(y - Y)}{dx}$$

quae eſt functio integra indeterminatarum x, l', l'', l''' etc. per $F(x, l', l'', l'''$ etc.$)$

vnde erit identice

$$1 + fx\,.\,(v - Y) + \varphi x\,.\,\frac{d(v - Y)}{dx} = 1 + F(x, \lambda', \lambda'', \lambda''' \text{ etc.})$$

Habebimus itaque aequationes identicas [1]

$$\varphi a\,.\,(a-b)\,(a-c)\,(a-d)\ldots\ldots = 1 + F(a, \lambda', \lambda'', \lambda''' \text{ etc.})$$
$$\varphi b\,.\,(b-a)\,(b-c)\,(b-d)\ldots\ldots = 1 + F(b, \lambda', \lambda'', \lambda''' \text{ etc.})$$
$$\varphi c\,.\,(c-a)\,(c-b)\,(c-d)\ldots\ldots = 1 + F(c, \lambda', \lambda'', \lambda''' \text{ etc.})$$

etc.

Suppo-

Supponendo itaque, productum ex omnibus

$$1 + F(a, l', l'', l''' \text{ etc.})$$
$$1 + F(b, l', l'', l''' \text{ etc.})$$
$$1 + F(c, l', l'', l''' \text{ etc.})$$
$$\text{etc.}$$

quod erit functio integra indeterminatarum a, b, c etc., l', l'', l''' etc. et quidem functio ſymmetrica reſpectu ipſarum a, b, c etc., exhiberi per

$$\psi(\lambda', \lambda'', \lambda''' \text{ etc.}, l', l'', l''' \text{ etc.})$$

e multiplicatione cunctarum aequationum [1] reſultabit aequatio identica noua [2]

$$\pi \varphi a . \varphi b . \varphi c \ldots = \psi(\lambda', \lambda'', \lambda''' \text{ etc.}, \lambda', \lambda'', \lambda''' \text{ etc.})$$

Porro patet, quum productum $\varphi a . \varphi b . \varphi c \ldots$ indeterminatas a, b, c etc. ſymmetrice inuoluat, inueniri poſſe functionem integram indeterminatarum l', l'', l''' etc. talem, quae per ſubſtitutiones $l' = \lambda'$, $l'' = \lambda''$, $l''' = \lambda'''$ etc. transeat in $\varphi a . \varphi b . \varphi c \ldots$ Sit t illa functio, eritque etiam identice [3]

$$pt = \psi(l', l'', l''' \text{ etc.}, l', l'', l''')$$

quoniam haec aequatio per ſubſtitutiones $l' = \lambda'$, $l'' = \lambda''$, $l''' = \lambda'''$ etc. in identicam [2] transit.

Iam ex ipſa definitione functionis F ſequitur, identice haberi

$$F(x, L', L'', L''' \text{ etc.}) = 0$$

Hinc etiam identice erit

$$1 + F(a, L', L'', L''' \text{ etc.}) = 1$$
$$1 + F(b, L', L'', L''' \text{ etc.}) = 1$$
$$1 + F(c, L', L'', L''' \text{ etc.}) = 1$$
$$\text{etc.}$$

et proin erit etiam identice

$$\psi(\lambda', \lambda'', \lambda''' \text{ etc.}, L', L'', L''' \text{ etc.}) = 1$$

adeoque etiam identice [4]

$$\psi(l', l'', l''' \text{ etc.}, L', L'', L''' \text{ etc.}) = 1$$

Quam-

Quamobrem e combinatione aequationum [3] et [4], et ſubſtituendo $l' = L'$, $l'' = L''$, $l''' = L'''$ etc. habebimus [5]

$$PT = 1$$

ſi per T denotamus valorem functionis t illis ſubſtitutionibus reſpondentem. Qui valor quum neceſſario fiat quantitas finita, P certo nequit eſſe $= 0$. *Q. E. D.*

10.

E praecedentibus iam perſpicuum eſt, quamlibet functionem integram Y vnius indeterminatae x, cuius determinans ſit $= 0$, decomponi poſſe in factores, quorum nullus habeat determinantem 0. Inueſtigato enim diuiſore communi altiſſimo functionum Y et $\frac{dY}{dx}$, illa iam in duos factores reſoluta habebitur. Si quis horum factorum *) iterum habet determinantem 0, eodem modo in duos factores reſoluetur, eodemque pacto continuabimus, donec Y in factores tales tandem reſoluta habeatur, quorum nullus habeat determinantem 0.

Facile porro perſpicietur, inter hos factores, in quos Y reſoluitur, ad minimum vnum reperiri debere ita comparatum, vt inter factores numeri, qui eius ordinem exprimit, binarius ſaltem non pluries occurrat, quam inter factores numeri m, qui exprimit ordinem functionis Y: puta, ſi ſtatuatur $m = k . 2^{\mu}$, denotante k numerum imparem, inter factores functionis Y ad minimum vnus reperietur ad ordinem $k' . 2^{\nu}$ referendus, ita vt etiam k' ſit impar, atque vel $\nu = \mu$, vel $\nu < \mu$. Veritas huius aſſertionis ſponte ſequitur

*) Reuera quidem non niſi factor iſte, qui eſt ille diuiſor communis, determinantem 0 habere poteſt. Sed demonſtratio huius propoſitionis hocce loco in quaſdam ambages perduceret; neque etiam hic neceſſaria eſt, quum factorem alterum, ſi et huius determinans euaneſcere poſſet, eodem modo tractare, ipſumque in factores reſoluere liceret.

tur inde, quod m eſt aggregatum numerorum, qui ordinem ſingulorum factorum ipſius Y exprimunt.

11.

Antequam vlterius progrediamur, expreſſionem quandam explicabimus, cuius introductio in omnibus de functionibus ſymmetricis disquiſitionibus maximam vtilitatem affert, et quae nobis quoque peropportuna erit. Supponamus, M eſſe functionem quamdam ex indeterminatis a, b, c etc., et quidem ſit μ multitudo earum, quae in expreſſionem M ingrediuntur, nullo reſpectu habito aliarum indeterminatarum, ſi quas forte implicet ipſa M. Permutatis illis μ indeterminatis omnibus quibus fieri poteſt modis tum inter ſe tum cum $m-\mu$ reliquis ex a, b, c etc., orientur ex M aliae expreſſiones ipſi M ſimiles, ita vt omnino habeantur

$$m\,(m-1)\,(m-2)\,(m-3)\,\ldots\ldots\,(m-\mu+1)$$

expreſſiones, ipſa M incluſa, quarum complexum ſimpliciter dicemus *complexum omnium M.* Hinc ſponte patet, quid ſignificet aggregatum omnium M, productum ex omnibus M etc. Ita e. g. π dicetur productum ex omnibus $a-b$, v productum ex omnibus $x-a$, v' aggregatum omnium $\frac{v}{x-a}$ etc.

Si forte M eſt functio ſymmetrica reſpectu quarundam ex μ indeterminatis, quas continet, iſtarum permutationes inter ſe functionem M non variant, quamobrem in complexu omnium M quilibet terminus pluries, et quidem $1.2.3\ldots\ldots\nu$ vicibus reperietur, ſi ν eſt multitudo indeterminatarum, quarum reſpectu M eſt ſymmetrica. Si vero M non ſolum reſpectu ν indeterminatarum ſymmetrica eſt, ſed inſuper reſpectu ν' aliarum, nec non reſpectu ν'' aliarum etc., ipſa M non variabitur ſiue binae e primis ν indeterminatis inter ſe permutentur, ſiue binae e ſecundis ν', ſiue binae e tertiis ν'' etc., ita vt ſemper

$$1.2.3\ldots\ldots\nu.\;1.2.3\ldots\ldots\nu'.\;1.2.3\ldots\ldots\nu''\text{ etc.}$$

permu-

permutationes terminis indenticis respondeant. Quare si ex his terminis identicis semper vnicum tantum retineamus, omnino habebimus

$$\frac{m(m-1)(m-2)(m-3)\ldots\ldots(m-\mu+1)}{1.2.3\ldots\ldots\nu.\ 1.2.3\ldots\ldots\nu'.\ 1.2.3\ldots\ldots\nu''\ \text{etc.}}$$

terminos, quorum complexum dicemus *complexum omnium M exclusis repetitionibus*, vt a *complexu omnium M admissis repetitionibus* distinguatur. Quoties nihil expressis verbis monitum fuerit, repetitiones admitti semper subintelligemus.

Ceterum facile perspicietur, aggregatum omnium M, vel productum ex omnibus M, vel generaliter quamlibet functionem symmetricam omnium M semper fieri functionem symmetricam indeterminatarum a, b, c etc., siue admittantur repetitiones, siue excludantur.

12.

Iam considerabimus, denotantibus u, x indeterminatas, productum ex omnibus $u-(a+b)x+ab$, exclusis repetitionibus quod per ζ designabimus. Erit itaque ζ productum ex $\frac{1}{2}m(m-1)$ factoribus his

$$\begin{array}{l}
u-(a+b)x+ab\\
u-(a+c)x+ac\\
u-(a+d)x+ad\\
\text{etc.}\\
u-(b+c)x+bc\\
u-(b+d)x+bd\\
\text{etc.}\\
u-(c+d)x+cd\\
\text{etc. etc.}
\end{array}$$

Quae functio quum indeterminatas a, b, c etc. symmetrice implicet, assignari poterit functio integra indeterminatarum u, x, l', l'', l''' etc.

l''' etc., per z denotanda, quae transeat in ζ, si loco indeterminatarum l', l'', l''' etc. substituantur λ', λ'', λ''' etc. Denique designemus per Z functionem solarum indeterminatarum u, x, in quam z transit, si indeterminatis l', l'', l''' etc. tribuamus valores determinatos L', L'', L''' etc.

Hae tres functiones ζ, z, Z considerari possunt tamquam functiones integrae ordinis $\frac{1}{2}m(m-1)$ indeterminatae u cum coëfficientibus indeterminatis, qui quidem coëfficientes erunt

pro ζ, functiones indeterminatarum x, a, b, c etc.

pro z, functiones indeterminatarum x, l', l'', l''' etc.

pro Z, functiones solius indeterminatae x.

Singuli vero coëfficientes ipsius z transibunt in coëfficientes ipsius ζ per substitutiones $l'=\lambda'$, $l''=\lambda''$, $l'''=\lambda'''$ etc. nec non in coëfficientes ipsius Z per substitutiones $l'=L'$, $l''=L''$, $l'''=L'''$ etc. Eadem, quae modo de coëfficientibus diximus, etiam de determinantibus functionum ζ, z, Z valebunt. Atque in hos ipsos iam propius inquiremus, et quidem eum in finem, vt demonstretur

THEOREMA. *Quoties non est $P=0$, determinans functionis Z certo nequit esse identice $=0$.*

13.

Perfacilis quidem esset demonstratio huius theorematis, si supponere liceret, Y resolui posse in factores simplices

$$(x-A)\,(x-B)\,(x-C)\,(x-D)\,\ldots\ldots$$

Tunc enim certum quoque esset, Z esse productum ex omnibus $u-(A+B)\,x+AB$, atque determinantem functionis Z productum e differentiis inter binas quantitatum

$$(A+B)\,x-AB$$
$$(A+C)\,x-AC$$
$$(A+D)\,x-AD$$
etc.

$(B+C)\,x-BC$
$(B+D)\,x-BD$
etc.
$(C+D)\,x-CD$
etc. etc.

Hoc vero productum identice euanescere nequit, nisi aliquis factorum per se identice fiat $=0$, vnde sequeretur, duas quantitatum A, B, C etc. aequales esse, adeoque determinantem P functionis Y fieri $=0$, contra hyp.

At seposita tali argumentatione, quam ad instar art. 6. a petitione principii proficisci manifestum est, statim ad demonstrationem stabilem theorematis art. 12. explicandam progredimur.

14.

Determinans functionis ζ erit productum ex omnibus differentiis inter binas $(a+b)\,x-ab$, quarum differentiarum multitudo est

$$\tfrac{1}{2}m\,(m-1)\,(\tfrac{1}{2}m\,(m-1)-1)=\tfrac{1}{4}\,(m+1)\,m\,(m-1)\,(m-2)$$

Hic numerus itaque indicat ordinem determinantis functionis ζ respectu indeterminatae x. Determinans functionis z quidem ad eundem ordinem pertinebit: contra determinans functionis Z vtique ad ordinem inferiorem pertinere potest, quoties scilicet quidam coëfficientes inde ab altissima potestate ipsius x euanescunt. Nostrum iam est demonstrare, in determinante functionis Z *omnes* certo coëfficientes euanescere non posse.

Propius considerando differentias illas, quarum productum est determinans functionis ζ, deprehendemus, partem ex ipsis (puta differentias inter binas $(a+b)\,x-ab$ tales, quae elementum commune habent) suppeditare

productum ex omnibus $(a-b)\,(x-c)$

e re

e reliquis vero (puta e differentiis inter binas $(a+b)x-ab$ tales, quarum elementa diuersa sunt) oriri

productum ex omnibus $(a+b-c-d)x-ab+cd$, exclusis repetitionibus.

Productum prius factorem vnumquemque $a-b$ manifesto $m-2$ vicibus continebit, quemuis factorem $x-c$ autem $(m-1)(m-2)$ vicibus, vnde facile concludimus, hocce productum fieri

$$=\pi^{m-2}\upsilon^{(m-1)(m-2)}$$

Quodsi ita productum posterius per ϱ designamus, determinans functionis ζ erit

$$=\pi^{m-2}\upsilon^{(m-1)(m-2)}\varrho$$

Denotando porro per r functionem indeterminatarum x, l', l'', l''' etc. eam, quae transit in ϱ per substitutiones $l'=\lambda'$, $l''=\lambda''$, $l'''=\lambda'''$ etc., nec non per R functionem solius x, eam, in quam transit r per substitutiones $l'=L'$, $l''=L''$, $l'''=L'''$ etc., patet determinantem functionis z fieri

$$=p^{m-2}y^{(m-1)(m-2)}r$$

determinantem functionis Z autem

$$=P^{m-2}Y^{(m-1)(m-2)}R$$

Quare quum per hypothesin P non sit $=0$, res iam in eo vertitur, vt demonstremus, R certo identice euanescere non posse.

15.

Ad hunc finem adhuc aliam indeterminatam w introducemus, atque productum ex omnibus

$$(a+b-c-d)w+(a-c)(a-d)$$

exclusis repetitionibus considerabimus, quod quum ipsas a, b, c etc. symmetrice inuoluat, tamquam functio integra indeterminatarum $w, \lambda', \lambda'', \lambda'''$ etc. exhiberi poterit. Denotabimus hanc

 functio-

functionem per $f(w, \lambda', \lambda'', \lambda'''$ etc.) Multitudo illorum factorum $(a+b-c-d)w+(a-c)(a-d)$ erit

$$= \tfrac{1}{2}m(m-1)(m-2)(m-3)$$

vnde facile colligimus fieri

$$f(0, \lambda', \lambda'', \lambda''' \text{ etc.}) = \pi^{(m-2)(m-3)}$$

et proin etiam

$$f(0, l', l'', l''' \text{ etc.}) = p^{(m-2)(m-3)}$$

nec non

$$f(0, L', L'', L''' \text{ etc.}) = P^{(m-2)(m-3)}$$

Functio $f(w, L', L'', L'''$ etc.) generaliter quidem loquendo ad ordinem

$$\tfrac{1}{2}m(m-1)(m-2)(m-3)$$

referenda erit: at in casibus specialibus vtique ad ordinem inferiorem pertinere potest, si forte contingat, vt quidam coëfficientes inde ab altissima potestate ipsius w euanescant: impossibile autem est, vt illa functio tota sit identice $= 0$, quum aequatio modo inuenta doceat, functionis saltem terminum vltimum non euanescere. Supponemus, terminum altissimum functionis $f(w, L', L'', L'''$ etc.), qui quidem coëfficientem non euanescentem habeat, esse Nw^ν. Si igitur substituimus $w = x - a$, patet $f(x-a, L', L'', L'''$ etc.) esse functionem integram indeterminatarum x, a, siue quod idem est, functionem ipsius x cum coëfficientibus ab indeterminata a pendentibus, ita tamen vt terminus altissimus sit Nx^ν, et proin coëfficientem determinatum ab a non pendentem habeat, qui non sit $= 0$. Perinde $f(x-b, L', L'', L'''$ etc.), $f(x-c, L', L'', L'''$ etc.) erunt functiones integrae indeterminatae x, tales vt singularum terminus altissimus sit Nx^ν, terminorum sequentium autem coëfficientes resp. a b, c etc. pendeant. Hinc productum ex m factoribus

$$f(x-a, L', L'', L''' \text{ etc.})$$
$$f(x-b, L', L'', L''' \text{ etc.})$$
$$f(x-c, L', L'', L''' \text{ etc.})$$
$$\text{etc.}$$

eri

erit functio integra ipſius x, cuius terminus altiſſimus erit $N^m x^{m\nu}$, dum terminorum ſequentium coëfficientes pendent ab indeterminatis a, b, c etc.

Conſideremus iam porro productum ex m factoribus his

$$f(x-a,\ l',\ l'',\ l'''\ \text{etc.})$$
$$f(x-b,\ l',\ l'',\ l'''\ \text{etc.})$$
$$f(x-c,\ l',\ l'',\ l'''\ \text{etc.})$$
$$\text{etc.}$$

quod quum ſit functio indeterminatarum, x, a, b, c etc., l', l'', l''' etc., et quidem ſymmetrica reſpectu ipſarum a, b, c etc., exhiberi poterit tamquam functio indeterminatarum $x, \lambda', \lambda'', \lambda'''$ etc. l', l'', l''' etc. per

$$\varphi(x,\ \lambda',\ \lambda'',\ \lambda'''\ \text{etc.},\ l',\ l'',\ l'''\ \text{etc.})$$

denotanda. Erit itaque

$$\varphi(x,\ \lambda',\ \lambda'',\ \lambda'''\ \text{etc.},\ \lambda',\ \lambda'',\ \lambda'''\ \text{etc.})$$

productum ex factoribus

$$f(x-a,\ \lambda',\ \lambda'',\ \lambda'''\ \text{etc.})$$
$$f(x-b,\ \lambda',\ \lambda'',\ \lambda'''\ \text{etc.})$$
$$f(x-c,\ \lambda',\ \lambda'',\ \lambda'''\ \text{etc.})$$
$$\text{etc.}$$

et proin indefinite diuiſibilis per ϱ, quum facile perſpiciatur, quemlibet factorem ipſius ϱ in aliquo illorum factorum implicari. Statuemus itaque

$$\varphi(x, \lambda', \lambda'', \lambda'''\ \text{etc.}, \lambda', \lambda'', \lambda'''\ \text{etc.}) = \varrho\psi(x, \lambda', \lambda'', \lambda'''\ \text{etc.})$$

vbi characteriſtica ψ functionem integram exhibebit. Hinc vero facile deducitur, etiam identice eſſe

$$\varphi(x, L', L'', L'''\ \text{etc.},\ L', L'', L'''\ \text{etc.}) = R\psi(x, L', L'', L'''\ \text{etc.})$$

Sed ſupra demonſtrauimus, productum e factoribus

$$f(x-a,\ L',\ L'',\ L'''\ \text{etc.})$$
$$f(x-b,\ L',\ L'',\ L'''\ \text{etc.})$$
$$f(x-c,\ L',\ L'',\ L'''\ \text{etc.})$$
$$\text{etc.}$$

quod

quod erit $= \varphi(x, \lambda', \lambda'', \lambda'''$ etc., L', L'', L''' etc.) habere terminum altissimum $N^m x^{m\nu}$; eundem proin terminum altissimum habebit functio $\varphi(x, L', L'', L'''$ etc., L', L'', L''' etc.), adeoque certo non est identice $= 0$. Quocirca etiam R nequit esse identice $= 0$, neque adeo etiam determinans functionis Z Q. E. D.

16.

Theorema. *Denotet $\varphi(u, x)$ *) productum ex quotcunque factoribus talibus, in quos indeterminatae u, x lineariter tantum ingrediuntur, siue qui sint formae*

$$\alpha + \beta u + \gamma x$$
$$\alpha' + \beta' u + \gamma' x$$
$$\alpha'' + \beta'' u + \gamma'' x$$

etc.: sit porro w alia indeterminata. Tunc functio

$$\varphi\left(u + w\frac{d\varphi(u, x)}{dx},\ x - w.\frac{d\varphi(u, x)}{du}\right) = \Omega$$

indefinite erit diuisibilis per $\varphi(u, x)$.

Dem. Statuendo

$$\varphi(u, x) = (\alpha + \beta u + \gamma x)\,\rho$$
$$= (\alpha' + \beta' u + \gamma' x)\,\rho'$$
$$= (\alpha'' + \beta'' u + \gamma'' x)\,\rho''$$
etc.

erunt ρ, ρ', ρ'' etc. functiones integrae indeterminatarum u, x, $\alpha, \beta, \gamma, \alpha', \beta', \gamma', \alpha'', \beta'', \gamma''$ etc. atque

$$d\varphi(u, x)$$

*) Vel nobis non monentibus quisque videbit, signa in art. praec. introducta restringi ad istum solum articulum, et proin significationem characterum φ, w praesentem non esse confundendam cum pristina.

$$\frac{d\varphi(u,x)}{dx} = \gamma\rho + (\alpha + \beta u + \gamma x).\frac{d\rho}{dx}$$
$$= \gamma'\rho' + (\alpha' + \beta' u + \gamma' x).\frac{d\rho'}{dx}$$
$$= \gamma''\rho'' + (\alpha'' + \beta'' u + \gamma'' x).\frac{d\rho''}{dx}$$
etc.

$$\frac{d\varphi(u,x)}{du} = \beta\rho + (\alpha + \beta u + \gamma x).\frac{d\rho}{du}$$
$$= \beta'\rho' + (\alpha' + \beta' u + \gamma' x).\frac{d\rho'}{du}$$
$$= \beta''\rho'' + (\alpha'' + \beta'' u + \gamma'' x).\frac{d\rho''}{du}$$
etc.

Subſtitutis hisce valoribus in factoribus, e quibus conflatur productum Ω, puta in

$$\alpha + \beta u + \gamma x + \beta w.\frac{d\varphi(u,x)}{dx} - \gamma w.\frac{d\varphi(u,x)}{du}$$
$$\alpha' + \beta' u + \gamma' x + \beta' w.\frac{d\varphi(u,x)}{dx} - \gamma' w.\frac{d\varphi(u,x)}{du}$$
$$\alpha'' + \beta'' u + \gamma'' x + \beta'' w.\frac{d\varphi(u,x)}{dx} - \gamma'' w.\frac{d\varphi(u,x)}{du}$$

etc. reſp.

hi obtinent valores ſequentes

$$(\alpha + \beta u + \gamma x)\,(1 + \beta w.\frac{d\rho}{dx} - \gamma w.\frac{d\rho}{du})$$
$$(\alpha' + \beta' u + \gamma' x)\,(1 + \beta' w.\frac{d\rho'}{dx} - \gamma' w.\frac{d\rho'}{du})$$
$$(\alpha'' + \beta'' u + \gamma'' x)\,(1 + \beta'' w.\frac{d\rho''}{dx} - \gamma'' w.\frac{d\rho''}{du})$$
etc.

qua-

quapropter Ω erit productum ex $\varphi(u, x)$ in factores

$$1 + \beta w. \frac{d\varrho}{dx} - \gamma w. \frac{d\varrho}{du}$$

$$1 + \beta' w. \frac{d\varrho'}{dx} - \gamma' w. \frac{d\varrho'}{du}$$

$$1 + \beta'' w. \frac{d\varrho''}{dx} - \gamma'' w. \frac{d\varrho''}{du}$$

etc. i. e. ex $\varphi(u, x)$ in functionem integram indeterminatarum u, $x, w, \alpha, \beta, \gamma, \alpha', \beta', \gamma', \alpha'', \beta'', \gamma''$ etc. *Q. E. D.*

17.

Theorema art. praec. manifesto applicabile est ad functionem ζ, quam abhinc per

$$f(u, x, \lambda', \lambda'', \lambda''' \text{ etc.})$$

exhiberi supponemus, ita vt

$$f\left(u + w. \frac{d\zeta}{dx}, x - w. \frac{d\zeta}{du}, \lambda', \lambda'', \lambda''' \text{ etc.}\right)$$

indefinite diuisibilis euadat per ζ: quotientem, qui erit functio integra indeterminatarum u, x, w, a, b, c etc., symmetrica respectu ipsarum a, b, c etc., exhibebimus per

$$\psi(u, x, w, \lambda', \lambda'', \lambda''' \text{ etc.})$$

Hinc concludimus, fieri etiam identice

$$f\left(u + w. \frac{dz}{dx}, x - w. \frac{dz}{du}, l', l'', l''' \text{ etc.}\right)$$
$$= z\psi(u, x, w, l', l'', l''' \text{ etc.})$$

nec non

$$f\left(u + w. \frac{dZ}{dx}, x - w. \frac{dZ}{du}, L', L'', L''' \text{ etc.}\right)$$
$$= Z\psi(u, x, w, L', L'', L''' \text{ etc.})$$

Quodsi itaque functionem Z simpliciter exhibemus per $F(u, x)$ ita vt habeatur

$$f(u, x, L', L'', L''' \text{ etc.}) = F(u, x)$$

eri

erit identice

$$F\left(u+w\cdot\frac{dZ}{dx},\ x-w\cdot\frac{dZ}{du}\right)=Z\psi(u,x,w,L',L'',L'''\text{ etc.})$$

18.

Si itaque e valoribus determinatis ipſarum u, x, puta ex $u=U$, $x=X$ prodire ſupponimus

$$\frac{dZ}{dx}=X',\ \frac{dZ}{du}=U'$$

erit identice

$$F(U+wX', X-wU')=F(U,X)\cdot\psi(U,X,w,L',L'',L'''\text{ etc.})$$

Quoties U' non euaneſcit, ſtatuere licebit

$$w=\frac{X-x}{U'}$$

vnde emergit

$$F\left(U+\frac{XX'}{U'}-\frac{X'x}{U'},\ x\right)=F(U,X)\cdot\psi\left(U,X,\frac{X-x}{U'},L',L'',L'''\text{ etc.}\right)$$

quod etiam ita enunciare licet:

Si in functione Z ſtatuitur $u=U+\dfrac{XX'}{U'}-\dfrac{X'x}{U'}$, tranſibit ea in

$$F(U,X)\cdot\psi\left(U,X,\frac{X-x}{U'},L',L'',L'''\text{ etc.}\right)$$

19.

Quum in caſu eo, vbi non eſt $P=0$, determinans functionis Z ſit functio indeterminatae x per ſe non euaneſcens, manifeſto multitudo valorum determinatorum ipſius x, per quos hic determinans valorem 0 nanciſci poteſt, erit numerus finitus, ita vt infinite multi valores determinati ipſius x aſſignari poſſint, qui determinanti illi valorem a 0 diuerſum concilient. Sit X talis valor ipſius x (quem inſuper *realem* ſupponere licet). Erit itaque

 deter-

determinans functionis $P(u, X)$ non $= 0$, vnde ſequitur, per theorema II. art. 6, functiones

$$F(u, X) \text{ et } \frac{\mathrm{d}F(u, X)}{\mathrm{d}u}$$

habere non poſſe diuiſorem vllum communem. Supponamus porro, exſtare aliquem valorem determinatum ipſius u, puta U (ſiue realis ſit, ſiue imaginarius i. e. ſub forma $g + h\sqrt{-1}$ contentus), qui reddat $F(u, X) = 0$, i. e. eſſe $F(U, X) = 0$. Erit itaque $u - U$ factor indefinitus functionis $F(u, X)$, et proin functio $\frac{\mathrm{d}F(u, X)}{\mathrm{d}u}$ certo per $u - U$ non diuiſibilis. Supponendo itaque, hanc functionem $\frac{\mathrm{d}F(u, X)}{\mathrm{d}u}$ nanciſci valorem U', ſi ſtatuatur $u = U$, certo eſſe nequit $U' = 0$. Manifeſto autem U' erit valor quotientis differentialis partialis $\frac{\mathrm{d}Z}{\mathrm{d}u}$ pro $u = U$, $x = X$: quodſi itaque inſuper pro iisdem valoribus ipſarum u, x valorem quotientis differentialis partialis $\frac{\mathrm{d}Z}{\mathrm{d}x}$ per X' denotemus, perſpicuum eſt per ea quae in art. praec. demonſtrata ſunt, functionem Z per ſubſtitutionem

$$u = U + \frac{XX'}{U'} - \frac{X'x}{U'}$$

identice euaneſcere, adeoque per factorem

$$u + \frac{X'}{U'}x - \left(U + \frac{XX'}{U'}\right)$$

indefinite eſſe diuiſibilem. Quocirca ſtatuendo $u = xx$, patet, $F(xx, x)$ diuiſibilem eſſe per

$$xx + \frac{X'}{U'}x - \left(U + \frac{XX'}{U'}\right)$$

adeoque obtinere valorem 0, ſi pro x accipiatur radix aequationis

$$xx + \frac{X'}{U'}x - \left(U + \frac{XX'}{U'}\right) = 0$$

i. e.

i. e. ſi ſtatuatur

$$x = \frac{-X' \pm \surd(4\,UU'U' + 4\,XX'U' + X'X')}{2\,U'}$$

quos valores vel reales eſſe vel ſub forma $g + h\surd -1$ contentos conſtat.

Facile iam demonſtratur, per eosdem valores ipſius x etiam functionem Y euaneſcere debere. Manifeſto enim φ (xx, x, λ', λ'', λ''' etc.) eſt productum ex omnibus $(x - a)$ $(x - b)$ excluſis repetitionibus, et proin $= v^{m-1}$: Hinc ſponte ſequitur

$$\varphi\,(xx,\ x,\ l',\ l'',\ l'''\ \text{etc.}) = y^{m-1}$$

$$\varphi\,(xx,\ x,\ L',\ L'',\ L'''\ \text{etc.}) = Y^{m-1}$$

ſiue $F(xx, x) = Y^{m-1}$, cuius itaque valor determinatus euaneſcere nequit, niſi ſimul euaneſcat valor ipſius Y.

20.

Adiumento disquiſitionum praecedentium reducta eſt *ſolutio* aequationis $Y = 0$, i. e. inuentio valoris determinati ipſius x, vel realis vel ſub forma $g + h\surd -1$ contenti, qui illi ſatisfaciat, ad ſolutionem aequationis $F(u, X) = 0$, ſiquidem determinans functionis Y non fuerit $= 0$. Obſeruare conuenit, ſi omnes coëfficientes in Y, i. e. numeri L', L'', L''' etc. ſint quantitates reales, etiam omnes coëfficientes in $F(u, X)$ reales fieri, ſiquidem quod licet pro X quantitas realis accepta fuerit. Ordo aequationis ſecundariae $F(u, X) = 0$ exprimitur per numerum $\frac{1}{2}\,m\,(m-1)$: quoties igitur m eſt numerus par formae $2^{\mu}\,k$, denotante k indefinite numerum imparem, ordo aequationis ſecundariae exprimitur per numerum formae $2^{\mu-1}\,k$.

In caſu eo vbi determinans functionis Y fit $= 0$, aſſignari poterit per art. 10. functio alia $\mathfrak{Y}$ ipſam metiens, cuius determinans non ſit $= 0$, et cuius ordo exprimatur per numerum formae $2^{\nu}\,k$, ita vt ſit vel $\nu < \mu$, vel $\nu = \mu$. Quaelibet ſolutio aequationis $\mathfrak{Y} = 0$ etiam ſatisfaciet aequationi $Y = 0$: ſolutio aequationis $\mathfrak{Y} = 0$ iterum redu-

reducetur ad ſolutionem alius aequationis, cuius ordo exprimetur per numerum formae $2^{\nu-1}k$.

Ex his itaque colligimus, generaliter ſolutionem cuiusuis aequationis, cuius ordo exprimatur per numerum parem formae $2^{\mu}k$, reduci poſſe ad ſolutionem alius aequationis, cuius ordo exprimatur per numerum formae $2^{\mu'}k$, ita vt ſit $\mu' < \mu$. Quoties hic numerus etiamnum par eſt, i. e. μ' non $= 0$, eadem methodus denuo applicabitur, atque ita continuabimus, donec ad aequationem perueniamus, cuius ordo exprimatur per numerum imparem; et huius aequationis coëfficientes omnes erunt reales, ſiquidem omnes coëfficientes aequationis primitiuae reales fuerunt. Talem vero aequationem ordinis imparis certo ſolubilem eſſe conſtat, et quidem per radicem realem, vnde ſingulae quoque aequationes antecedentes ſolubiles erunt, ſiue per radices reales ſiue per radices formae $g + h\sqrt{-1}$.

Euictum eſt itaque, functionem quamlibet Y formae $x^m - L'x^{m-1} + L''x^{m-2} -$ etc. vbi L', L'' etc. ſunt quantitates determinatae reales, inuoluere factorem indefinitum $x - A$, vbi A ſit quantitas vel realis vel ſub forma $g + h\sqrt{-1}$ contenta. In caſu poſteriori facile perſpicitur, Y nanciſci valorem 0 etiam per ſubſtitutionem $x = g - h\sqrt{-1}$, adeoque etiam diuiſibilem eſſe per $x - (g - h\sqrt{-1})$, et proin etiam per productum $xx - 2gx + gg + hh$. Quaelibet itaque functio Y certo factorem indefinitum realem primi vel ſecundi ordinis implicat, et quum idem iterum de quotiente valeat, manifeſtum eſt, Y in factores reales primi vel ſecundi ordinis reſolui poſſe. Quod demonſtrare erat propoſitum huius commentationis.

PRAECIPUORUM INDE A NEUTONO CONATUUM, COMPOSITIONEM VIRIUM DEMONSTRANDI, RECENSIO.

AUCTORE

CAROLO JACOBI.

Cum II. Tabul. aen.

GOTTINGAE

APUD RUDOLPHUM DEUERLICH

MDCCCXVIII.

VIRIS CLARISSIMIS,

ILLUSTRISSIMIS, AMPLISSIMIS,
FAUTORIBUS SUMME VENERANDIS,
PRAECEPTORIBUS PIE COLENDIS,

BERNHARDO DE LINDENAU,

CAROLO DIEDERICO DE MUENCHOW,

FRIDERICO KRIES,

HASCE STUDIORUM PRIMITIAS

CONSECRAT

A U C T O R.

Nomina auctorum.

I. Quorum demonstrationes expositae sunt:

II. Quorum demonstrationes exponere quidem partim haud licitum, partim haud necessarium fuit, quorum autem mentio tamen facta est:

E r r a t a.

p. 2 lin. 25 legatur praestet pro praestare
p. 6 — 15 — quem — quam.
p. 8 — 11 loco commatis inter $\frac{(AB)^2}{AD}$ et AG ponendum est signum aequalitatis
p. 8 — 25 legatur CE pro CB
p. 12 — 30 — moniusse pro monuisse
p. 13 — 13 — $\frac{1}{2^n}$ pro $\frac{1}{2n}$
p. 15 — ult. AQ pro AO
p. 16 — 24 — CB. sin φ' pro CB. sin φ
p. 24 — ult. — primum pro mihi
p. 25 — 21 — AI pro AB
p. 27 — 21 — dato pro data
p. 29 — 10 — 2AD pro AB, AC
—— — 31 — IG pro AG
—— — — — AI pro AB
p. 31 — 11 — est pro sit
—— — — — AB, AD pro AF, AG
—— lin. 26 — AP :: sin. RAQ : sin. PAR : sin PAQ pro AQ :: sin RAQ : sin QAP
—— lin 28 — ex praecedentibus pro praecedentibus
—— lin. 28 et 29 AH : AI : AG pro AI AH :: AG
—— lin. 30 deleatur: sin. PAR
p. 36 signum # e linea 10 transponendum est in lin. 9 inter AD et B'C
—— lin. 9 inter B'C et AR ponendum est signum ||

p. 39	sub fin.	legatur	dividenda pro divenda.
p. 41	lin. 9	—	$R_{m-1} + R_m$ pro $R_{m-1} \cdot R_m$
——	— 10	—	${}^{2n-1}R_{m-1}$: pro ${}^{2n-}R_{m-1}$
p. 42	— 1	—	$\frac{n\pi}{2^{m-1}}$ pro $\frac{n\pi}{2^{m+1}}$
p. 43	— 2	—	mCm pro MCm
p. 48	— 2	—	quum pro quam
p. 51	— 18	—	$B e^{-\alpha\sqrt{K}}$ pro $B e^{\alpha - \sqrt{K}}$
p. 60	— 11	—	MH pro MB
p. 61	— ult.	—	1804 pro 1814
p. 62	— 6	—	constitutae pro constituae

Cetera, quae levioris momenti sunt, benevolus lector ipse agnoscat atque corrigat.

PRAEMITTENDA QUAEDAM.

§. 1.

Quum omnes fere hominum artes, omnisque doctrina ac disciplina ad varias humanae naturae necessitates praecipue spectent, vel quum, ut animi nostri vires excitentur, irritamentis, iisque saepissime externis, indigeamus, eas potissimum scientias, quae plurima ad ea, quae cuique maxime sunt necessaria, praebenda et praestanda conferunt, tractari atque excoli, per se satis apparet. Jam sexcenties matheseos, quod maximam hominibus utilitatem adtulerit, prosperrimo successu multis rebus, in vita communi obviis, immo toti fere physicae adplicata fuerit, laudes sunt praedicatae. Mechanica, seu scientia de motu corporum, jure meritoque ad potiores matheseos, quam vocant, adplicatae partes refertur. Itaque jam inde ab antiquis temporibus multi deinceps viri, iique saepe ingenii praestantissimi, pertractandae atque excolendae huic scientiae operam navarunt. Incredibile eſt dictu, quantopere Archimedis, Galilei, Neutoni, Euleri, Lagrangii aliorumque virorum operâ hujus scientiae exactissima cognitione progressi simus.

§. 2.

Natura animi humani ita comparata eſt, ut, si quis primam curam et cogitationem in rem aliquam conferat, in singulis ac specialibus, quae ei offeruntur, perpendendis acquiescat. Temporis demum progressu, his singulis varie inter se conferendis atque nectendis, ad rerum proprietates magis universas ac generales accedit. Item animo omnino excultiore opus eſt, ut quis rerum, quas jam diu fortasse notas habet, caussas explorare studeat. Hinc intelligitur, quomodo factum sit, ut plura mechanicae theoremata multum antea cognita sint, quam cuidam leges, ex quibus haec omnia deduci, immo secundum quas ampliari atque dilatari possint, universas explorare in mentem inciderit. Quibus de mechanicae principiis summi demum viri, Leibnitius, Wolfius, Bernoullius, Lambertus, Riccatus, Alembertus, Eulerus, Lagrangius, Kaestnerus, Karstenius, Salimbenus, Ferronus aliique magni geometrae disquisitiones instituerunt. Multum de his principiis, sed multo magis de motuum caussis, seu de viribus inter geometras, et praesertim inter Italos, est disputatum. Quorum quidem omnium expositio idonea atque apta, quantumvis esset utilis, partim tamen ad propositum nostrum haud conveniret, partim, ut ingenue fatear, tironis vires longe excederet.

§. 3.

Quocunque autem modo geometrae de his rebus inter se dissideant, ejus tamen mechanicae partis, quae de virium aequilibrio agit, tres potissimum propositiones esse fundamentales, inter omnes fere constat. Quavis earum, tanquam fundamento, cetera omnia staticae theoremata superstrui possunt. Sed ne ab iis, quae hic prosequimur, nimium aberremus, in unam tantummodo ex his tribus, in illam scilicet, quam compositioem vel parallelogrammum virium vocant, inquirere nunc possumus.

Quae quidem doctrina, una vel altera denominatione in libris staticis et dynamicis fere omnibus obvia, consistit in eo, ut, viribus, quotcunque libuerit, una corpus quoddam sollicitantibus, unam omnino esse vim, quae sola eundem, quem illae conjunctim agentes, effectum praestare, sumatur. In determinanda autem cum directione, tam quantitate ejusmodi potentiae omnis haec doctrina versatur.

§. 4.

Quum omnes autores statici punctum id, in quod duae vires una agant, secundum diagonalem moveri, ideoque punctum ad eundem, sive vires actiones suas conjunctim, sive singulatim exseruerint, locum ferri contendant, haec libenter uti vera accipimus. Veri atque congrui quid, ut ita dicam, in eo conspicimus, quod duae ejusmodi vires, etsi altera alterius actionem imminuit, eundem tamen effectum praestant, h. e. quod punctum conjuncta ipsarum actione ad eundem locum, ad quem singulis deinceps agentibus latum fuisset, movetur. Hinc theorema nostrum satis diu, etsi non rigida demonstratione munitum, non solum notum esse, sed etiam ad alias ejus ope propositiones probandas adhiberi potuisse intelligitur.

§. 5.

Quod attinet ad originem propositionis nostrae, secundum ea, quae summus geometra *a*) refert, prima ejus vestigia apud Galileum *b*) reperiuntur. Idem vero Italus geometra aliique ne suspicabantur quidem, quanti momenti theorema nostrum sit, et quam facile ab eo plures, ni omnes staticae propositiones dededuci possint. Ipsius plani inclinati theoriae, quae proxime ad compositionem virium accedit, exponendae tunc temporis theorema nostrum haud adhibitum est. Multo satis post Petrus Varingonius omnia certe ea staticae theoremata, quae ad aequilibrium machinarum pertinent, hac ipsa nostra propositione superstrui posse ostendit; multoque serius Dan. Bernoullius primus demonstrationem ejusdem theorematis magis rigidam conficere tentavit. Cujus quidem viri exemplum aliis secutis, plures ejusmodi demonstrationes accepimus, quas omnes mox cognoscemus.

§. 6.

Quaedam nunc de his demonstrationibus, generatim spectatis, praecipue vero de Kantiana disserere mihi licitum sit. Mathesis adplicata, uti nomen satis indicat, ea est scientia, quae de mathesi variis naturae externae rebus, quatenus ipsae aut ad calculum, aut ad constructionem geometricam revocari possunt, adplicanda agit. Quam quidem disciplinam a mathesi pura distare ac differre, per se satis apparet. Paucis vero, qua-

---

a) Lagrange mecanique analytique; ab init. Verbotinus totus hic locus iterum legitur in libro: Montucla histoire des mathemat. Tom III. p. 608. sq.

b) Galileo opere. Bologna 1556. Tom II; Dialoghi p. 190.

nam in re hoc discrimen positum sit, exponere, haud inconveniens esse mihi videtur. Matheseos nimirum purae principia vel axiomata, quibus omnia superstruuntur, ita comparata sunt, ut ex ipso nostro intellectu, eoque solo prodierint, vel ut mens nostra, cujusque alius rei ratione plane nulla habita, secundum ipsius tantummodo naturam atque indolem haec sibi finxerit et constituerit. Itaque non solum haec ipsa principia, sed etiam omnia ea, ad quae iisdem rite adhibendis pervenitur, intellectui nostro ita accommoddata esse, ut contrarium eorum, quae ibi pronuntiantur, ne cogitari quidem possit, omnino necesse est. Hinc illa perspicuitas atque evidentia, quâ omnia gaudent, quae mathesis nos docet.

§. 7.

Ex his ipsis vero jure colligendum est, hanc evidentiam veritatemque necessariam non amplius locum habere, quum praeter principia vere mathematica simul et alia spectentur, quae non a sola mente nostra statuta, seu potius ab ea sola, ut ita dicam, genita sunt, vel, quod idem est, cum mathesis externae naturae rebus adplicetur. Tum enim et universarum naturae legum, quibus ejusmodi res vel corpora obnoxia sunt, et variarum, quibus gaudent, proprietatum multorumque aliorum, quae, licet plane non geometrica sint, aut philosophia, aut experientia nos docet, ratio omnino est habenda. Tum propositiones, quae neque calculo, neque consructione geometrica demonstrari possunt, in subsidium vocari debent. Quodsi enim v. c. in propositionem hanc: " Vis duarum aequalium media, si ejus directionem respicias, angulum, quem illae comprehendunt, bifariam secat. " si, inquam, in hanc propositionem diligentius inquirimus, mox neque ipsum axioma esse vere geometricum, neque ex his deduci, vel sola eorum ope demonstrari posse videbimus. Attamen omnes eos auctores staticos, qui hanc propositionem, tanquam axioma acceperunt, minime reprehendendos esse puto. Ibi enim omnia, quae ad determinandam resultantis directionem aliquid conferre possunt, utrimque ita inter se sunt aequalia, ut nulla reperiri queat caussa, quâ ipsa haec directio propius unam, quam alteram virium componentium accedat. Eadem, quae de hac propositione diximus, de multis aliis, non vere mathematicis, sed tamen in mathesi adplicata accipiendis, dici possunt. Ex his autem matheseos adplicatae propositiones, universe spectatas, non eodem, quo matheseos purae theoremata, sensu ac modo, vel non plane geometrice demonstrari posse, patet. Est igitur omnino, ut Kantio, compositionem motuum rigore plane vereque geometrico a se demonstratam esse, dicenti, non statim fidem praebeamus. Postquam infra autem ipsum Kantii argumentum exposuerim, spero, fore ut, hanc demonstrationem ejusmodi rigore haud gaudere, ostendere possim.

§. 8.

Pauca quaedam denique de discrimine inter compositionem virium et compositionem motuum adjecerim.

Multi auctores statici, has duas notitiones haud inter se distare, sumsisse videntur. Itaque, una cum compositione motuum demonstrata virium quoque compositionem probatam esse, existimarnnt. Quantum autem equidem video, res non ita se habet. Quum enim sine dubio plures vires, secundum diversas directiones in corpus vel punctum quoddam una agentes concipi possint, merito quoque, quaenam sit corporis, hoc modo ad motum sollicitati, directio et celeritas, disquiritur. Unusquisque autem, si quis eidem corpori eodem tempore plures secundum diversas directiones motus tribueret, hoc plane absurdum esse, intelligit. Quodsi igitur de compositione motuum sermo est, hoc tantummodo quaeri potest, quinam sit motus ille, quo solo corpus ad eundem perveniret spatii locum, ad quem pluribus singulis deinceps motibus latum fuisset? Quae vero tunc respondenda sint, per se ita apparet, ut nullis disquisitionibus, nullâque demonstratione opus sit. Hoc autem ipso compositionem virium nondum esse demonsratam, non minus clarum atque perspicuum est.

Pars commentationis prior.

Demonstrationes eae, quarum auctores compositionem virium, ut fundamentalem magis staticae, quam mechanicae propositionem probandam sibi sumunt, ideoque motus, a viribus adhibitis efficiendi, saepissime nullam fere rationem habent.

Liber primus.

Autores, qui theorema nostrum sine ulla alius staticae propositionis ope demonstrare student.

§. 9.

Principia vel axiomata, quibus aliis aliae harum demonstrationum nituntur, haeccine sunt:

1) Quarumvis potentiarum loco aliae, illis aequivalentes, substitui possunt.

2) Plures potentiae, plane inter se conspirantes, uni potentiae, summae earum aequali, aequipollentes habendae sunt.

3) Potentia duarum aequalium media angulum, quam hae comprehendunt, bifariam secat.

4) Duae vires nonnisi aequales ac plane repugnantes sunt inter se in aequilibrio.

5) Item duae potentiae, in aequilibrio positae, aequales et inter se repugnantes sint necesse est.

6) Aequilibrium, quod inter plures constat potentias, aut addendis, aut auferendis et ipsis in aequilibrio viribus, haud tollitur.

7) Aequilibrium, in quo plures versantur potentiae, etiam inter omnes illas vires, quae, secundum similes directiones agentes, quodammodo illis sunt proportionales locum habere oportet.

8) Actio cujusdam potentiae semper sibi constat, quocunque directionis suae loco ipsa adplicata concipiatur.

9) Vires omnino in aequilibrio esse nequeunt eae, quae corpus seu punctum, in quod agunt, omnino omnes ad eandem spatii partem *) movere tendunt.

Sectio prima.

Demonstrationes geometricae, atque geometrico-analyticae.

Classis prima.

Demonstrationes principiis vel axiomatibus **) 1. 2. 3. 4. 6 *supersructae.*

Cap. I.

Argumentum Bernoullianum ***).

§. 10.

Theor. Quodsi plures vires, punctum quoddam sollicitantes, inter se in aequilibrio versantur, potentias etiam eas, quae, quodammodo illis proportionales, secundum easdem directiones agunt, in aequilibrio esse necesse est.

---

*) Ad eandem spatii partem plures vires corpus quoddam movere dicuntur, dum omnes, sicuti v. c AB, AD, AC etc. (fig. 1.) ab eadem lineae rectae CF parte sunt adplicatae.

**) Auctores ipsi haec axiomata modo rite pronuntiaverunt, modo tacite suppleri voluere.

*** Dan. Bernoullii examen principiorum mechanicae; v. Comment. Acad. Petrop 1728 Tom I. p. 126 sqq.

Demonstr. Quum enim vires, duplo, triplo etc. deinceps auctas concipiamus, his sane incrementis, et ipsis inter se aequilibrantibus — sit venia verbo — aequilibrium tolli plane nequit. Eadem omnino, dum ab his viribus, quarum quamvis in tantasdem partes aequales divisam ponamus, ejusmodi partes deinceps auferuntur, valere debent.

§. 11.

Theor. Vis ea AD (fig. 1.), quae duabus aequalibus rectangulisque AB, AC, aeqnivalet, si ejus quantitatem respicias, per diagonalem quadrati exhibetur.

Demonstr. Ducatur EF perpendicularis ad AD fiatque $EA = \frac{(AB)^2}{AD}$, $AG = AF$. Quum vero sit $BAD = DAC = 45°$, ideoque $EAB = BAD = CAF$, potentia AB duabus AE, AG, itemque AC viribus AG, AF aequivaleus habenda est. Itaque potentia AD viribus his: 2AG, AE, AF aequipolleat necesse est, vel cum AE, AF semet ipsas invicem destruant, $AD = 2AG = \frac{2(AB)^2}{AD}$, et hinc $(AD)^2 = 2(AB)^2$

Coroll. Potentia igitur duabus aequalibus ac rectangulis aequivalens, tam quantitatis quam directionis respectu per diagonalem exprimitur.

§. 12.

Theor. Quum potentia CF (fig. 2) duabus rectangulis, sed inaequalibus CD, CE aequipolleat, aequationem hanc, $(CF)^2 = (CD)^2 + (CE)^2$ locum habere necesse est.

Demonstr. Ducatur et nunc BA perpendicularis ad CF; deinde sit $CG = \frac{(CD)^2}{CF}$, et $CH = \frac{(CE)^2}{CF}$, denique $CB = CA = \frac{CD.CE}{CF}$. His ita positis, CD duabus CG, CB et CB aliis duabus CH, CA aequivalere necesse est; unde patet potentiam CF hisce aequipollere potentiis: CH, CG, CB, CA, vel, quum CA, CB, sint inter se aequales ac repugnantes $CF = \frac{(CD)^2}{CF} + \frac{(CE)^2}{CF}$, seu $(CF)^2 = (CD)^2 + (CE)^2$

§. 13.

Theor. Quodsi vis quaedam AD (fig. 3.) duabus aequalibus AB, AC aequivalet, atque AE, AF duae aliae vires sunt aequales, quae, et ipsae potentiae AD aequipollentes, angulos BAD, CAD bifariam secant (positis $AB = AC = a$, $AE = AF = x$, $AD = b$) aequationem hanc $x = b \sqrt{(\frac{a}{2a+b})}$ prodire necesse est.

Demonstr. Posito enim $AG = AH = AL = \frac{x^2}{b}$, AE duabus AG, AH, et AF aliis AH, AL aequipollet; porro sit $AM = \frac{b.AG}{a} = \frac{x^2}{a}$, hinc ergo AM viribus AG, AL, ideoque AD potentiis AM, 2AH aequivalet, habebimus itaque $b = \frac{x^2}{a} + \frac{2x^2}{b}$, unde elicimus $x = b \sqrt{(\frac{a}{2a+b})}$.

§. 14.

Quum AB, AC (fig. 4.) duae sint vires aequales ac rectangulae, ducta AD perpendiculari ad BC, binas vires, AG, AH, item AE, AF, etc. angulos BAD, GAD etc. bifariam secantes, eidem potentiae 2AD, cui AB, AC aequipollent, aequivalere necesse est.

Demonstr. Postquam enim ex theoremate precedente valor virium AG, AH determinatus fuerit, habebimus

$$AG = AH = \frac{a\sqrt{2}}{\sqrt{(2+\sqrt{2})}}$$

Idem vero valor geometricus duabus AG, AH, angulos ABD, ADC bisecantibus, statuendus est; ergo potentiae AG, AH potentiae 2AD aequivalent. Eadem facile pro AE, AF aliisque binis ejusmodi viribus probari possunt.

Coroll. Binis igitur viribus aequalibus, uno horumce angulorum: 1 R, ½ R, ¼ R, ⅛ R etc. in punctum quoddam agentibus, vis earum media, tam quantitatis, quam directionis respectu habito, diagonalem exaequat.

§. 15.

Quodsi vires aequales AB, AC (fig. 5.) potentiae BF, per lineam AC in duas partes aequales BL, LF divisae, aequivalent, lineis DE ad BF, et AD, CE ad DE perpendicularibus ductis, BA duabus BD, BL et BC duabus BE, BL aequipolleant necesse est.

Demonstr. Quodsi enim res non sic se haberet, BA duabus aliis v. c. Bd, Bl, et BC viribus Be, Bl aequipollentes ponamus; hinc ergo BF viribus Bd, Be, 2Bl aequivalere sequitur; quod quidem absurdum; alteram igitur virium potentiae BA aequipollentium, vim BL aequare necesse est; hinc autem alteram esse potentiam BD jure colligimus.

Coroll. In omnibus igitur rectangulis iis, quae lineis aut AB, aut AG, aut AE (v. fig. ad §. 14.) tanquam diagonalibus circumscripta, et quorum alterum latus est AD, dum per easdem lineas vires exhibentur, vis mediae et quantitas et directio determinata est.

§. 16.

Theor. Viribus aequalibus BA, BE (fig. 6.), itemque aliis aequalibus BC, BD uni potentiae 2BL aequivalentibus, vires quoque BF, BG aequales, angulos ABM, NBE bifariam secantes, eidem potentiae 2BL aequipollere necesse est.

Demonstr Productis lineis BC, BD, ita ut sit BM=BN=BE, MN, PR ipsi AE et AP, MO, QN, RE, ipsi BS parallelae ducantur. Ex precedentibus potentiam 2BS viribus BM, BN aequivalere patet; itaque si BU duabus BA, BM, et BW duabus BE, BN aequipollere ideoque angulos ABM, NBE bisecare ponitur, duas BU, BW uni potentiae 2BL + 2BS aequivalere necesse est. Resolutis autem BM in duas BO, BS, et BA in duas BP,

BL aequipollentes, hanc habemus aequationem

$$BU = \sqrt{((BP + BO)^2 + (BL + LS)^2)}.$$

Quum vero, uti vidimus, potentiae BU, BW uni potentiae 2BL + 2BS, aequivaleant, et si earum directionem respicias cum duabus BF, BG coincidant, vim duarum BF, BG mediam esse = X posito, $\frac{BU}{2BL + 2BS} = \frac{BF}{X}$ (1) esse debet. Qua quidem aequatione quantitas X determinari potest. Quem in finem AB = a, BC = b, AC = c statuamus. Ex ipsa constructione nostra statim hae prodeunt aequationes:

$$BO = MS = \frac{a^3 - ab^2 - ac^2}{2bc}$$

$$BP = AL = \frac{a^2 - b^2 + c^2}{2c}$$

$$BL = \sqrt{\left(\frac{2b^2c^2 + 2a^2b^2 + 2a^2c^2 - a^4 - b^4 - c^4}{2bc}\right)} \text{ et hinc}$$

$$BU = \frac{\sqrt{(a^3b + ab^3 + 2a^2b^2 - abc^2)}}{b}.$$

Dum autem BAF et BFZ angulos inter se aequales reddamus, ex triangulorum BAF et BZF similitudine aequatio haec $BF = \frac{\sqrt{(a^3b + ab^3 + 2a^2b^2 + abc^2)}}{a + b}$ deducitur; substitutis autem in aequatione (1) quantitatum BU, 2BL + 2BS et BF valoribus supra repertis, hanc habebimus aequationem

$$X = \frac{\sqrt{(2b^2c^2 + 2a^2b^2 + 2a^2c^2 - a^4 - b^4 - c^4)}}{c} = 2BL.$$

§. 17.

Theor. Duae vires aequales AG, AH (fig. 7.), quopiam angulo in punctum quoddam A concurrentes, uni potentiae, quae tam quantitatis, quam directionis respectu habito, diagonalem aequat, aequivaleant omnino necesse est.

Demonstr. Quum enim supra, duas vires AB, AC, dum sint inter se aequales ac rectangulae, diagonali AK aequipollere, idemque pro viribus AE, AF: angulos BAD, DAC bisecantibus, valere demonstratum sit, et quum detur progressio haec in infinitum, liquet non posse exhiberi duas potentias aequales intra terminos AB, AC concurrentes in B et terminatas a linea BC, quae non aequivaleant potentiae AK. Duplicatis vero angulis, inter AD et quamcunque AE, seu AG etc. comprehensis, propositio manifesta quoque fit de illis potentiis, quae terminos AB, AC transgrediuntur.

§. 18.

Quae huc usque pro potentiis aequalibus ostendimus, facile viribus in aequalibus ac rectangulis, et inde quibuspiam binis viribus accommodari possunt. Quomodo ad vires rectangulas extendantur omnino ex iis quae (§. 15.) probavimus patet; eadem vero etiam pro quibuspiam viribus valere nunc videbimus. Sint enim binae ejusmodi vires AB, AC (fig. 8.). Alterâ earum AC in duas rectangulas AE, AF resolutâ ductisque EC, BG, DG, AD, quisque, vires AE, AG eundem, quem etiam AB, AC, praestituras esse effectum, intelligit. Vis autem duarum AE, AG media quum sit diagonalis AD, eadem et potentiis AE, AB aequipollere debet; ergo, quod AD utriusque parallelogrammi EG, CB est diagonalis, quarumlibet binarum virium resultantis tam quantitas quam directio est determinata.

§. 19.

Epicrisis.

Autor noster, uti primus, qui hanc virium compositionem rigidius, quam antea, evincere conatus fuerit, omnino laudandus, multumque laudatus est. Omnis haec ejus demonstratio, quantopere evidentia, perspicuitas, rigorque geometricus curae ei fuerit, satis ostendit, Tanto magis autem optandum fuisset, ut eventus operae nostri responderit. Sed quantum equidem video hoc nostri argumentum plura desideranda relinquit *).

---

*) Postquam jam diu haec scripseram, non sine voluptate virum doctissimum Alembertum eadem fere contra hoc argumentum moniusse cognovi.

Nam quum haec demonstratio propositionis Staticae fundamentalis jam a tironibus, prima hujus scientiae elementa adeuntibus, cognosci atque intelligi debeat, calculus iste satis impeditus, quo noster in posteriori praecipiue parte utitur, jure reprehendi potest. Insuper tota demonstratio tanta prolixitate laborat, ut in librum, elementa staticae exhibentem, recipi nequeat. Deinde me non intelligere fateor, quomodo noster aequationem: $BU = \sqrt{([PB + BO]^2 + [BA + BS]^2)}$ nactus sit. Ni enim fallor ponendum ei fuisset: $BU = \sqrt{(BP^2 + BO^2 + BL^2 + BS^2)}$. Sed, quod maximum est, theorema, quod (§. 17.) legimus, debito rigore non est demonstratum. Ea enim, quae noster ibi probavit, non valent, nisi anguli, quo vires componentes concurrunt, quantitas hujus est formae: $\frac{1}{2n}$ R. Idem vero jam antea (§. 14.) probaverat noster; duae igitur postremae propositiones (§§. 16. 17.) ad id, quod noster petiit, adsequendum nihil contulerunt.

Cap. II.

Argumentum a Lamberto traditum *).

§. 20.

Theor. Quum peripheriam ABDE (fig. 9.) in tres partes aequales divisam AB, AD, BD concipiamus, tres vires, per radios CA, CD, CB exhibitas, unaque punctum C sollicitantes, in aequilibrio esse contenditur.

Demonstr. Quum enim hae vires ita inter se comparatae sint, ut, quae pro una valeant, cuivis ceterarum omnino accommodari possint, si unius trium harum virium actione punctum

---

*) J. H. Lambert's Beyträge zum Gebrauche der Mathematik. 1771. Tom. II. p. 444 sqq.

C vere moveretur, duas alias simul eundum effectum producere necesse esset; ergo punctum eodem temporis momento secundum diversas directiones ferretur; quod quidem absurdum. --- Quis igitur est, qui potentiam CE, ipsi CB aequalem, sed repugnantem, eandem, quam CA, CD conjunctim exserunt, actionem exercituram esse dubitet? Ex quibus autem, virium compositionem re vera locum habere, rite colligitur. Ductis AE et DE, ACDE esse parallelogrammum, cujus diagonalis sit CE, statim intelligitur; his ergo positis, vel hoc rerum statu, compositio virium breviter atque evidenter demonstrari potest.

Coroll. Eadem, quae de ternis viribus dicta sunt, ad plura facillime extendi posse, per se clarum est.

§. 21.

Theor. Ternis viribus, quae punctum quoddam una sollicitant, in aequilibrio versantibus, omnes quoque eas, quae, secundum easdem directiones agentes, quodammodo illis sunt proportionales, inter se aequilibrari necesse est.

Demonstratio est omnino eadem, quam jam supra (§. 10.) legimus.

§. 22.

Theor. Quum potentia CD (fig. 10.) duabus CB, CA, inter se rectangulis aequipolleat, aequationem hanc $(CD)^2 = (CB)^2 + (AC)^2$ locum habere necesse est.

Demonstratio haud discrepat ab ea, quam Bernoullius (§. 12.) pro eodem theoremate tradidit.

Coroll. 1. Idem, quod apud Bernoullium legitur.

Coroll. 2. Sit angulus $ABC = \phi$; hinc nobis erunt aequationes

$$CB = CD \cos \phi$$
$$CA = CD \sin \phi.$$

Scholion. Angulum ABC littera ϕ, alterum BCD littera ω nobis denotet; illam autem brevitatis caussa angulum hypothenusalem, hunc angulum directorem adpellemus.

§. 23.

Theor. Quodsi, dum angulus director est ω, angulus hypothenusalis sit φ, itemque dum ang. dir. ω', angul. hypoth. φ', etiam, dum angulus direct. $\omega + \omega'$, angulum hypothenusalem $\varphi + \varphi'$ esse necesse est.

Demonstr. Resolutis enim viribus CD, cd (fig. 11.) in binas laterales CB, CA et Cb, Ca, ita quidem, ut sit $DCA = \omega$, $dCA = \omega'$, dum $CD = Cd = 1$ hae nobis erunt aequationes,

$$CA = \cos\varphi \qquad Ca = \cos\varphi'$$
$$CB = \sin\varphi \quad \text{et} \quad Cb = \sin\varphi'$$

Sit porro $C\delta = Cd$ et $\delta CD = dCA$, ideoque $\delta CA = \omega + \omega'$; ducatur Ce perpendicularis ad CD; fiat

$$C\varepsilon = Ca = \cos\varphi'$$
$$Ce = Cb = \sin\varphi'$$

resolvantur, $C\varepsilon$ in duas $C\varkappa$, $C\varkappa'$, Ce in alias $C\gamma$, Cg et $C\delta$ in duas $C\beta$, $C\alpha$; denique ducantur $\delta\varepsilon$, δe, $\beta\delta$.

His ita constitutis, quum sint $eCB = DCA = \omega$, et $\delta C\varepsilon = dCA = \omega'$, hasce nanciscimur aequationes:

$$C\varkappa = C\varepsilon \cos\varphi = Ca \cos\varphi = \cos\varphi' \cos\varphi$$
$$C\gamma = Ce \sin\varphi = Cb \sin\varphi = \sin\varphi' \sin\varphi,$$

hinc ergo
$$C\varkappa - C\gamma = C\alpha = \cos\varphi' \cos\varphi - \sin\varphi' \sin\varphi$$
$$= \cos(\varphi + \varphi')$$

Item habebimus
$$C\varkappa' = C\varepsilon \sin\varphi = \cos\varphi' \sin\varphi$$
$$Cg = Ce \cos\varphi = \sin\varphi' \cos\varphi$$

ergo $C\varkappa' + Cg = C\beta = \sin(\varphi + \varphi')$.

§. 24.

Quum igitur angulis ω, ω', $\omega + \omega'$ abscissae AP, AQ, AR (fig. *), angulis vero φ, φ', $\varphi + \varphi'$, ordinatae PM, QN, RL respondeant, ducta LK ipsi AR parallela, quoniam $AP = QR = TL$, ideoque $PM = TN$ atque eadem ratione $SM = QN$, linea AMNL curva esse nequit. Quodsi enim esset, ducta recta AmnL, $Pm = Tn$, et $Qn = Sm$ haberemus, quae aequationes non nisi puncta bina M, m, N, n coincidant locum habere possunt, itaque hae erunt aequationes

$$\frac{AP}{PM} = \frac{AQ}{QN} = \frac{AR}{RL}, \text{ vel } \frac{\omega}{\varphi} = \frac{\omega'}{\varphi'} = \frac{\omega + \omega'}{\varphi + \varphi'}.$$

Posito igitur, esse $\varphi = n\omega$, etiam $\varphi' = n\omega'$, $\varphi + \varphi' = n(\omega + \omega')$, $\varphi + \varphi' + \varphi'' = n(\omega + \omega' + \omega'')$ etc. esse debent. Tres anguli ω, ω', ω'' si sint ita inter se comparati, ut sit $\omega + \omega' + \omega'' = 90°$, habebimus

$$\sin(\varphi + \varphi' + \varphi'') = 1$$
$$\cos(\varphi + \varphi' + \varphi'') = 0$$

ergo $\varphi + \varphi' + \varphi'' = 90° = \omega + \omega' + \omega''$ et hinc $n = 1$, ideoque $\varphi = \omega$, $\varphi' = \omega'$, $\varphi'' = \omega''$.

Quum igitur anguli BCD, CBA sint omnino inter se aequales, vis binarum rectangularum media tam quantitatis quam directionis habito respectu aequet diagonalem necesse est.

§. 25.

Aequalitas binorum angulorum, ω, φ, vel ω', φ', vel $\omega + \omega'$, $\varphi + \varphi'$, hoc quoque modo probari potest.

Vires tres una in punctum C (fig. 12.) agentes sint inter se in aequilibrio. Productis AC, CB ita ut, $C\alpha = CA$, et $C\varepsilon = CB$, potentiisque CD in Cd, $C\delta$, et CB in Cb, $C\beta$ aequivalentes resolutis

$$BC\alpha = \omega$$
$$DC\alpha = \omega'$$
$$DC\varepsilon = \omega''$$

ideoque $\omega + \omega' + \omega'' = 180°$ esse ponatur. Ceterum iisdem denotationibus retentis, erunt aequationes

$$C\beta = CB \cos\varphi,\quad C\delta = CD \cos\varphi'$$
$$Cb = CB \sin\varphi,\quad Cd = CD \sin\varphi'$$

Itaque, quoniam est $Cb = Cd$ et $C\alpha = C\delta + C\beta$

$$CB \sin\varphi' = CD \sin\varphi'$$
$$CA = CB \cos\varphi + CD \cos\varphi'$$ habere debemus; unde facile deducitur

$$\cos\varphi = \frac{(CA)^2 + (CB)^2 - (CD)^2}{2AC.\ BC}$$

$$\cos\varphi' = \frac{(CA)^2 + (CD)^2 - (CB)^2}{2AC.\ CD}$$

$$\cos\varphi'' = \frac{(CB)^2 + (CD)^2 - (CA)^2}{2BC.\ DC}$$

Ex eo autem tres angulos φ, φ', φ'' tribus trianguli cujusdam angulis, cujus latera sint AC, BC, DC, aequales, ideoque $\varphi + \varphi' + \varphi'' = 180°$ esse patet.

Etsi igitur $\varphi + \varphi' + \varphi'' = n(\omega + \omega' + \omega'')$ ponatur, ex iis tamen, quae modo demonstravimus, n. 180° = 180° ideoque n = 1 esse jure colligitur. Itaque et ω, ω', ω'' trianguli angulos aequant; ergo quaevis potentia, cum duabus aliis in aequilibrio versans, omnino diagonalem exaequat.

§. 26.

Quae pro viribus rectangulis demonstrata sunt, facile, uti supra vidimus, aliis quibuspiam viribus accommodari possunt.

Cap. III.

Argumentum ab Eytelwino allatum *).

§. 27.

Potentia quadam duabus inter se rectangulis P, Q aequipollente, aequationem hanc $R^2 = P^2 + Q^2$ nobis esse necesse est.

In demonstrando hoc theoremate noster Bernoullium omnino sequutus est v. Supr. §. 12.

§. 28.

Theor. Quodsi angulo directori ω angulus hypothenusalis φ, respondeat, ejusmodi angulo 2ω angulum hyp. quoque 2φ respondere necesse est.

---

*) Eytelwein's Grundlehren der Statik und Mechanik fester Körper, Tom. I. ab init. Gilbert's Annalen der Physik, XVIII. Th. p. 181 sqq. — Quod argumentum ab iis, quae jam exposuimus, eo quidem discrepat, quod propositionem, quam auctores illi in primis theorematibus evincere conati sunt, tanquam axioma pronuntiaverit. Nihilominus tamen hanc nostri demonstrationem jure ad hanc classem referri puto.

Demonstr. Potentiam P (fig. 13.) vim mediam, eamque in duas vires rectangulas p, q, secundum directiones GF, GM agentes, ita, ut sit $DGM = \omega$, ideoque $CGM = 2\omega$, resolutam concipiamus. Simili modo Q in duas p′, q′ vires resolvatur.

His ita positis, sponte hae prodeunt aequationes

$$p = \frac{P^2}{R},\ q = \frac{P.Q}{R},\ p' = \frac{PQ}{R},\ q' = \frac{Q^2}{R}.$$

Duarum autem virium P, Q, loco potentiis quatuor p, q, p′, q′ substitutis, dum $p - q' = P'$ et $q + p' = Q'$ posuerimus, has habebimus aequationes $P' = R(\cos\varphi^2 - \sin\varphi^2) = R\cos. 2\varphi$, $Q' = 2R\cos\varphi.\sin\varphi = R.\sin 2\varphi$.

§. 29.

Theor. Quodsi ea, quae modo pronunciavimus, pro angulis ω, φ atque $n\omega$, $n\varphi$ locum habent, pro angulis quoque $(n+1)\,\omega$, $(n+1)\,\varphi$ eadem valere necesse est.

Demonstr. Vires laterales, quarum anguli ω, φ, esse P, Q, potentias autem eas, quibus anguli $n\omega$, $n\varphi$, P′, Q′ esse ponamus. Eodem, quo antea, modo potentia P′ in duas vires p, q rectangulas, quarum altera v. c. p cum ipsa potentia P angulum ω, ideoque cum potentia R angulum $(n+1)\,\omega$ constituit, itemque Q′ in duas ejusmodi potentias p′, q′ resolvatur; hinc, dum $p - q' = P''$, et $q + p' = Q''$ ponamus, has nanciscimur aequationes:

$$P'' = \frac{PP' - QQ'}{R},\quad Q'' = \frac{QP' + PQ'}{R}.$$

Est autem $\dfrac{PP' - QQ'}{R} = R\,(\cos\varphi.\cos n\varphi - \sin\varphi.\sin n\varphi)$

$$= R\cos.(n+1)\,\varphi$$

$$QP' + PQ' = R\,[\sin.\varphi.\cos.n\varphi + \sin.n\varphi.\cos\varphi]$$
$$= R\sin.(n+1)\,\varphi.$$

Coroll. Quum autem, uti cognovimus, ratio, in qua angulos ω, φ, $n\omega$, $n\varphi$ constitutos esse sumsimus, revera, dum $n = 2$ ponatur, locum habeat, eandem pro quibuscumque valoribus, litterae n attributis, locum habere rite colligitur.

§. 30.

Quodsi igitur binae vires, quarum anguli directores atque hypotheunsales ω, et φ potentiae R aequipollent, binae aliae vires, quibus eadem potentia R aequivalet, dum anguli dir. et hyp. sint $n\omega$, et $n\varphi$, inter se aequilibrari debent. Posito igitur esse $n\omega = \omega'$ et $n\varphi = \varphi'$, habebimus $\frac{\omega}{\varphi} = \frac{\omega'}{\varphi'}$.

Quae quidem aequatio cum rata sit; quicunque valores quantitati φ tribuantur, ratio, quam φ et ω subeunt, nobis est nota, simulac ratio, quae inter φ' et ω' intercedit, pro quopiam, quantitati φ' assignato, valore enotescit. Quisque autem, dum $\omega' = 45°$, etiam $\varphi' = 45°$ intelligit; itaque est $\frac{\omega'}{\varphi'} = 1$, hinc etiam $\frac{\omega}{\varphi} = 1$, h. e. $\omega = \varphi$.

Angulus igitur director angulo hyp. aequalis sit omnino necesse est. Ex his vero vim duarum rectangularum mediam, si tam ejus quantitatem quam directionem respicias, omnino diagonalem aequare, jure meritoque concludimus.

§. 31.

Quomodo, quae pro viribus rectangulis sunt demonstrata, ad quaspiam alias AD, AE (fig. 14.) extendantur, nunc videamus.

Constructo parallelogrammo ADFE, CB, EG, DH perpendiculares ad diagonalem, atque EB, DC eidem diagonali parallelae ducantur. Nunc AD in duas AC, AH et AE in alias AB, AG resolutas esse ponamus. Quum autem vires AC, AB, quae inter se aequales ac plane repugnantes sint, plane sese destruant AD, AE uni potentiae AG + AH, h. e. AF aequipollent.

§. 32.

E p i c r i s i s.

Unusquisque hanc, quam modo exposuimus, demonstrationem, generatim spectatam, proxime ad precedentem (§. 20

sqq.) accedere cernit. Itaque de utriusque ambitu, tenore atque rigore una tantummodo disceptatione opus esse arbitratus sum.

Utriusque demonstrationis auctores in exploranda resultantis quantitate Bernoullianam methodum jure sequuntur. Eytelwinus nimirum ex dissertis suis verbis hanc methodum a Bernoullio sibi sumsit. Lambertus vero ipse illam invenisse putandus est, cum, se non, si Bernoullianam demonstrationem, etsi prolixam, satis tamen rigidam, prius cognoverit, novam meditatum fuisse dixerit. In determinanda autem resultantis directione, ambo viam, a Bernoulliana plane diversam, inierunt. Quonam successu ab iis hoc factum sit, nunc videamus. Cardo utriusque hujus demonstrationis in eo versatur, ut aequalitas inter angulum directorem et hypothenusalem demonstretur. Quod primum ad Lambertum attinet, quantum equidem video, neque unum, neque alterum ejus conamen, hanc aequalitatem probandi, ita comparatum est, ut nihil desiderandum relinquat. Argumentum enim, quo noster, lineam AMNL omnino non esse curvam probare studet, eo nititur, ut; quoniam AP $=$ TL, etc. ordinatas quoque PM et TN etc. aequales esse contendat. Quod quidem haud verum. Nam si AMNL, sicuti noster ipse primum sumit, revera esset curva, ab altera parte concavam, ab altera autem esse convexam necesse esset; itaque ab utraque parte abscissis aequalibus omnino aequales respondere ordinatas, minime oportet; imo conditionibus, quas noster ponit, fieri plane nequit. Eodem modo altera, quam auctor ad idem demonstrandum init, ratio, me quidem judice, lectori haud satis facit.

Quum enim nostro, nîl nisi resultantis quantitas sit nota, ipse non solum potentiam CB in duas rectangulas, Cd, Cδ, sed etiam plures alias, illi aequales v. c. CB′, CB″ etc. (vid. fig. 12.) resolvi posse, omnino concedere nobis debet. Eadem pro altera potentia CD valent. Tunc autem pluribus virium paribus, etsi diversas haberent directiones, eadem tamen esset resultans. Quod quidem locum habere nequit.

§. 33.

Eytelwinus aequalitatem inter angulum directorem atque hypothenusalem pro quibuscunque binis viribus universe a se demonstratam esse contendit. Quod quidem haud verum esse puto. Quum nimirum auctor dissertis verbis literâ n nummerum quendam integrum significari dixerit, atque omnino hac tantummodo conditione omnia, a nostro demonstrata, valeant, sine dubio, ut ea, quae de aequatione $\frac{\omega}{\varphi} = \frac{\omega'}{\varphi'}$ disseruit, tam universe spectata, vera rectaque essent, aut, quicunque valores quantitati ω tribuantur, semper omnino aequationem $\omega = \frac{45}{n}$ locum habere, aut eadem, quae, dum quantitati n integrorum numerorum valores vindicantur, valeant, etiam tunc, cum eâdem quantitate fractio, vel quantitas quaedam irrationalis denotetur, valere probandum ei fuisset.

Quod attinet ad ambitum duarum harum demonstrationum argumento Bernoulliano sine dubio sunt praeferendae. Nihilo minus tamen et ipsae nimia longitudine premuntur. Eytelwinus ipse argumentum Lamberti multo prolixius esse dicit, quam ut in librum elementorum staticae recipi posset. Pro mea autem sententia ipsius demonstratio illam brevitate parum praecellit. Ceterum methodus, generatim spectata, quam hi duo auctores usurparunt, sine dubio planior atque expeditior, quam Bernoulliana, judicanda est.

Cap. IV.

Argumentum a Scarella adlatum *).

§. 34.

In parte demonstrationis priori auctor, etsi pauca quaedam modo mutaverit, modo addiderit, in universum tamen metho-

*) J. B. Scarellae physica generalis methodo mathem. tractata. Tom. II. Brixiae 1756. p. 13 sqq.

dum Bernoullianam sequitur. Quare ea, quae ad determinandam resultantis quantitatem protulit, jure omitti hic possunt.

§. 35.

At directionis quoque respectu duarum virium mediam per diagonalem exhiberi, hac fere ratione probare noster tentavit.

Quodsi duarum virium rectangularum, sed inaequalium DA, DC (fig. 15.), ita quidem, ut DA > DC, resultanti non eadem, quae et diagonali DB rectanguli CA, esset directio, ab alterutra hujus diagonalis parte sitam esse illam, h. e. aut secundum Dc, aut secundum Db agere necesse esset. Quum prius autem illud sumamus, hoc iis, quae antea demonstrata sunt, omnino repugnat. Quum enim, viribus tanquam aequalibus assumtis, harum resultantis directionem quoque cum diagonali coincidere, ideoque corpus nostrum, duabus viribus una agentibus, inde a puncto D versus rectam AB aeque, ac si potentia DA sola egisset, auferri videremus; quum ergo hoc respectu potentia DC, quamvis ex ejus actione corpus secundum directionem, a DA diversam, moveri nititur, alterius DA actionem haud imminuere dici possit, hanc actionis imminutionem multo minus tunc, quum sit DC < DA, locum habere necesse est. Itaque corpus et nunc non minus, quam spatio DA, inde a D versus AB amoveri oportet. Sed hoc ipsum non fieret, si corporis directio esset Ac. Sed non magis corpus, hoc modo sollicitatum, secundum directionem Db moveri potest. Quum enim tunc corpus majori, quam DA, spatio, versus AB moveretur, ideoque majori, quam si potentia DA sola egisset, tanquam caussa hujus rei potentia DC spectari deberet. Quod quidem omnino absurdum. Itaque duarum inaequalium DA, DC, resultantis directio a neutra diagonalis DB parte sita esse potest, ergo cum hac ipsa coincidere debet.

§. 36.

E p i c r i s i s.

Quamquam, quibus noster directionem resultantis determinare studuit, praeferenda omnino sunt iis, quae multi alii, ut eundem scopum adtingerent, tentarunt, et quamquam multis fortasse lectoribus, haec tanquam facilia atque expedita sese commendent, non deerunt tamen, qui totam hanc demonstrandi rationem non esse geometricam, et omnia, solâ ejus ope probata, magis verisimilitudine, quam veritate geometrica gaudere contendant.

Cap. V.

Demonstratio a Venino tradita *).

§. 37.

Quum duae vires inaequales, eaeque rectangulae DA, DC (fig. 15.), una punctum quoddam sollicitent, eandem exserunt actionem, quam quatuor aliae vires, quarum duae DT, DO latera sunt quadrati, circa DA circumscripti, duae autem DH, De latera ejusmodi parallelogrami, cujus diagonalis DC, producunt.

Demonstr. Posito enim esse $DE = DT + De$
et $DF = DO - DH$

hinc nonciscimur $DE = \dfrac{AD + DC}{\sqrt{2}}$

$$DF = \frac{AD - DC}{\sqrt{2}}$$

Ducta igitur BF ipsi DE parallela, rectangulo DE. DF eandem, quae rectangulo AD. DC, esse diagonalem, facile probari potest. Quum enim inde a puncto B ducatur Bf perpendicularis ad DE, quoniam DCM triangulum tam aequicrurum quam rectangulum, ideoque etiam BfM ejusmodi est triangulum, puncta E, f coincidere necesse est; ita habebimus

$$Df = DM + Mf = DC.\sqrt{2} + \frac{AD - DC}{\sqrt{2}} = \frac{AD + DC}{\sqrt{2}}$$

*) Venini nouvelle demonstration du principe de la composition des forces. v. Journal des Sçav. année 1764.

ergo Df = DE, et hinc duobus rectangulis eadem est diagonalis. Itaque vim duabus AD, DC aequipollentem, secundum eandem directionem, quae et potentiae duarum DF, DE mediae est, agere oportet. Qua quidem directione angulum ADC quodammodo secari, non minus, quam, eandem directionem tanto propius directionem ejus potentiae accedere, quae quanto magis alterius quantitatem excedat, evidens atque perspicuum est.

§. 38.

Ratio igitur sinuum angulorum, quibus vis media ad duas componentes inclinatur, tanquam functio rationis, in qua hae duae potentiae laterales positae sunt, spectanda est; sive illa sinuum ratio huic inversae virium rationi aequalis, sive major, sive minor eâ sit. Quum ipsam esse majorem ponamus, punctum D virium DA, DC actione secundum directionem quandam inter AD et DB sitam v. c. Db moveri debet; eadem caussa idem punctum, viribus DF, DE sollicitantibus, secundum directionem, angulum BDE quodammodo secantem, v. c. Dc ferri oportet. Itaque a duobus virium paribus, eandem actionem exserentibus, punctum quoddam inde ab eodem loco secundum diversas directiones moveretur. Quod quidem fieri nequit. Simili plane modo rationem sinuum, quam rationem virium componentium inversam, non esse minorem probari potest; itaque altera haec ratio alteri omnino aequalis sit necesse est; h. e. vis, duabus DA, DC aequipollens, non solum quantitatis, sed etiam directionis respectu habito diagonalem aequare debet.

§. 39.

E p i c r i s i s.

Autor non sine caussa de directione tantummodo resultantis duarum virium inaequalium ac rectangularum determinanda agit. Hac enim semel explorata cetera omnia sponte inde fluunt. Sed et noster, uti plures alii, hanc directionem non debito rigore determinasse mihi videtur. Jam Alembertus *)

---

*) Opuscules mathematiques. Tom. I, p. 170.

quaedam contra hanc nostri demonstrationem monuit. Dixit nimirum ex eo, quod semel haec ratio virium inversa major, aut minor, quam ratio sinuum sit, colligi plane non posse, idem pro omnibus omnino binis viribus locum esse habiturum. Equidem quoque, ut ingenue fatear, ab initio, sed aliis praecipue caussis, huic nostri demonstrationi rigorem geometricum vindicari non posse putavi. Sed quantum equidem nunc video, nullius momenti sunt ea, quae auctori objici possent. Itaque hoc ejus argumentum plurimis lectoribus satisfacere persuasum mihi habeo.

Cap. VI.

Argumentum ab Alemberto traditum *).

§. 40.

Quodsi tres vires aequales una in punctum ita agunt, ut quilibet angulorum, quos binae comprehendunt sit = 120°, punctum vel corpus illud in aequilibrio versatur.

Demonstratio est eadem, quam supr. (§. 20.) legimus.

§. 41.

Quodsi duae vires aequaeles AB, AC (fig. 16.), aequipollent uni potentiae AD, eadem pro potentiis aequalibus Ab, Ac, angulos BAD, CAD bifariam secantibus, valere necesse est.

Demonstr. Nam si res non sic se haberet, Ab, Ac potentiae AO > AD aequivalentes ponantur; rhombus ALbl construatur; fiatque AB : Ab :: Ab : AO; ergo AL > AI esse debet; sit Ao = AI; itaque Ab his duabus Ao, AI aequipolleat necesse est. Item Ac aequivaleat duabus Ao, AK; itaque Ab, Ac viribus his AI, AK, 2Ao aequipollent. Quoniam vero AI, AK po-

---

*) D'Alembert opuscules mathematiques, Tom. I. p. 169 sqq.

tentiae 2Ai aequivalent, Ab, Ac uni potentiae $2Ai + 2Ao$ aequivalere oportet. Praeterea autem, cum sit $Ib > AI$, etiam $IG > Ai$ esse debet; atqui etiam $Al > Ao$, ergo $2Ai + 2Ao < 2Al + 2lG$, h. e. $< AD$ omnino esse oportet. Hoc igitur modo vires Ab, Ac viribus inaequalibus simul aequivalerent; quod omnino absurdum; simili ratione potentiam duarum Ab, Ac mediam non minorem quam AD esse probari potest; ergo potentiae AD omnino est aequalis.

Coroll. 1. Itaque vis duarum virium Ab, Ac, per diagonalem rhombi exhibetur.

Coroll. 2. Ea quae de viribus Ab, Ac demonstravimus, de omnibus binis potentiis, quae unum horumce angulorum: $\frac{BAC}{4}$, $\frac{BAC}{8}$ vel universe $\frac{BAC}{2^n}$ comprehendunt, valere facile intelligitur.

Coroll. 3. Quibuslibet binis potentiis aequalibus angulum quendam hujus formae $\frac{120^\circ}{2^n}$ inter se comprehendentibus, vis una aequipollet, quae diagonalem plane exaequat.

§. 42.

Theor. Quodsi virium duarum AB, AC (fig. 17.) resultans diagonali AD aequalis est, deinde si vis duarum aliarum aequalium Ab, Ac media per diagonalem 2Ag exhibetur, denique si $BAb' = BAb$, et AB duabus Ab, Ab′ aequipollet, eademque de altera AC valent, vim, duarum Ab′, Ac′ mediam per diagonalem 2Ag′ exhiberi necesse est.

Demonstr. Quum enim ipsa nostra constructione vires tam AB, AC potentiis Ab, Ab′, Ac, Ac′ quam Ab, Ac uni potentiae 2Ag aequipollentes statuerimus, vires Ab′, Ac′ potentiae 2gG, vel, cum sit $Ag' = gG$, potentiae 2Ag′ aequipollere debent.

Coroll. 1. Itaque, re generatim spectata, si duae vires aequales quempiam angulum, A, comprehendentes diagonali aequivalent, eademque de duobus aliis virium paribus, quorum alterum b, alterum A—b angulos constituit, valent, tunc quoque, cum duae ejusmodi vires aequales angulo $2A - b$ concurrant, quae pronuntiavimus, locum habere necesse est.

Coroll. 2. Quum igitur, uti supra vidimus, resultans binarum virium, quarum angulus $\frac{120^\circ}{2^n}$, per diagonalem exhibeatur, eadem pro potentia earum, quae angulum $\frac{m.\ 120^\circ}{2^n}$ comprehendunt, media valere facile intelligitur.

§. 43.

Theor. Inter omnes binas potentias eae, quae minimum constituunt angulum, maximae potentiae aequipollent.

Demonst. Fiat $ad' = ad$ (fig. 18.) et $ae' = ae$. Si ad', ac una agentes ponantur, vis earum media angulum Nad' quodammodo secare debet; item vim duabus ab, ae' aequipollentem angulum Mae' in quaspiam duas partes dividere necesse est. Quae vires duae cum sint inter se aequales, secundum directionem aR agere omnino debent. Itaque vis media X', cui eadem directio est, $> x$, ideoque etiam $X > x$ esse debet.

§. 44.

Theor. Dato quopiam angulo BAC (fig. 19.), alius omnino hujus formae $\frac{q.\ 120^\circ}{2^n}$ angulus inveniri potest, ita ut uterque aut plane sit inter se aequalis, aut alter alterum minus, quam data, quantumvis parva, quantitate k excedat.

Demonstr. Primum enim fractionem $\frac{120^\circ}{2^n}$, ejus denominatore magis magisque aucto, a quoque data valore superari posse intelligitur; deinde facillime quantitatis q is valor reperitur, quo assumto $(q+1)\frac{120^\circ}{2^n} > BAC$, sed $q.\frac{120^\circ}{2^n} < BAC$ redditur; itaque habebimus $(q+1)\frac{120^\circ}{2^n} - q\frac{120^\circ}{2^n} > BAC - q.\frac{120^\circ}{2^n}$

vel $\frac{120^\circ}{2^n} > BAC - q.\frac{120^\circ}{2^n}$, tanto magis igitur $k > BAC - q.\frac{120^\circ}{2^n}$. Simili ratione habemus

$$(q+1)\frac{120^\circ}{2^n} - BAC < (q+1)\frac{120}{2^n} - q\frac{120}{2^n}$$
$$< \frac{120^\circ}{2^n}.$$

ergo $(q+1)\frac{120}{2^n} - BAC < k$.

Coroll. Neutiquam igitur angulus GAD, qui < BAC, itemque alius, FAE qui > BAC, ita ut uterque ab angulo BAC, minus quam data, quantumvis exigua, hujus formae $q.\frac{120^\circ}{2^n}$ quantitate superetur, inveniri nequit.

Coroll. 2. Quodsi ergo AH est rhombi ABHC diagonalis, si AF = AG = AB = AD = AE = AC atque, anguli GAD, FAE ejus sunt indolis, ut universe per quantitatem $\frac{q.\ 120}{2^n}$ exhibeantur, diagonales rhomborum sub AG, AD et AF, AE constructorum, tantum, quantum libuerit, ad diagonalem accedere sumi potest.

§. 45.

Duabus potentiis aequalibus, quopiam angulo punctum quoddam una sollicitantibus, omnino diagonalis aequipollet.

Demonstr. Si enim vim earum mediam AR > AH diagonalem poneremus, atque duarum virium AG, AD, angulo quodam $\frac{p.\ 120^\circ}{2^n} <$ BAC concurrentium, vim mediam diagonalem minus quam lineâ HR superare conciperemus, duarum AG, AD resultans major quam virium AB, AC potentia media esset. Quod quidem praecedentibus plane repugnat. Simili ratione AR < AH esse nequire probatur; ergo omnino AR = AH.

§. 46.

Quae huc usque pro viribus iis, quae sunt inter se aequales, probavimus, facile ad potentias quodammodo inaequales transferri possunt.

Quum enim vires AG, AD, AH, AD (fig. 20.) esse ponamus, quarum binae angulo recto punctum A sollicitant, et quae ita inter se comparatae sunt, ut AH = AG sit, vim omnium mediam 2AD esse, satis apparet. Secundum ea, quae Bernoullius demonstravit, vires binarum ejusmodi mediae diagonales AB, AC exaequant; sint autem earum directiones AE, AF. Tunc omnino AE, AF eundem, quem et AB, AC, effectum producerent; quod quidem fieri nequit, nisi puncta D et K coincidant; ita autem AE, AB, et AF, AC coincidere necesse est.

Quomodo omnia theoremata, pro viribus rectangulis demonstrata, quibuslibet aliis potentiis accommodari possint supra vidimus.

§. 47.

E p i c r i s i s.

Quodsi auctor ipse hanc suam demonstrationem facilem atque simplicem praedicat, pro mea sententia, haec laus hactenus tantum ei tribuenda est, quatenus non nisi aliquot planimetriae theoremata in subsidium vocat. Quum enim in ejusmodi simplicitate recte dijudicanda ambitus quoque argumenti rationem habeas, quae, me judice, omnino est habenda, ab hac parte simplicitas atque facilitas demonstrationis nostrae laudari nequit; nullâ aliâ certe earum, quae saepius nimiae prolixitatis accusatae sunt, ipsa praecellit. — Quantum equidem video rigori geometrico haud alienum fuisset, si noster in §. 41, figuram ALbl esse rhombum, demonstravisset. Quum enim lineae bL, ipsi AG parallelae, eo, quod punctum b transire sumebatur, plane esset directio determinata, insuper AL = bL esse, probandum fuit.

Quae auctor eadem theorematis hujus parte colligit, scilicet rectam AG, cum lb = AL > AB sit, majorem quam Ai esse, ut essent vera, lineam Ii = bG, aut Ii > bG esse noster evincere debuisset. Quod vero, pro mea sententia non solum probari nequit, sed etiam saepius vere non locum habet. Praecipue autem ea nostro, quae in corollario primo, theoremati (§. 42.) adjecto, pronuntiavit, adsentire non possum. Nervus enim theorematis illius probandi sine dubio in eo consistit, ut Ab, Ab′ latera sint rhombi, cujus diagonalis AB. Itaque non nisi tunc, cum vires in hac ratione inter se sint positae, minime vero cum, uti noster dicit, vires quaepiam sint, ea, quae autor hoc corollario contendit, valent. Hoc autem corollario primo, quod dolendum! corollarium secundum, imo tota demonstrationis pars posterior tanquam fundamento superstructa est. Quo quidem labefiente tota demonstratio corruere debet.

Classis secunda.

Demonstrationes axiomatibus 4. 5. 6. 8 *supersructae.*

Caput unicum.

Argumentum Salimbenianum *).

§. 48.

Quamquam omnia, quae noster in his staticae elementis protulit arctissime inter se cohaerent, haec tamen hic exponi plane nequeunt. Itaque tantummodo ea, quae maxime ad compositionem virium pertinent, referam.

Postquam nimirum auctor rigore vere Euclideo plura staticae theoremata, praecipue autem hoc: „quum inde a puncto

---

*) Leonardo Salimbeni Saggio di un nuovo corso di elementi di statica v. Memorie di matematica è fisica della Società Ital. Tom. V. p. 426 sqq.

quodam D, in directione unius trium inter se aequilibrantium virium P, Q, R, v. c. R sumto (fig. 21.), ceteris viribus ducantur parallelae DB, DC; analogiam hanc R:Q:P::AD:AC:AB locum habere necesse est" nimium prolixa demonstratione ostenderit, hoc fere modo pergit.

§. 49.

Quodsi trium virium, in punctum quoddam A (fig. 22.) concurrentium, atque in eodem plano sitarum, quaevis ad eam spatii partem, quae illi, ad quam ceterae punctum sollicitant, opposita est, corpus vel punctum urget, et si, dum inde a puncto, in directione unius illarum sito, ceteris ducantur parallelae, sit, P:Q:T::AF:AC:AG, hae vires in aequibibrio sint necesse est.

Demonstr. Quum enim vires P, Q una punctum A permeent, quaepiam vis, quae, idem punctum transiens, cum his aequilibratur, esse debet. Quae quidem potentia sit T. Sed non secundum directionem AH, sed secundum aliam quandam v. c. AE agere eam ponamus. Productâ HA ad G, ductaque GF ipsi AC parallela, ex praecedentibus est. P : Q : T : : AF : AC : AG Sed per hyp. est P : Q : : AB : AC, ergo AB = AF; quae quidem aequatio locum habere nequit, nisi AH et AE coincidant.

Coroll. Eadem, quae pro potentia, cum illis aequilibrante demonstravimus, pro ea quoque, quae iisdem illis aequipollet, valent.

§. 50.

Quum tres vires AP, AQ, AR (fig. 23.), in punctum A concurrentes, inter se aequilibrentur, hancce analogiam AR : AQ : AQ : : sin. RAQ : sin QAP locum habere necesse est.

Demonstr. Ductis enim GI et GH ipsis AP, AQ parallelis, praecedentibus erit: AP : AQ : AR : : AH : AI : AG: est autem AI AH : : AG : : sin. c : sin b : sin a ergo etiam AH · AI : AG : : sin QAR : sin PAR : sin. PAR : sin PAQ.

Coroll. Quodsi igitur potentia AS secundum directionem AK aequipollet, hanc esse anafogiam AP : AQ : AS : : sin. QAK : sin PAK : sin PAQ jure hinc concluditur.

§. 51.

Quum ad directiones trium virium AP, AQ, AR (fig. 24.), inter se aequilibrantium, ducantur perpendiculares, quae satis productae triangulum EGF constituunt, hanc analogiam EG : GF : EF : : AP : AQ : AR esse contenditur.

Demonstr. Ductis inde a puncto D, libere sumto DC, DB ipsis AP, AQ parallelis AP : AQ : AR : : AB : AC : AD esse debet. Quoniam vero BAD = GEF, atque DAC = EFG, etiam EGF = ACD esse oportet, itaque AP : AQ : AR : : sin EFG : sin GEF : sin EGF ideoque AP : AQ : AR : : GE : GF : EF esse oportet.

§. 52.

Quum, datis trium, quae inter se aequilibrari debent, virium directionibus BK, CH (fig. 25.), DE, ipsarum autem virium una tantummodo nobis sit nota, ceterae duae ita sumendae sunt, ut, si IG, IH lineis DE, CH, parallelae ducantur sit analogia haec: AI : AG : AH : : AR : AP : AQ.

Demonstratio nostri theorematis sponte ex iis, quae supr. §. 49. probavimus, fluit.

§. 53.

Probl. Duabus AP, AQ (fig. 26.), quae punctum A transeunt, viribus datis, reperiatur vis ea AR, quae cum illis aequilibretur.

Solut. Constructo parallelogrammo ABDC, AR in directione RD ita sumatur, ut sit AD : AB : AC : : AR : AQ : AP. Eadem vis AR quemadmodum cum potentiis AP, AQ aequilibratur, ita potentia AD, ipsi aequalis sed repugnans, iisdem illis aequipolleat necesse est. Quam quidem solutionem esse ratam ex precedentibus intelligitur.

§. 54.

Probl. Datis tribus potentiis AP, AQ, AR (fig. 27.), quarum binarum summa major, quam tertia est, inveniantur directiones, secundum quas hae vires agentes, inter se aequilibrentur.

Solut. Constructo parallelogrammo AHGI, ita ut sit AR: AQ : AP :: AG : AH : AI; potentiae AR secundum AD, AQ secundum AH et AP secundum AI agant.

His ita constitutis, vires illas aequilibrari ex prioribus patet.

§. 55.

Epicrisis.

Noster in his staticae elementis summa opera id agit, ut methodum vere Euclideam sequatur, omnesque suas propositiones satis rigide demonstret. Ipsis igitur praemittenda in difinitiones, postulata et axiomata dividit. Ceterum puto hypothesin, quam attulit, eam: „vires, una in corpus quoddam adplicatae, non inter se aequilibrari possunt, si omnes ad eandem spatii partem corpus vel punctum sollicitant" non majore frui evidentia, quam plures propositiones, quas noster demonstrandas sibi sumsit. Laudanda omnino est nostri diligentia, cura, ac perspicuitas, quam in his suis demonstrationibus, quae non nisi aliquot planis geometriae theorematibus superstructae sunt, consectatur. Eorundum autem elementorum ambitum multo esse majorem, quam debeat, quisque satis intelligit. Tanta enim est prolixitas, ut non sine labore satis magno ad finem perveniri possit. Quod attinet ad rigorem, quantum equidem video, nihil contra has demonstrationes moneri potest.

Classis tertia.

Demonstrationes axiomatibus 1. 2. 3. 8 nitentes.

Caput unicum.

Argumentum a viro doctissimo Duchayla adlatum *).

§. 56.

Theor. Quodsi vis duarum media non solum cum hae vires per p et m, sed etiam cum per p et n exhibeantur, diagonalem parallelogrammi, sub his constructi, exaequat, idem, dum vires laterales sint p et m+n, easdemque obtineant directiones, locum habere necesse est.

Demonstr. Si (fig. 28.) AB = p, AE = m, et EC = n esse ponimus, vires p, et m+n per rectas AB, AC exhibentur. Incolumi autem potentiae m+n actione, fieri potest, ut potentiam n vel EC puncto E adplicatam esse concipiamus. Quum autem potentiam, duabus m, p aequivalentem, directionis suae respectu, cum diagonali AF coincidere sumserimus, hanc ipsam vim, a puncto A ad F transpositam, secundum directionem FK agere concipi potest. Resolvatur nunc, quod omnino concedendum est, potentia AF in duas FH, FG, ita, ut sit FH = AB et FG = AE; alteram earum FH puncto E adplicatam esse ponamus. Sed cum duabus p, n aequivalentem cum diagonali ED coincidere sumatur, vires ED, FG inde a punctis E, F ad punctum D transferri possunt; duabus igitur ED, FG, vel tribus EF, EC, FG aequipollentem punctum D transire necesse est. Hae autem vires omnino potentias AB, AC, vel p, m+n exhibent; itaque his quoque aequivalens idem punctum D permeare

---

*) Legitur haec demonstratio in hisce libris: Poisson traité de Mecanique, Par. 1811. Tom. I. p. 475 sq. — Francœur elemens de Statique 1812. ab init — Correspondance de l'ecole polytechnique.

debet; quum illa autem punctum quoque A transeat, cum diagonali coincidere omnino debet.

§. 57.

Ex his vero, quae modo probavimus, et ex axiomate tertio, potentiam duabus viribus, ita inter se comparatis, ut sit P:Q :: m:n (m et n nummeros quospiam integros denotent) aequivalentem, diagonalem omnino aequare facile colligi potest. Ponamus enim esse p = n = 1, ac deinceps m = 1, m = 2 etc. Primum igitur demonstrata quum pro viribus aequalibus 1 et 1 valeant, eadem pro viribus quoque 2 et 1, 3 et 1, et universe N et 1 locum habere oportet. Itaque si nunc p = N esse ponitur, quoniam, quae contendimus, pro potentiis, N et 1 valeant, etiam pro N et 2, N et 3, et generatim pro N et M valere necesse est.

§. 58.

Quae pro viribus commensurabilibus sic demonstrata sunt, facile et incommensurabilibus accommodari possunt.

Potentiam enim, duabus ejus modi viribus aequivalentem, cum diagonali non coincidere ponamus; sit igitur ejus directio v. c. AD (fig. 29.). Lineâ D′B′ ipsi DB parallela ducta, AC in partes aequales, quarum quaevis < BB′ dividatur, ita, ut si in recta AB inde a puncto A ejusmodi partes sumantur, unum certe punctorum, partes illas determinantium, intra B et B′ situm sit. Quum vero potentiae, duabus commensurabilibus AE, AC aequivalenti, directio secundum AF omnino sit vindicanda, et quo magis altera virium lateralium decrescat, dum eadum maneat altera, eo propius earum resultantem directionis respectu majorem accedere necesse sit, potentiam, duabus AB, AC aequivalentem, secundum directionem AD′ agere omnino non posse intelligitur. Eadem vero ratione non aliam quandam ei esse directionem probatur; itaque ipsam cum diagonali coincidere oportet.

§. 59.

At quantitatis quoque respectu habito vim duarum mediam diagonalem aequare, demonstrari potest.

Sint enim (fig. 30.) AB, AC duae vires componentes, fiatque parallelogrammum $ABDC$. Quum ex praecedentibus resultantem cum diagonali coincidere pateat, vis quaedam AR, secundum directionem DAD' agens, cum duabus AB, AC aequilibrari debet; immo quaevis trium virium, circa punctum A in aequilibrio versantium, aequalis sed repugnans potentiae, ceteris duabus aequipollenti, esse debet. Itaque si $AB' = AB$, et BAB linea recta, AB' duarum AC, AR media est habenda. Quum autem sit $AB' ⋕ DC$, etiam AD, $B'C$ ideoque $B'C$, AR est. Dum ducatur $B'D'$ ipsi AC parallela, ⋕ $ACB'D'$ parallelogrammum hoc modo prodit. Quum autem vim, duabus AR, AC aequipollentem, secundum directionem AB' agere necesse sit, $AD = AR$ omnino esse debet. Itaque, cum sit $AD' = AR = B'C = AD$, vis duarum media omnino diagonalem exaequat.

§. 60.

E p i c r i s i s.

Quae quidem nostri demonstratio tam facilis, tam brevis, tamque expedita est, ut ab hac parte permultis aliis antecellat. Inprimis auctor in determinanda resultantis directione methodum multo magis brevem atque expeditam, quam omnes fere alii, usurpavit. Tanto magis eo doleo, quod in ipsa hac demonstrationis parte priore non omnia, ut mihi quidem videtur, rigore geometrico satis munita sunt. Equidem enim nostrum axioma 7. nimium extendisse, eoque abusum fuisse puto. Nam axiomate illo nihil aliud exprimitur nisi id: „actio cujusdam potentiae eadem omnino manet, quocunque directionis suae loco vel puncto ipsam adplicatam esse concipiamus."

Quodsi nimirum ex. gr. pondus quoddam filo vel re quadam alia corpori alicui nexum est, idque vi quadam ad motum sollicitat, actionem hujus potentiae, cujuscunque longitudinis filum illud sit, semper sibi constare contenditur. Omnino igitur nostro, potentiam, duabus AB, AE aequivalentem, quopiam directionis suae AFK loco adplicatam poni, et ubique ejusmodi loci in duas, ex quibus composita est, vires iterum resolvi, minime vero potentiam HF a puncto F ad punctum E transferri posse concedendum est. Hac enim transpositione potentia HF in punctum plane aliud quam antea, agere incipit; quod quidem axiomati 7. omnino repuguat. Nostri igitur argumentum omnibus nummeris esse absolutum dici non potest.

Classis quarta.

Demonstrationes axiomatibus 1, 2 et 3 superstructae.

Cap. I.

*Argumentum a cl. Araldo traditum *).*

§. 61.

Duarum virium aequalium rectangularumque media quantitatis quoque respectu per diagonalem exhibetur. Sit enim duarum AB, AC media major, quam diagonalis earum quadrati AD. Eandem rationem, dum et AB, AC in binas aequales atque rectangulas resolverentur, locum habere necesse esset; ergo AB, AC aequivalerent potentiis minoribus, quam latera ipsarum quadrati, v. c. AM′, AO′, AN′, AO′, vel potius 2AO′; quod quidem hypothesi nostrae, qua duarum AB, AC media major quam diagonalis sit, omnino repugnat. Eadem ratione quum resultantem non minorem, quam diagonalem esse demonstrari possit, utramque inter se aequalem esse oportet.

§. 62.

Quae pro potentiis aequalibus modo probavimus in vires quoque inaequales DA, DC facile extendi possunt. Angulo enim DAC (fig. 15.) lineâ DE bifariam secto, et non solum ad hanc

---

*) Araldi sul principio dell' equipollenza v. Memorie dell' instituto nazionale Italiano, Tom, I. P. 1. Bologna 1806. p. 415.

ipsam DE recta OH, sed etiam ad utramque lineis AO, CH et AT, Ce perpendicularibus ductis, potentia DA duarum DO, DT, altera autem DC virium DH, De resultans haberi potest; ducantur BF, Bf perpendiculares. Quum autem sit Df = DT + De et DF = DO — DH virium DF, Df media plane eadem, quae et duarum DA, DC esse debet. Itaque quum utrique rectangulo Ff, AC una eademque sit diagonalis, hoc tantummodo probandum est, hanc duarum potentiis DA, DC et DF, Df aequivalentium, aequalitatem nullo modo locum habere posse, nisi hae vires mediae per diagonalem exhibeantur.

§. 63.

Quodsi vero etiam illas cum diagonali non coincidere sumamus, ab eadem tamen parte diagonalis esse sitas necesse est. Sit earum directio inter lineas DB, Df.

Dum ergo duo virium paria DF, Df, et DA, DC primum singulatim, deinde una secundum directiones DD′, DC′ agere ponamus (fig. A), ex hypothesi nostra duarum DF, Df mediam inter DB, Df, virium autem DA, DC mediam inter DB′, DC′ sitam, angulosque, ab utraque parte cum diagonalibus DB, DB′ efformatos aequales esse oportet; vis igitur ea, quae duabus his aequipollet, secundum ipsam diagonalem directa est. Fiat autem DC = FC et DA = fD′; ex hac ipsa constructione DB, B′B″ duorum rectangulorum omnino aequalium sunt diagonales; ergo DB ≠ B′B″; ideoque rectangulo C′D′, et rhombo B′B eadem est diagonalis DB″; resultans igitur quatuor virium DF, Df, DA, DC secundum diagonalem ejus rectanguli, cujus alterum latus DA + Df, alterum vero DF + DC, directa est. Ex ipsa igitur nostra hypothesi, qua duarum DA, DC mediam non cum diagonali coincidere ponimus, duas tamen alias esse vires DD′, DC′, secundum easdem directiones agentes, quarum resultans secundum diagonalem directa sit, rite colligere possumus.

§. 64.

Quodpiam par virium DD′, DC′ (fig. A) nobis sit datum; diagonali illarum rectanguli rhombi infiniti, quorum unus DBB″B′, circumscripti concipiantur. Omnino autem potentias has

DD′, DC′ tanquam e binis viribus Df, DA, et DC, DF compositas spectare, imo potentiam DA cum altera DC, vimque Df cum vi DF conjugare licet. Ex hoc ipso autem necessario harum quatuor virium resultantem, ideoque etiam duarum DD′, DC′ mediam secundum diagonalem DB″ directam esse sequitur.

§. 65.

Quantitatis quoque respectu duarum ejusmodi mediam exaequare diagonalem simili plane, quo modo antea, ratione demonstratur. — Quomodo, quae pro viribus rectangulis probata sunt, facile quibuspiam aliis accomodentur, saepius jam vidimus.

E p i c r i s i s.

§. 66.

Quod quidem argumentum pro mea sententia multis, quae inter magnam illam ejusmodi demonstrationum turbam reperiuntur, praeferendum est. Primum enim quod attinet ad ejus ambitum atque tenorem, non nimia sane prolixitate premitur, et non nisi aliquot planimetriae theorematum auxilio utitur. Deinde si ad ejus rigorem respicias hoc quoque respectu, plurima, tanquam bene munita placent. Attamen, quantum equidem video, rigori geometrico haud alienum fuisset, si auctor nos docuisset, quomodo quaevis duarum potentiarum quarumpiam DD′, DC′ in binas alias vires divenda sit, ita ut non solum inter singulas has novas potentias, sed etiam inter omnes in universum ratio illa quaesita intercedat.

Classis quinta.

Demonstrationes principiis vel axiomatibus 1, 2, 3, 7 superstructae.

Cap. I.

*Demonstratio a Cl. Wachtero tradita *).*

§. 67.

Quemadmodum duarum potentiarum aequalium P', P'', quarum directiones o et x, media R' secundum directionem $\frac{1}{2}$ x, ita potentia R'', duabus, alteri P' aequalibus P''', P^{IV}, quarum directiones y et z, aequivalens, secundum directionem $y + \frac{1}{2} z$ agit. Loco igitur potentiarum, P', P'', P''', P^{IV} (dum $y = \frac{1}{2}[x - z]$) vis ipsis aequipollens $R' + R''$ substitui potest. Duarum ergo, viribus P', P''' et P'', P^{IV} aequivalentium R''', R^{IV}, quae inter se aequales, quarumque alteri directio $\frac{1}{4}(x - z)$, alteri vero, $\frac{1}{2}(x + z) + \frac{1}{4}(x - z)$, eadem, quae et quatuor virium P', P'', P''', P^{IV} est resultans $R' + R''$. Qua ex mutua virium harum ratione suppeditantur nobis aequationes, quae virium, R', R'', R''', quarum directiones notae, quantitati determinandae inservire possunt. Quodsi nimirum effectum duarum virium, quae, unitati aequales, angulo quodam α in punctum agunt, per $2\varphi(\alpha) = R$ exhibeamus, et brevitatis caussa $P' = P'' = P''' = P^{IV} = 1$ ponamus, has nanciscimur aequationes:

I. $2\varphi(x) = R'$; III. $2\varphi\frac{1}{2}(x - z) = R'''$

II. $2\varphi(z) = R''$; IV. $R'''.\ 2\varphi\frac{1}{2}(x + z) = R' + R''$.

Dum vero $x = 180° = \pi$, et $z = 0$ esse sumamus, inde $R' = 0$ et $R'' = 2$ prodire quisque intelligit. Quibus valoribus in aequationes nostras (III.) et (IV.) substitutis, hae aequationes emergunt:

$$2\varphi\left(\frac{\pi}{2}\right) = R''' = R_1, \text{ et } R'''.\ 2\varphi\left(\frac{\pi}{2}\right) = R_1.\ 2\varphi\left(\frac{\pi}{2}\right) = R_1.\ R_1 = 2.$$

---

*) Frid. Ludov. Wachter commentatio de elementis, quae ad corporum cœlestium revolutionem spectant etc. Gœttingae 1815. p. 55 sqq.

Accepto z $=$ o et $x = \frac{\pi}{2}$, habebimus, $R_2 . 2\varphi\left(\frac{\pi}{2^2}\right) = R_2 . R_2 = 2 + R1 = 2 + \sqrt{2}$, et sic ulterius progrediendo $2\varphi\left(\frac{\pi}{2^3}\right) \ldots . 2\varphi\left(\frac{\pi}{2^m}\right) = R^m$ eliciuntur. Posito esse $z = o$ et $x = \frac{\pi}{2^{m-1}}$, hinc obtinemus $R_m . 2\varphi\left(\frac{\pi}{2^m}\right) = R_m . R_m = 2 + R_{m-1}$. Ad inveniendam potentiam ${}^{2n+1}R_{m+1}$, duabus aliis, angulum $\frac{(2n+1)\pi}{2^{m+1}}$ constituentibus, aequivalentem, tribuamus quantitati z valorem $\frac{\pi}{2^m}$, alteri vero x hos deinceps valores: $\frac{\pi}{2^{m-1}}, \frac{2\pi}{2^{m-1}} \ldots \frac{n\pi}{2^{m-1}}$

Hoc modo suppeditantur nobis hae aequationes:

$$R^{m+1} . 2\varphi\left(\frac{3\pi}{2^{m+1}}\right) = R_{m+1} . {}^3R_{m+1} = R_{m-1} . R_m \text{ et perinde}$$

$$^{2n-}R_{m+1} . 2\varphi\left[\frac{(2n+1)\pi}{2^{m+1}}\right] = {}^{2n-1}R_{m+1} . {}^{2n+1}R_{m+1} = {}^nR_{m-1} + R_m \text{ (A).}$$

Quum autem litteris m, n omnes diversi valores inde a o usque ad ∞ tribui possint, angulum $\frac{\pi}{2^m}$, in infinitum eum bisecando, minorem quam quempiam angulum datum reddere possumus, quo deinceps continuo multiplicando, angulus $\frac{(2n+1)\pi}{2^{m+1}}$ ad quemlibet datum x quam proxime accedens haberi potest. Itaque quarumlibet duarum potentiarum aequalium, quemlibet angulum inter se constituentium, resultantis effectus in nostra aequatione (A) exhibetur.

Est autem 2 cos. x. cos z $=$ cos. $(x + z) +$ cos $(x - z)$ ergo, $x = \frac{(2n-1)\pi}{2^{m+1}}$ et $z = \frac{(2n+1)\pi}{2^{m+1}}$ esse posito, 2 cos. $\frac{(2n-1)\pi}{2^{m+1}}$.

$2\cos.\frac{(2n+1)\pi}{2^{m+1}} = 2\cos.\frac{n\pi}{2^{m+1}} + 2\cos.\frac{\pi}{2^m}$ (I.) Sed quum modo antea haberemus ${}^{2n-1}R_{m+1}\cdot{}^{2n+1}R_{m+1} = {}^{n}R_{m-1} + R_m$ (II.) hinc ${}^{2n+1}R_{m+1} = 2\cos.\frac{(2n+1)\pi}{2^{m+1}} = 2\cos. x$ (III.) esse jure meritoque colligimus. Resultans igitur duarum aequalium virium diagonali rhombi, sub illis constructi, omnino aequalis est.

§. 68.

Epicrisis.

Quae quidem demonstratio, dum ad ejus ambitum tenoremque spectes, sine dubio laudanda est. Quod autem ad rigorem spectat, pro mea sententia non omnia ita comparata sunt, ut totum argumentum omnibus nummeris absolutum dici possit. Quum enim, uti auctor ipse dicit, m, n nonnisi nummeros integros denotent, formula illa $\frac{(2n+1)\pi}{2^{m+1}}$ omnes omnino angulos a o usque ad ∞ minime complectitur. Itaque a nostro probata non tam late patent, quam ipse ea patere sumsit. Ceterum fortasse etiam sunt, qui nostro, ex aequationibus (I.) et (II.) necessario fluere ac deduci aequationem (III.) qui contenderit, non adsentiant.

Caput II.

*Argumentum a viro clarissimo Foncenex *) traditum.*

§. 69.

Sit (fig. 30.) mCM angulus ita comparatus, ut sit $\frac{mCM}{90^\circ} = \frac{1}{v}$ (v quendam numerum integrum denotet); anguli ACM, BCM

---

*) Sur les principes fontamentaux de la mechanique v. Melanges de philos. et de mathem. de la Soc. roy. de Turin. T. II. p. 404 sq. 1760—61.

sint inter se aequales, iique $= n. MCm$; deinde sit $MCm = ACa = aCa' = BCb = bCb'$. Nunc vim duarum mediam, angulo MCm concurrentium, quarum quaevis $= a$, esse $= ka$; potentiam iisdem duabus, angulum vero mCm comprehendentibus, aequivalentem $= pa$; porro, cum eaedem BCA angulo concurrant, vim earum mediam $= p^n a$; si ejusmodi angulus aCb, aequipollentem potentiam $= p^{n+1} a$, denique duarum ejusmodi potentiarum, angulum a'Cb' inter se constituentium, mediam $= p^{n+2} a$ esse ponamus.

Quum autem a'CA, BCb', mCm inter se aequales sint, vires a'C, AC uni potentiae, quae secundum directionem Ca agit, et quae $= ka$, aequipollent; eademque pro viribus CB, Cb' valent. Viribus autem Ca, Cb potentia $p^{n+1} a$ aequivalet; itaque binarum virium ka vis media est $= kp^{n+1} a$. Quum ergo duabus CA, CB potentia $= p^n a$, viribus autem Ca', Cb' potentia $= p^{n+2}$ aequivaleant, erit nobis haec aequatio: $p^{n+2} a + p^n a = kp^{n+1} a$, et hinc $p^{n+2} - kp^{n+1} + p^n = o$.

Itaque universe habebimus $p^n = Dx^n + Ey^n$, dum scilicet x, y duae sunt radices hujus aequationis: $u^2 - ku + 1 = o$. Erit ergo

$$p^n = D\left[\frac{k}{2} + \sqrt{\left(\frac{k^2}{4} - 1\right)}\right]^n + E\left[\frac{k}{2} - \sqrt{\left(\frac{k^2}{4} - 1\right)}\right]^n.$$

Quum vero $k = 2\cos\alpha$ esse ponamus, hinc nonciscimur

$[\cos\alpha + \sqrt{(\cos\alpha^2 - 1)}]^n = \cos n\alpha + \sqrt{-1}.\ \sin n\alpha$ et

$[\cos\alpha - \sqrt{(\cos\alpha^2 - 1)}]^n = \cos. n\alpha - \sqrt{-1}.\ \sin. n\alpha.$; unde

$p^n = (D + E)\cos. n\alpha + (D - E)\sqrt{-1}.\ \sin n\alpha.$, vel

$p^n = F\cos n\alpha + G\sqrt{-1}.\ \sin. n\alpha$

Si autem $n = o$ esse ponitur, hinc prodit $p^n = 2$, ideoque etiam $F = 2$; dum sumas $n = 1$, erit (p. hyp.) $p^n = k = 2\cos\alpha$ itaque $2\cos\alpha = 2\cos\alpha + G\sin\alpha$ ergo $G = o$, ideoque $p^n = 2\cos. n\alpha$ esse debet. Ceterum dum $n = v$ esse ponimus h. e. dum angulus, cui resultans n. MCm respondet $= 180°$, omnino $p^v = o$ esse debet; ergo $2\cos. v\alpha = o$ unde accipitur $v\alpha = \frac{\pi}{4}$, ergo $a = \frac{\pi}{4v}$ ideoque $p^n = 2\cos\frac{n\pi}{4v} = 2\cos\frac{ACB}{2}$.

§. 70.

Epicrisis.

Quodsi ambitum ac tenorem hujus demonstrationis respicias, omnino laudanda est. Quod attinet vero ad rigorem geometricum merito quaeri potest: quonam jure noster $k = 2 \cos \alpha$ esse sumserit? Equidem non video, quomodo haec aequatio ex ceteris, quae auctor adtulit, sit deducenda.

Sectio secunda.

Demonstrationes analyticae.

Classis sexta.

Argumenta, quae axiomatibus 1. 2. 3. nituntur.

Caput I.

Demonstratio Alembertana prior *).

§. 71.

AB, AC (fig. 32.) sint duae vires, punctum A una sollicitantes. Ponatur esse $AC = a$, $AB = b$, vim illarum mediam $AF = z$, $FAC = u$, $BAC = \alpha$. Ductis lineis AD, Ac ita, ut sit pars anguli CAc dimidia $CAD = m$, duas vires Ab, Ac, quarum,

*) Demonstration de la composition des forces par d'Alembert v. Memoires de l'acad. des Sc. de Paris année 1769.

eodem angulo, quo AB, AC, concurrentium, altera $Ac = a$, altera $Ab = b$, una cum viribus AB, AC agere concipiamus. His ita positis unusquisque non solum vires, utrique pari aequipollentes, omnino aequales esse, sed etiam vim duarum AF, Af mediam, secundum directionem AD agentem, eundem praestituram esse effectum, quem resultantes virium AC, Ac et AB, Ab, secundum eandem directionem punctum A sollicitantes, producant, facile intelligit. Est igitur aequatio

$$a.\varphi(m) + b.\varphi(\alpha + m) = z\varphi(u + m).$$

§. 72.

Quodsi vero virium (fig. 35.) AC, Ac coincidere directiones, simulque duas vires AB′, Ab′, ita inter se comparatas, ut sit $AB' = Ab' = AB = b$, et $BAB' = bAb' = 2m'$ praeter alias punctum A sollicitare ponimus, vis omnium harum media, quae secundum directionem AE agat necesse est, ita exhiberi potest:

$$2a + b\varphi(m'). \varphi(\alpha + m').$$

Quum autem sint AF, Af resultantes virium AB, AC et Ab, Ac, vires, AF, Af et AB′ [illegible] potentiis aequivalentes, has esse necesse est: $z\varphi(u) + b\varphi(\alpha + 2m')$. Habebimus igitur hanc aequationem: $2a + b\varphi(m'). \varphi(\alpha + m') = z\varphi(u) + b\varphi(\alpha + 2m')$ (I.)

§. 73.

Supra autem, quicunque valor quantitati m attribuatur, omnino hanc esse aequationem: $a\varphi(m) + b\varphi(\alpha + m) = z\varphi(u + m)$ vidimus; unde, si $m = o$ esse sumas, patet fore

$$2a + b\varphi(\alpha) = z\varphi(u) \text{ et hinc}$$

$$\varphi(m'). \varphi(\alpha + m') = \varphi(\alpha) + \varphi(\alpha + 2m')$$

vel, si $\alpha + m' = \delta$, $\varphi(\delta - m') + \varphi(\delta + m') = \varphi(m'). \varphi(\delta)$

Quae quidem aequatio non nisi hac conditione, ut sit

$$\varphi(\delta - m') + \varphi(\delta + m') = e^{\alpha \sqrt{A}} + e^{-\alpha \sqrt{A}}$$

locum habere potest.

Quum autem, si $\alpha = 90°$, eâque sola conditione, sit $\varphi(\alpha) = o$ hinc $\sqrt{A} = \sqrt{-1}$, et $\varphi(\alpha) = 2 \cos \alpha$ esse rite colligitur.

§. 74.

Ex praecedentibus autem est $z = \frac{a\varphi(m) + b\varphi(\alpha + m)}{\varphi'(u+m)}$ et $\varphi(m) = 2\cos m$. Itaque, cum quantitati m successive alium aliumque valorem tribuas, primum vero $m = 0$ statuas, haec erit æquatio: $\frac{a.\cos m + b\cos(\alpha + m)}{\cos(u+m)} = \frac{a + b.\cos\alpha}{\cos u.}$, unde facile elicitur $\frac{b}{a} = \frac{\sin u}{\sin(\alpha - u)}$.

Quae quidem aequatio quum locum habere nequeat nisi duarum virium a, b, media secundum directionem diagonalis agat, eâ ipsâ directio hujus potentiae est determinata. Potentia ipsa cum sit $= \frac{a}{\cos.\ u} + \frac{b.\cos\alpha}{\cos u}$, hinc facile deducitur: $z = \frac{b.\sin\alpha}{\sin u}$ Itaque potentiam quarundam duarum media diagonalem omnino aequare necesse est.

§. 75.

E p i c r i s i s.

Quum doctrinam de compositione virium jam in primis staticae elementis obviam esse necesse sit, demonstratio hujus theorematis satis idonea atque apta, me judice, ita comparata esse debet, ut ab iis, qui his elementis primam operam dant, intelligi possit *). Hoc igitur nostri argumentum, ceteraque omnia, ad hanc classem referenda, ab hac parte, quod analysin sublimiorem in subsidium vocant autores, non omnino absoluta judicari possunt. Quod attinet ad brevitatem, ceteris autoris, eandem propositionem demonstrandi, pluribusque aliorum virorum ejusmodi conatibus, hic nostri est praeferendus. Itaque, quum autori ipsi haec sua demonstratio haud satisfecerit, immo quum

*) Ipse noster in libro suo: traité de Dynamique 1743, dicit: un Principe (composition des mouvemens), qui etant l'un des premiers de la Mechanique doit necessairement être appuyé sur des preuves simples et faciles.

non multo post aliam, et ipsam analyseos sublimioris theorematibus superstructam, eamque multo prolixiorem tradiderit, hanc nostram non satis geometrico rigore munitam esse existimandum est. Quantum equidem video auctor in hunc rigorem peccat, dum ex eo, quod, si $\alpha = 90°$, $\varphi(\alpha) = 0$ sit, necessario esse oportere $\sqrt{A} = \sqrt{-1}$, igiturque $\varphi(\alpha) = 2\cos\alpha$ colligi posse contendit. Quum nimirum anguli recti cosinus sit $= 0$, jure quidem, si, dum $\alpha = 90°$, $\varphi(\alpha) = 0$ sit, $\varphi(\alpha) = 2\cos\alpha$ esse *posse*, minime vere hunc valorem *necessario* ei tribuendum esse statui potest.

Cap. II.

Argumentum Alembertanum posterius *).

§. 76.

Quum duae vires rectangulae AB, AC (fig. 34.) una punctum sollicitent, directionem potentiae earum mediae tam diu, quam diu ratio AC : AB h. e. $\sin x : \cos x$ sibi constet, eandem omnino manere unus quisque intelligit. Haec igitur directio tanquam functio illius rationis, quam literâ z denotemus, spectari potest; hinc erit $\sin x : \cos. x = \text{tang}\, x = \varphi(z)$

Quodsi ergo $AB = a$, et $AC = b$ esse atque duas vires na, nb secundum directiones AC, AV agere, ponimus, $QAC = BAD$, ideoque $DAQ = 90°$ esse oportet. Quum vero AD' omnium virium harum esse mediam concipiamus, ex iis, quae modo disseruimus, hae nobis erunt aequationes:

$$\text{tang}\,(x + x') = \varphi\left(\frac{b + na}{a - nb}\right) = \varphi\left(\frac{z + n}{1 - nz}\right)$$

hinc ergo $\dfrac{\text{tg}x + \text{tg}x'}{1 - \text{tg}x.\ \text{tg}x'} = \varphi\left(\dfrac{z + n}{1 - nz}\right)$; et loco $\text{tg}x$ quantitatis

*) d'Alembert nouvelle demonstration du parallelogramme des forces v. opuscules mathem. Tom. VI. p. 360 sq.

ipſius valore ſubſtituto: $\operatorname{tang} x' = \frac{\varphi\left(\frac{z+n}{1-nz}\right) - \varphi(z)}{1+\varphi(z).\,\varphi\left(\frac{z+n}{1-nz}\right)}$

§. 77.

Potentiam autem, secundum directionem AD agentem, quam $= y$ esse ponamus, sine dubio $AQ = ny$ esse debet; hinc ergo

$$\operatorname{tg} x' = \varphi\left(\frac{ny}{y}\right) = \varphi(n)$$

Duobus his quantitatis $\operatorname{tg} x'$ valoribus inter se comparandis accipimus: $\frac{\varphi(z)+\varphi(u)}{1-\varphi(z).\,\varphi(u)} = \varphi\left(\frac{z+n}{1-nz}\right)$, cujus aequationis ope $\varphi(z)$ determinari potest. Quodsi igitur ipsa semel secundum z tanquam variabilem, semelque secundum n differentiatur, has aequationes nanciscimur:

$$\frac{1+\varphi(u)^2}{[1-\varphi(z).\,\varphi(u)]^2}.\,\frac{d\varphi(z)}{dz} = d.\varphi\left(\frac{z+n}{1-nz}\right).\,\frac{1+n^2}{(1-nz)^2}$$

$$\frac{1+\varphi(z)^2}{[1-\varphi(z)\,\varphi(u)]^2}.\,\frac{d\varphi(n)}{dn} = d\varphi\left(\frac{z+n}{1-nz}\right).\,\frac{1+z^2}{(1-nz)^2}$$

§. 78.

Sed ut conditionibus hujus aequationis satisfiat, esse

$$\frac{d.\,\varphi(z)}{1+\varphi(z)^2} = a.\,\frac{dz}{1+z^2} \quad (1) \quad \text{et}$$

$$\frac{d.\,\varphi(n)}{1+\varphi(n)^2} = a.\,\frac{dn}{1+n^2} \quad (2)$$

(a quantitatem quandam constantem innuit) ponamus omnino necesse est. Qua quidem aequatione quantitati $\varphi(z)$, valor tangentis trigonometricae tribuitur; nimirum, uti vidimus

$$\varphi(z) = a.\operatorname{tg} z.$$

esse debet. Quum autem pro rei natura $\varphi(z)$ in eadem ratione, qua z vel $\frac{b}{a}$, crescat, dum altera duarum potentiarum, b, quantitate g augetur, altera vero eadem manet, vim earum mediam directionis suae respectu angulum CAD secare necesse est; itaque omnino $D'AB > DAB$. Ceterum quantitatem $\varphi(z)$ tam diu futuram esse positivam, quam diu ipsa z positiva sit, satis apparet. Dum autem $z = 1$ esse sumimus, etiam $\varphi(z) = 1$ esse debet; tunc enim est $b = a$ h. e. vis media angulum BAC bifariam secat. Quibus conditionibus ut satisfiat in aequationibus supra repertis (1) et (2) aut $a = 1$ aut $a = 1 + 4r$ sumi debet. Nullo enim alio modo, dum $z = 1$, etiam $\varphi(z) = 1$ esse potest.

Quodsi igitur $a = 1 + 4r$, simulque angulum, cujus tangens z, paullo majorem quam $\frac{90^\circ}{1 + 4r}$, minorem vero, quam 90°, angulum vero $\frac{90}{1 + 4r} + \alpha$ ita comparatum, ut $(1 + 4r)\alpha < 270^\circ$, esse ponamus, tangentem anguli hujus $\left(\frac{90^\circ}{1 + 4r} + \alpha\right)(1 + 4r)$ quantitatem esse negativam omnino necesse est; ita igitur, dum z augeretur, $\varphi(z)$ neque cresceret, neque positiva esset; ergo aequatio $a = 1 + 4r$ locum habere nequit; ergo $a = 1$, hinc vero $\varphi(z) = z$ ideoque $tg\ x = z = \frac{b}{a}$ esse, h. e. vis duarum media, quoad directionem omnino cum diagonali coincidere debet.

§. 79.

E p i c r i s i s.

In demonstranda virium compositione eam praecipue partem, quae de directione resultantis determinanda agit, difficultatibus premi, ideoque merito, ceteris ommissis, hanc solam partem tractari, uti noster fecit, jam alias monitum est. Num vere et quomodo noster hanc directionem determinaverit nunc videamus. Primum quod attinet ad usum calculi differentialis atque integralis jam ad alterum nostri argumentum verba feci. Ceterum ipse noster, hanc suam demonstrationem non tanta, quanta debeat, simplicitate ac facilitate gaudere, ideoque alteri, quam modo antea cognovimus, demonstrationi suae posthabendam esse dicit. Praeterea omnia debito rigore demonstrata esse, equidem contendere non ausim. Conditiones enim, quas noster collocat, nimirum dum angulum, cujus tangens z paulo majorem quam $\frac{90}{1+4r}$, minorem autem quam $90°$, porro, angulum $\left(\frac{90}{1+4r}+\alpha\right)(1+4r)$ non majorem quam $270°$ esse sumit, minime esse necessarias, ideoque nostri demonstrationem non necessario veram, unusquisque inficias ire nequit.

Cap. III.

Argumentum a geometra Foucenex traditum *).

§. 80.

Quum potentia z duabus aequalibus $= a$, quae angulum α inter se constituunt, aequipolleat, summi posse $z = a\,\varphi(\alpha)$ satis adparet.

Sit aequatio $\varphi(\alpha) = y$. Cujus quantitatis y ad inveniendum valorem lineae Cm, Cm′, Ca, Ca′, Cb, Cb′ ita ducantur (fig. 31.), ut, si $ACB = \alpha$, $mCM = m'CM = ACa = BCb = aCa' = bCb' = \frac{d\alpha}{2}$; ergo etiam $ACa' = BCb' = mCm' = \delta\alpha$,

$$aCb = \alpha + \delta\alpha$$
$$a'Cb' = \alpha + 2\delta\alpha$$

esse oportet. Dum autem angulus ACB in aCb, y in $y + dy$, et dum aCb in a′Cb′, $y + dy$ in $y + 2dy + d^2y$ mutatur.

---

*) Daviet de Foucenex sur les principes fondamentaux de la mechanique v. Melanges de philos. et de mathem. de la Soc. roy. de Turin. Tom. II. 1760—61. p. 399 sqq.

Itaque si $y + dy = y'$, et $y + 2dy + d^2y = y''$, deinde $dy = ud\alpha$, et, dum $\alpha = o$, $u = V$ esse ponimus, si α in m'Cm matatur, $y = 2 + Vd\alpha$ esse debet.

§. 81.

Quodsi igitur quatuor vires Ca', CA, Cb', CB una punctum C sollicitant, vim earum mediam, secundum directionem CM agentem, esse $= a(y + y'')$ necesse est. Quum autem in locum virium a'C, AC, et CB, Cb' duae aliae, quarum quaelibet $= a(2 + Vd\alpha)$, quibusque una potentia, secundum directionem CM agens, $= ay'(2 + Vd\alpha)$ aequivalet, substitui possint, hinc facile aequatio haeccine $y + y'' = y'(2 + Vd\alpha)$ deducitur, et suffectis in locum y', y'' valoribus supra statutis $d^2y = yVd\alpha + Vdy.d\alpha$ ergo quoque $d^2y = yVd\alpha$ nanciscimur.

Quum autem y quantitas sit finita, sine dubio V infinita, eaque ejusdem, cujus et $d\alpha$, ordinis esse debet. Itaque, si $V = kd\alpha$ esse ponimus, $d^2y = ykd\alpha^2$ (1) esse debet; cujus aequationis integralis, universe spectata haec est:

$$y = Ae^{\alpha\sqrt{K}} + Be^{-\alpha\sqrt{K}} \quad (2)$$

ergo

$$dy = \sqrt{K}\left(Ae^{\alpha\sqrt{K}} + Be^{\alpha - \sqrt{K}}\right) d\alpha \quad (3)$$

Quum nunc in aequationibus (2) et (3) $\alpha = o$ esse sumamus, inde nobis erit $A + B = 2$ et $dy = \sqrt{(k)}.(A - B)\, d\alpha$. Verum, si $\alpha = o$, est quoque, uti vidimus, $dy = Vd\alpha = Kd\alpha^2$, ergo $\sqrt{K}.\, d\alpha = A - B$, ergo etiam $A - B = o$. Hinc autem $A = B$, ideoque $y = e^{\alpha\sqrt{k}} + e^{-\alpha\sqrt{k}} = 2\cos(\alpha\sqrt{-k})$.

Dum autem $\alpha = \frac{\pi}{2}$ esse ponimus, est $y = o$, ergo $\cos\frac{\pi}{2}\sqrt{-k} = o$; hinc quoque $\frac{\pi}{2}\sqrt{-k} = \frac{\pi}{4}(2\mu + 1)$ [μ quendam nummeram integrum denotat]; unde patet, fore $\sqrt{-k} = \frac{2\mu + 1}{2}$ ergo $y = 2\cos.\left(\frac{2\mu + 1}{2}\alpha\right)$. Liquet autem, z, ideoque etiam y, dum $\alpha < 2R$, quantitates esse positivas; quae conditio omnino locum habere nequiret, nisi $m = o$; itaque est $2 \cos \frac{\alpha}{2} = \phi(\alpha) = y$.

Coroll. Quodsi igitur tam quantitatem, quam directionem potentiae duabus aequalibus aequivalentis respicias, ipsam diagonalem aequare necesse est.

§. 82.

Eadem, quae pro viribus aequalibus modo demonstravimus, etiam de inaequalibus iisque primum rectangulis valere, sic ostenditur.

Sint ejusmodi vires CA, CB (fig. 35.), earumque resultantis directio CD; recta FCE ita ducta, ut $FCB = BCD$, ideoque etiam $ECA = ACD$, potentia CB in duas alias aequales, secundum directiones CD, CF, itemque CA in duas ejusmodi secundum CE, CD resolvatur. Ex praededentibus quaevis potentiarum, quibus BC aequipollet $= \frac{BC}{2 \cos. DCB}$; illarum autem, quarum vis media est AC, quaelibet $= \frac{AC}{2 \cos ACD}$ esse debet. Ita quatuor nobis sunt vires, quarum duae secundum directionem CD conspirant, duae autem plane sibi repugnant. Quum duarum CA, CB mediae directionem CD esse a nobis positum sit, duas illas vires repugnantes inter se aequales esse omnino necesse est. Qua ex re patet, fore $\frac{AC}{2 \cos. ACD} = \frac{BC}{2 \cos. DCB}$ et

$$\frac{AC}{2 \cos. ACD} + \frac{BC}{2 \cdot \cos DCB} = CD.$$

Dum in locum quantitatis BC, ejus valorem, e priori aequatione elicitum, in posteriori sufficias, prodibit $CD = \frac{CA}{\cos. ACD}$ et hinc nobis erunt hae analogiae

$$\cos. ACD : \sin ACD :: AC : AB$$
$$\text{et } \sin. DCB : 1 :: AC : CD$$

quarum illâ directio, hac vero quantitas resultantis determinatur. =

Quae quidem demonstrata facile viribus, quodammodo in aequalibus accommodari possunt.

§. 83.

E p i c r i s i s.

Methodum fere novam calculi differentialis atque integralis ad demonstrandam virium compositionem adhibendi hîc noster usurpavit. Qua in re ipsum magnam sollertiam ingeniique acumen praebuisse nemo inficiari potest. Nihilominus tamen non sine satis magno, ut ita dicam adparatu, atque sumtu, nostrum priori demonstrationis parte ad id, quod petit, pervenisse concedi debet. Ceterum — si ea, quae equidem sentio, ad alios transferre licet — noster lectori non plane satisfacit, dum, quod $A - B = \sqrt{k}.\, d\alpha$, $A - B = 0$ esse contendit. Desideramus saltem atque optamus, ut auctor aliâ, quam hic factum est via, hanc aequationem, quae maximi est momenti, invenerit.

Denique quod attinet ad rigorem nostrae demonstrationis geometricum, quaedam contra eum monenda esse mihi videntur. Nimirum ex eo, quod $y = 2\cos\left(\frac{\mu + 1}{2}\alpha\right)$, atque y, dum $\alpha < 2R$, quantitas esse debeat positiva, nondum $\mu = 0$ esse necessario sequitur. Inter infinitum enim valorum numerum, qui quantitatibus μ et α tribui possunt, permulti sane ita comparati sunt, ut $\frac{2\mu + 1}{2}\alpha < 90^\circ$

ideoque $\frac{2\mu + 1}{2}\alpha$ quantitas sit positiva. Quum autem in hac aequatione $\mu = 0$, nervus probandi positus sit, atque pars demonstrationis posterior hac priore omnino superstructa sit, toti hinc argumento absolutum rigorem vindicari non posse videmus atque intelligimus.

Cap. IV.

Argumentum a summo geometra Laplacio traditum *).

§. 84.

Quum x, y duae vires inter se rectangulae sint, quae una quoddam punctum sollicitant, quarumque resultans est z, trium harum potentiarum quantitatem multifariam variari posse, dum directio potentiae z eadem maneat, per se satis patet. Universe igitur, cum angulus, quem vis media et componentium altera v. c. x inter se comprehendunt, sit $= \alpha$, ponere possumus

$$x = z\,\varphi(\alpha) \text{ et } y = z\,\varphi(\tfrac{1}{2}\pi - \alpha).$$

Quodsi vero potentiam x, tanquam resultantem duarum rectangularum x', x'', quarum illa cum potentia z coincidit, spectamus, eâdem, qua antea, ratione nobis erit $x' = x\,\varphi(\alpha) = \frac{x^2}{z}$

$$x'' = x\,\varphi\left(\frac{\pi}{2} - \alpha\right) = \frac{x.\,y}{z}$$

Altera potentia simili modo resoluta, habebimus

$$y' = y\,\varphi\left(\frac{\pi}{2} - \alpha\right) = \frac{y^2}{z}$$

$$y'' = y\,\varphi(\alpha) = \frac{x.\,y}{z.}$$

Itaque in locum potentiarum x, y, vires hae:

$$\frac{x^2}{z},\ \frac{y^2}{z},\ \frac{x.\,y}{z},\ \frac{x.\,y}{z};$$

ergo his et illis eadem est resultans. Sed ex ipsa nostra constructione potentias duas aequales $\frac{x.\,y}{z}$, $\frac{x.\,y}{z}$ plane sibi repugnare, ideoque inter se aequilibrari satis liquet; unde erit nobis aequatio $z^2 = x^2 + y^2$ h. e. vis duarum x, y media quantitatis respectu habito diagonalem rectanguli x. y aequat.

---

*) Laplace mecanique celeste. Tom. I. abinit.

§. 85.

Ad determinandam resultantis directionem, x in quantitatem $x+dx$, dum y sibi constet, variari concipiamus. Ita quidem angulus α quantitate $d\alpha$ decrescit. Resoluta autem potentia dx, in duas rectangulas dx', dx'', quarum illa secundum directionem potentiae z agit, duae potentiae $z+dx'$ et dx'' rectangulae, quarum resultantem z' quantitate innuamus, una punctum idem sollicitant; habebimus ergo $dx''=z'\varphi\left(\frac{\pi}{2}-d\alpha\right)$. Itaque quantitatis $\frac{\pi}{2}-d\alpha$ functio infinite parvum quid exhibere, ideoque hujus formae $-kd\alpha$ esse debet; ergo $\frac{dx''}{z'}=-kd\alpha$ [k quantitatem quandam constantem, haud ab α pendentem innuit].

Quum autem vires dx'', dx, angulum $=\left(\frac{\pi}{2}-\alpha\right)$ comprehendant, atque z' non nisi infinite parvo quodam a quantitate z differat, erit aequatio

$dx''=dx\,\varphi\left(\frac{\pi}{2}-\alpha\right)=\frac{y\,dx}{z}$, ergo $d\alpha=-\frac{y\,dx}{kz^2}$

Simili ratione, quum y in $y+dy$ varietur, dum x eundem valorem servet, habebimus $dy''=dy\,\varphi(\alpha)=\frac{x.\,dy}{dz}$

ergo $d\left(\frac{\pi}{2}-\alpha\right)=-\frac{x\,dy}{kz}$, ideoque $d\alpha=\frac{x.\,dy}{kz^2}$

Itaque quum x, y una variabiles esse sumatur, erit aequatio

$$kd\alpha=\frac{x\,dy-y\,dx}{x^2+y^2}$$

Integrando accipimus tang. $(k\alpha+\varrho)=\frac{y}{x}$ [ϱ quampiam quantitatem constantem innuit], vel $x=z.\cos.(k\alpha+\varrho)$.
Hac in aequatione quum ad determinandas k, et ϱ quantitates, $y=0$ esse ponamus, habebimus $x=z$ et $\alpha=0$ itaque $\cos\varrho=1$ ideoque $x=z.\cos(k\alpha)$.

Quodsi vero $x = o$ esse sumimus, inde erit $z = y$ et $\alpha = \frac{1}{2}\pi$; quum vero tunc $\cos(k\alpha) = o$ esse debeat, quantitati k hanc esse formam $2n + 1$, necesse est.

Habebimus ita $x = o$, dum $\frac{\frac{1}{2}\pi}{2n+1} = \alpha$; cum autem, uti vidimus, etiam sit $x = o$, si $\alpha = \frac{1}{2}\pi$, omnino $k = 1$, ideoque $x = z \cos \alpha$ esse oportet. Itaque potentia duabus rectangulis aequipollens, et si ejus directionem respicias diagonalem aequat.

§. 86.

Jure meritoque igitur vis quaelibet in duas alias, quae per latera rectanguli, illi tanquam diagonali circumscripti, exhibentur; itemque quaevis potentia in tres alias, quibus id parallelepipedum, cujus ipsa diagonalis est, determinatur, resolvi potest. Quodsi igitur a, b, c coordinatae rectangulae sunt, potentiae, cujus exordium cum exordio coordinatarum coincidat, respondentes, per quantitatem $\sqrt{(a^2 + b^2 + c^2)}$ ipsa potentia exhibetur; dum per a, b, c vires indicantur, in quas illa resolvi potest. Quum autem a', b', c' sint coordinatae alius ejusmodi potentiae, $a + a'$, $b + b'$, $c + c'$ coordinatas harum duarum resultanti respondentes esse omnino necesse est. Eaedem vero coordinatae quum exhibeant vires eas laterales, in quas potentia illa media resolvi potest, ipsa diagonalem parallelepipedi sub illis constructi aequare debet.

Quo quidem modo tam quantitas, quam directio quarumpiam virium determinari potest *).

---

*) Cl. Burckhardt in versione libri Laplaciani „Mecanique celeste" p. 6 et ipse demonstrationem adtulit, quae fere haec est:

Quum ratio, quae tribus viribus x, y, z (componentibus et compositae) intercedit, constans sit, atque angulorum, quos illae inter sese constituunt, quantitas ab hac mutua ratione pendeat, rationem binarum omnino virium, functione anguli, ab ipsis constituti, datam nobis esse satis elucet. Angulis igitur, quibus vis media versus componentes inclinatur, per litteras ϑ, et λ denotatis, haec nobis erit aequatio $z = x\,\varphi(\vartheta) + y\,\varphi(\lambda)$

Cap. V.

Argumentum a Poissonio adlatum *).

§. 87.

Quum duae vires aequales, una in punctum quoddam agentes, angulum $2x$ inter se comprehendant, utramque vero $= P$, iisque aequipollentem $= R$ esse ponamus, aequationem $R = P\,\varphi(x)$ prodire jam supra vidimus.

Lineis mA', mA'', mB', mB'' ita ductis, ut $AmA' = AmA'' = BmB' = BmB'' = z$, potentia P in duas aequales vires secundum directiones mA', mA'' agentes resolvatur; sit utraque ejusmodi potentia $= Q$; unde erit aequatio $P = Q\,\varphi(z)$.

Simili modo et altera potentia P resoluta, quum duabus secundum mA', mB' agentibus aequipollentem $= Q'$, et aliarum duarum, secundum mA'', mB'' sollicitantium, mediam $= Q''$ esse positum sit, hasce habemus aequationes:

$$Q' = Q\,\varphi(x - z)$$
$$Q'' = Q\,\varphi(x + z)$$
$$R = Q' + Q''$$

et hinc $\varphi(x).\,\varphi(z) = \varphi(x - z) + \varphi(x + z)$

Quoniam vero si x, y secundum directiones plane contrarias agunt, est

$$\vartheta = 0°$$
$$\lambda = 180°$$
$$\&\ z = x - z$$

unde rite haec aequatio deducitur

$$z = x \cos.\,\vartheta + y \cos\lambda$$

Sed ipsa haec aequatio potentiam z diagonalem parallelogrammi, cujus latera x, y, atque angulum, quo sese secant, $(\vartheta + \lambda)$ esse satis indicat. — Quae quidem demonstratio si non minus rigida, quam brevis atque expedita esset, ceteris omnibus sine dubio palmam praeriperet. Sed ab ipso hoc rigore, quantum equidem video, haud parum abest. Ex iis enim quae auctor sumsit, omnino hae duae aequationes $z = x\,\varphi(\vartheta)$
$z = y\,\varphi(\lambda)$
prodeunt; quomodo autem inde aequatio illa

$$z = x\,\varphi(\vartheta) + y\,\varphi(\lambda)$$

deduci possit, nemo sane intelligit.

*) Poisson traité de Mecanique. Tom. I. ab init.

§. 88.

Ex hac aequatione valor quantitatis $\varphi(x)$, vel, quo idem adsequimur, $\varphi(z)$, ut eliciatur, haec fieri oportet. Evolvantur quantitates $\varphi(x+z)$ et $\varphi(x-z)$ fecundum theorema Taylorianum, ita ut sit

$$\varphi(z) = 2\left[1 + \frac{d^2\varphi(x)}{dx^2.\varphi(x)}\cdot\frac{z^2}{1.2} + \frac{d^4\varphi(x)}{dx^4.\varphi(x)}\cdot\frac{z^4}{1.2.3.4} + \text{etc.}\right]$$

Quum autem $\varphi(z)$ quantitatem x non continere necesse sit, eandem in quantitatibus $\frac{d^2\varphi(x)}{dx^2.\varphi(x)}$, $\frac{d^4\varphi(x)}{dx^4.\varphi(x)}$ etc. non occurrere omnino oportet. Hae igitur quantitates constantes esse, vel haud a variabilibus x, z pendere debent. Statuta igitur aequatione $\frac{d^2\varphi(x)}{dx^2} = b\,\varphi(x)$, inde identidem differentiando derivatur $\frac{d^4\varphi(x)}{dx^4} = b\,\frac{d^2\varphi(x)}{dx^2} = b^2\varphi(x)$ etc. et hinc, dum $b = -a^2$ esse ponamus,

$$\varphi(z) = 2\left[1 - \frac{a^2z^2}{2} + \frac{a^4.z^4}{2.3.4} - \frac{a^6z^6}{2.3.4.5.6} + \text{etc.}\right] = 2\cos.(az)$$

unde, dum in locum quantitatis z sufficitur x, erit

$$\varphi(x) = 2\cos.(ax)$$

ideoque $R = 2P.\cos.(ax)$

Ad determinandum valorem quantitatis a, ipsam ab x haud pendere memineris. Posito autem esse $x = 90°$, erit $R = 0$, ergo $\cos(a.90°) = 0$. Quae quidem aequatio a quendam nummerum inparem denotare satis indicat; simul vero $a = 1$ esse contenditur. Nam si $a > 1$, v. c. $a = 5$ esset, $R = 0$, dum $x = \frac{90°}{5}$, esse deberet. Quod quidem fieri nequit; ergo $R = 2P\cos x$. Quomodo haec, pro viribus aequalibus demonstrata, ad vires inaequales extendantur jam alias vidimus *).

---

*) Demonstrationem theorematis nostri eam, quam attulit Francœur in libro suo: Elemens de Statique. Paris 1812., plane eandem esse, quam modo cognovimus, auctor ipse fatetur. Jure igitur hic omitti potest.

§. 89.

Epicrisis.

Quae duae demonstrationes a multis aliis, vel potius ab omnibus, quas hucusque exposuimus, haud parum differunt. Methodi, quas autores in demonstrando nostro theoremate calculi differentialis et integralis ope sequuntur, plane sunt novae. Utra methodus sit praeferenda, multi fortasse quaerunt. Quamquam cuique suae sint virtutes, equidem tamen eam, quam Poissonius usurpavit, Laplacii methodo praeferre velim. Utriusque autem demonstrationis auctores summum ingenii acumen summamque sollertiam ostenderunt. Demonstrationes ipsae inter omnes, quas cognovimus, praecipue rigore geometrico eminent.

Liber secundus.

Demonstrationes aliis staticae theorematibus superstructae.

Classis septima.

Argumenta, quae vectis theoria nituntur.

Cap. I.

Argumentum Kaestnerianum.

§. 90.

Postquam auctor ope axiomatis: „vectis, cui paribus inde ab hypomochlio distantiis aequales vires adplicatae sunt, aequilibratur,“ haec theoremata probare tentavit:

Item ea, quae Lagrange, Prony aliique geometrae de compositione virium scripserunt, ommitti debere puto. Quae quidem doctrina in horum virorum libris arctius cum principiis, quibus totam mechanicam superstruere student, cohaeret, quam ut hîc rite explicari possit.

1) Quilibet vectis DB, vel DC (fig. 37 et 38.), si P.DA = Q.AB vel p.DA = Q.AC, in aequilibrio versatur, eademque de vecte angulari (fig. 39.) valent.

2) Vectem ACB, quum duae vires P, Q (fig. 40.), in ejus brachia oblique agentes, ita comparatae sint, ut, ductis CE, CD perpendicularibus, sit: CD : CE :: Q : P, aequilibrari oportet, — ubi, inquam, haec probare conatus est, hoc fere modo pergit:

Quodsi potentias, P, Q vecti ACB (fig. 40.), eique mobili, adplicatas, tanquam inde a puncto M, quo earum directiones concurrunt, agentes spectamus, punctum C secundum directionem CM moveri omnino patet. Ductis ergo CG || MQ et CH || MP, erit: P : Q :: MG : MB, h. e. si potentiae MG, MH una in punctum M agunt, vis earum mediae directio cum diagonali parallelogrammi coincidit. Potentia igitur ea, quae huic potentiae aequalis est, ipsi vero repugnat, cum duabus MG, MH aequilibretur necesse est.

Quodsi igitur MT, MV, Mc (fig. 41.), tres sunt vires, inter se aequilibrantes, et directionem potentiae Mc cum diagonalis parallelogrammi MTCV coincidere sumitur, etiam Mv tanquam duabus MT, Mc aequivalens spectari potest; itaque Mv secundum directionem diagonalis par. McvT agere debet. Hoc autem modo quum sit MC = Mc, vim, duabus aequipollentem, omnino diagonalem aequare oportet.

§. 91.

Inter alios, qui eandem methodum sequuti sunt, auctores memorandi sunt: Karsten *), Pasquich **), Lorenz ***), Ferroni †), Peyrard ††), Schmidt †††) aliique. Omnes autem horum virorum demonstrationes exponere partim locus non per-

*) Lehrbegr. der gesammten Math. III. p. 40 sq.
**) Opuscula statico-mechanica. II. p. 35 sq.
***) Grundriſs der ges. Math. II. p. 31 sq.
†) Memorie di M. et di F. della Soc. Ital. Tom. X. P. II. p. 481 sq.
††) Statique geometrique v. Bezout cours de mathematiques. IVme partie. p. 30 sqq.
†††) Anfangsgr. der math. Wissensch. Frankf. 1806. Th. II. ab init.

mittit, partim haud necessarium est. Unam igitur instar omnium cognovisse sufficiat.

§. 92.

Omnia haec argumenta laudanda sunt, quod non nisi aliquot geometriae theoremata satis plana in subsidium vocant. Plura autem eorum, maximeque Ferronianum, maxima prolixitate premuntur. Ceterum methodum eam, qua, plures certe auctores, illa, quae pro viribus vectisque brachiis inter se commensurabilibus probavere, ad res easdem incommensurabiles extendant, non esse geometricam, vel rigori geometrico non consentaneam, negari nequit.

Caput II.

Argumentum a viro doctissimo Marini traditum *).

§. 93.

Auctor totam hanc suam demonstrationem hocce theoremate superstruit: quodsi vecti rectilineo DB (fig. 37.) duae vires P, Q, ab eadem parte normales adplicantur, ita ut $P.DA = Q.AB$, punctoque A vis L, quae et ipsa normalis secundum directionem plane contrariam agit, atque est $= P + Q$, huic vecti neque motus rotatus, neque progressivus tribui potest.

Ex hoc theoremate facile hae propositiones deducuntur:

1) Potentiae L actione sublata, vectis secundum directionem virium P, Q moveretur. Itaque directio duarum harum mediae punctum A, circa quod ipsae aequilibrantur, permeat.

2) Quum alia quaedam potentia S puncto vectis cuidam adplicetur, haec cum altera P in aequilibrio versatur, dum $CA.S = DA.P$. Potentiae igitur S, Q relate ad punctum A eun-

---

*) Aloysii Marini tentamen de motu composito. Romae 1814.

dem omnino effectum praestant; sed resultans duarum, circa A aequilibrantium, modo per P + Q, modo per P + S exhibetur, prouti aut unam aut alteram adplicatam concipias.

3) Binae vires, quarum altera secundum directionem, vecti normalem, altera secundum obliquam agit, dum in ratione perpendicularium, a quopiam vectis puncto in earum directiones demissarum, inversa constituae sunt, in aequilibrio esse debent.

4) Eadem illa ratio duas ejusmodi vires subeat necesse est, si utraque secundum directionem, vecti obliquam, adplicata est.

5) Duae vires aequales P, O, quae, vecti GS (fig. **) in puncto F adhibitae, cum vi quadam normali Q aequilibrantur, angulos SFO, PFC aequales efformant. Quavis earum in duas laterales U, N et u, n resoluta, quarum altera cum vectis directione coincidat, altera ad hanc sit perpendicularis, ex ipsa rerum natura hae duae sunt aequationes: $U = u$; et $N = n$; ideoque U, u semet ipsas invicem destruere oportet. Ceteras N, n, quum sit $N + n = 2N$, cum potentia 2Q circa C aequilibrari necesse est; hinc autem $N.FC = Q.CG = P.CA$. Sed his ipsis aequationibus ratio indicatur, quae inter vim compositam alteramque componentium intercedere debet. Simulac enim P mutatur in 2P, 3 P etc. etiam N, non mutata ejus directione, 2N, 3N etc. evadere necesse est; duae igitur potentiae in ratione directa sunt positae.

Quum vero, quantitate manente eâdem, angulus, quem P, N inter sese constituunt, mutetur, simul et potentiam N mutari oportet. Itaque N tam a quantitate potentiae P, quam ab angulo, quo versus P inclinatur, quemque nuncupemus x, dependet, meritoque igitur poni potest;

$$N = P\varphi(x)$$
$$U = P(90° - x)$$

§. 94.

His propositionibus praemissis, corpus quoddam, in puncto B versans (fig. ***), in quod duae potentiae rectangulae G, M una agant, quarum mutua ratio per rectas BD, BC indicatur, hoc, inquam, corpus secundum diagonalem ferri BA rectanguli DC probare possumus.

1) Corporis moti directio eadem est, quae diagonalis BA.

Ducta enim recta TU alteri BA perpendiculari, potentiisque duabus P, Q, quae, viribus G, M aequales, secundum directiones omnino contrarias agunt, in punctis F, E adplicatis, has quatuor vires vel potius duas binarum resultantes inter se aequilibrari oportet. Est autem $BD.DA = CA.BC$, vel $G.DA = M.AC$, ideoque $P.DA = Q.AC$; potentiae ergo P, Q circa punctum A in aequilibrio versantur itaque quum duarum G, M, media punctum B transeat, haec ipsa secundum BA directa omnino esse debet.

2) Sed et quantitas resultantis per diagonalem exhibetur.

Quavis enim duarum P, Q in duas alias, U, S, et T, L rectangulas resolutâ, duarum P, Q media, tanquam quatuor virium S, U, T, L resultans spectari potest; ergo, postquam $CBA = x$ resultantemque $= R$ esse posuerimus, hasce habebimus aequationes:

$$M = R.\varphi(x) \qquad T = M.\varphi(90° - x)$$
$$G = R.\varphi(90° - x) \qquad U = G.\varphi(x)$$
$$L = M.\varphi(x) \qquad S = G.\varphi(90° - x)$$

unde, eliminando quantitates $\varphi(x)$ et $\varphi(90° - x)$, hae nobis aequationes oriuntur:

$$L = \frac{M^2}{R}; \; T = \frac{M.G}{R}; \; U = \frac{M.G}{R}; \; S = \frac{G^2}{R}$$

et hinc facile $R^2 = M^2 + G^2$.

§. 95.

E p i c r i s i s.

Quae quidem demonstratio pro mea sententia ceteris hujus classis omnibus, permultisque aliis ejusmodi argumentis praeferenda est. Quod enim primum adtinet ad ejus ambitum atque tenorem haud eâ, quâ multâ alia, prolixitate premitur, et non nisi quaedam matheseos elementaris theoremata in subsidium vocat. Sed, quod maximum est, rigore sane geometrico haec nostri demonstratio gaudet. Ea enim, quibus auctor totum argumentum superstruit, ab aliis geometris probata fuere; ipse autem quae probanda sibi sumsit, re vera illorum ope demonstravit.

Pars commentationis posterior.

Demonſtrationes eae, in quibus motus, a viribus adhibitis efficiendi, ratio omnino habetur.

Classis octava.

Argumenta, quorum auctores theorema noſtrum ita demonſtrare ſtudent, ut vires earumque actiones nobis, ut ita dicam, ante oculos ponant, v. c. fidibus elaſticis adhibitis.

Demonſtratio a Vincentio Riccato tradita *).

§. 96.

Auctor his theorematibus:

1) Quum fides quaedam elastica AS (fig. 42.) vi quadam AB, corpus A, nonnisi secundum directionem AD mobile, sollicitet, potentiam AH, quae lineâ perpendiculari determinatur, potentiae AB aequipollere necesse est.

2) Quum AS, AT (fig. 43.) duae una in corpus, secundum directionem AD tantummodo mobile, adplicatae sint fides, eundemque, quem vires AB, AC, praestent effectum, lineâ DK = AH assumta, tota potentia AD duabus his chordis aequipollet.

*) Vincenzo Riccati dialoghi delle force vive etc. Bologn. 1749. p. 208 sqq. — Commentariorum Bononiens. T. II. P. I. p. 373 sq. Ceterum multa quoque de hac re disputavit: J. Bapt. Scarella in libro suo: Physica generalis. Tom. I. p. 434 sq., quae tamen hic satis explicari atque dijudicari nequeunt.

Coroll. Ductis CF, EB (fig. 44.) lineae AD et EA, AF alteri BH parallelis, sine dubio per AN = AF — AE. vis exprimitur ea, quae corpus motum a directione AD detorquere nititur. Itaque si AE = AF punctum A sine ulla resistentia tubum vel canalem AD permeat.

His, inquam, propositionibus compositionis virium demonstrationem hoc fere modo noster superstruere conatur:

Quodsi duae fides elasticae AS, AT (fig. 44.) una in punctum A agunt, lineis BD, CD ita ductis, ut fiat parallelogrammum ABDC, potentiam, duabus AB, AC aequivalentem, tam quantitatis, quam directionis liberae respectu diagonalem AD aequare necesse est.

Simulac enim punctum, viribus AB, AC una in id agentibus, secundum certam directionem moveri non est coactum, viam usurpabit omnino eam, in qua vires, quae illud a directione antea necessaria amovere, uti vidimus, conabantur, invicem sese destruunt, h. e. ubi BH = CK. Item actionem hujusmodi potentiae AD singularum actionum, a viribus AB, AC praestitarum, summae aequalem esse satis liquet. Utrique autem conditioni omnino non satisfieri potest, nisi sit ABCD parallelogrammum ejusque diagonalis AD.

§. 97.

Epicrisis.

Ipse noster declarat, in hunc potissimum finem hanc compositionis ac resolutionis motus demonstrationem a sese esse traditam, ut principium illud naturae primarium, aequalitatem scilicet inter caussam et effectum *), nostro hoc theoremate, dummodo res eâ, qua debeat, ratione tractetur, haud tolli probet atque ostendat. Quodsi enim, inquit, vis duarum media, uti omnes auctores statici ac mechanici inter se consentiunt, diagonalem parallelogrammi aequat, ejusmodi compositione ac reso-

*) Non sine caussa ipsis nostri verbis: „aequalitas inter caussam et effectum," usus sum.

lutione virium, dum duo parallelogrammi latera ejusdem diagonalem omnino superent, aequalitas inter caussam et effectum minime servatur. In plerisque igitur theorematis nostri demonstrationibus, graviter huc usque peccatum est. Statim autem quaedam monere mihi liceat. Quantum equidem enim video, verba nostri, „aequalitas inter caussam et effectum," sunt ambigua. Primum enim ita intelligi possunt, ut caussa quaevis effectui, quem gignit, omnino aequalis, vel potius res plane eadem, quae ipsius effectus, esse debeat. Sed haec verba, sic intellecta, principium, vel legem naturae universae primariam innuere, quis est qui dicat? Quum autem verbis nostri hunc tribuamus sensum: effectus, quos caussae aequales praestant, ceteris paribus aequales esse necesse est" et plures alias compositionis virium demonstrationes huic principio non repugnare equidem credo. Nimirum denominatio „compositio virium" non ita urgenda est, ut vim duarum mediam ex his vere esse compositam, h. e. potentiarum singularum summae aequalem esse putemus. Quod quidem nullus fere *) omnium, qui hanc rem tractarunt, dixit; immo dum vim duarum mediam diagonalem aequare contenderunt, his verbis nihil aliud intellexerunt, nisi hoc: si duae vires quopiam angulo una punctum quoddam sollicitant, *hoc rerum ſtatu* eundem, quem potentia una, per diagonalem exhibita, effectum praestant. Quid igitur de quorundam sententia, fides elasticas rem esse unicam, quâ loco virium adhibita, earum compositio rite possit demonstrari, judicandum sit, facile intelligi potest. Immo hunc ejusmodi chordarum usum singularibus premi difficultatibus, equidem puto. Nam si duas fides una in punctum A agere ponitur, ipsas, dum contrahantur, corpus secundum directionem diagonalis movere noster dicit. Quae quidem fidium contractio cum maxima sit, dum corpusculum in eo directionis puncto, quo fidium directiones cum illa angulos constituunt rectos, versatur, ut corpusculum alterius moveatur, ipsae chordae extendantur necesse est. Ita autem, secundum ipsa ea, quae noster dixit, punctum A vi, qua-

*) Demonstrationes eorum, qui revera hoc contenderunt, mox cognoscemus.

cum moveri nititur, privatur, nec spatium, quod noster statuit, percurrere potest.

Deinde quamvis negari nequit fidis elasticae actionem, universe spectatam, ab ejus contractione pendere, hinc tamen, quantum equidem video, duarum chordarum AB, AH, particulis aequalibus Ap, Aa contractarum, actiones, dum AB. Ap = AH. Aa, omnino esse aequales haud necessario sequitur. Ceterum aequatio AB. Ap = AH. Aa non nisi tunc vera est, cum Aa, Ap lineae sint infinite parvae. Noster enim arcum circularem ap tanquam lineam rectam spectat. Quod quidem, pro mea sententia, demonstrationis rigorem omnino impedit.

Nota. Argumentum Jacobi Riccati *), qui partim Bernoullium, partim Vincentium Riccatum sequutus est, ideoque nihil plane novi attulit, jure ommitti hic potest.

Classis nona.

Auctores ii, qui compositionem virium et composit. motuum unam eandemque rem esse arbitrantur.

§. 98.

Satis nota sunt ea, quae Neutonus multique cum eo alii ad propositionem: „punctum A, a duabus viribus AB, AC (fig. 45.) una sollicitatum, per diagonalem AD fertur“ probandam protulerunt. Innummerabiles fere sunt demonstrationes — si modo hac voce hic uti licet — in hanc classem referendae. Gravesande, Belidor, Musschenbroeck, Wolf, Pascoli, Saverien, de la Caille, Mako, Ferguson, Hennert, Martin, d'Antoni, Brisson, Mariano Fontana, multique alii, quorum nomina referre hic non licet, hanc methodum, tanquam facillimam sequuti sunt. Sed praecipue notandus est Savioli, qui propositionem, sane inexpectatam, ipsi demonstrationi praemittit. Ope nimirum theore-

*) Jacopo Riccati opere. Tom. II. p. 365 sqq.

matis hujus: „si potentiae cuidam AD (fig. 46.) altera AB, quae cum illa angulum constituit rectum, supervenit, punctum A haud secus versus lineam DC || AB movebitur, quam si potentiae AB actionem plane non expertus fuisset" noster corpus, duabus viribus AB, AC (fig. 47.) sollicitatum, secundum diagonalem AD moveri probare conatur.

Quid de omnibus hujusmodi argumentis sit judicandum, duo viri clarissimi, Bernoullius *), atque Lambertus **) satis ostenderunt. Itaque nunc longa verborum serie in eorum rigorem aliaque inquirere Ilias sane post Homerum esset.

Classis decima.

Argumenta eorum, qui compositionem tantummodo motuum, minime vero virium demonstrari posse dicunt.

Cap. I.

*Argumentum Kantianum ***).*

§. 99.

Theor. Motuum duorum compositio ita tantummodo intelligi potest, ut alterum eorum in spatio absoluto corpus ipsum re vera sequi, alterius autem loco spatium relativum secundum directionem oppositam moveri ponamus.

Nam etsi etiam corpus utrique motui satisfacere sumamus, hi tamen non ad lineas AB, AC (fig. 49.), sed ad alias tantum,

---

*) Commentar. Acad. Petropol. Tom. I. p. 127.

**) Beyträge zum Gebrauche der Mathem. II. Th. p. 448 sq.

***) Metaphysische Anfangsgründe der Naturwissenschaft. 1786. p. 13 sq.

his ipsis parallelas, fieri possunt. Itaque alterum motum alterius mutationem, h. e. deflectionem a directione data efficere ponendum esset. Quod quidem compositionis virium notioni repugnat.

At si motum corporis secundum AC vere locum habere, simul vero spatium relativum celeritate AB, secundum directionem huic oppositam moveri ponamus, lineâ AC, in aliquot v. c. tres partes aequales divisa, dum corpus per spatium AE, ipsum spatium relativum et una cum eo punctum E per Ee = MA fertur, item, dum corpus per totam lineam AC, punctum C per Cc = AB movetur.

Ita autem idem omnino effectus gignitur, ac si corpus A tribus variis tempusculis per spatia Em, Fn, CD = AM, AN, AB latum fuisset. Elapso igitur tempore statuto quum corpus A in puncto D versetur, anteaque singula deinceps diagonalis puncta occupaverit, hac ipsa diagonali tam quantitas quam directio motus compositi exhibetur.

Schol. Argumentum Schultzianum *) plane non discrepat ab eo, quod modo legimus; ommitti igitur hic potest.

§. 100.

E p i c r i s i s.

De principiis, quibus totum hoc demonstrandi genus nititur, jam supra (§§. 6 sq.) quaedam diximus. Itaque nunc videamus, utrum auctores principiorum illorum ope vere ea demonstrarint, quae probanda sibi sumserunt. Quum celeritas, uti omnes, ni fallor, consentiunt, nihil aliud sit, quam facultas, qua corpus quoddam certo tempore per certum spatium moveri possit, et quum celeritas eo major habeatur, quo breviore tempore per idem spatium corpus feratur, equidem non intelligo, quomodo noster, eo, quod corpus eodem tempore per duplum, quam antea, spatium moveatur, celeritatem ejus duplo auctam esse, necessario non sequi, dicere potuerit. Sed haec etsi

*) Schultz Anfangsgr. der reinen Mechanik. Königsb. 1804.

nostro concedantur, eo tamen ejus demonstratio nondum omnibus difficultatibus liberatur. Ipse enim quantitates eas, quarum aequalitas constructione geometrica demonstrata sit, omnino tam similes, quam aequales esse debere ait; et ejusmodi constructione compositionem motuum a se demonstratam esse putat. Motum igitur, ex duobus compositum, motibus componentibus esse omnino aequalem oporteret. Haberemus ergo aequationem $AD = AB + BC$; haec ipsa autem aequatio, uti jam in primis geometriae elementis demonstratur, locum habere nequit. Itaque ea, ad quae noster hac ipsa sua demonstratione pervenit, ceteris, ab eo statutis, repugnant.

Cap. II.

Argumentum Alembertanum *).

§. 101.

Auctor SO, TP (fig. 50.) tanquam columnas mobiles, inter quas planum NCDM moveatur, spectat, et simultaneae duarum virium AB, AC, actioni omnino satisfieri, si pro AB columnis SO, TP motus secundum directionem BA atque celeritate AB, pro AC autem plano NCDM motus secundum CA celeritateque AC tribueretur, contendit. Facillime igitur noster hoc modo, corpus a duabus viribus sollicitatum, secundum diagonalem moveri, probavisse putat. — Hoc autem non re vera factum esse ex multis aliis, quae jam ad alias ejusmodi demonstrationes reprehendimus, praecipue autem e corollario primo satis adparet. Quid enim judicandum sit de argumento, cujus auctor, ut quae in corollariis proponit, non iis, in ipso argumento pronuntiatis, repugnent, parallelogrammum construere omnino coactus est, cujus diagonalis haud minor sit, quam duo ejus latera constitu-

*) Traité de dynamique. Paris 1743. p. 22 sq.

tiva, quid, inquam, de hujusmodi argumento judicandum sit, omnes sane, et non nisi primis geometriae elementis imbuit, sciunt.

Classis undecima.

*Argumentum a viro cl. Fontaine adlatum *).*

§. 102.

Ea, quibus argumentum, tanquam principiis, nititur, haec fere sunt:

1) Corpus quoddam M (fig. 51.), secundum directionem BC, celeritate AC latum, ut inde a puncto A non ad punctum C, sed celeritate AD ad punctum D moveatur, vim quandam, cujus directio lineae CD est parallela, in corpus, dum in puncto A versatur, agere necesse est.

2) Quum vis ea, qua corpus ejusmodi mutationi resistit, partim ab hujus materiae quantitate, partim a discrimine duarum celeritatum — alterius nimirum, qua ab initio corpus ferebatur, alteriusque, quam mutatione accepit — pendeat, corporis M, modo memorati, potentiam, quae hoc corpus secundum directionem AD moveatur haud sinit, hac quantitate M.CD exhiberi ponere possumus.

3) Quodsi igitur haec potentia, M.CD vi alia, huic aequali, sed contraria destruitur, corpus M inde a puncto A ad D movebitur. Fieri enim non potest, quin corpus nostrum, ubi in puncto A actionem potentiae M.CD expertum fuerit, secundum AD ferri ponamus.

---

*) Fontaine traité de calcul differentiel et integral. Paris 1770. p. 306 sqq.

§. 103.

His autem ita constitutis, corpus quoddam M, celeritate quadam AC secundum AQ praeditum, in quod autem eodem temporis momento, vis altera M. AE (fig. 52.) agat, secundum directionem AD, diagonalem parallelogrammi ACDE moveri, facile demonstrari potest.

Pro natura enim rei nunc corpus, cui modo antea celeritatem AC tribuimus, quiescere quidem, sed eodem, quo in A versatur, momento potentiam M. AC in id agere sumere omnino possumus. Conjunctis igitur harum duarum virium M. AC et M. AE actionibus, corpus secundum diagonalem ferri necesse est.

§. 104.

E p i c r i s i s.

Quod quidem argumentum eo laudandum est, quod auctor ejus viam, antea nondum tentatam, ineundo, argumentum non nimis prolixum compositionis virium conficere tentavit. Sed et in hoc tentamine sicuti in multis aliis, quae huc usque cognovimus, hanc ipsam compositionem magis temere sumtam, quam rigide demonstratam esse, non inficiandum. Unusquisque enim totius argumenti cardinem in eo versari, quod directio potentiae (fig. 51.), cujus actione corpus secundum AD moveatur, lineae CD sit parallela intelligit. Sed hanc ipsam propositionem sine ulla demonstratione noster accepit. Itaque toti argumento rigor geometricus minime vindicandus est.

Tab. I.

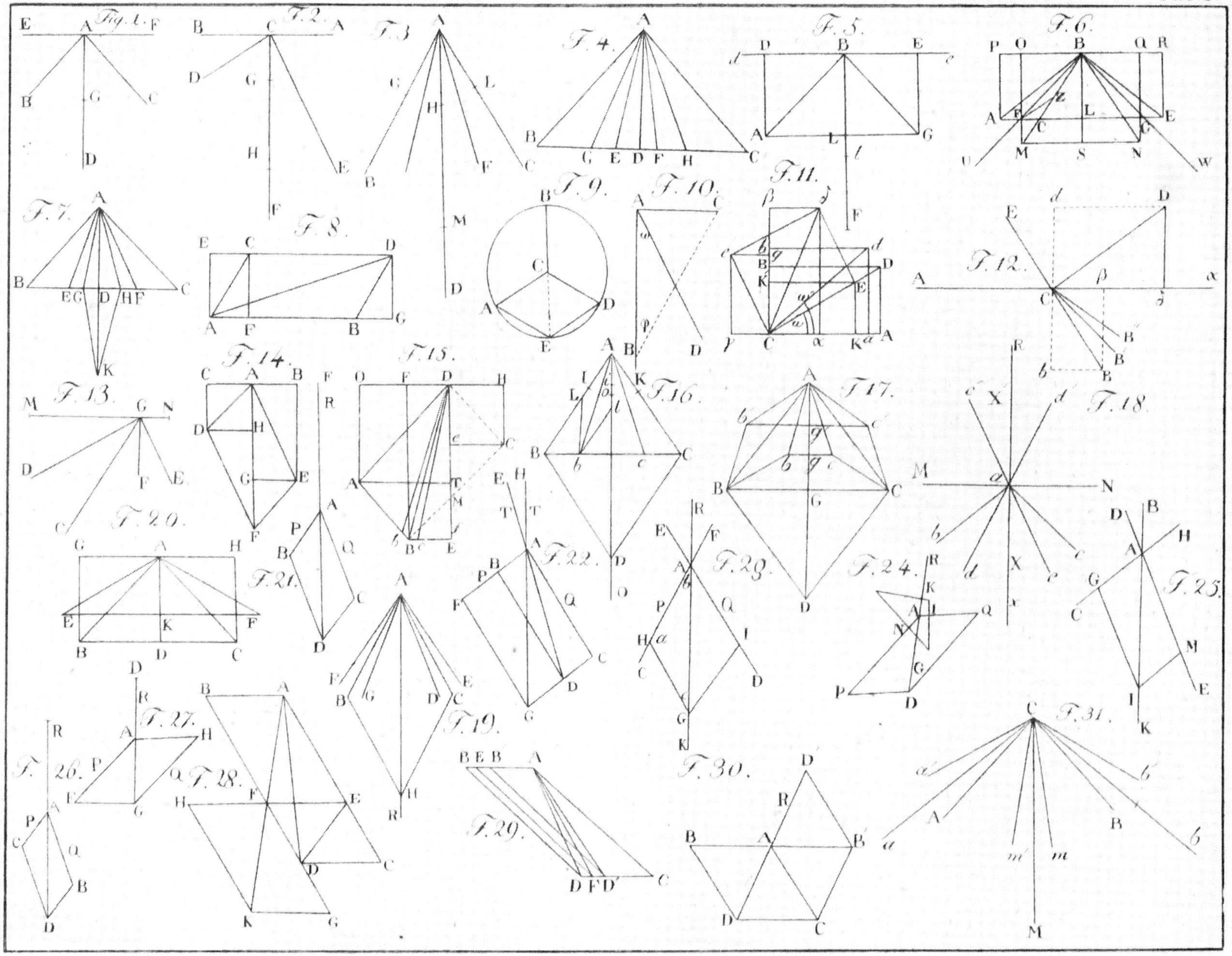

Tab. II.

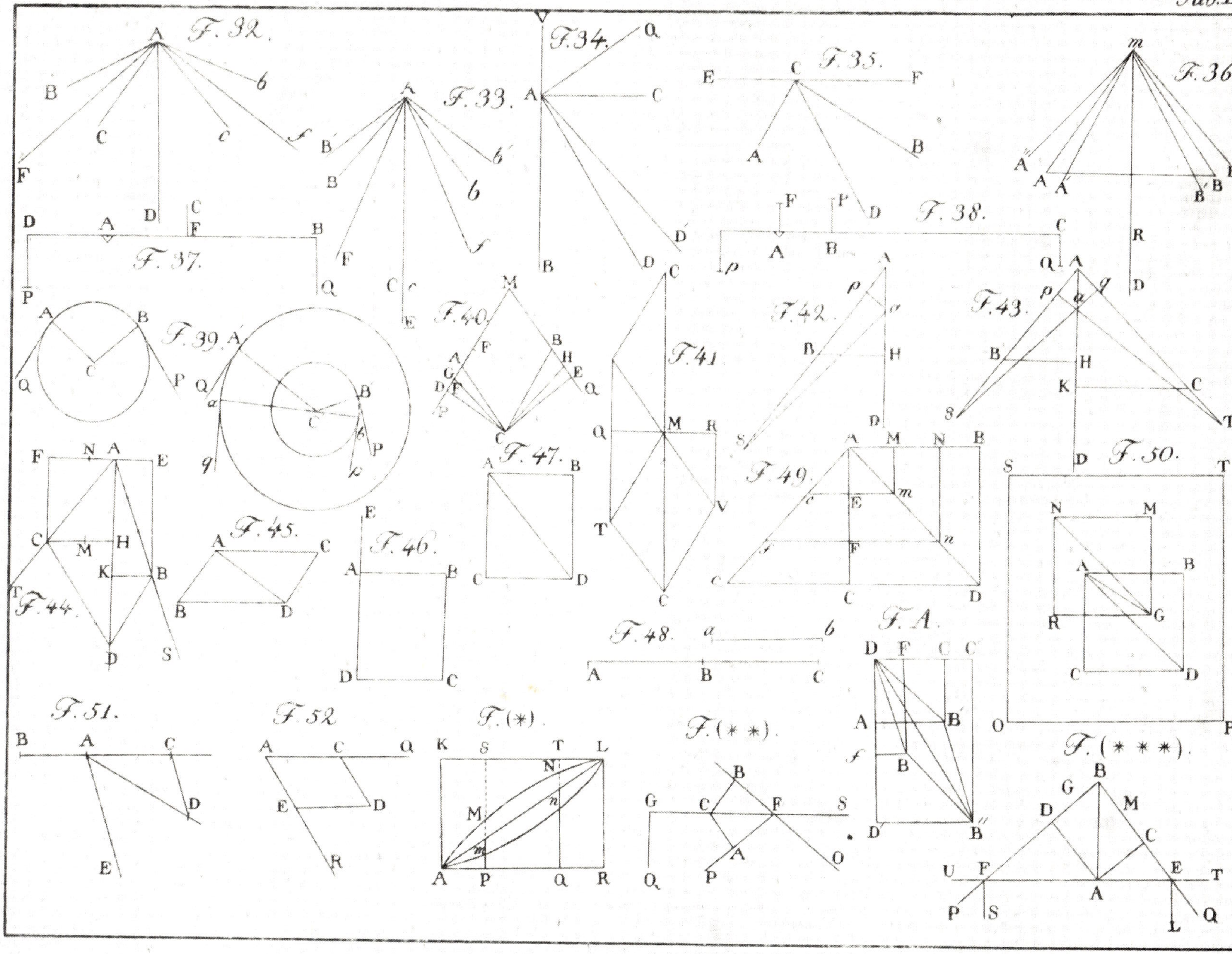
F. 32.
F. 33.
F. 34.
F. 35.
F. 36.
F. 37.
F. 38.
F. 39.
F. 40.
F. 41
F. 42.
F. 43.
F. 44.
F. 45.
F. 46.
F. 47.
F. 48.
F. 49.
F. 50.
F. A.
F. 51.
F. 52
F. (*).
F. (**).
F. (***).